Agonizing Love

THE GOLDEN ERA OF ROMANCE COMICS

MICHAEL BARSON

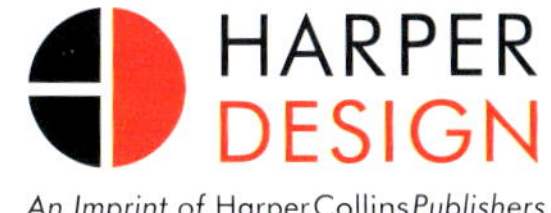
HARPER DESIGN
An Imprint of HarperCollinsPublishers

HarperCollins books may be purchased for educational, business, or sales promotional use. For information please write: Special Markets Department, HarperCollins*Publishers*, 10 East 53rd Street, New York, NY 10022.

First published in 2011 by:
Harper Design
An Imprint of HarperCollins*Publishers*
10 East 53rd Street
New York, NY 10022
Tel: (212) 207-7000
Fax: (212) 207-7654
harperdesign@harpercollins.com
www.harpercollins.com

Distributed throughout the world by:
HarperCollins*Publishers*
10 East 53rd Street
New York, NY 10022
Fax: (212) 207-7654

Library of Congress
Cataloging-in-Publication Data

Barson, Michael.
Agonizing love / Michael Barson.
p. cm.
ISBN 978-0-06-180734-3 (pbk.)
1. Romance comic books, strips, etc.—United States—History and criticism.
2. Comic book covers—United States. I. Title.

PN6725.B3723 2010
741.5'3543—dc22

2009021580

Design by Tom Manning

Printed in China
First Printing, 2011

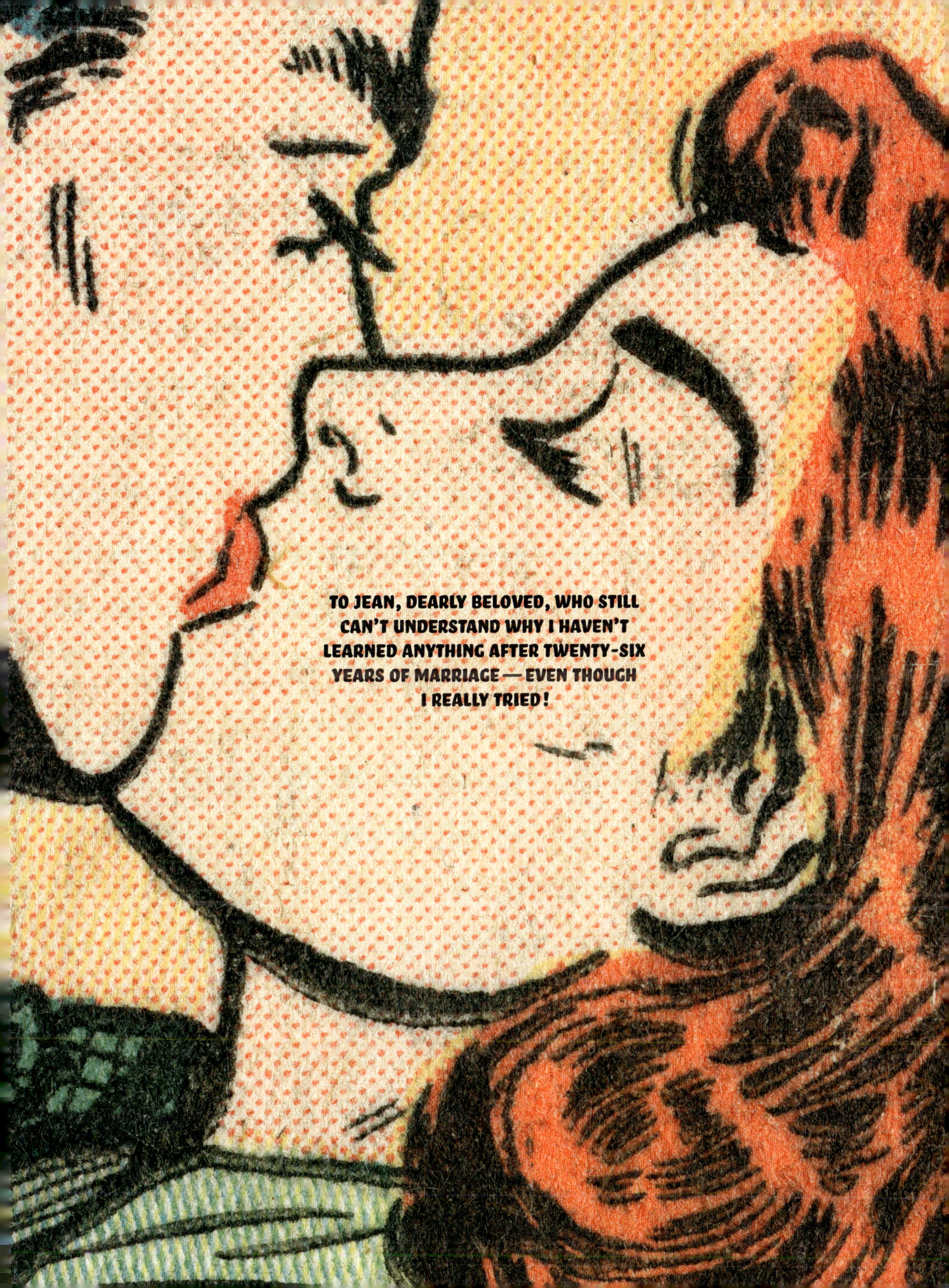

TO JEAN, DEARLY BELOVED, WHO STILL CAN'T UNDERSTAND WHY I HAVEN'T LEARNED ANYTHING AFTER TWENTY-SIX YEARS OF MARRIAGE — EVEN THOUGH I REALLY TRIED!

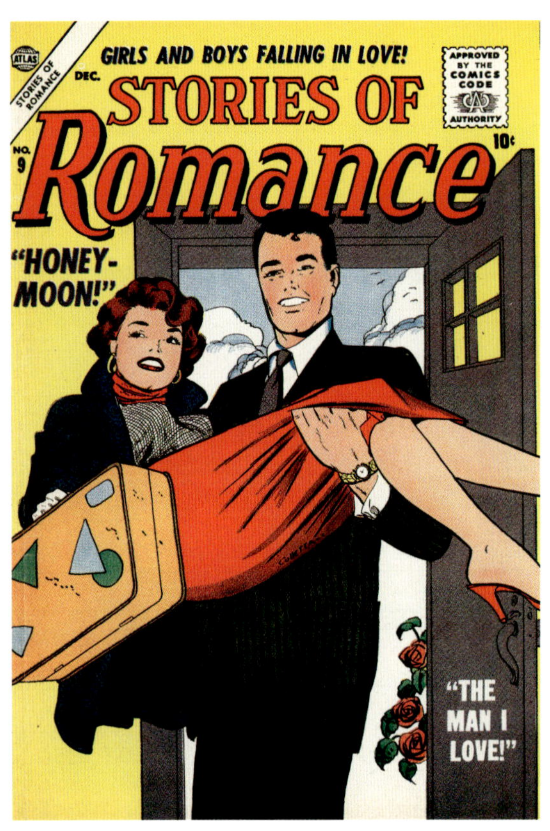

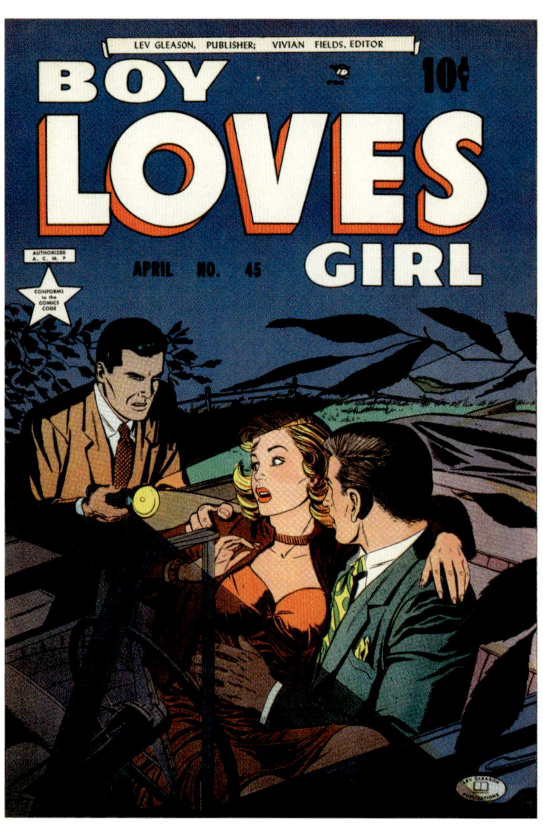

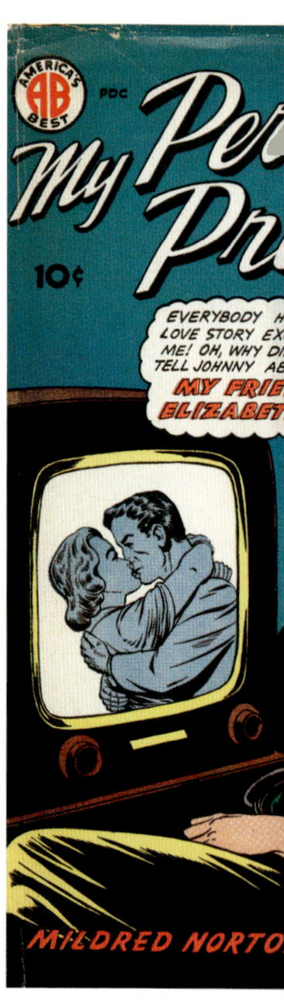

"MARRIAGE TAKES A SPECIAL TALENT, LIKE ACTING. MONOGAMY REQUIRES GENIUS."

— WARREN BEATTY

Page 3: detail from **LOVELORN** #23, March 1952; This page, from left to right: **STORIES OF ROMANCE** #9, December 1956; **BOY LOVES GIRL** #45, April 1954; **MY PERSONAL PROBLEM** #3, May 1958; Opposite: **BRIDE'S SECRETS** #4, September–October 1954; **BRIDES ROMANCES** #7, September 1954

Contents

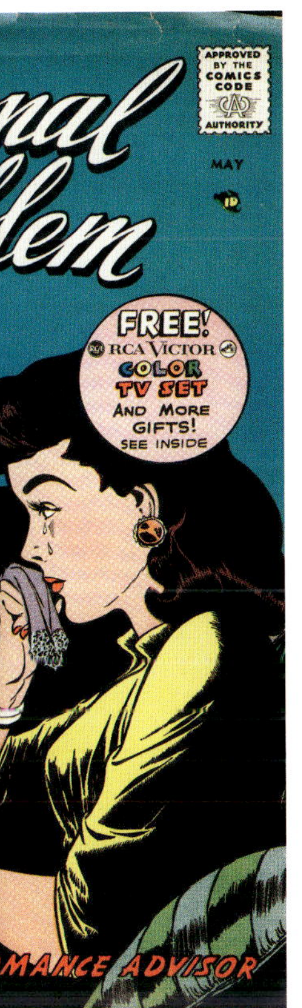
APPROVED BY THE COMICS CODE AUTHORITY
MAY
FREE! RCA VICTOR COLOR TV SET AND MORE GIFTS! SEE INSIDE

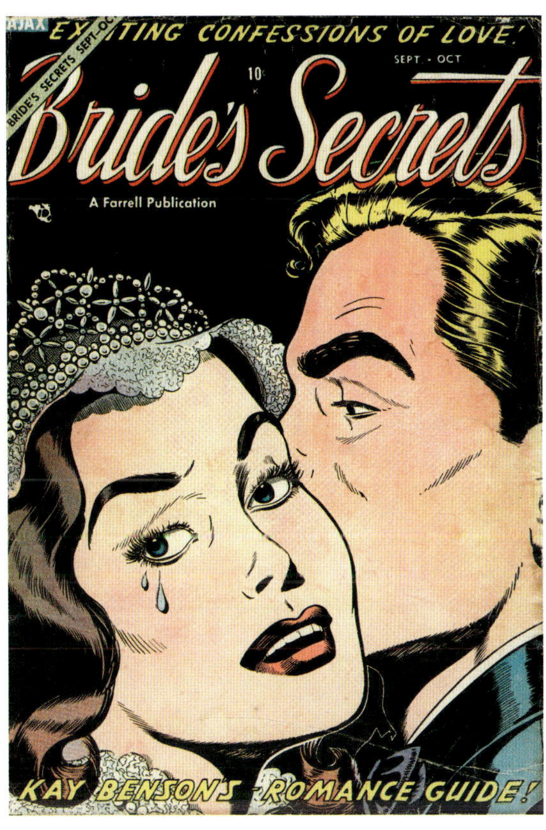
AJAX
EXCITING CONFESSIONS OF LOVE!
SEPT • OCT
10¢
Bride's Secrets
A Farrell Publication
KAY BENSON'S ROMANCE GUIDE!

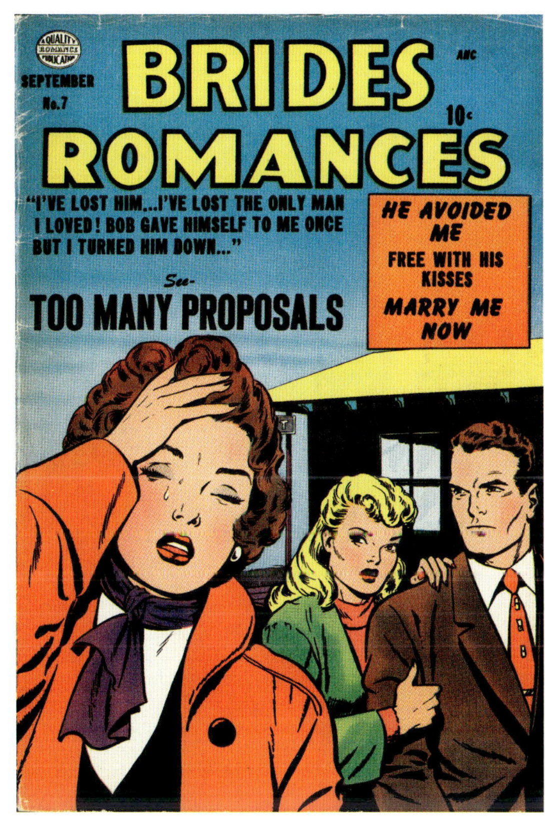
SEPTEMBER
No.7
BRIDES ROMANCES
10¢
"I'VE LOST HIM...I'VE LOST THE ONLY MAN I LOVED! BOB GAVE HIMSELF TO ME ONCE BUT I TURNED HIM DOWN..."
See-
TOO MANY PROPOSALS
HE AVOIDED ME
FREE WITH HIS KISSES
MARRY ME NOW

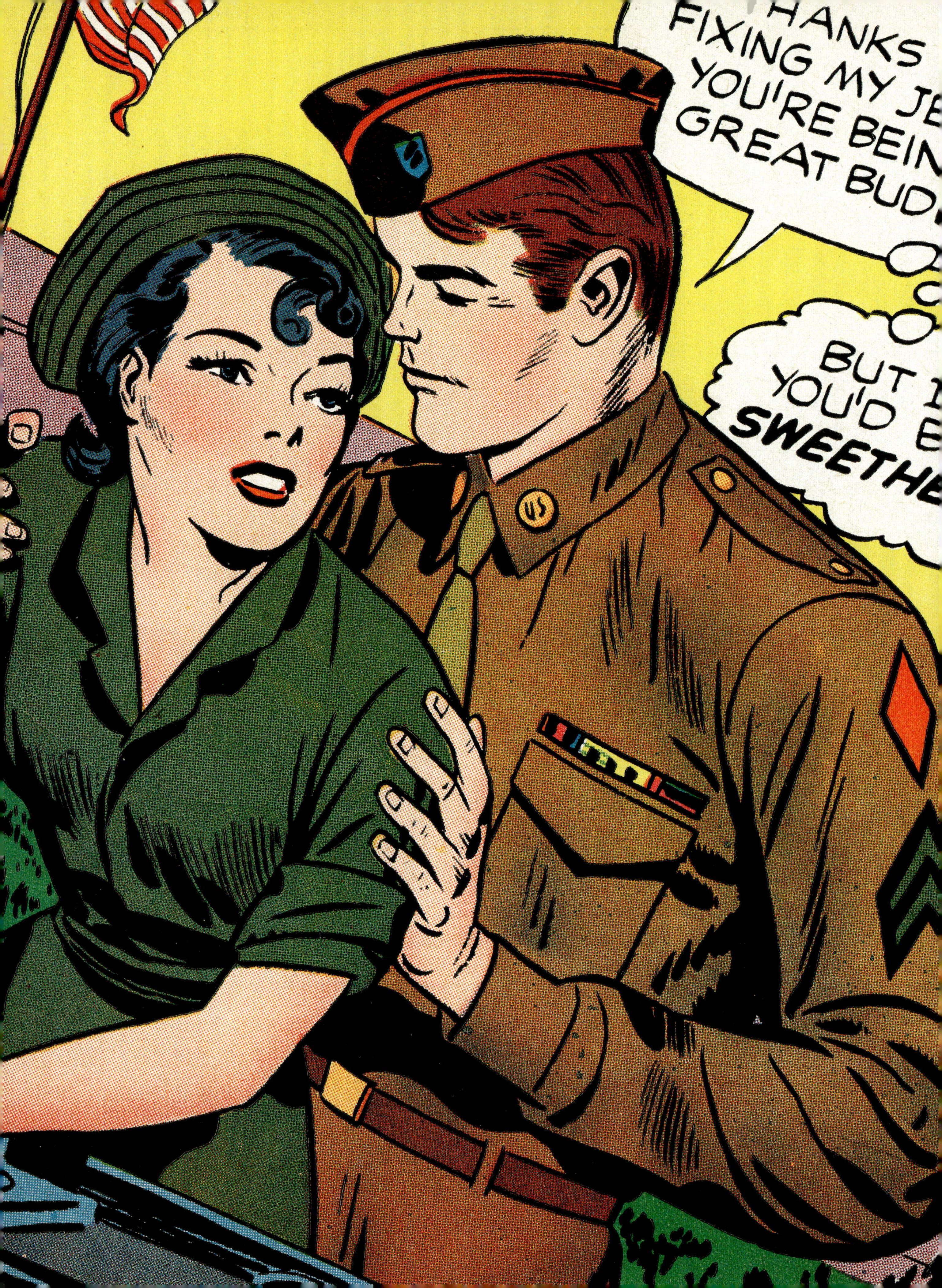
HANKS
FIXING MY JE
YOU'RE BEIN
GREAT BUD
BUT I
YOU'D B
SWEETHE

Introduction

WHAT WE TALK ABOUT WHEN WE TALK ABOUT LOVE (COMICS)

WE MIGHT AS WELL admit it from the get-go: for all of our cultural sophistication, for all of the wonderful technological innovations that seemingly appear every few months, for all of the accrued wisdom passed down and across the generations (those li'l life lessons gleaned from our moms and dads and BFFs)—we *still* don't know a tinker's damn about how love and romance really work. Experts? Don't make me laugh. At best, let's give ourselves a C– for everything we have managed to learn in this key area over, say, the last six hundred years. But we all agree that the concepts of love and romance do exist—we know that, individually and collectively, beyond a doubt. Why should love and romance remain such a puzzle—too elusive for anyone who is being honest to fully comprehend, to parse, to *decode*? That is why we are willing to spend about 70 percent of our waking hours (and 96 percent of our sleeping ones) exerting enormous effort to plumb those mysteries. We want—we *need*—to solve this age-old puzzle. (Hey, the Cold War is over—we should have plenty of time now!) It's more than a little embarrassing to still remain so much in the dark after all these centuries of accumulated experience, feverish research, and imparted wisdom. Isn't it?

Today we are able to avail ourselves (or perhaps you, dear reader, can, anyway—my wife has yet to provide me with her permission) of scientifically perfected dating services such as Match.com and eHarmony.com, along with dozens of others that are even more targeted and specialized. These widely embraced pathways to a more perfect kind of love and romance—that is, a kind that doesn't make you want to kill yourself three weeks into the affair—share a common dedication to the proposition that if you just take the randomness out of the dating equation—if you just nail down all of those external and internal factors that matter most to you about the other person's makeup—why, nirvana should be a slam dunk every time. Right?

Alas, no. Finding true love doesn't really work out that way. If it did, *Sex and the City* would never have existed. So the fact remains that, for untold millions, the search for true love and romance goes on. Maybe it never will be. So why aren't we any smarter than all those Internet-deprived generations who came before us? Why, with all the advantages we have over our ancestors in terms of pure knowledge (biochemical, technological, Twitter, Facebook—you name it), aren't we any more successful in navigating those treacherous shoals of love and romance? In short: why are we still so dumb?

That burning question is the theme of the book you now hold in your hands, *Agonizing Love*. Agonizing love is, after all, the only kind of love we have been raised to expect and accept in our From Here to Eternity—and Step on It! culture. And this book—a collection of the best of romance comic stories, covers, advertising, and art from the genre's heyday, the late 1940s through the late 1950s—is testimony to that endless pursuit.

A BRIEF HISTORY OF THE RISE AND FALL OF LOVE COMICS

The first love comics were published in 1947, and the last of the genre went out of print with *Young Love* #126 in 1977. According to Michelle Nolan's book *Love on the Racks*, a fine and exhaustive study on this exquisite genre, there were some 147 different love comics titles being published in 1950—one of every four comic books then reaching the newsstands! At the height of their popularity, love comics sold millions of copies each month, month after month. While it's true this tidal wave of tears and ultimate triumph receded fairly quickly, the staggering sales statistics are an irrefutable indication that the craze hijacked the comic book readers of our great nation. This was a mania that would be replayed a few years later in another, far more ubiquitous mass medium, when the TV industry was overwhelmed by Westerns for the latter half of the 1950s.

There can be little doubt that the vast majority of romance comics were purchased by females—not only girls, but also young and maybe even middle-aged women. Just think of all the guidance the comics provided! Could we ever hope to quantify all the broken hearts that these four-color dramas surely forestalled? But we are getting ahead of ourselves. First, the stage must be set for the Love Comics Revolution of 1947.

In pre–World War II America, young women came to understand that, to ever fully grasp the elusive nature of true romance, they would have to immerse themselves in a veritable ocean of romantic entertainments—the popular culture that was constantly lapping the shores of our proud if unabashedly tawdry culture. And so, rolling up their sleeves and cuffs, these millions of girls and young women gamely waded in.

They soaked up the popular music of the day—the tunes made famous by the likes of the ultra-smooth, frighteningly urbane Bing Crosby, and that skinny young tyro from Hoboken, Frank Sinatra. They listened to radio soap operas such as *The Guiding Light* and *The Brighter Day* that dramatized romantic situations. They watched serious romance and romantic comedies by the score, with alluring pairings such as Cary Grant and Katharine Hepburn (*Bringing Up Baby*, *The Philadelphia Story*), Errol Flynn and Olivia de Havilland (*Captain Blood*, *The Adventures of Robin Hood*), Gary Cooper and Jean Arthur (*Mr. Deeds Goes to Town*, *The Plainsman*), Clark Gable and Joan Crawford (*Possessed*, *Dancing Lady*), Fred Astaire and Ginger Rogers (*Top Hat*, *Swing Time*), Jean Harlow and Gable (*Red Dust*, *Wife vs. Secretary*), William Powell and Myrna Loy (*Libeled Lady*, *The Thin Man*), Nelson Eddy and Jeanette MacDonald (*Rose-Marie*, *Maytime*)—the list of classic romantic couples of the 1930s goes on and on.

Female readers also consumed reams of romantic fiction, making it a hugely successful genre, and in those days it could easily be found both in the form of inexpensive hardcover books and their lower-class brethren, pulp magazines. Though long extinct and today forgotten by all but pockets of historians, collectors, and octogenarians, the pulps proudly populated newsstands throughout the first half of the twentieth century, and were available in a wide range of genres: crime, horror, science fiction, Western, hero—and, of course, romance.

To rattle off just a very few of the 140 or so love pulps that were published at one point or another during the past century, one could choose from this tasty array: *Sweetheart Stories*, *Ranch Romances*, *I Confess*, *Love Book*, *All-Story Love Tales*, *Love Story Magazine*, *Popular Love*, *Thrilling Love*, *Gay Love Stories*, *Rangeland Romances*, *Life Romances*, *Exciting Love*, *Complete Love*, and *Street & Smith's Love Story Magazine Illustrated*. Females were clearly the audience for these publications, and they also read what were called confession magazines—*True Story*, *True Confessions*, *Life Story*, and so on—by the cubic ton.

One medium that young women of that time did not bother delving into, however, was the four-color world of the comic book. For in those days, both prior to and during World War II, comic books were almost the exclusive province of young boys and young girls. There were the superhero books, of course—the tales of Batman, Superman, Captain America, the Human Torch, Plastic Man, and others. But with the possible exception of the wildly kinky Wonder Woman stories, there wasn't much among them likely to command the attention of a typical 1940s female. Nor did the hugely popular "funny animal" genre—stories featuring characters such as Donald Duck, Mickey Mouse, and Bugs Bunny—

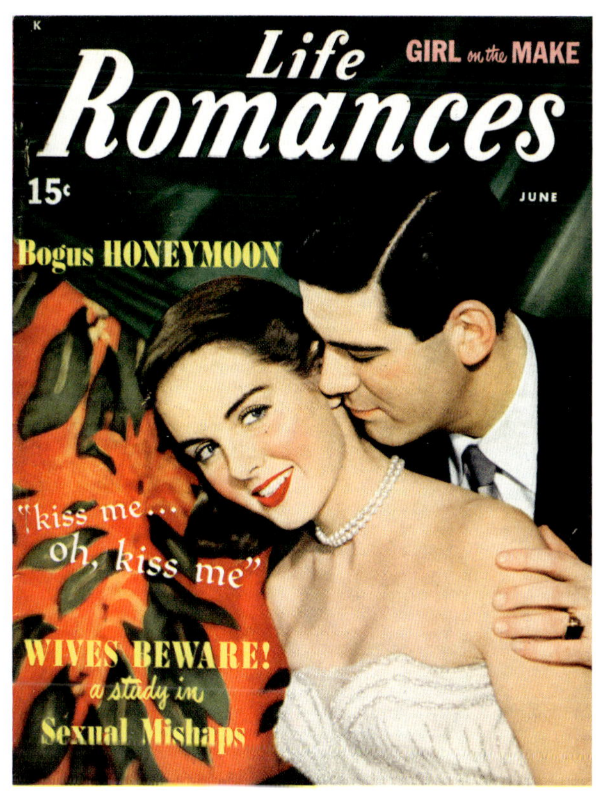

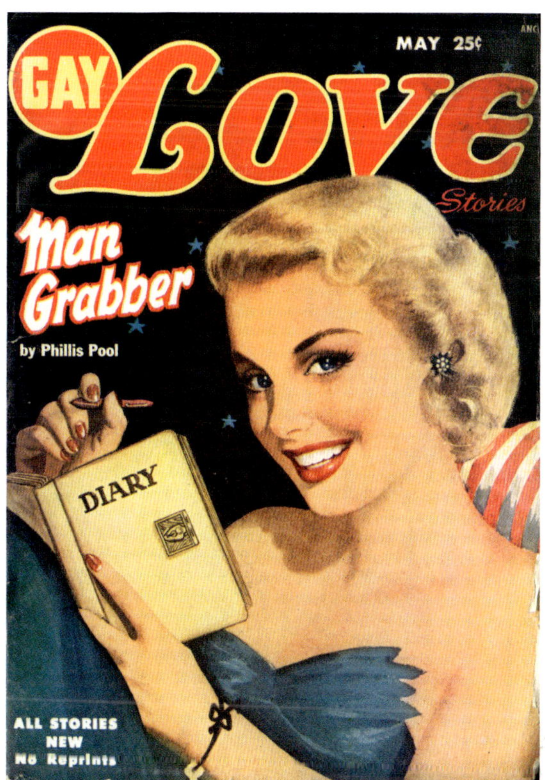

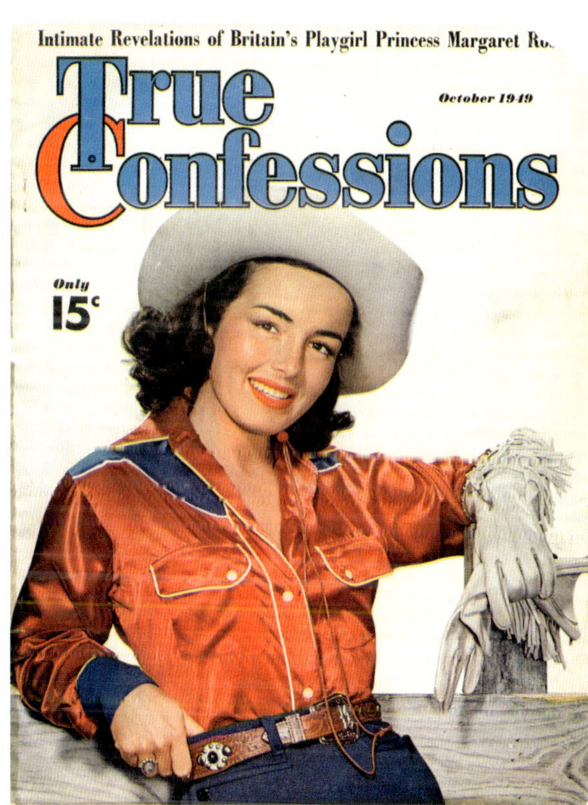

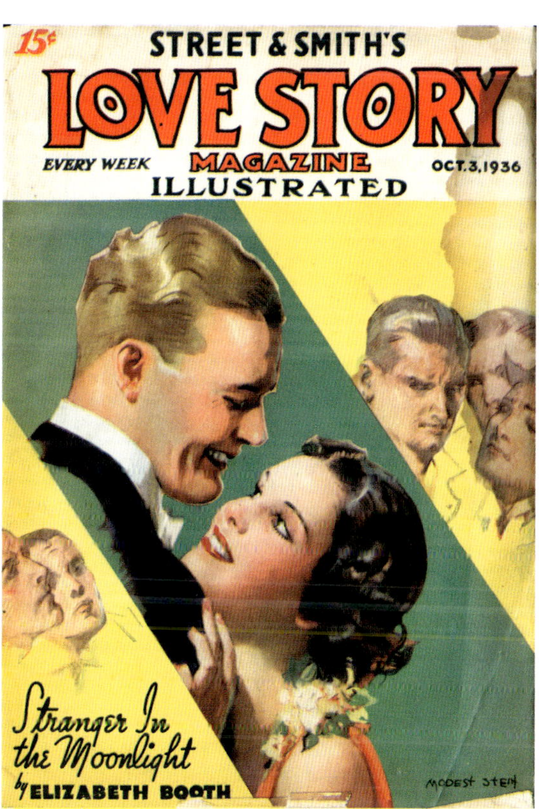

Page 6:
TRUE LOVE PROBLEMS AND ADVICE ILLUSTRATED
#38, March 1956

Clockwise from top left:
LIFE ROMANCES
Volume 2, #2, June 1950

GAY LOVE
May 1953

STREET & SMITH'S LOVE STORY MAGAZINE ILLUSTRATED
October 3, 1936

TRUE CONFESSIONS
October 1949

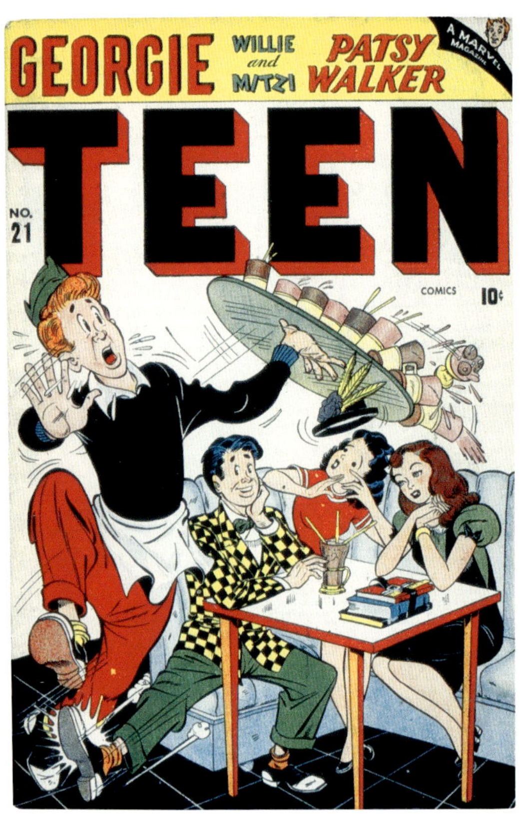

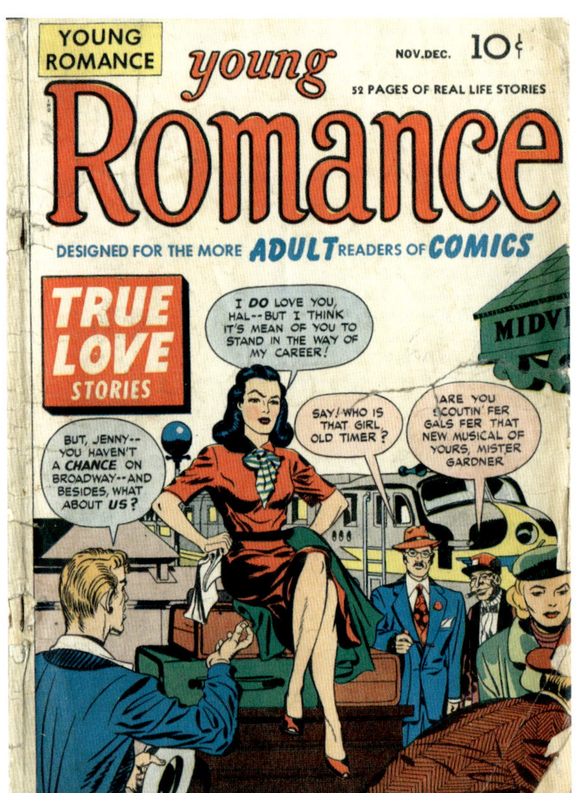

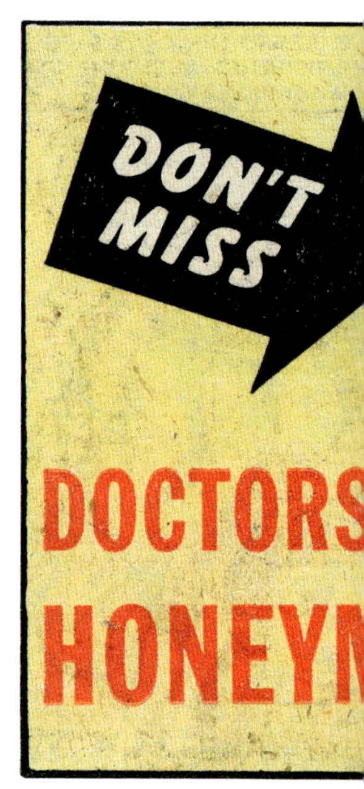

have much to say to a healthy girl over the age of eleven. So that left very little aimed at that distaff readership, with the notable exception of the *Archie* line of benign teen misadventures.

Created in 1939 by Bob Montana, a student at Haverhill High School in Massachusetts (where he famously doodled the characters who became the *Archie* gang on the classroom blackboard before the teacher arrived), the first *Archie* strip appeared as a backup feature in *Pep Comics* #22 (December 1941). Such was the character's popularity that Archie Andrews soon became the cover feature of *Pep*, displacing erstwhile star the Shield, a patriotic superhero of no particular distinction. Archie was given his own comic book in 1943, which in turn led to a host of spin-offs—*Archie's Girls Betty and Veronica*, *Archie's Pal Jughead*, *Archie's Rival Reggie* (to name but a few)—throughout the 1940s and on into the '50s and '60s. An empire had been born.

Archie's principal interests in the town of Riverdale were two almost identical knockouts, Betty Cooper (the faithful, good-girl blonde) and Veronica Lodge (the rich, manipulative, raven-haired temptress). Archie's inability to choose between the two is one of the longest-running gags in the history of comics. Archie also had two male friends, the insufferable Reggie Mantle (his chief rival for Veronica's attention) and the primeval Jughead, the purest embodiment of the id ever to stroll through the pages of a comic book. (He probably grew up to become *Seinfeld*'s Cosmo Kramer.)

Partly inspired by the popular Andy Hardy movies that Mickey Rooney had been making for MGM since 1937, the *Archie* comics were essentially about the humorous aspects of teen life, of which romance was just one element. Even so, they seemed to appeal equally to both boys and girls, since the stories represented both viewpoints as often as not. (If anything, Betty and Veronica got the upper hand over the doltish lads in the majority of the stories.) But for all their mass appeal and all the millions of female readers the series could claim, in the end the *Archie* comics were about comedy. The mild-mannered stories never even pretended to have a single serious thought in their red-thatched heads. And if there was one defining characteristic of the stories in the love comics genre that would soon be coming on the scene, it was that they took themselves very, very seriously—or at least gave a persuasive imitation of doing so.

Which brings us to 1947, when the first love comic book, *Young Romance*, debuted on newsstands. *Young Romance* was conceived by the

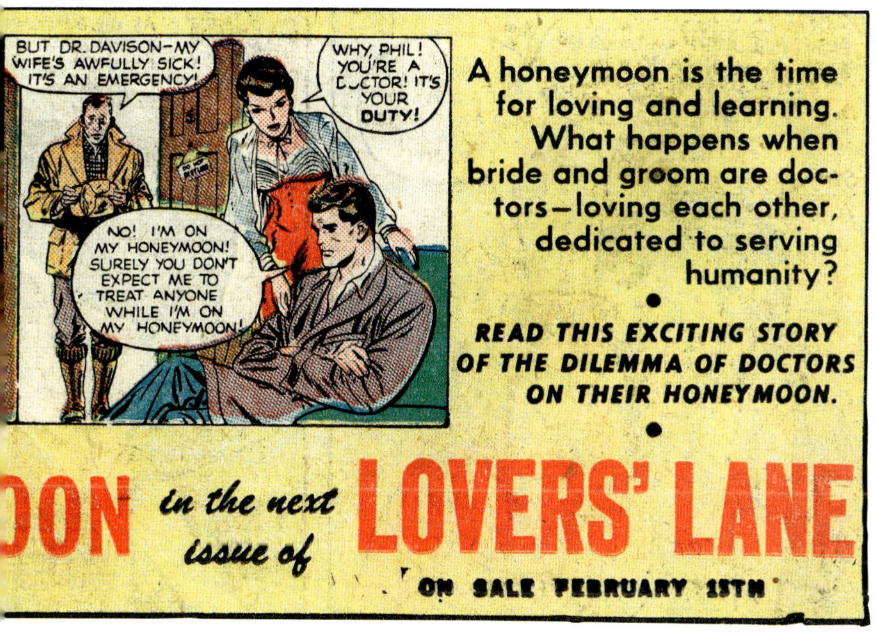

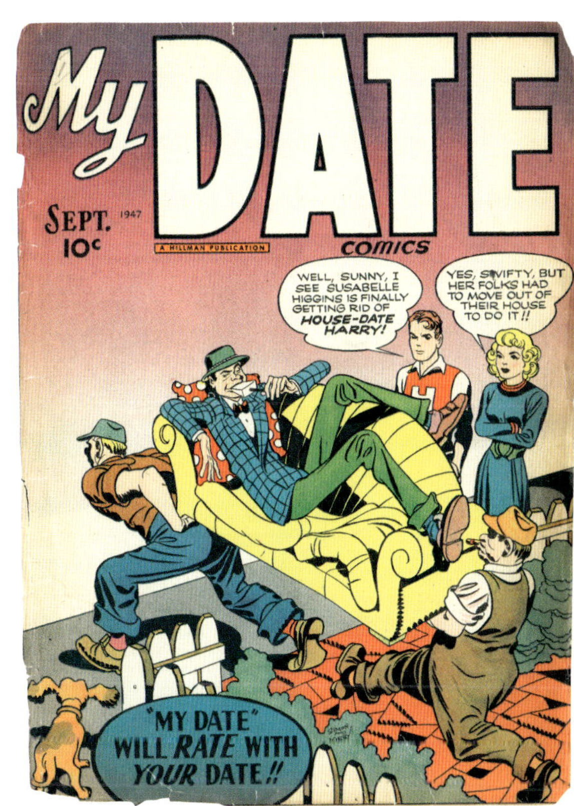

legendary tandem of Joe Simon and Jack Kirby, who had famously created the patriotic hero Captain America in 1941, then went on to conceive such popular superhero strips as *The Newsboy Legion*, *Boy Commandos*, *Manhunter*, and *The Sandman* during World War II. Following the war, Simon and Kirby had reentered a very crowded comic book marketplace by diving into a hodgepodge of projects. One of the most interesting was a little title called *My Date*, created for the second-banana comic book publisher Hillman. *My Date* was a less cartoony version of the *Archie* line. The stories centered on high spirited teenagers and their constant dating dramas, all occurring in teens' natural habitats, like jalopies, diners, and dances in the school gym.

But the presentation of *My Date*, while less overtly cartoony than the hugely popular *Archie* comics, still emphasized humor. The genius of Joe Simon was to add a whole other sensibility that had been foreign to the comic-book universe up to that point. Like so many tipping points of genius in humankind's history, in retrospect Joe Simon's intuitive leap seems almost telementary. Romance magazines—known widely as confession magazines, as embodied by the Fawcett empire's longtime field leader *True Confessions*—were multiplying on postwar newsstands at an incredible rate, like so many slumming bunny rabbits, along with an amalgam of romantic paperback books, pulp and digest magazines, and even hardcover books. Simon saw there was an absence of love comics from the multimillion-selling comic-book world of 1947, a gaping black hole that he detailed in his entertaining 1990 memoir, *The Comic Book Makers*. In it, he described his eureka moment:

> It had long been a source of wonder to me that so many adults were reading comic books designed for children, and now I was finding myself increasingly wondering why there was such a dearth of comic book material for the female population. Women factory workers, housemaids, housewives, and teenage girls.... I wondered how they would accept a comic book version of the popular *True Story* magazine, with youthful, emotional, yet wholesome stories supposedly told in the first person by love-smitten teenagers. Visually, the magazine love stories seemed a natural conversion for comic books.

And so Simon mocked up the first cover of what he christened *Young Romance*, giving it an irresistible slug above the title: "Designed for the More Adult Readers of Comics." He showed the cover to erstwhile partner Jack Kirby, who also

Pages 10–11, from left to right:
TEEN COMICS #21, April 1947

YOUNG ROMANCE #2, November–December 1947

LOVERS' LANE #3, February 1950, house ad

MY DATE #2, September 1947

was freelancing at the time, and on the spot the two renewed their partnership. They devised a formula for their new baby—the first-person confessional mode, following the approach of the true-confession-style magazines—executed a handful of stories, and took the results to Maurice Rosenfeld and Teddy Epstein, the general managers of Crestwood, a small magazine and comic-book publishing house. Simon and Kirby then took their next bold step. Going against industry practice of being paid upfront, they negotiated to be paid for their work at the back end, out of the eventual sales profits—of which they would claim an as-yet-unheard-of share of 50 percent. After much negotiation, the Crestwood owners agreed to these terms, and *Young Romance* was launched.

The first issue (September–October 1947), which featured art and stories by Simon and Kirby, along with a very talented supporting cast, was a bimonthly. The debut, a print run that Simon recalls was in the neighborhood of 350,000 copies, sold out completely, unheard of during those newsstand-glutted days. The print run of subsequent issues was soon increased to a cool million copies per issue—and still issues of *Young Romance* sold at an unprecedented pace. Love was in the air!

Such was the genius of Simon and Kirby that almost all of the themes that would predominate in this genre for the next fifteen years or so were introduced in these first issues of their groundbreaking creation. Jealousy? Check. Betrayal? Double check. Suffocating mothers-in-law? Too many to count! To those evergreens you may add such tasty themes as greed, narcissism, class struggles, and prejudice (this last a Simon and Kirby specialty that most other publishers steered clear of). *Young Romance* was like a four-color laboratory that dramatized case studies in other-directed behavior, neuroses, and dysfunctional relationships between and among lovers, friends, coworkers, parents, siblings, and those pesky in-laws (this last area being my personal favorite, in the spirit of unbridled confession).

While they were riding high, Simon and Kirby launched a companion magazine, *Young Love*, in early 1949, the delectably melodramatic contents of which were indistinguishable from *Young Romance*. *Young Love* was another immediate success. By then, though, Crestwood's pot of gold had come to the attention of competing publishers: by early 1949 the company had plenty of competition on the newsstands. Joe Simon estimated in his memoir that as many as six hundred imitation publications were launched in the first years following the advent of *Young Romance*, but comic-book historian Richard Howell offers the more precise number of 527 in his excellent introduction to the Simon and Kirby anthology *Real Love*.

Though I have not been fortunate enough to sample or even see all 527 of these titles, I have read enough vintage romance comic books over the years to know that, like every other form of popular culture, some were quite good, some were just okay, and some—perhaps even the majority—were unabashedly dreadful. Poignant or pointless, they were consumed in record numbers, month after month, year after year.

There is not world enough and time to list more than a representative number of the romance comics that rode the wake of the success of *Young Romance*. But restricting the focus to the key word "love," consider this array that nested in the newsstand racks between 1949 and 1954: *Love Adventures*, *Love and Marriage*, *Love at First Sight*, *Love Classics*, *Love Confessions*, *Love Diary*, *Love Experiences*, *Love Journal*, *Loveland*, *Love Lessons*, *Love Letters*, *Love Life*, *Lovelorn*, *Love Memories*, *Love Mystery*, *Love Romances*, *Lovers*, *Lovers' Lane*, *Love Scandals*, *Love Secrets*, *Love Stories*, *Love Tales*, and *Love Trails*. Many of these comics replaced the publishers' forays into other categories, such as superhero, crime, and teen, as everyone wanted to double-down where the dice were hottest. (My favorite conversion was Fawcett making its long-running superhero title *Captain Midnight* into *Sweethearts* with issue #68.)

Of course, by crowding onto the gravy train, the publishers sowed the seeds of their own undoing, glutting the market to the point where even the assembled legions of female comic-book readers couldn't keep all of these love publications afloat. To paraphrase Cole Porter, the love comics affair was too hot not to cool down. So cool down it did, to the point where, by 1953, the love comics industry was actually suffering a recession. Even Simon and Kirby had to move on to other ventures during this market correction. Nonetheless, even though the shake-out reduced the number of romance titles to a fraction of what had been on the newsstands from 1949 to 1950, dozens of titles still went to press every month.

Through the remainder of the '50s and into the early '60s, love comics still commanded enough of an audience to be financially viable, but their market share continued to shrink, for reasons that remain something of a mystery to this day. Was it the advent of teen culture magazines like *16* and *Dig*? But those had more to do with rock 'n' roll than anything involving the heart, really. True, the superhero category, which could barely claim a pulse for much of the early and mid-1950s, was given a second life when DC Comics introduced a new space-age incarnation of *The Flash* in 1956; it caught on and quickly led to a whole new generation of costumed characters on the newsstands. By the end of the decade, the once moribund superhero genre was again thriving, with the likes of Green Lantern, the Challengers of the Unknown, the Justice League of America, and Adam Strange. But it's not likely that young women were lured away from their romance titles by the likes of these garishly clad crime fighters. Nor had some other medium come into being to lure away that female readership, the way that television had siphoned off the audience for radio programs in the early '50s, or the way that the advent of the paperback book drove the pulp magazine business into extinction.

Nonetheless, the love comics industry was sputtering badly by the mid-1960s, losing much of its ability to connect with its core audience seemingly overnight. The '60s may have been one of the most exciting, tumultuous, and progressive decades in humankind's history to date, but you would never have known it from the tear-drenched issues of *Young Love* and *Girls' Romances* clogging up the comic-book racks. Romance comics weren't keeping up with the times, and their efforts to weave in stories with themes touching on current events and the counterculture were almost universally laughable. No matter how many headbands and tie-dyed T-shirts appeared on the characters in those pages, readers must have been able to sense that something inauthentic was afoot back at the storyboard. Feminism, Woodstock, interracial romance, rock 'n' roll, pot—the purveyors of the love comic tried to incorporate seemingly relevant issues, events, and pop culture into the stories, yet all the efforts came across as bogus—and fell flat. The titles that once had sold a cool million copies per issue were now limping along with circulations below 150,000, which in the late '60s translated into grounds for cancellation. As the '60s gave way to the '70s, the cancellations began and never stopped until *Young Love* went out of business in 1977. And just like that, the halcyon era of the romance comic book had come to an end, its like perhaps never to be seen again.

In the thirty-odd years since love comics went the way of the dinosaur, some wonderful pop culture has emerged, in media ranging from films to music to books to magazines to, of course, the Internet. Except for the Internet, all these other media had happily flourished alongside romance comics during their glory decades, and vice versa.

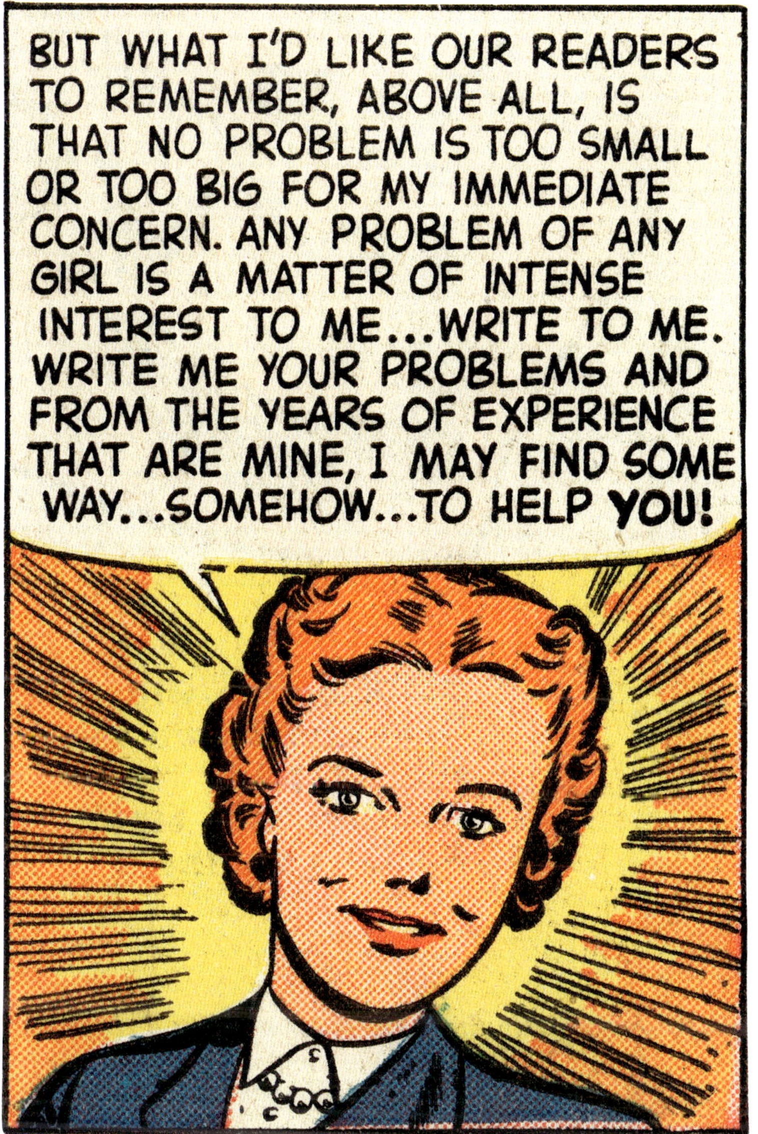

LOVE LESSONS
#4, April 1950, advice column detail

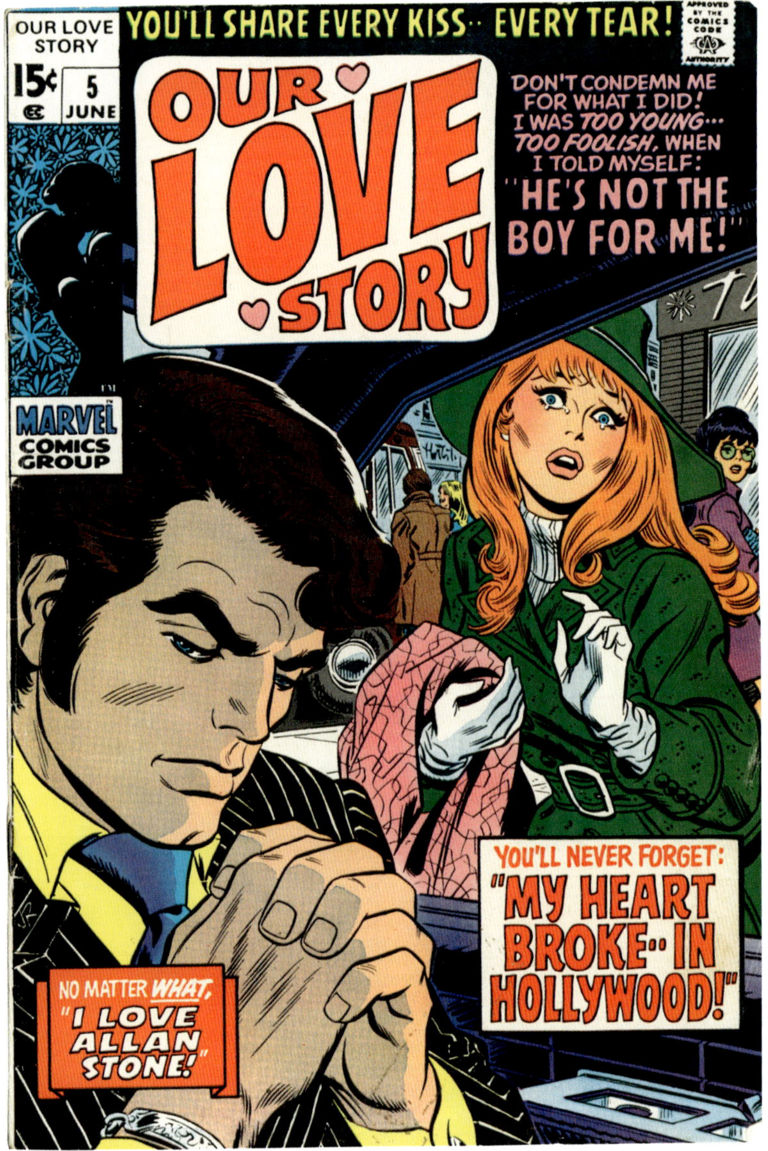

This page:
OUR LOVE STORY
#5, June 1970

Page 15:
UNKNOWN ISSUE
circa 1950

Pages 16–17:
MY OWN ROMANCE
Unknown issue, circa 1950

There is no reason to assume that any of those popular entertainments, individually or collectively, led to the piteous demise of the love comics. But if not—then what was to blame? The question haunts me—particularly once I have moved past my third beer.

And so, this lonely nation—and all of our sister lonely nations around the globe—still needs help figuring out that persistent mystery of the ages: what makes a good romance tick? But even as the answer continues to elude us—and by "us" I mean you, dear reader, since as mentioned earlier I have been married and in a state of constant ecstasy for over a quarter century now—one thought recurs: why do fools fall in love? And once in love, why can't they learn not to muck it up fifteen minutes after it ignites? That is a rhetorical question, of course, but in all honesty, if we had a few hundred different love comics back out there on the newsstands, it might do something to help us poor fools find our way.

ABOUT THIS BOOK

The contents of *Agonizing Love* fall primarily into the ten-year period from 1947 to 1957, which most fans would agree constitutes the golden age of the now lost and sorely missed category of romance comics. The majority of the book features an array of wonderful covers or key stories—or both—that appear in more than a hundred different issues I have culled from my still-growing collection. It would seem there are about 5,500 more issues I still need to make any claim to thorough knowledge of this delightful genre, but please do not mention that quest to my wife, whose patience has been tested beyond science's ability to measure it. I also couldn't resist including a good representation of the peripheral materials that graced so many issues: the advice columns and letters pages, the mini-story object lessons presented by the often fictional house psychologist, the colorful ads—both for fashion (to use the word loosely) and personal grooming products, and for the publisher's current and upcoming love comics. In some cases, these little tidbits prove to be more entertaining than the "main course" of stories they surround. And educational too!

Because so much of retro pop culture is appreciated and then immediately dismissed as mere camp, let me assure readers that my affection for these little four-color morality plays is genuine. I can also say that my fondness isn't based on cheap nostalgia, since these weren't the comics I was reading in my formative years (roughly age six to age fifty-six). At that time, I was all about superhero stuff, war comics, and *Turok, Son of Stone*. But once these romance comics came to my attention, long after their era had passed, I helplessly responded to their often daffy immediacy and power. It is my hope that some of you looking at *Agonizing Love* enjoy the same visceral reaction, even if you are a half century removed from the culture that gave them birth. I can't help but feel that this would be a better world if I could saunter into a newsstand and see, in all their glory, nestled there between the latest issues of *GQ*, *People*, and *Entertainment Weekly*, some bright, shiny issues of *Teen-Age Romances*, *My Secret Marriage*, and *Untamed Love* begging for my dime. Hell, make it a dollar.

Well, I can dream, can't I?

—*Michael Barson*

AMERICA'S MOST THRILLING WESTERN ROMANCES

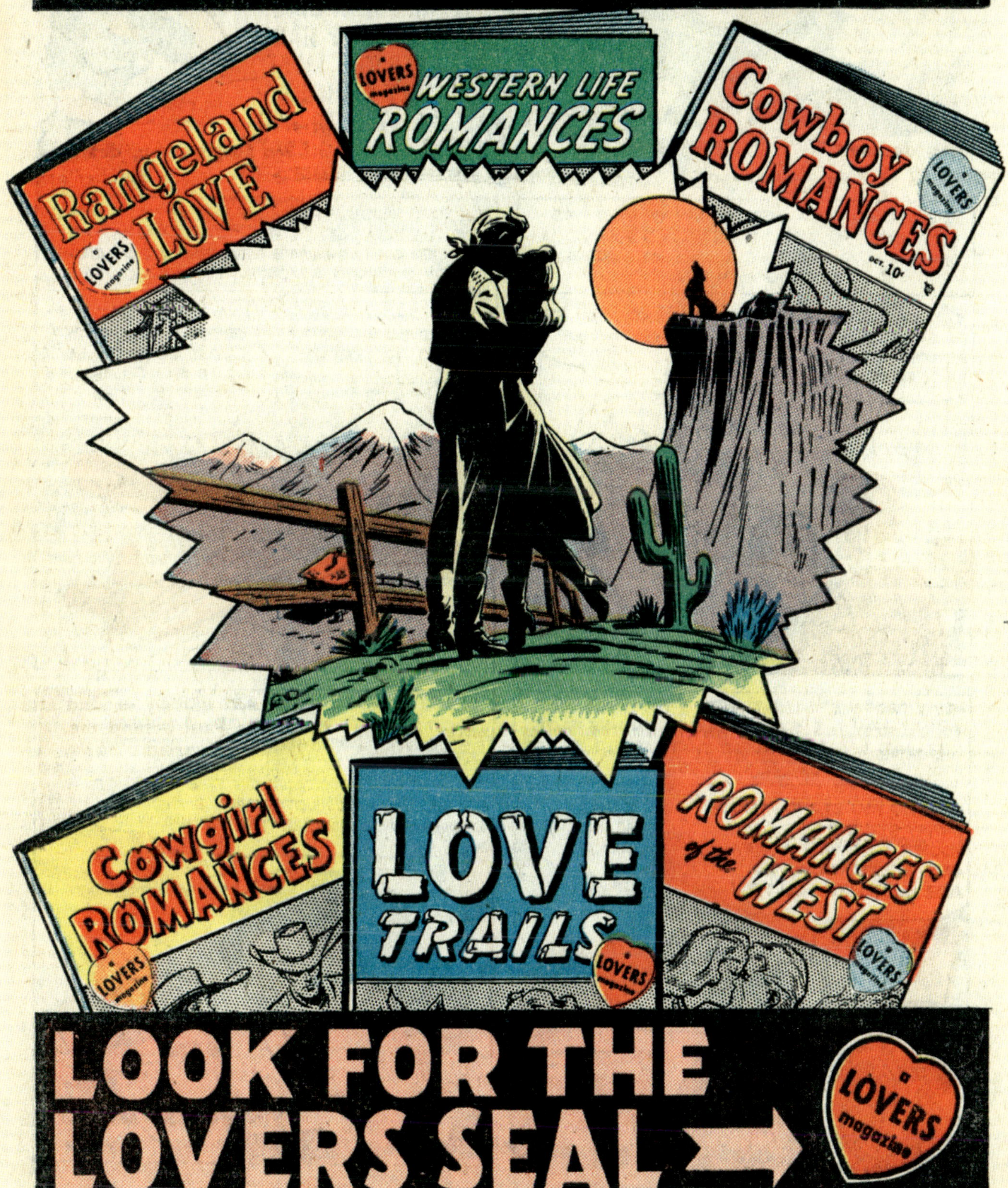

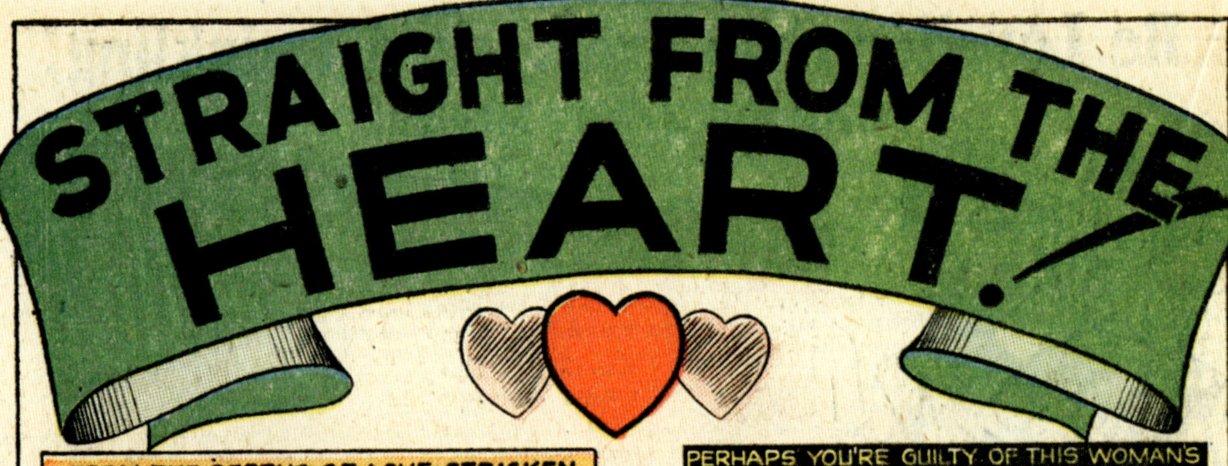

FROM THE DEPTHS OF LOVE-STRICKEN HEARTS COME THESE LETTERS, AND FROM EDITORS WITH YEARS OF COUNSELING EXPERIENCE COME THE ANSWERS. READ THIS COLUMN CAREFULLY, THOROUGHLY... IT IS COMPILED FOR YOU!

A STUDENT FROM NEW YORK CITY ASKS ABOUT A PROM DATE:

Dear Editors,
I'm 20, and a sophomore in college. I've just met a girl whom I like a lot, but she is 21 and a senior. We don't go to the same school and I would like to ask her to our next prom. I'm afraid she'll refuse because of the difference in our ages. How about it?
H.L.O.

DEAR H.L.O.
LET'S FACE FACTS: THE WAR HAS FLOODED OUR COLLEGES WITH FRESHMEN RANGING FROM EIGHTEEN TO THIRTY. THIS GIRL SHOULD BE BIG ENOUGH TO OVERLOOK THE DIFFERENCE IN YOUR SCHOLASTIC STATUS.

AS FAR AS YOUR AGE IS CONCERNED, A YEAR'S DIFFERENCE MIGHT HAVE MADE YOU THINK TWICE IN YOUR TEENS--BUT AT TWENTY YOU ARE SURELY MATURE ENOUGH TO SHOW A GIRL OF TWENTY-ONE A GOOD TIME.

IF YOU THINK SHE LIKES YOU, THE ODDS ARE IN YOUR FAVOR. SHE PROBABLY HASN'T EVEN THOUGHT ABOUT THE THINGS THAT ARE WORRYING YOU... SO TAKE YOUR CHANCE, AND GIVE HER A BID BEFORE SOMEONE ELSE DOES!

PERHAPS YOU'RE GUILTY OF THIS WOMAN'S FAULT!

Dear Editors,
I'm 26 and very lonely. I've gone with lots of men, but I never seem to be able to hold them. I have just lost a man I loved very much. I brood day and night over it. I'm terribly anxious to be married, and I'm not getting any younger. Can you help me?
J. B.

DEAR J.B.
YOUR LETTER CONTAINS THE CLUE TO YOUR FAILURE IN FINDING A MAN. WE SUSPECT THAT YOU ARE TOO EAGER TO LEAD MEN TO THE ALTAR. TAKE YOUR HEART OFF YOUR SLEEVE, AND KEEP 'EM GUESSING ABOUT YOUR FEELINGS UNTIL THEY PRESENT THE SUBJECT FOR DISCUSSION. THIS FORMULA IS WEARY WITH AGE—BUT STILL TRUE!

HERE'S A LETTER FROM A TEEN-AGER IN OMAHA, NEBRASKA:

Dear Editor,
I'm a girl 17 and I think I'm old for my age. I'm crazy about Jim, the boy I go with, and we spend most of our free time together. We want to go steady, but my parents forbid it. Everyone at our school does, and I can't understand why they don't approve.
M.W.

DEAR M.W.

JIM IS PROBABLY A VERY WONDERFUL BOY. BUT THERE ARE LOTS OF OTHER WONDERFUL BOYS, TOO. YOUR PARENTS WANT YOU TO MEET AND DATE THESE BOYS, AND EXPAND YOUR SOCIAL HORIZON. THEY DON'T WANT YOU TO CONFINE YOURSELF TO ONE BOY DURING THE TIME WHEN YOU SHOULD BE DATING DOZENS OF THEM--AND THEY ARE RIGHT. THE MORE BOYS YOU KNOW NOW, THE BETTER EQUIPPED YOU'LL BE TO CHOOSE THE RIGHT HUSBAND, WHEN THE TIME COMES!

HOW DO YOU FEEL ABOUT THIS WIDELY-DISCUSSED PROBLEM?

Dear Editors,

I'm going to marry a wonderful girl in a few months, but there's one thing we're not settled on. My salary is good enough to support us comfortably, but she wants to go on working after we're married. I don't think she should. Which of us is right?

G.T.R.

DEAR G.T.R.

YOU'RE FACING A COMMON POST-WAR PREDICAMENT, AS YOU PROBABLY KNOW. HOW YOU SETTLE IT DEPENDS UPON THE FACTS OF YOUR INDIVIDUAL CASE. THE REASONS WHY YOUR FIANCÉE WANTS TO BE A WORKING WIFE--ADDED INCOME, SOMETHING TO DO UNTIL YOU HAVE CHILDREN, TO NAME A COUPLE--ARE AS VALID AS YOUR OJECTIONS.

YOUR FIRST PROBLEM IS BEFORE YOU-TALK IT OUT SENSIBLY AND TRY TO COME TO A CONCLUSION OR, PERHAPS, A COMPROMISE (A PART-TIME JOB, FOR INSTANCE)-AND GOOD LUCK!

A CONFUSED GIRL FROM BOISE, IDAHO, WRITES...

Dear Editor:

I went with a man for two years, and our romance was ideal. He never mentioned marriage, but I thought it was understood. I was stunned when I saw an announcement of his marriage to another woman in the paper a few months ago. Now he writes that he wants to see me and explain everything. I don't know what to do.

C.P.

DEAR C.P.

YOU CAN NEVER RECAPTURE YOUR IDEAL LOVE LIFE WITH THIS MAN BECAUSE HE IS MARRIED. YET YOU ARE TOYING WITH THE IDEA OF SEEING HIM AGAIN!

IN THE FIRST PLACE, A MAN WHO SIDESTEPS A BREAKOFF AND DISAPPEARS IS OBVIOUSLY UNTRUSTWORTHY. SECONDLY, IF YOU ARE STILL ATTRACTED TO HIM, YOU WOULD BE PLAYING WITH DYNAMITE IF YOU AGREED TO A MEETING! WE URGENTLY ADVISE YOU TO IGNORE HIS PLEAS AND FIND A NEW, TRUE HEART INTEREST.

HERE'S AN INTERESTING LETTER FROM CLEVELAND, OHIO.

Dear Editors,

I was married to my wife for one year, then we separated and she told me she was going to begin divorce proceedings. I returned to my home a month ago to find new work and to try to accustom myself to living without her. Now she writes that she wants to see me and talk things over. She said nothing of our divorce. I love her very much but she is emotionally unstable, and I'm beginning to feel that in the long run I'd be better off without her. What should I do?

J.B.A.

DEAR J.B.A.

IF YOU TRULY LOVE YOUR WIFE, AND THERE IS A CHANCE OF RECONCILIATION, DON'T GIVE UP! A YEAR IS A SHORT TIME IN WHICH TO JUDGE YOUR MARRIAGE. PERHAPS YOU WERE THE CAUSE OF HER "EMOTIONAL INSTABILITY." WOMEN NEED CONSTANT REASSURANCE OF THEIR HUSBANDS' LOVE...

YOU BOTH HAVE UNDOUBTEDLY MADE MISTAKES, BUT NOW YOU'VE HAD TIME TO COOL OFF AND CONSIDER YOUR LIFE TOGETHER. SEARCH YOUSELF. IF YOU HAVE ANY LOVE LEFT FOR HER, GO BACK--AND TRY AGAIN!

WE LOVE TO RECEIVE YOUR LETTERS... TO CONSIDER YOUR PROBLEMS... AND TRY TO HELP YOU SOLVE THEM. WRITE US TODAY!

***MY OWN ROMANCE
SUITE 1404
350 FIFTH AVENUE
NEW YORK 1, NEW YORK***

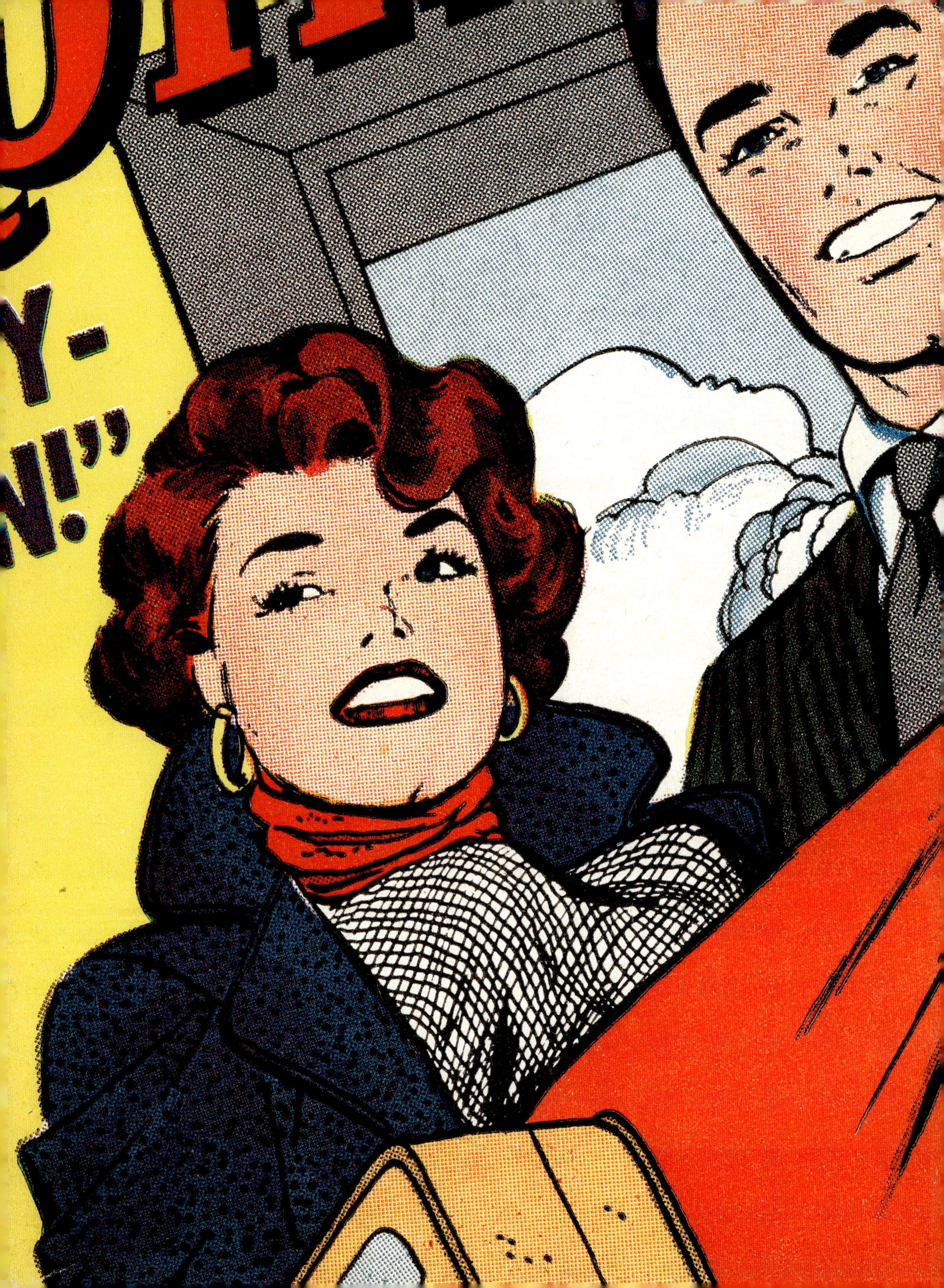

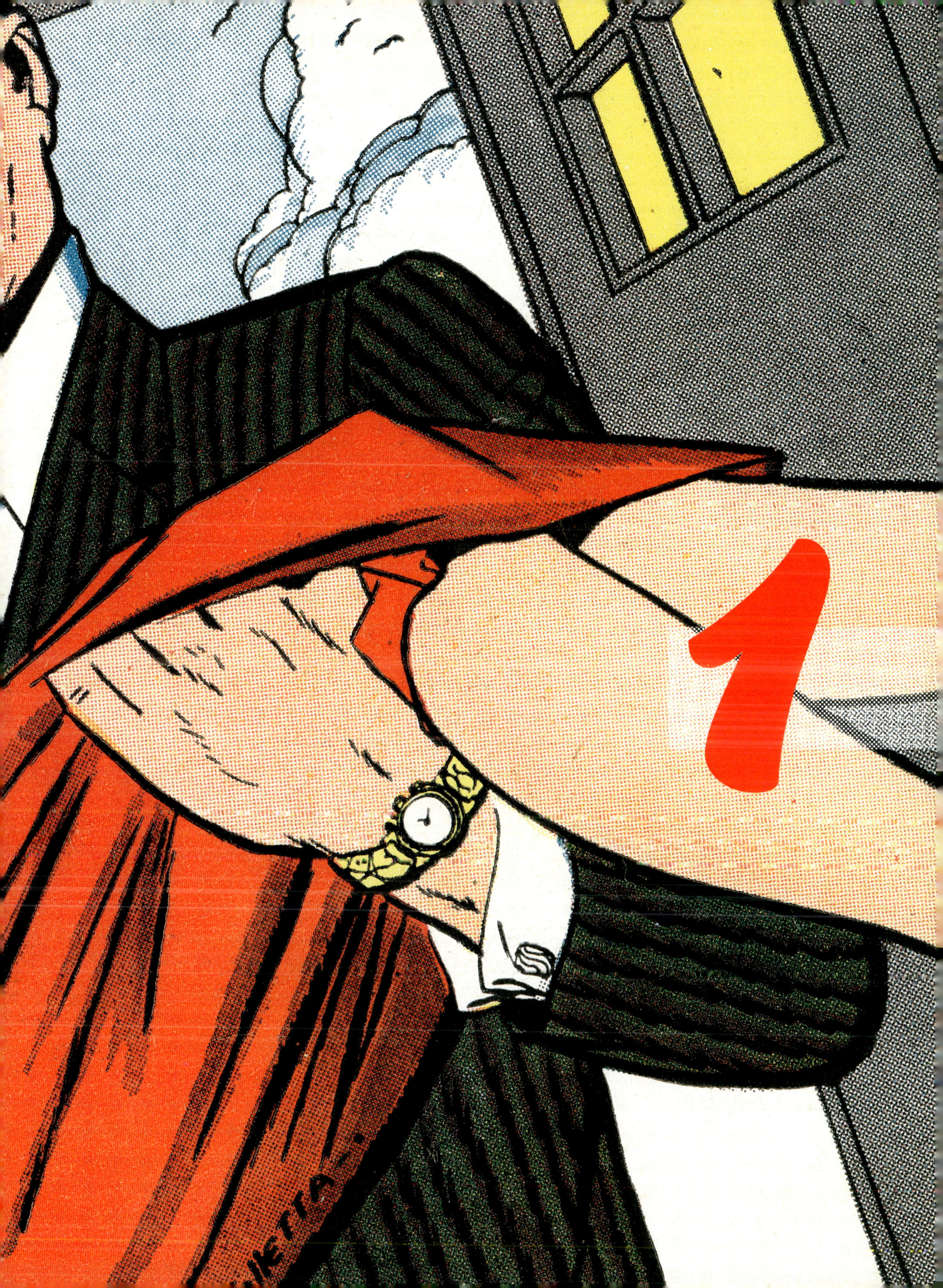
1

With Open Arms!

BLISS

THERE IS A TIME in every romance when both lovers are in complete accord, with the world perfectly aligned in every respect, as if the cosmos has no greater concern than to synchronize its billions of moving pieces to ensure that the absolute perfection of a young couple's love can be sustained to infinity—and beyond!

Now, those of us with a little bit of experience know that the real duration of that perfect state lasts for approximately a half hour in the middle of the night. Or maybe one particular morning. After that, the Love Boat may start to collide with some shoals. Then, inevitably, it begins to take on water, and that's when the bailing begins in earnest. But the wonderful thing about romance comics is that in their pages time can be made to stand still so that those precious few moments of bliss can be suspended, to feel as if they are lasting an eternity—or at least as long as it takes to renew your driver's license. In this section are a number of covers and stories that capture the very moment of joyful wedding unions, several weeks before the invoices from the caterer, the florist, and the jazz quartet (among others too numerous to mention) arrive, marking the beginning of a new stage of eternity. Here, too, are depictions of more than a few engagement celebrations—after all, one must take bliss wherever one can find it, and as often as one can.

Did all these hard-won engagements lead to marriage in the lives of those characters? Nothing of the sort. And did all those happy comic-book couples whose engagements led to a marriage ceremony remain in a blissful state forever and ever—amen? Please. We all know better than that.

Fortunately, the seven or eight pages allotted to most of the stories means there was only so much each tale could even aspire to portray. Sometimes it was full-on bliss. Sometimes it was post-bliss. And sometimes it was the absolute dregs of despair. These themes are all well represented in the pages of *Agonizing Love*—we don't call it "agonizing" for nothing!

But first, we want you to warm up with these happy images—all the better to pull the rug out from under you a bit later. So here comes "I'll Never Forget You!" "His Kiss!" "Madly in Love!" and "Forever After!" to transport you. (Just remember to pack your exclamation points for the honeymoon!!!)

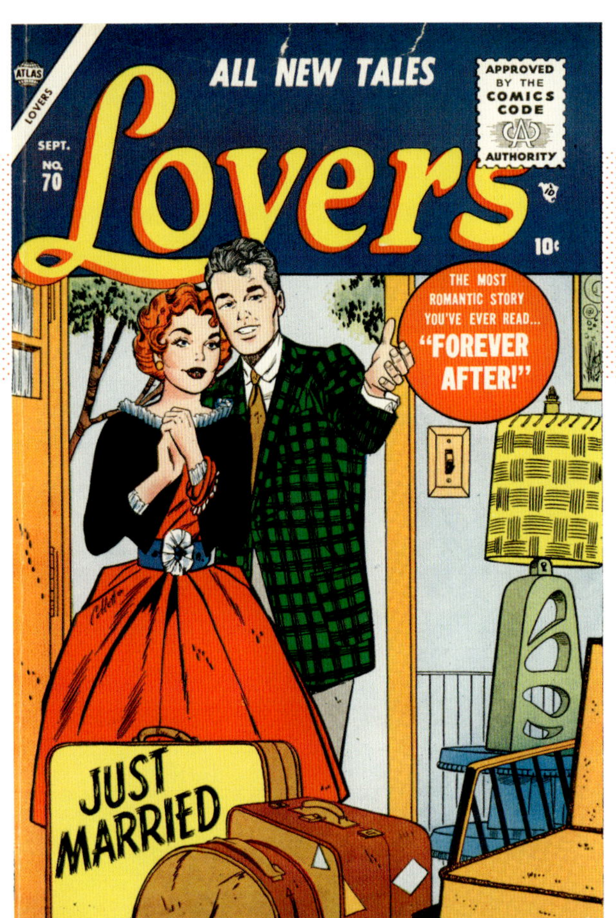
ALL NEW TALES
APPROVED BY THE COMICS CODE AUTHORITY
SEPT.
NO. 70
Lovers
10¢
THE MOST ROMANTIC STORY YOU'VE EVER READ... "FOREVER AFTER!"
JUST MARRIED

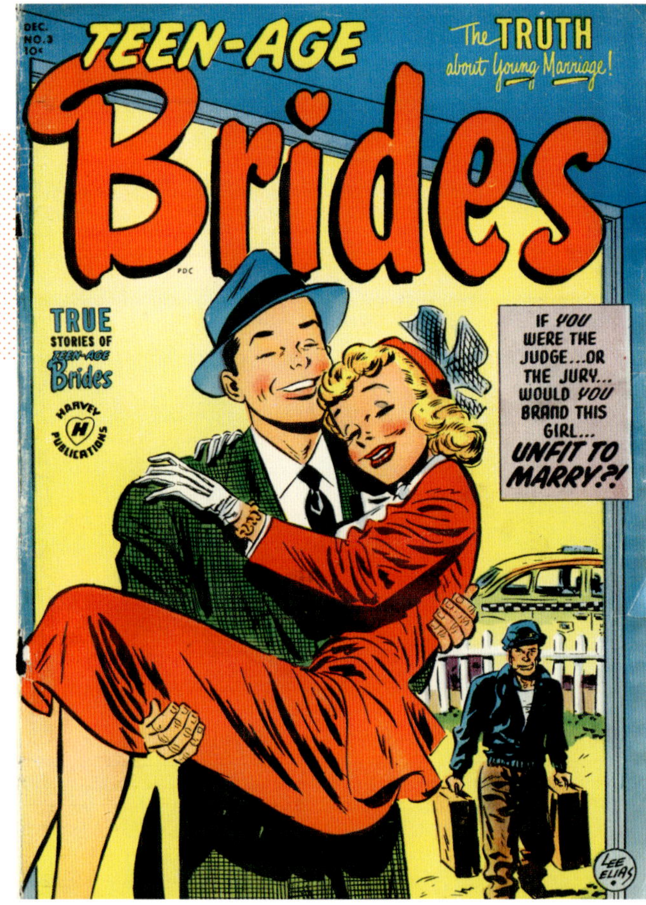
DEC. NO. 3 10¢
TEEN-AGE
Brides
The TRUTH about Young Marriage!
TRUE STORIES OF TEEN-AGE Brides
HARVEY PUBLICATIONS
IF YOU WERE THE JUDGE...OR THE JURY... WOULD YOU BRAND THIS GIRL... UNFIT TO MARRY?!

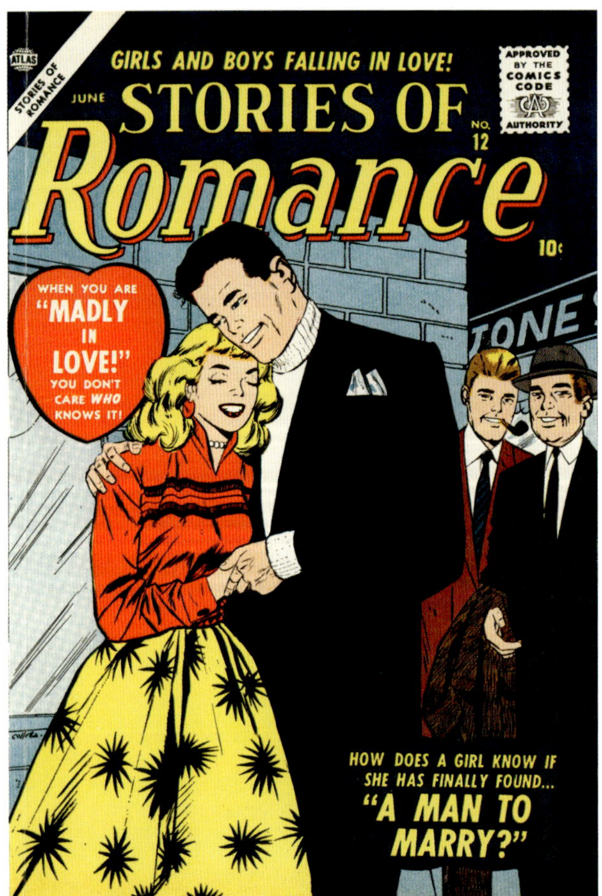
GIRLS AND BOYS FALLING IN LOVE!
APPROVED BY THE COMICS CODE AUTHORITY
JUNE
STORIES OF
NO. 12
Romance
10¢
WHEN YOU ARE "MADLY IN LOVE!" YOU DON'T CARE WHO KNOWS IT!
HOW DOES A GIRL KNOW IF SHE HAS FINALLY FOUND... "A MAN TO MARRY?"

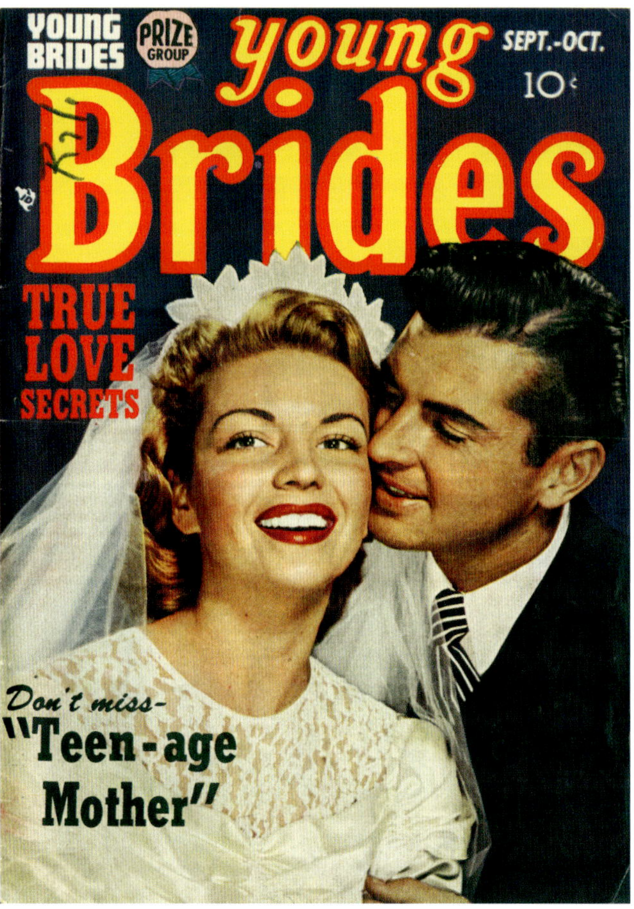
YOUNG BRIDES
PRIZE GROUP
young
SEPT.-OCT.
10¢
Brides
TRUE LOVE SECRETS
Don't miss-
"Teen-age Mother"

"HE TAUGHT ME HOUSEKEEPING; WHEN I DIVORCE I KEEP THE HOUSE."
— ZSA ZSA GABOR

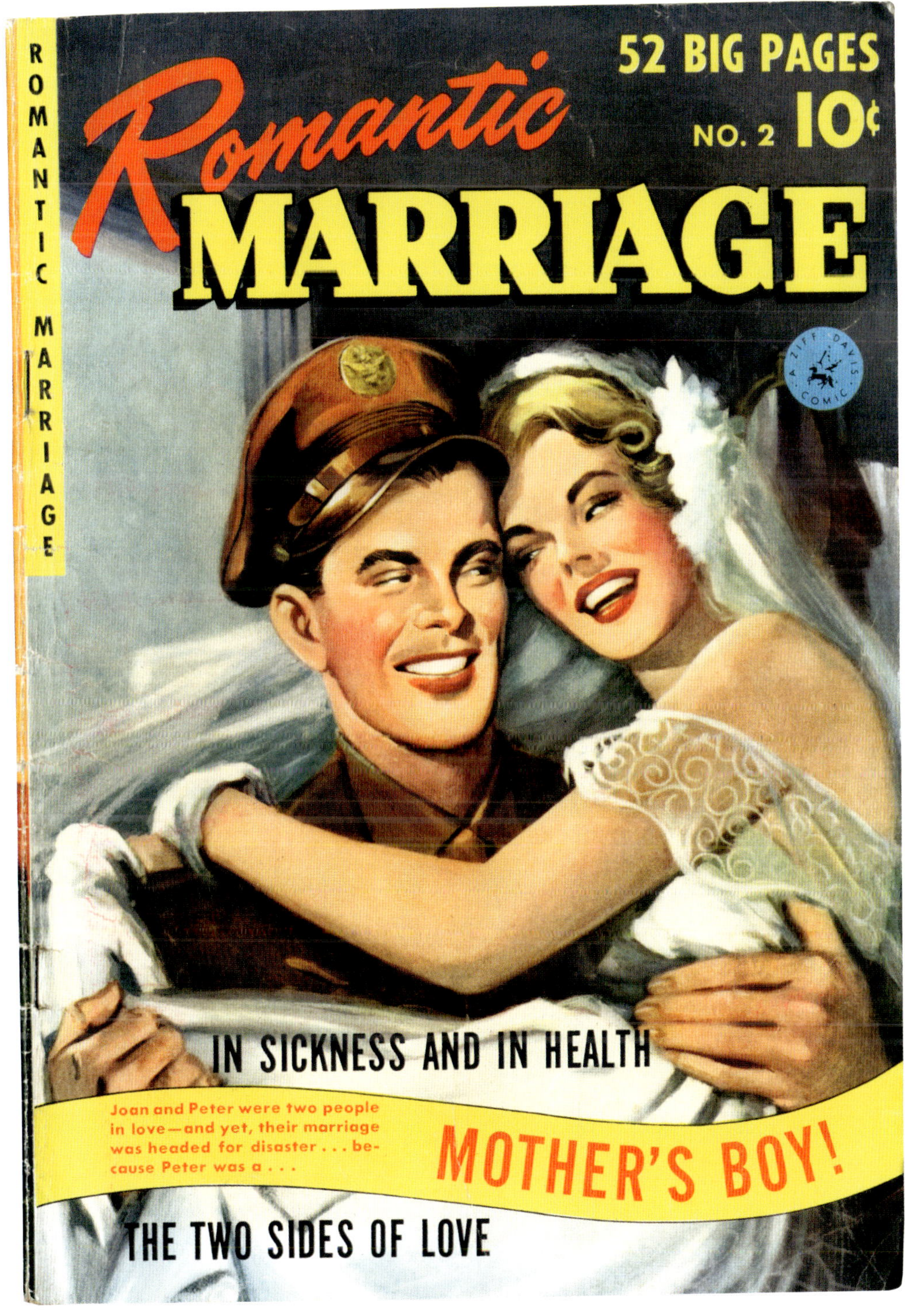

Pages 18–19: **STORIES OF ROMANCE** #9, December 1956, cover detail

Page 22, clockwise from top left: **LOVERS** #70, September 1955

TEEN-AGE BRIDES #3, December 1953

YOUNG BRIDES #1, September–October 1952

STORIES OF ROMANCE #12, June 1957

This page: **ROMANTIC MARRIAGE** #2, 1950

Below, from left to right:
TRUE TALES OF LOVE
#27, December 1956

LOVE ROMANCES
#52, October 1955

Page 25:
MY OWN ROMANCE
#53, August 1956, cover detail

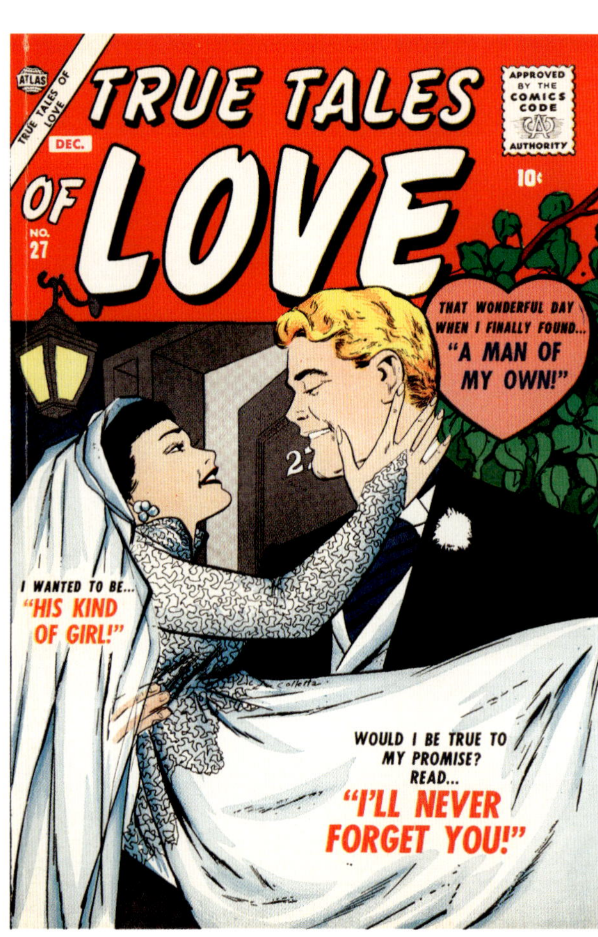

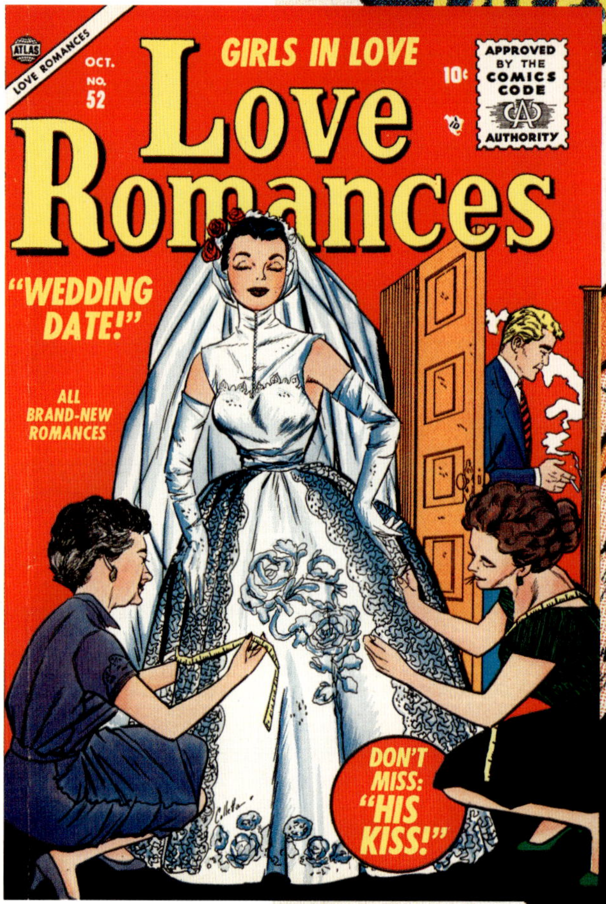

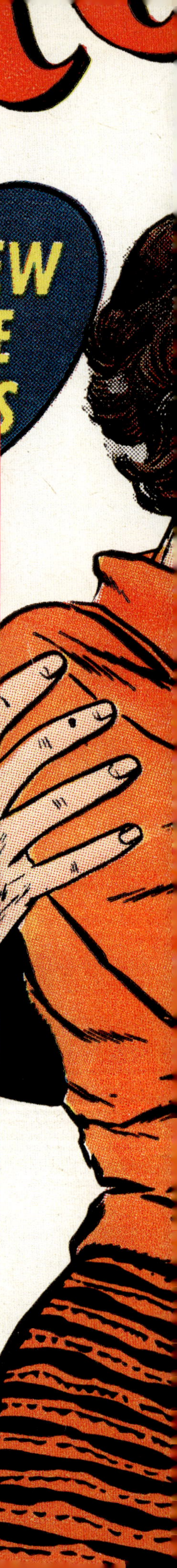

"TO KEEP YOUR MARRIAGE BRIMMING WITH LOVE IN THE LOVING CUP, WHENEVER YOU'RE WRONG, ADMIT IT, WHENEVER YOU'RE RIGHT, SHUT UP."
— OGDEN NASH

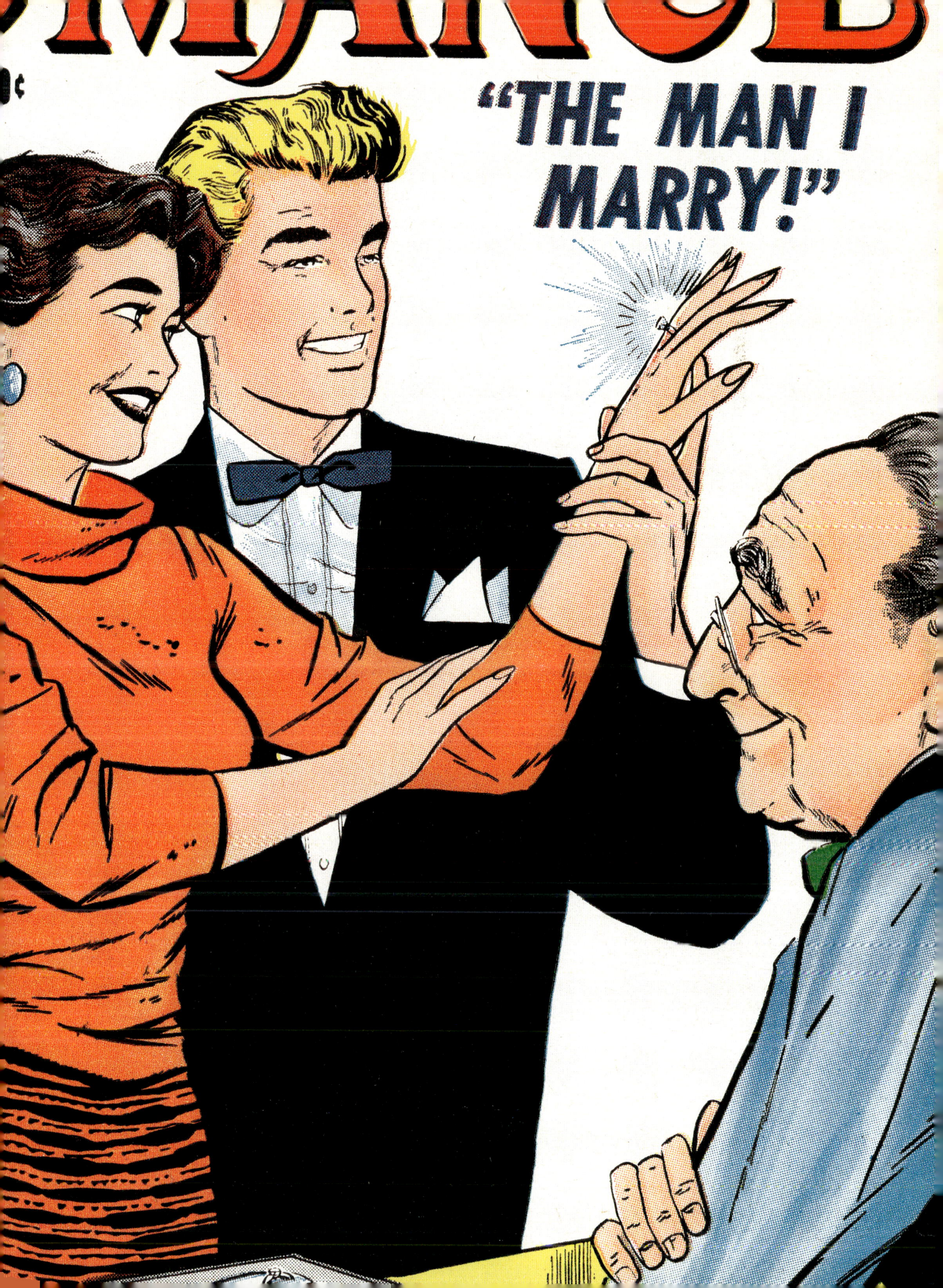
"THE MAN I MARRY!"

LOVE LETTERS

BE POPULAR WITH THE OPPOSITE SEX

BY DEVELOPING A GOOD CHARACTER!

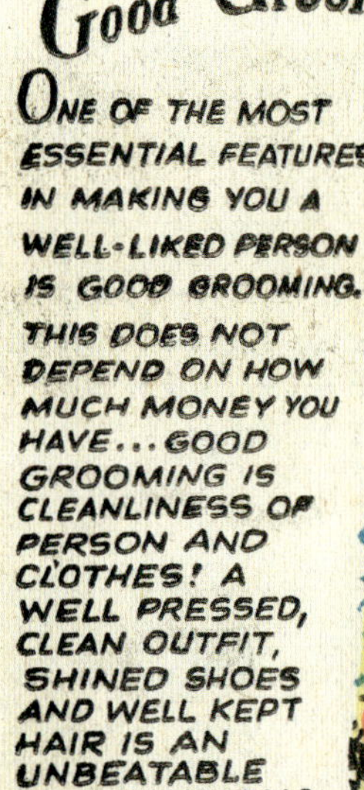

Good Grooming!

ONE OF THE MOST ESSENTIAL FEATURES IN MAKING YOU A WELL-LIKED PERSON IS GOOD GROOMING. THIS DOES NOT DEPEND ON HOW MUCH MONEY YOU HAVE... GOOD GROOMING IS CLEANLINESS OF PERSON AND CLOTHES! A WELL PRESSED, CLEAN OUTFIT, SHINED SHOES AND WELL KEPT HAIR IS AN UNBEATABLE COMBINATION!

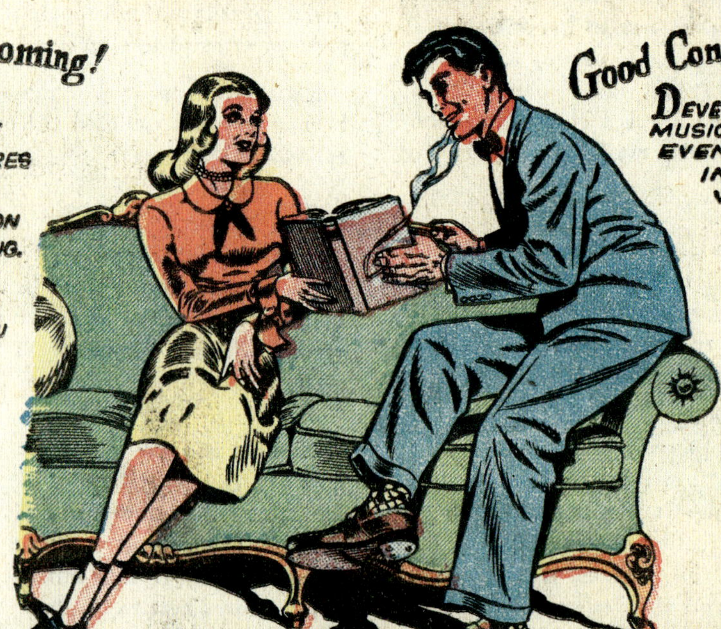

Good Conversation!

DEVELOP A LIKING FOR MUSIC, ARTS, CURRENT EVENTS ETC.... A KEEN INTEREST IN THESE WILL SHARPEN YOUR MIND AND FURNISH YOU WITH A VAST RESERVOIR OF GOOD TOPICS FOR CONVERSATION... TOO OFTEN LACK OF SOMETHING TO TALK ABOUT HAS RUINED MANY A PROSPECTIVE ROMANCE... EVEN MANY A MARRIAGE HAS BEEN RUINED BY SUCH BOREDOM.

CULTURE IS A NECESSARY REQUISITE FOR SUCCESS IN ALL WALKS OF LIFE!

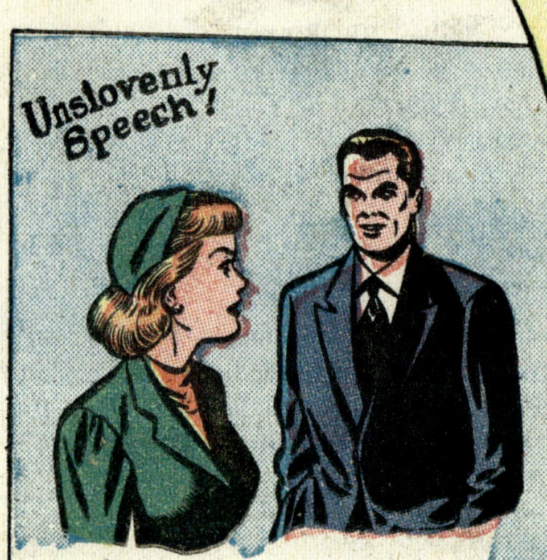

Unslovenly Speech!

YOUR DICTION AND VOCABULARY BRAND YOU! SLOVENLY SPEECH MARKS YOU AS A BOORISH, UNEDUCATED PERSON... A SHRILL VOICE IN A GIRL OR A LOUD BOISTEROUS VOICE IN A BOY ARE THE MOST OFFENSIVE MANNERS OF SPEECH... AND INDICATES A SLOPPY CHARACTER!

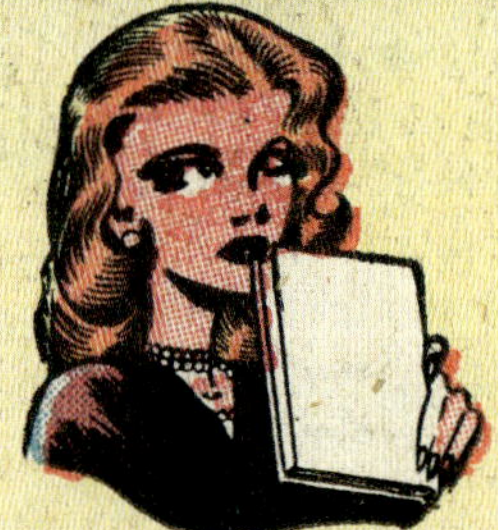

Attend church regularly! Nothing molds character like religion.. A strong belief and faithful interest in your religion is the greatest comfort in times of stress... "There are no athiests in foxholes"--- a statement out of the past war is very true!

DON'T BECOME A PATHOLOGICAL LIAR... DON'T MAKE DATES AND BREAK THEM... BE HONEST WITH YOURSELF AS WELL AS WITH OTHERS!

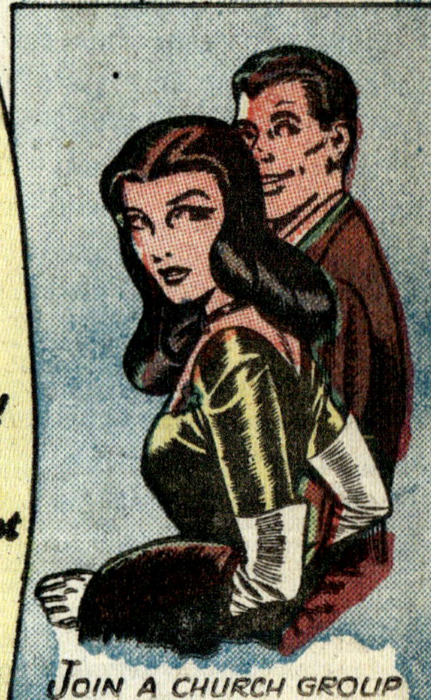

JOIN A CHURCH GROUP FOR WHOLESOME COMPANIONSHIP.. HERE YOU'LL AVOID THE UNDESIRABLE CROWD OFTEN FOUND IN LOW ORDER SOCIAL CLUBS! THE PEOPLE YOU ASSOCIATE WITH CAN INFLUENCE YOUR ENTIRE FUTURE...

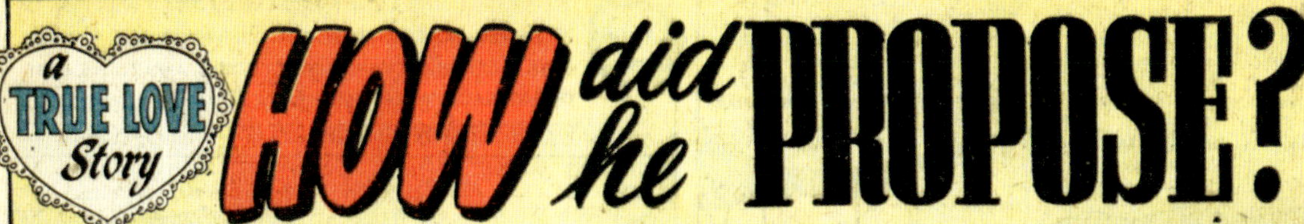

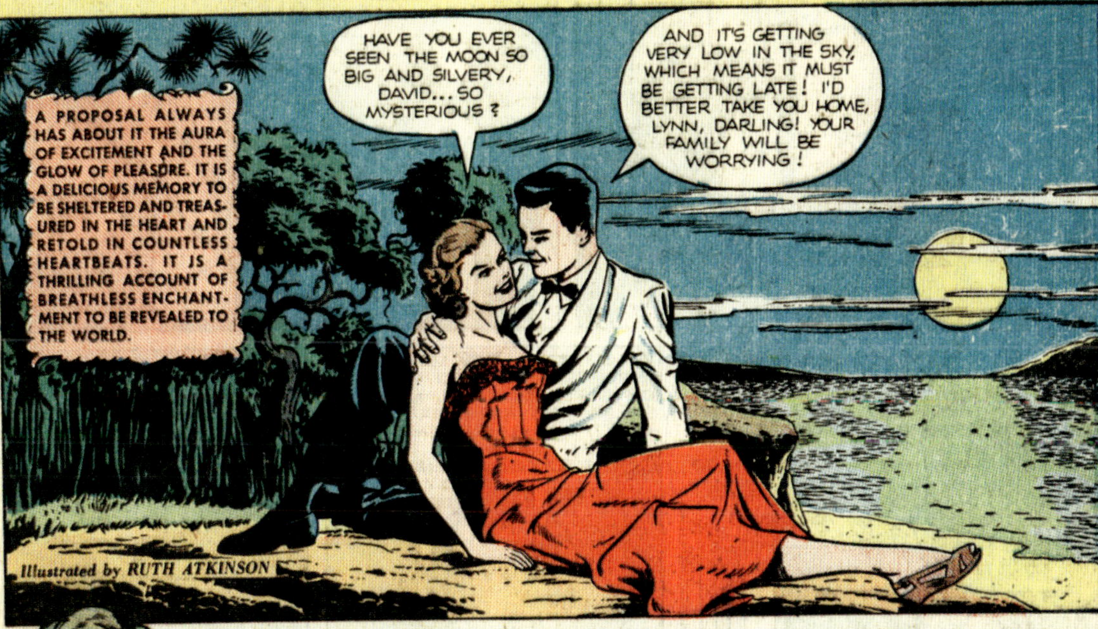

THE INSTANT I MET DAVID DILLON I KNEW HE WAS THE ONE MAN IN THE WORLD FOR ME. AND I KNEW HE LOVED ME, TOO, FOR SOON AFTER WE MET HE STOPPED GOING OUT WITH OTHER GIRLS. EVERYTHING SEEMED PERFECT, EXCEPT FOR ONE THING—NOT ONCE IN ALL THE MONTHS WE DATED HAD HE EVER SPOKEN OF MARRIAGE. ON EACH DATE I WOULD HOPE FOR THOSE ALL-IMPORTANT WORDS, BUT IN VAIN.

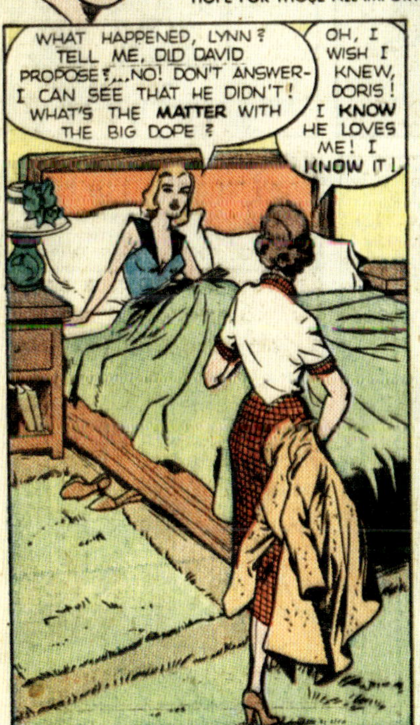

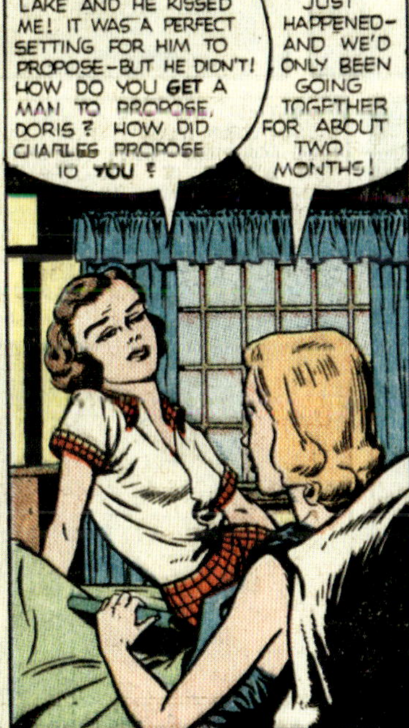

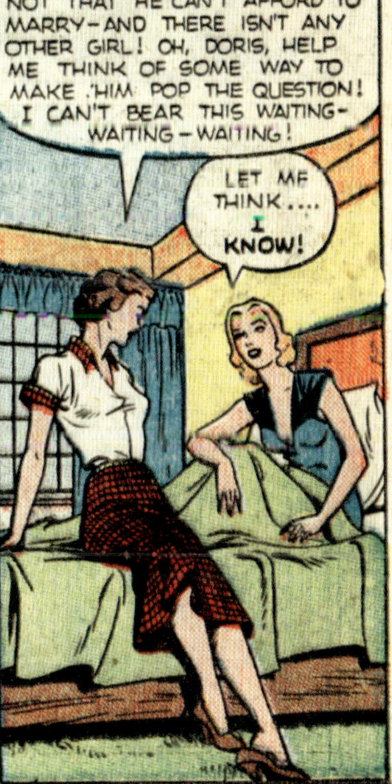

Page 26:
LOVE LETTERS
#9, May 1951

This page:
LOVERS' LANE
#3, February 1950

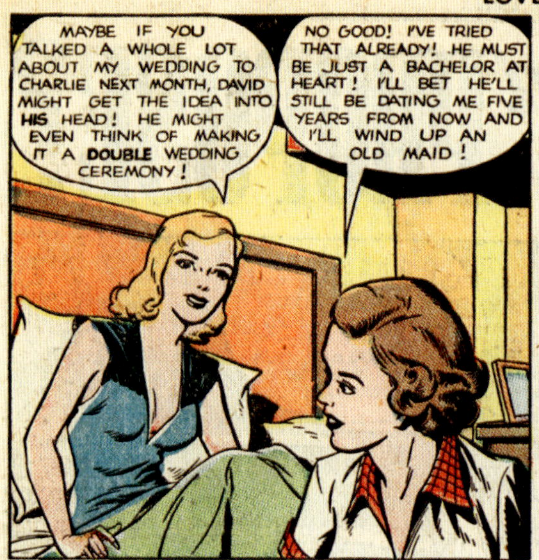
MAYBE IF YOU TALKED A WHOLE LOT ABOUT MY WEDDING TO CHARLIE NEXT MONTH, DAVID MIGHT GET THE IDEA INTO **HIS** HEAD! HE MIGHT EVEN THINK OF MAKING IT A **DOUBLE** WEDDING CEREMONY!
NO GOOD! I'VE TRIED THAT ALREADY! HE MUST BE JUST A BACHELOR AT HEART! I'LL BET HE'LL STILL BE DATING ME FIVE YEARS FROM NOW AND I'LL WIND UP AN OLD MAID!

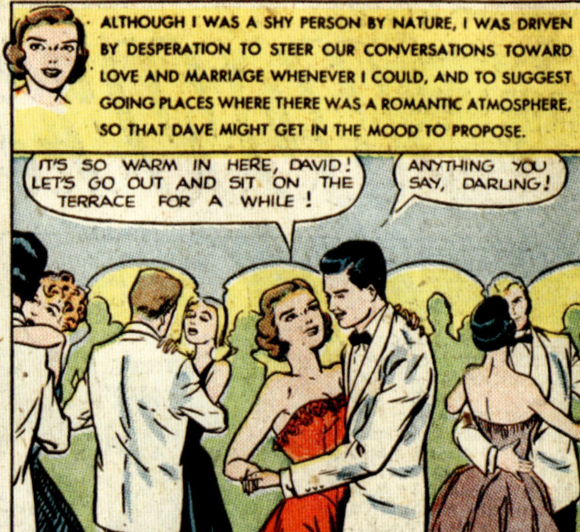
ALTHOUGH I WAS A SHY PERSON BY NATURE, I WAS DRIVEN BY DESPERATION TO STEER OUR CONVERSATIONS TOWARD LOVE AND MARRIAGE WHENEVER I COULD, AND TO SUGGEST GOING PLACES WHERE THERE WAS A ROMANTIC ATMOSPHERE, SO THAT DAVE MIGHT GET IN THE MOOD TO PROPOSE.
IT'S SO WARM IN HERE, DAVID! LET'S GO OUT AND SIT ON THE TERRACE FOR A WHILE!
ANYTHING YOU SAY, DARLING!

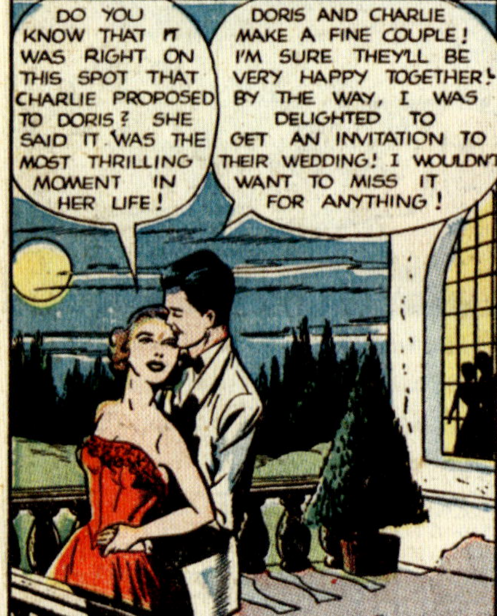
DO YOU KNOW THAT IT WAS RIGHT ON THIS SPOT THAT CHARLIE PROPOSED TO DORIS? SHE SAID IT WAS THE MOST THRILLING MOMENT IN HER LIFE!
DORIS AND CHARLIE MAKE A FINE COUPLE! I'M SURE THEY'LL BE VERY HAPPY TOGETHER! BY THE WAY, I WAS DELIGHTED TO GET AN INVITATION TO THEIR WEDDING! I WOULDN'T WANT TO MISS IT FOR ANYTHING!

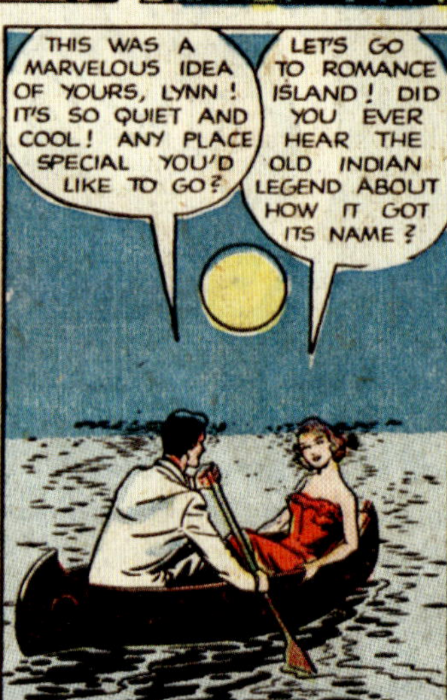
THIS WAS A MARVELOUS IDEA OF YOURS, LYNN! IT'S SO QUIET AND COOL! ANY PLACE SPECIAL YOU'D LIKE TO GO?
LET'S GO TO ROMANCE ISLAND! DID YOU EVER HEAR THE OLD INDIAN LEGEND ABOUT HOW IT GOT ITS NAME?

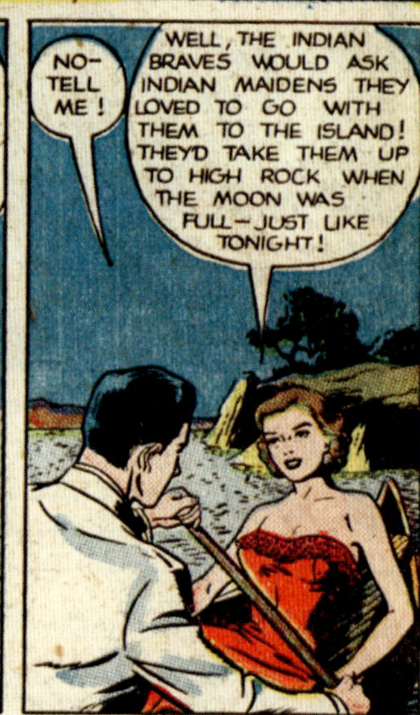
NO- TELL ME!
WELL, THE INDIAN BRAVES WOULD ASK INDIAN MAIDENS THEY LOVED TO GO WITH THEM TO THE ISLAND! THEY'D TAKE THEM UP TO HIGH ROCK WHEN THE MOON WAS FULL—JUST LIKE TONIGHT!

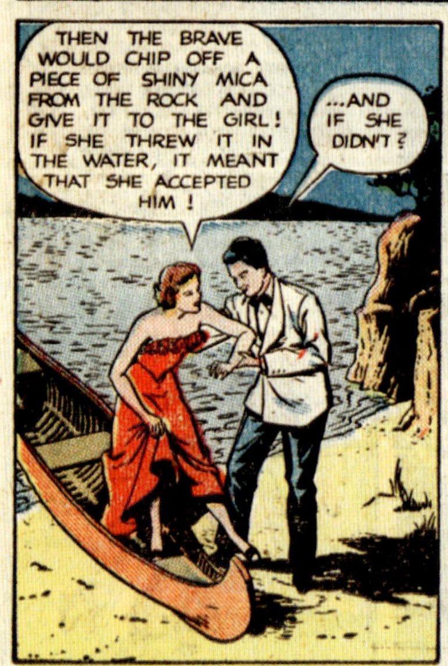
THEN THE BRAVE WOULD CHIP OFF A PIECE OF SHINY MICA FROM THE ROCK AND GIVE IT TO THE GIRL! IF SHE THREW IT IN THE WATER, IT MEANT THAT SHE ACCEPTED HIM!
...AND IF SHE DIDN'T?

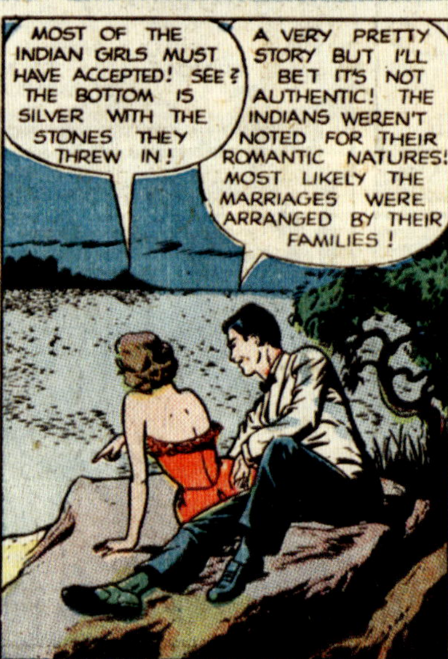
MOST OF THE INDIAN GIRLS MUST HAVE ACCEPTED! SEE? THE BOTTOM IS SILVER WITH THE STONES THEY THREW IN!
A VERY PRETTY STORY BUT I'LL BET IT'S NOT AUTHENTIC! THE INDIANS WEREN'T NOTED FOR THEIR ROMANTIC NATURES! MOST LIKELY THE MARRIAGES WERE ARRANGED BY THEIR FAMILIES!

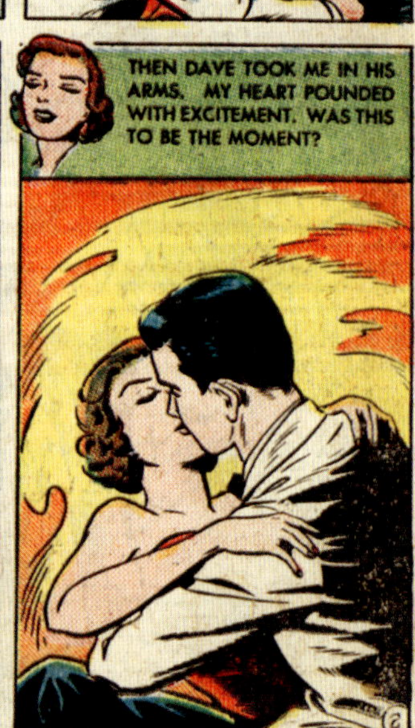
THEN DAVE TOOK ME IN HIS ARMS. MY HEART POUNDED WITH EXCITEMENT. WAS THIS TO BE THE MOMENT?
2

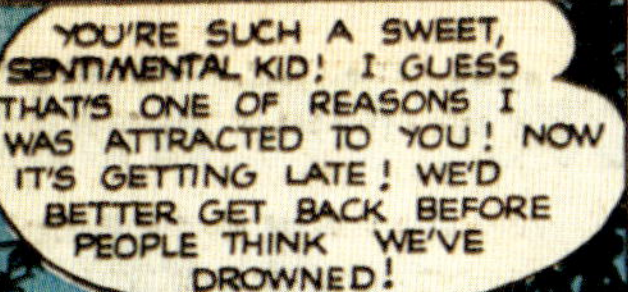
YOU'RE SUCH A SWEET, SENTIMENTAL KID! I GUESS THAT'S ONE OF REASONS I WAS ATTRACTED TO YOU! NOW IT'S GETTING LATE! WE'D BETTER GET BACK BEFORE PEOPLE THINK WE'VE DROWNED!
SO SOON! WE-WE JUST GOT HERE!

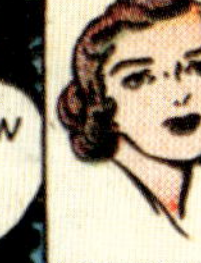
FINALLY THE DAY OF DORIS' WEDDING ARRIVED. I FELT HAPPY FOR HER, BUT OTHERWISE THE OCCASION MADE ME FEEL SAD. WHY COULDN'T I BE GETTING MARRIED, TOO?

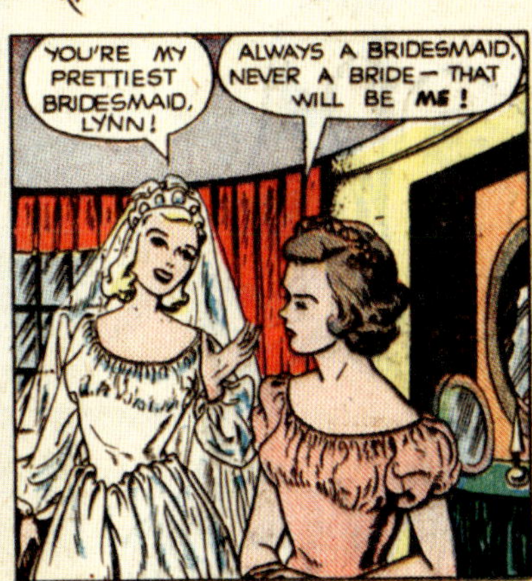
YOU'RE MY PRETTIEST BRIDESMAID, LYNN!
ALWAYS A BRIDESMAID, NEVER A BRIDE—THAT WILL BE ME!

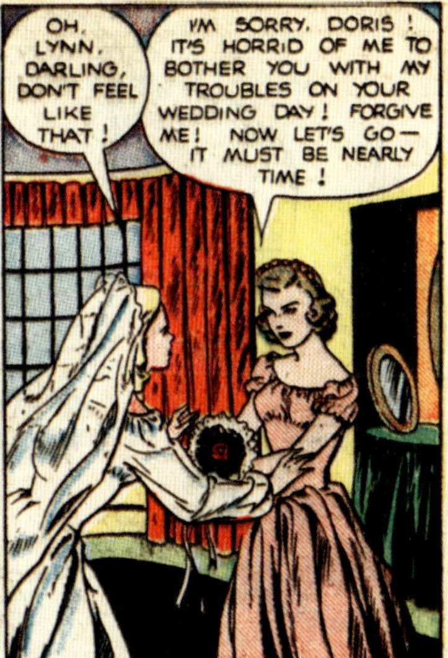
OH, LYNN, DARLING, DON'T FEEL LIKE THAT!
I'M SORRY, DORIS! IT'S HORRID OF ME TO BOTHER YOU WITH MY TROUBLES ON YOUR WEDDING DAY! FORGIVE ME! NOW LET'S GO—IT MUST BE NEARLY TIME!

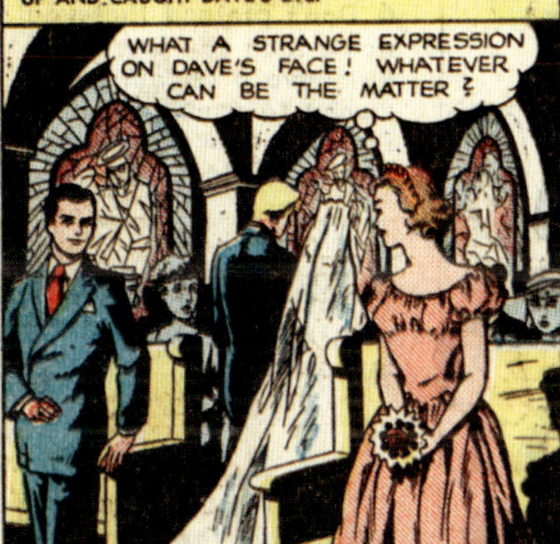
DORIS' WEDDING WAS BEAUTIFUL. I ALMOST FELT LIKE CRYING WHEN I HEARD THE LOW VOICES OF CHARLIE AND DORIS SAYING "I DO!" AND THEN IT WAS OVER AND THEY WERE GOING UP THE AISLE TOGETHER. I LOOKED UP AND CAUGHT DAVE'S EYE.
WHAT A STRANGE EXPRESSION ON DAVE'S FACE! WHATEVER CAN BE THE MATTER?
LYNN! LYNN, I MUST TALK TO YOU—NOW! THIS VERY MINUTE!
NOW? BUT CAN'T YOU WAIT TILL WE LEAVE THE CHURCH?

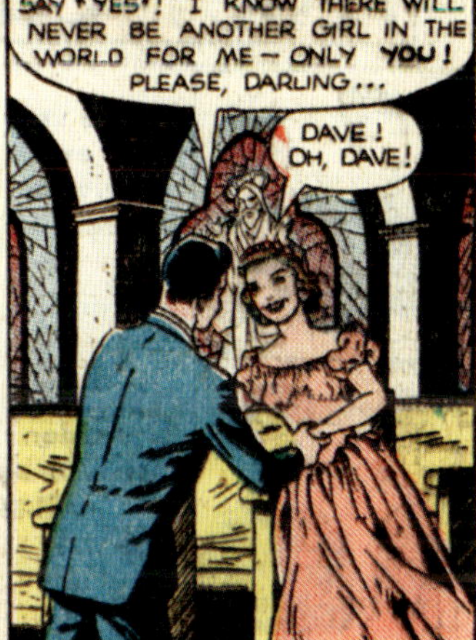
THIS CAN'T WAIT! LYNN DARLING, I LOVE YOU! I WANT YOU TO MARRY ME! YOU MUST SAY "YES!" I KNOW THERE WILL NEVER BE ANOTHER GIRL IN THE WORLD FOR ME—ONLY YOU! PLEASE, DARLING...
DAVE! OH, DAVE!

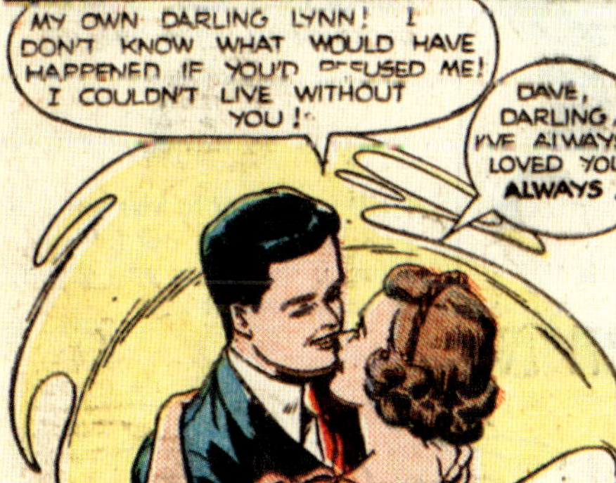
I COULD SCARCELY ANSWER DAVE! I COULDN'T BELIEVE MY EARS! DAVE HAD PROPOSED TO ME! SUDDENLY—AND WITHOUT ANY WARNING—HE'D UTTERED THE WORDS I'D BEEN HOPING AND DREAMING HE'D SAY. WEAKLY I ANSWERED AND HE CRUSHED ME IN HIS ARMS.
MY OWN DARLING LYNN! I DON'T KNOW WHAT WOULD HAVE HAPPENED IF YOU'D REFUSED ME! I COULDN'T LIVE WITHOUT YOU!
DAVE, DARLING, I'VE ALWAYS LOVED YOU! ALWAYS!
BUT, WHY—HOW—HOW DID YOU HAPPEN TO PROPOSE TO ME AT THIS TIME? WHAT MADE YOU DO IT SO SUDDENLY?
DARLING, WHEN I SAW YOU IN THE CHURCH, LOOKING ALMOST LIKE A BRIDE YOURSELF, I BEGAN TO IMAGINE IT WAS YOU AND I STANDING IN FRONT OF THE MINISTER! I COULD HARDLY WAIT TO ASK YOU TO BE MY BRIDE!
...AND THAT IS HOW DAVE PROPOSED TO ME!

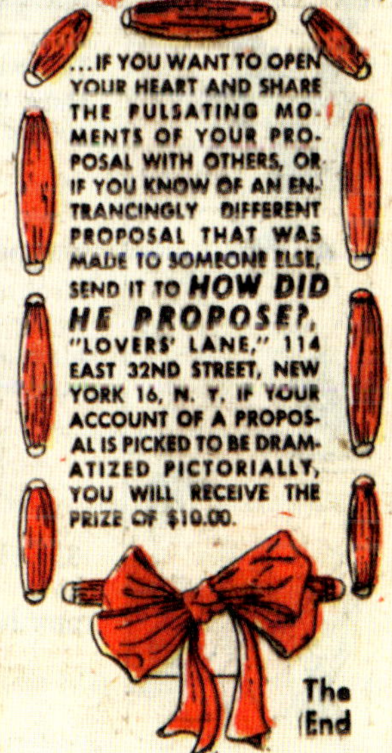
...IF YOU WANT TO OPEN YOUR HEART AND SHARE THE PULSATING MOMENTS OF YOUR PROPOSAL WITH OTHERS, OR IF YOU KNOW OF AN ENTRANCINGLY DIFFERENT PROPOSAL THAT WAS MADE TO SOMEONE ELSE, SEND IT TO HOW DID HE PROPOSE?, "LOVERS' LANE," 114 EAST 32ND STREET, NEW YORK 16, N. Y. IF YOUR ACCOUNT OF A PROPOSAL IS PICKED TO BE DRAMATIZED PICTORIALLY, YOU WILL RECEIVE THE PRIZE OF $10.00.
The End

ARE YOU READY FOR MARRIAGE?
A Game of MAKE-BELIEVE

OF COURSE YOU WANT TO MARRY! IT'S YOUR CONSTANT DREAM, YOUR DESIRE FOR THE FUTURE! WELL, LET'S PRETEND THAT THE MAN OF YOUR DREAMS IS REALLY YOURS, THAT THE HONEYMOON IS OVER, AND YOU AND YOUR HUSBAND ARE STARTING OUT ON THE ROAD TO A HAPPY MARRIAGE! NOW THERE'S THE CATCH! ARE YOU, AS A NEW BRIDE, MATURE ENOUGH AND UNDERSTANDING ENOUGH TO MAKE THE KIND OF WIFE YOUR HUSBAND DESIRES? WILL YOU HELP HIM IN HIS CAREER—OR HINDER HIM? WILL YOU BUILD A HAPPY HOME—OR A BROKEN ONE? THAT'S WHAT YOU WANT TO KNOW—AND HERE IS YOUR ANSWER, IN THIS THOUGHT-PROVOKING QUIZ! HERE ARE TEN SITUATIONS THAT YOU WILL ALMOST INEVITABLY FACE AT ONE TIME OR ANOTHER! THERE ARE THREE POSSIBLE SOLUTIONS FOR EACH PROBLEM! CHOOSE THE ONE YOU THINK IS RIGHT, ADD UP YOUR SCORE, THEN TURN THE PAGE UPSIDE-DOWN TO SEE WHETHER YOU ARE READY FOR MARRIAGE!

DARLING, CAN'T YOU CUT **DOWN** ON OUR **EXPENSES** A **LITTLE** BIT ? LOOK! HERE'S A BILL FOR TWO NEW HATS!

I **NEVER** WOULD HAVE MARRIED YOU IF I'D THOUGHT YOU WERE GOING TO BE SO **STINGY**!

1

YOUR HUSBAND COMPLAINS ABOUT THE MONEY YOU ARE SPENDING, SO . . .

A. YOU START TO CRY AND CALL HIM AN OLD SKINFLINT!

B. YOU SAY, "DEAR, WHY DON'T WE START A BUDGET SO WE CAN SEE WHERE OUR MONEY GOES?"

C. YOU TELL HIM YOU'LL SEE WHAT YOU CAN DO—AND THEN GO TO YOUR FATHER SECRETLY FOR EXTRA SPENDING MONEY!

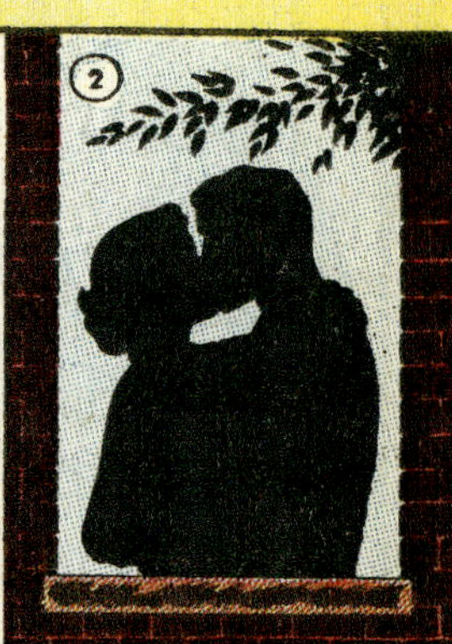

YOUR HUSBAND WHISPERS, "COME CLOSER, DARLING, AND LET ME TELL YOU HOW MUCH I LOVE YOU," AND YOU ANSWER . . .

A. "DON'T, YOU'RE MUSSING MY NEW HAIR-DO!

B. OF COURSE, DEAR! IT'S SO HEAVENLY TO BE TOGETHER!

C. I HAVEN'T GOT TIME FOR THAT SORT OF THING. I'VE GOT TO WASH THE DISHES."

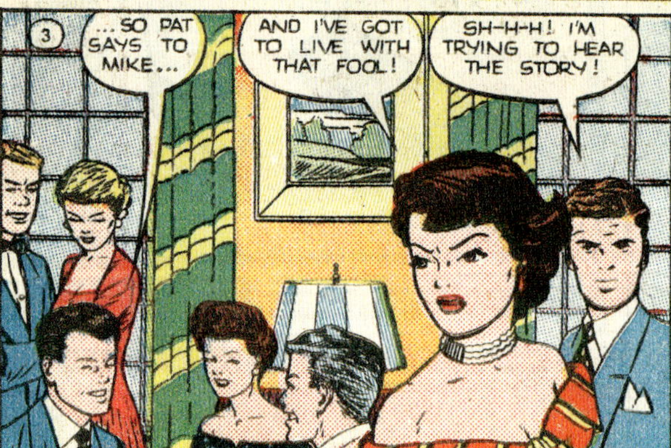

WHEN YOUR HUSBAND TELLS HIS FAVORITE, OFT-REPEATED JOKE TO YOUR GUESTS, DO YOU . . .

A. REMARK IN A STAGE WHISPER, "THERE HE GOES AGAIN! AND HE THINKS IT'S FUNNY!"

B. LEAD THE LAUGHTER AFTER THE STORY HAS BEEN TOLD!

C. INTERRUPT TO CORRECT HIM WHENEVER HE ISN'T TELLING THE STORY THE BEST WAY!

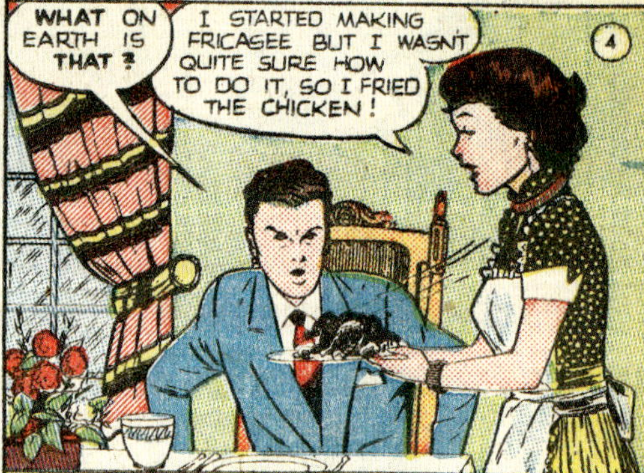

AFTER YOU'VE SLAVED FOR THREE HOURS PREPARING DINNER, YOUR HUSBAND SAYS! "BUT *THIS* ISN'T THE WAY MY *MOTHER* FIXED CHICKEN!" DO YOU SAY . . .

A. "WHY DON'T YOU GO BACK AND EAT HERS THEN!

B. I SPENT THREE HOURS IN THAT HOT KITCHEN FIXING THIS DINNER (SOB)—AND YOU DON'T EVEN APPRECIATE IT!

C. SHE'S A WONDERFUL COOK, DEAR! THE NEXT TIME I WRITE, I'LL ASK HER HOW *SHE* FIXES CHICKEN!"

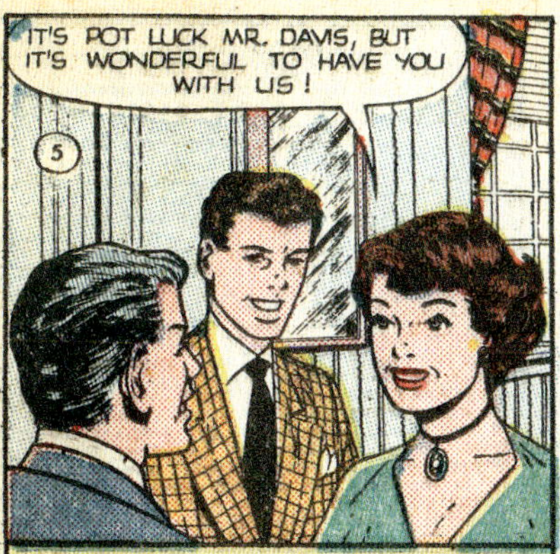

AT 5 P.M. YOUR HUSBAND PHONES TO SAY HE'S BRINGING AN IMPORTANT CUSTOMER HOME TO DINNER! YOU HAD PLANNED ON HASH, SO . . .

A. YOU TELL HIM TO CANCEL THE INVITATION!

B. YOU BLOW THE WEEK'S FOOD BUDGET, BY HAVING DINNER BROUGHT IN BY A CATERER!

C. YOU SHOW THE GUEST BOTH YOUR HOSPITALITY AND YOUR INGENUITY BY PREPARING DINNER FROM YOUR STOCK OF EASY-TO-PREPARE BUT DELICIOUS EMERGENCY RESERVES!

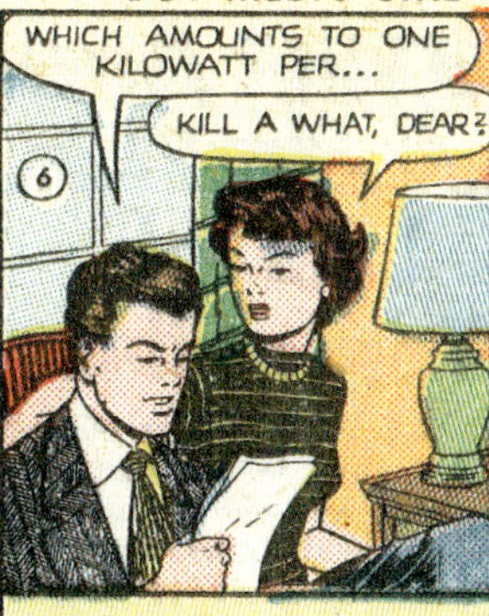

THE JOB YOUR HUSBAND HAS IS GREEK TO YOU, BUT WHEN HE STARTS TO TALK ABOUT WHAT HAPPENED DURING THE DAY . . .

A. YOU LISTEN SYMPATHETICALLY AND ASK A FEW INTELLIGENT QUESTIONS!

B. YOU GO TO THE KITCHEN, CALLING OVER YOUR SHOULDER, "SO YOU CLOSED THAT BIG DEAL—THAT DOESN'T GET THE DINNER ON THE TABLE!"

C. YOU PLAY DUMB BY ASKING CONSTANTLY, "WHAT DO YOU MEAN? WHAT'S A CONTRACT?"

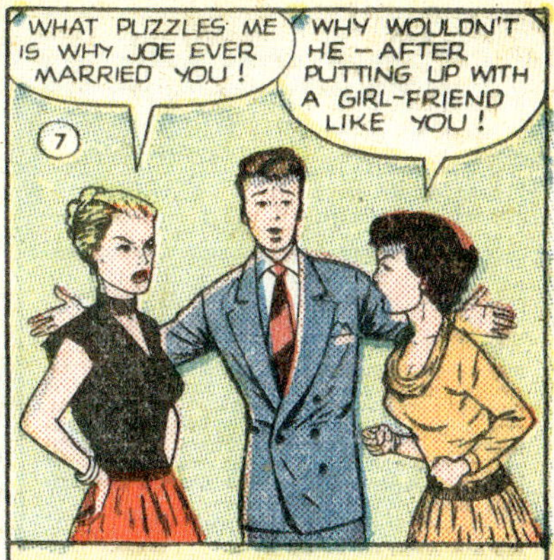

YOUR HUSBAND'S OLD FLAME ARRIVES IN TOWN! YOU *FIX HER* GOOSE BY . . .

A. INVITING HER TO YOUR HOUSE, THEN APPEARING AT YOUR CHARMING BEST IN DRESS AND MANNER.

B. REFUSING TO SEE HER—AND INTERFERING WITH YOUR HUSBAND'S DESIRE TO SEE HER FOR THE SAKE OF OLD TIMES!

C. SAYING, "I DON'T SEE HOW YOU COULD HAVE *EVER* GONE OUT WITH A BAG LIKE THAT!"

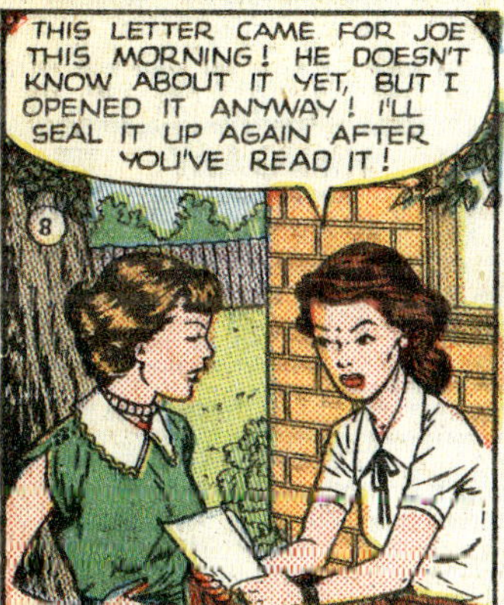

AN IMPORTANT LOOKING LETTER FOR YOUR HUSBAND ARRIVES! YOU'RE CURIOUS AND EXCITED, BUT DO YOU . . .

A. OPEN IT TO READ IT, THEN PUT IT BACK AND RESEAL IT?

B. PHONE YOUR HUSBAND TO TELL HIM THE LETTER HAS ARRIVED, THEN OPEN IT IF HE ASKS YOU TO?

C. OPEN IT, LEAVE IT ON THE HALL TABLE, THEN TELL YOUR NEXT DOOR NEIGHBOR ABOUT IT!

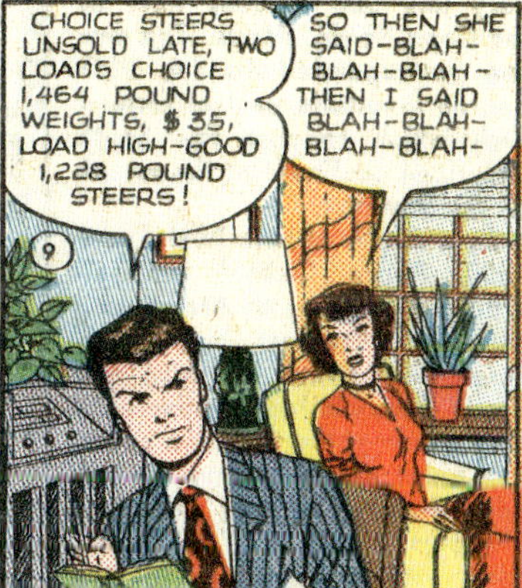

YOUR HUSBAND LIKES TO HEAR THE CATTLE REPORTS ON THE RADIO! THEY BORE YOU TO TEARS, SO . . .

A. WITHOUT A WORD, YOU FLICK OFF THE RADIO SWITCH!

B. YOU TRY TO INTEREST HIM IN SOME THING ELSE BY TALKING CONSTANTLY ON A WIDE VARIETY OF SUBJECTS!

C. YOU EITHER LISTEN QUIETLY, OR ELSE GO ABOUT OTHER JOBS IN THE HOUSE!

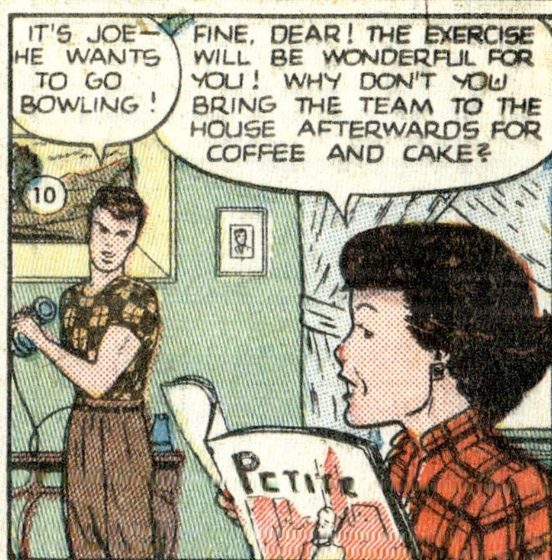

YOUR HUSBAND WOULD LIKE TO GO TO A STAG PARTY WITH THE BOYS NEXT TUESDAY, AND YOU TELL HIM . . .

A. "OF COURSE, DEAR! I MIGHT GO TO A MOVIE WITH MARGIE SO I WON'T MISS YOU TOO MUCH, IF THAT'S ALL RIGHT!

B. YOU DON'T LOVE ME ANY MORE! (SOB) YOU WANT TO LEAVE ME ALONE!

C. IF YOU LIKE THAT MOTH-EATEN GANG OF YOURS, GO RIGHT AHEAD!

IF YOU WANT TO KNOW WHETHER OR NOT YOU ARE READY FOR MARRIAGE, CHECK THE BOTTOM PANEL FOR YOUR SCORE. PLACE IN FRONT OF A MIRROR, READ IT AND YOU WILL GET YOUR ANSWER.

WHAT IS YOUR SCORE? IF YOU HAD THE CORRECT ANSWER 8 TIMES OUT OF 10, YOU DON'T HAVE TO WORRY—YOU'LL BE THE KIND OF A WONDERFUL WIFE A MAN NEEDS! FROM 6 TO 8, WATCH OUT! YOU'LL REALLY HAVE TO MAKE AN EFFORT IF YOU WANT TO HOLD YOUR HUSBAND! AND FOR ANY SCORE UNDER 6—YOU'D BETTER GROW UP! STEER CLEAR OF MARRIAGE UNTIL YOU'VE LEARNED TO SHARE, TO TRUST, TO LOVE!

HERE ARE THE CORRECT ANSWERS!

1 . . . . B
2 . . . . B
3 . . . . B
4 C
5 C
6 . . . . A
7 . . . . A
8 . . . . B
9 C
10 . . . A

BOY MEETS GIRL
#3, June 1950

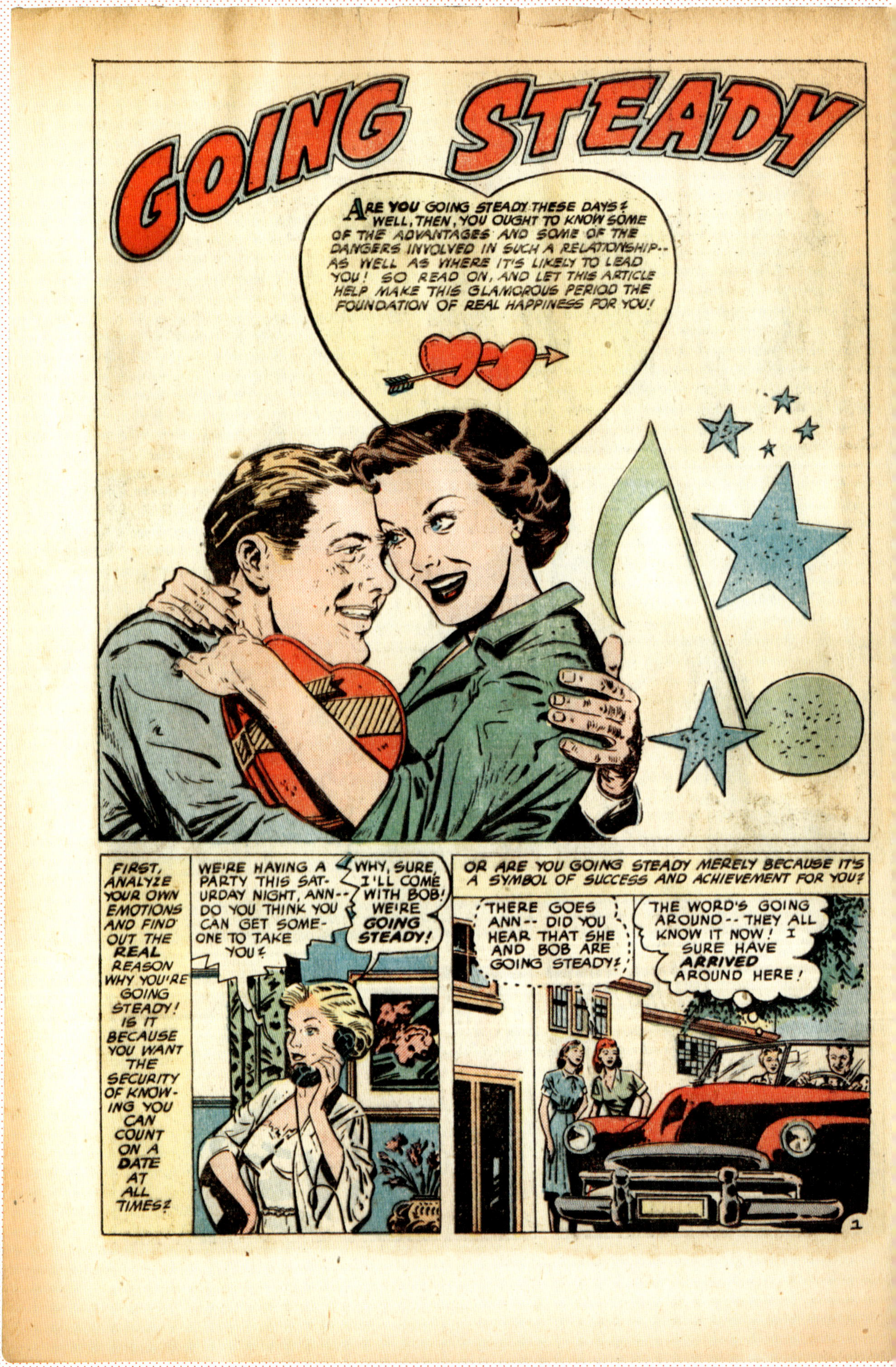

GOING STEADY

ARE YOU GOING STEADY THESE DAYS? WELL, THEN, YOU OUGHT TO KNOW SOME OF THE ADVANTAGES AND SOME OF THE DANGERS INVOLVED IN SUCH A RELATIONSHIP-- AS WELL AS WHERE IT'S LIKELY TO LEAD YOU! SO READ ON, AND LET THIS ARTICLE HELP MAKE THIS GLAMOROUS PERIOD THE FOUNDATION OF REAL HAPPINESS FOR YOU!

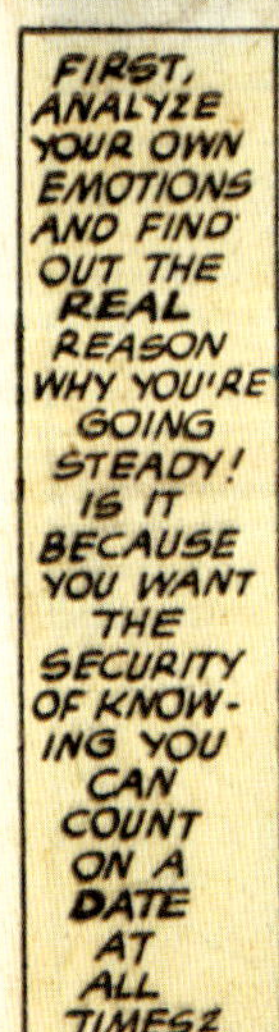

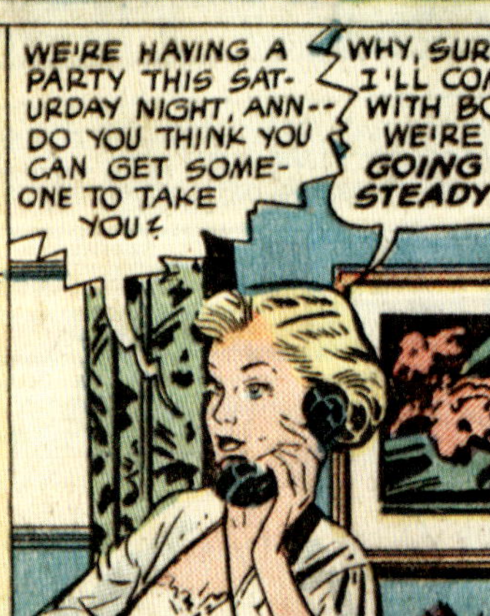

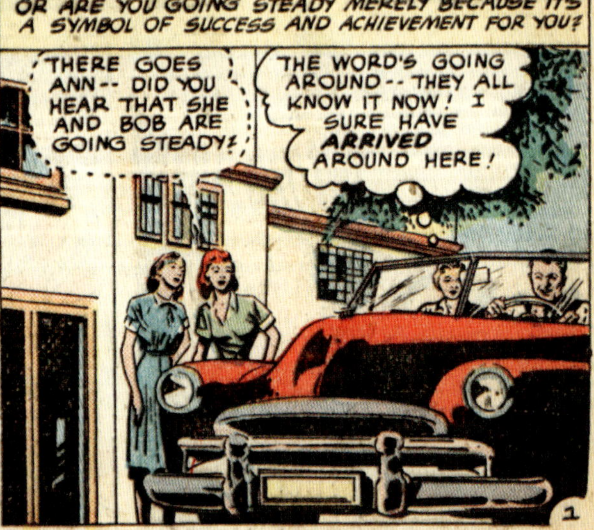

SOME COUPLES JUST DRIFT INTO GOING STEADY AFTER A FEW DATES TOGETHER-- BECAUSE THEIR FRIENDS AUTOMATICALLY START PAIRING THEM OFF IN THEIR THINKING!

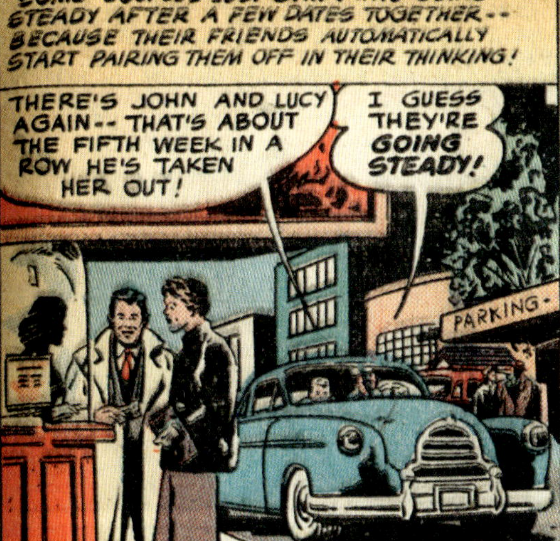

THUS, WHAT WAS ACTUALLY JUST A CASUAL SERIES OF DATES TURNED INTO SOMETHING FAR DIFFERENT AS A RESULT OF THE PRESSURE OF SOCIAL OPINION!

SAY, JOHN, WE'RE HAVING A SHINDIG AND WE NEED ANOTHER COUPLE! YOU CAN BRING LUCY, CAN'T YOU?

ER... YEAH, I GUESS SO!

SO HERE WE HAVE A RELATIONSHIP KEPT ALIVE BECAUSE THE HABIT OF GOING TOGETHER WAS CEMENTED BY PUBLIC OPINION! FAR TOO MANY OF SUCH ACCIDENTAL PAIRINGS-OFF END UP AT THE ALTAR-- RESULTING IN A MARRIAGE THAT SHOULD NEVER HAVE BEEN!

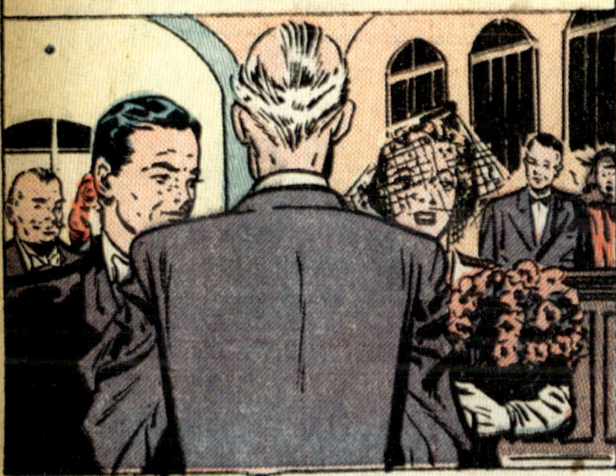

ALL OF THESE ARE INADAQUATE REASONS FOR GOING STEADY! IF YOU SETTLE PREMATURELY ON ANY ONE PERSON BEFORE YOU HAVE A CHANCE TO KNOW YOUR OWN MIND, YOU MAY MISS OUT ON FINDING THE REAL ONE-AND-ONLY!

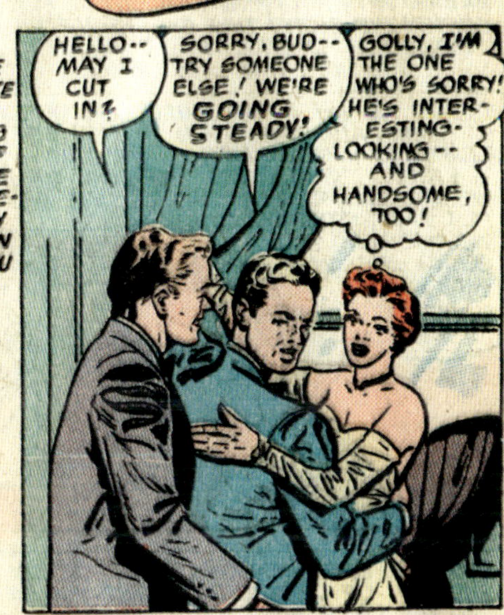

THUS, BY STARTING TO GO STEADY TOO EARLY, YOU'LL HAVE LESS OF AN OPPORTUNITY TO EXPLORE THE FIELD-- AND YOU'LL BE BLINDING YOURSELF TO OTHER POSSIBILITIES WHO MIGHT HAVE MADE YOU MUCH HAPPIER...

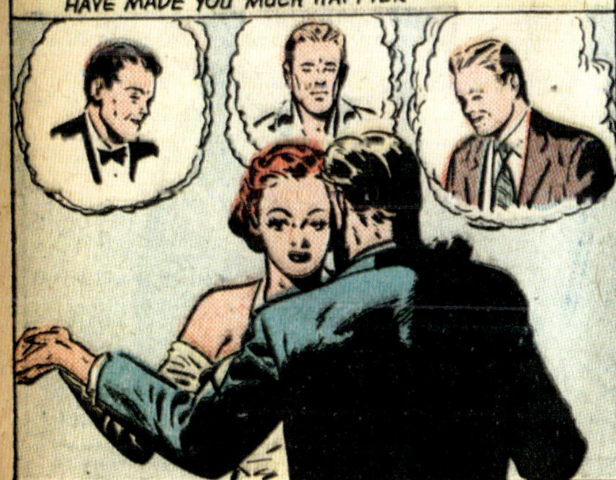

IF YOU FINALLY DECIDE YOU'VE MADE A MISTAKE ABOUT YOUR CHOICE OF A STEADY, DON'T MAKE THE MISTAKE EVEN WORSE BY DELAYING THE BREAK TOO LONG! YOU'LL BE KINDER TO HIM IN THE LONG RUN BY TELLING HIM THE TRUTH NOW!

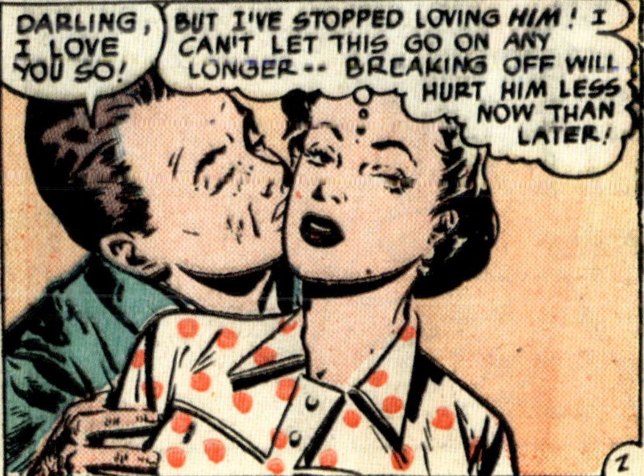

LOVELORN
#17, September 1951

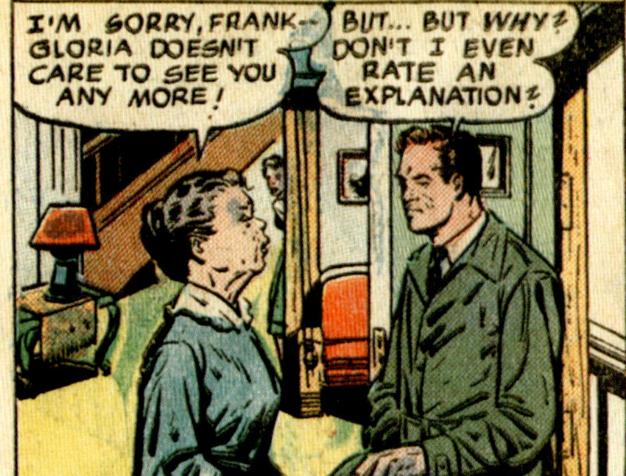

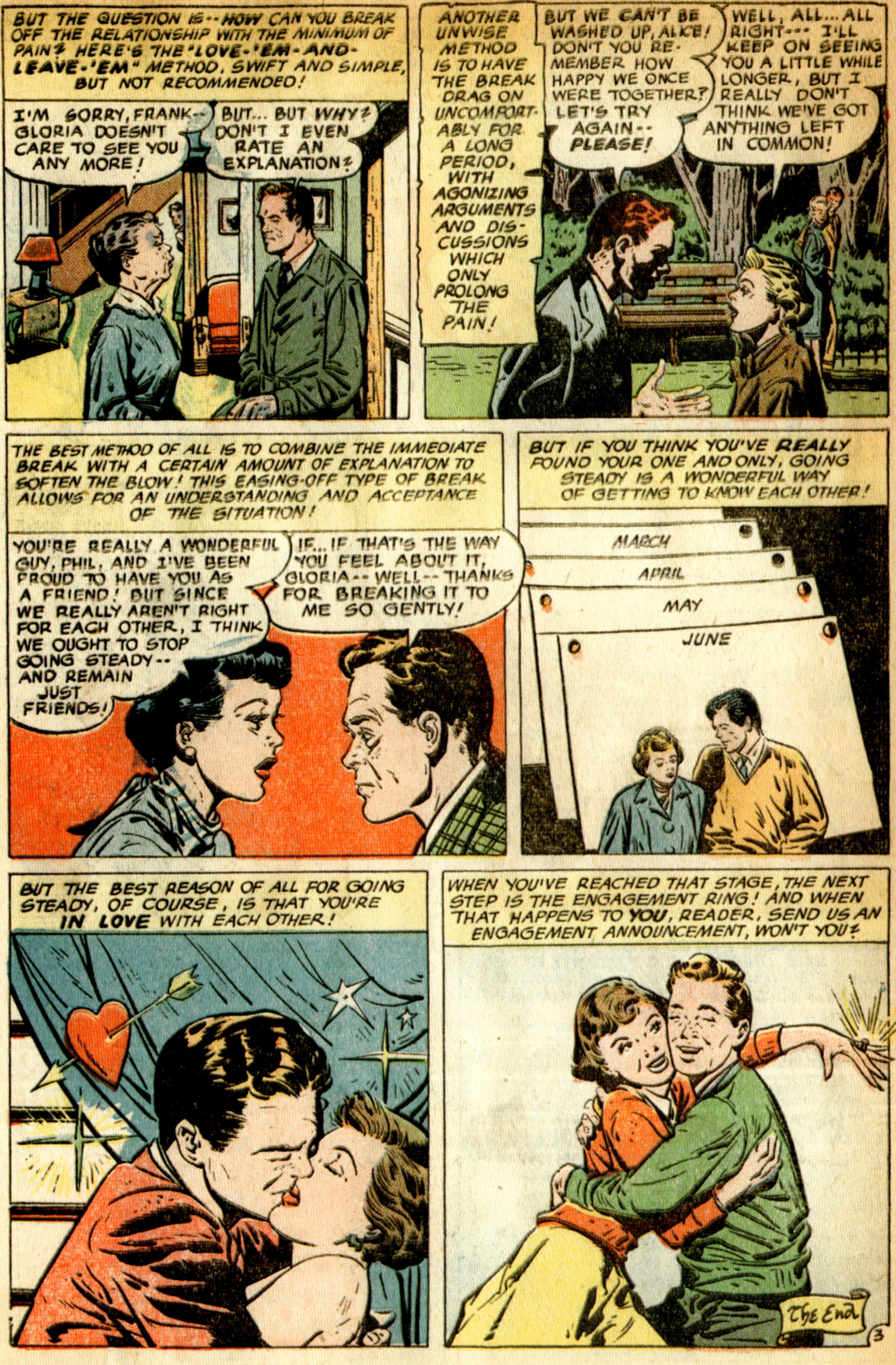

ANOTHER UNWISE METHOD IS TO HAVE THE BREAK DRAG ON UNCOMFORTABLY FOR A LONG PERIOD, WITH AGONIZING ARGUMENTS AND DISCUSSIONS WHICH ONLY PROLONG THE PAIN!

BUT WE CAN'T BE WASHED UP, ALICE! DON'T YOU REMEMBER HOW HAPPY WE ONCE WERE TOGETHER? LET'S TRY AGAIN-- PLEASE!

WELL, ALL... ALL RIGHT--- I'LL KEEP ON SEEING YOU A LITTLE WHILE LONGER, BUT I REALLY DON'T THINK WE'VE GOT ANYTHING LEFT IN COMMON!

THE BEST METHOD OF ALL IS TO COMBINE THE IMMEDIATE BREAK WITH A CERTAIN AMOUNT OF EXPLANATION TO SOFTEN THE BLOW! THIS EASING-OFF TYPE OF BREAK ALLOWS FOR AN UNDERSTANDING AND ACCEPTANCE OF THE SITUATION!

YOU'RE REALLY A WONDERFUL GUY, PHIL, AND I'VE BEEN PROUD TO HAVE YOU AS A FRIEND! BUT SINCE WE REALLY AREN'T RIGHT FOR EACH OTHER, I THINK WE OUGHT TO STOP GOING STEADY-- AND REMAIN JUST FRIENDS!

IF... IF THAT'S THE WAY YOU FEEL ABOUT IT, GLORIA-- WELL-- THANKS FOR BREAKING IT TO ME SO GENTLY!

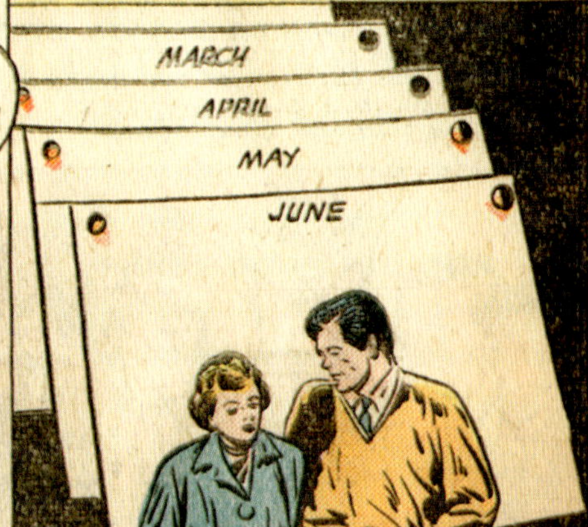

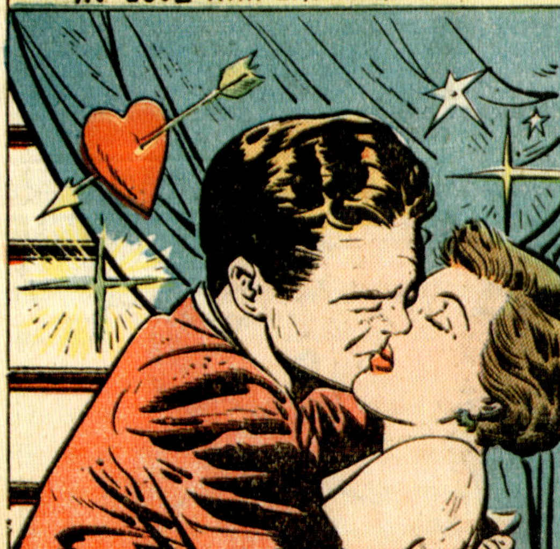

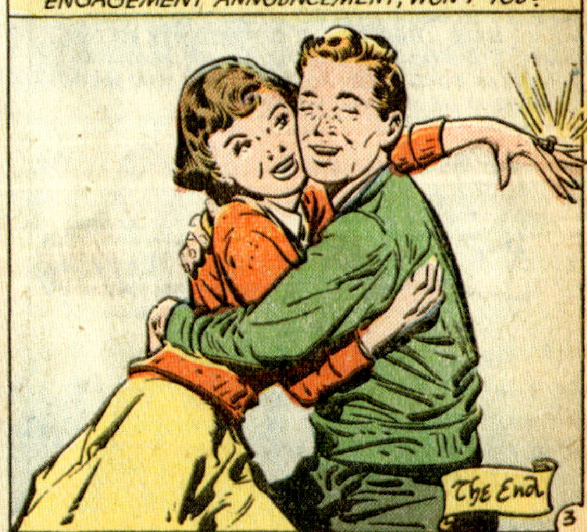

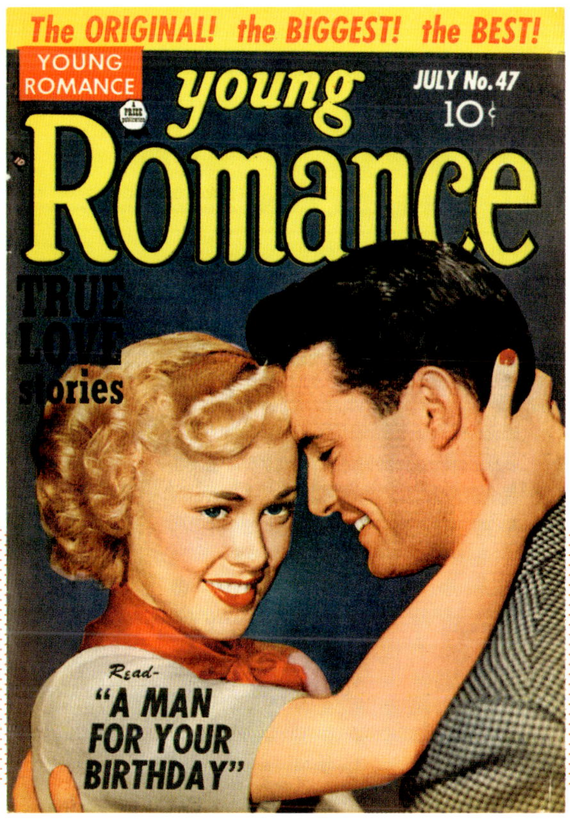

Twenty Peerless Love Story Titles

One of the eternal truisms about comic books is that more often than not, the covers were often the best part of an issue, far superior to the stories themselves. (The same could be said about movie posters of 1940s and '50s versus the actual movies.) Even so, one of the most unappreciated elements of romance comic books are the wonderful titles of the stories themselves. While it is true that many of these titles may have promised a drama that was never fully delivered, it is equally true that a great many story titles contained enough poetry to evoke an emotional response all on their own. Then, too, some of those titles were just so shamelessly goofy they qualify as unforgettable on that basis alone. Here is a short list of twenty story titles that transport me into sheer rhapsody. (Then again, I may have a rather low threshold for achieving rhapsody.)

This page:
YOUNG ROMANCE
#47, July 1952

"I WAS ENGAGED TO A PUPPET"
"HASH HOUSE QUEEN"
"MEN WERE MY GUINEA PIGS"
"I HATED BEING A WOMAN!"
"MY HEART BECAME A WASTELAND"
"I LOVED A WEAKLING"
"SUDDENLY—I WAS MARRIED"
"BEHIND THE ROMANTIC CURTAIN"
"THIS MAN I LOVED WAS A MAMA'S BOY!"
"I WAS A COAL MINE CINDERELLA"
"LOVE OF A LUNATIC"
"TENDERFOOT SWEETHEART"
"I SPELLED KI$$E$ THE WRONG WAY"
"DID I GIVE MY LIPS TOO FREELY?"
"THE BRIDE WORE BUCKSKIN"
"WORLD WITHOUT MEN"
"I WAS A PROFITEER!"
"COWTOWN CASANOVA"
"I GAVE BOYS THE GREEN LIGHT"
"COMMUNIST KISSES"

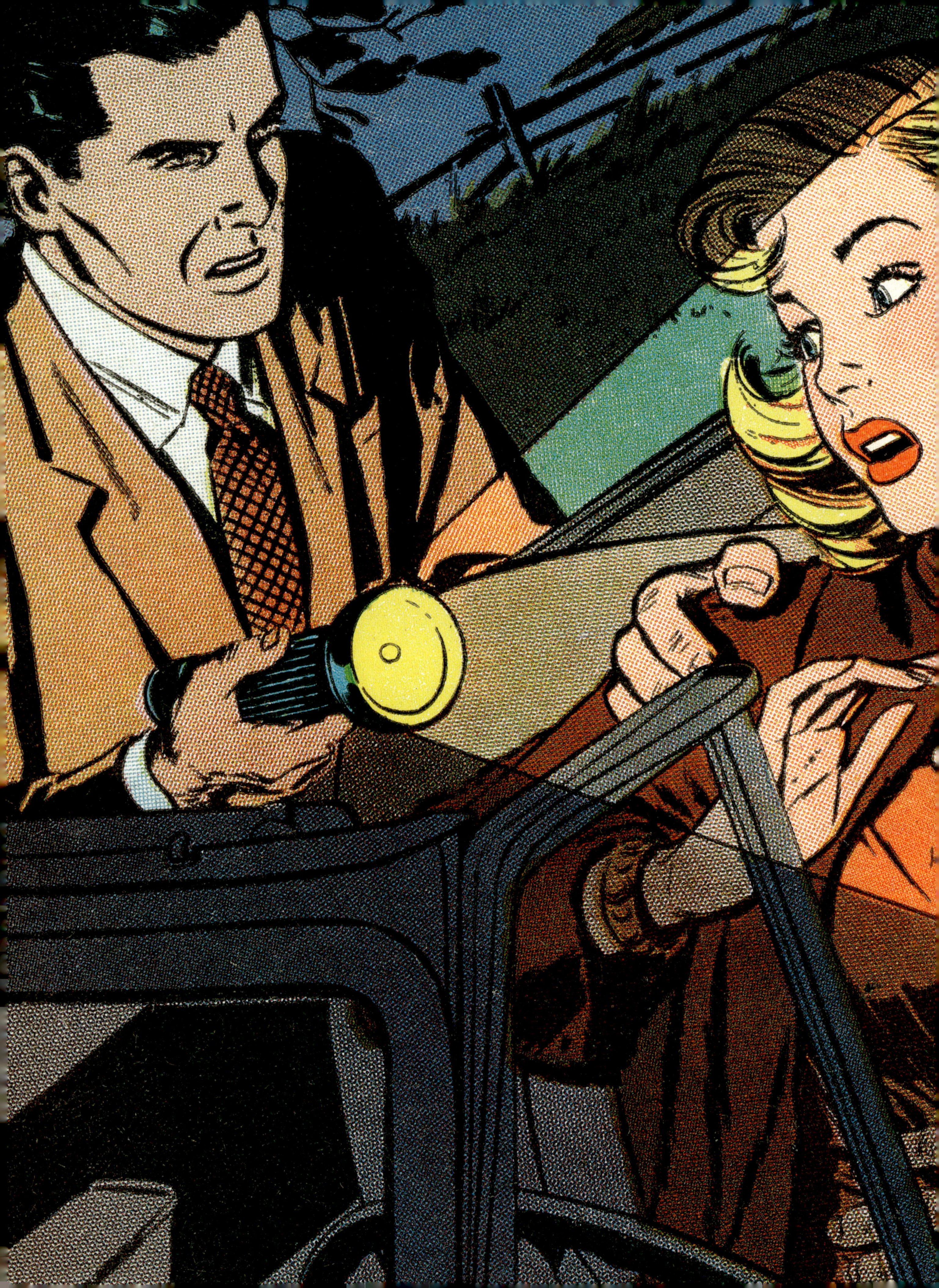

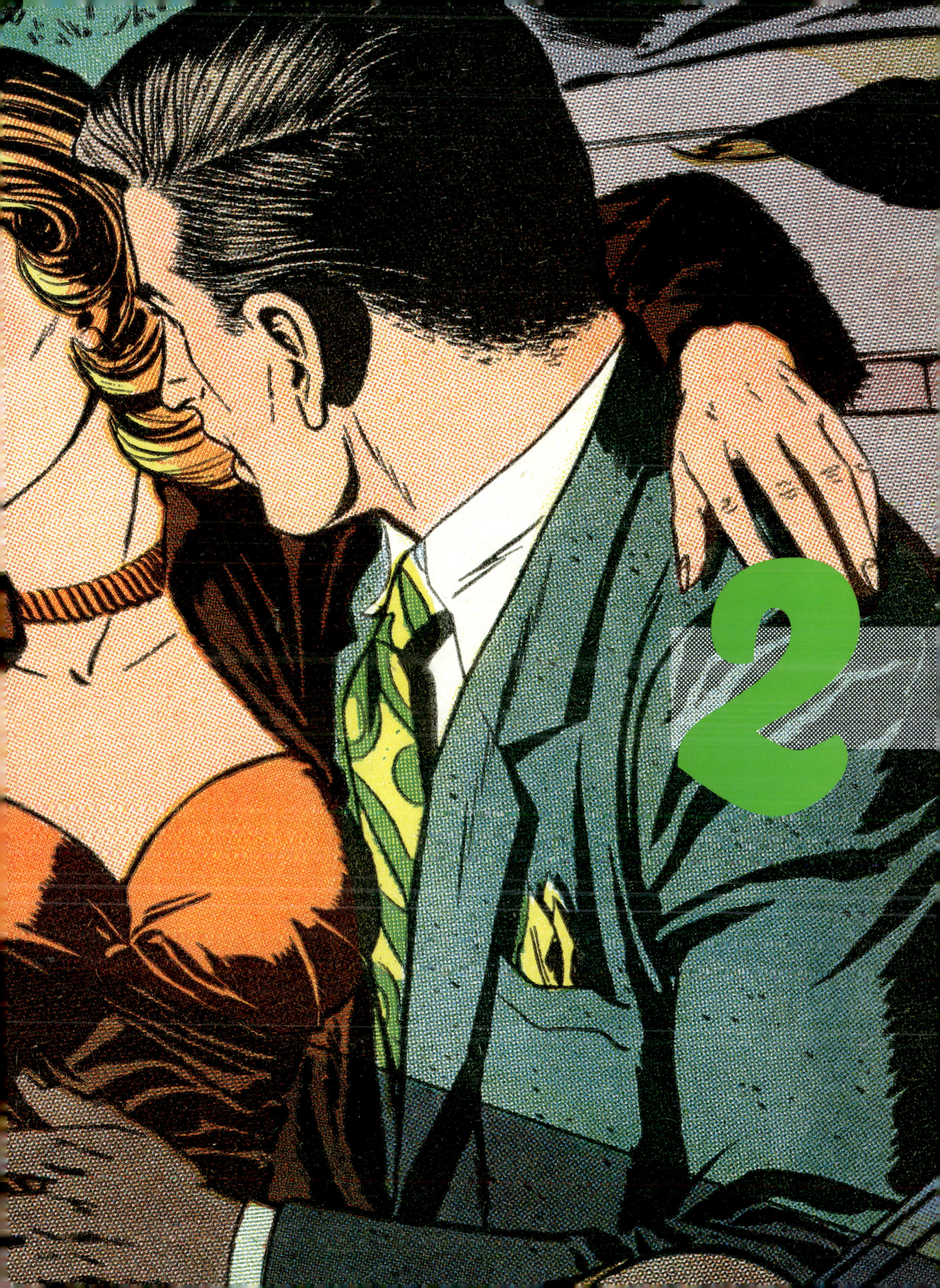
2

Love Vampire

JEALOUSY AND BETRAYAL

WHEN IT COMES to naming a human emotion that tops the list for unflattering, petty, immature behavior, you'd have to think long and hard to come up with a better fit than jealousy. Let's face it, most of us cannot resist indulging in the shameful practice of taking pleasure from the train wrecks in the emotional lives of others—after all, it distracts us from our own miseries, selfish people that we are! The vintage romance comics sampled here prove to be especially adept at dramatizing in miniature the rise, the development, and then the resolution of a situation that may or may not have had its roots in an actual dalliance or betrayal of another kind.

This is something of a marvel, compared to how long and messy the experience of jealousy and betrayal in a relationship may prove to be in real life. And don't forget—there were three or four complete stories in each issue of a typical love comic during this peak period, meaning that three or four highly complex situations were both presented and then resolved, all for a mere ten cents. Such a satisfying deal!

As the covers and stories in this section make clear, there are few situations more dramatic than someone caught either in the throes of a major fit of jealousy, or in the moment of recognizing a cutting betrayal. Or both! Here, evocative stories such as "Flame of Jealousy," "I Craved His Kisses!" and "With Hate in My Heart," as well as the cover to *Love Tales* #44—"So THIS is what you've been doing behind my back?"—illustrate exactly how the classic love comics catered to our worst eavesdropping impulses while also, in the end, providing so many rewarding cathartic moments.

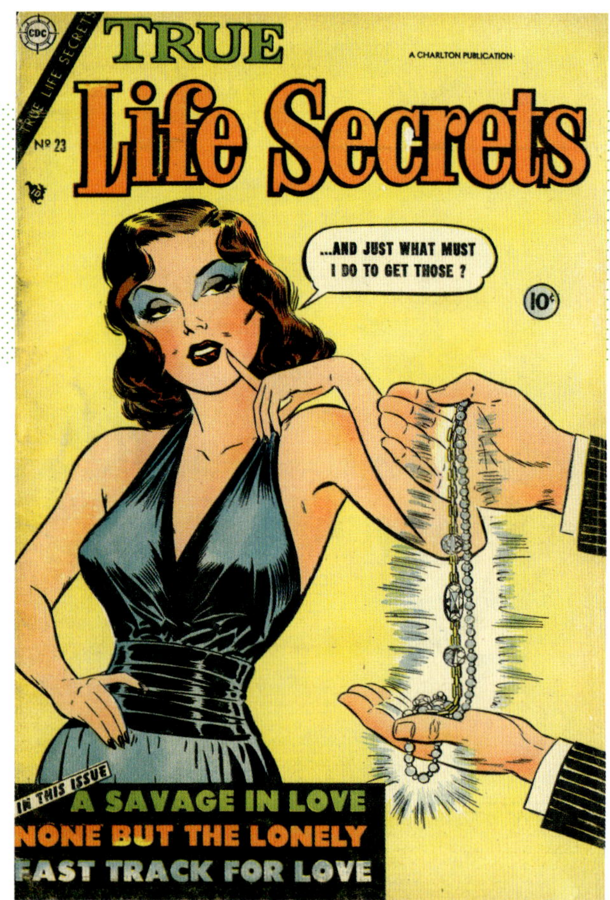
TRUE Life Secrets
A CHARLTON PUBLICATION
TRUE LIFE SECRETS
Nº 23
...AND JUST WHAT MUST I DO TO GET THOSE ?
10¢
IN THIS ISSUE
A SAVAGE IN LOVE
NONE BUT THE LONELY
FAST TRACK FOR LOVE

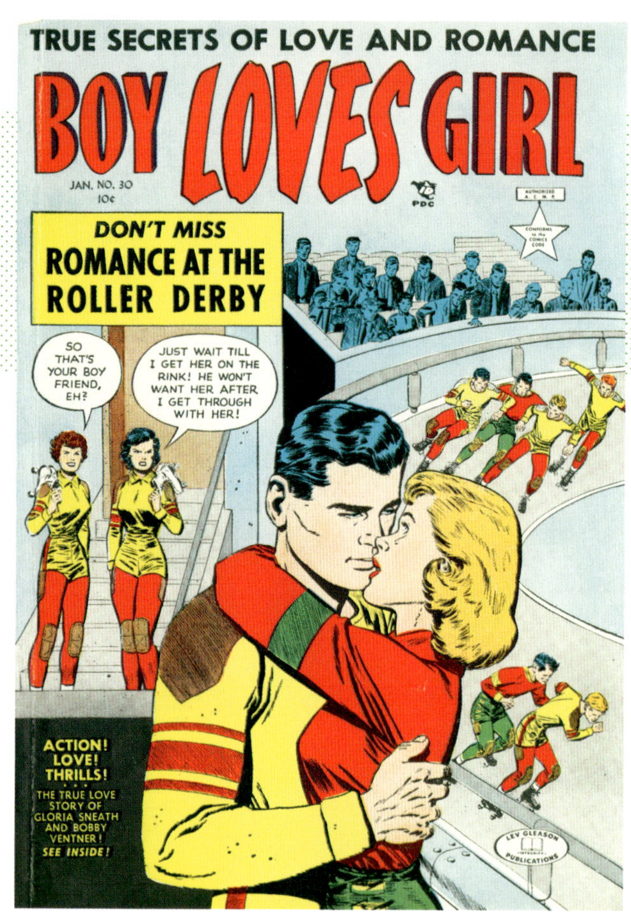
TRUE SECRETS OF LOVE AND ROMANCE
BOY LOVES GIRL
JAN. NO. 30
10¢
DON'T MISS
ROMANCE AT THE ROLLER DERBY
SO THAT'S YOUR BOY FRIEND, EH?
JUST WAIT TILL I GET HER ON THE RINK! HE WON'T WANT HER AFTER I GET THROUGH WITH HER!
ACTION! LOVE! THRILLS!
THE TRUE LOVE STORY OF GLORIA SNEATH AND BOBBY VENTNER!
SEE INSIDE!
LEV GLEASON PUBLICATIONS

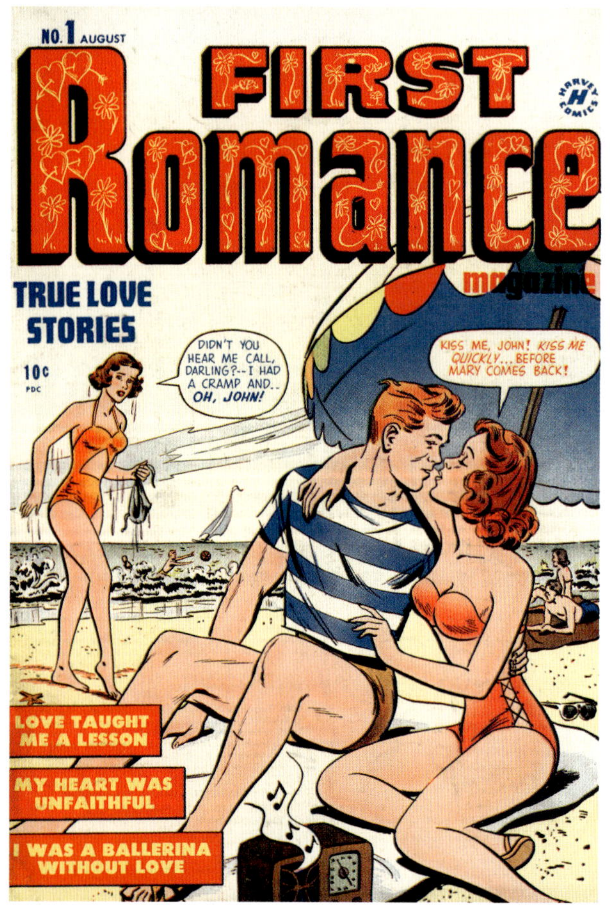
NO. 1 AUGUST
FIRST Romance magazine
TRUE LOVE STORIES
10¢
DIDN'T YOU HEAR ME CALL, DARLING?--I HAD A CRAMP AND.. OH, JOHN!
KISS ME, JOHN! KISS ME QUICKLY... BEFORE MARY COMES BACK!
LOVE TAUGHT ME A LESSON
MY HEART WAS UNFAITHFUL
I WAS A BALLERINA WITHOUT LOVE

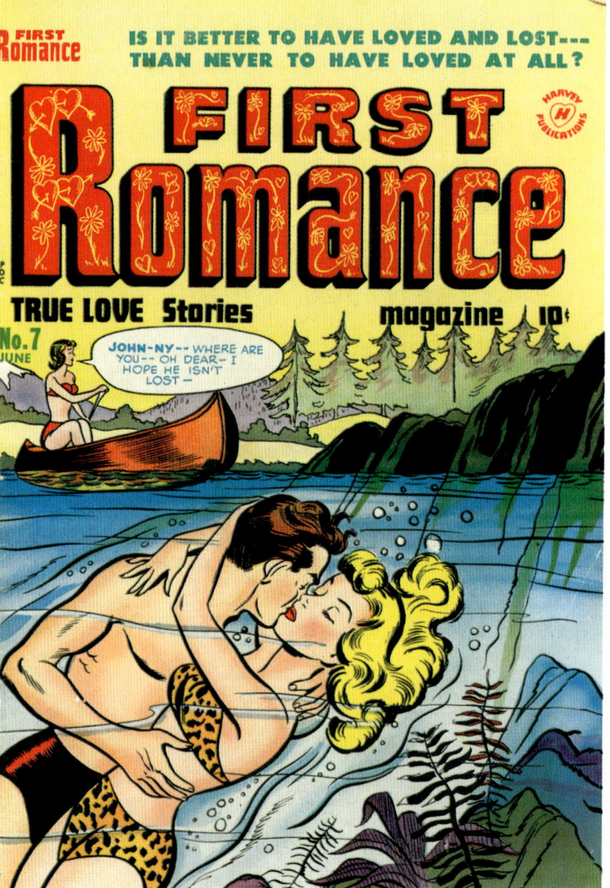
FIRST Romance
IS IT BETTER TO HAVE LOVED AND LOST--- THAN NEVER TO HAVE LOVED AT ALL?
FIRST Romance
TRUE LOVE Stories
magazine 10¢
No. 7 JUNE
JOHN-NY-- WHERE ARE YOU-- OH DEAR-- I HOPE HE ISN'T LOST--

“IF YOU WANT TO SACRIFICE THE ADMIRATION OF MANY MEN FOR THE CRITICISM OF ONE, GO AHEAD, GET MARRIED.”
— KATHARINE HEPBURN

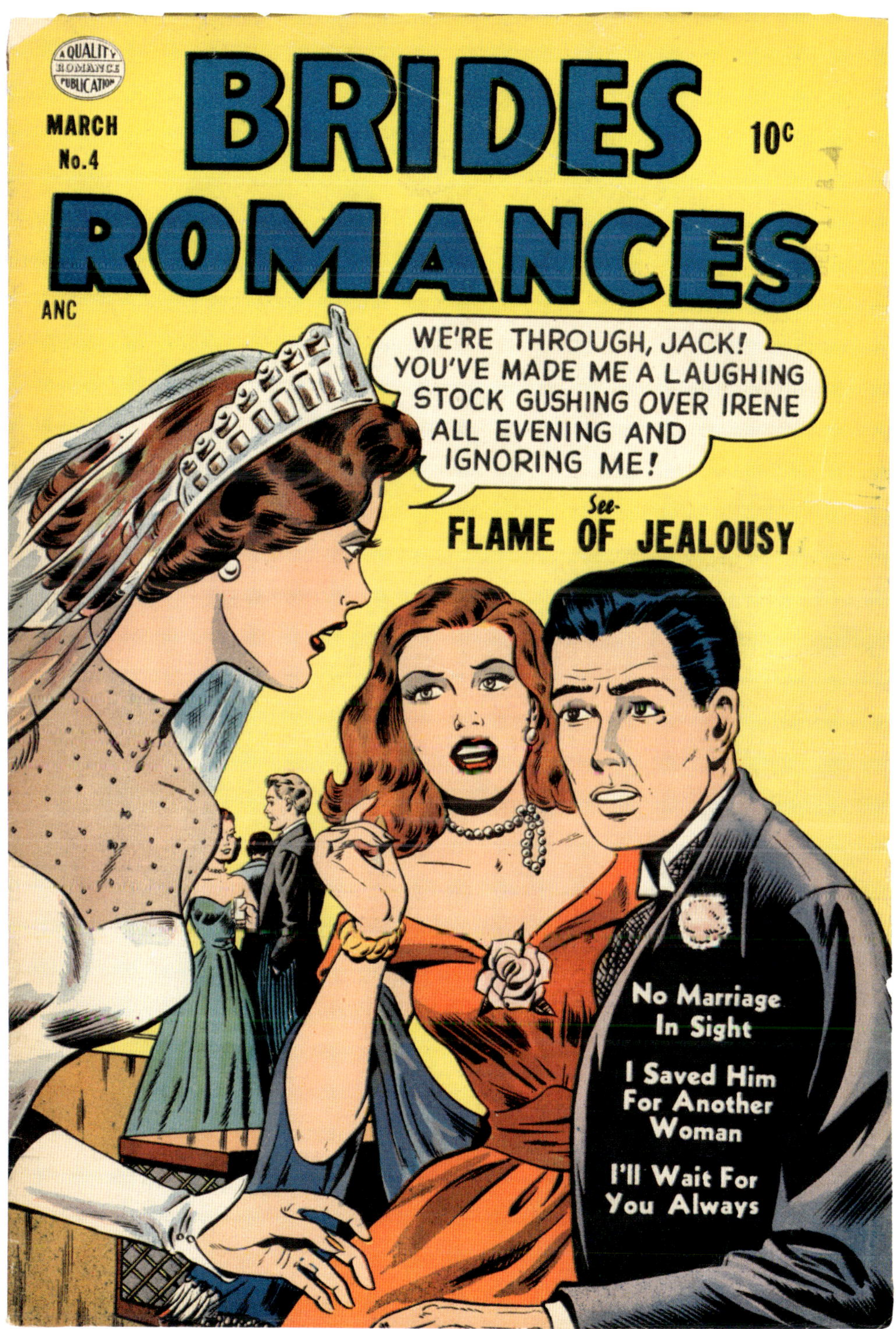

Pages 36–37:
TRUE LIFE SECRETS
#45, April 1954, cover detail

Page 40, clockwise from top left:
TRUE LIFE SECRETS
#23, November–December 1954

BOY LOVES GIRL
#30, January 1953

FIRST ROMANCE
#7, June 1951

FIRST ROMANCE
#1, August 1949

This page:
BRIDES ROMANCES
#4, March 1954

Below, from left to right:
FIRST LOVE
#12, May 1951

FIRST LOVE
#14, September 1951

Opposite:
LOVE TALES
#44, January 1951, cover detail

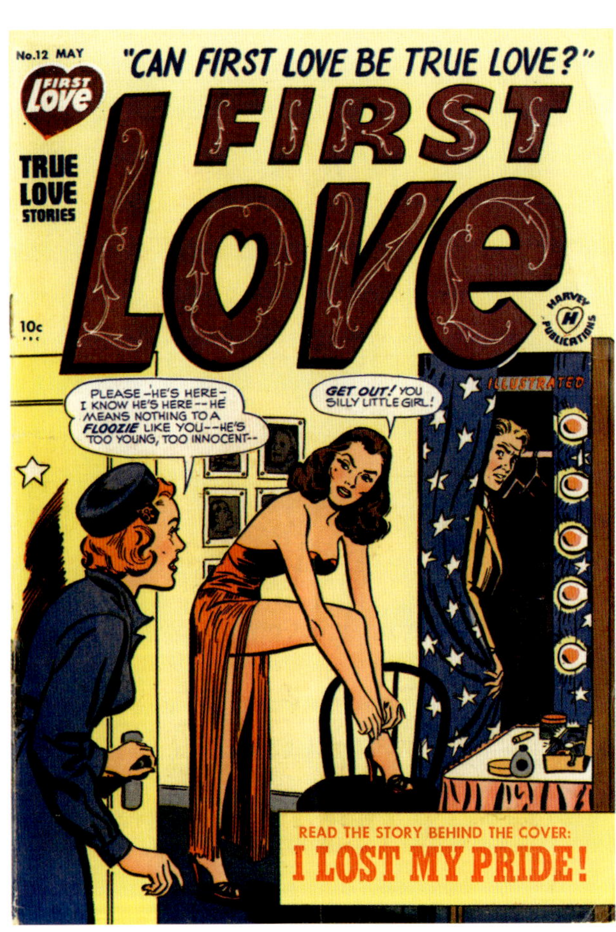

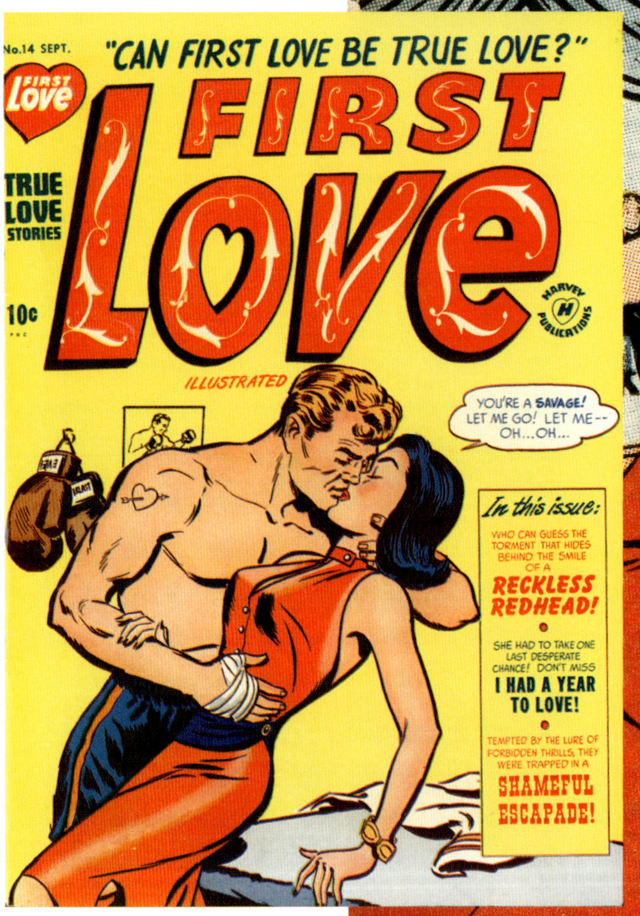

"IT WAS PARTIALLY MY FAULT THAT WE GOT DIVORCED... I TENDED TO PLACE MY WIFE UNDER A PEDESTAL."

— WOODY ALLEN IN HIS 1964 MONOLOGUE "I HAD A ROUGH MARRIAGE"

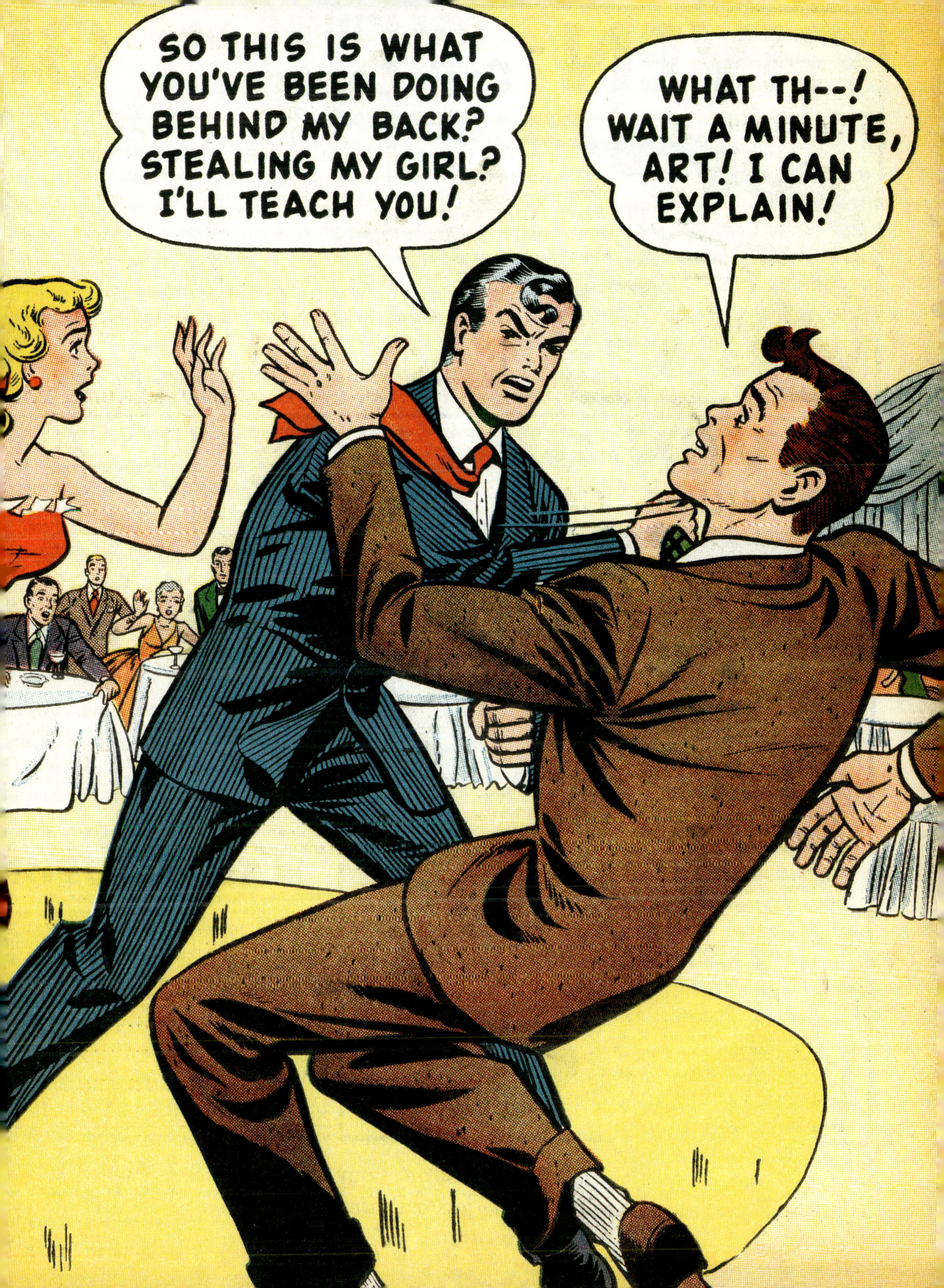
SO THIS IS WHAT YOU'VE BEEN DOING BEHIND MY BACK? STEALING MY GIRL? I'LL TEACH YOU!
WHAT TH--! WAIT A MINUTE, ART! I CAN EXPLAIN!

Clockwise from top:
YOUNG LOVE
Volume 2, #7
September 1950,
splash page

LOVERS' LANE
#38, January 1954

GIRLS IN LOVE
#52, March 1956

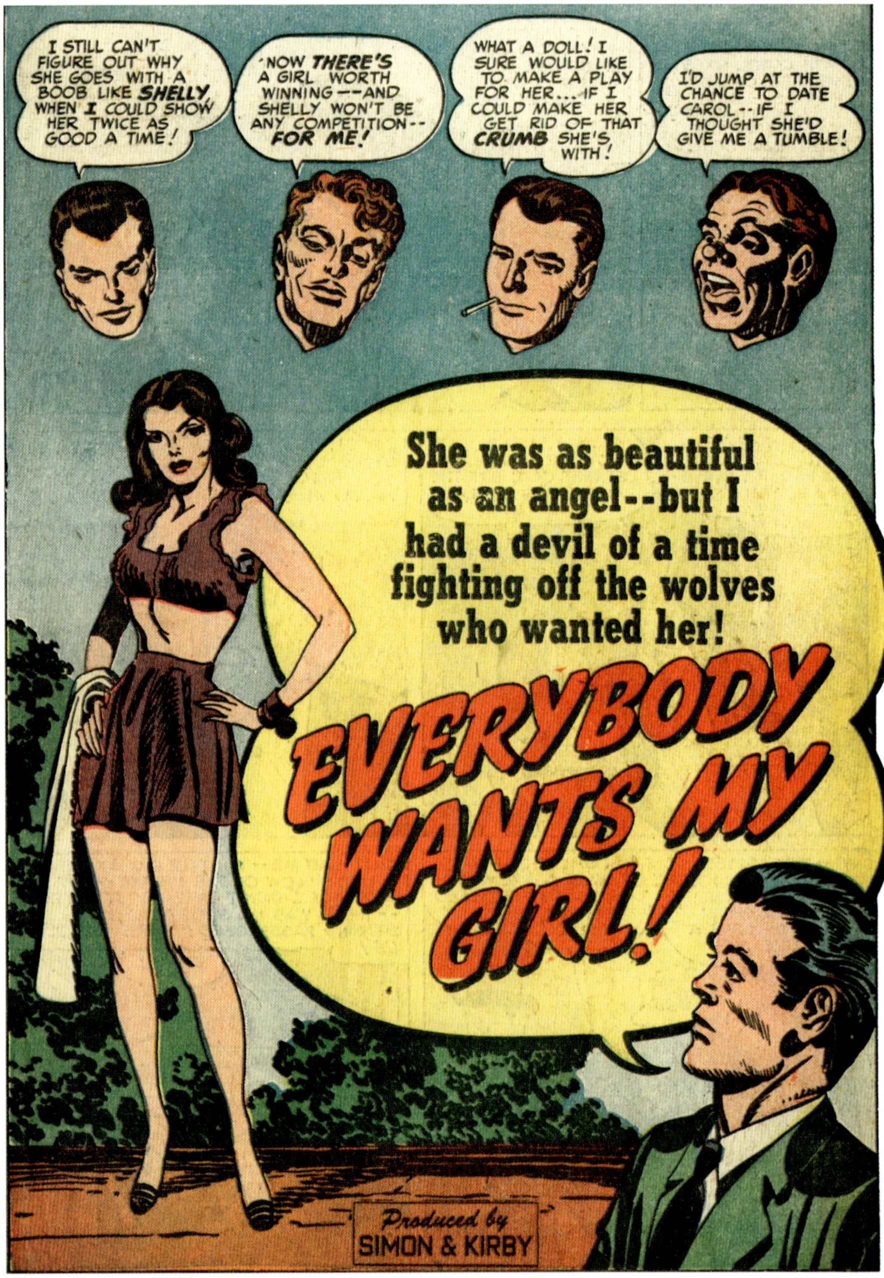

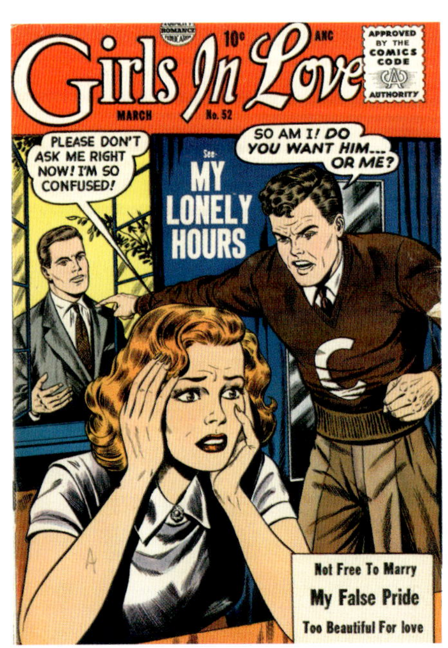

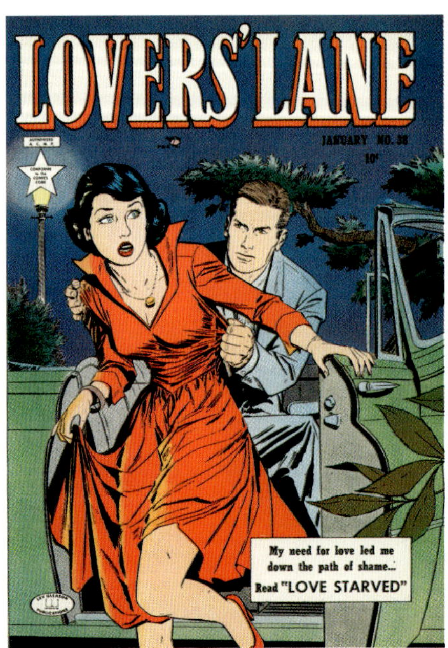

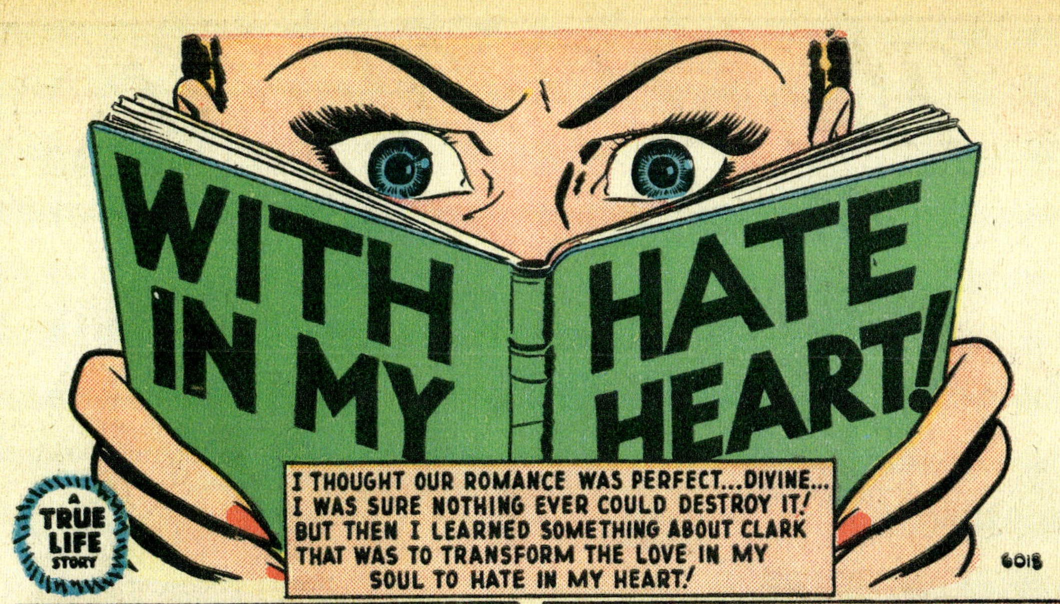

AMBITION! I KNOW ALL ABOUT IT--HOW IT CAN BE A GOOD THING, OR A BAD THING! HOW IT CAN CREATE JEALOUSY AND TEAR TWO PEOPLE APART, OR CAN BE A BOND BRINGING TWO PEOPLE TOGETHER AND MAKING SECURE THEIR LOVE! AND I KNOW THAT IT CAN BRING UNHAPPINESS IF YOU MAKE ONE VITAL MISTAKE-- FOR I MADE THAT MISTAKE!

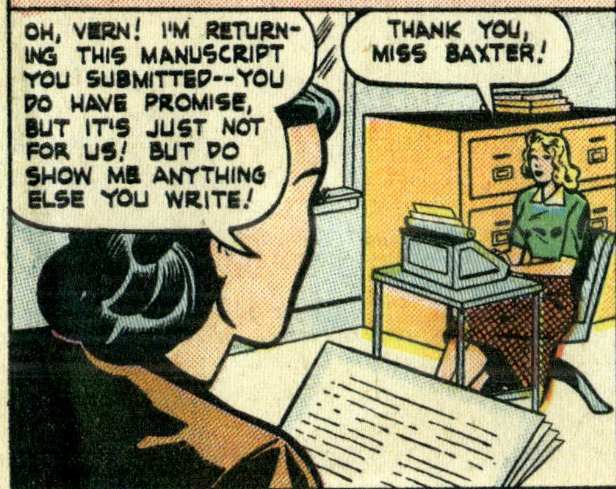

MISS BAXTER WAS MY BOSS AT THE PUBLISHING FIRM WHERE I WORKED-- SHE KNEW OF MY DRIVING AMBITION TO WRITE, AND HAD CONSENTED TO READ MY MANUSCRIPT HERSELF! I'D WORKED FOR MONTHS ON IT, AND EVEN HER VERDICT DIDN'T STOP ME--I TOOK IT TO ANOTHER PUBLISHER...

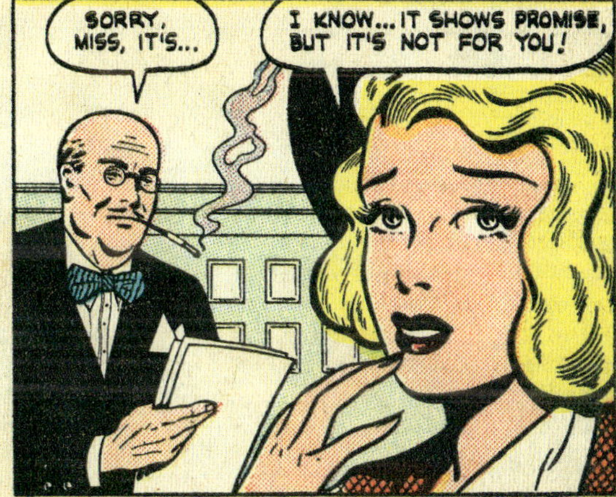

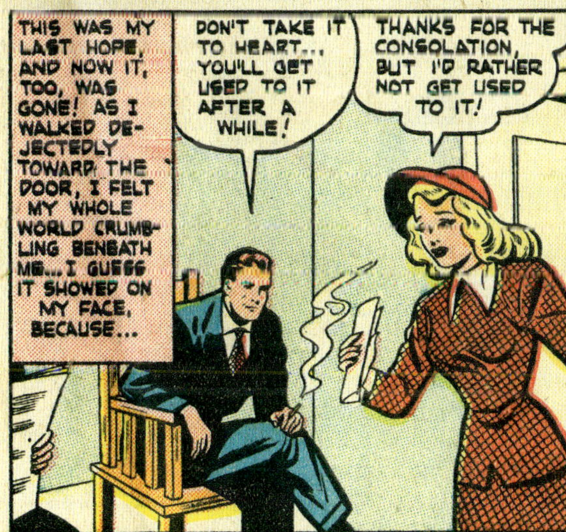

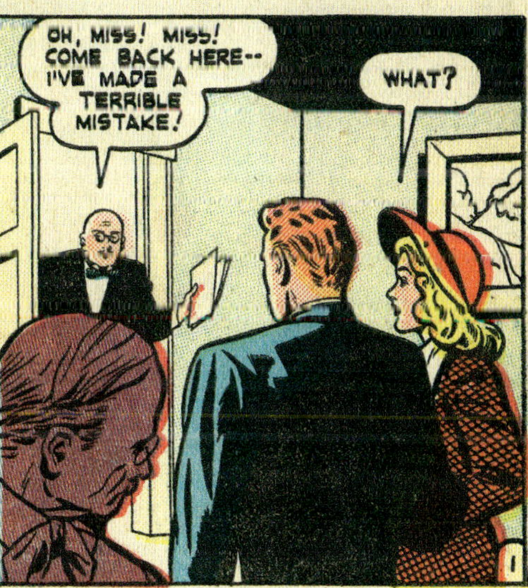

LOVE TALES
#39, December 1949

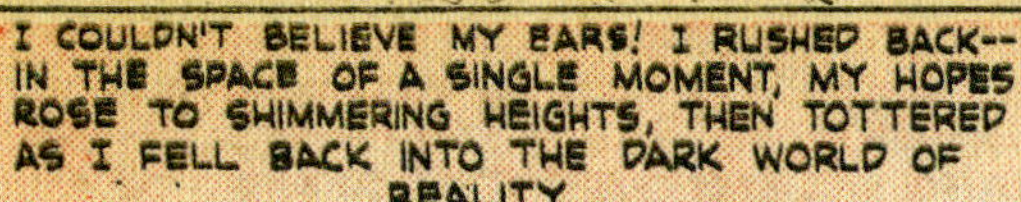
I COULDN'T BELIEVE MY EARS! I RUSHED BACK-- IN THE SPACE OF A SINGLE MOMENT, MY HOPES ROSE TO SHIMMERING HEIGHTS, THEN TOTTERED AS I FELL BACK INTO THE DARK WORLD OF REALITY...

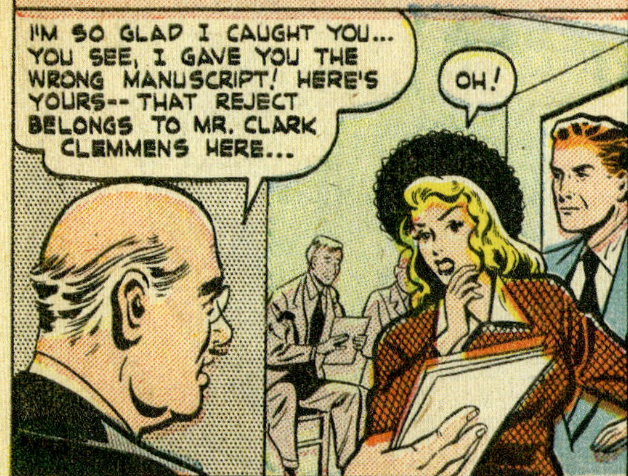
I'M SO GLAD I CAUGHT YOU... YOU SEE, I GAVE YOU THE WRONG MANUSCRIPT! HERE'S YOURS-- THAT REJECT BELONGS TO MR. CLARK CLEMMENS HERE...
OH!

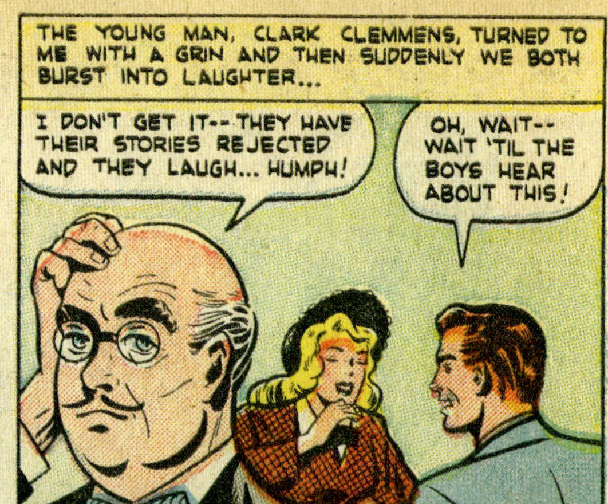
THE YOUNG MAN, CLARK CLEMMENS, TURNED TO ME WITH A GRIN AND THEN SUDDENLY WE BOTH BURST INTO LAUGHTER...
I DON'T GET IT-- THEY HAVE THEIR STORIES REJECTED AND THEY LAUGH... HUMPH!
OH, WAIT-- WAIT 'TIL THE BOYS HEAR ABOUT THIS!

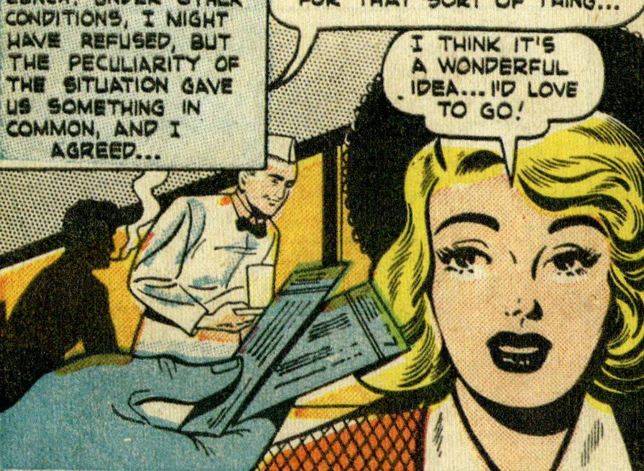
I THOUGHT WE'D NEVER STOP LAUGHING ABOUT IT! AFTER THE PUBLISHER DISAPPEARED BEHIND A DOOR, CLARK ASKED ME TO JOIN HIM AT LUNCH! UNDER OTHER CONDITIONS, I MIGHT HAVE REFUSED, BUT THE PECULIARITY OF THE SITUATION GAVE US SOMETHING IN COMMON, AND I AGREED...
SAY, LOOK, LET'S NOT TALK ABOUT OUR REJECTIONS! IT WASN'T MY FIRST, AND THERE WILL PROBABLY BE MORE... I'VE A BETTER IDEA! I'VE GOT TWO TICKETS TO A CONCERT! I DON'T KNOW IF YOU ARE FOR THAT SORT OF THING...
I THINK IT'S A WONDERFUL IDEA... I'D LOVE TO GO!

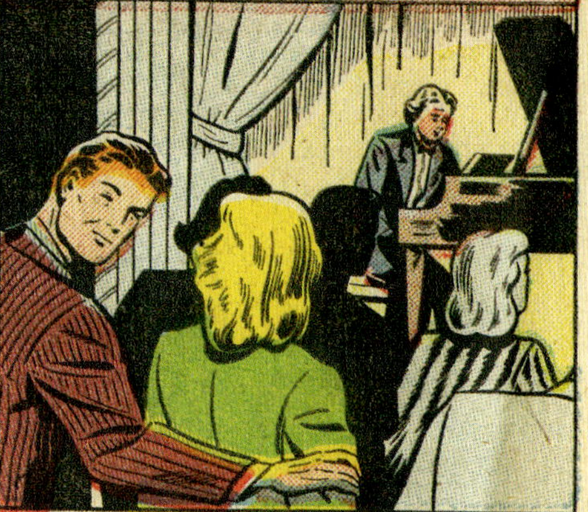
CLARK PICKED ME UP AFTER WORK... WE HAD DINNER, AND THEN WENT TO THE CONCERT! SOMEHOW, BEING WITH HIM, I FORGOT ABOUT MY REJECTION... IT WAS THE FIRST TIME I'D FELT THAT QUICK RESPONSE TO A MAN'S VOICE, HIS SMILE... I HAD IGNORED EVERYTHING BUT MY WRITING FOR SO LONG!

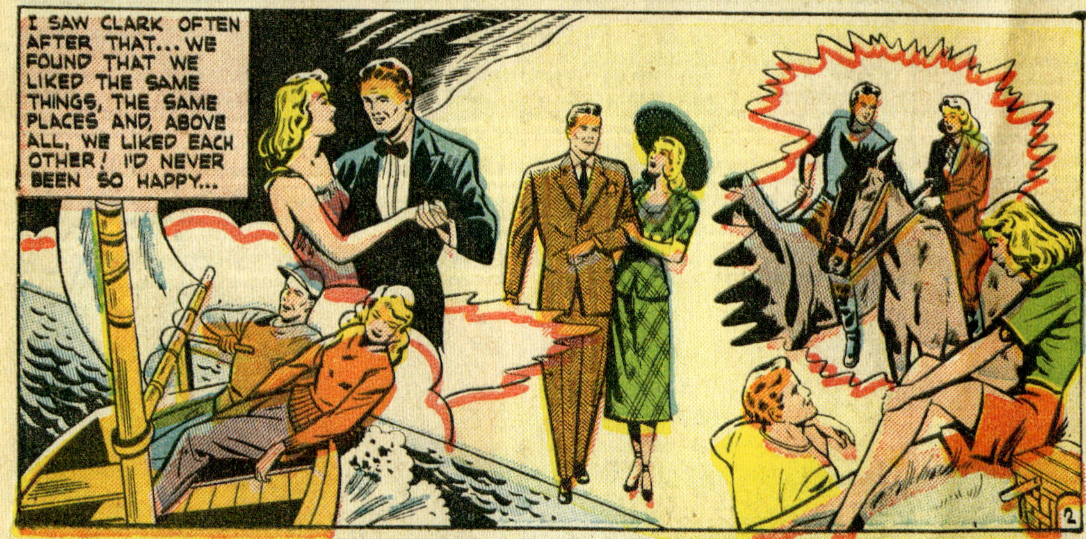
I SAW CLARK OFTEN AFTER THAT... WE FOUND THAT WE LIKED THE SAME THINGS, THE SAME PLACES AND, ABOVE ALL, WE LIKED EACH OTHER! I'D NEVER BEEN SO HAPPY...
2

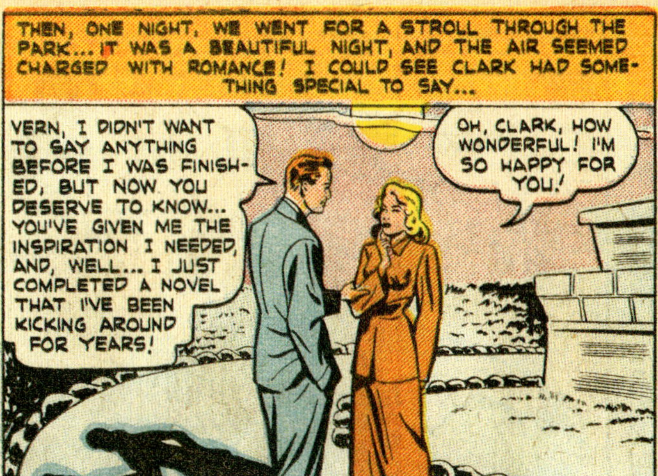
THEN, ONE NIGHT, WE WENT FOR A STROLL THROUGH THE PARK... IT WAS A BEAUTIFUL NIGHT, AND THE AIR SEEMED CHARGED WITH ROMANCE! I COULD SEE CLARK HAD SOMETHING SPECIAL TO SAY...
VERN, I DIDN'T WANT TO SAY ANYTHING BEFORE I WAS FINISHED, BUT NOW YOU DESERVE TO KNOW... YOU'VE GIVEN ME THE INSPIRATION I NEEDED, AND, WELL... I JUST COMPLETED A NOVEL THAT I'VE BEEN KICKING AROUND FOR YEARS!
OH, CLARK, HOW WONDERFUL! I'M SO HAPPY FOR YOU!

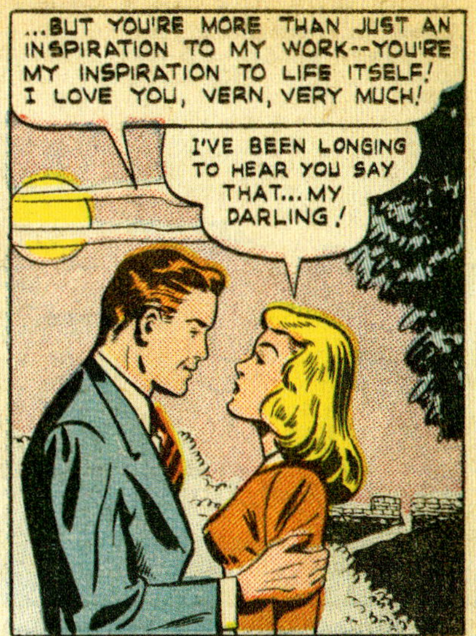
...BUT YOU'RE MORE THAN JUST AN INSPIRATION TO MY WORK--YOU'RE MY INSPIRATION TO LIFE ITSELF! I LOVE YOU, VERN, VERY MUCH!
I'VE BEEN LONGING TO HEAR YOU SAY THAT... MY DARLING!

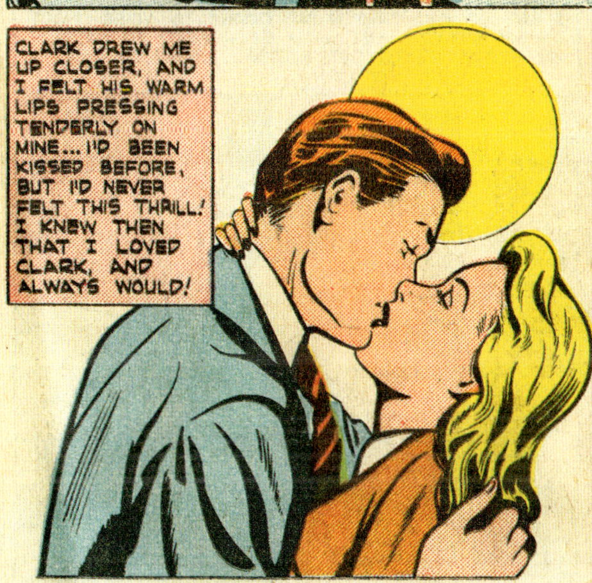
CLARK DREW ME UP CLOSER, AND I FELT HIS WARM LIPS PRESSING TENDERLY ON MINE... I'D BEEN KISSED BEFORE, BUT I'D NEVER FELT THIS THRILL! I KNEW THEN THAT I LOVED CLARK, AND ALWAYS WOULD!

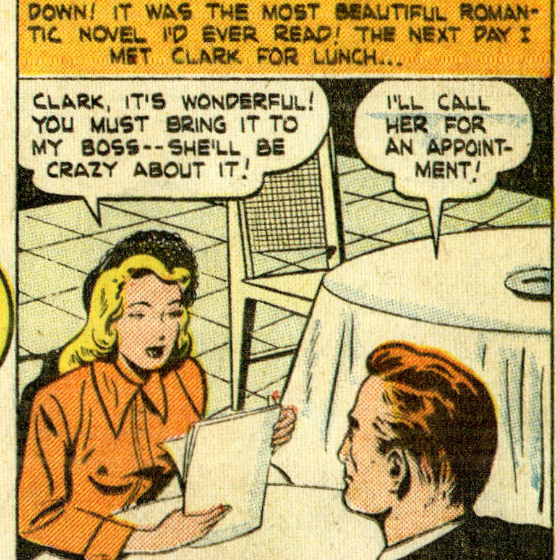
I STAYED UP MOST OF THE NIGHT READING CLARK'S MANUSCRIPT--I COULDN'T PUT IT DOWN! IT WAS THE MOST BEAUTIFUL ROMANTIC NOVEL I'D EVER READ! THE NEXT DAY I MET CLARK FOR LUNCH...
CLARK, IT'S WONDERFUL! YOU MUST BRING IT TO MY BOSS--SHE'LL BE CRAZY ABOUT IT!
I'LL CALL HER FOR AN APPOINTMENT!

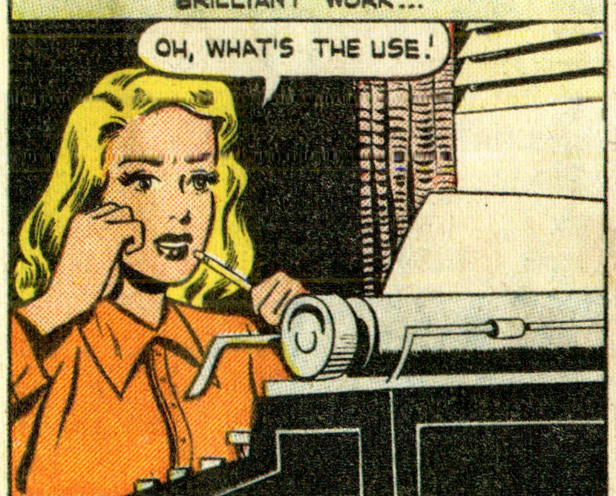
BEFORE I'D MET CLARK, I'D SPENT EVERY AVAILABLE MOMENT AT MY TYPEWRITER. NOW I DUSTED IT OFF, THINKING HIS WORK WOULD SPUR ME ON! INSTEAD IT HAD AN OPPOSITE EFFECT... NOTHING I WROTE SEEMED TO MATCH UP TO CLARK'S BRILLIANT WORK...
OH, WHAT'S THE USE!

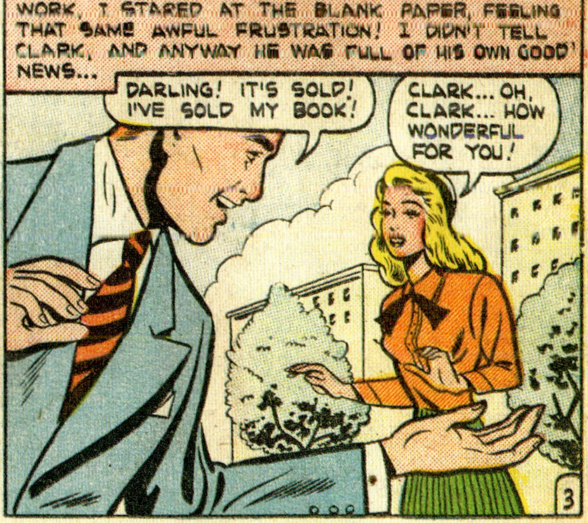
I KEPT TRYING, BUT EACH TIME I SAT DOWN TO WORK, I STARED AT THE BLANK PAPER, FEELING THAT SAME AWFUL FRUSTRATION! I DIDN'T TELL CLARK, AND ANYWAY HE WAS FULL OF HIS OWN GOOD NEWS...
DARLING! IT'S SOLD! I'VE SOLD MY BOOK!
CLARK... OH, CLARK... HOW WONDERFUL FOR YOU!
3

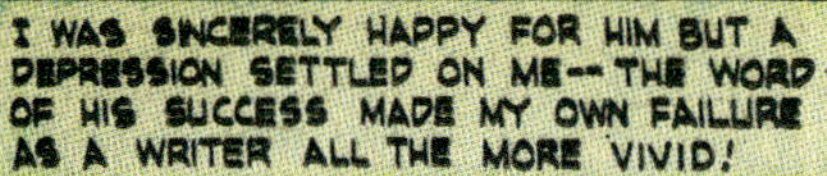
I WAS SINCERELY HAPPY FOR HIM BUT A DEPRESSION SETTLED ON ME-- THE WORD OF HIS SUCCESS MADE MY OWN FAILURE AS A WRITER ALL THE MORE VIVID!

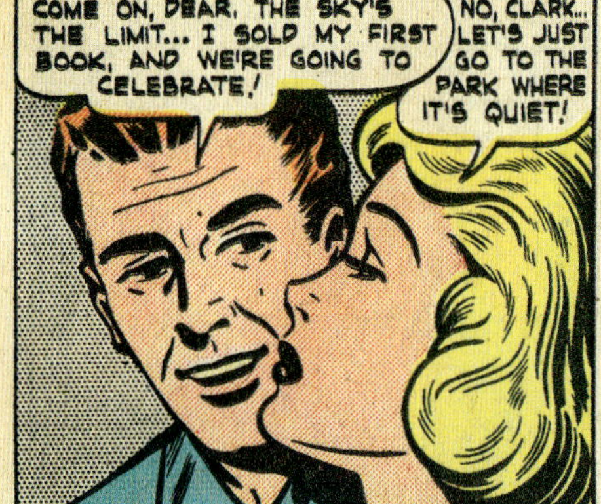
COME ON, DEAR, THE SKY'S THE LIMIT... I SOLD MY FIRST BOOK, AND WE'RE GOING TO CELEBRATE!
NO, CLARK.. LET'S JUST GO TO THE PARK WHERE IT'S QUIET!

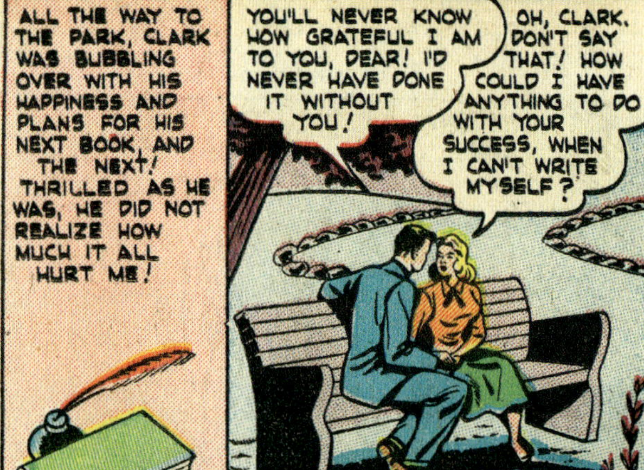
ALL THE WAY TO THE PARK, CLARK WAS BUBBLING OVER WITH HIS HAPPINESS AND PLANS FOR HIS NEXT BOOK, AND THE NEXT! THRILLED AS HE WAS, HE DID NOT REALIZE HOW MUCH IT ALL HURT ME!
YOU'LL NEVER KNOW HOW GRATEFUL I AM TO YOU, DEAR! I'D NEVER HAVE DONE IT WITHOUT YOU!
OH, CLARK, DON'T SAY THAT! HOW COULD I HAVE ANYTHING TO DO WITH YOUR SUCCESS, WHEN I CAN'T WRITE MYSELF?

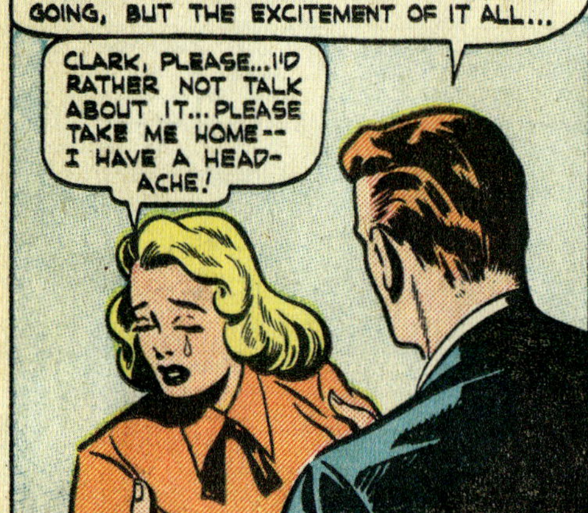
I WAS ASHAMED OF WHAT I SAID-- I HAD NO RIGHT TO SPOIL HIS DAY FOR HIM! YET IT WAS TRUE AND I HAD NO CONTROL OVER THE WAY I FELT...
I'M SORRY, DEAREST... I'M A SELFISH FOOL! I MEANT TO ASK HOW YOUR STORY WAS GOING, BUT THE EXCITEMENT OF IT ALL...
CLARK, PLEASE...I'D RATHER NOT TALK ABOUT IT...PLEASE TAKE ME HOME-- I HAVE A HEAD-ACHE!

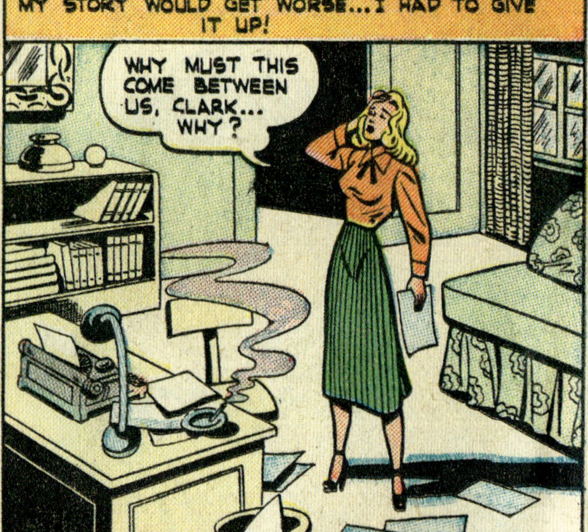
I SAT UP ALL THAT NIGHT TRYING TO WORK IT OUT OF MY SYSTEM, YET WITH EACH WORD I'D WRITE, MY STORY WOULD GET WORSE...I HAD TO GIVE IT UP!
WHY MUST THIS COME BETWEEN US, CLARK... WHY?

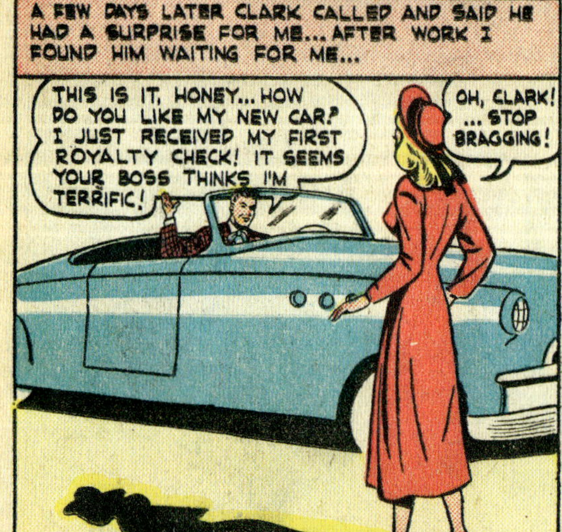
A FEW DAYS LATER CLARK CALLED AND SAID HE HAD A SURPRISE FOR ME... AFTER WORK I FOUND HIM WAITING FOR ME...
THIS IS IT, HONEY... HOW DO YOU LIKE MY NEW CAR? I JUST RECEIVED MY FIRST ROYALTY CHECK! IT SEEMS YOUR BOSS THINKS I'M TERRIFIC!
OH, CLARK! ...STOP BRAGGING!

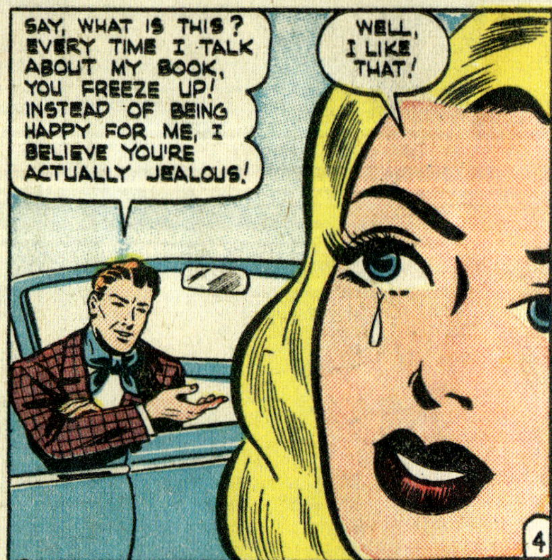
SAY, WHAT IS THIS? EVERY TIME I TALK ABOUT MY BOOK, YOU FREEZE UP! INSTEAD OF BEING HAPPY FOR ME, I BELIEVE YOU'RE ACTUALLY JEALOUS!
WELL, I LIKE THAT!
4

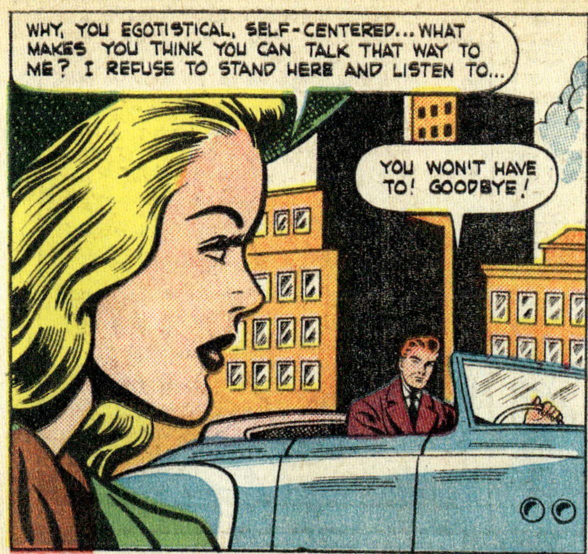

I RAN ALL THE WAY HOME AND CRIED BITTERLY! MY HEART ACHED WITH A PAIN THAT CAN ONLY COME WITH REPENTANCE... EVERY WORD CLARK HAD SAID WAS TRUE... YET FOR SOME REASON, I COULDN'T ADMIT IT TO HIM! MAYBE IT WAS FALSE PRIDE, BUT WHATEVER IT WAS, IT HAD COST ME MY FIRST LOVE -- CLARK'S "GOODBYE" HAD BEEN FIRM, AND FINAL!

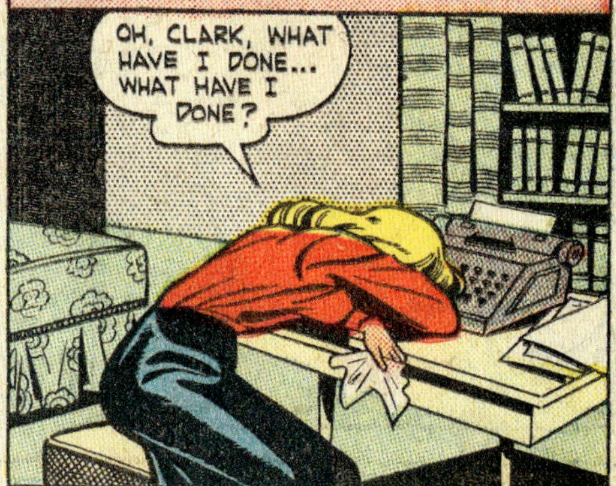

FOR DAYS AFTERWARDS, I SEEMED TO BE LIVING IN A VOID! I QUIT MY JOB TO AVOID BUMPING INTO CLARK! I COULDN'T FACE HIM, YET HE WAS IN MY THOUGHTS WHEREVER I'D GO! I COULDN'T FORGET HIM FOR A MOMENT...

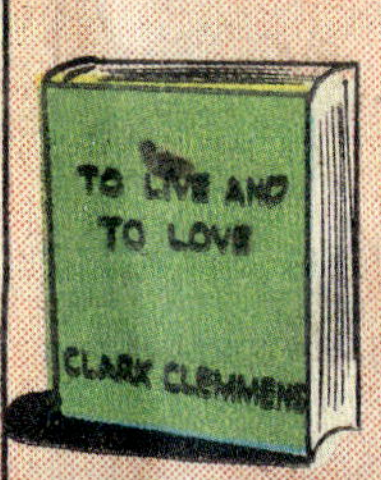

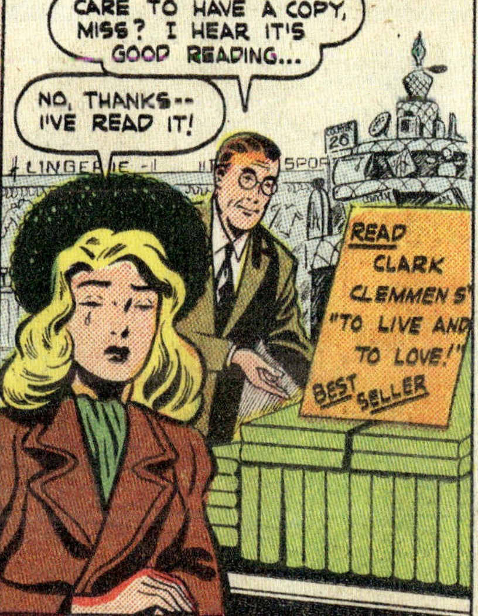

I WALKED BACK TO MY ROOM, NOT KNOWING WHAT TO DO WITH MYSELF! THERE HAD TO BE A WAY OUT OF ALL THIS! THEN SUDDENLY...

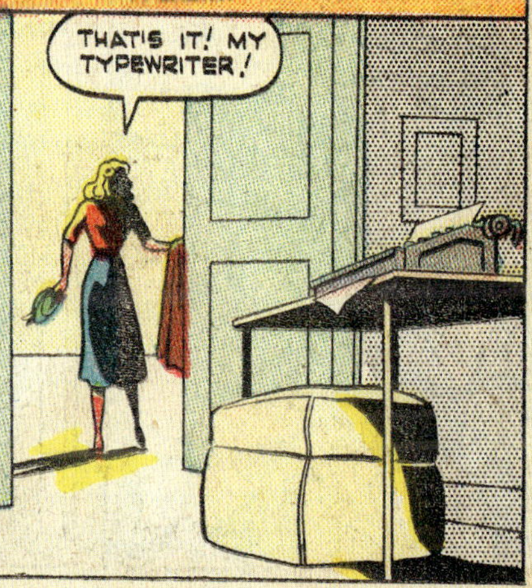

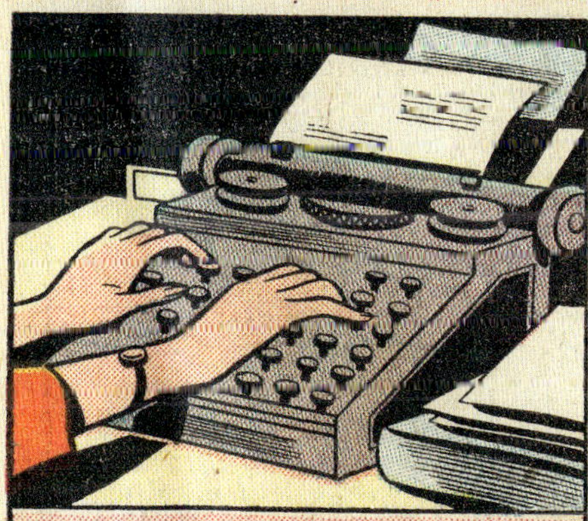

I HAD TO FIND AN OUTLET FOR MY FEELINGS, AND I TURNED TO THE ONLY WAY I KNEW... THE WORDS FLOWED FREELY, FOR THIS WAS A STORY I KNEW TOO WELL! I BURIED MY HEART DEEP IN THE PAGES...

I CAN'T REMEMBER HOW MANY DAYS OR WEEKS IT TOOK TO FINISH IT... I DECIDED TO LET MY OLD BOSS, MISS BAXTER, READ IT, AND SEE WHAT SHE THOUGHT! WHEN I GOT TO THE OFFICE, I SAW HER--ARM IN ARM WITH CLARK!

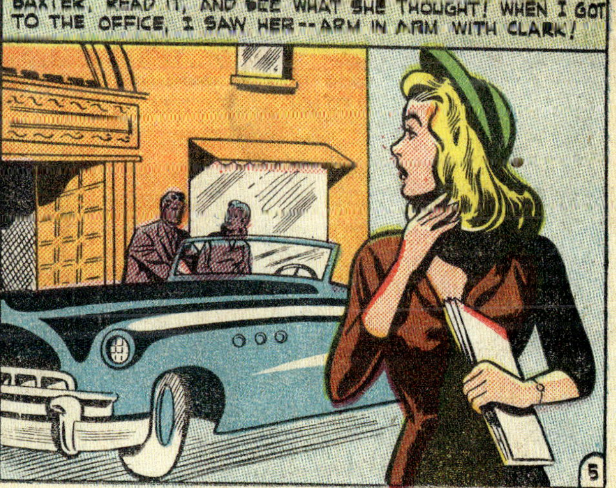

5

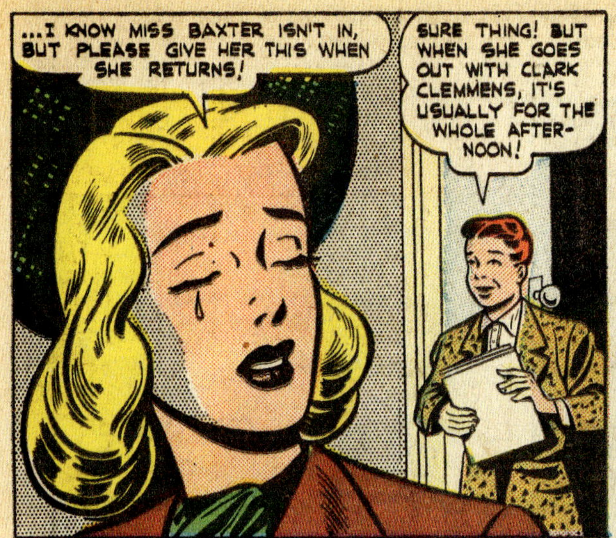
...I KNOW MISS BAXTER ISN'T IN, BUT PLEASE GIVE HER THIS WHEN SHE RETURNS!
SURE THING! BUT WHEN SHE GOES OUT WITH CLARK CLEMMENS, IT'S USUALLY FOR THE WHOLE AFTER-NOON!

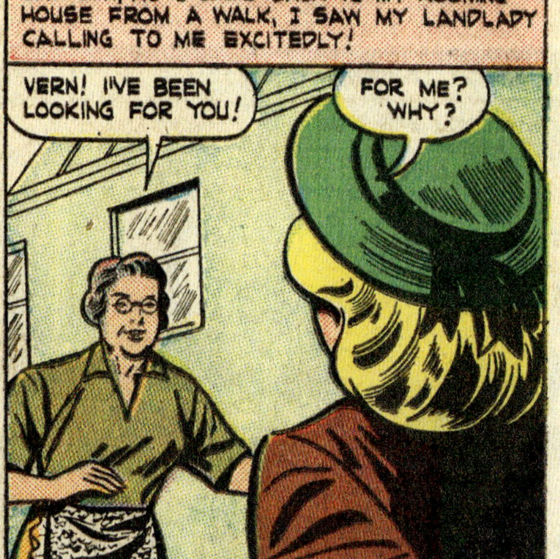
I DIDN'T HEAR ANYTHING FOR DAYS! THEN ONE DAY, AS I CAME BACK TO MY ROOMING HOUSE FROM A WALK, I SAW MY LANDLADY CALLING TO ME EXCITEDLY!
VERN! I'VE BEEN LOOKING FOR YOU!
FOR ME? WHY?

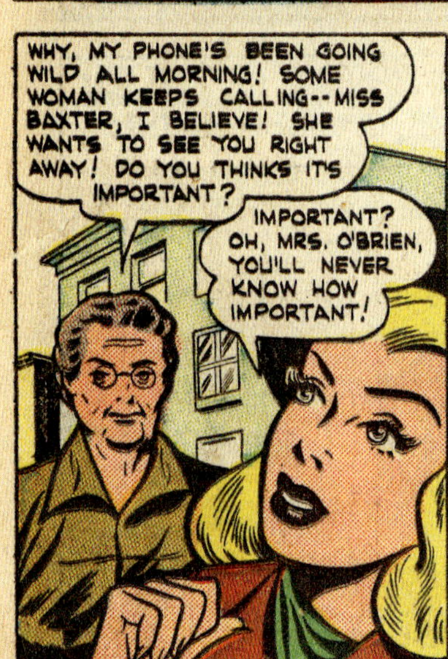
WHY, MY PHONE'S BEEN GOING WILD ALL MORNING! SOME WOMAN KEEPS CALLING--MISS BAXTER, I BELIEVE! SHE WANTS TO SEE YOU RIGHT AWAY! DO YOU THINKS IT'S IMPORTANT?
IMPORTANT? OH, MRS. O'BRIEN, YOU'LL NEVER KNOW HOW IMPORTANT!

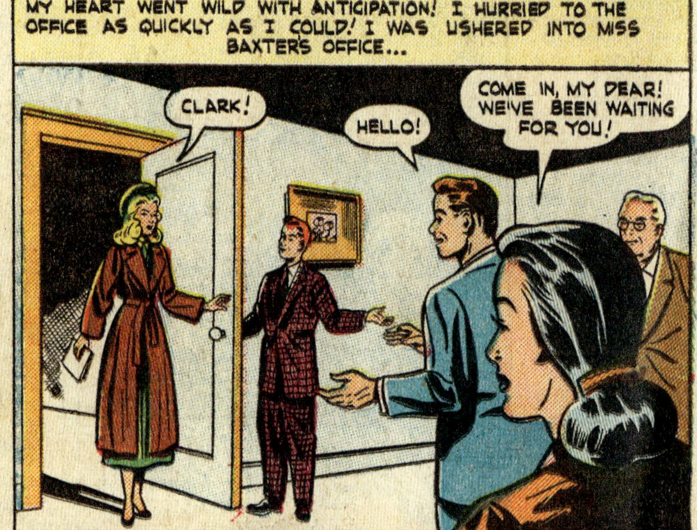
MY HEART WENT WILD WITH ANTICIPATION! I HURRIED TO THE OFFICE AS QUICKLY AS I COULD! I WAS USHERED INTO MISS BAXTER'S OFFICE...
CLARK!
HELLO!
COME IN, MY DEAR! WE'VE BEEN WAITING FOR YOU!

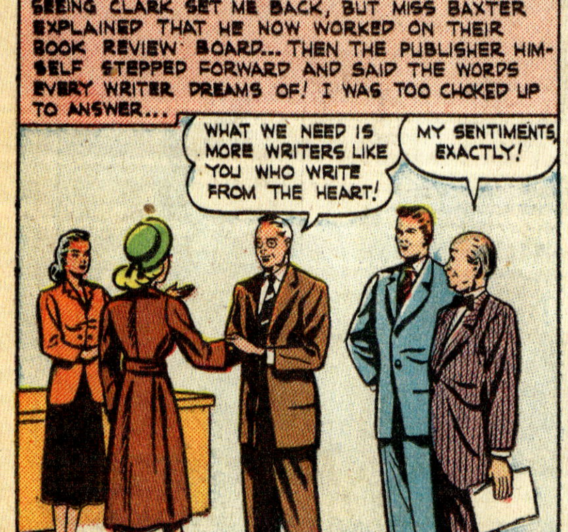
SEEING CLARK SET ME BACK, BUT MISS BAXTER EXPLAINED THAT HE NOW WORKED ON THEIR BOOK REVIEW BOARD... THEN THE PUBLISHER HIM-SELF STEPPED FORWARD AND SAID THE WORDS EVERY WRITER DREAMS OF! I WAS TOO CHOKED UP TO ANSWER...
WHAT WE NEED IS MORE WRITERS LIKE YOU WHO WRITE FROM THE HEART!
MY SENTIMENTS, EXACTLY!

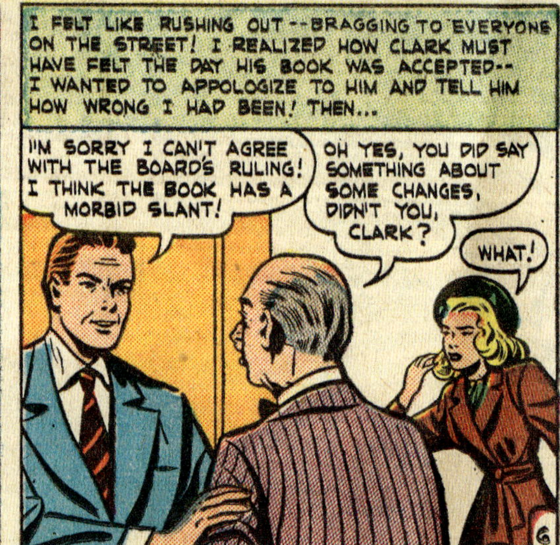
I FELT LIKE RUSHING OUT--BRAGGING TO EVERYONE ON THE STREET! I REALIZED HOW CLARK MUST HAVE FELT THE DAY HIS BOOK WAS ACCEPTED--I WANTED TO APPOLOGIZE TO HIM AND TELL HIM HOW WRONG I HAD BEEN! THEN...
I'M SORRY I CAN'T AGREE WITH THE BOARD'S RULING! I THINK THE BOOK HAS A MORBID SLANT!
OH YES, YOU DID SAY SOMETHING ABOUT SOME CHANGES, DIDN'T YOU, CLARK?
WHAT!
6

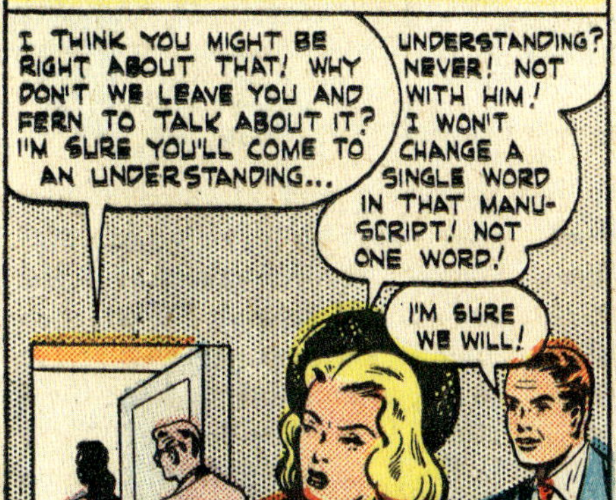
I FELT THE BLOOD RUSH TO MY HEAD, AND IT WAS ALL I COULD DO TO CONTROL MYSELF! NOW HE WAS THE ONE WHO WAS JEALOUS! I HAD TO TURN AWAY! I HEARD MISS BAXTER AND THE OTHER MEN START TO LEAVE THE ROOM...
I THINK YOU MIGHT BE RIGHT ABOUT THAT! WHY DON'T WE LEAVE YOU AND FERN TO TALK ABOUT IT? I'M SURE YOU'LL COME TO AN UNDERSTANDING...
UNDERSTANDING? NEVER! NOT WITH HIM! I WON'T CHANGE A SINGLE WORD IN THAT MANUSCRIPT! NOT ONE WORD!
I'M SURE WE WILL!

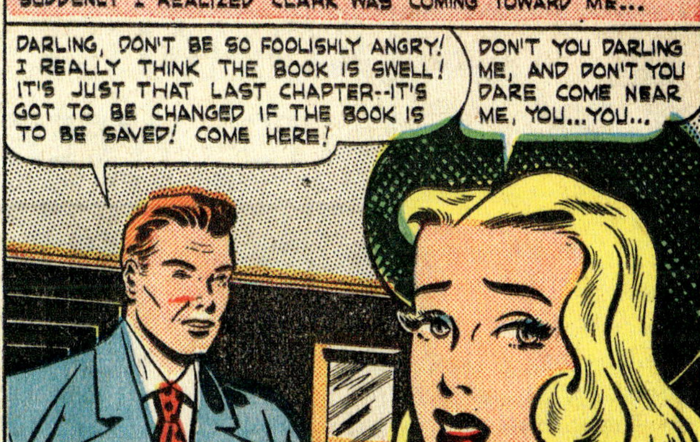
THE DOOR CLOSED BEHIND HER, AND WE WERE ALONE... SUDDENLY I REALIZED CLARK WAS COMING TOWARD ME...
DARLING, DON'T BE SO FOOLISHLY ANGRY! I REALLY THINK THE BOOK IS SWELL! IT'S JUST THAT LAST CHAPTER--IT'S GOT TO BE CHANGED IF THE BOOK IS TO BE SAVED! COME HERE!
DON'T YOU DARLING ME, AND DON'T YOU DARE COME NEAR ME, YOU...YOU...

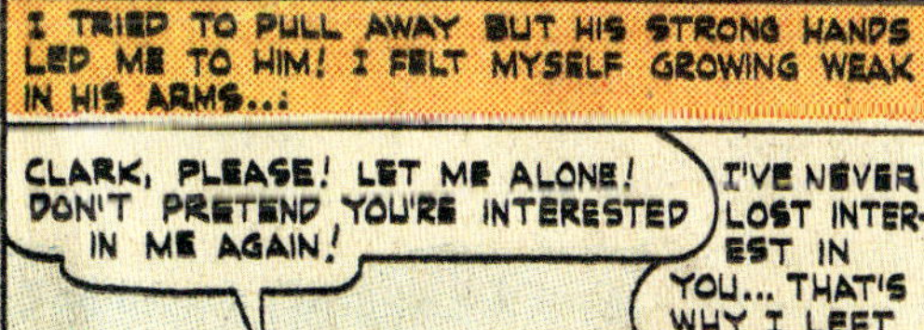
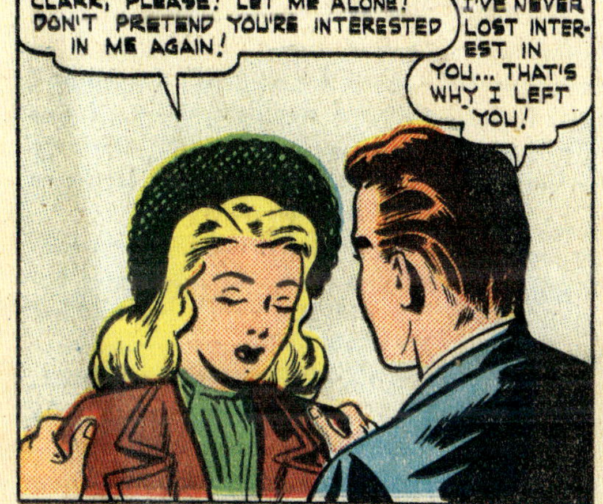
I TRIED TO PULL AWAY BUT HIS STRONG HANDS LED ME TO HIM! I FELT MYSELF GROWING WEAK IN HIS ARMS...
CLARK, PLEASE! LET ME ALONE! DON'T PRETEND YOU'RE INTERESTED IN ME AGAIN!
I'VE NEVER LOST INTEREST IN YOU... THAT'S WHY I LEFT YOU!

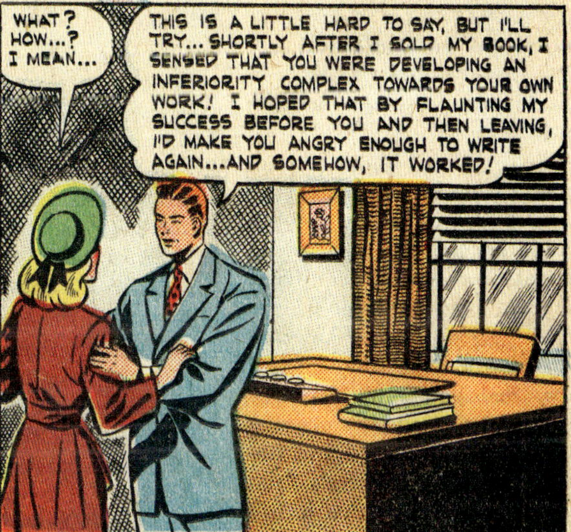
WHAT? HOW...? I MEAN...
THIS IS A LITTLE HARD TO SAY, BUT I'LL TRY... SHORTLY AFTER I SOLD MY BOOK, I SENSED THAT YOU WERE DEVELOPING AN INFERIORITY COMPLEX TOWARDS YOUR OWN WORK! I HOPED THAT BY FLAUNTING MY SUCCESS BEFORE YOU AND THEN LEAVING, I'D MAKE YOU ANGRY ENOUGH TO WRITE AGAIN...AND SOMEHOW, IT WORKED!

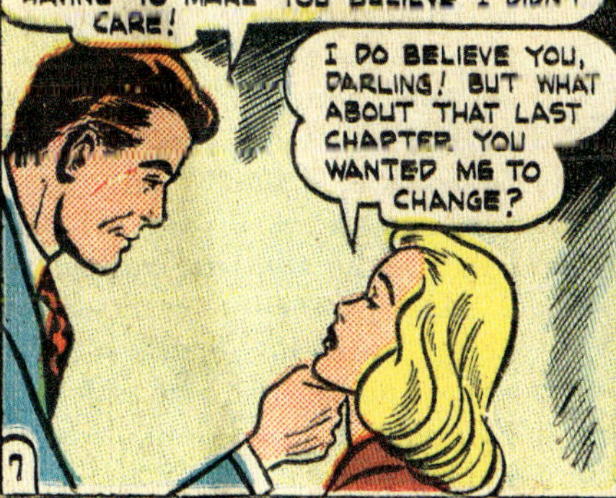
CLARK'S WORDS STRUCK HOME! I COULD SEE NOW WHAT A FOOL I'D BEEN ALL ALONG! CLARK PULLED ME CLOSER... I TRIED TO PULL AWAY, MURMURING SOMETHING ABOUT MISS BAXTER...
OH, DARLING... I'VE NEVER LOVED ANYONE ELSE BUT YOU... AND IT WAS TORTURE HAVING TO MAKE YOU BELIEVE I DIDN'T CARE!
I DO BELIEVE YOU, DARLING! BUT WHAT ABOUT THAT LAST CHAPTER YOU WANTED ME TO CHANGE?
7

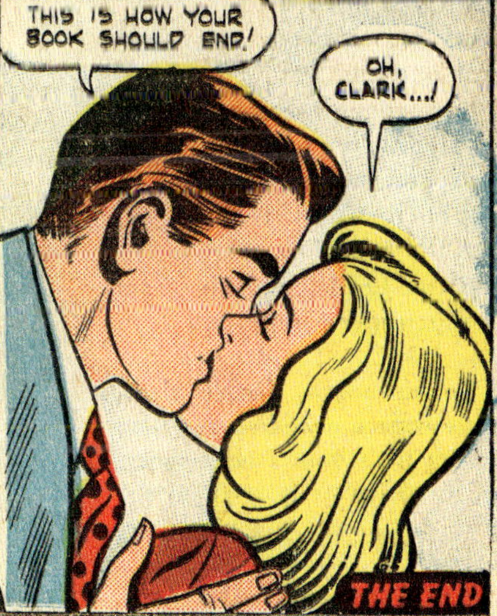
CLARK HELD MY FACE UP TO HIS! ONCE AGAIN I KNEW THE SPELL OF HIS KISS, AND OUR HEARTS SANG OUT OUR SONG OF LOVE... I KNEW THEN THAT LOVE, LIKE THE SANDS OF TIME, COULD NOT BE STOPPED FOR LONG!
THIS IS HOW YOUR BOOK SHOULD END!
OH, CLARK...!
THE END

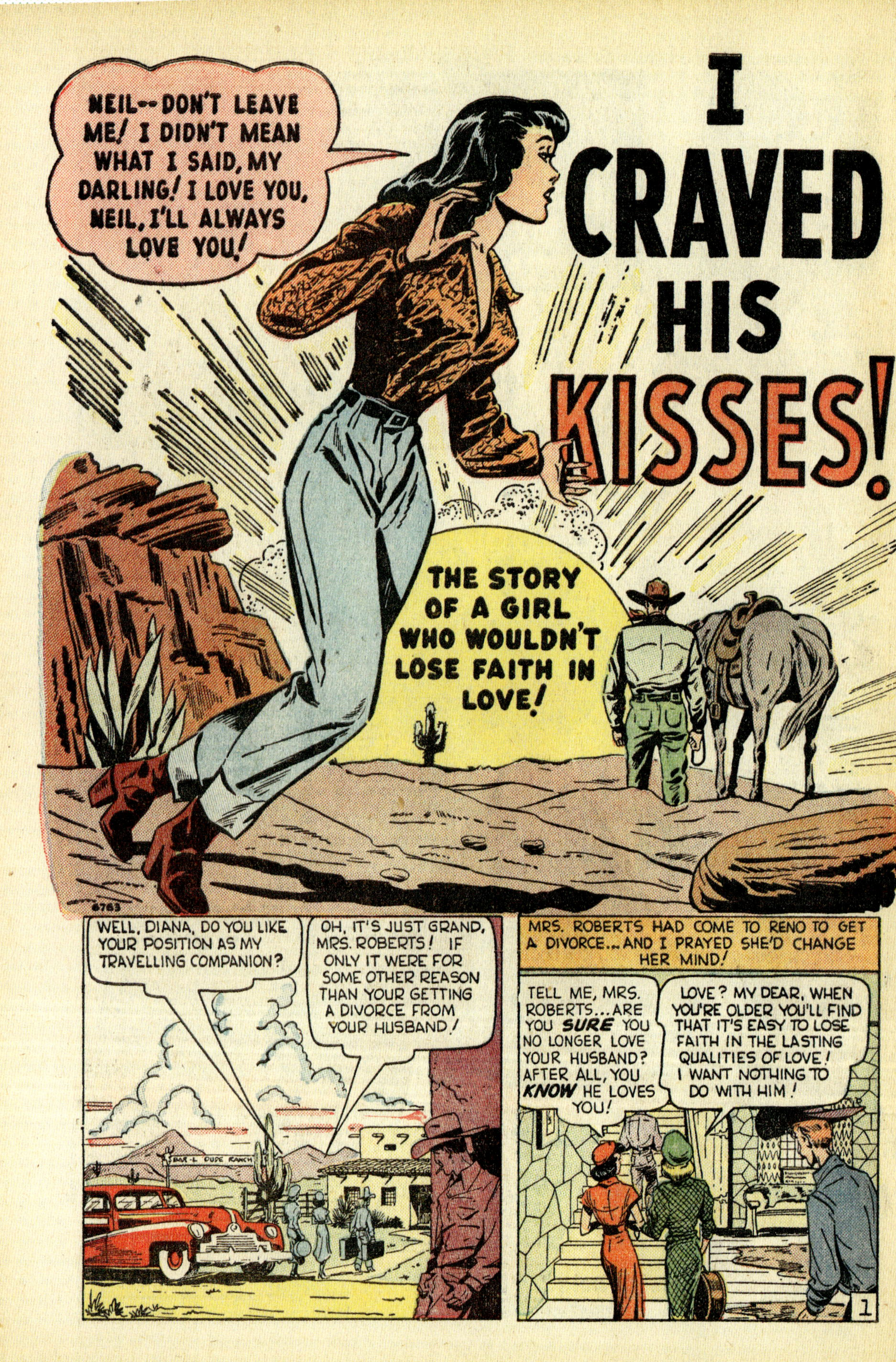
I CRAVED HIS KISSES!
NEIL--DON'T LEAVE ME! I DIDN'T MEAN WHAT I SAID, MY DARLING! I LOVE YOU, NEIL, I'LL ALWAYS LOVE YOU!
THE STORY OF A GIRL WHO WOULDN'T LOSE FAITH IN LOVE!
WELL, DIANA, DO YOU LIKE YOUR POSITION AS MY TRAVELLING COMPANION?
OH, IT'S JUST GRAND, MRS. ROBERTS! IF ONLY IT WERE FOR SOME OTHER REASON THAN YOUR GETTING A DIVORCE FROM YOUR HUSBAND!
MRS. ROBERTS HAD COME TO RENO TO GET A DIVORCE... AND I PRAYED SHE'D CHANGE HER MIND!
TELL ME, MRS. ROBERTS... ARE YOU SURE YOU NO LONGER LOVE YOUR HUSBAND? AFTER ALL, YOU KNOW HE LOVES YOU!
LOVE? MY DEAR, WHEN YOU'RE OLDER YOU'LL FIND THAT IT'S EASY TO LOSE FAITH IN THE LASTING QUALITIES OF LOVE! I WANT NOTHING TO DO WITH HIM!
1

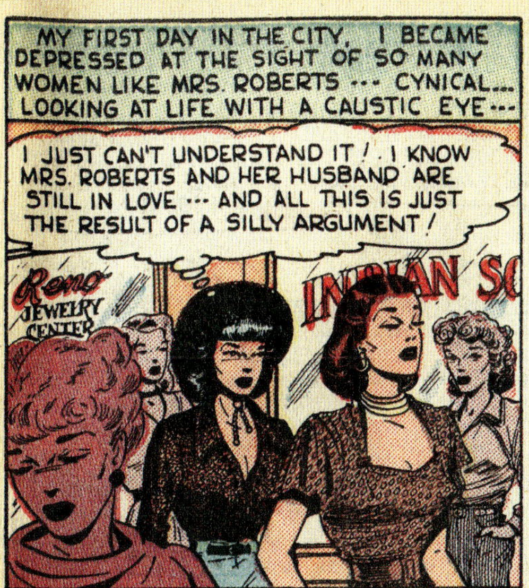

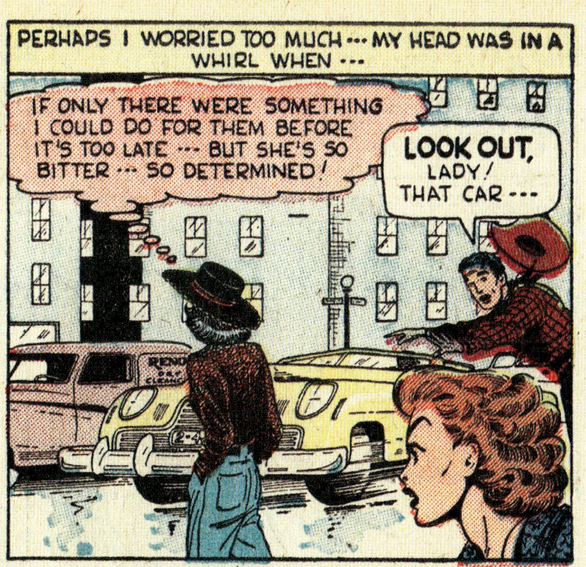

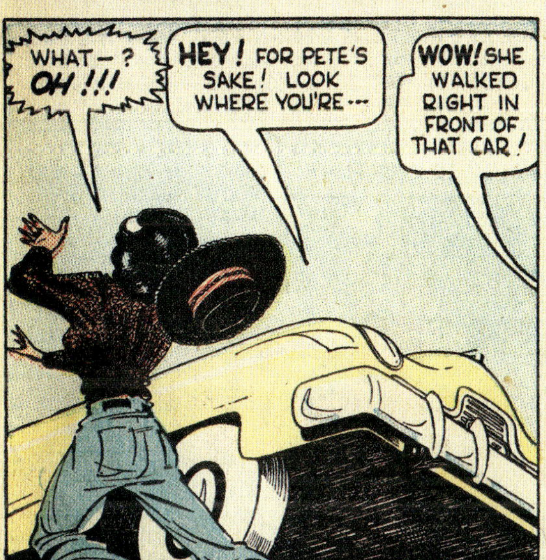

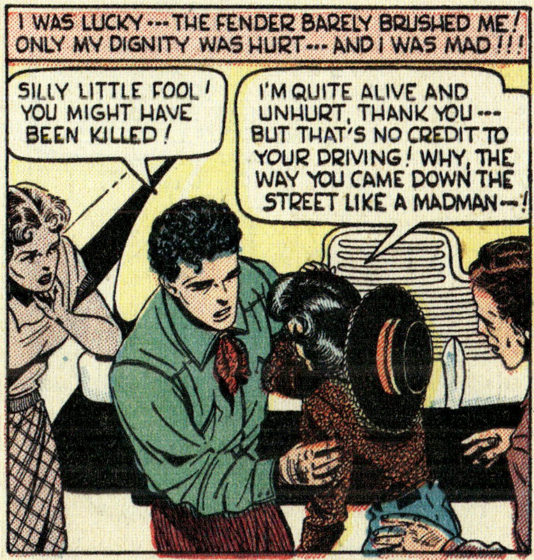

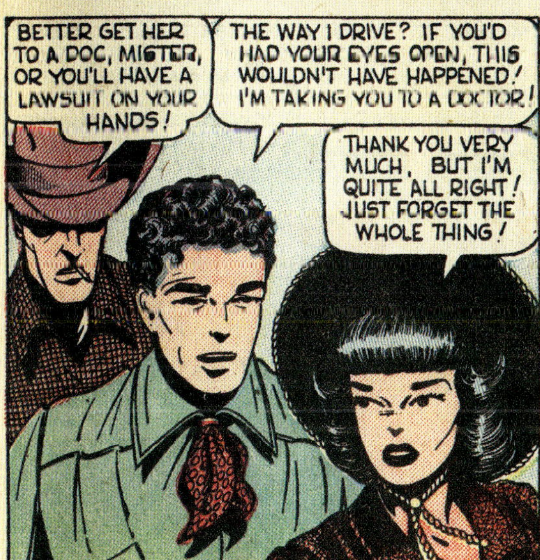

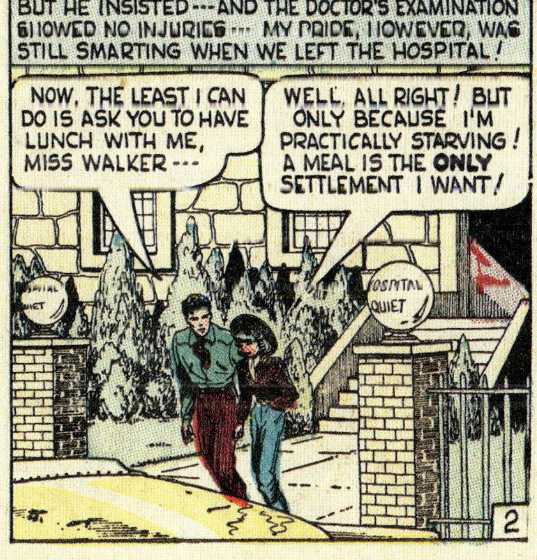

BEST LOVE
#36, April 1950
Art by Bill Everett

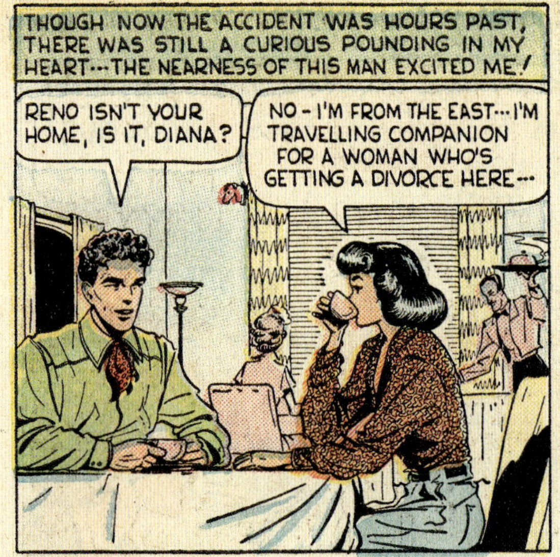
THOUGH NOW THE ACCIDENT WAS HOURS PAST, THERE WAS STILL A CURIOUS POUNDING IN MY HEART---THE NEARNESS OF THIS MAN EXCITED ME!
RENO ISN'T YOUR HOME, IS IT, DIANA?
NO - I'M FROM THE EAST---I'M TRAVELLING COMPANION FOR A WOMAN WHO'S GETTING A DIVORCE HERE---

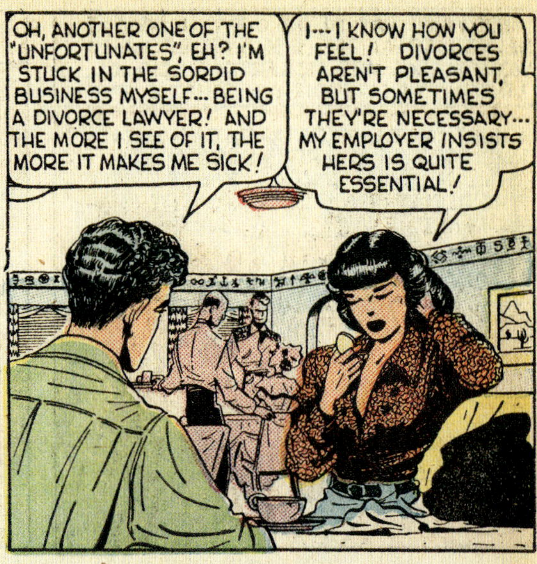
OH, ANOTHER ONE OF THE "UNFORTUNATES", EH? I'M STUCK IN THE SORDID BUSINESS MYSELF---BEING A DIVORCE LAWYER! AND THE MORE I SEE OF IT, THE MORE IT MAKES ME SICK!
I---I KNOW HOW YOU FEEL! DIVORCES AREN'T PLEASANT, BUT SOMETIMES THEY'RE NECESSARY---MY EMPLOYER INSISTS HERS IS QUITE ESSENTIAL!

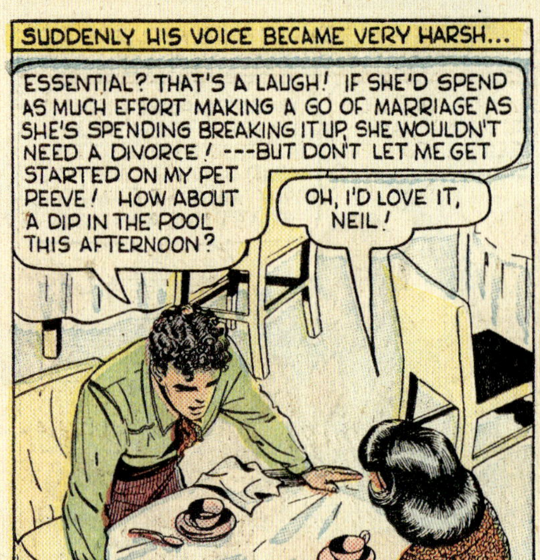
SUDDENLY HIS VOICE BECAME VERY HARSH...
ESSENTIAL? THAT'S A LAUGH! IF SHE'D SPEND AS MUCH EFFORT MAKING A GO OF MARRIAGE AS SHE'S SPENDING BREAKING IT UP, SHE WOULDN'T NEED A DIVORCE! ---BUT DON'T LET ME GET STARTED ON MY PET PEEVE! HOW ABOUT A DIP IN THE POOL THIS AFTERNOON?
OH, I'D LOVE IT, NEIL!

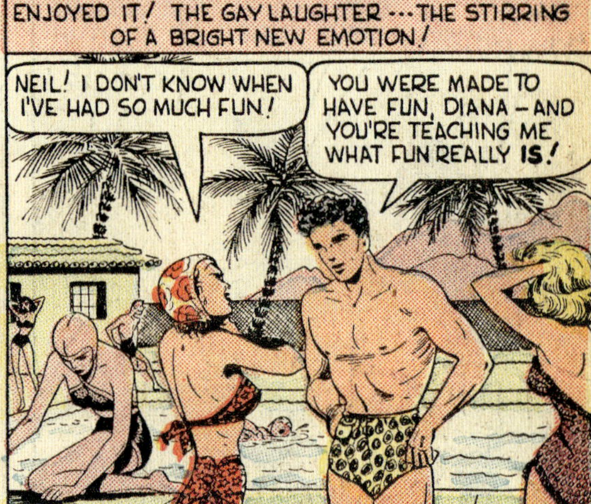
THAT WAS JUST THE BEGINNING! SOON THE POOL BECAME OUR FAVORITE RENDEZVOUS---AND HOW WE ENJOYED IT! THE GAY LAUGHTER---THE STIRRING OF A BRIGHT NEW EMOTION!
NEIL! I DON'T KNOW WHEN I'VE HAD SO MUCH FUN!
YOU WERE MADE TO HAVE FUN, DIANA - AND YOU'RE TEACHING ME WHAT FUN REALLY **IS**!

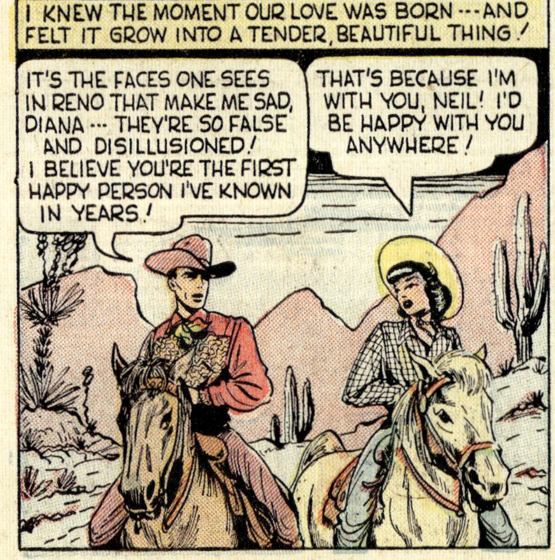
I KNEW THE MOMENT OUR LOVE WAS BORN---AND FELT IT GROW INTO A TENDER, BEAUTIFUL THING!
IT'S THE FACES ONE SEES IN RENO THAT MAKE ME SAD, DIANA--- THEY'RE SO FALSE AND DISILLUSIONED! I BELIEVE YOU'RE THE FIRST HAPPY PERSON I'VE KNOWN IN YEARS!
THAT'S BECAUSE I'M WITH YOU, NEIL! I'D BE HAPPY WITH YOU ANYWHERE!

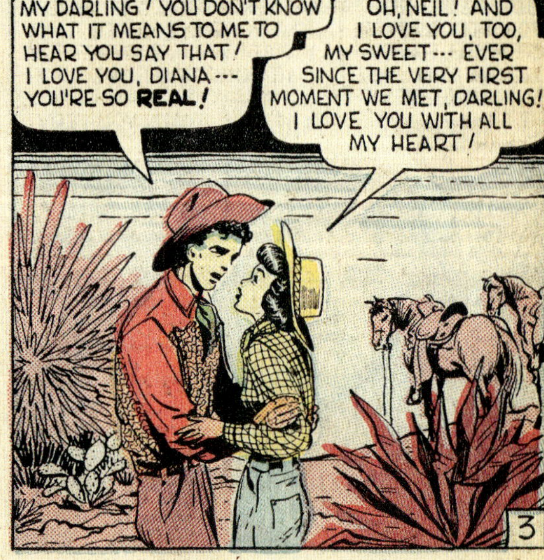
MY DARLING! YOU DON'T KNOW WHAT IT MEANS TO ME TO HEAR YOU SAY THAT! I LOVE YOU, DIANA--- YOU'RE SO **REAL**!
OH, NEIL! AND I LOVE YOU, TOO, MY SWEET--- EVER SINCE THE VERY FIRST MOMENT WE MET, DARLING! I LOVE YOU WITH ALL MY HEART!
3

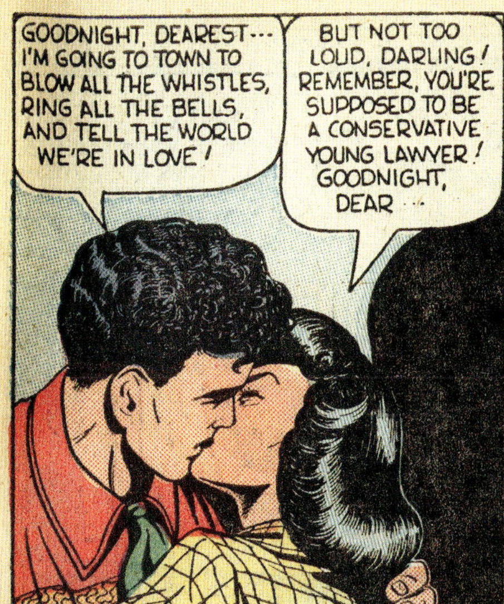
GOODNIGHT, DEAREST--- I'M GOING TO TOWN TO BLOW ALL THE WHISTLES, RING ALL THE BELLS, AND TELL THE WORLD WE'RE IN LOVE!
BUT NOT TOO LOUD, DARLING! REMEMBER, YOU'RE SUPPOSED TO BE A CONSERVATIVE YOUNG LAWYER! GOODNIGHT, DEAR ...

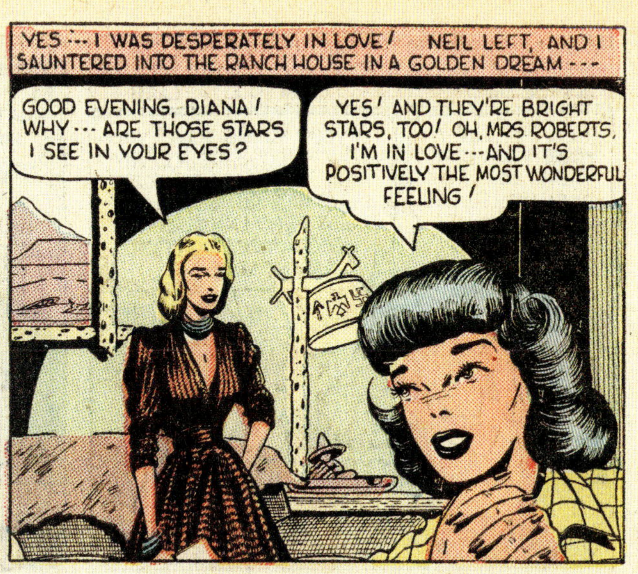
YES --- I WAS DESPERATELY IN LOVE! NEIL LEFT, AND I SAUNTERED INTO THE RANCH HOUSE IN A GOLDEN DREAM ---
GOOD EVENING, DIANA! WHY --- ARE THOSE STARS I SEE IN YOUR EYES?
YES! AND THEY'RE BRIGHT STARS, TOO! OH, MRS ROBERTS, I'M IN LOVE --- AND IT'S POSITIVELY THE MOST WONDERFUL FEELING!

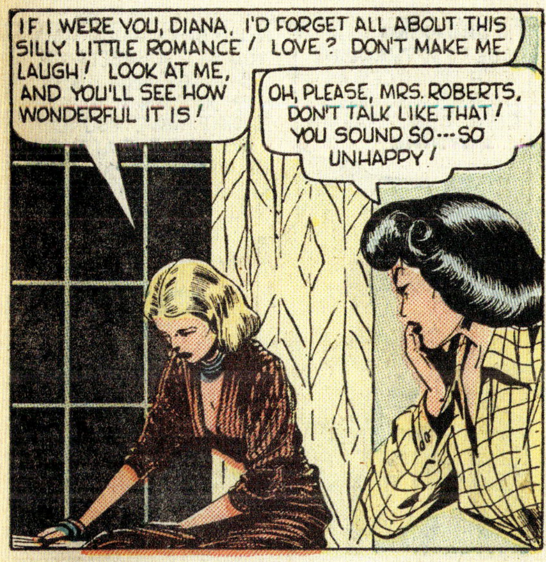
IF I WERE YOU, DIANA, I'D FORGET ALL ABOUT THIS SILLY LITTLE ROMANCE! LOVE? DON'T MAKE ME LAUGH! LOOK AT ME, AND YOU'LL SEE HOW WONDERFUL IT IS!
OH, PLEASE, MRS. ROBERTS, DON'T TALK LIKE THAT! YOU SOUND SO --- SO UNHAPPY!

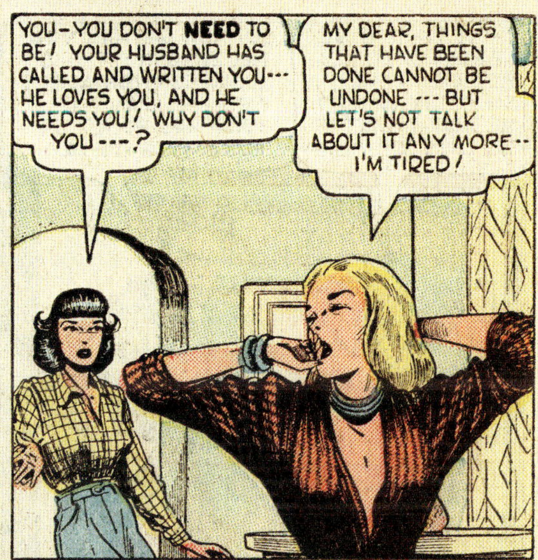
YOU - YOU DON'T NEED TO BE! YOUR HUSBAND HAS CALLED AND WRITTEN YOU--- HE LOVES YOU, AND HE NEEDS YOU! WHY DON'T YOU ---?
MY DEAR, THINGS THAT HAVE BEEN DONE CANNOT BE UNDONE --- BUT LET'S NOT TALK ABOUT IT ANY MORE -- I'M TIRED!

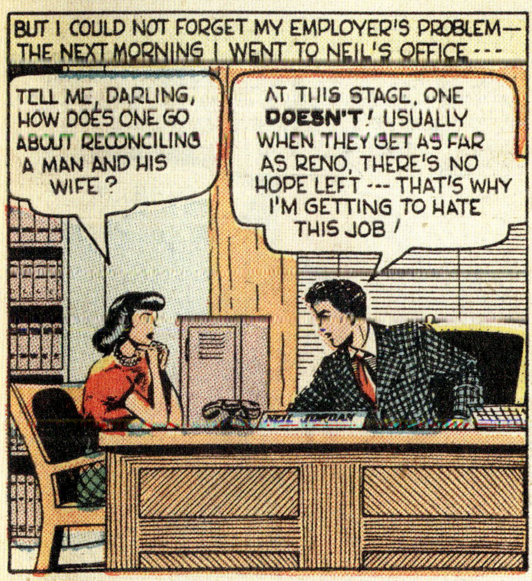
BUT I COULD NOT FORGET MY EMPLOYER'S PROBLEM— THE NEXT MORNING I WENT TO NEIL'S OFFICE ---
TELL ME, DARLING, HOW DOES ONE GO ABOUT RECONCILING A MAN AND HIS WIFE?
AT THIS STAGE, ONE DOESN'T! USUALLY WHEN THEY GET AS FAR AS RENO, THERE'S NO HOPE LEFT --- THAT'S WHY I'M GETTING TO HATE THIS JOB!

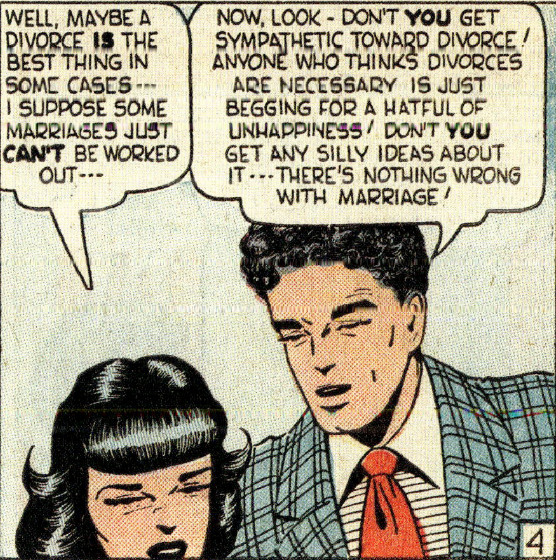
WELL, MAYBE A DIVORCE IS THE BEST THING IN SOME CASES --- I SUPPOSE SOME MARRIAGES JUST CAN'T BE WORKED OUT---
NOW, LOOK - DON'T YOU GET SYMPATHETIC TOWARD DIVORCE! ANYONE WHO THINKS DIVORCES ARE NECESSARY IS JUST BEGGING FOR A HATFUL OF UNHAPPINESS! DON'T YOU GET ANY SILLY IDEAS ABOUT IT --- THERE'S NOTHING WRONG WITH MARRIAGE!
4

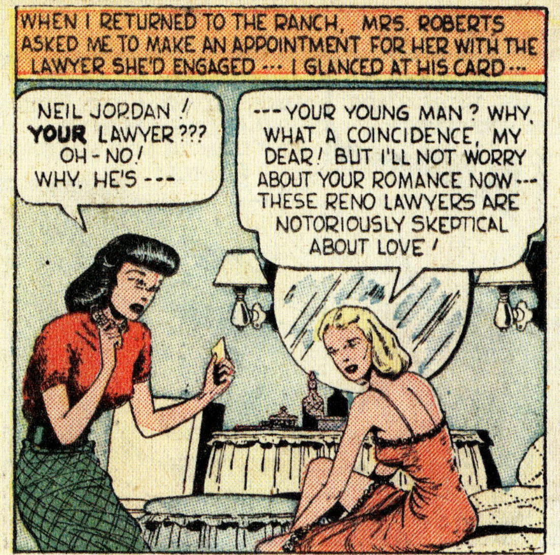
WHEN I RETURNED TO THE RANCH, MRS. ROBERTS ASKED ME TO MAKE AN APPOINTMENT FOR HER WITH THE LAWYER SHE'D ENGAGED --- I GLANCED AT HIS CARD ---
NEIL JORDAN! YOUR LAWYER??? OH - NO! WHY, HE'S ---
--- YOUR YOUNG MAN? WHY, WHAT A COINCIDENCE, MY DEAR! BUT I'LL NOT WORRY ABOUT YOUR ROMANCE NOW --- THESE RENO LAWYERS ARE NOTORIOUSLY SKEPTICAL ABOUT LOVE!

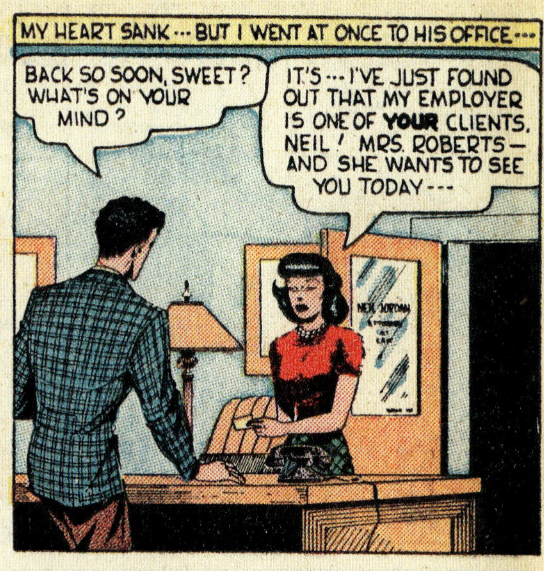
MY HEART SANK --- BUT I WENT AT ONCE TO HIS OFFICE ---
BACK SO SOON, SWEET? WHAT'S ON YOUR MIND?
IT'S --- I'VE JUST FOUND OUT THAT MY EMPLOYER IS ONE OF YOUR CLIENTS, NEIL! MRS. ROBERTS — AND SHE WANTS TO SEE YOU TODAY ---

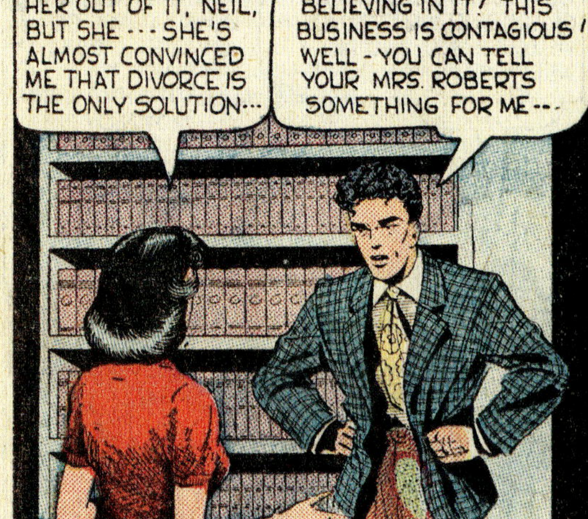
I - I'VE TRIED TO TALK HER OUT OF IT, NEIL, BUT SHE --- SHE'S ALMOST CONVINCED ME THAT DIVORCE IS THE ONLY SOLUTION ---
SO! NOW SHE HAS YOU BELIEVING IN IT! THIS BUSINESS IS CONTAGIOUS! WELL - YOU CAN TELL YOUR MRS. ROBERTS SOMETHING FOR ME ---

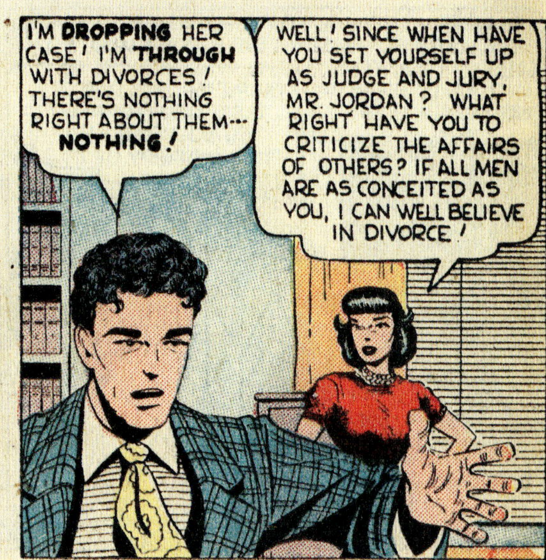
I'M DROPPING HER CASE! I'M THROUGH WITH DIVORCES! THERE'S NOTHING RIGHT ABOUT THEM --- NOTHING!
WELL! SINCE WHEN HAVE YOU SET YOURSELF UP AS JUDGE AND JURY, MR. JORDAN? WHAT RIGHT HAVE YOU TO CRITICIZE THE AFFAIRS OF OTHERS? IF ALL MEN ARE AS CONCEITED AS YOU, I CAN WELL BELIEVE IN DIVORCE!

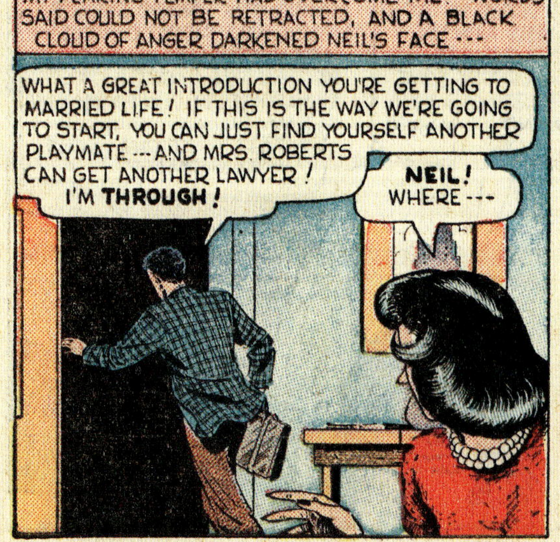
MY FLARING TEMPER HAD OVERCOME ME! WORDS SAID COULD NOT BE RETRACTED, AND A BLACK CLOUD OF ANGER DARKENED NEIL'S FACE ---
WHAT A GREAT INTRODUCTION YOU'RE GETTING TO MARRIED LIFE! IF THIS IS THE WAY WE'RE GOING TO START, YOU CAN JUST FIND YOURSELF ANOTHER PLAYMATE --- AND MRS. ROBERTS CAN GET ANOTHER LAWYER! I'M THROUGH!
NEIL! WHERE ---

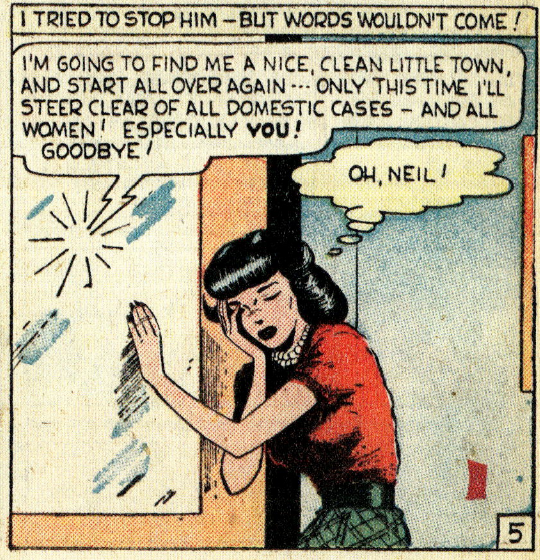
I TRIED TO STOP HIM — BUT WORDS WOULDN'T COME!
I'M GOING TO FIND ME A NICE, CLEAN LITTLE TOWN, AND START ALL OVER AGAIN --- ONLY THIS TIME I'LL STEER CLEAR OF ALL DOMESTIC CASES — AND ALL WOMEN! ESPECIALLY YOU! GOODBYE!
OH, NEIL!
5

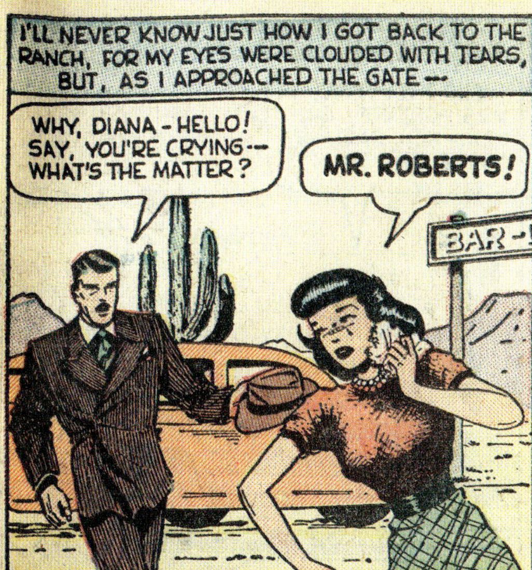
I'LL NEVER KNOW JUST HOW I GOT BACK TO THE RANCH, FOR MY EYES WERE CLOUDED WITH TEARS, BUT, AS I APPROACHED THE GATE ---
WHY, DIANA - HELLO! SAY, YOU'RE CRYING -- WHAT'S THE MATTER?
MR. ROBERTS!
BAR-

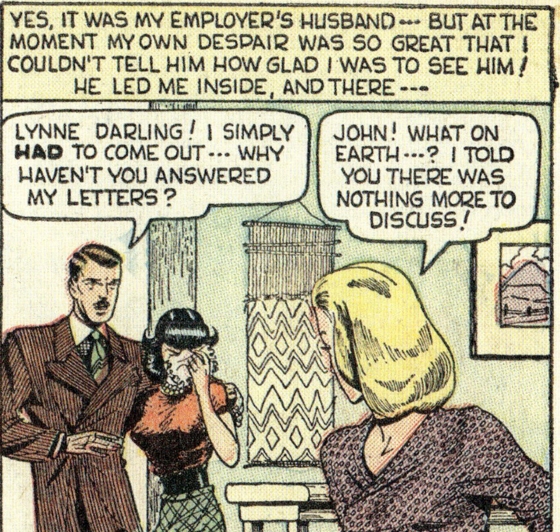
YES, IT WAS MY EMPLOYER'S HUSBAND --- BUT AT THE MOMENT MY OWN DESPAIR WAS SO GREAT THAT I COULDN'T TELL HIM HOW GLAD I WAS TO SEE HIM! HE LED ME INSIDE, AND THERE ---
LYNNE DARLING! I SIMPLY HAD TO COME OUT --- WHY HAVEN'T YOU ANSWERED MY LETTERS?
JOHN! WHAT ON EARTH ---? I TOLD YOU THERE WAS NOTHING MORE TO DISCUSS!

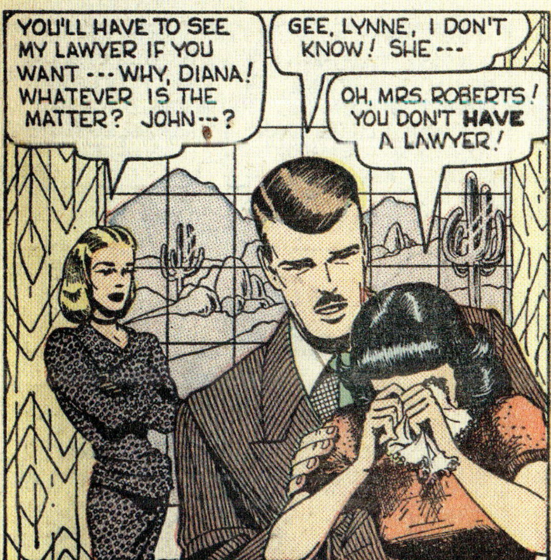
YOU'LL HAVE TO SEE MY LAWYER IF YOU WANT --- WHY, DIANA! WHATEVER IS THE MATTER? JOHN ---?
GEE, LYNNE, I DON'T KNOW! SHE ---
OH, MRS. ROBERTS! YOU DON'T HAVE A LAWYER!

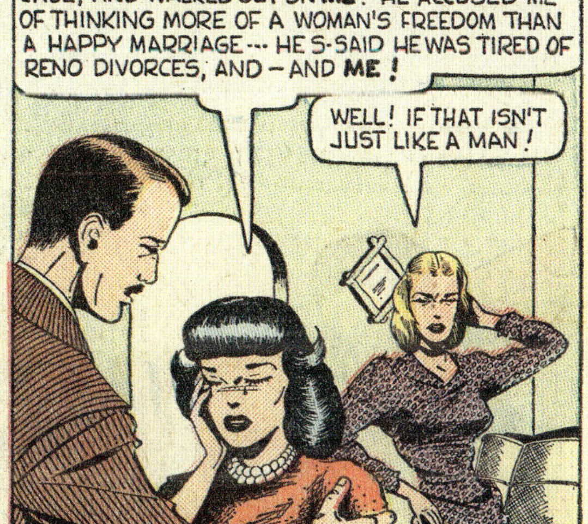
IT'S - IT'S NEIL JORDAN! HE'S DROPPED YOUR CASE, AND WALKED OUT ON ME! HE ACCUSED ME OF THINKING MORE OF A WOMAN'S FREEDOM THAN A HAPPY MARRIAGE --- HE S-SAID HE WAS TIRED OF RENO DIVORCES, AND - AND ME!
WELL! IF THAT ISN'T JUST LIKE A MAN!

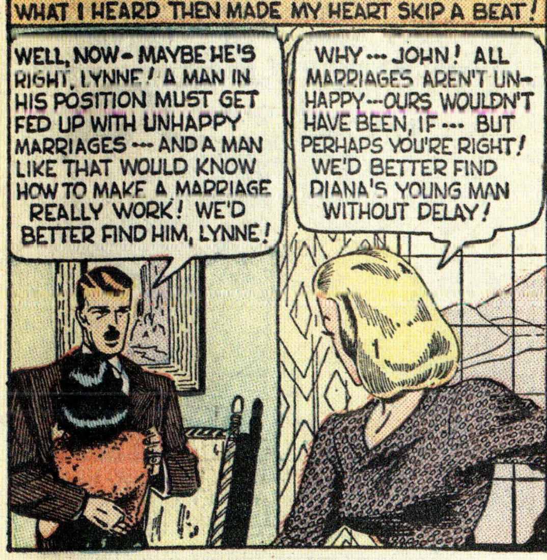
WHAT I HEARD THEN MADE MY HEART SKIP A BEAT!
WELL, NOW - MAYBE HE'S RIGHT, LYNNE! A MAN IN HIS POSITION MUST GET FED UP WITH UNHAPPY MARRIAGES --- AND A MAN LIKE THAT WOULD KNOW HOW TO MAKE A MARRIAGE REALLY WORK! WE'D BETTER FIND HIM, LYNNE!
WHY --- JOHN! ALL MARRIAGES AREN'T UN-HAPPY---OURS WOULDN'T HAVE BEEN, IF --- BUT PERHAPS YOU'RE RIGHT! WE'D BETTER FIND DIANA'S YOUNG MAN WITHOUT DELAY!

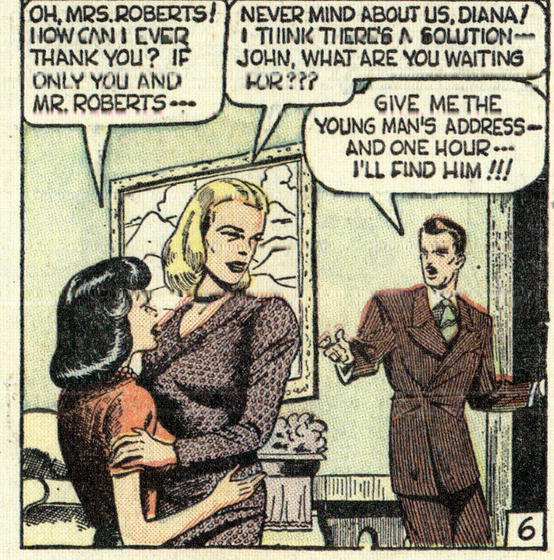
OH, MRS. ROBERTS! HOW CAN I EVER THANK YOU? IF ONLY YOU AND MR. ROBERTS ---
NEVER MIND ABOUT US, DIANA! I THINK THERE'S A SOLUTION --- JOHN, WHAT ARE YOU WAITING FOR???
GIVE ME THE YOUNG MAN'S ADDRESS -- AND ONE HOUR --- I'LL FIND HIM!!!
6

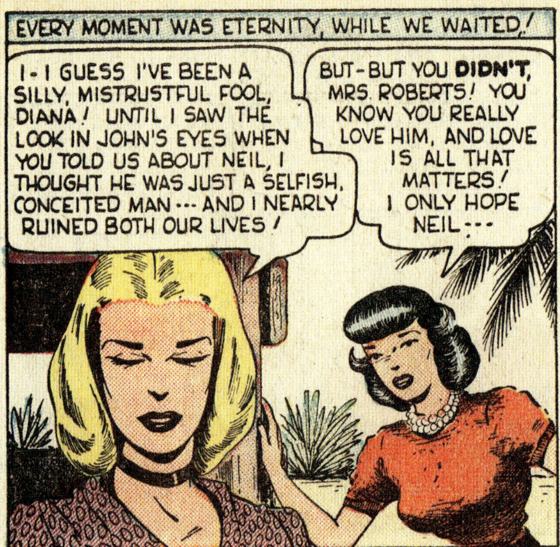
EVERY MOMENT WAS ETERNITY, WHILE WE WAITED!
I-I GUESS I'VE BEEN A SILLY, MISTRUSTFUL FOOL, DIANA! UNTIL I SAW THE LOOK IN JOHN'S EYES WHEN YOU TOLD US ABOUT NEIL, I THOUGHT HE WAS JUST A SELFISH, CONCEITED MAN --- AND I NEARLY RUINED BOTH OUR LIVES!
BUT-BUT YOU **DIDN'T**, MRS. ROBERTS! YOU KNOW YOU REALLY LOVE HIM, AND LOVE IS ALL THAT MATTERS! I ONLY HOPE NEIL---

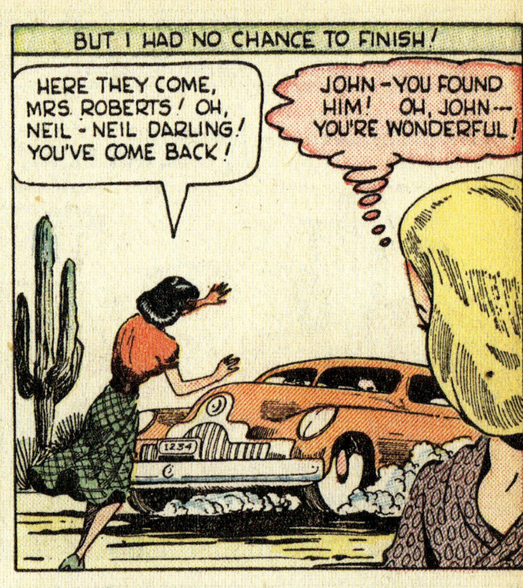
BUT I HAD NO CHANCE TO FINISH!
HERE THEY COME, MRS. ROBERTS! OH, NEIL - NEIL DARLING! YOU'VE COME BACK!
JOHN --YOU FOUND HIM! OH, JOHN--- YOU'RE WONDERFUL!
1254

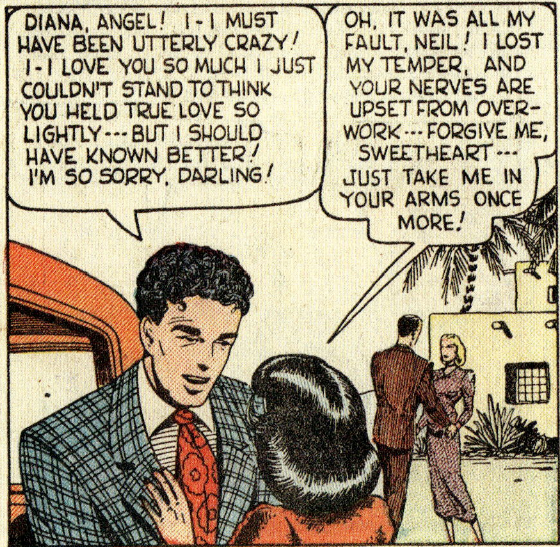
DIANA, ANGEL! I-I MUST HAVE BEEN UTTERLY CRAZY! I-I LOVE YOU SO MUCH I JUST COULDN'T STAND TO THINK YOU HELD TRUE LOVE SO LIGHTLY--- BUT I SHOULD HAVE KNOWN BETTER! I'M SO SORRY, DARLING!
OH, IT WAS ALL MY FAULT, NEIL! I LOST MY TEMPER, AND YOUR NERVES ARE UPSET FROM OVER-WORK--- FORGIVE ME, SWEETHEART--- JUST TAKE ME IN YOUR ARMS ONCE MORE!

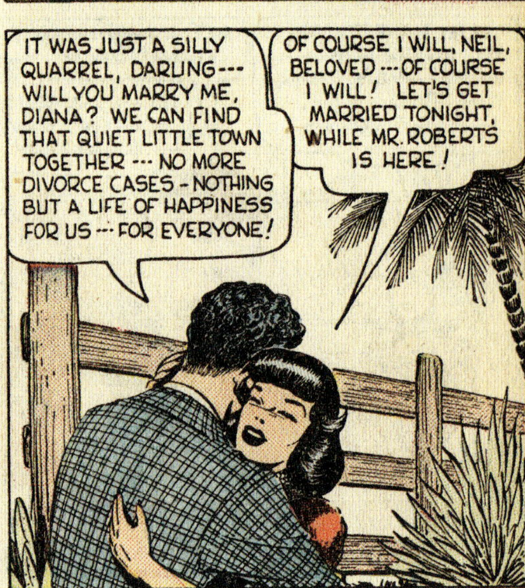
IT WAS JUST A SILLY QUARREL, DARLING--- WILL YOU MARRY ME, DIANA? WE CAN FIND THAT QUIET LITTLE TOWN TOGETHER --- NO MORE DIVORCE CASES - NOTHING BUT A LIFE OF HAPPINESS FOR US --- FOR EVERYONE!
OF COURSE I WILL, NEIL, BELOVED --- OF COURSE I WILL! LET'S GET MARRIED TONIGHT, WHILE MR. ROBERTS IS HERE!

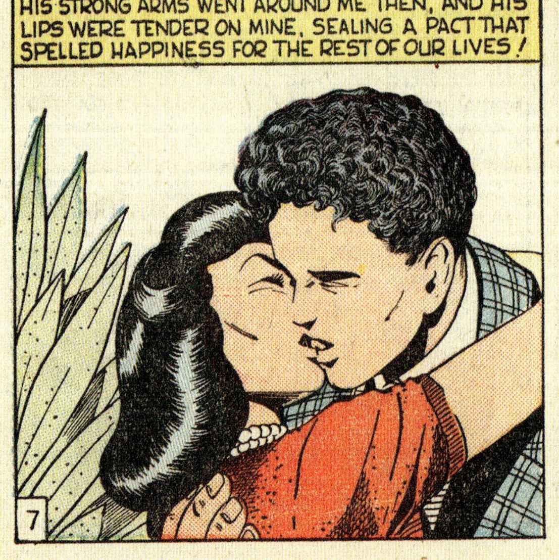
HIS STRONG ARMS WENT AROUND ME THEN, AND HIS LIPS WERE TENDER ON MINE, SEALING A PACT THAT SPELLED HAPPINESS FOR THE REST OF OUR LIVES!
7

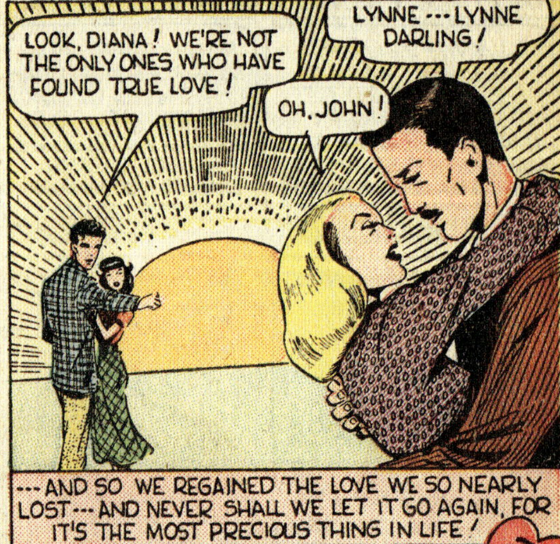
LOOK, DIANA! WE'RE NOT THE ONLY ONES WHO HAVE FOUND TRUE LOVE!
LYNNE --- LYNNE DARLING!
OH, JOHN!
--- AND SO WE REGAINED THE LOVE WE SO NEARLY LOST--- AND NEVER SHALL WE LET IT GO AGAIN, FOR IT'S THE MOST PRECIOUS THING IN LIFE!
The End

I SHOULD HAVE KNOWN FROM THE BURNING INTENSITY OF JACK LINTER'S KISSES THAT HE LOVED ME---AND ME ALONE? YET WHY WAS I DRIVEN INTO A JEALOUS FRENZY EVERY TIME HE SO MUCH AS SPOKE TO ANOTHER GIRL? TOO LATE I LEARNED THAT NOT EVEN HEARTBREAK CAN QUENCH THE ---

Flame of Jealousy

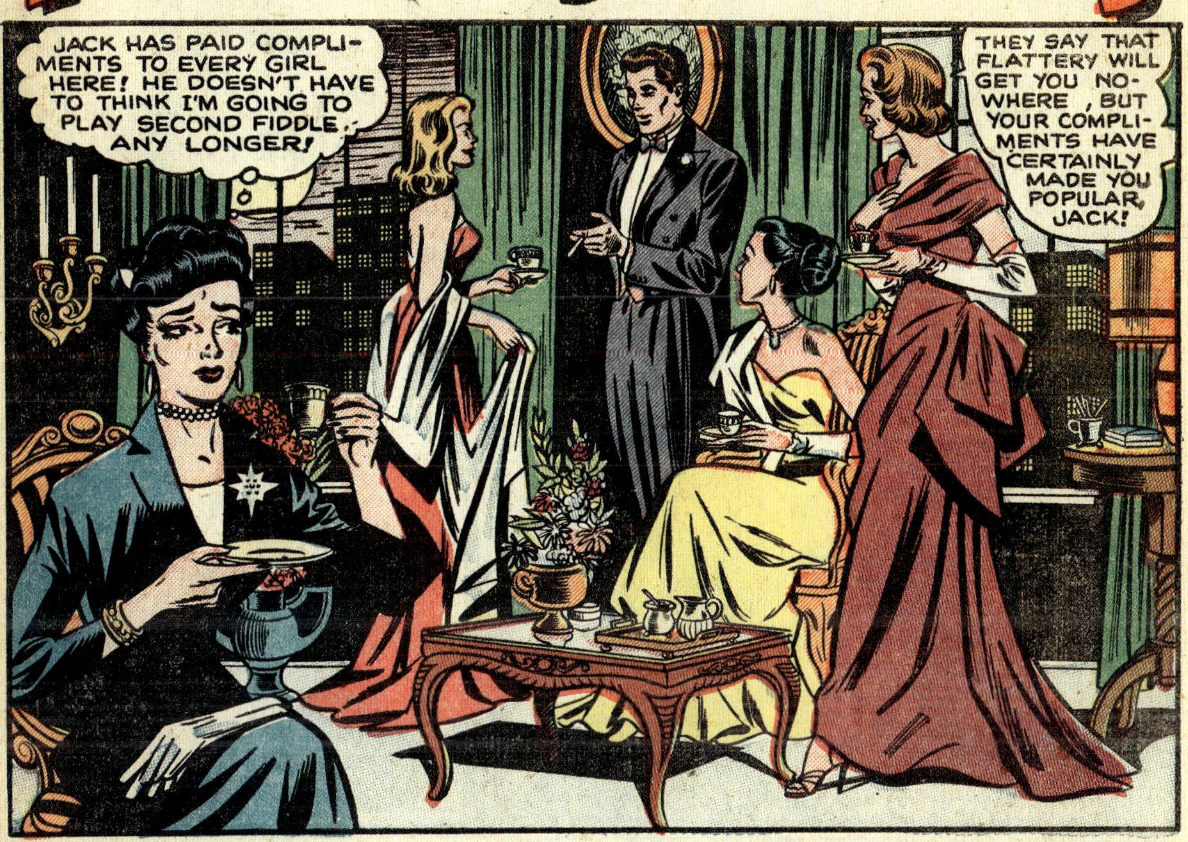

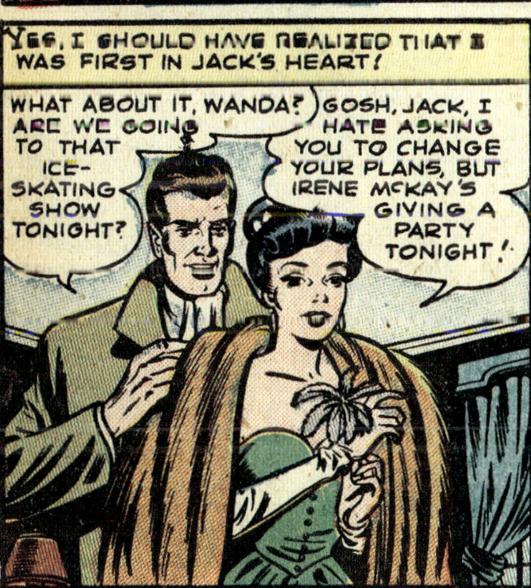

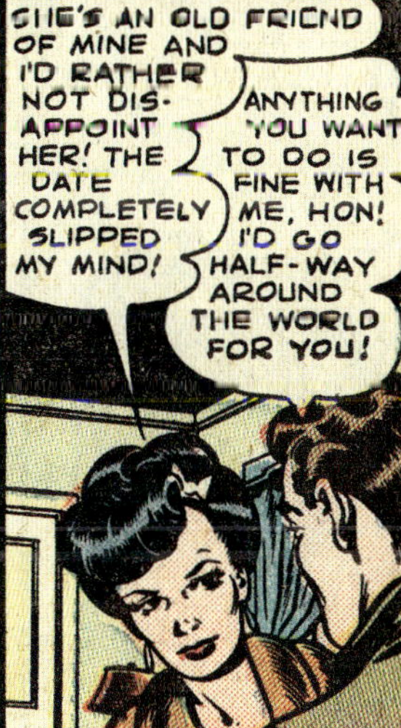

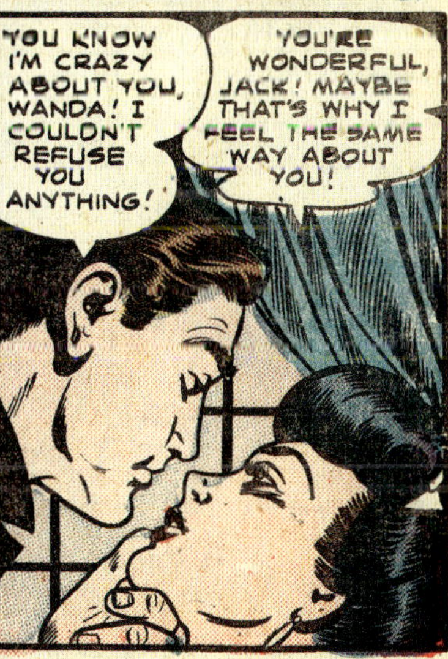

BRIDES ROMANCES
#4, March 1954

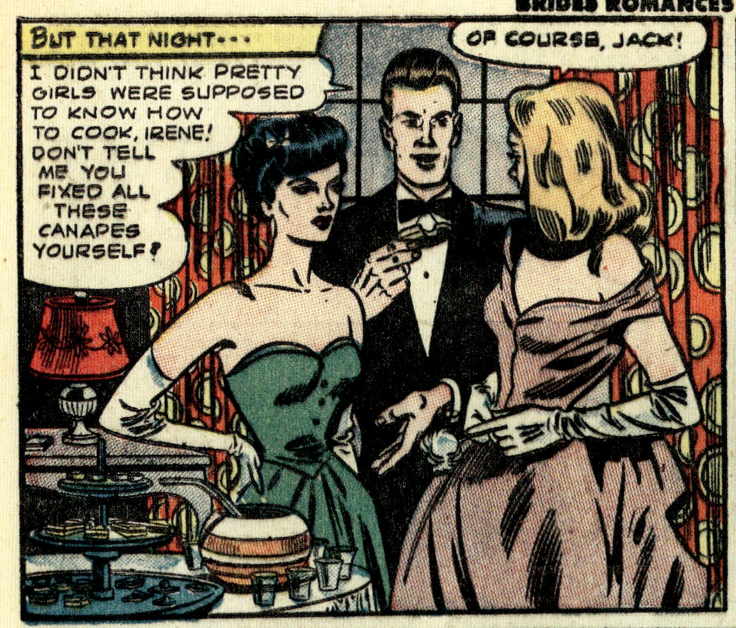

BUT THAT NIGHT---
I DIDN'T THINK PRETTY GIRLS WERE SUPPOSED TO KNOW HOW TO COOK, IRENE! DON'T TELL ME YOU FIXED ALL THESE CANAPES YOURSELF?
OF COURSE, JACK!

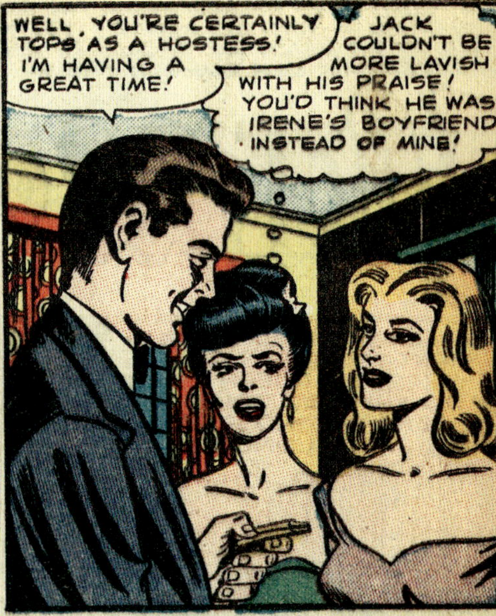

WELL, YOU'RE CERTAINLY TOPS AS A HOSTESS! I'M HAVING A GREAT TIME!
JACK COULDN'T BE MORE LAVISH WITH HIS PRAISE! YOU'D THINK HE WAS IRENE'S BOYFRIEND INSTEAD OF MINE!

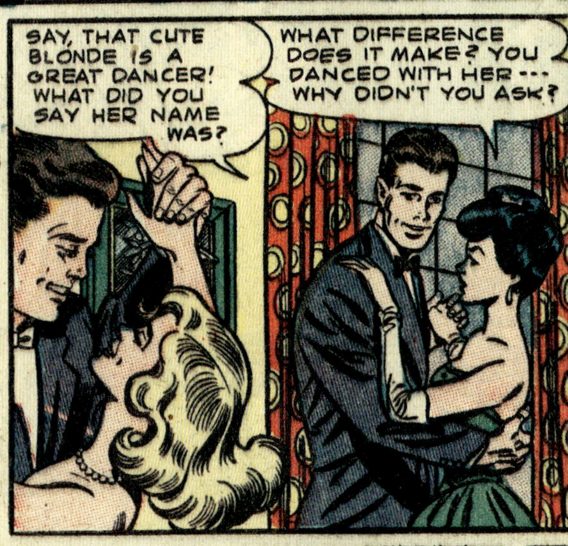

I SHOULD HAVE REALIZED THAT JACK WAS JUST BEING HIS NATURAL FRIENDLY SELF, BUT EVERY-TIME HE PAID ANOTHER GIRL A COMPLIMENT, RESENTMENT WELLED UP IN ME! THAT EVENING IT SEEMED THAT EVERY GIRL GOT HER SHARE OF HIS ATTENTION!
SAY, THAT CUTE BLONDE IS A GREAT DANCER! WHAT DID YOU SAY HER NAME WAS?
WHAT DIFFERENCE DOES IT MAKE? YOU DANCED WITH HER --- WHY DIDN'T YOU ASK?

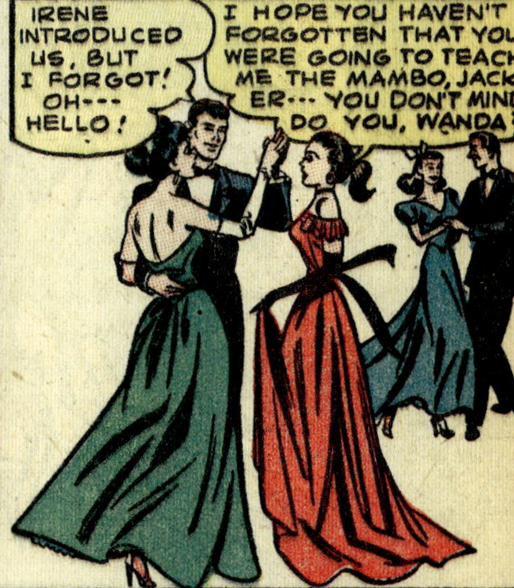

IRENE INTRODUCED US, BUT I FORGOT! OH--- HELLO!
I HOPE YOU HAVEN'T FORGOTTEN THAT YOU WERE GOING TO TEACH ME THE MAMBO, JACK! ER--- YOU DON'T MIND, DO YOU, WANDA?

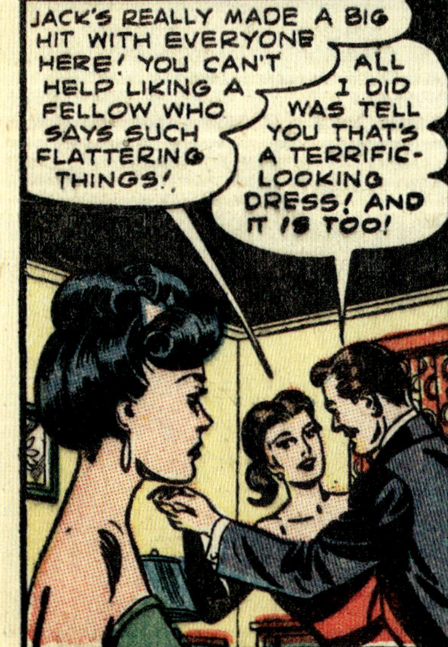

JACK'S REALLY MADE A BIG HIT WITH EVERYONE HERE! YOU CAN'T HELP LIKING A FELLOW WHO SAYS SUCH FLATTERING THINGS!
ALL I DID WAS TELL YOU THAT'S A TERRIFIC-LOOKING DRESS! AND IT IS TOO!

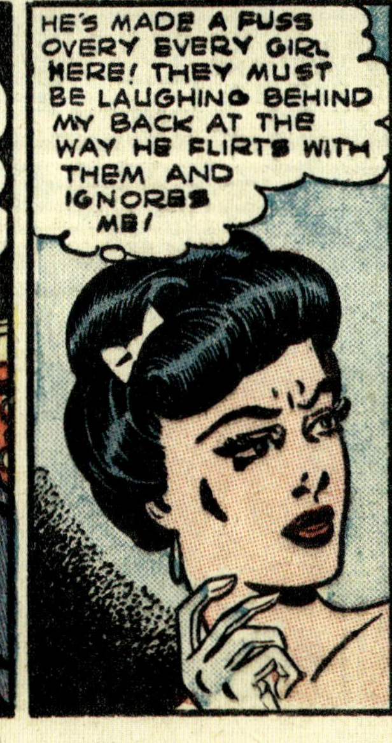

HE'S MADE A FUSS OVERY EVERY GIRL HERE! THEY MUST BE LAUGHING BEHIND MY BACK AT THE WAY HE FLIRTS WITH THEM AND IGNORES ME!

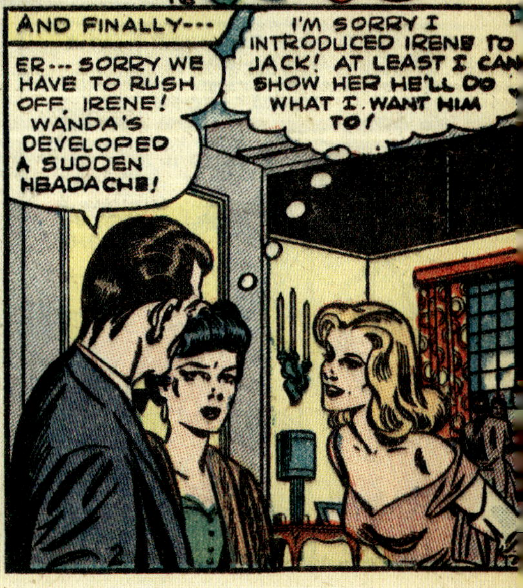

AND FINALLY---
ER--- SORRY WE HAVE TO RUSH OFF, IRENE! WANDA'S DEVELOPED A SUDDEN HEADACHE!
I'M SORRY I INTRODUCED IRENE TO JACK! AT LEAST I CAN SHOW HER HE'LL DO WHAT I WANT HIM TO!

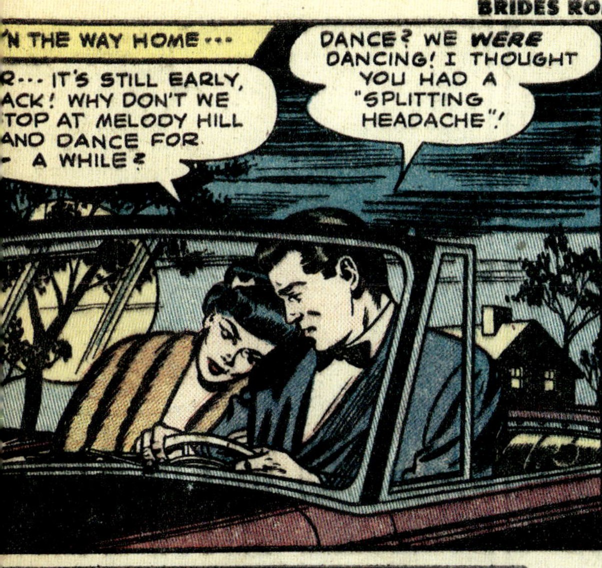

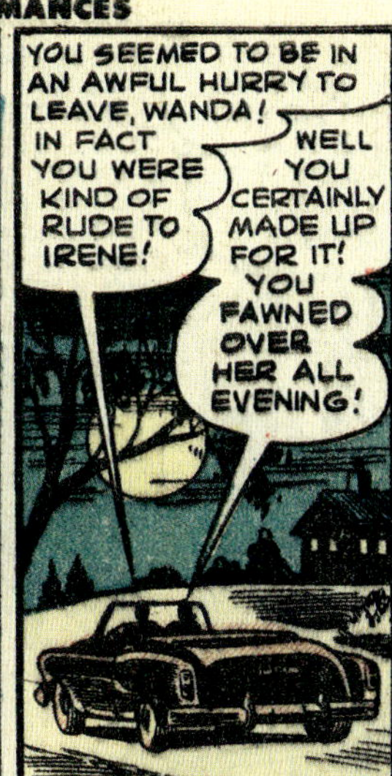

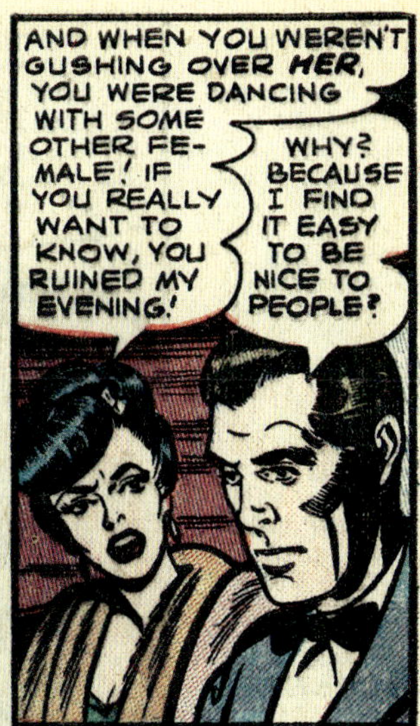

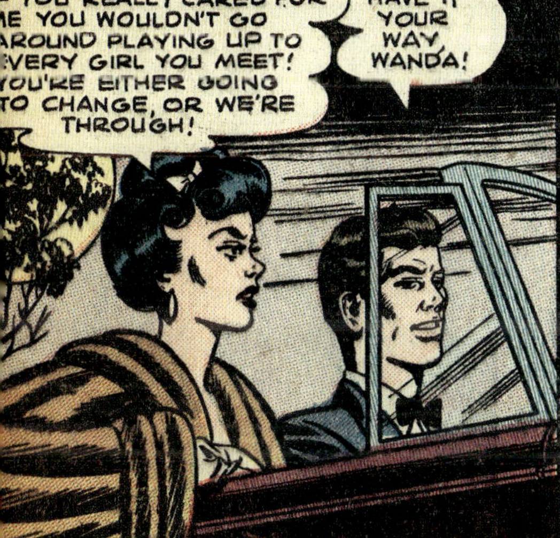

I HAD BEEN SO POSITIVE THAT JACK WOULD APOLOGIZE AND CHANGE HIS WAYS TO PLEASE ME! INSTEAD, HE DROVE ME HOME IN GRIM SILENCE AND LEFT ME WITH ONLY A CURT "GOOD-NIGHT"! CONVINCED THAT I WAS RIGHT, I WAS FURIOUS WITH HIM!

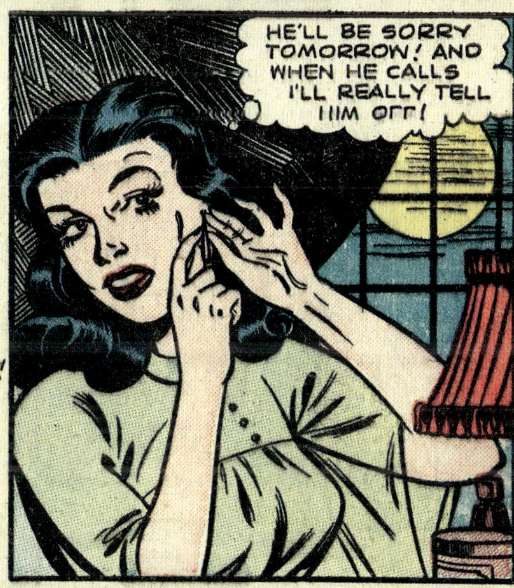

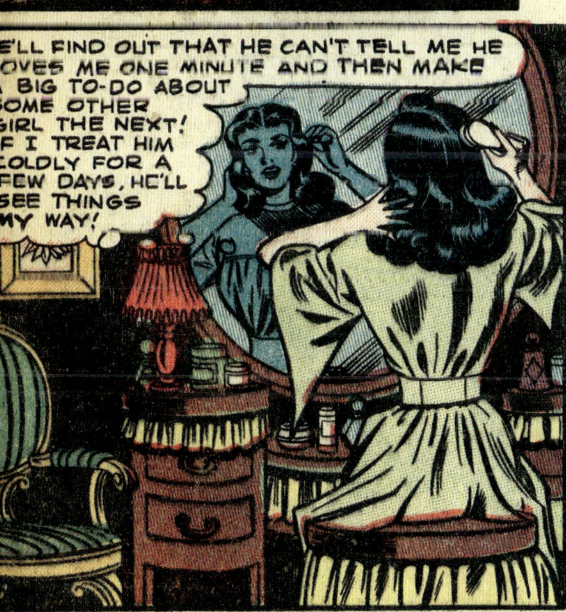

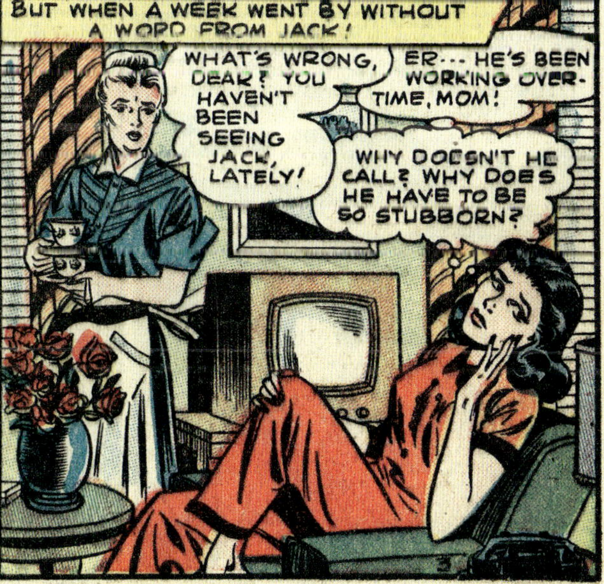

SEVERAL LONELY WEEKS DRAGGED BY BEFORE I REALIZED THAT JACK HAD TAKEN MY ULTIMATUM SERIOUSLY! HE WAS THROUGH WITH *ME!* HURT AND ANGRY, UNABLE TO SWALLOW MY PRIDE LONG ENOUGH TO CALL HIM, I DECIDED TO LET OTHER MEN HELP ME FORGET!

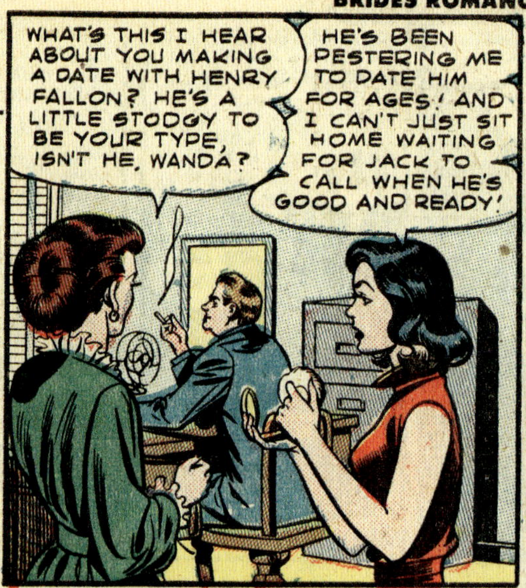

THAT NIGHT!

I DON'T KNOW HOW I RATED AN EVENING WITH THE PRETTIEST GIRL AT THE OFFICE! DID I TELL YOU YOU'RE LOOKING MIGHTY LOVELY TONIGHT, WANDA?

WHY --- THAN YOU' ...NK

HENRY MAY NOT BE TOO INTERESTIN BUT AT LEAS HE GIVES AL HIS ATTENTIO TO ME'

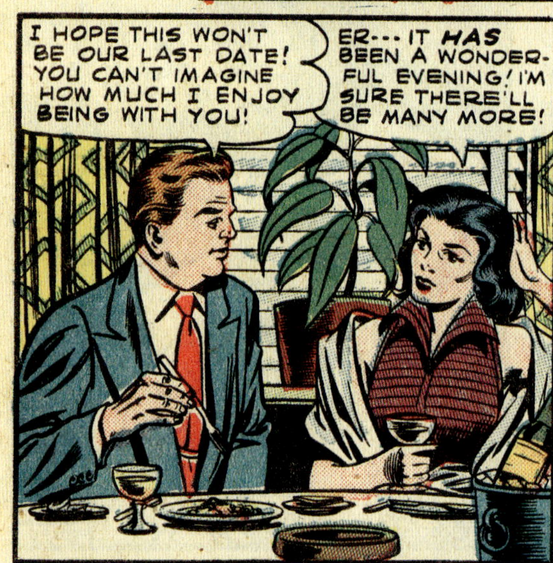

ACTUALLY, COMPARED WITH JACK, HENRY FALLON WAS A TERRIFIC BORE! BUT MY VANITY CRIED OUT FOR COMPLIMENTS AND ON THAT FIRST DATE HENRY WENT OUT OF HIS WAY TO FEED MY EGO! BUT ON A DOUBLE-DATE A FEW DAYS LATER

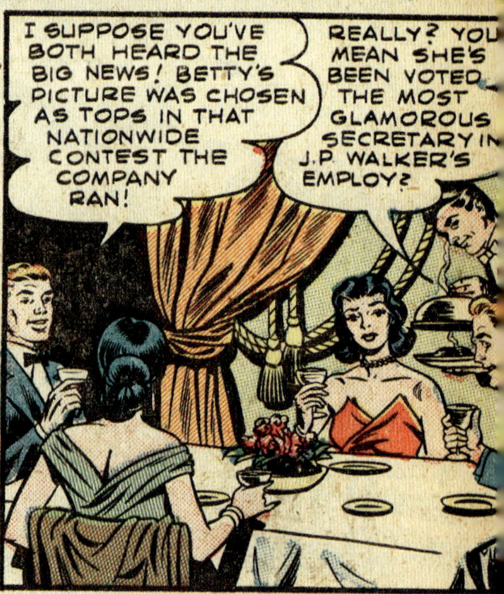

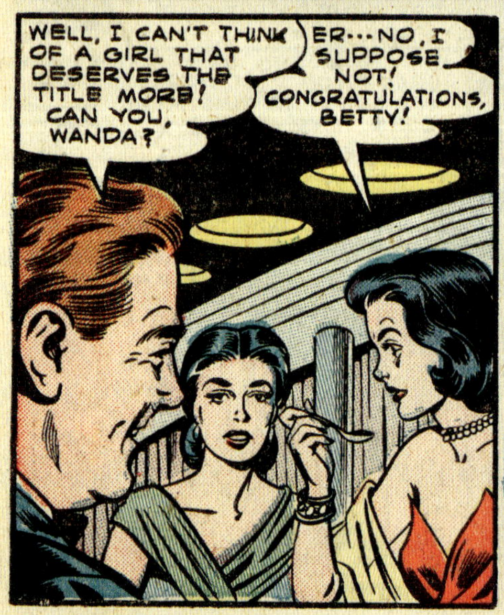

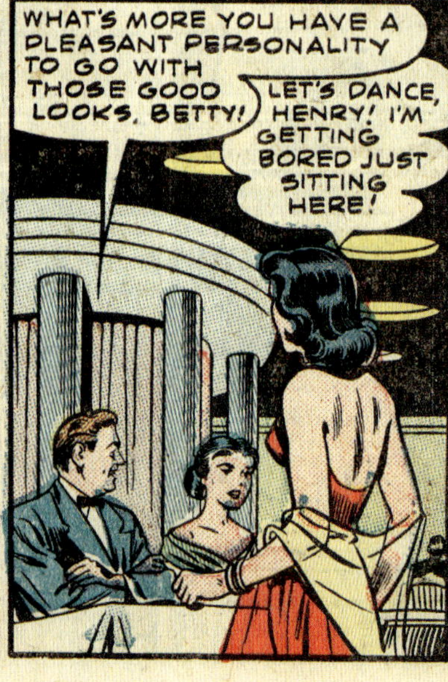

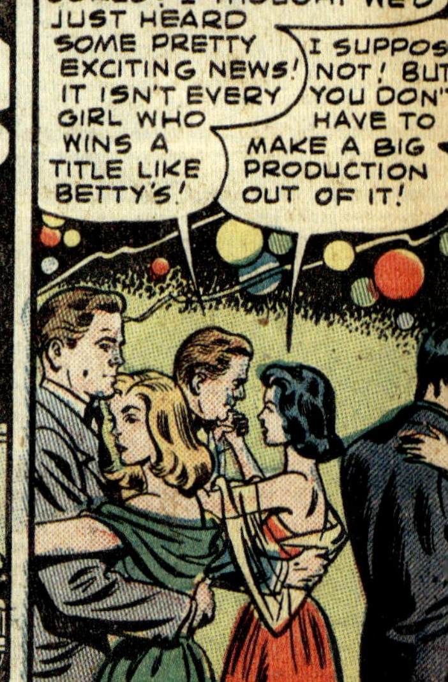

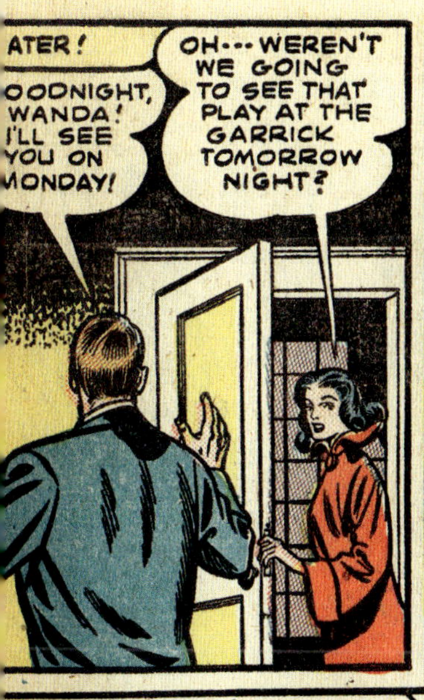

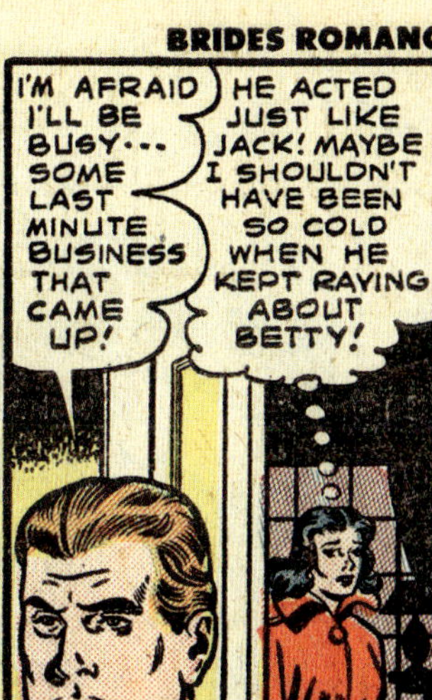

TWICE I HAD RESENTED ANOTHER GIRL TAKING THE LIMELIGHT FROM ME, AND TWICE THE RESULT HAD BEEN THE SAME! I WASN'T HURT BY THE FACT THAT HENRY FALLON HAD COOLED TOWARD ME, BUT MY LONELINESS AFTER THAT ONLY MADE MY BREAK WITH JACK MORE PAINFUL! AND TO MAKE THINGS WORSE---

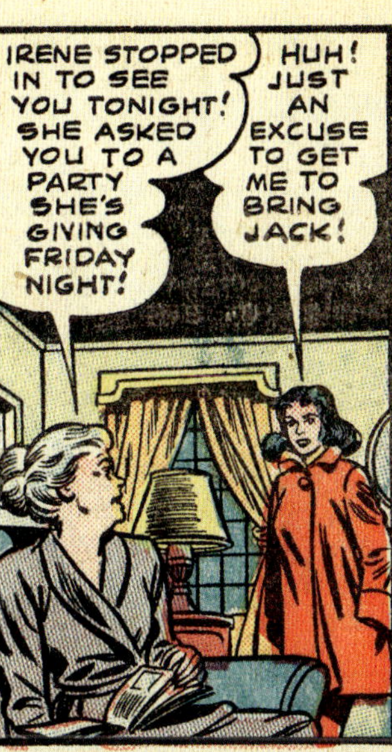

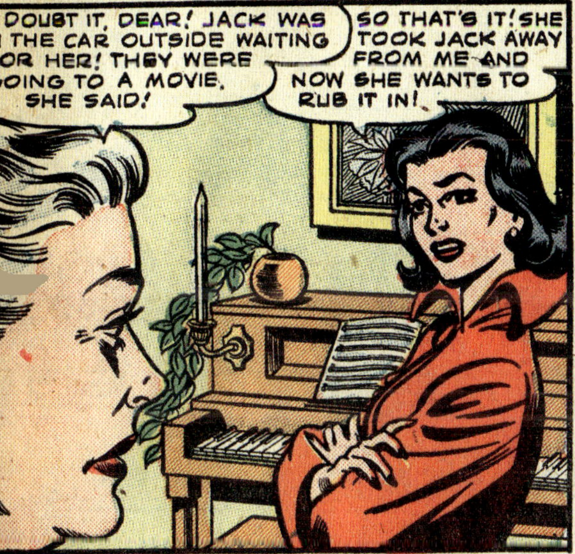

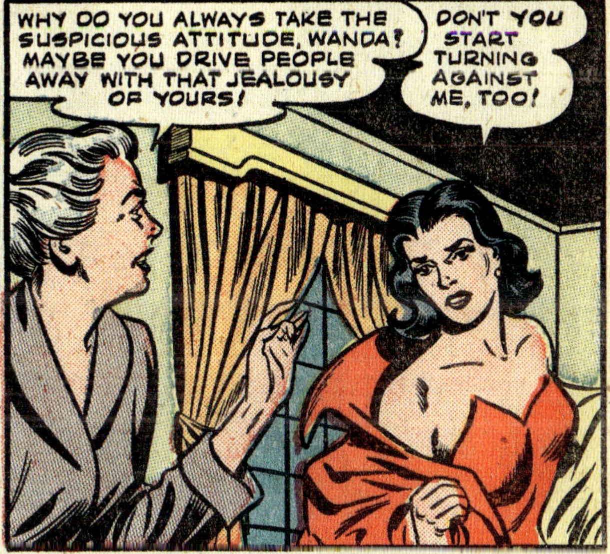

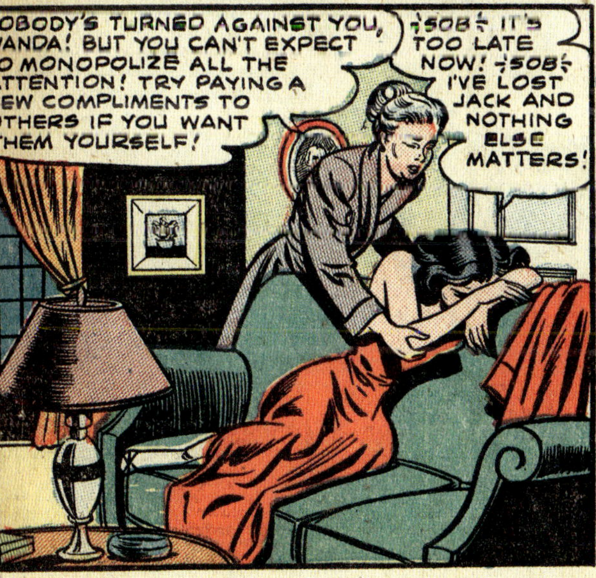

IT WAS ONLY BECAUSE I WANTED DESPERATELY TO SEE JACK THAT I FORCED MYSELF TO GO TO IRENE'S PARTY ON FRIDAY NIGHT! AND EVEN THEN I WENT WITH A CHIP ON MY SHOULDER!

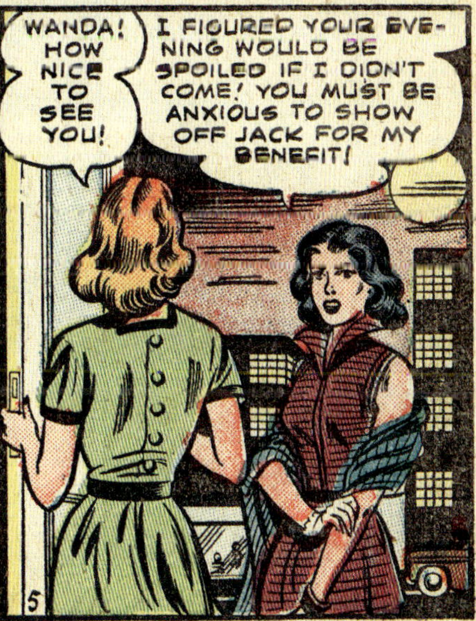

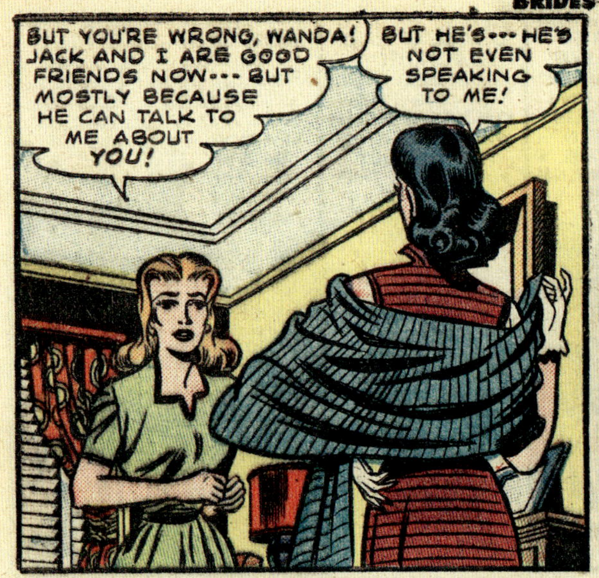

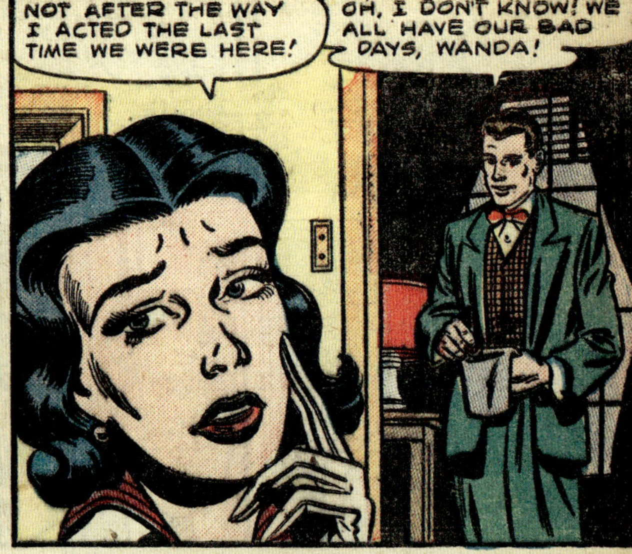

I HAD EXPECTED AN ICY RECEPTION FROM IRENE AND JACK! INSTEAD, THEY GREETED ME AS ONLY REAL FRIENDS CAN--- AND SUDDENLY I REALIZED THAT BEING KIND TO PEOPLE WAS A PART OF JACK'S MAKE-UP! I HAD TURNED AGAINST THE MAN I LOVED FOR THE VERY QUALITY THAT HAD ENDEARED HIM TO ME IN THE FIRST PLACE!

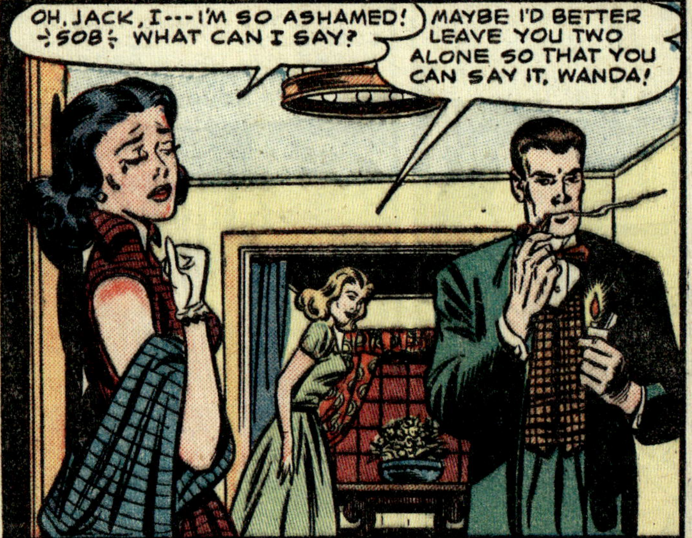

I'VE BEEN SO VAIN AND THOUGHTLESS! I SHOULD HAVE BEEN PROUD OF YOU, JACK, FOR THE PLEASANT THINGS YOU SAID TO MY FRIENDS!

I'M HOPING YOU WERE JEALOUS BECAUSE YOU'RE VERY MUCH IN LOVE WITH ME, WANDA!

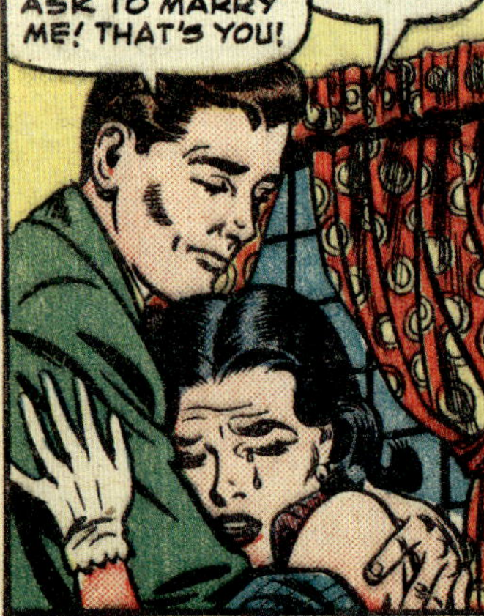

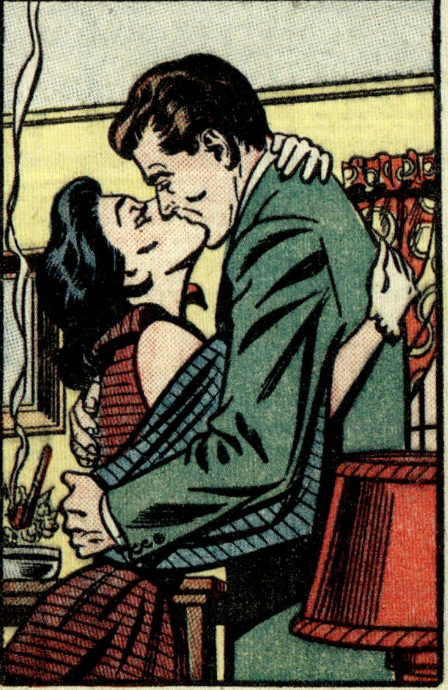

HAD I LEARNED MY LESSON? I PROVED THAT I HAD A FEW MONTHS LATER AT OUR WEDDING!

IRENE SURE LOOKS PRETTY IN THAT BRIDESMAID'S GOWN, DOESN'T SHE, MRS. LINTER?

ADORABLE, MR. LINTER! JUST ADORABLE!

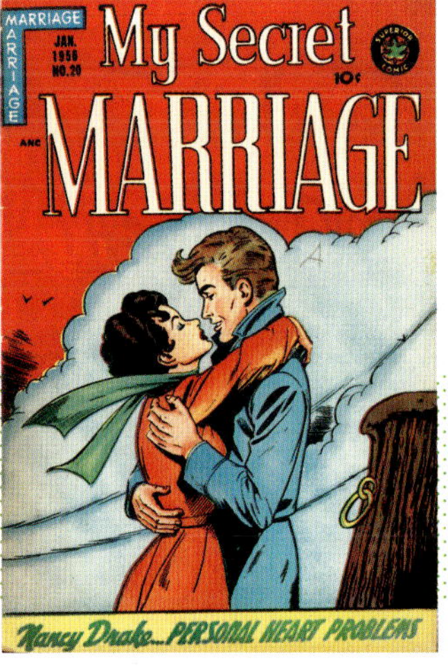

My Oh Mys

WHY LOVE COMICS FEED OUR INNER NARCISSIST

So much happened on the global scale in 1949—to cite just one literally earth-shattering example, the Russians decided to explode their first atomic bomb in August of that year. But in the hermetically sealed world of comic-book publishing, there was one trend that trumped all the others by a clear margin, and that was the explosion of romance comic books on America's newsstands. Prior to 1949 there had been only a few dozen romance comic book titles in the wake of the September 1947 debut of Simon and Kirby's groundbreaking *Young Romance*. Even in the first half of 1949, things remained fairly quiet on the love comics front. But then, in the second half of 1949, there was a boom—118 different love comic titles hit the newsstands—that would continue into 1950, making the romance comic genre the hottest in the biz, hands down.

One of the oddities of this sudden outburst of new titles is that a great many of them brandished the personal pronoun "my" in the title. No reason in particular for this choice is going to be suggested here—it's a perfectly good word, after all, and provides a certain degree of immediacy that suits a love comic just fine—but as the list that follows illustrates, more than half of the love comics bearing "my" in their titles first appeared during 1949. Another minor oddity is that many of these were published by the Fox publishing company, one of the cheesier of the day's comic-book houses.

While several of those "my" comics failed to last more than one or two issues, they do carry a certain kind of poetry when you string them all together. Can't you see—it's all about me! Call it the poetry of the suffering narcissist—though, in actuality, the stories that appeared in these books were neither more nor less narcissistic than those in any other contemporary love comics.

And away we go!

This page:
MY SECRET MARRIAGE
#20, January 1956

MY CONFESSIONS (DEBUTED IN 1949)
MY DESIRE (1949)
MY DIARY (1949)
MY EXPERIENCE (1949)
MY GREAT LOVE (1949)
MY INTIMATE AFFAIR (1950)
MY LIFE (1948)
MY LOVE (1949)
MY LOVE AFFAIR (1949)
MY LOVE LIFE (1949)
MY LOVE MEMOIRS (1949)
MY LOVE SECRET (1949)
MY LOVE STORY (1949)
MY LOVE STORY (1956)
MY OWN ROMANCE (1949)
MY PAST (1949)
MY PERSONAL PROBLEM (1955)
MY PRIVATE LIFE (1950)
MY REAL LOVE (1952)
MY ROMANCE (1948)
MY ROMANTIC ADVENTURES (1956)
MY SECRET (1949)
MY SECRET AFFAIR (1949)
MY SECRET CONFESSION (1955)
MY SECRET LIFE (1957)
MY SECRET MARRIAGE (1953)
MY SECRET ROMANCE (1950)
MY SECRET STORY (1949)

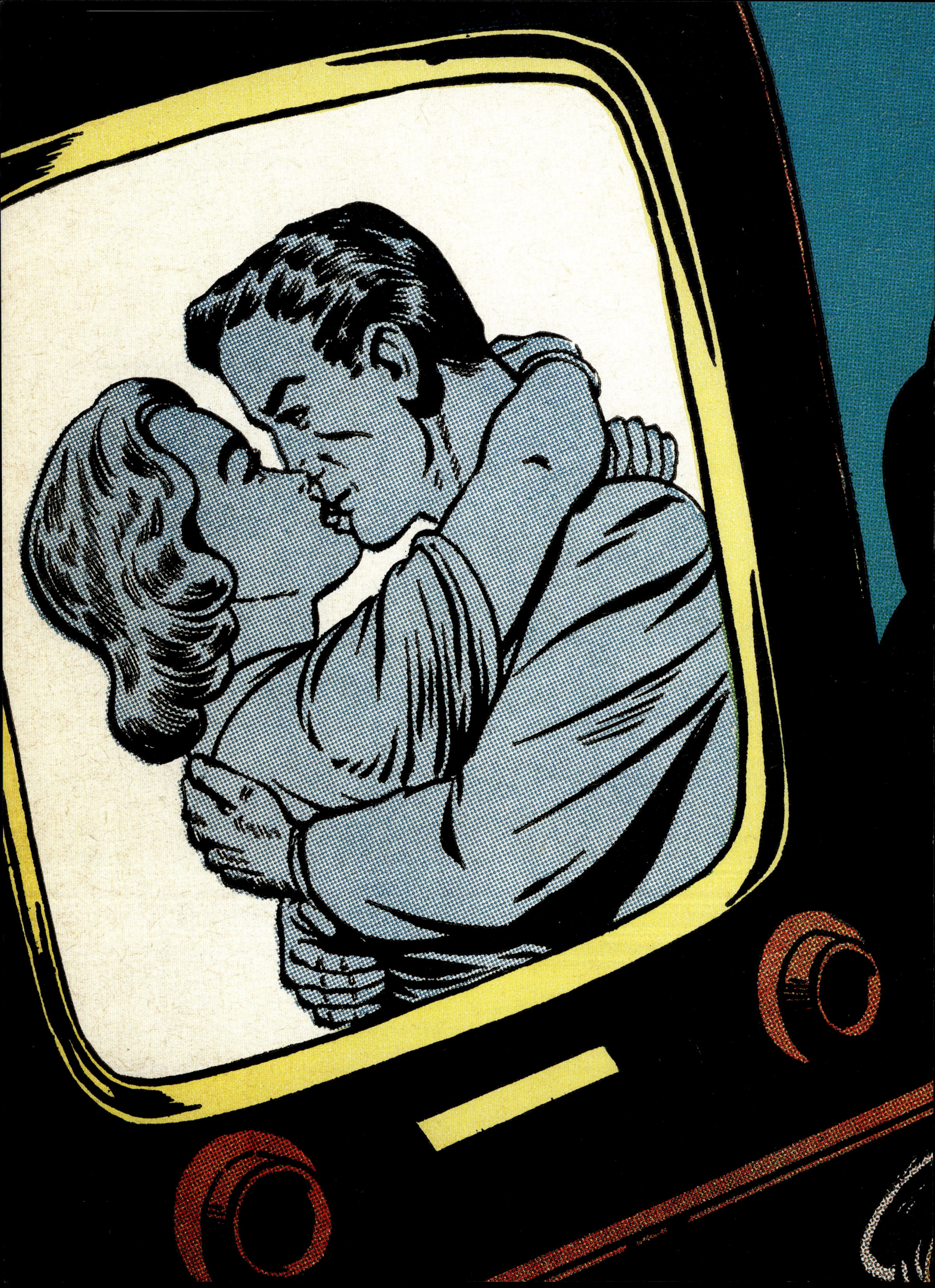

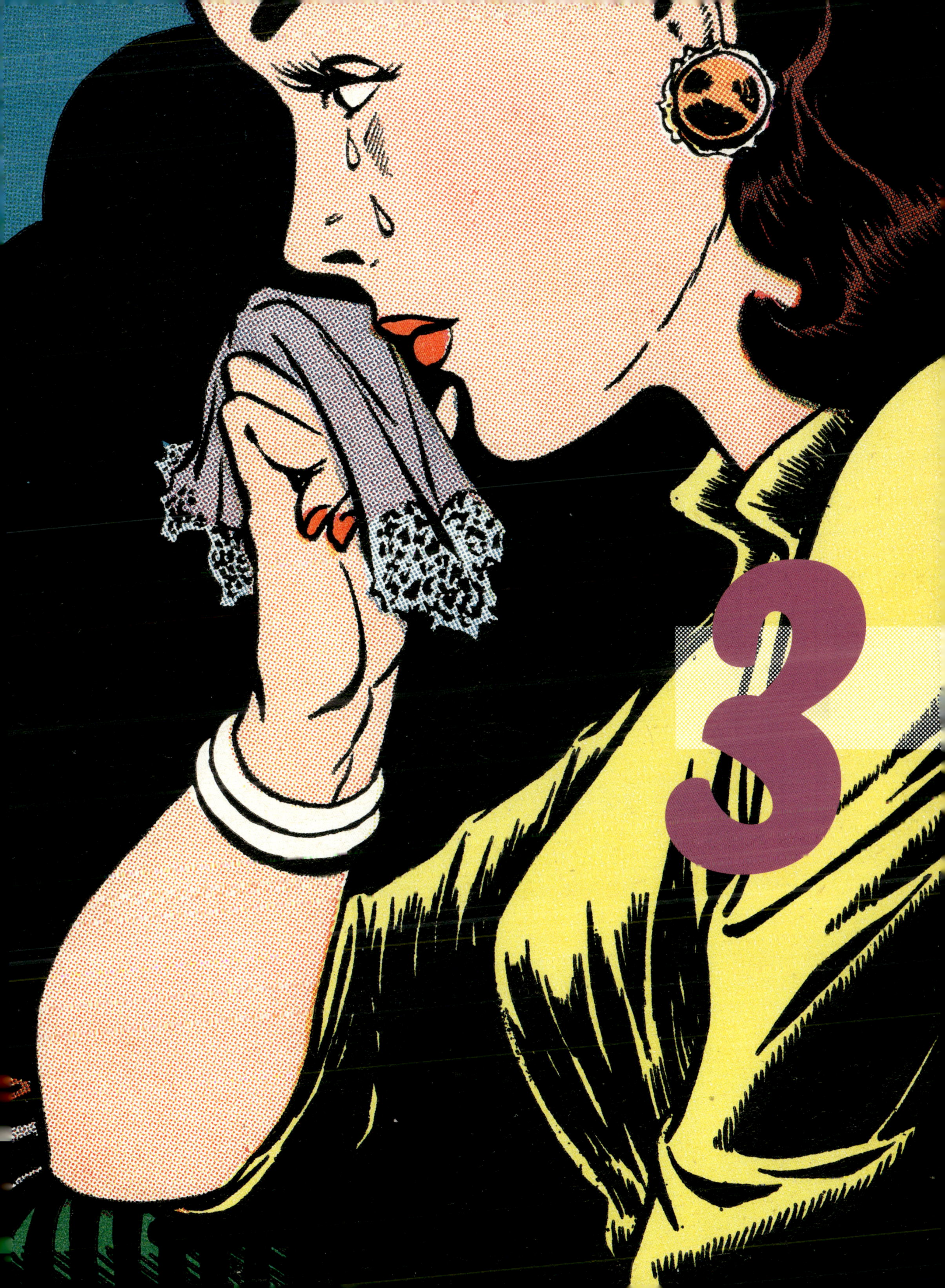
3

It Was Too Late for Love

DESPAIR

ALL THOSE who have ever loved and lost—which at last count would number approximately 4.6 billion people worldwide—have experienced that awful feeling in the pit of their stomach, the kind that whispers in their ear, "Go ahead—step in front of that bus right now—it'll only hurt for a moment—then blessed peace!" Happily, though, most of us never quite got around to locating a bus that was traveling at just the right speed at just the right moment in just the right place, so we survived our broken hearts long enough for them to heal, eventually. Just in case you're wondering, the average time for a broken heart to mend has proven to be seven months, two weeks, and three days—give or take a couple of years.

But before the healing can happen, one must wallow in despair. And to celebrate that excruciating emotion, we are providing in this section such pitiable tales as "Wrong Bridegroom," "The Trail of the Purple Sage," and "The Man in My Dreams." Painful as it may be to share in these experiences, the sensitive reader can take heart in the knowledge that, at least 95 percent of the time, the protagonists in these romantic tales experience salvation. Just like we do in real life—only your percentage may tally closer to an 8.4.

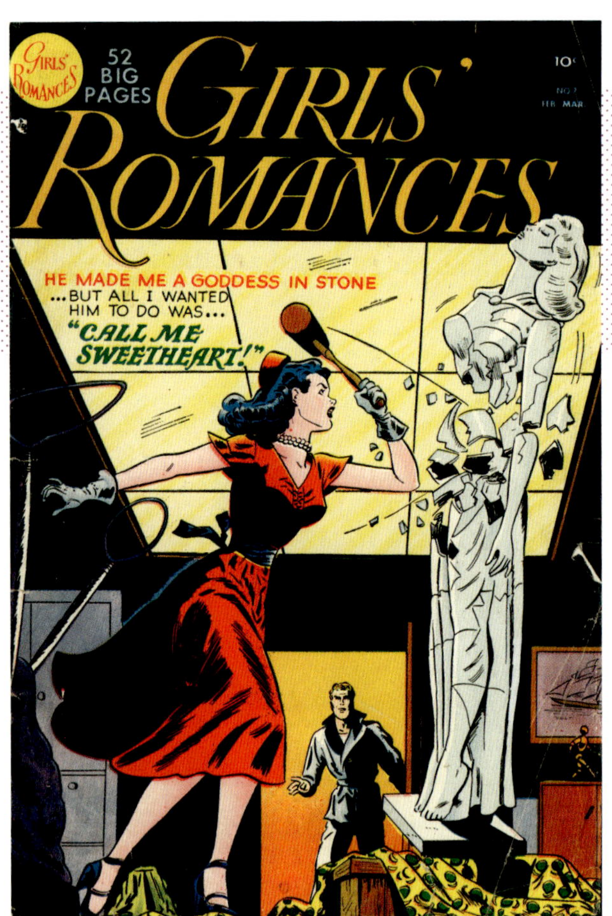
GIRLS' ROMANCES
52 BIG PAGES
GIRLS' ROMANCES
10¢
HE MADE ME A GODDESS IN STONE
...BUT ALL I WANTED HIM TO DO WAS...
"CALL ME SWEETHEART!"

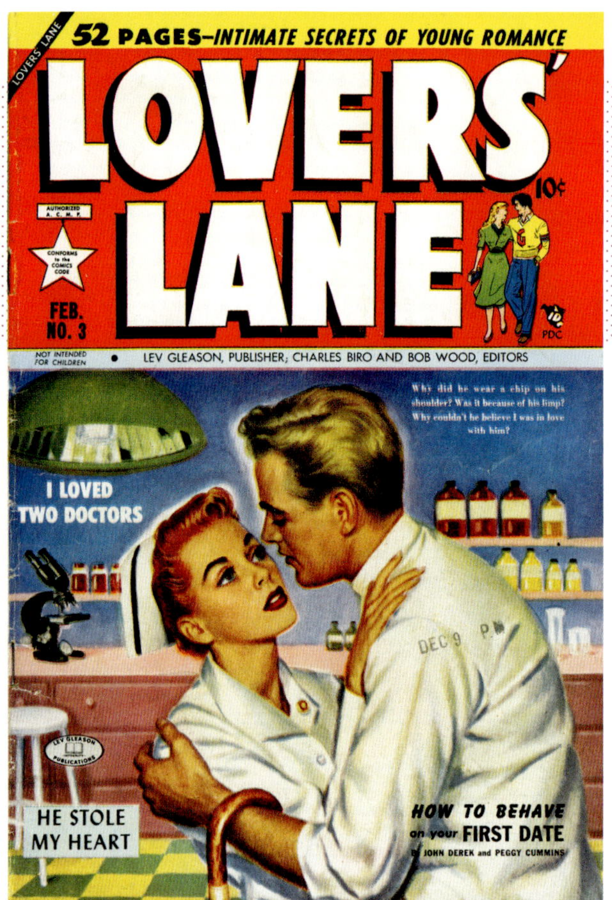
52 PAGES–INTIMATE SECRETS OF YOUNG ROMANCE
LOVERS' LANE
10¢
FEB. NO. 3
NOT INTENDED FOR CHILDREN
LEV GLEASON, PUBLISHER; CHARLES BIRO AND BOB WOOD, EDITORS
Why did he wear a chip on his shoulder? Was it because of his limp? Why couldn't he believe I was in love with him?
I LOVED TWO DOCTORS
HE STOLE MY HEART
HOW TO BEHAVE on your FIRST DATE
By JOHN DEREK and PEGGY CUMMINS

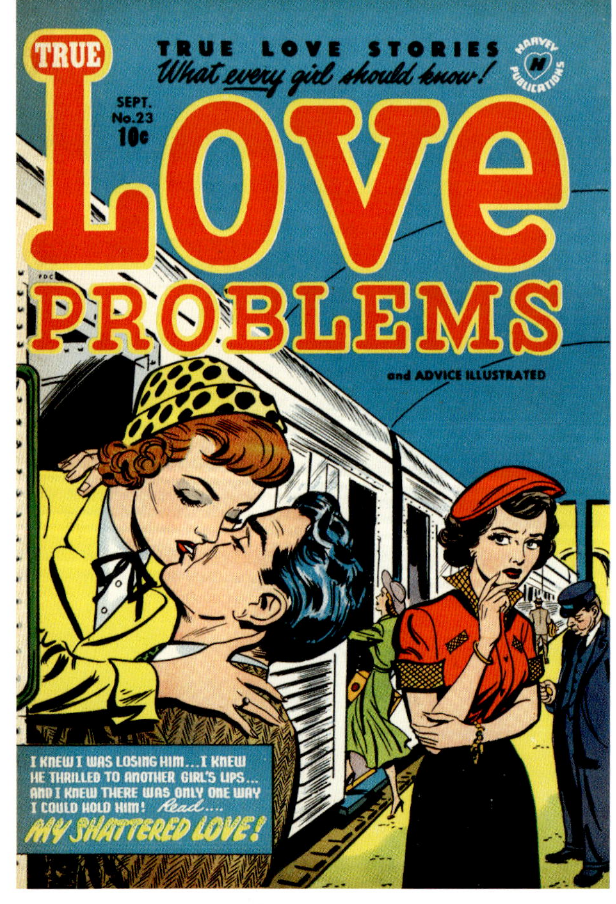
TRUE
TRUE LOVE STORIES
What every girl should know!
HARVEY PUBLICATIONS
SEPT. No.23
10¢
Love
PROBLEMS
and ADVICE ILLUSTRATED
I KNEW I WAS LOSING HIM...I KNEW HE THRILLED TO ANOTHER GIRL'S LIPS... AND I KNEW THERE WAS ONLY ONE WAY I COULD HOLD HIM! Read....
MY SHATTERED LOVE!

"I AM A VERY COMMITTED WIFE. AND I SHOULD BE COMMITTED, TOO—FOR BEING MARRIED SO MANY TIMES."

— ELIZABETH TAYLOR

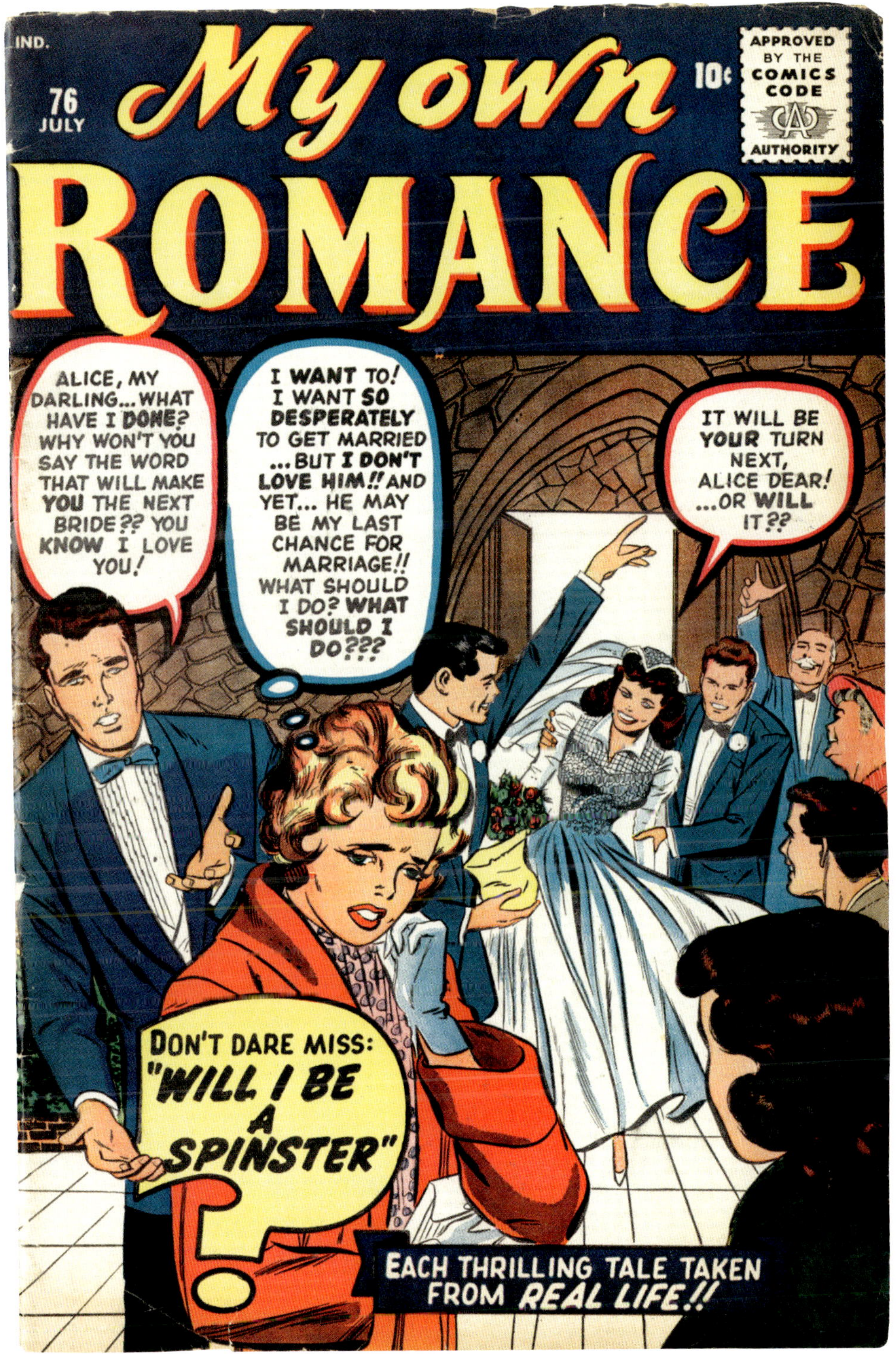

Pages 66–67:
MY PERSONAL PROBLEM
#3, May 1958, cover detail

Page 70, clockwise from top left:
GIRLS' ROMANCES
#7, February–March 1951

LOVERS' LANE
#3, February 1950

TRUE LOVE PROBLEMS
#23, September 1953

This page:
MY OWN ROMANCE
#76, July 1960

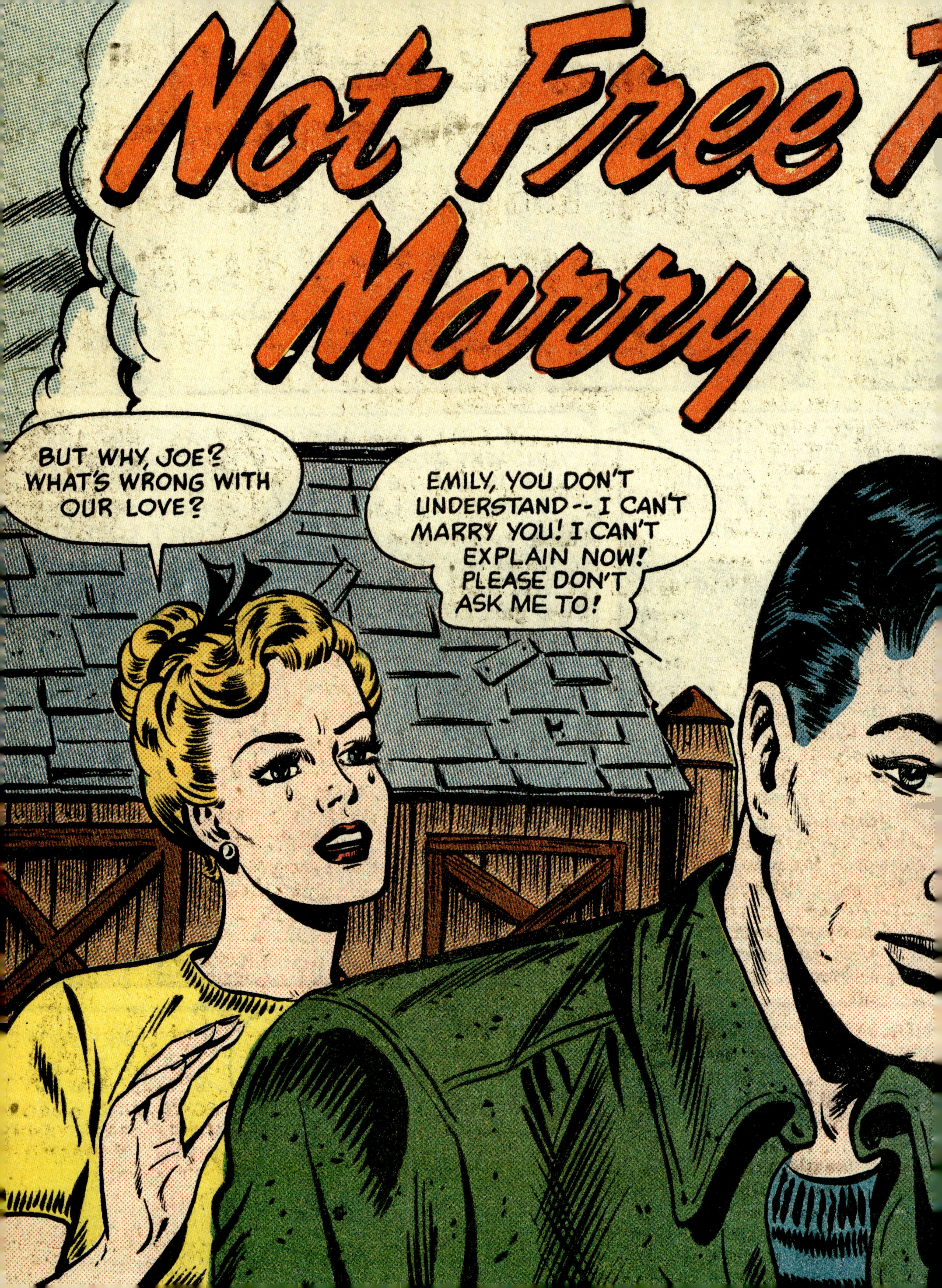
Not Free To Marry
BUT WHY, JOE? WHAT'S WRONG WITH OUR LOVE?
EMILY, YOU DON'T UNDERSTAND -- I CAN'T MARRY YOU! I CAN'T EXPLAIN NOW! PLEASE DON'T ASK ME TO!

Page 72:
GIRLS IN LOVE
#52, March 1956, story detail

Below, from left to right:
ALL TRUE ROMANCE
#34, June 1958

YOUNG ROMANCE
#8, November–December 1948

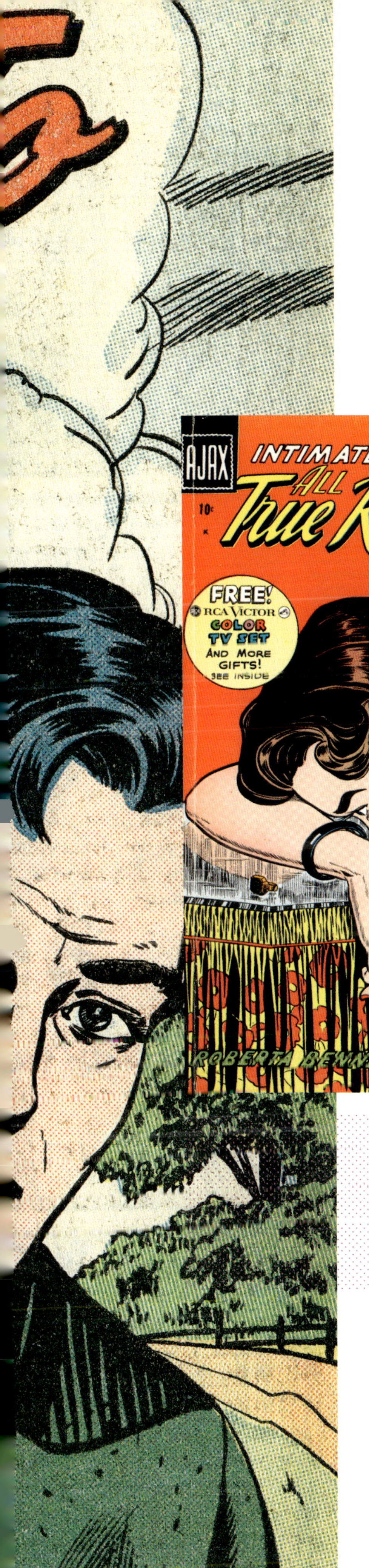

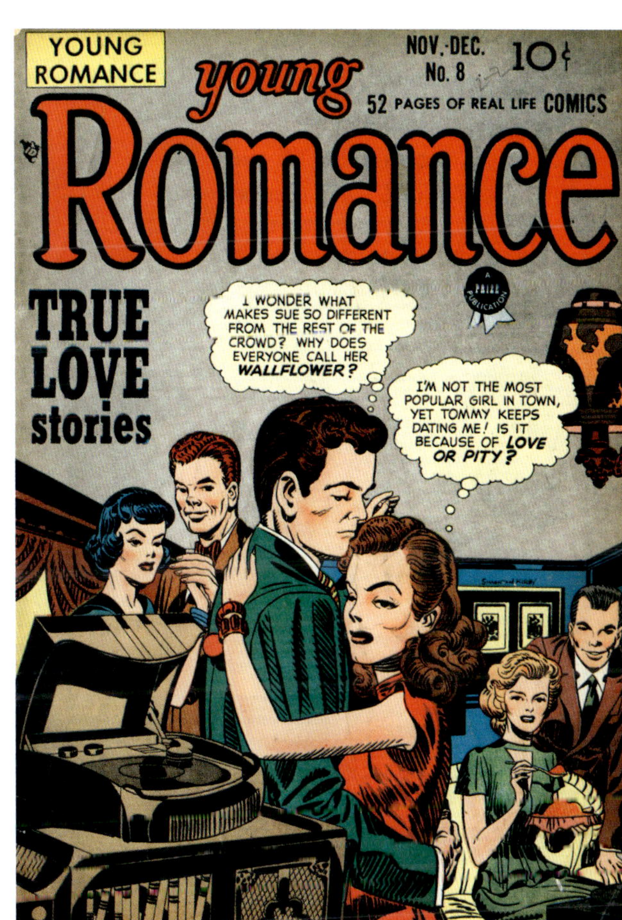

"A TV HOST ASKED MY WIFE, 'HAVE YOU EVER CONSIDERED DIVORCE?' SHE REPLIED, 'DIVORCE NEVER, MURDER OFTEN.'"

— CHARLTON HESTON, IN A 1999 NEWSPAPER INTERVIEW

This page, from left to right:
BOY LOVES GIRL
#33, April 1953

BEST LOVE
#35 (or 36),
April 1950,
splash page

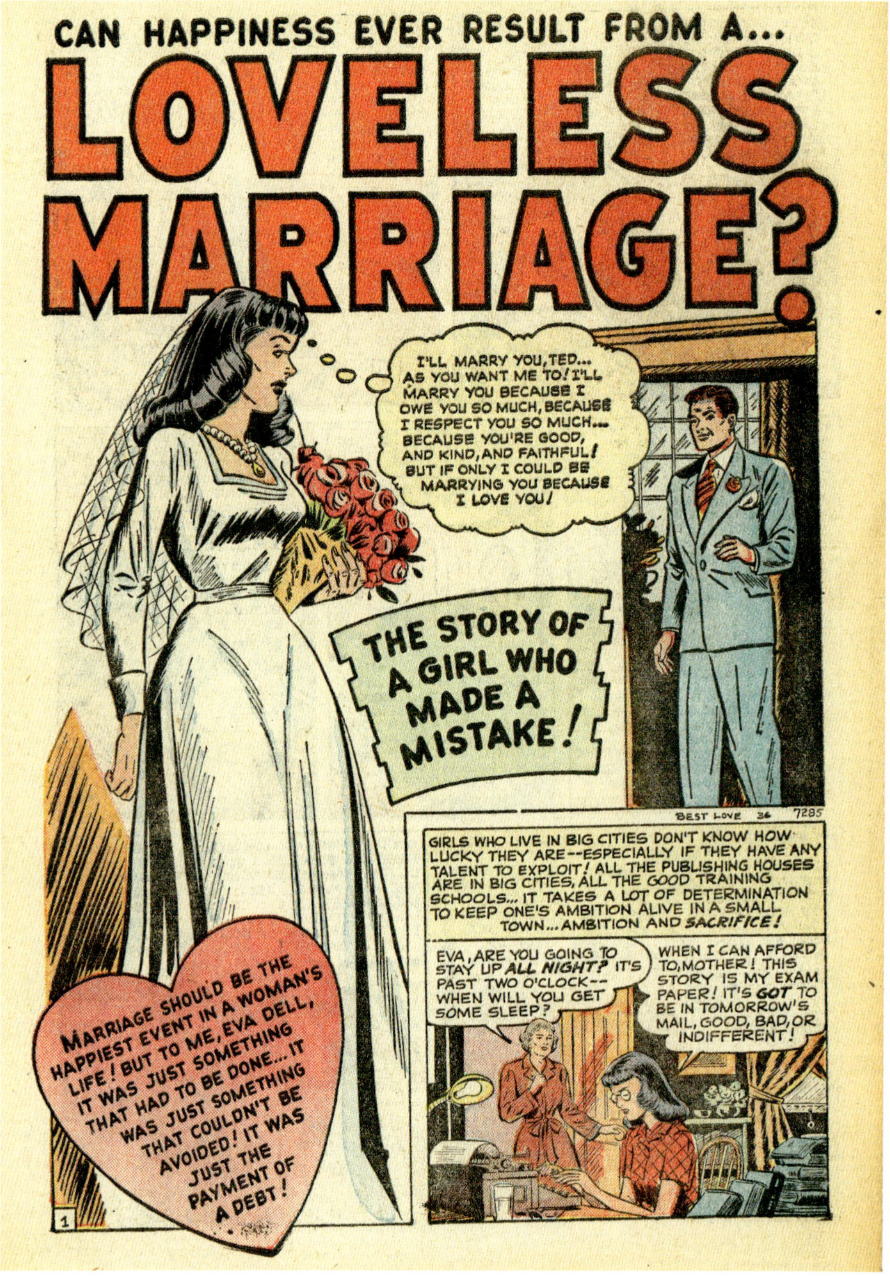

CAN HAPPINESS EVER RESULT FROM A...

LOVELESS MARRIAGE?

I'LL MARRY YOU, TED... AS YOU WANT ME TO! I'LL MARRY YOU BECAUSE I OWE YOU SO MUCH, BECAUSE I RESPECT YOU SO MUCH... BECAUSE YOU'RE GOOD, AND KIND, AND FAITHFUL! BUT IF ONLY I COULD BE MARRYING YOU BECAUSE I LOVE YOU!

THE STORY OF A GIRL WHO MADE A MISTAKE!

MARRIAGE SHOULD BE THE HAPPIEST EVENT IN A WOMAN'S LIFE! BUT TO ME, EVA DELL, IT WAS JUST SOMETHING THAT HAD TO BE DONE... IT WAS JUST SOMETHING THAT COULDN'T BE AVOIDED! IT WAS JUST THE PAYMENT OF A DEBT!

BEST LOVE 36 7285

GIRLS WHO LIVE IN BIG CITIES DON'T KNOW HOW LUCKY THEY ARE--ESPECIALLY IF THEY HAVE ANY TALENT TO EXPLOIT! ALL THE PUBLISHING HOUSES ARE IN BIG CITIES, ALL THE GOOD TRAINING SCHOOLS... IT TAKES A LOT OF DETERMINATION TO KEEP ONE'S AMBITION ALIVE IN A SMALL TOWN... AMBITION AND *SACRIFICE!*

EVA, ARE YOU GOING TO STAY UP *ALL NIGHT?* IT'S PAST TWO O'CLOCK--WHEN WILL YOU GET SOME SLEEP?

WHEN I CAN AFFORD TO, MOTHER! THIS STORY IS MY EXAM PAPER! IT'S *GOT* TO BE IN TOMORROW'S MAIL, GOOD, BAD, OR INDIFFERENT!

1

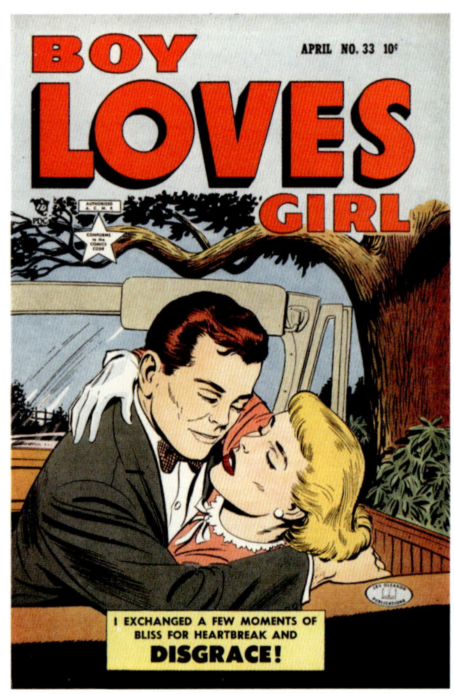

"HOW CAN A WOMAN BE EXPECTED TO BE HAPPY WITH A MAN WHO INSISTS ON TREATING HER AS IF SHE WERE A PERFECTLY NORMAL HUMAN BEING?"

—— **OSCAR WILDE**

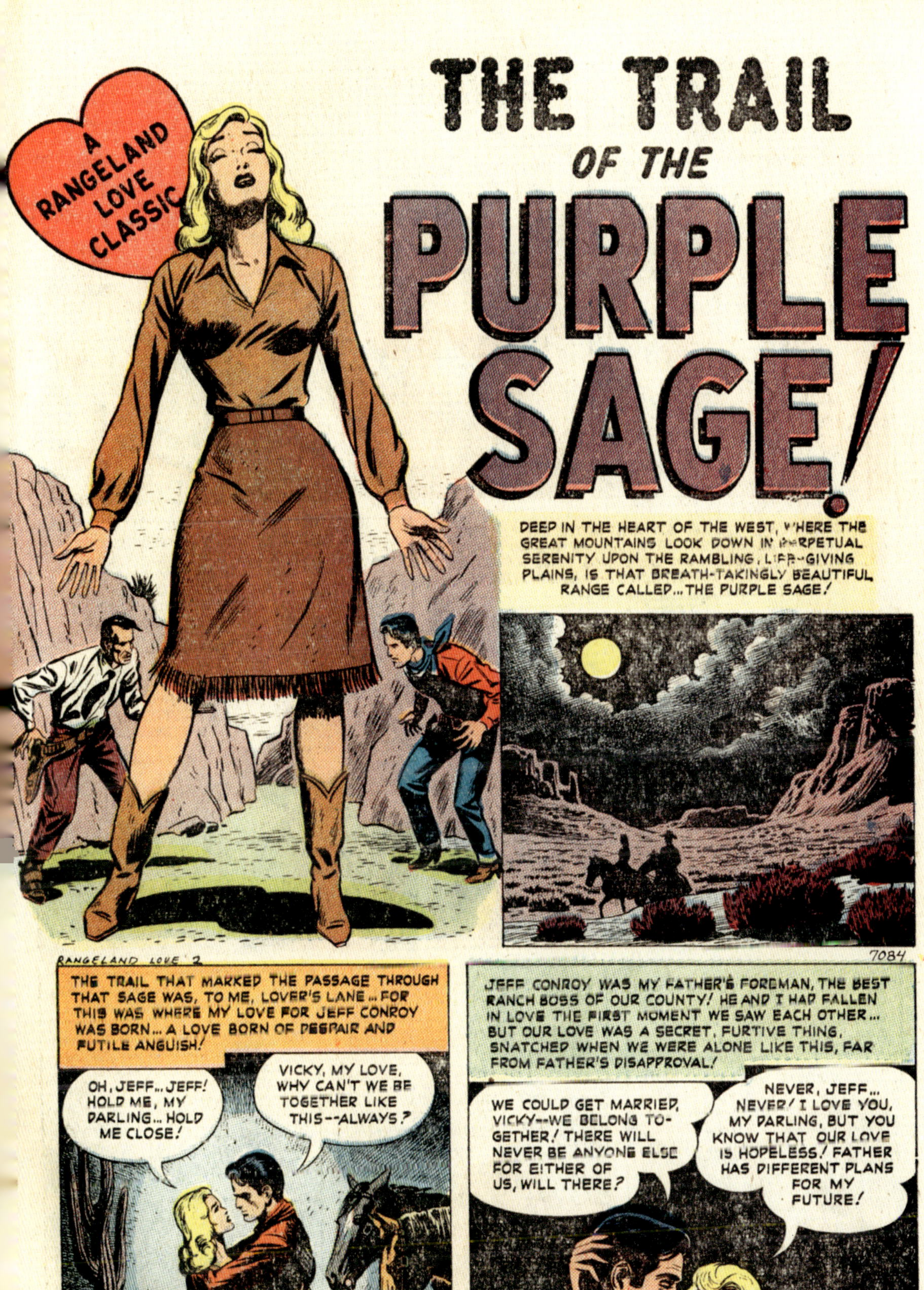

RANGELAND LOVE
#2, March 1950
Art by Russ Heath

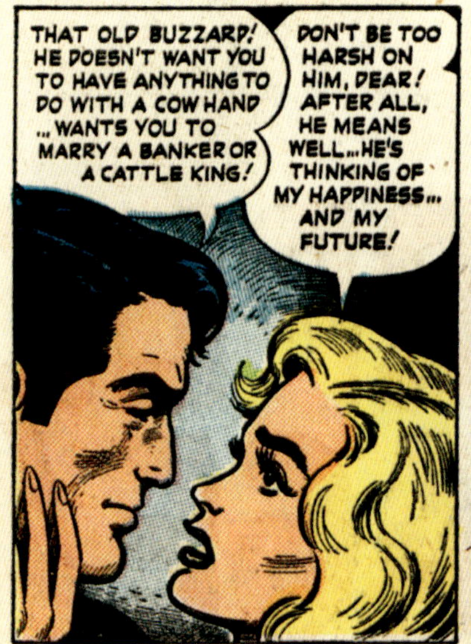
THAT OLD BUZZARD! HE DOESN'T WANT YOU TO HAVE ANYTHING TO DO WITH A COW HAND ...WANTS YOU TO MARRY A BANKER OR A CATTLE KING!
DON'T BE TOO HARSH ON HIM, DEAR! AFTER ALL, HE MEANS WELL...HE'S THINKING OF MY HAPPINESS... AND MY FUTURE!

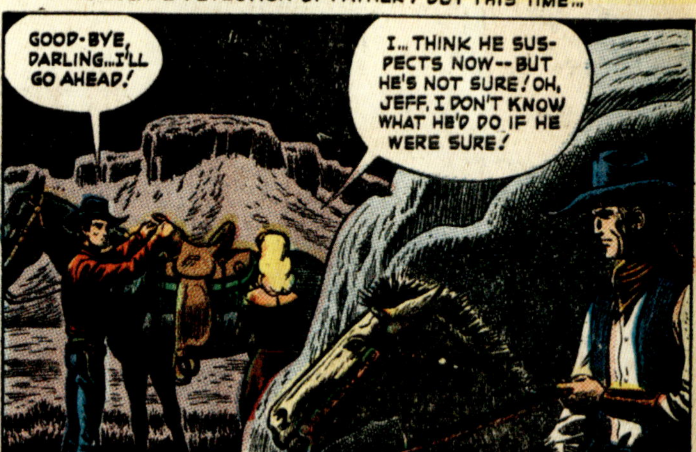
JEFF AND I OFTEN STOLE AWAY TO OUR SECRET MEETING PLACE--THE TRAIL OF THE PURPLE SAGE! THERE WE HELD EACH OTHER, WHISPERING OUR HOPES! WE ALWAYS WENT BACK TO THE RANCH SEPARATELY, TO ESCAPE DETECTION BY FATHER! BUT THIS TIME...
GOOD-BYE, DARLING...I'LL GO AHEAD!
I...THINK HE SUSPECTS NOW--BUT HE'S NOT SURE! OH, JEFF, I DON'T KNOW WHAT HE'D DO IF HE WERE SURE!

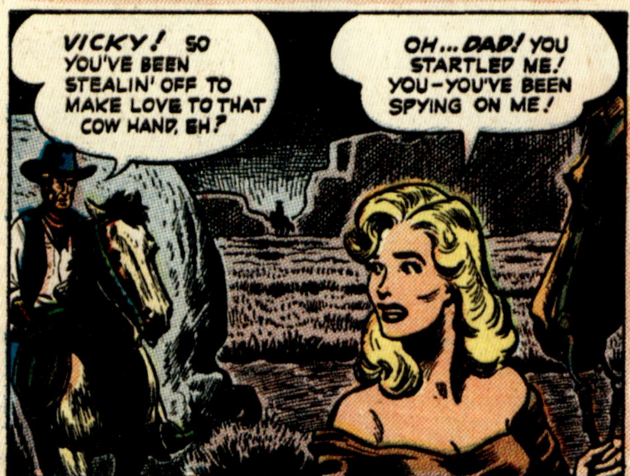
I WATCHED JEFF, TALL AND STRAIGHT IN THE SADDLE, RIDE AWAY AND MY HEART WENT WITH HIM...HE WAS SO WONDERFUL...SO GOOD! THEN...WHEN JEFF WAS GONE, MY FATHER'S VOICE CRACKED THE STILLNESS--AND MY HEART!
VICKY! SO YOU'VE BEEN STEALIN' OFF TO MAKE LOVE TO THAT COW HAND, EH?
OH...DAD! YOU STARTLED ME! YOU-YOU'VE BEEN SPYING ON ME!

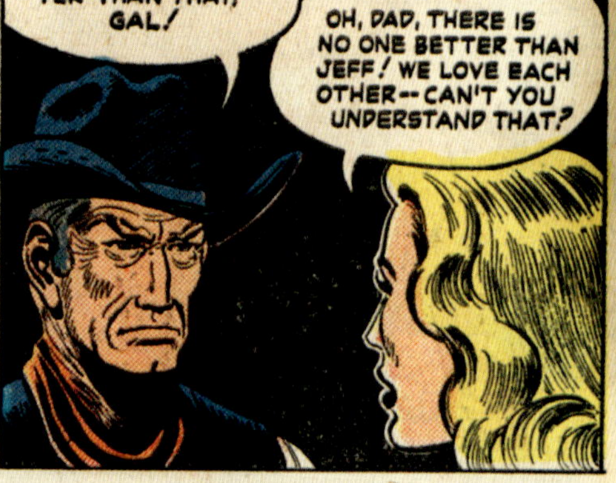
LISTEN, DAUGHTER, DON'T PLAY INNOCENT WITH ME...YOU KNOW WHAT I'M TALKING ABOUT...YOU AND JEFF HAVE BEEN SEEING EACH OTHER IN SECRET! DO YOU THINK I RAISED MY DAUGHTER TO FALL IN LOVE WITH A COMMON COWPOKE? I MEAN FOR YOU TO HAVE BETTER THAN THAT, GAL!
OH, DAD, THERE IS NO ONE BETTER THAN JEFF! WE LOVE EACH OTHER--CAN'T YOU UNDERSTAND THAT?

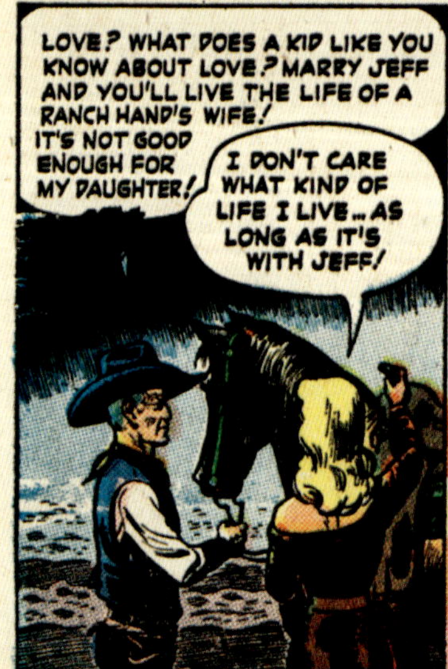
LOVE? WHAT DOES A KID LIKE YOU KNOW ABOUT LOVE? MARRY JEFF AND YOU'LL LIVE THE LIFE OF A RANCH HAND'S WIFE! IT'S NOT GOOD ENOUGH FOR MY DAUGHTER!
I DON'T CARE WHAT KIND OF LIFE I LIVE...AS LONG AS IT'S WITH JEFF!

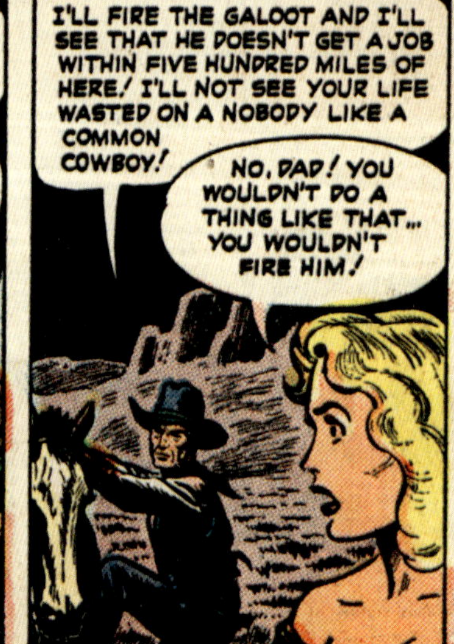
I'LL FIRE THE GALOOT AND I'LL SEE THAT HE DOESN'T GET A JOB WITHIN FIVE HUNDRED MILES OF HERE! I'LL NOT SEE YOUR LIFE WASTED ON A NOBODY LIKE A COMMON COWBOY!
NO, DAD! YOU WOULDN'T DO A THING LIKE THAT... YOU WOULDN'T FIRE HIM!

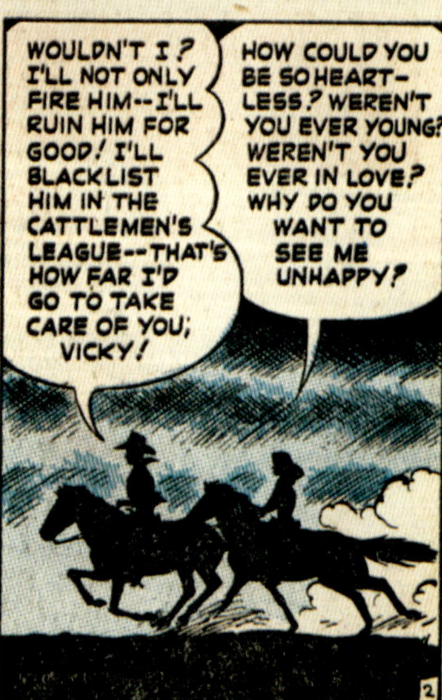
WOULDN'T I? I'LL NOT ONLY FIRE HIM--I'LL RUIN HIM FOR GOOD! I'LL BLACKLIST HIM IN THE CATTLEMEN'S LEAGUE--THAT'S HOW FAR I'D GO TO TAKE CARE OF YOU, VICKY!
HOW COULD YOU BE SO HEARTLESS? WEREN'T YOU EVER YOUNG? WEREN'T YOU EVER IN LOVE? WHY DO YOU WANT TO SEE ME UNHAPPY?
2

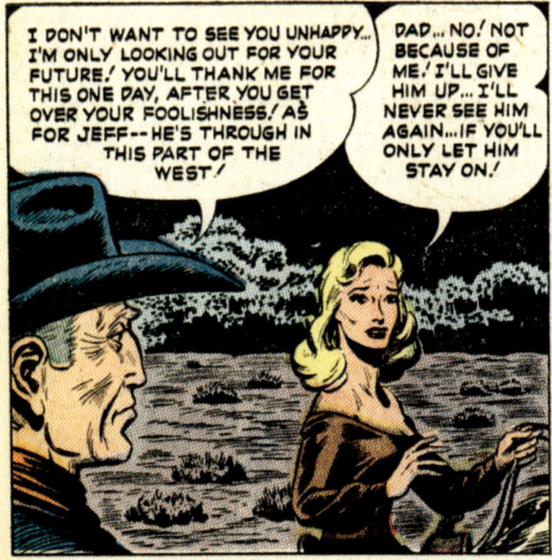
I DON'T WANT TO SEE YOU UNHAPPY... I'M ONLY LOOKING OUT FOR YOUR FUTURE! YOU'LL THANK ME FOR THIS ONE DAY, AFTER YOU GET OVER YOUR FOOLISHNESS! AS FOR JEFF-- HE'S THROUGH IN THIS PART OF THE WEST!
DAD... NO! NOT BECAUSE OF ME! I'LL GIVE HIM UP... I'LL NEVER SEE HIM AGAIN... IF YOU'LL ONLY LET HIM STAY ON!

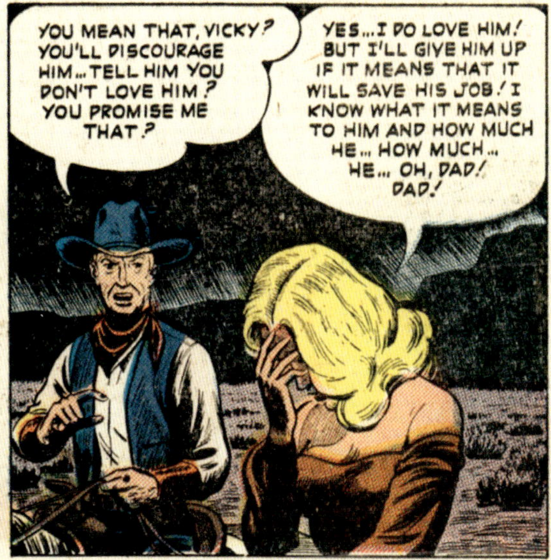
YOU MEAN THAT, VICKY? YOU'LL DISCOURAGE HIM... TELL HIM YOU DON'T LOVE HIM? YOU PROMISE ME THAT?
YES... I DO LOVE HIM! BUT I'LL GIVE HIM UP IF IT MEANS THAT IT WILL SAVE HIS JOB! I KNOW WHAT IT MEANS TO HIM AND HOW MUCH HE... HOW MUCH... HE... OH, DAD! DAD!

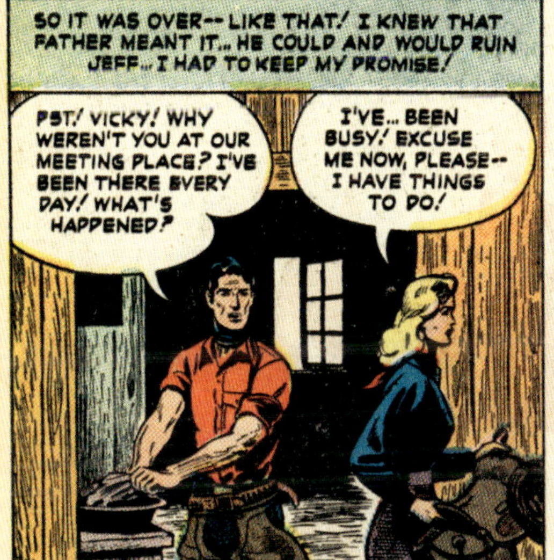
SO IT WAS OVER-- LIKE THAT! I KNEW THAT FATHER MEANT IT... HE COULD AND WOULD RUIN JEFF... I HAD TO KEEP MY PROMISE!
PST! VICKY! WHY WEREN'T YOU AT OUR MEETING PLACE? I'VE BEEN THERE EVERY DAY! WHAT'S HAPPENED?
I'VE... BEEN BUSY! EXCUSE ME NOW, PLEASE-- I HAVE THINGS TO DO!

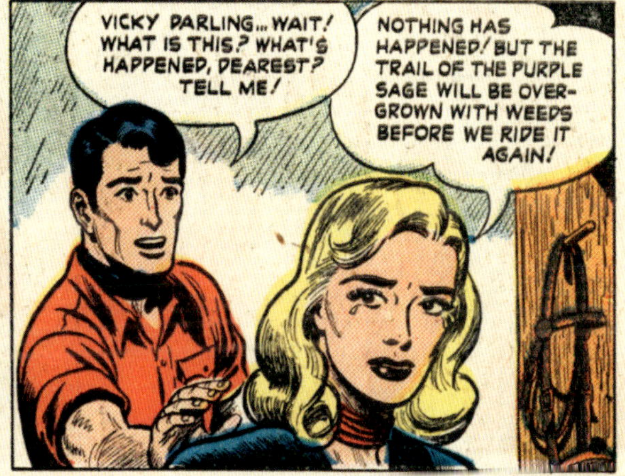
THERE WAS A SHARP PAIN IN HIS EYES... AS MUCH AS THERE WAS IN MY HEART! TO SUDDENLY ENCOUNTER COLDNESS-- WHERE HE HAD KNOWN THE WARMTH OF LOVE--WAS BEYOND HIS UNDERSTANDING!
VICKY DARLING... WAIT! WHAT IS THIS? WHAT'S HAPPENED, DEAREST? TELL ME!
NOTHING HAS HAPPENED! BUT THE TRAIL OF THE PURPLE SAGE WILL BE OVERGROWN WITH WEEDS BEFORE WE RIDE IT AGAIN!

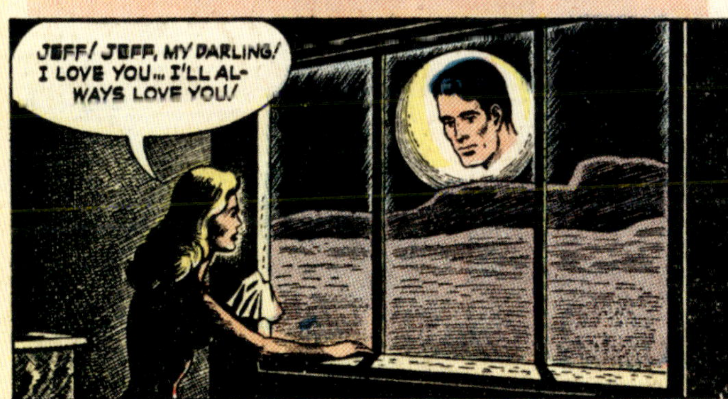
IN THE DAYS THAT FOLLOWED WE BOTH CARRIED OUR SECRET BURDEN! AS FAR AS I WAS CONCERNED, LIFE WAS OVER! WAS I DOING THE RIGHT THING? SHOULD I HAVE DEFIED FATHER AND GONE OFF WITH JEFF... NO MATTER WHAT CAME? I ONLY KNEW THAT JEFF WAS A PROUD MAN, PROUD OF HIS JOB... HE HAD NEVER BEEN FIRED... I COULDN'T SPOIL THAT FOR HIM... NO MATTER WHAT HAPPENED! BUT AT NIGHT, WHEN THE MOON CAST ITS GLOW OVER THE PURPLE SAGE... MY HEART CRIED OUT...
JEFF! JEFF, MY DARLING! I LOVE YOU... I'LL ALWAYS LOVE YOU!

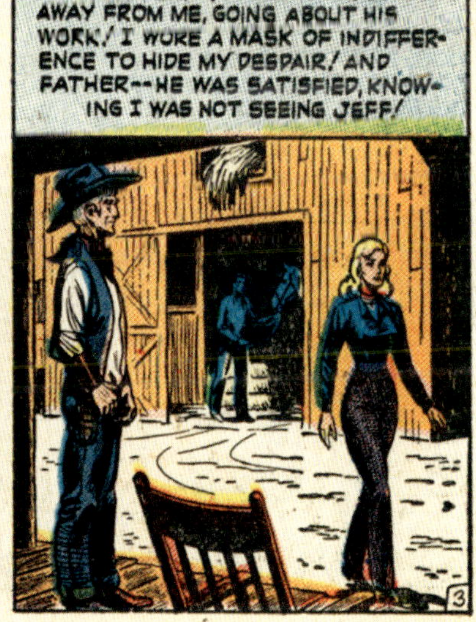
JEFF, BITTER, HEARTBROKEN, STAYED AWAY FROM ME, GOING ABOUT HIS WORK! I WORE A MASK OF INDIFFERENCE TO HIDE MY DESPAIR! AND FATHER--HE WAS SATISFIED, KNOWING I WAS NOT SEEING JEFF!
3

WAS I WRONG? I DIDN'T KNOW! BUT I WAS MISERABLE AVOIDING THE MAN I LOVED, TRYING TO MAKE HIM THINK I NO LONGER CARED FOR HIM! THEN, ONE DAY, A STRANGER CAME TO THE RANCH... TALL, DARK, GOOD LOOKING IN A SOMBER SORT OF WAY! FATHER SEEMED GLAD TO SEE HIM!

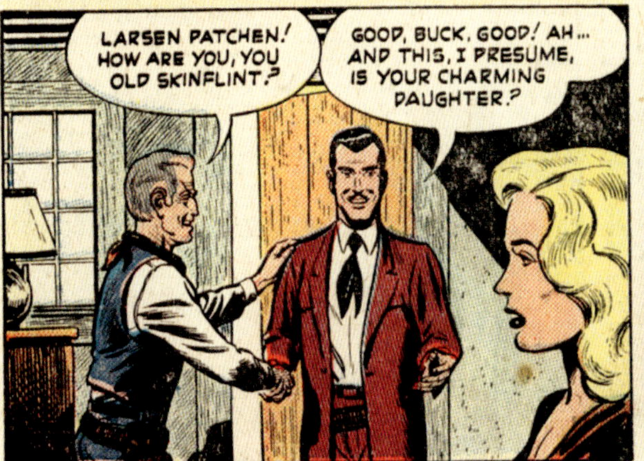

I DIDN'T LIKE HIM--HE WAS TOO SLICK, TOO WELL DRESSED, HIS TONGUE TOO OILY!

YES, THIS IS VICKY! ER, VICKY, THIS IS LARSEN PATCHEN, AN OLD FRIEND I HAVEN'T SEEN IN TEN YEARS! WHAT HAVE YOU BEEN DOING, LARSEN?

WELL, I'M AN INVESTMENT BROKER, BUCK! AS A MATTER OF FACT, THAT'S WHY I'M HERE... I'M INTERESTED IN YOUR RANCH... AND ITS WATER HOLE!

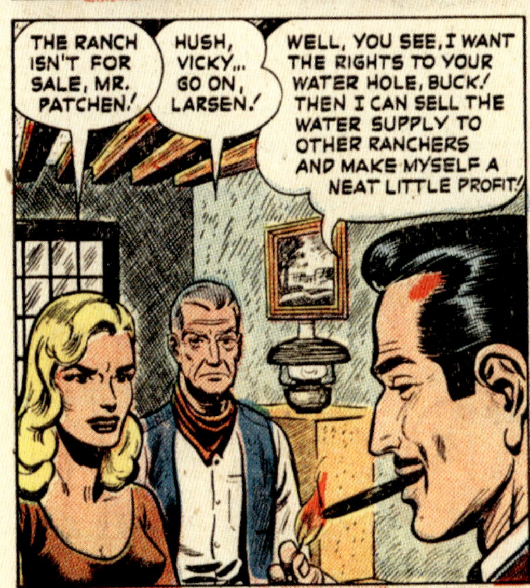

WHAT? WHY... THAT'S RANGE-LAND ROBBERY!

NOW, VICKY, YOU MUSTN'T SAY THAT... GOSH, ALL BUSINESSMEN DO THOSE THINGS! LARSEN, HERE, IS A FINE MAN! SORRY, THOUGH, LARSEN--THE PLACE ISN'T FOR SALE! ER... HOW ABOUT STAYING FOR SUPPER?

DELIGHTED, THOUGH I'M SORRY YOU WON'T SELL, BUCK!

WHILE LARSEN WASHED UP, I HAD A SHOWDOWN WITH FATHER! I HAD GUESSED AT WHY HE WAS SO NICE TO THIS OILY INTRUDER--NOW HE ADMITTED IT...

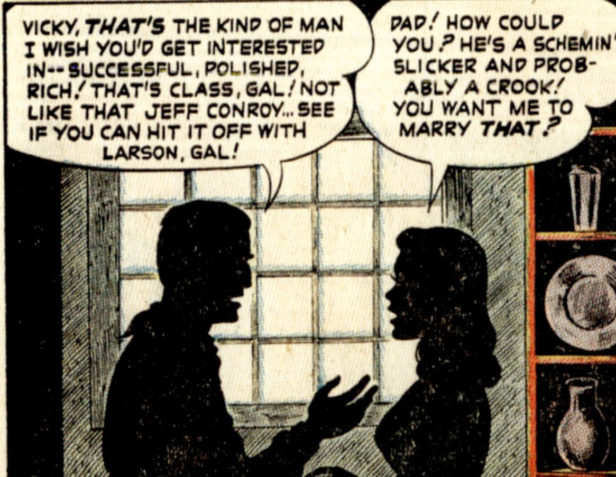

BUT DAD KEPT PUSHING ME ON LARSEN ALL THROUGH SUPPER, ENCOURAGING HIM TO TALK ABOUT HIMSELF--WHICH HE DID WITH A VENGEANCE!

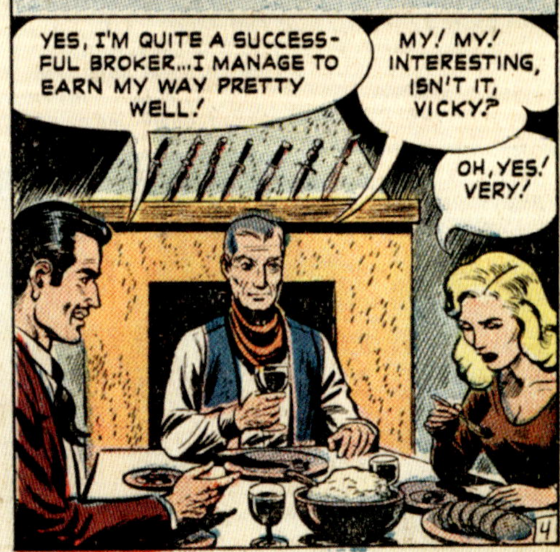

FATHER FELL ALL OVER HIMSELF TRYING TO MAKE LARSEN LOOK ATTRACTIVE TO ME, TO MY EMBARRASSMENT! IN A LITTLE WHILE IT BECAME OBVIOUS TO THE BROKER AND HE ASKED ME TO GO FOR A RIDE WITH HIM!

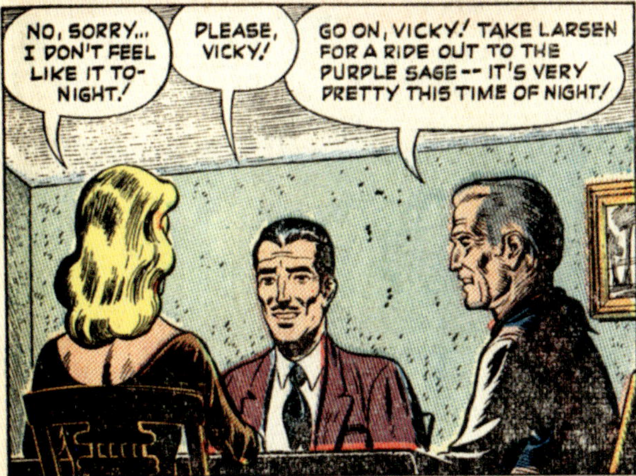

THE PURPLE SAGE! FATHER, HOW CAN YOU SUGGEST SUCH A THING! YOU... KNOW WHAT IT'S MEANT TO ME!

I WANT IT TO MEAN MUCH MORE TO YOU, VICKY! COME... PLEASE!

GO ON! THE HORSES ARE SADDLED!

SO I LET MYSELF BE FORCED TO GO FOR A RIDE WITH LARSEN PATCHEN... IT WOULD HAVE BROKEN FATHER'S HEART IF I HAD NOT GONE! AS FOR ME--I HAD NO HEART LEFT TO BREAK!

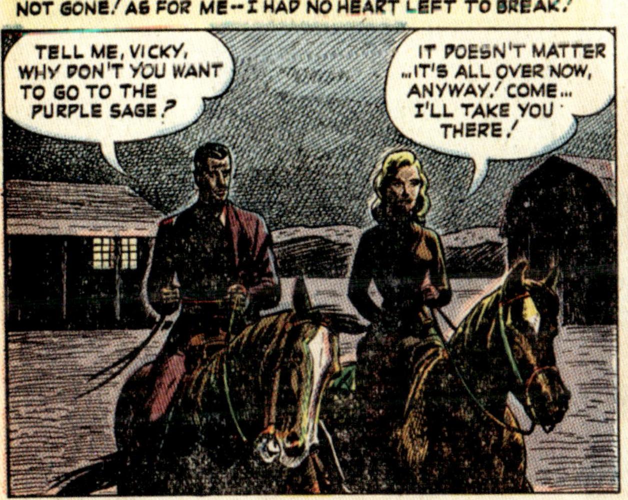

AS WE RODE OUT, I CAME FACE TO FACE WITH JEFF STANDING QUIETLY AGAINST THE FENCE... A SAD, BITTER JEFF! FOR AN INSTANT OUR EYES MET, THOUGH WE DIDN'T SAY A WORD!

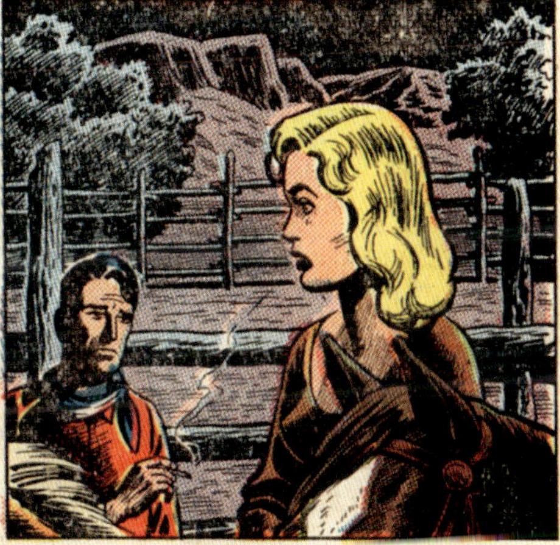

THEN LARSEN AND I RODE ON, AND I HAD TO FIGHT BACK MY TEARS! I KNEW WHAT JEFF WAS THINKING...

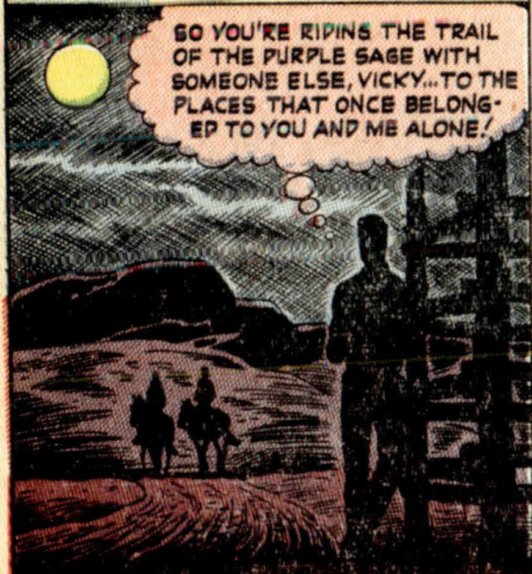

I COULD TELL THAT NOW WE WERE REALLY THROUGH! I WAS PROFANING A SACRED PLACE BY TAKING LARSEN TO THE PURPLE SAGE... AND I WAS PROFANING OUR LOVE!

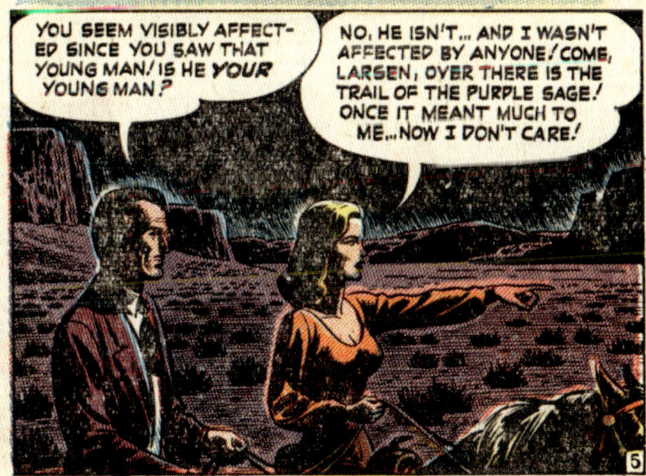

I WAS SILENT AND WITHDRAWN DURING THAT RIDE.. I FELT THAT I HAD BETRAYED EVERYTHING THAT I HELD DEAR! LARSEN FOLLOWED, AS SILENT AS I!

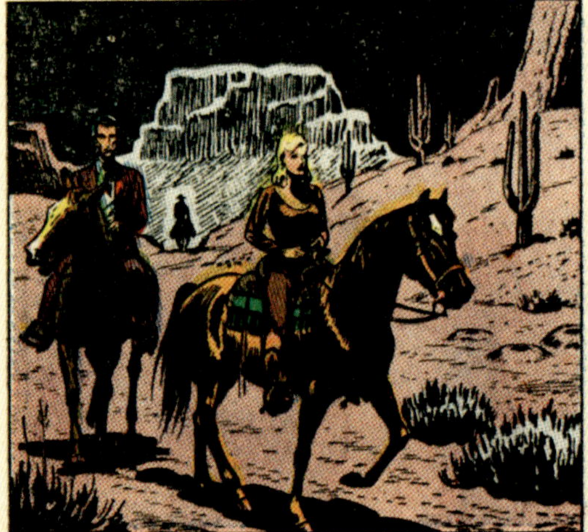

I DIDN'T LOOK BACK...IF I HAD, I WOULD HAVE SEEN ANOTHER RIDER FOLLOWING BOTH OF US AS I BLINDLY RODE TO THE SECRET PLACE KNOWN ONLY TO JEFF AND ME! THEN LARSEN SPURRED HIS HORSE AND CAUGHT UP WITH ME...

THIS IS QUITE A REMOTE SPOT--IT SEEMS FAR AWAY FROM THE WORLD!

IT IS... FAR AWAY... VERY FEW PEOPLE KNOW OF THIS PLACE! SHALL WE GO BACK NOW?

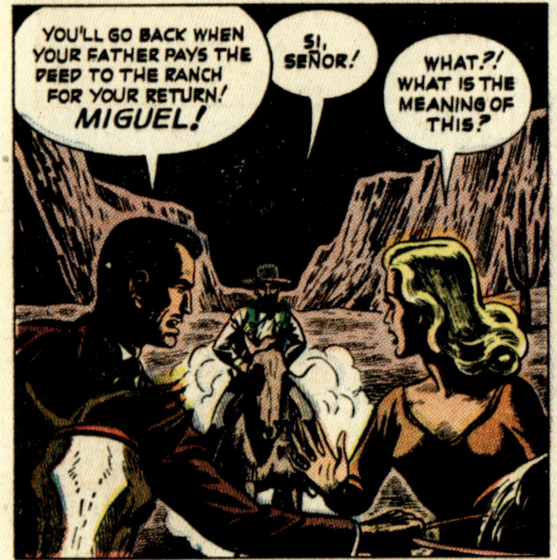

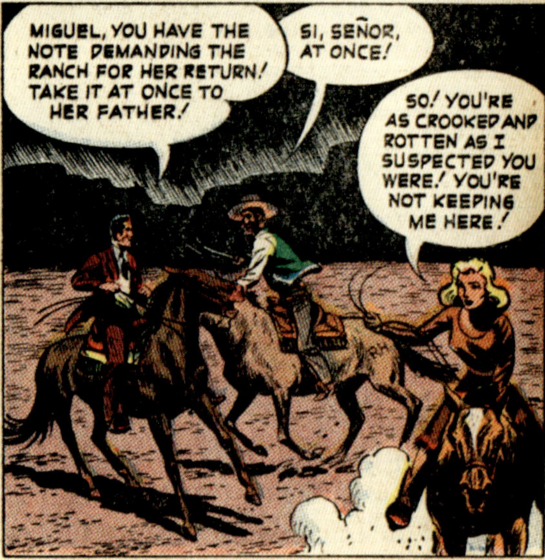

I MADE A SUDDEN WILD RUSH TO ESCAPE BUT LARSEN WAS FAST AND STRONG--HE SWEPT ME OFF MY HORSE, CRUSHED ME TO HIM UNTIL I COULDN'T BREATHE!

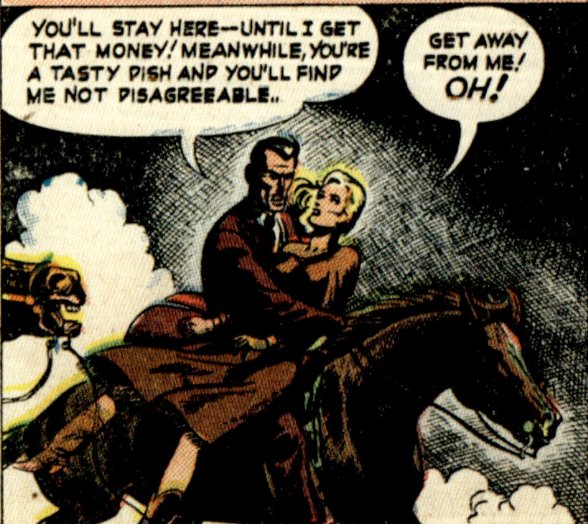

SO I WAS LARSEN'S PRISONER AT THE RENDEZVOUS OF MY LOVE AND JEFF'S! MEANWHILE, MIGUEL DELIVERED THE RANSOM NOTE TO FATHER...

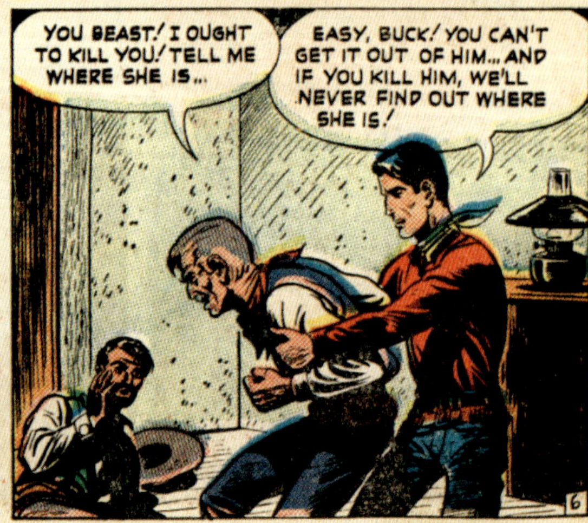

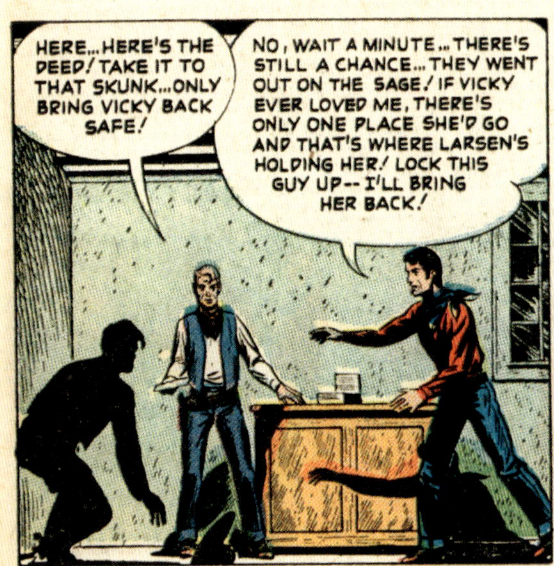
HERE...HERE'S THE DEED! TAKE IT TO THAT SKUNK...ONLY BRING VICKY BACK SAFE!
NO, WAIT A MINUTE...THERE'S STILL A CHANCE...THEY WENT OUT ON THE SAGE! IF VICKY EVER LOVED ME, THERE'S ONLY ONE PLACE SHE'D GO AND THAT'S WHERE LARSEN'S HOLDING HER! LOCK THIS GUY UP--I'LL BRING HER BACK!

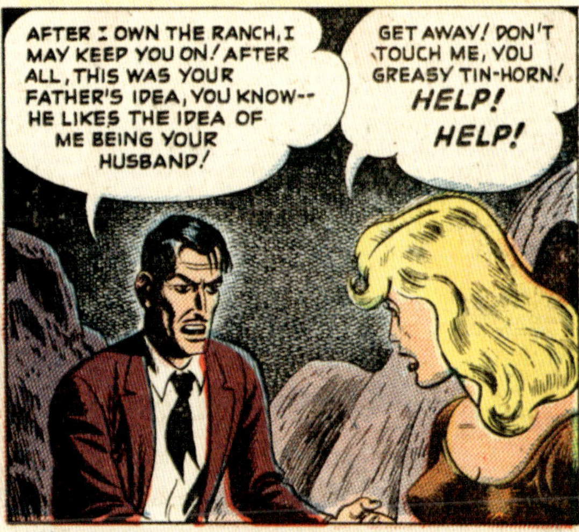
MEANWHILE, FRIGHTENED, I WAS BACKED UP AGAINST A BOULDER AS LARSEN'S EYES GLOWED WITH GREED...
AFTER I OWN THE RANCH, I MAY KEEP YOU ON! AFTER ALL, THIS WAS YOUR FATHER'S IDEA, YOU KNOW--HE LIKES THE IDEA OF ME BEING YOUR HUSBAND!
GET AWAY! DON'T TOUCH ME, YOU GREASY TIN-HORN! HELP! HELP!

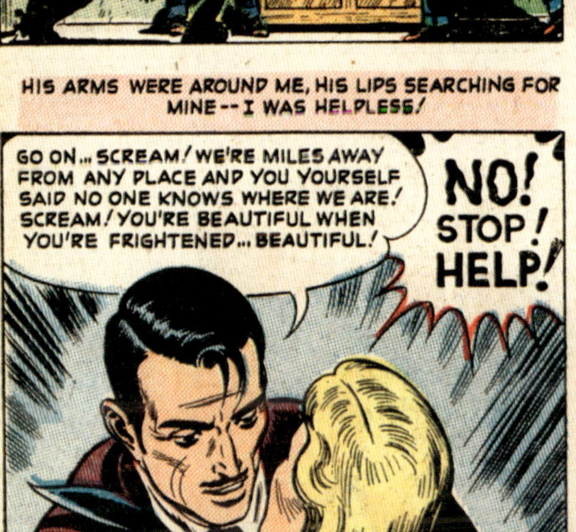
HIS ARMS WERE AROUND ME, HIS LIPS SEARCHING FOR MINE--I WAS HELPLESS!
GO ON...SCREAM! WE'RE MILES AWAY FROM ANY PLACE AND YOU YOURSELF SAID NO ONE KNOWS WHERE WE ARE! SCREAM! YOU'RE BEAUTIFUL WHEN YOU'RE FRIGHTENED...BEAUTIFUL!
NO! STOP! HELP!

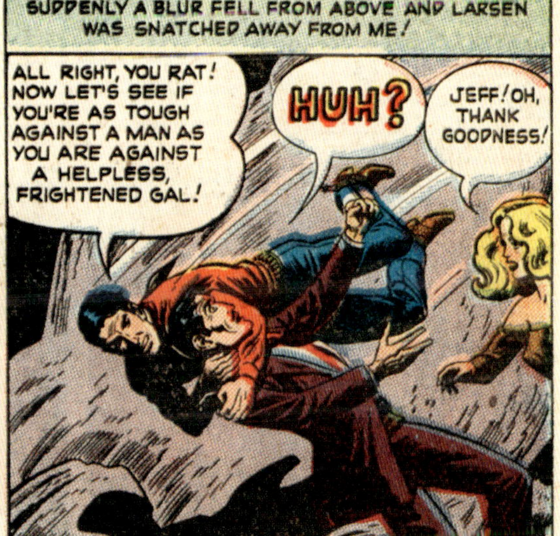
SUDDENLY A BLUR FELL FROM ABOVE AND LARSEN WAS SNATCHED AWAY FROM ME!
ALL RIGHT, YOU RAT! NOW LET'S SEE IF YOU'RE AS TOUGH AGAINST A MAN AS YOU ARE AGAINST A HELPLESS, FRIGHTENED GAL!
HUH?
JEFF! OH, THANK GOODNESS!

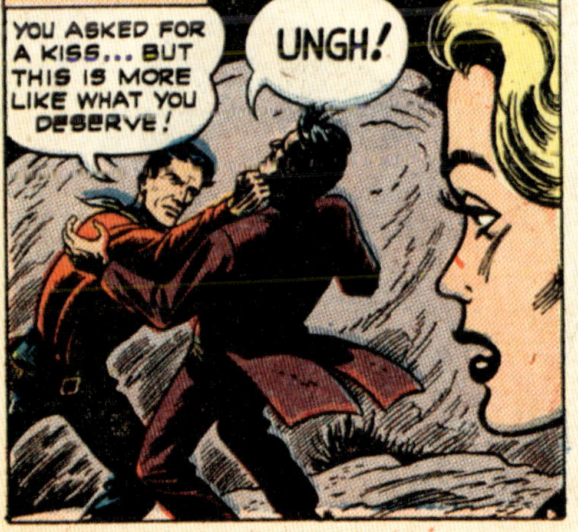
THE BATTLE WAS SHORT BUT VIOLENT! THE BEATING LARSEN'S FACE TOOK FROM JEFF'S FISTS LEFT THE CROOK A HULKING MASS OF LIMP FLESH!
YOU ASKED FOR A KISS... BUT THIS IS MORE LIKE WHAT YOU DESERVE!
UNGH!

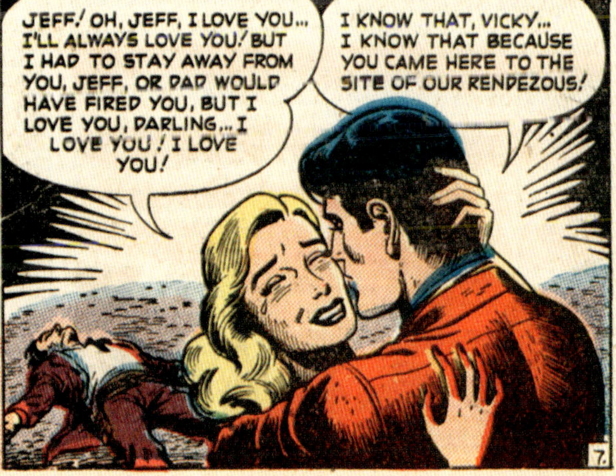
THEN IT WAS OVER AND I WAS CLOSE IN JEFF'S ARMS WHERE I BELONGED! SAFE AT LAST, MY HEART SINGING ONCE AGAIN, I POURED OUT THE TRUTH TO HIM!
JEFF! OH, JEFF, I LOVE YOU... I'LL ALWAYS LOVE YOU! BUT I HAD TO STAY AWAY FROM YOU, JEFF, OR DAD WOULD HAVE FIRED YOU, BUT I LOVE YOU, DARLING... I LOVE YOU! I LOVE YOU!
I KNOW THAT, VICKY... I KNOW THAT BECAUSE YOU CAME HERE TO THE SITE OF OUR RENDEZOUS!
7

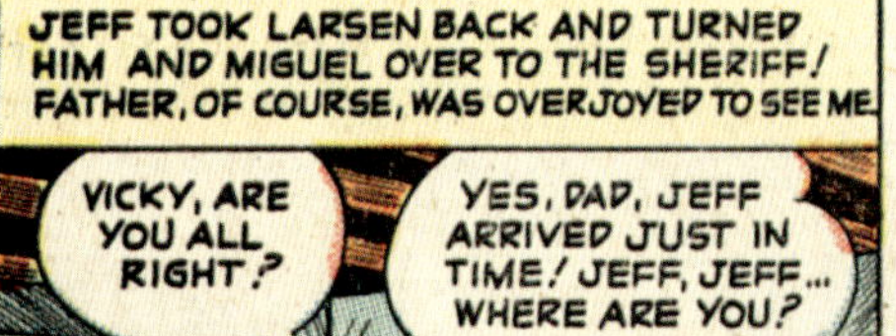
JEFF TOOK LARSEN BACK AND TURNED HIM AND MIGUEL OVER TO THE SHERIFF! FATHER, OF COURSE, WAS OVERJOYED TO SEE ME.

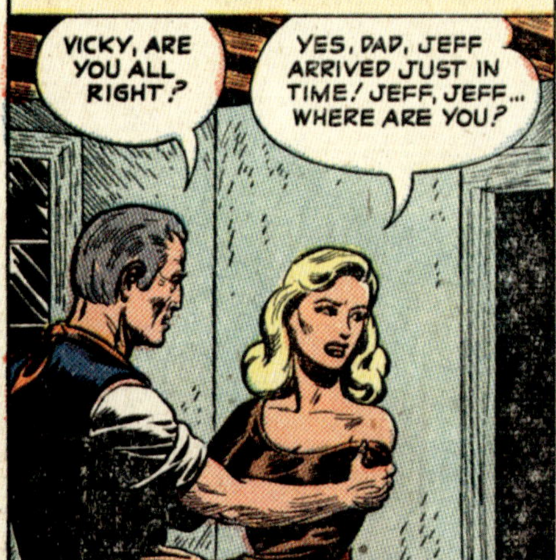
VICKY, ARE YOU ALL RIGHT?
YES, DAD, JEFF ARRIVED JUST IN TIME! JEFF, JEFF... WHERE ARE YOU?

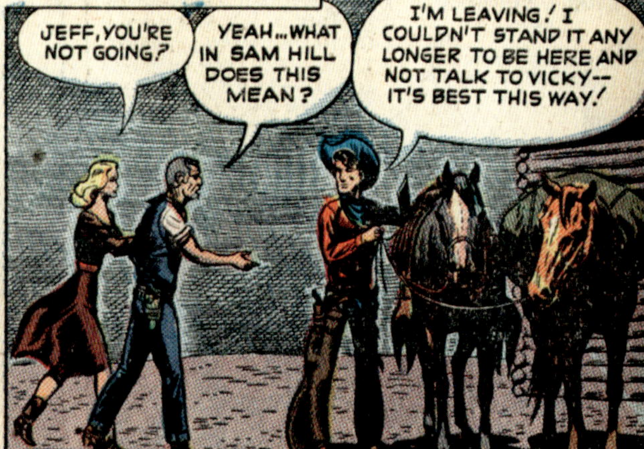
HE HADN'T FOLLOWED ME INTO THE HOUSE AFTER THE SHERIFF TOOK THE TWO CROOKS AWAY! NOW FATHER AND I LOOKED OUTSIDE AND THERE HE WAS, HIS PACK ON HIS HORSE, READY TO LEAVE!
JEFF, YOU'RE NOT GOING?
YEAH...WHAT IN SAM HILL DOES THIS MEAN?
I'M LEAVING! I COULDN'T STAND IT ANY LONGER TO BE HERE AND NOT TALK TO VICKY-- IT'S BEST THIS WAY!

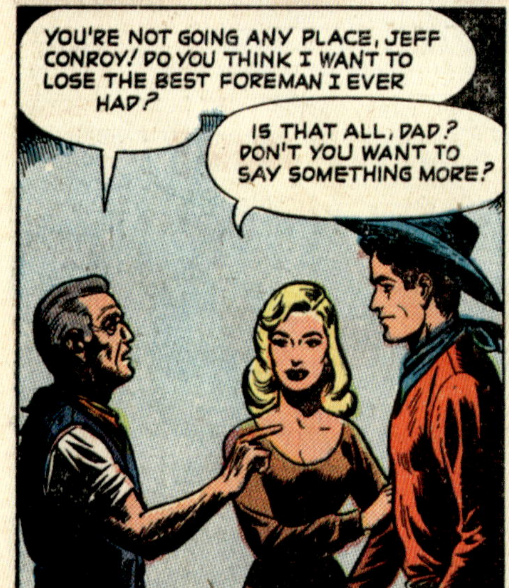
YOU'RE NOT GOING ANY PLACE, JEFF CONROY! DO YOU THINK I WANT TO LOSE THE BEST FOREMAN I EVER HAD?
IS THAT ALL, DAD? DON'T YOU WANT TO SAY SOMETHING MORE?

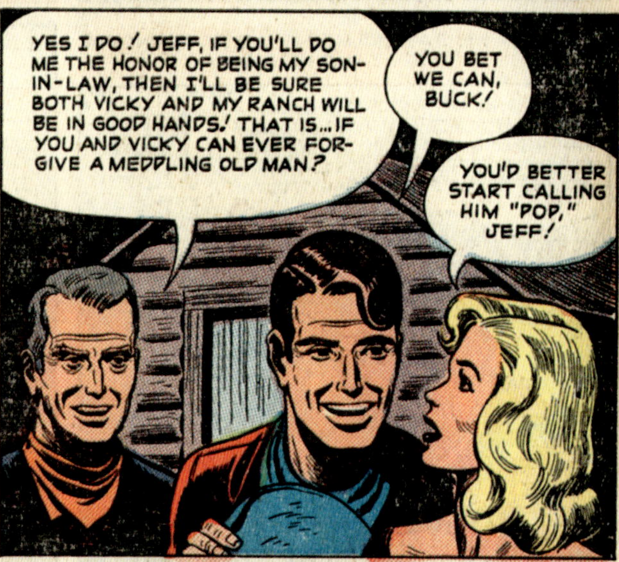
YES I DO! JEFF, IF YOU'LL DO ME THE HONOR OF BEING MY SON-IN-LAW, THEN I'LL BE SURE BOTH VICKY AND MY RANCH WILL BE IN GOOD HANDS! THAT IS...IF YOU AND VICKY CAN EVER FORGIVE A MEDDLING OLD MAN?
YOU BET WE CAN, BUCK!
YOU'D BETTER START CALLING HIM "POP," JEFF!

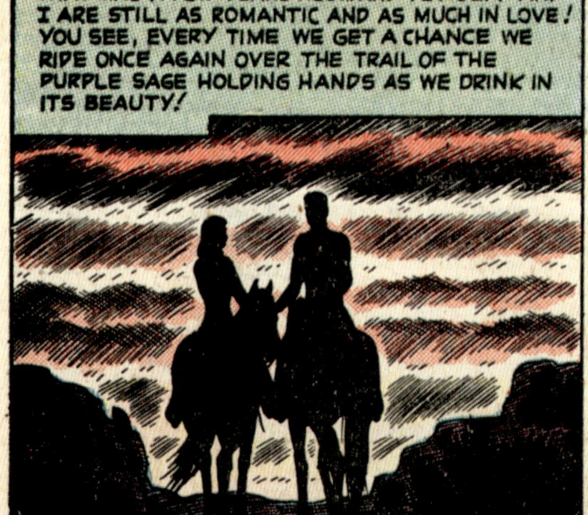
THAT WAS A FEW YEARS AGO...AND YET JEFF AND I ARE STILL AS ROMANTIC AND AS MUCH IN LOVE! YOU SEE, EVERY TIME WE GET A CHANCE WE RIDE ONCE AGAIN OVER THE TRAIL OF THE PURPLE SAGE HOLDING HANDS AS WE DRINK IN ITS BEAUTY!
8

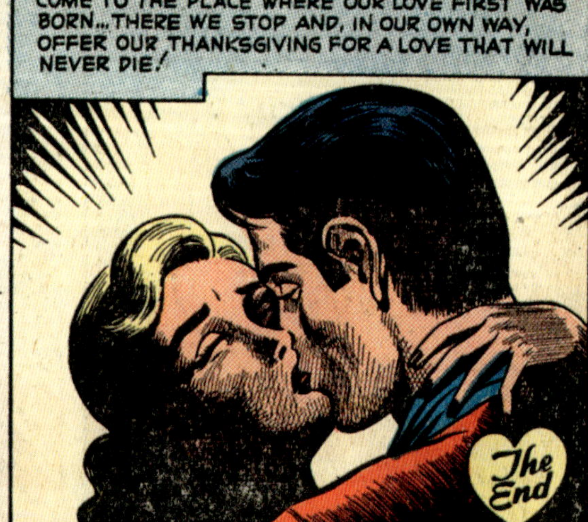
AND THEN, WHEN WE REACH ITS END, WHEN WE COME TO THE PLACE WHERE OUR LOVE FIRST WAS BORN...THERE WE STOP AND, IN OUR OWN WAY, OFFER OUR THANKSGIVING FOR A LOVE THAT WILL NEVER DIE!
The End

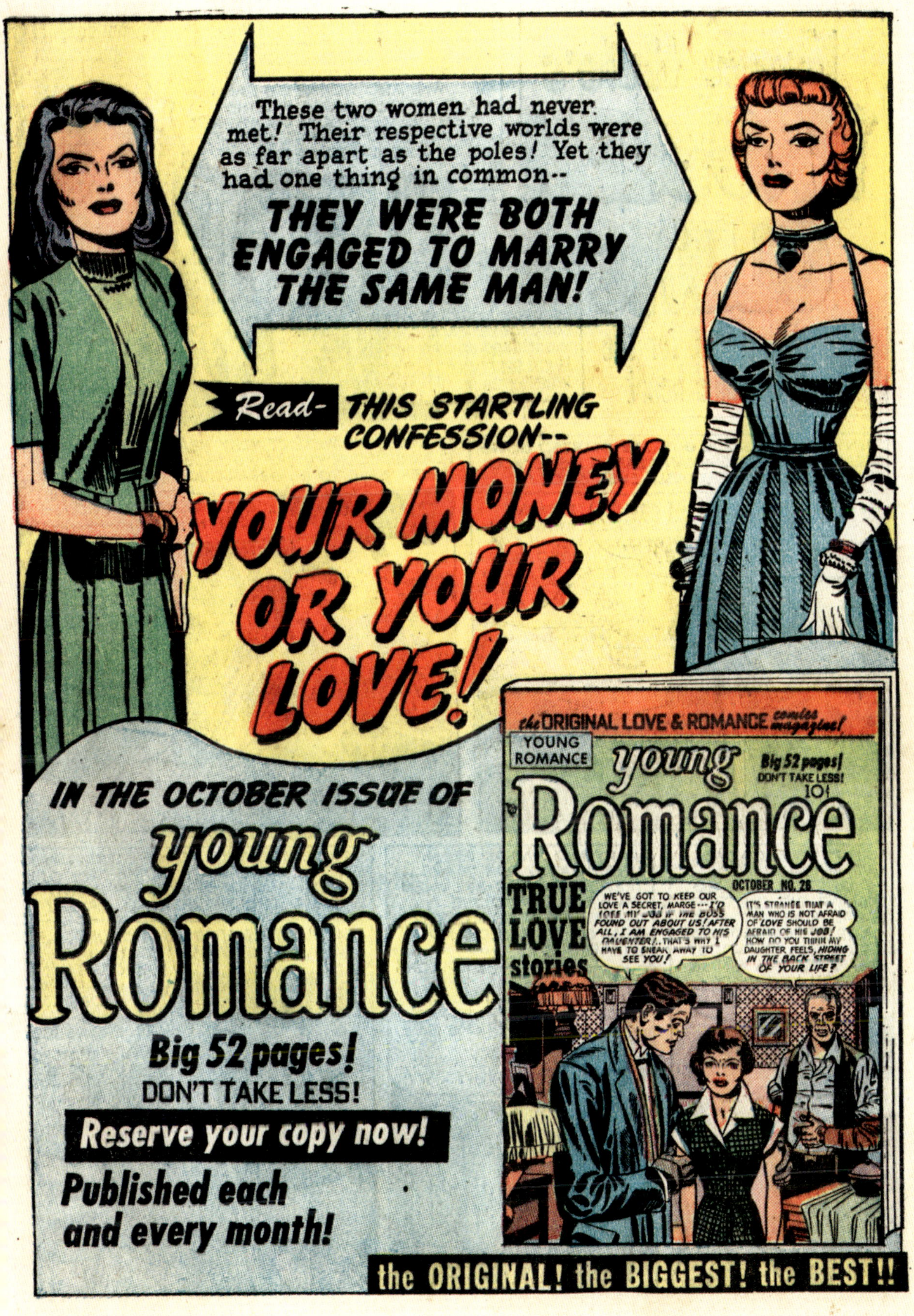

YOUNG LOVE
Volume 2, #7,
September 1950

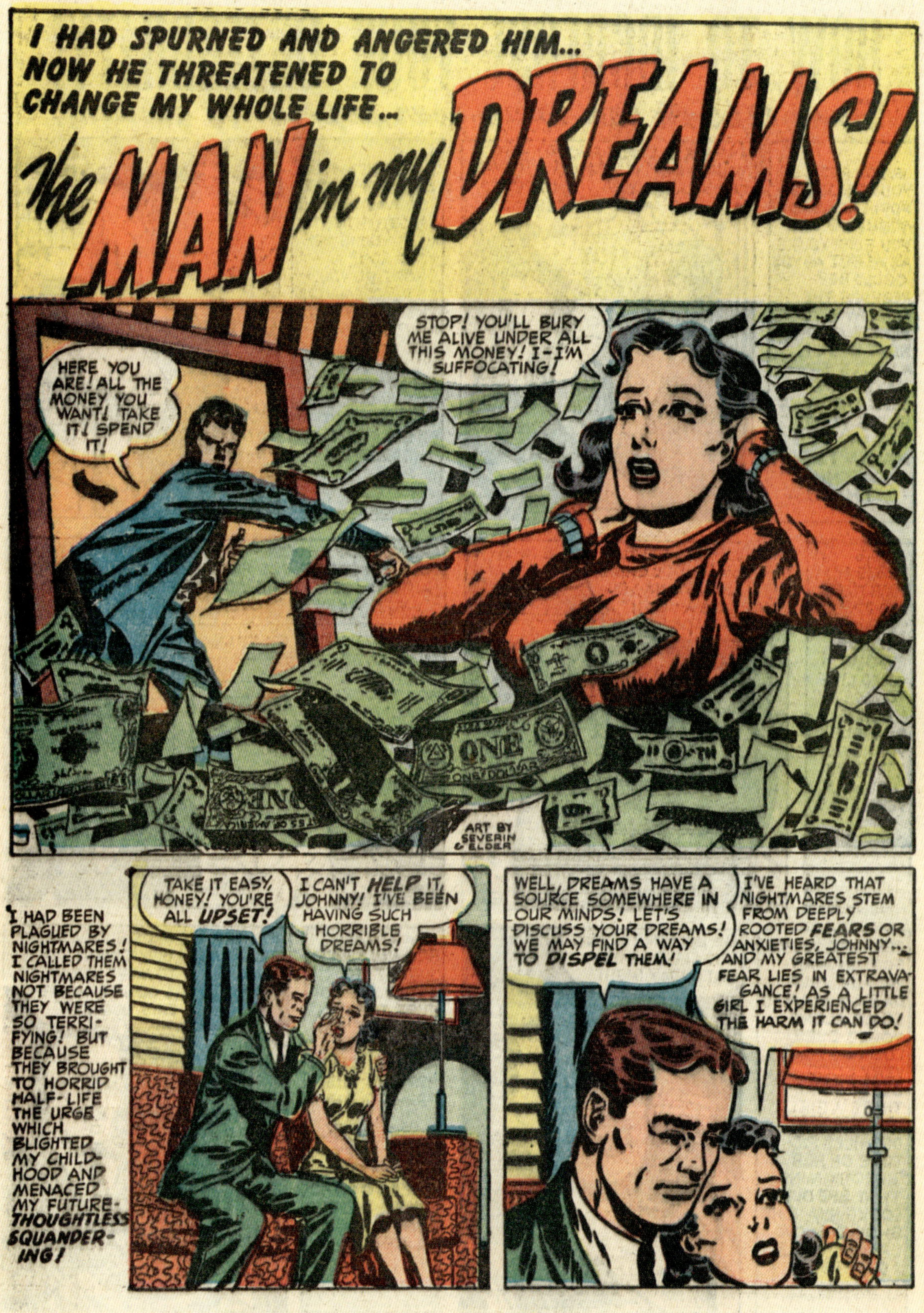

I HAD SPURNED AND ANGERED HIM... NOW HE THREATENED TO CHANGE MY WHOLE LIFE...

The MAN in my DREAMS!

HERE YOU ARE! ALL THE MONEY YOU WANT! TAKE IT! SPEND IT!

STOP! YOU'LL BURY ME ALIVE UNDER ALL THIS MONEY! I-I'M SUFFOCATING!

ART BY SEVERIN ELDER

I HAD BEEN PLAGUED BY NIGHTMARES! I CALLED THEM NIGHTMARES NOT BECAUSE THEY WERE SO TERRIFYING! BUT BECAUSE THEY BROUGHT TO HORRID HALF-LIFE THE URGE WHICH BLIGHTED MY CHILDHOOD AND MENACED MY FUTURE-***THOUGHTLESS SQUANDERING!***

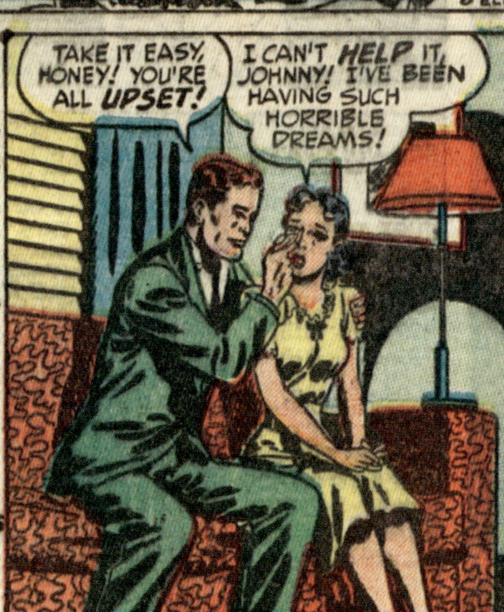

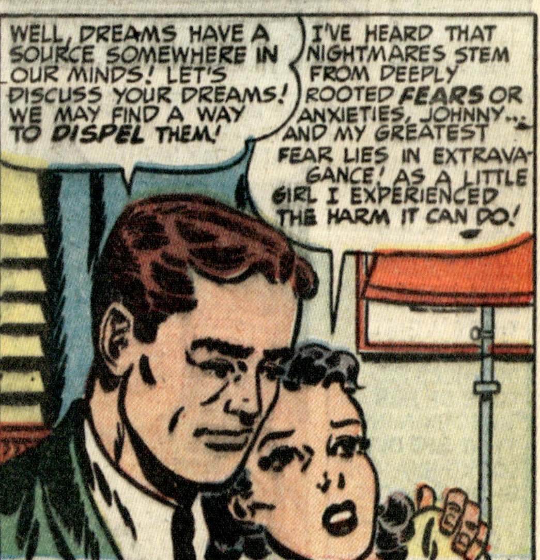

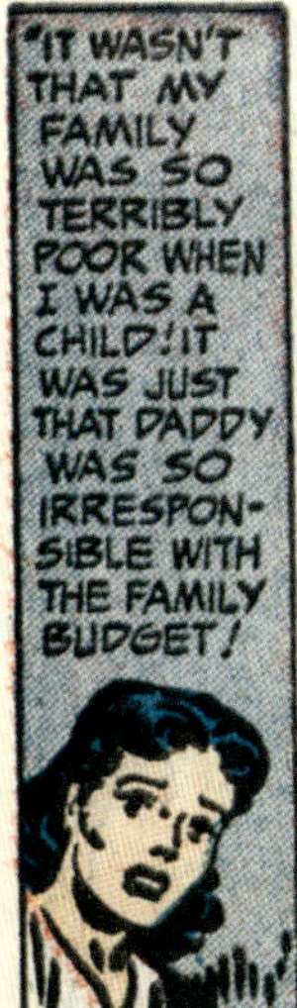

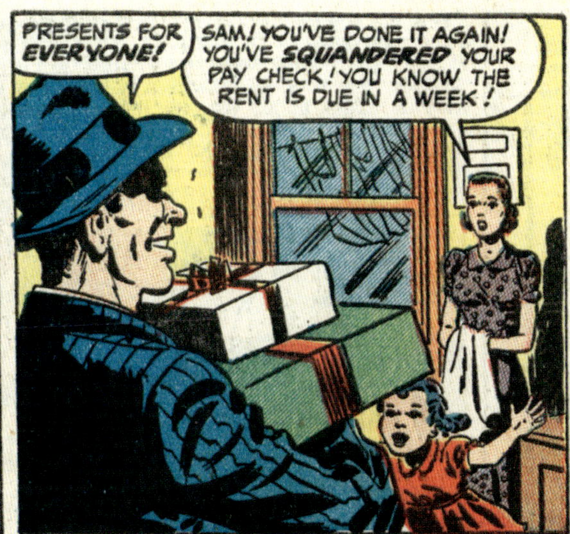

"DADDY EARNED A FAIR SALARY...BUT WE WERE NEVER ABLE TO SAVE BECAUSE OF HIS CAPRICIOUS WAYS...HE WAS ALWAYS BUYING **UNNECESSARY** AND IMPRACTICAL ITEMS WE COULD DO WITHOUT!

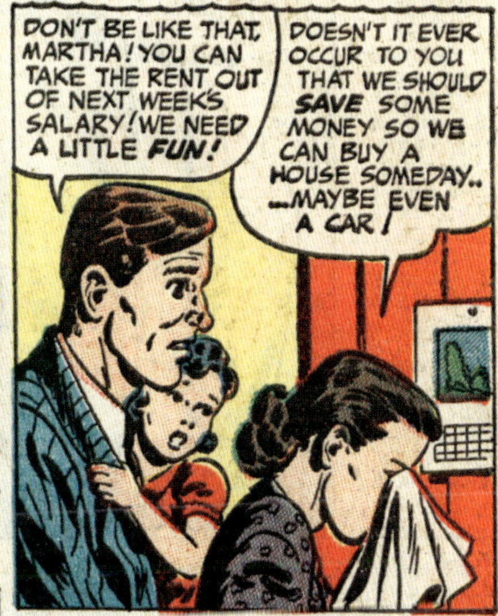

"THAT WAS THE SITUATION! DAD LIVED ONLY FOR THE PRESENT...ALLOWING THE FUTURE TO TAKE CARE OF ITSELF! HE INSISTED WE ENJOY THE GOOD TIME WE COULDN'T AFFORD... WE DID...IN POVERTY... AS I GREW... SO DID MY DETERMINATION TO FIND **SECURITY!**

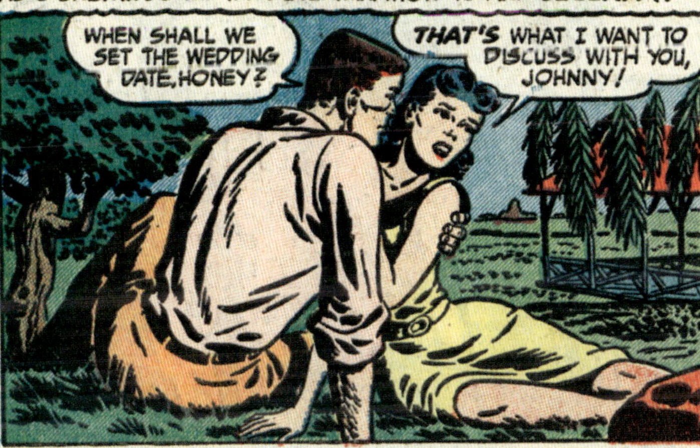

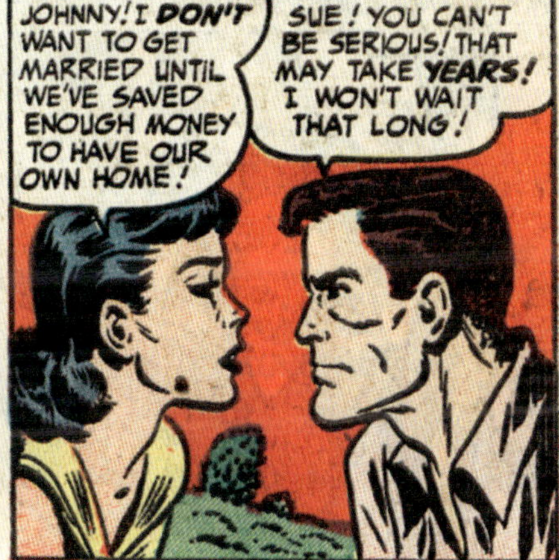

"THE LOOK ON YOUR FACE ALMOST MADE ME CRY! I WANTED TO THROW MYSELF INTO YOUR ARMS AND TELL YOU I'D MARRY YOU RIGHT AWAY! BUT MY PRIDE STOPPED ME! I WANTED MORE FROM LIFE THAN MY MOTHER HAD! AND I WAS INTENT ON GETTING IT!

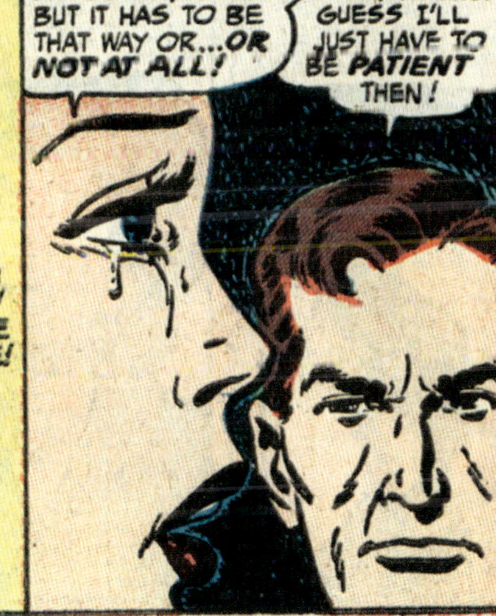

"YOU WERE USED TO SPENDING MONEY FREELY AND IT WAS DIFFICULT FOR YOU TO SAVE SO MUCH! BUT GRADUALLY, YOU ADJUSTED YOURSELF TO MY WAY OF THINKING!

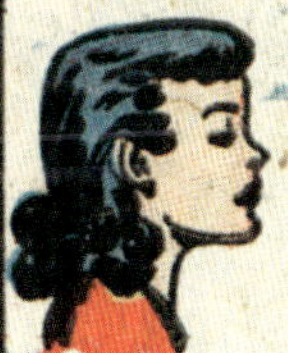

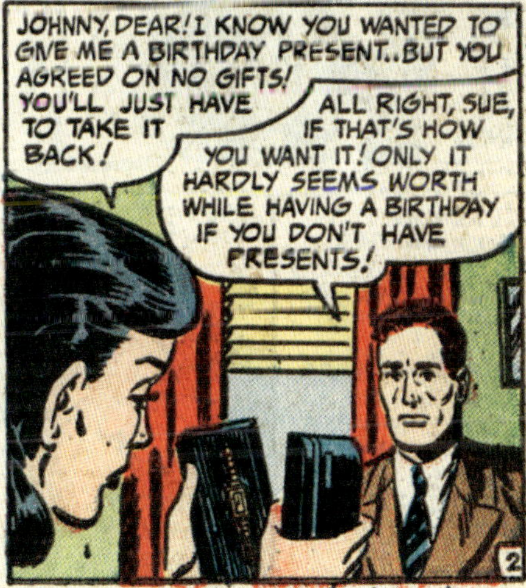

YOUNG LOVE
Volume 2, #2
April 1950

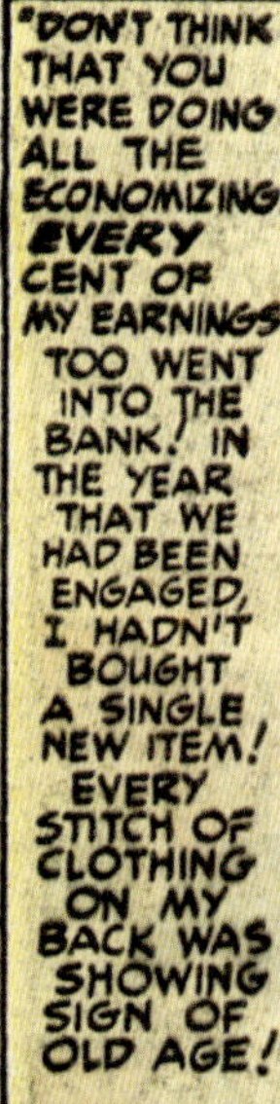

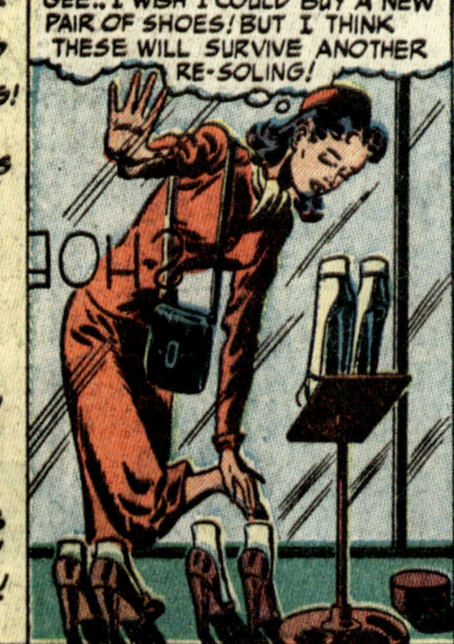

"YES, WE SACRIFICED A LOT! BUT OUR BANK ACCOUNT WAS GROWING! I DIDN'T FEEL WE SHOULD WASTE MONEY ON ENTERTAINMENT, EITHER! SO WE CONFINED OURSELVES TO ONE MOVIE A WEEK! AND ON OTHER NIGHTS TOOK LONG WALKS! IT WAS ON THESE STROLLS THAT I FIRST NOTICED YOU LOOKING **LONGINGLY** AT THE BEAUTIFULLY DRESSED WOMEN!

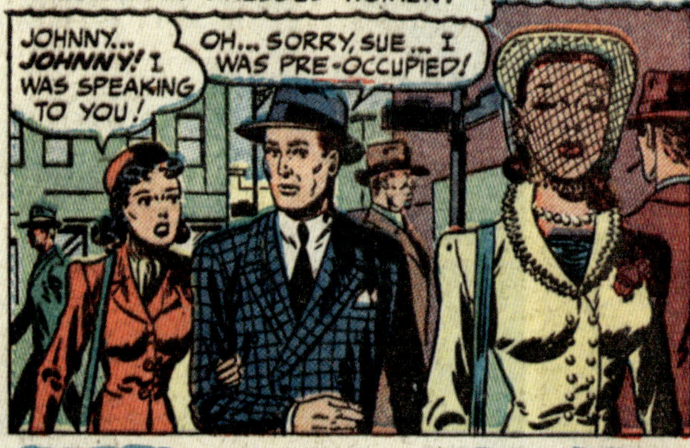

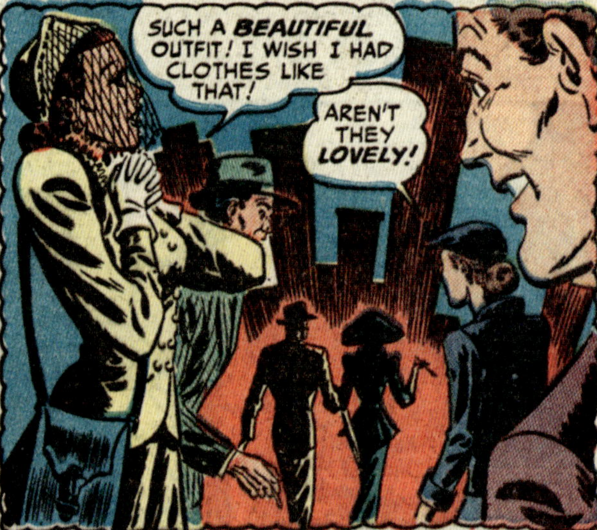

"THAT NIGHT I BEGAN HAVING MY STRANGE DREAMS! I DREAMED THAT YOU AND I WERE WALKING DOWN THE SAME STREET... ONLY THIS TIME, I WAS VERY EXPENSIVELY, IF **GAUDILY** DRESSED!

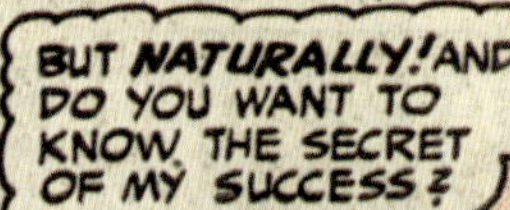

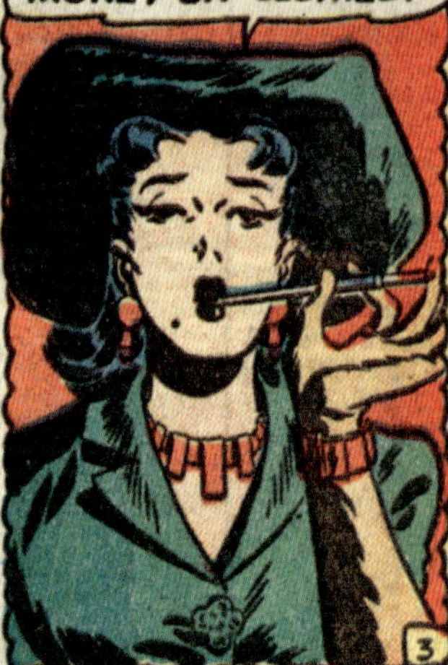

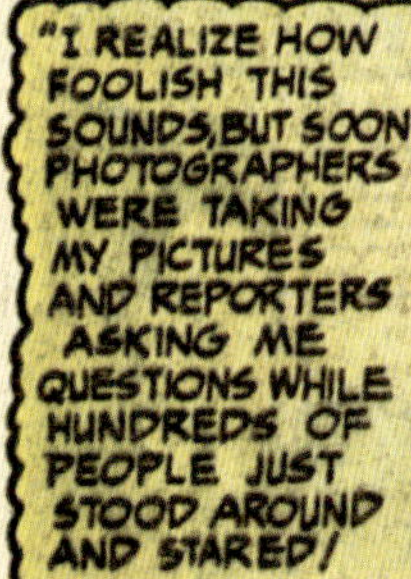

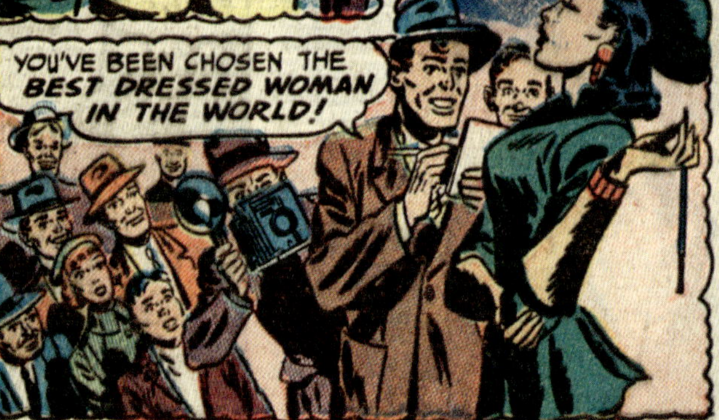

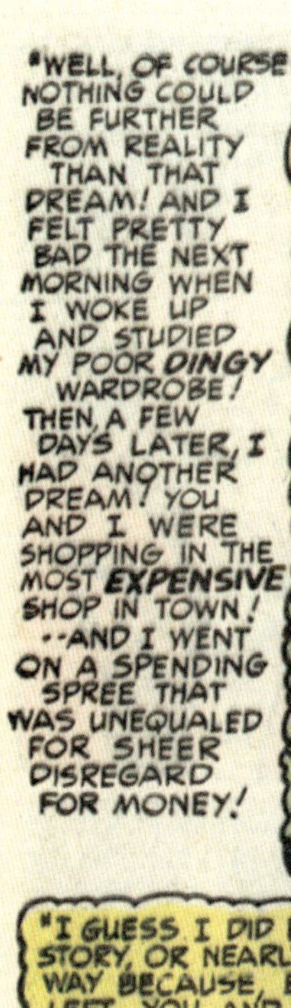
"WELL, OF COURSE NOTHING COULD BE FURTHER FROM REALITY THAN THAT DREAM! AND I FELT PRETTY BAD THE NEXT MORNING WHEN I WOKE UP AND STUDIED MY POOR DINGY WARDROBE! THEN, A FEW DAYS LATER, I HAD ANOTHER DREAM! YOU AND I WERE SHOPPING IN THE MOST EXPENSIVE SHOP IN TOWN! --AND I WENT ON A SPENDING SPREE THAT WAS UNEQUALED FOR SHEER DISREGARD FOR MONEY!

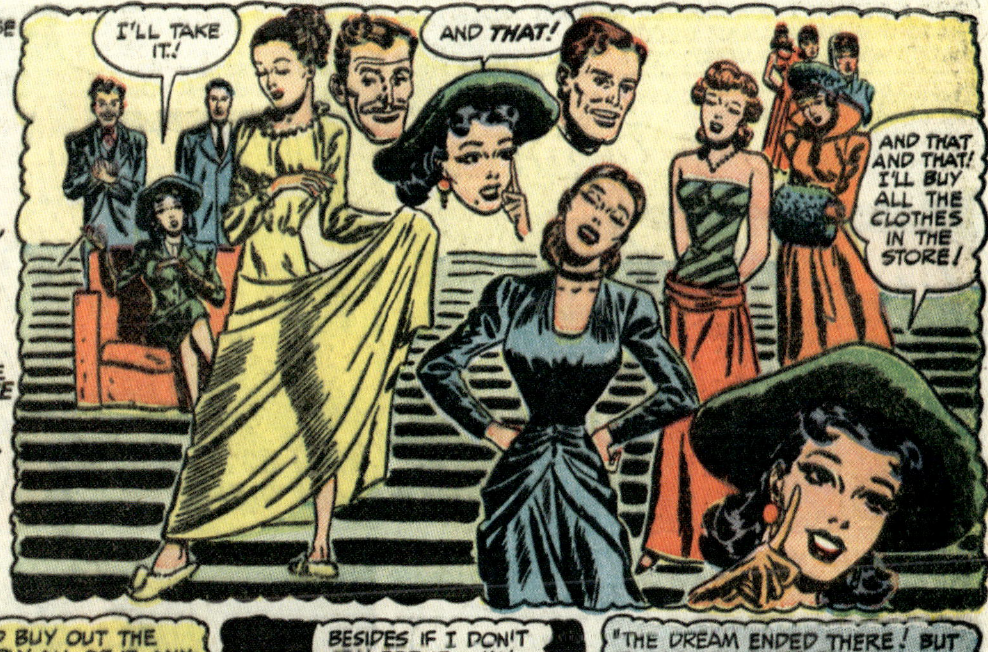
I'LL TAKE IT.!
AND THAT!
AND THAT AND THAT! I'LL BUY ALL THE CLOTHES IN THE STORE!

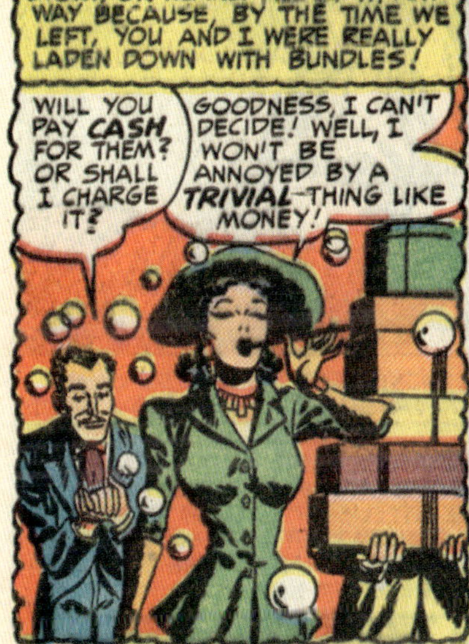
"I GUESS I DID BUY OUT THE STORY, OR NEARLY ALL OF IT, ANY-WAY BECAUSE, BY THE TIME WE LEFT, YOU AND I WERE REALLY LADEN DOWN WITH BUNDLES!
WILL YOU PAY CASH FOR THEM? OR SHALL I CHARGE IT?
GOODNESS, I CAN'T DECIDE! WELL, I WON'T BE ANNOYED BY A TRIVIAL THING LIKE MONEY!

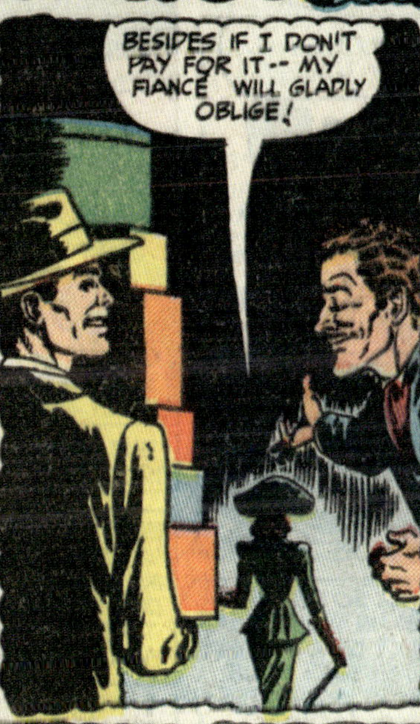
BESIDES IF I DON'T PAY FOR IT-- MY FIANCE WILL GLADLY OBLIGE!

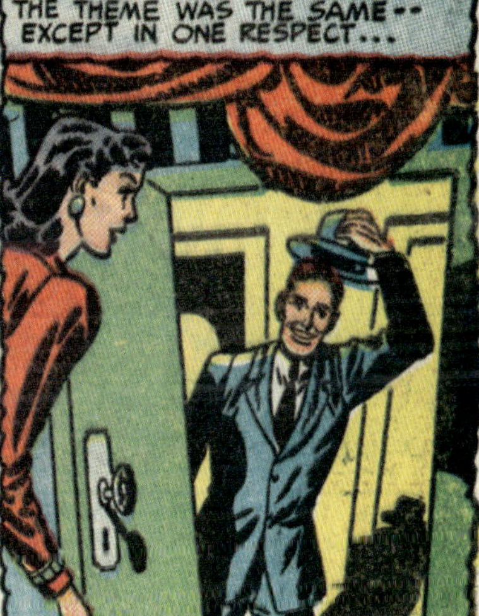
"THE DREAM ENDED THERE! BUT IT WAS FOLLOWED BY STILL ANOTHER THE NEXT NIGHT! THE SETTING WAS DIFFERENT! BUT THE THEME WAS THE SAME-- EXCEPT IN ONE RESPECT...

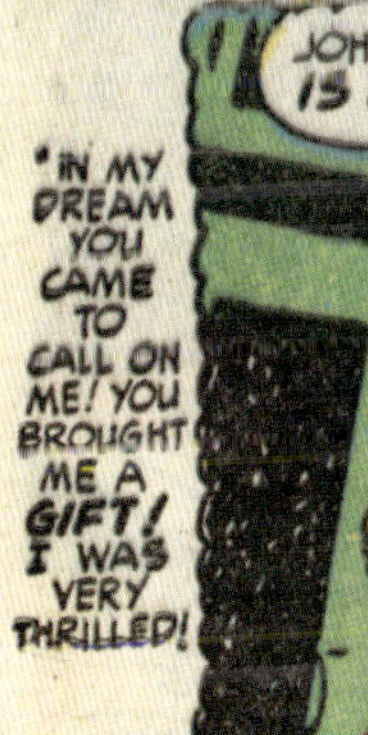
"IN MY DREAM YOU CAME TO CALL ON ME! YOU BROUGHT ME A GIFT! I WAS VERY THRILLED!

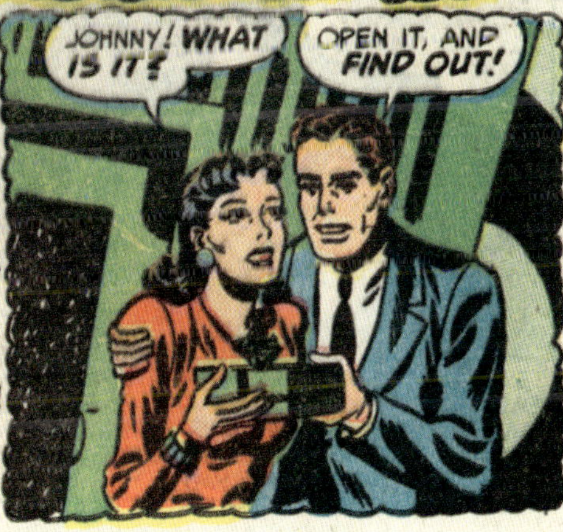
JOHNNY! WHAT IS IT?
OPEN IT, AND FIND OUT!

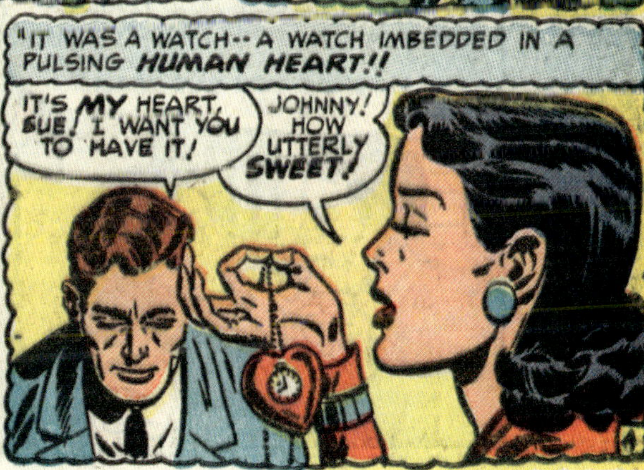
"IT WAS A WATCH-- A WATCH IMBEDDED IN A PULSING HUMAN HEART!!
IT'S MY HEART, SUE! I WANT YOU TO HAVE IT!
JOHNNY! HOW UTTERLY SWEET!

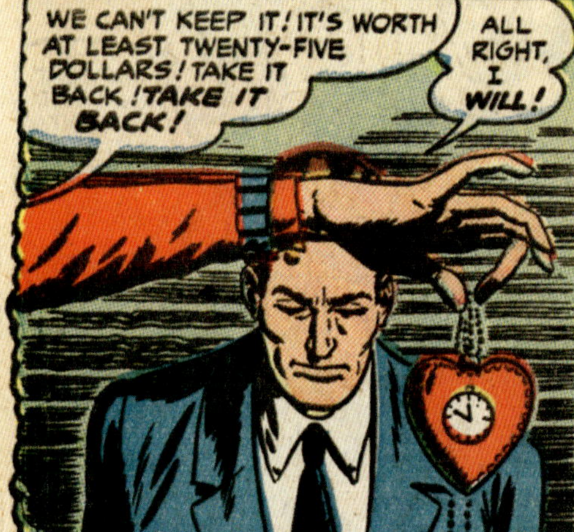

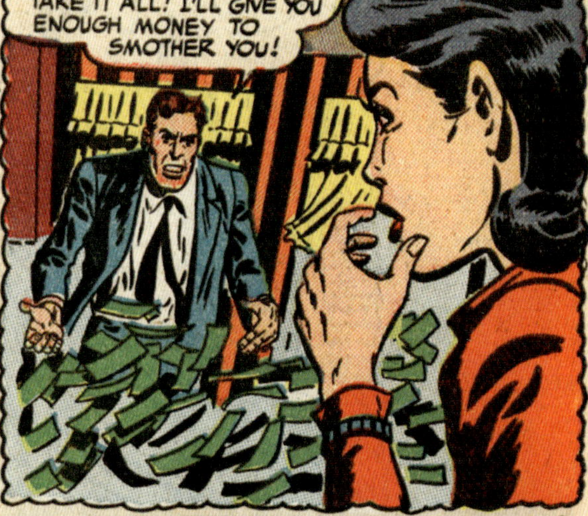

"THAT WAS HOW I AWOKE...GASPING AND THRASHING VIOLENTLY ABOUT! I WAS SO FRIGHTENED I BEGAN TO CRY!

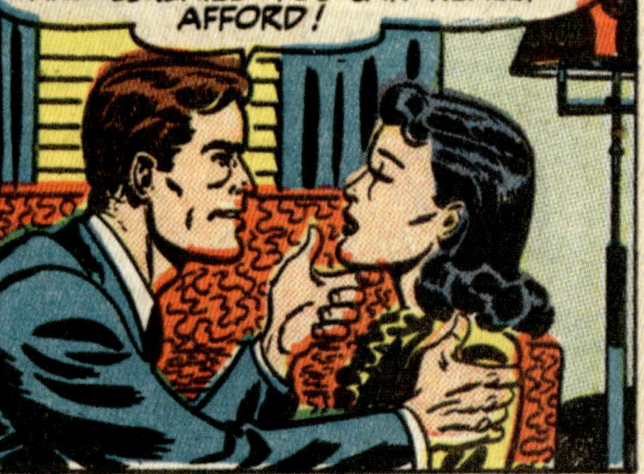

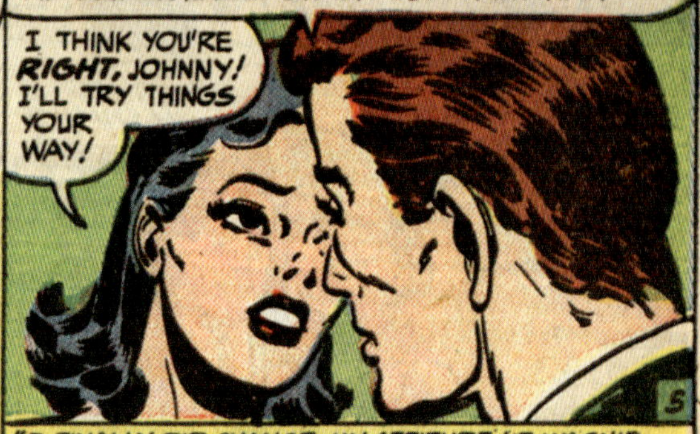

BOY MEETS GIRL

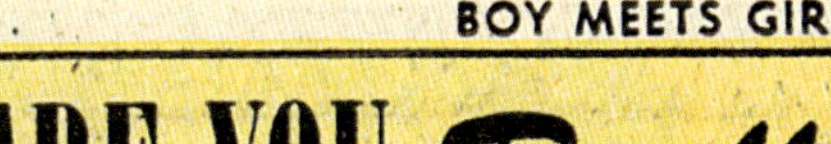

ARE YOU *Really in* LOVE?

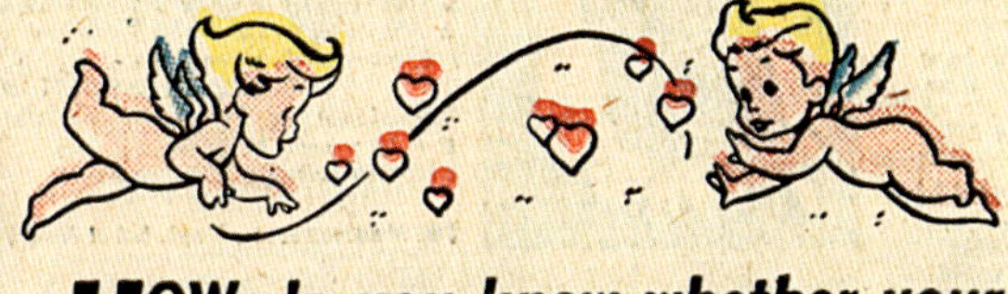

HOW do you know whether your current heartbeat is the one-and-only? Can it be love...this great excitement you feel...or is it only another crush? Here are a dozen questions to help you decide for yourself if you are REALLY IN LOVE!

Are you willing to give up all other men friends if and when HE asks you to do so?
YES_____ NO_____

Do you feel excitement and delight in HIS company?
YES_____ NO_____

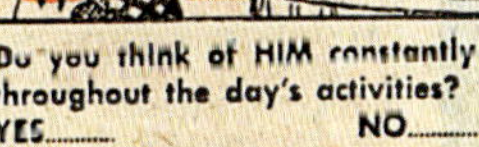

Do you think of HIM constantly throughout the day's activities?
YES_____ NO_____

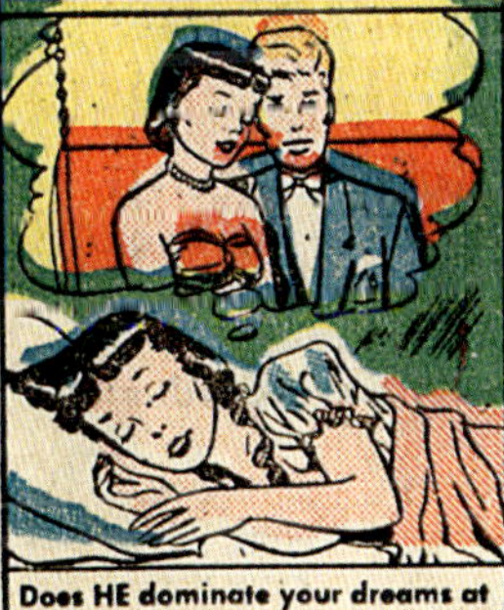

Does HE dominate your dreams at night?
YES_____ NO_____

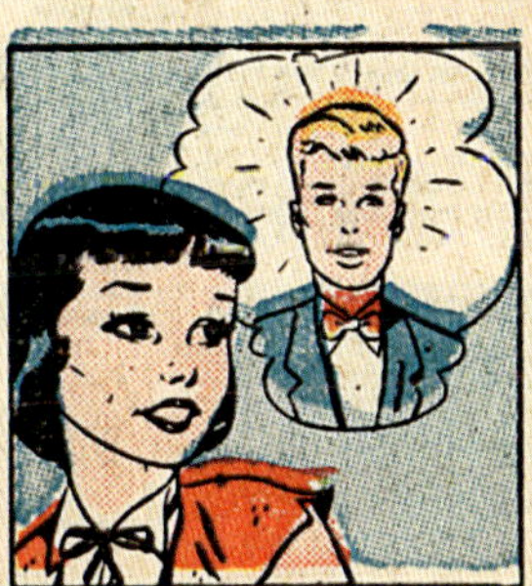

Do you think HE is the handsomest man in the world?
YES_____ NO_____

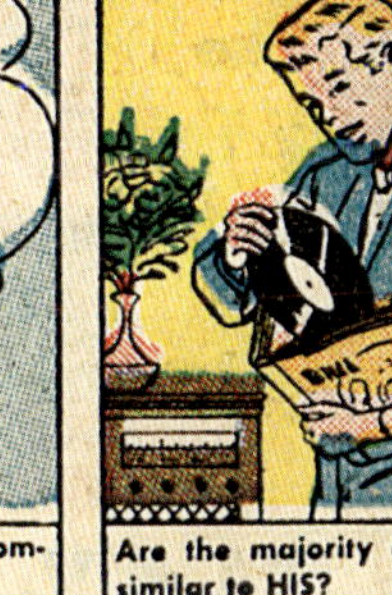

Are the majority of your tastes similar to HIS?
YES_____ NO_____

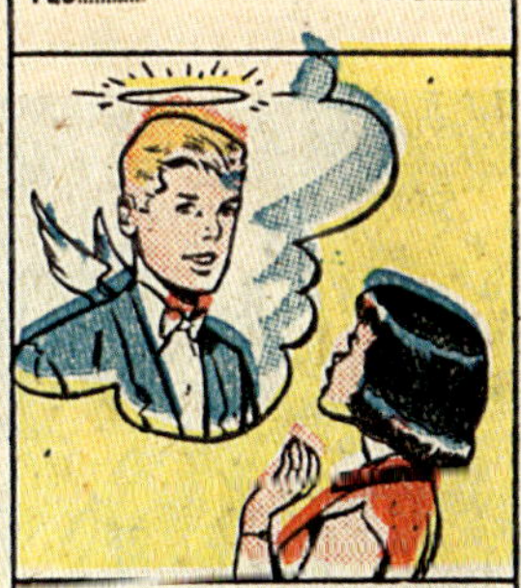

Does HE seem perfect to you in every way?
YES_____ NO_____

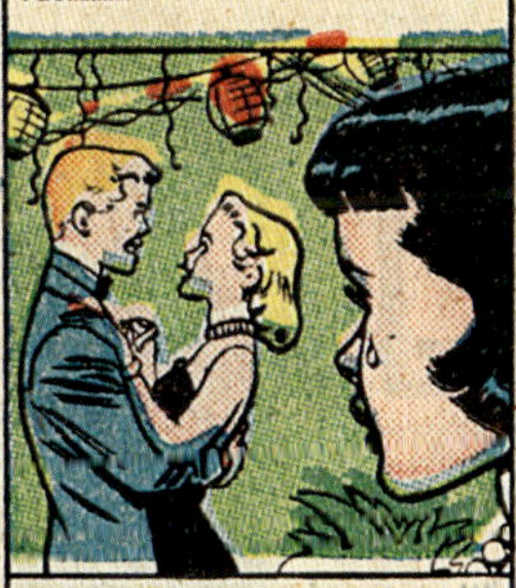

Are you deeply hurt when HE shows marked attention to another girl?
YES_____ NO_____

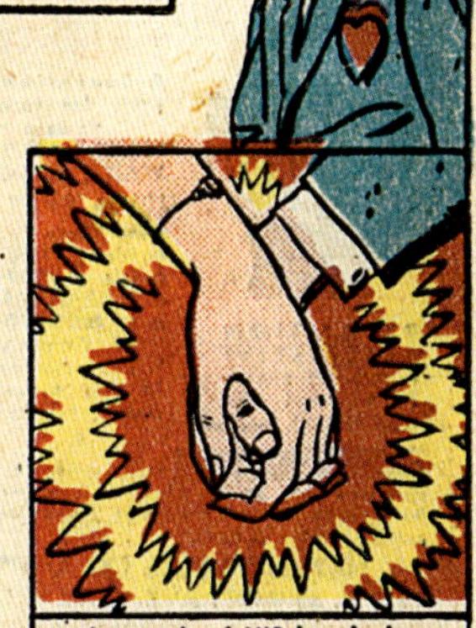

Is the touch of HIS hand always thrilling?
YES_____ NO_____

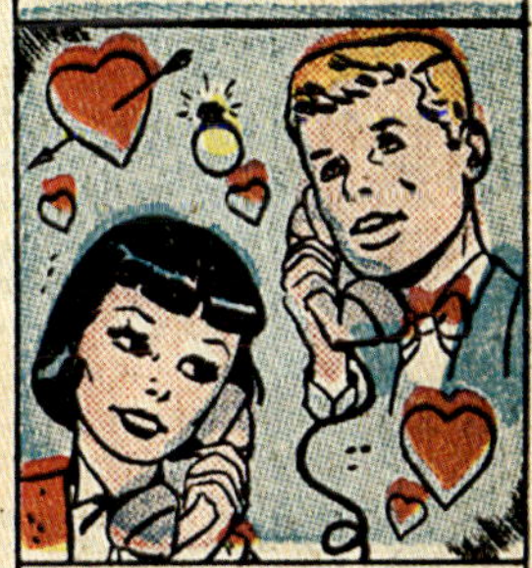

Does the sound of HIS voice thrill you every time you hear it?
YES_____ NO_____

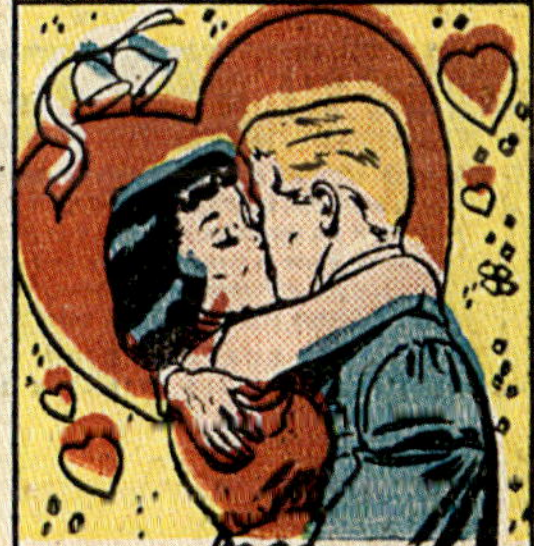

If HE has kissed you . . . was that kiss a soul-shaking experience?
YES_____ NO_____

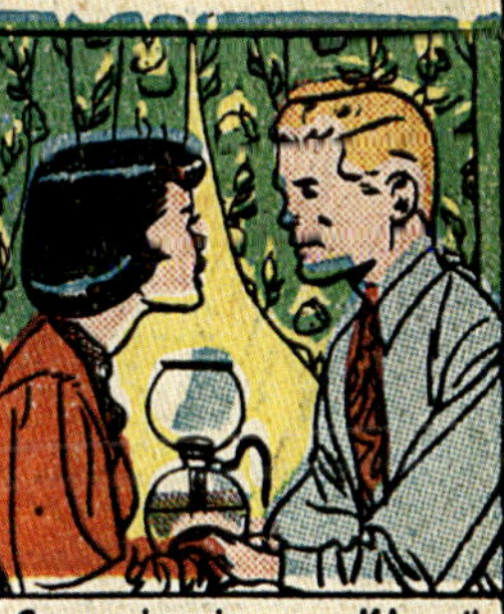

Can you imagine yourself happily spending the rest of your life with HIM?
YES_____ NO_____

Check off your answers, then score yourself one point for each yes. Now total your score. 10 to 12 indicates you are REALLY IN LOVE. 7 to 9 shows a very high susceptibility to the man in question, but what you feel isn't real love as yet. Anything below 7 and it's NOT the real thing. But don't give up—there's a man for every maid...remember?

BOY MEETS GIRL
#1, February 1950

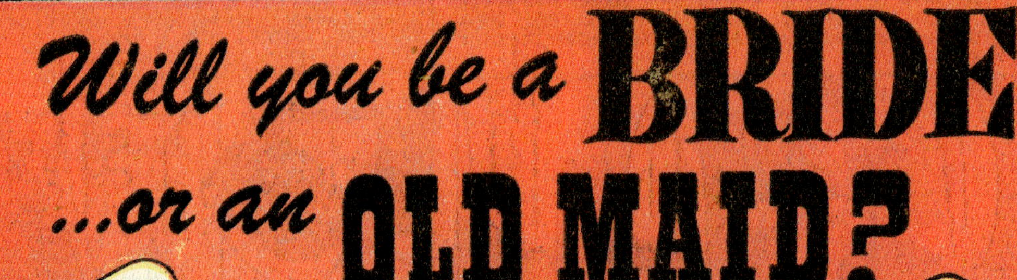

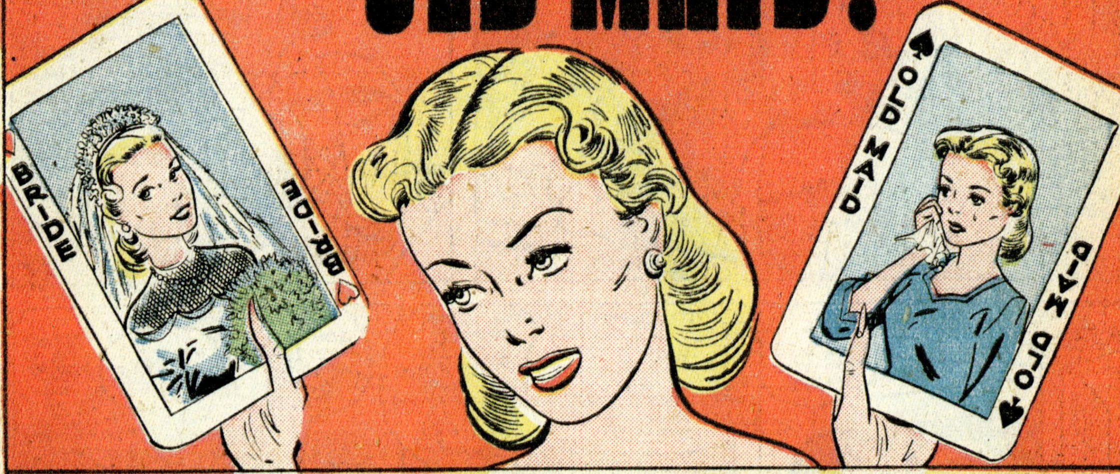

EVERYONE TRIES TO GET A GLIMPSE OF THE FUTURE. SOME DO IT WITH CRYSTAL BALLS, OTHERS BY READING PALMS. THE MODERN WAY IS BY GIVING YOURSELF A TEST, AND HERE WE OFFER A SET OF QUESTIONS TO HELP YOU ANSWER THAT PERSISTENT DOUBT IN YOUR HEART . . WILL YOU BE A BRIDE OR AN OLD MAID? OF COURSE THERE IS NO SURE WAY OF PREDICTING THE FUTURE. IT IS LOCKED IN MYSTERY . . . BUT THERE ARE CERTAIN SIGNPOSTS THAT INDICATE THE DIRECTION YOU ARE TAKING . . TOWARDS MARRIAGE OR AWAY FROM IT.

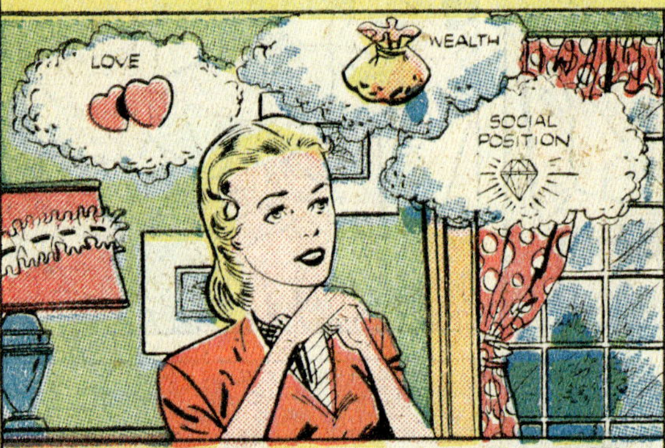

DO YOU BELIEVE LOVE IS THE ONLY REAL BASIS FOR MARRIAGE?
YES.... NO....

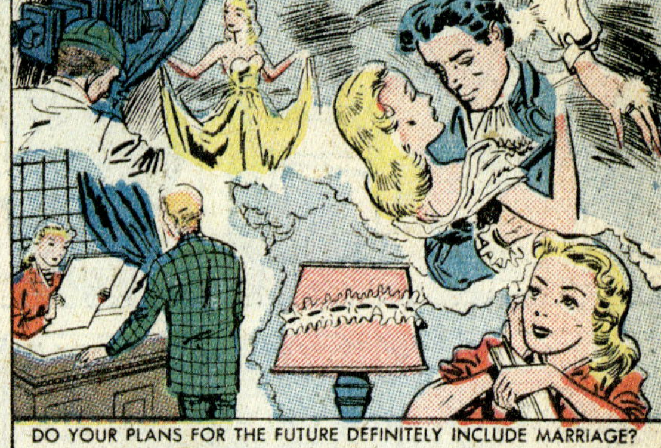

DO YOUR PLANS FOR THE FUTURE DEFINITELY INCLUDE MARRIAGE?
YES.... NO....

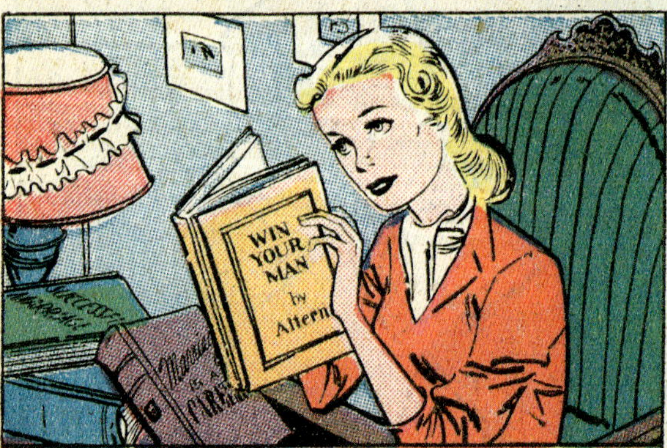

ARE YOU WILLING TO MAKE AN INTELLIGENT EFFORT TO REALIZE YOUR DREAM OF MARRIAGE? YES NO

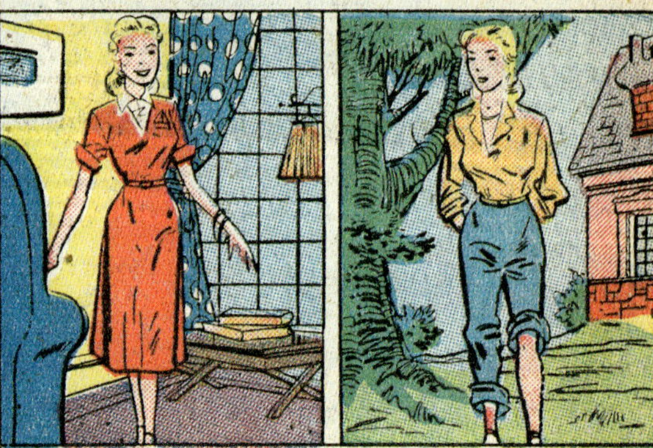

DO YOU KEEP YOURSELF WELL-GROOMED AND ATTRACTIVELY DRESSED?
YES.... NO....

BOY MEETS GIRL

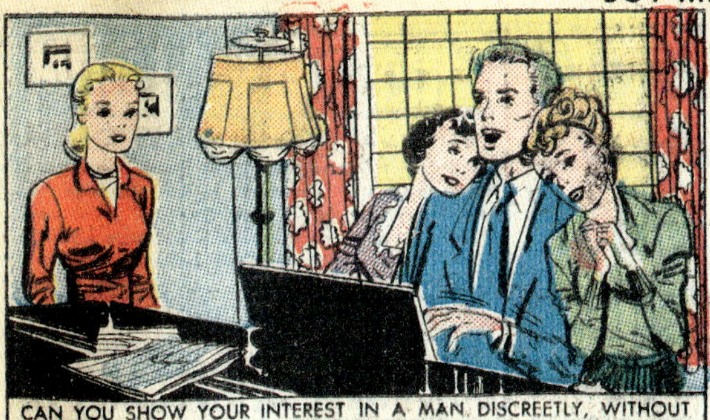

CAN YOU SHOW YOUR INTEREST IN A MAN DISCREETLY, WITHOUT PUSHING YOURSELF INTO HIS ATTENTION? YES.... NO....

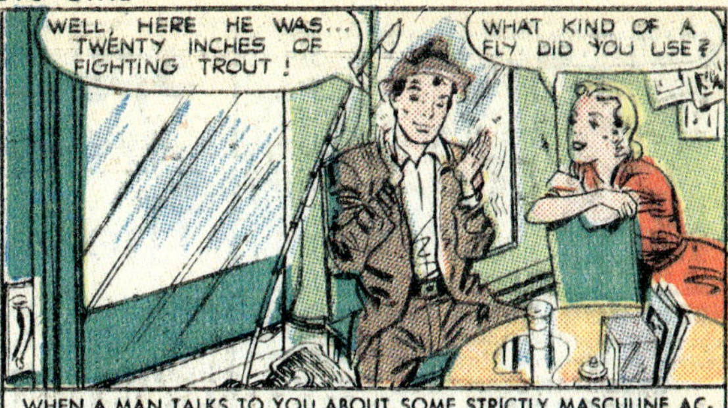

WHEN A MAN TALKS TO YOU ABOUT SOME STRICTLY MASCULINE ACTIVITY, LIKE FISHING, CAN YOU LISTEN WITH INTEREST AND ANIMATION? YES.... NO....

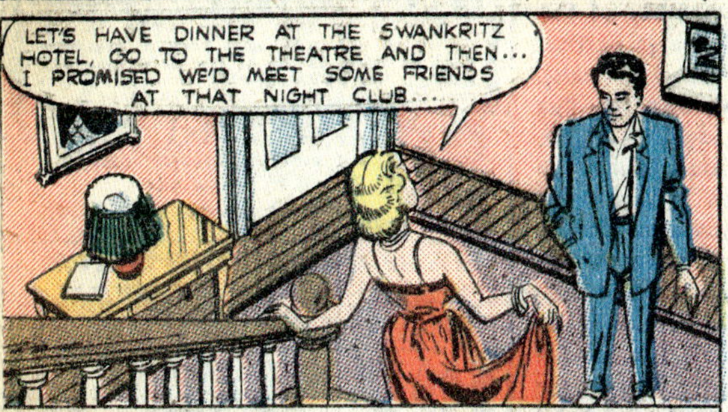

DO YOU CONSIDER A MAN'S FINANCES WHEN YOU MAKE THE PLANS FOR THE EVENING? YES.... NO....

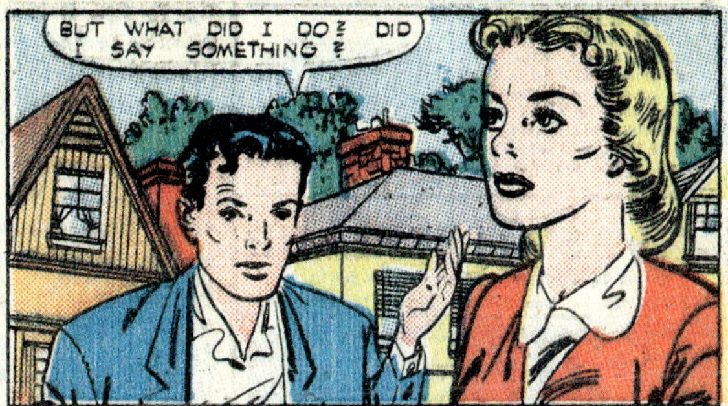

DO YOU EXPECT A MAN TO CATER TO YOUR MOODS ALL THE TIME? YES.... NO....

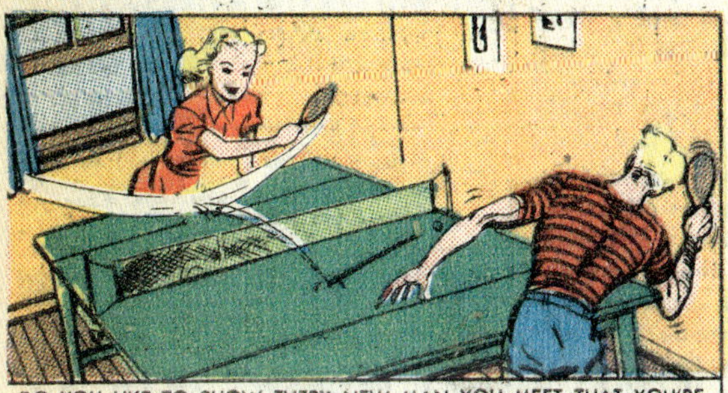

DO YOU LIKE TO SHOW EVERY NEW MAN YOU MEET THAT YOU'RE SMARTER AND MORE ACCOMPLISHED THAN HE IS? YES.... NO....

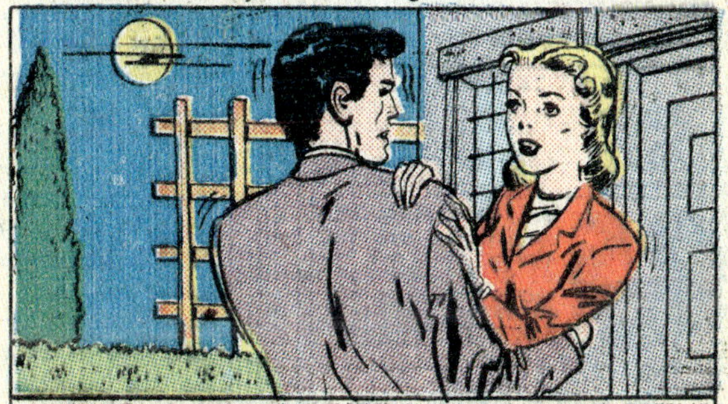

ARE YOU OUTRAGED AND OFFENDED WHEN A MAN WANTS TO KISS YOU? YES.... NO....

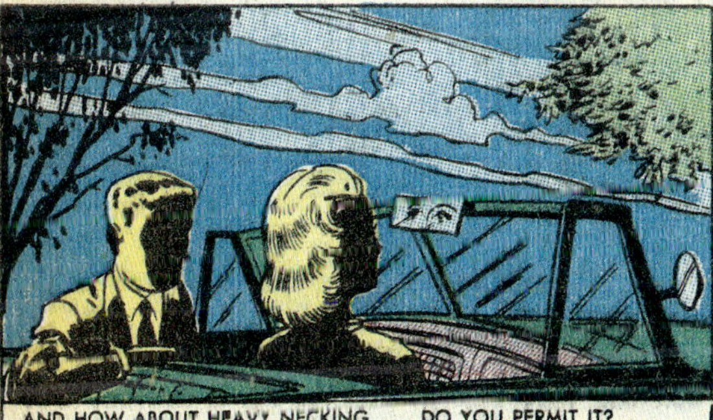

AND HOW ABOUT HEAVY NECKING . . . DO YOU PERMIT IT? YES.... NO....

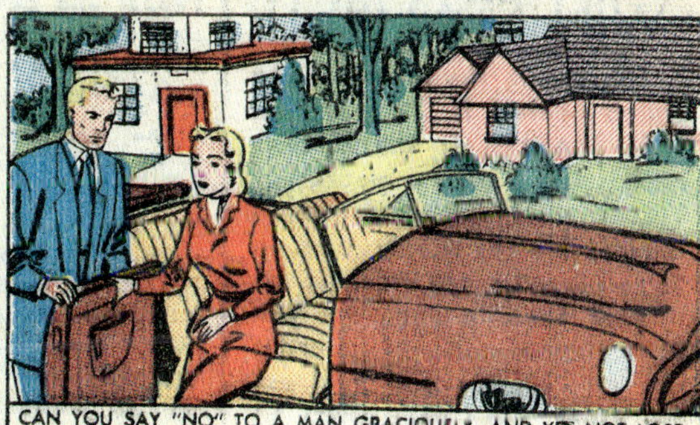

CAN YOU SAY "NO" TO A MAN GRACIOUSLY, AND YET NOT LOSE HIS FRIENDSHIP? YES.... NO....

—KEY—

1 THRU 7 ALSO 12 } ANSWERS SHOULD BE YES

8 THRU 11 } ANSWERS SHOULD BE NO

IF YOU CAN HONESTLY ANSWER THE YES'S AND NO'S CORRECTLY, YOU HAVE A PERFECT SCORE . . . YOU'LL SURELY BE A BRIDE

SIX OUT OF 8 ON THE YES'S AND ALL THE NO'S CORRECT . . . AND YOUR CHANCES OF BEING A BRIDE ARE GOOD, BUT YOU NEED A LITTLE MORE HOME-WORK.

LESS THAN 6 ON THE YES'S AND LESS THAN 4 ON THE NO'S . . . AND YOU'LL HAVE TO DO A REAL ALTERATION JOB ON YOURSELF IF YOU REALLY WANT TO BE A BRIDE INSTEAD OF AN OLD MAID.

BOY MEETS GIRL
#2, April 1950

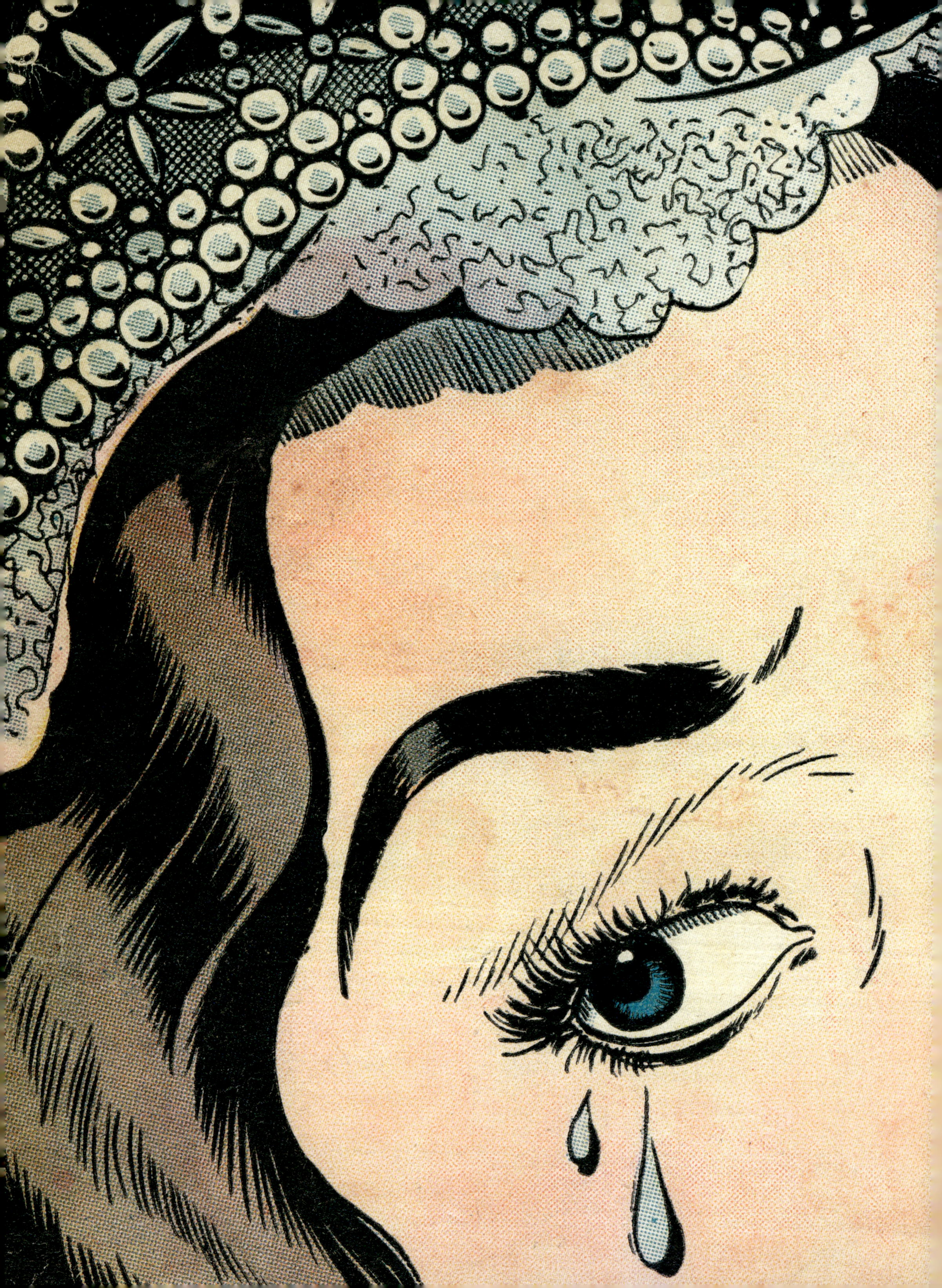

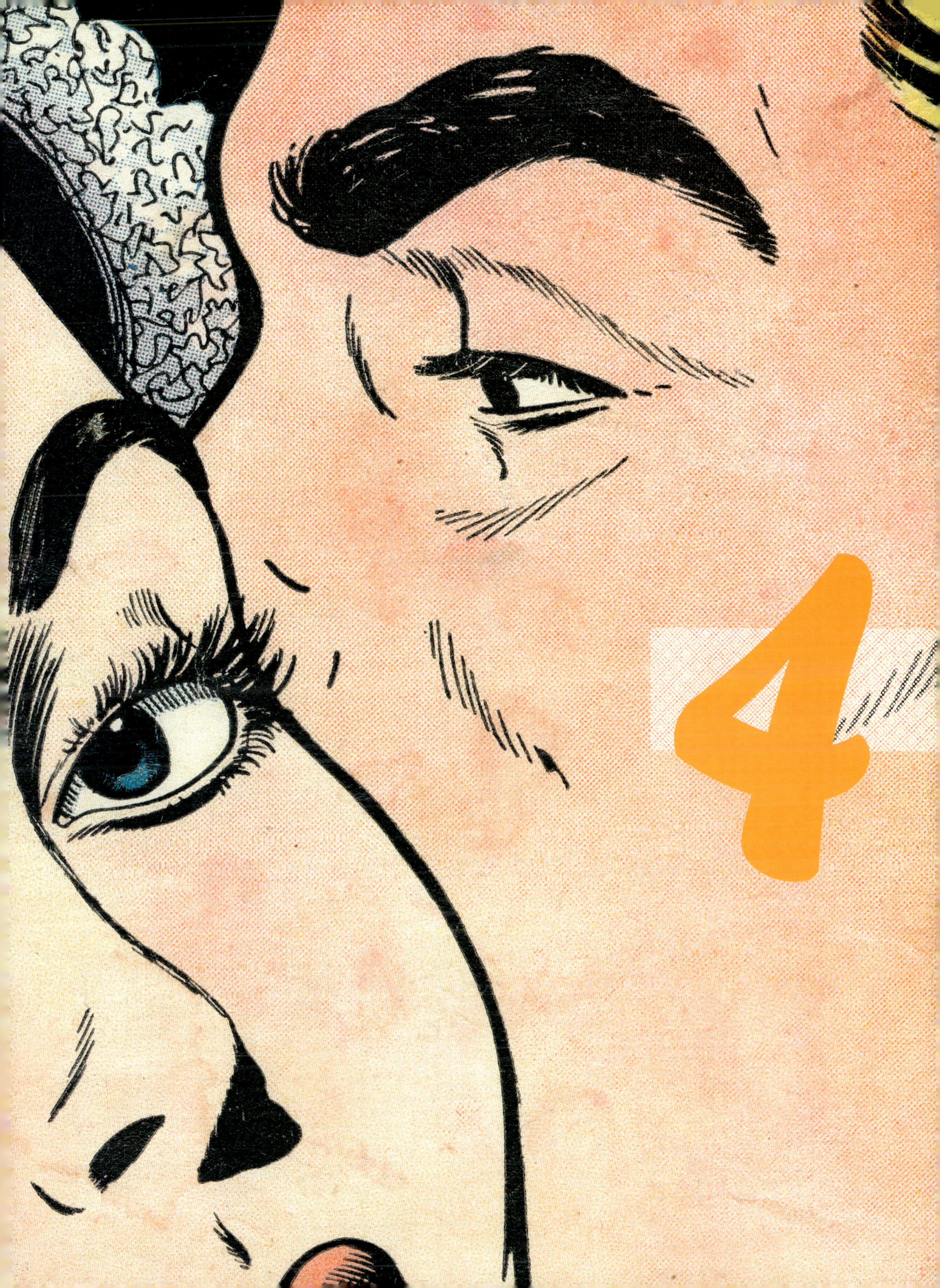
4

Heartbreak on My Honeymoon

MARRIAGE HELL

DEAR READER, you may not yet be betrothed, but please pause a moment to learn from those of us who are: the road to a lasting, fulfilling, storybook marriage can be paved with many a pothole. (Did I just write "can be"? It is to laugh!) And so, in this section of *Agonizing Love*, we examine several of the most dangerous and destructive of those potholes, some of which can prove to be the size of a meteor crater.

Here is where we present dramatic conflicts with mothers-in-law (and certainly, fathers-in-law too — they just don't get the same PR attention as the moms), as shown in stories like "Mother's Boy" and "I Was Engaged to a Puppet." We examine how damaging it can be when one learns of a mate's (or maybe your own) crippling flaw, as in "Married to His Work" and "Was I a Wicked Wife?" And we delve into those moments of self-examination that those who wear a ring experience every now and again — generally along the order of, "Why exactly did I think I wanted to marry this jerk??!!??"— as embodied in stories such as "Kisses Came Second" and "A Spot in the Sun."

Not that you shouldn't eagerly pursue the path to marriage. By all means, go for it! But you will be ever so much better prepared if you are able to take away with you the lessons shared here. These comics may be a half century or more old, but their wisdom remains timeless.

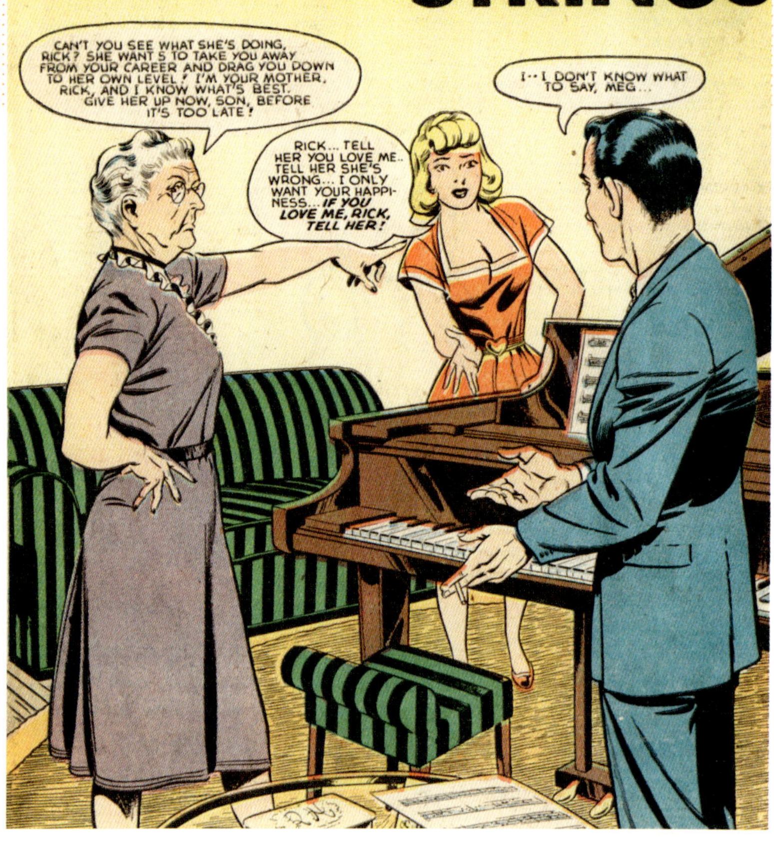
COULD I EVER HOPE TO MARRY RICK, OR WAS THE SILVER CORD THAT TIED HIM TO HIS MOTHER STRONGER THAN THE GOLDEN BOND OF OUR LOVE? WOULD I EVER TEAR HIM AWAY FROM
Mama's APRON STRINGS
CAN'T YOU SEE WHAT SHE'S DOING, RICK? SHE WANTS TO TAKE YOU AWAY FROM YOUR CAREER AND DRAG YOU DOWN TO HER OWN LEVEL! I'M YOUR MOTHER, RICK, AND I KNOW WHAT'S BEST. GIVE HER UP NOW, SON, BEFORE IT'S TOO LATE!
RICK... TELL HER YOU LOVE ME.. TELL HER SHE'S WRONG... I ONLY WANT YOUR HAPPINESS... IF YOU LOVE ME, RICK, TELL HER!
I... I DON'T KNOW WHAT TO SAY, MEG...

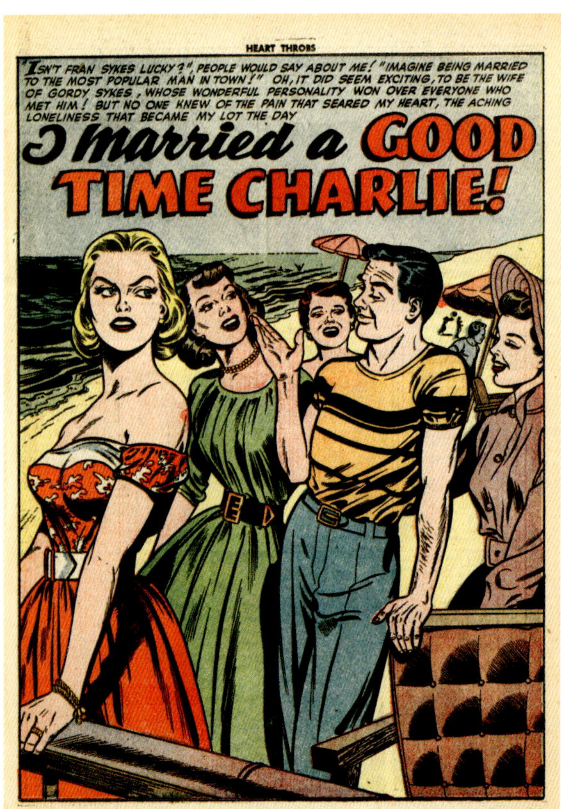
HEART THROBS
"ISN'T FRAN SYKES LUCKY?", PEOPLE WOULD SAY ABOUT ME! "IMAGINE BEING MARRIED TO THE MOST POPULAR MAN IN TOWN!" OH, IT DID SEEM EXCITING, TO BE THE WIFE OF GORDY SYKES, WHOSE WONDERFUL PERSONALITY WON OVER EVERYONE WHO MET HIM! BUT NO ONE KNEW OF THE PAIN THAT SEARED MY HEART, THE ACHING LONELINESS THAT BECAME MY LOT THE DAY
I Married a GOOD TIME CHARLIE!

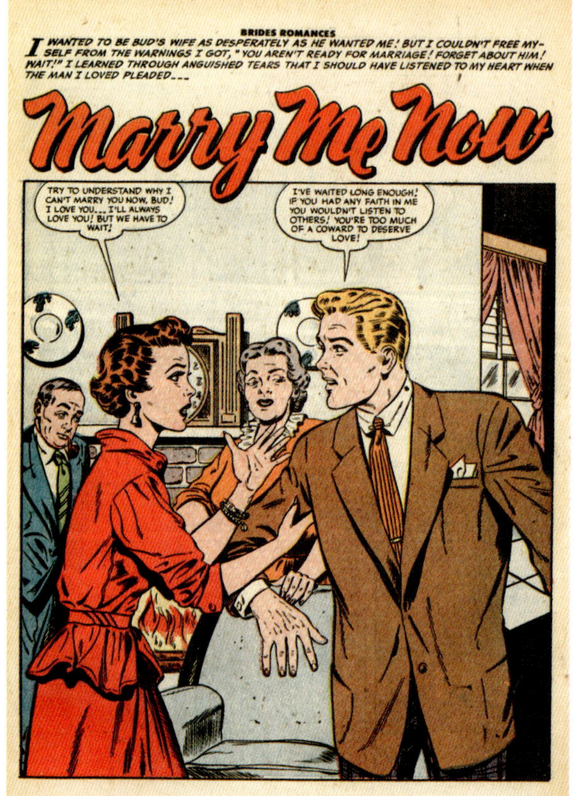
BRIDES ROMANCES
I WANTED TO BE BUD'S WIFE AS DESPERATELY AS HE WANTED ME! BUT I COULDN'T FREE MYSELF FROM THE WARNINGS I GOT, "YOU AREN'T READY FOR MARRIAGE! FORGET ABOUT HIM! WAIT!" I LEARNED THROUGH ANGUISHED TEARS THAT I SHOULD HAVE LISTENED TO MY HEART WHEN THE MAN I LOVED PLEADED---
Marry Me Now
TRY TO UNDERSTAND WHY I CAN'T MARRY YOU NOW, BUD! I LOVE YOU... I'LL ALWAYS LOVE YOU! BUT WE HAVE TO WAIT!
I'VE WAITED LONG ENOUGH! IF YOU HAD ANY FAITH IN ME YOU WOULDN'T LISTEN TO OTHERS! YOU'RE TOO MUCH OF A COWARD TO DESERVE LOVE!

"I'D MARRY AGAIN IF I FOUND A MAN WHO HAD FIFTEEN MILLION DOLLARS, AND WOULD SIGN OVER HALF TO ME, AND GUARANTEE THAT HE'D BE DEAD WITHIN A YEAR."

— BETTE DAVIS

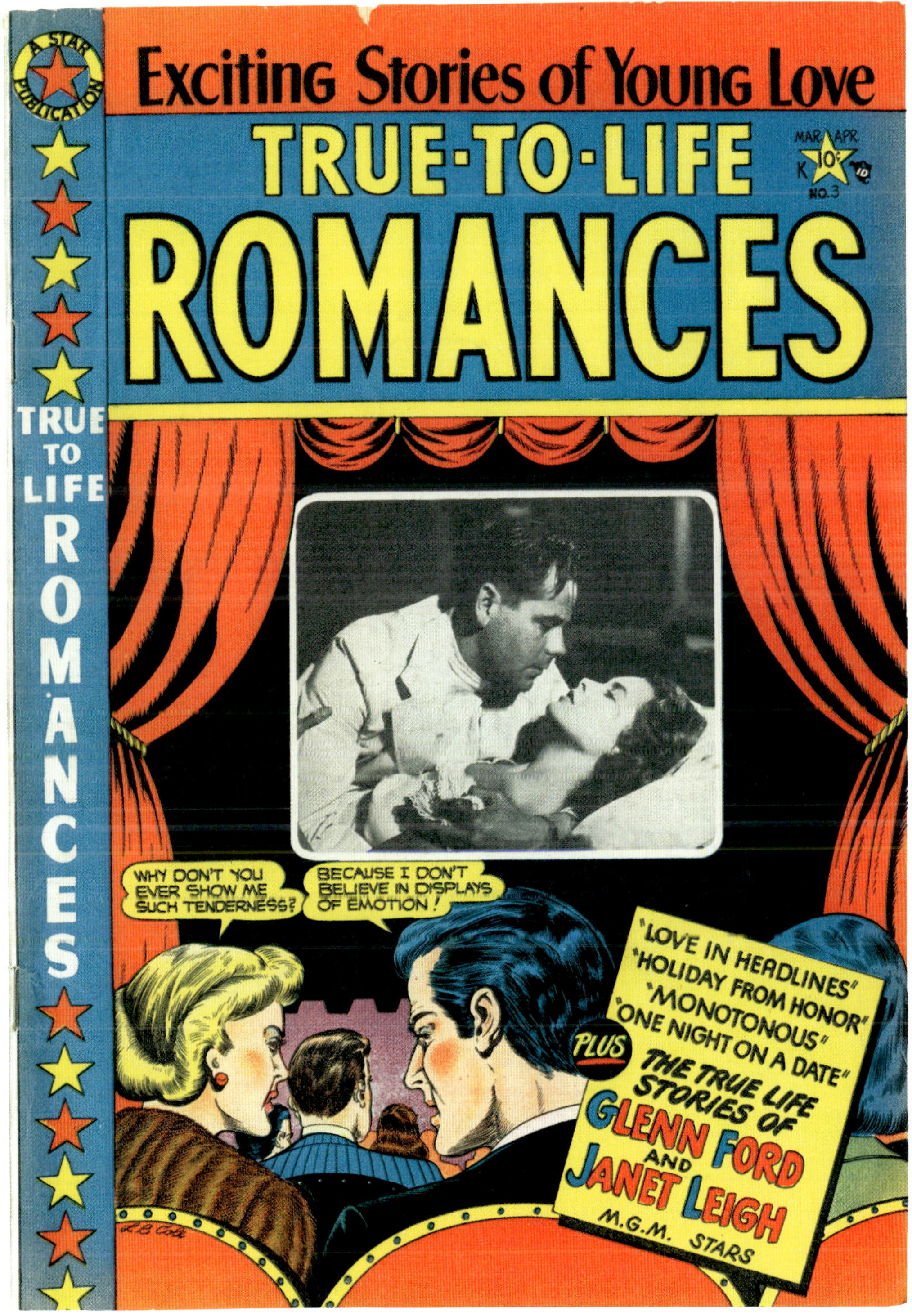

Pages 92–93: **BRIDE'S SECRETS** #4, September–October 1954, cover detail

Page 96, clockwise from top right: **DARLING LOVE** #2, December–January 1950, splash page

BRIDES ROMANCES #7, September 1954, splash page

HEART THROBS #11, June 1952, splash page

This page: **TRUE-TO-LIFE ROMANCES** #3, March–April 1950

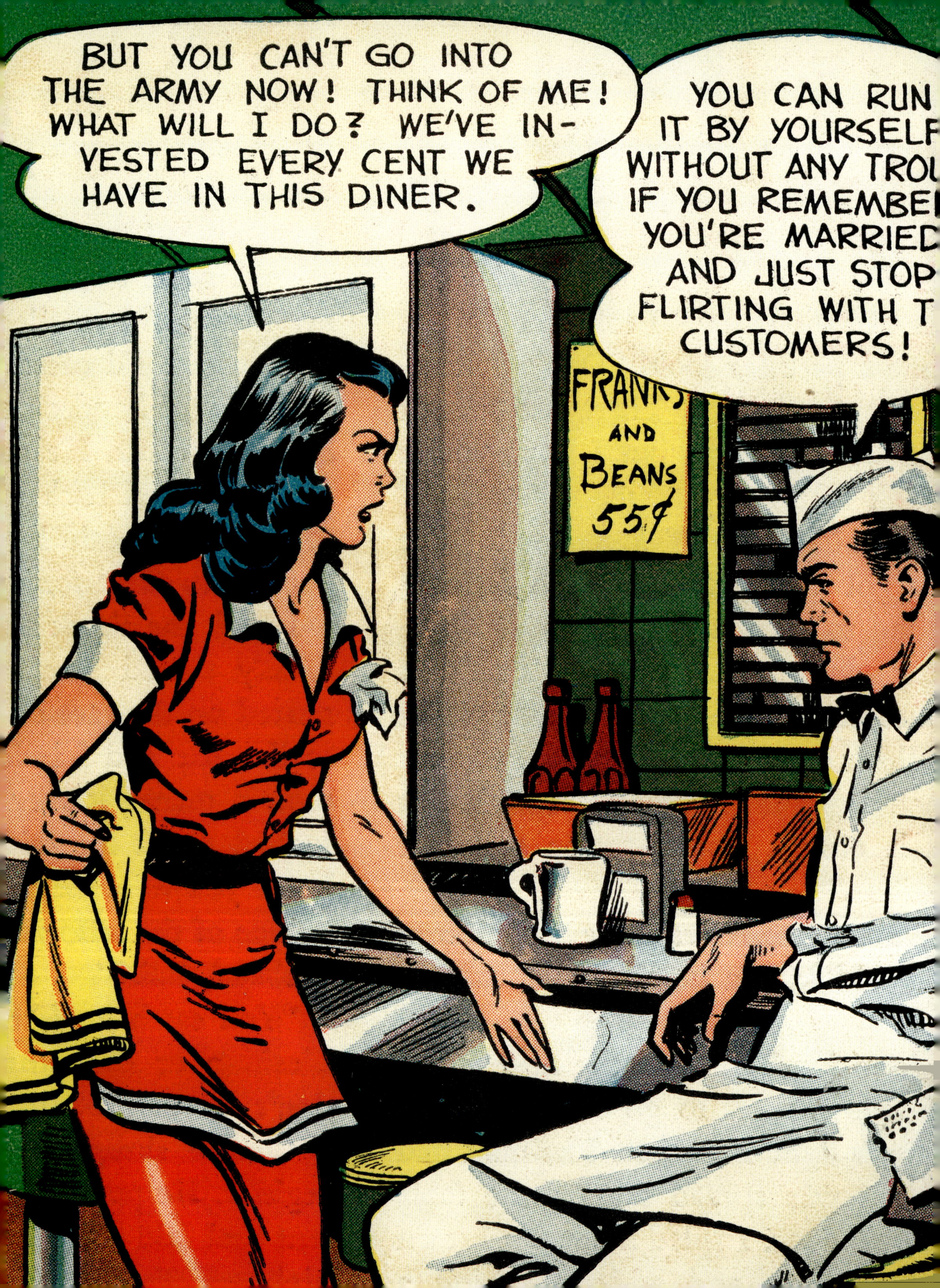

BUT YOU CAN'T GO INTO THE ARMY NOW! THINK OF ME! WHAT WILL I DO? WE'VE INVESTED EVERY CENT WE HAVE IN THIS DINER.
YOU CAN RUN IT BY YOURSELF WITHOUT ANY TROU IF YOU REMEMBE YOU'RE MARRIED AND JUST STOP FLIRTING WITH T CUSTOMERS!
FRANKS AND BEANS 55¢

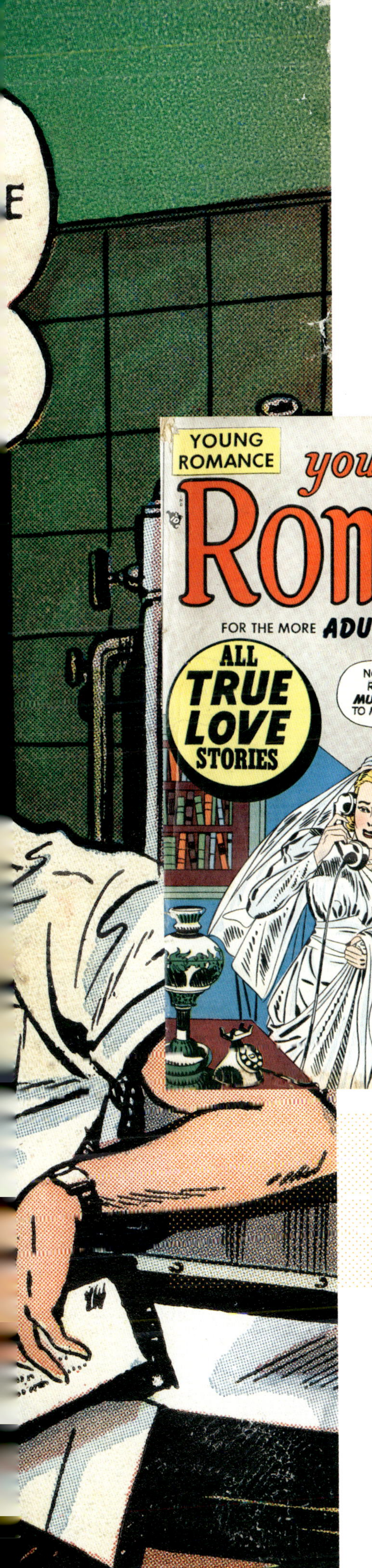

Page 98:
WARTIME ROMANCES
#7, April 1952, cover detail

Below, from left to right:
YOUNG ROMANCE
#3, January–February 1948

YOUNG ROMANCE
#9, January–February 1949

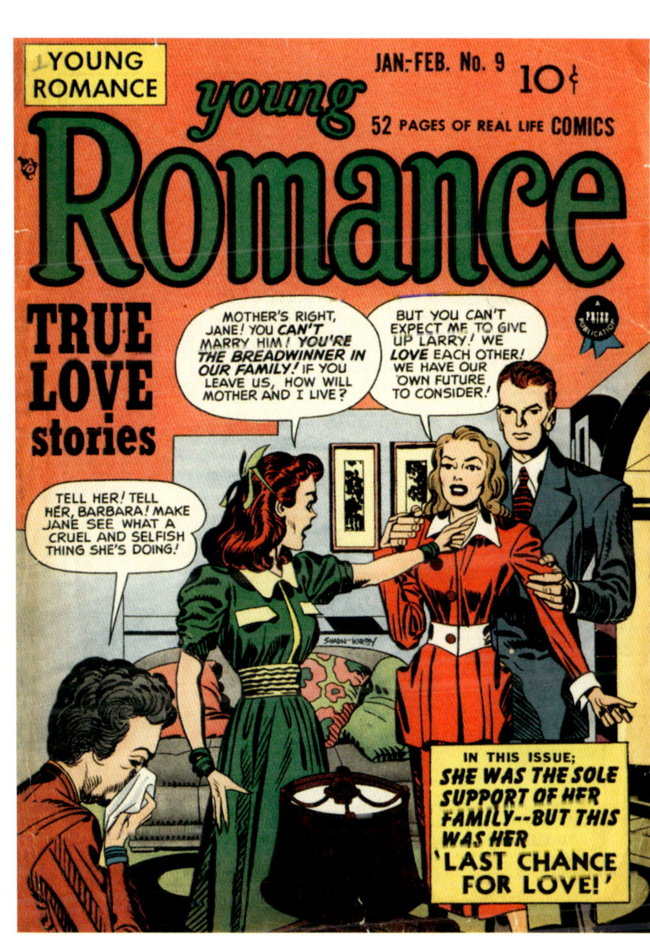

"THE ONLY PERSON WHO LISTENS TO BOTH SIDES OF A HUSBAND AND WIFE ARGUMENT IS THE WOMAN IN THE NEXT APARTMENT."
— SAM LEVENSON, "YOU CAN SAY THAT AGAIN, SAM!"

LOVE ALONE ISN'T ENOUGH TO MAKE A SUCCESSFUL MARRIAGE. LIKE A BLOOMING FLOWER, A NEW MARRIAGE MUST BE TREATED WITH CARE, NURTURED, AND TENDED...AND THE WEEDS THAT THREATEN IT, MUST BE UPROOTED, OR THE FLOWER DIES... BECAUSE, A MARRIAGE LIKE A FLOWER, NEEDS...

a SPOT in the SUN

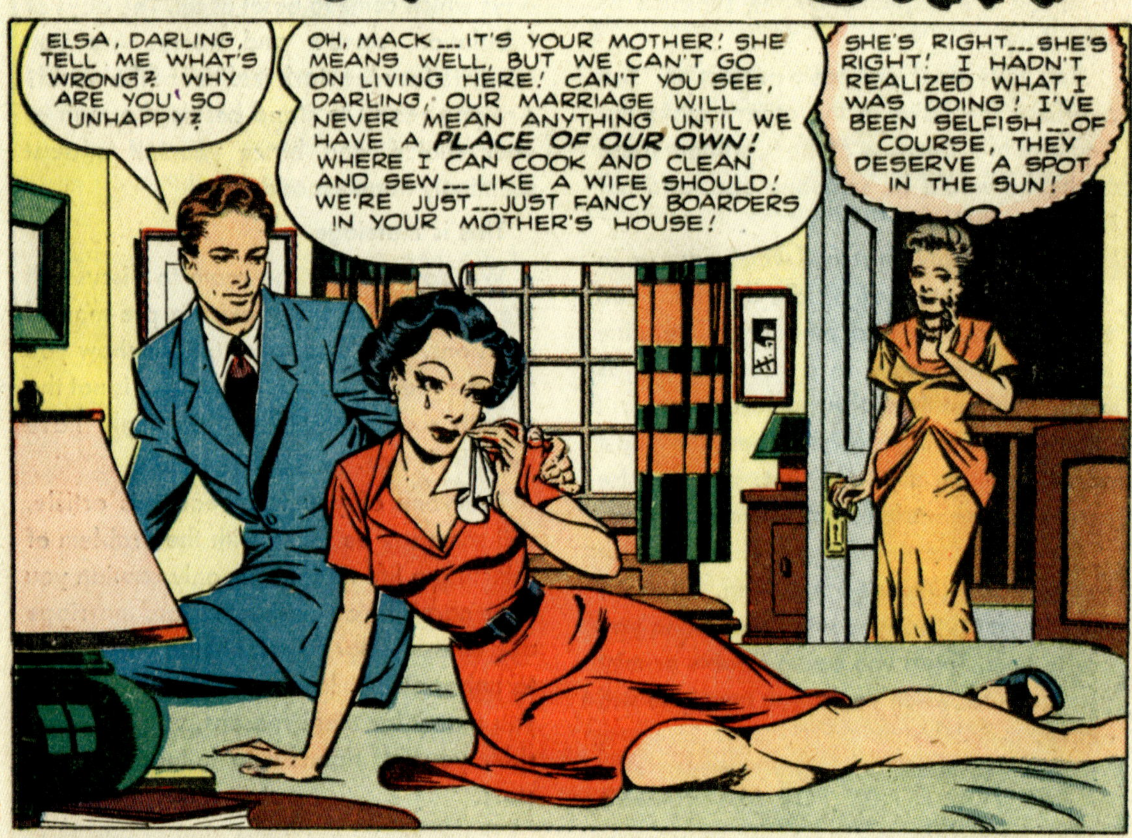

"MACK AND HIS MOTHER SHOULD BE ALONG ANY MINUTE NOW... SHE'S COMING TO SEE OUR NEW HOME! AND AS I STAND HERE, WAITING FOR THEM... A PARADE OF THOUGHTS GOES THROUGH MY MIND... FOR THE TRAIL THAT LED US HERE WAS FILLED WITH PITFALLS!"

"IT GOES BACK THREE YEARS TO THE NIGHT THAT I FIRST MET MACK! I LOVED MACK, AND MY GREATEST MOMENT WAS THE EVENING WE SAT ON A LONELY BENCH, IN A DESERTED PARK..."

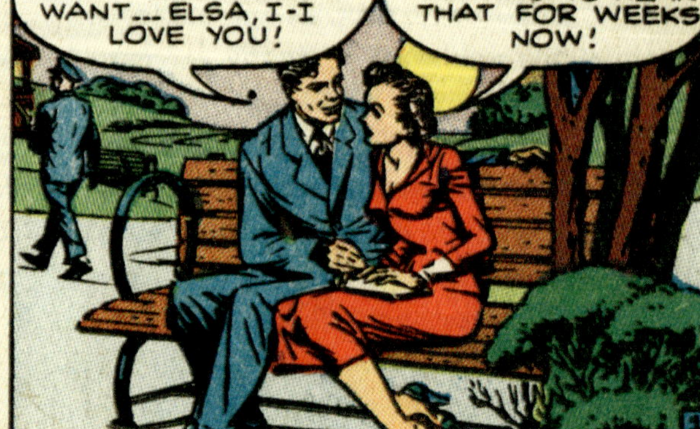

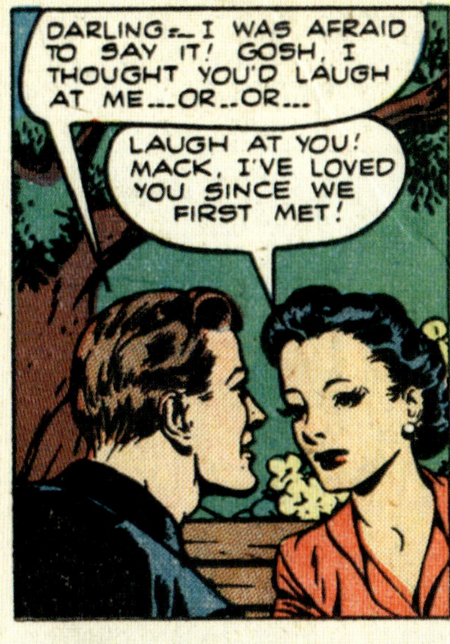

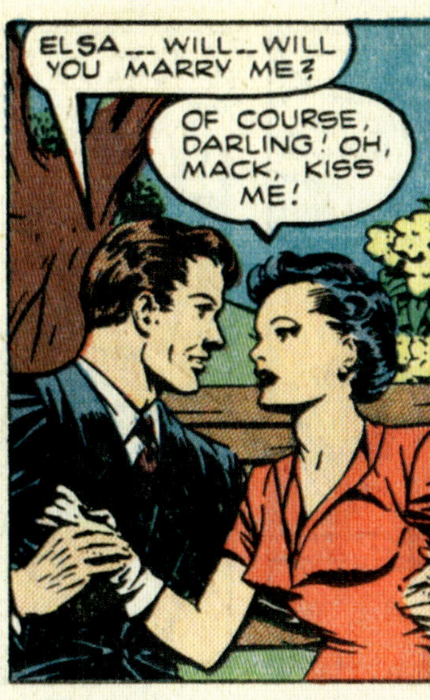

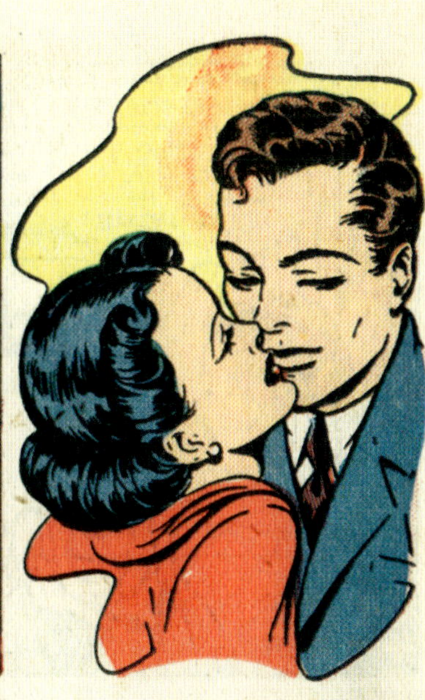

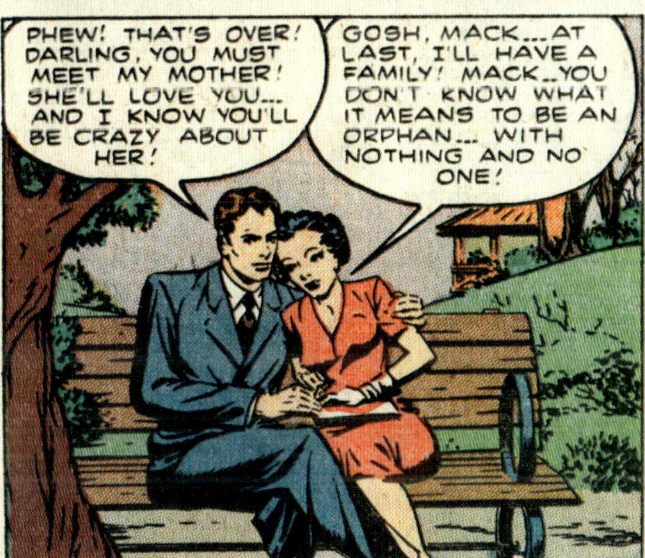

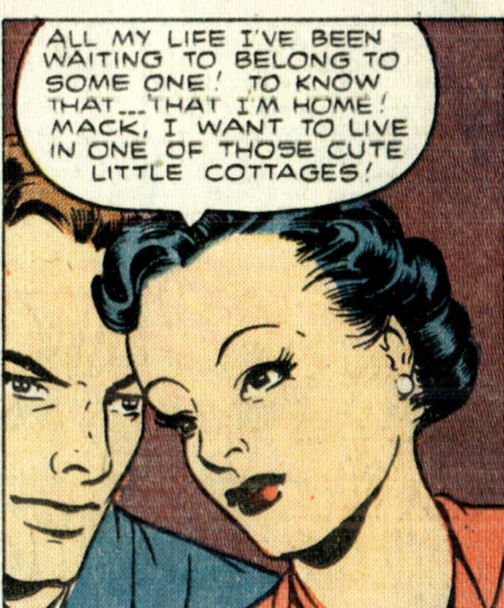

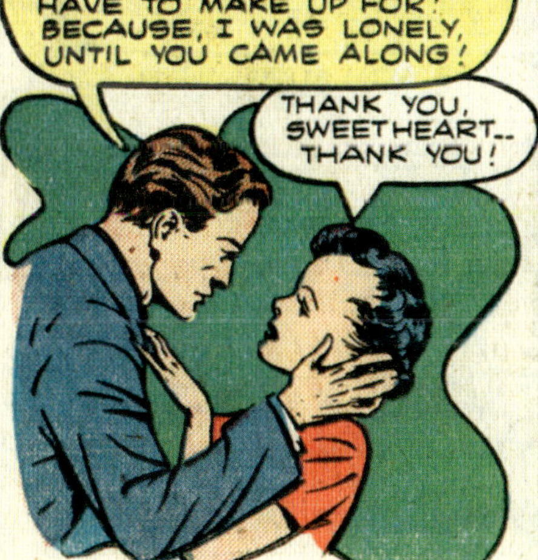

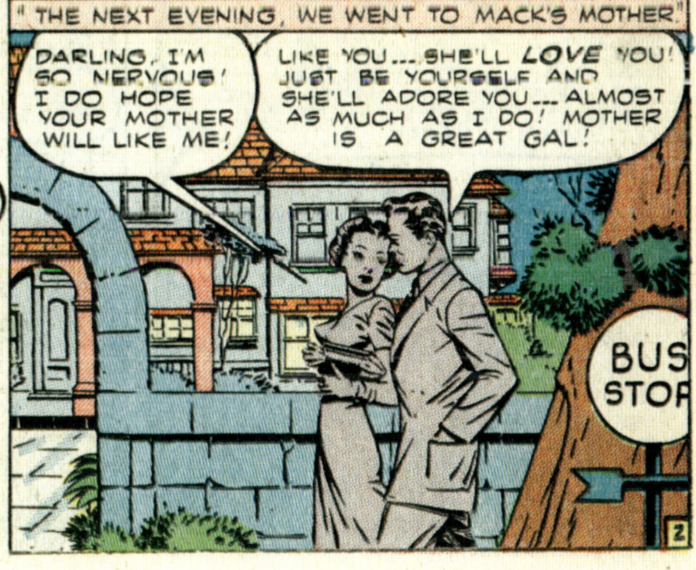

LOVE DIARY
#5, March 1950

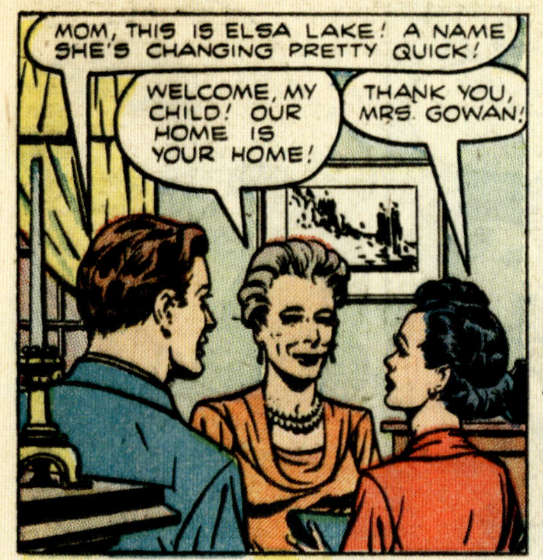

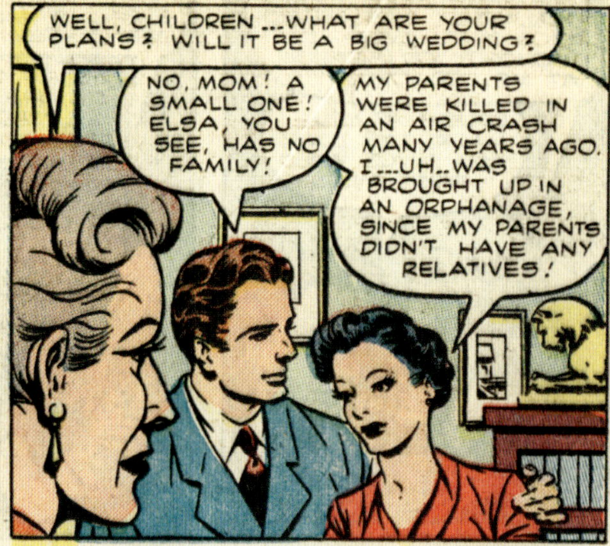

YOU'RE NOT ALONE ANY LONGER, MY DEAR! YOU HAVE MACK AND ME! I HAD HOPED THAT MACK WOULD MARRY INTO A FINE, WELL-KNIT FAMILY! BUT SINCE YOU'RE HIS CHOICE ... YOU'RE MINE, TOO!

THAT'S VERY SWEET OF YOU!

"AS SHE KEPT TALKING, I REALIZED WITH A SINKING HEART, THAT SHE INTENDED TO DOMINATE OUR MARRIAGE, AS SHE HAD DOMINATED MACK'S LIFE ... BECAUSE THAT WAS APPARANT, TOO ..."

WHERE DO YOU INTEND TO LIVE? THERE'S A HOUSING SHORTAGE, YOU KNOW!

I'M TALKING TO A REALTOR TOMORROW! I THINK WE'LL TAKE A NEW COTTAGE ALONG THE LAKE!

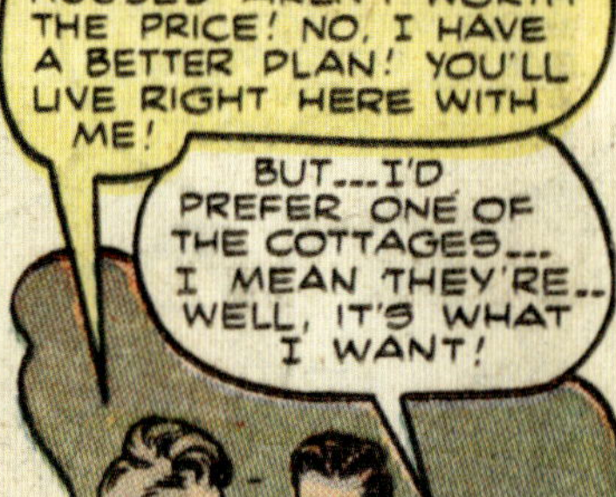

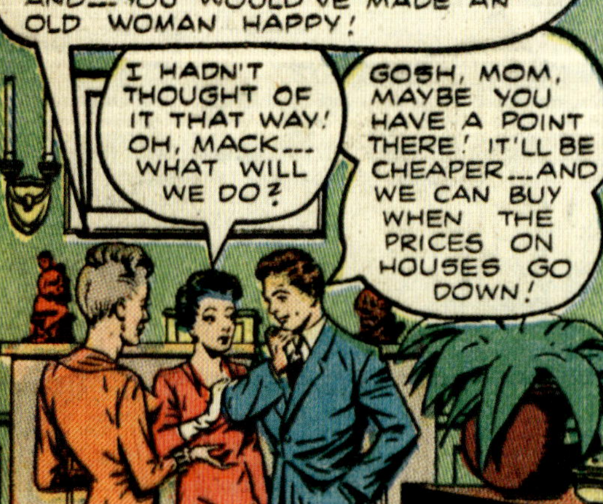

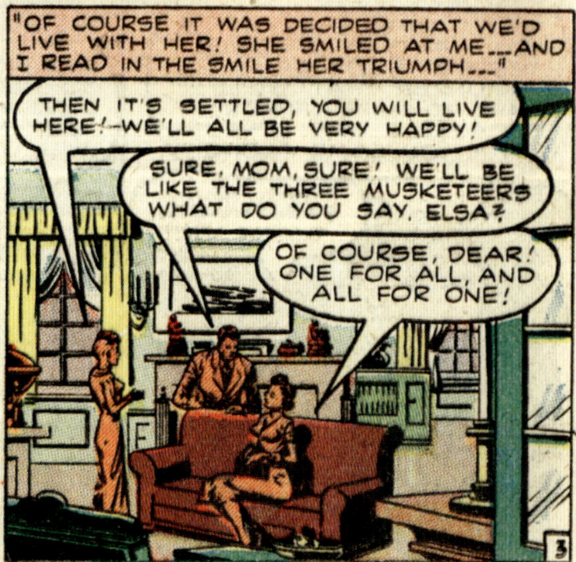

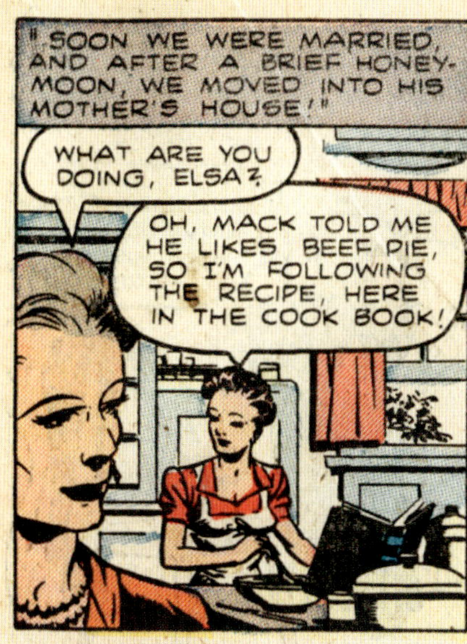
"SOON WE WERE MARRIED, AND AFTER A BRIEF HONEY-MOON, WE MOVED INTO HIS MOTHER'S HOUSE!"
WHAT ARE YOU DOING, ELSA?
OH, MACK TOLD ME HE LIKES BEEF PIE, SO I'M FOLLOWING THE RECIPE, HERE IN THE COOK BOOK!

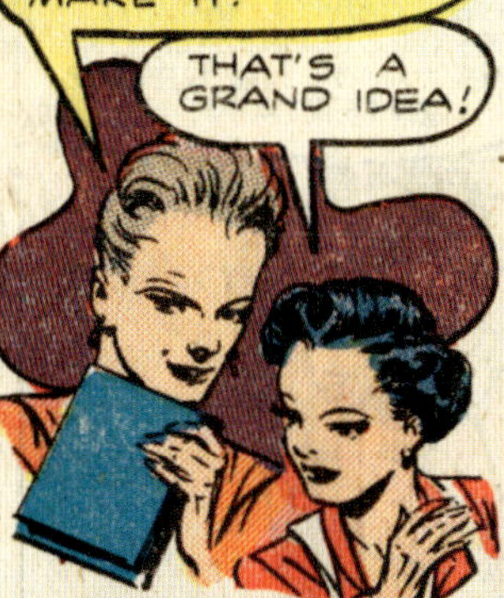
LAND SAKES, CHILD! SURELY I KNOW BETTER THAN ANYONE HOW MY SON LIKES HIS BEEF PIE! HERE, YOU DO THE COOKING, AND I'LL TELL YOU EXACTLY HOW TO MAKE IT!
THAT'S A GRAND IDEA!
"SHE TOLD ME WHAT TO PUT INTO IT... AND I CARRIED OUT HER INSTRUCTIONS! IT WAS FUN COOKING FOR MACK! THIS WAS THE FIRST MEAL I'D EVER ATTEMPTED..."
WHY DID WE PUT SO MUCH TABASCO SAUCE IN IT, MRS. GOWAN?
MACK *LIKES* IT HOT! THE SPICIER THE BETTER!

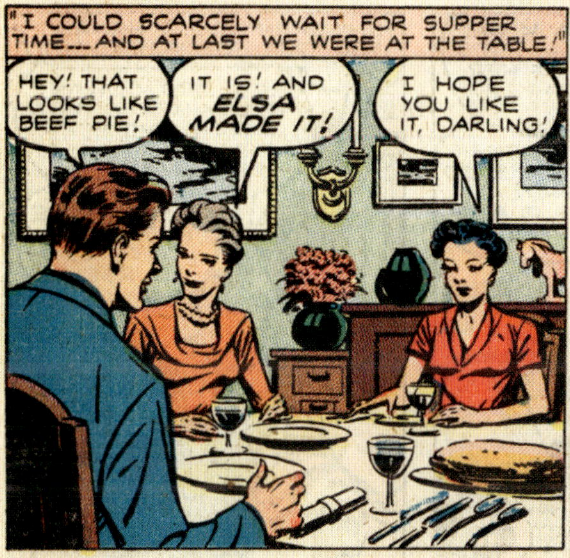
"I COULD SCARCELY WAIT FOR SUPPER TIME... AND AT LAST WE WERE AT THE TABLE!"
HEY! THAT LOOKS LIKE BEEF PIE!
IT IS! AND *ELSA MADE IT!*
I HOPE YOU LIKE IT, DARLING!

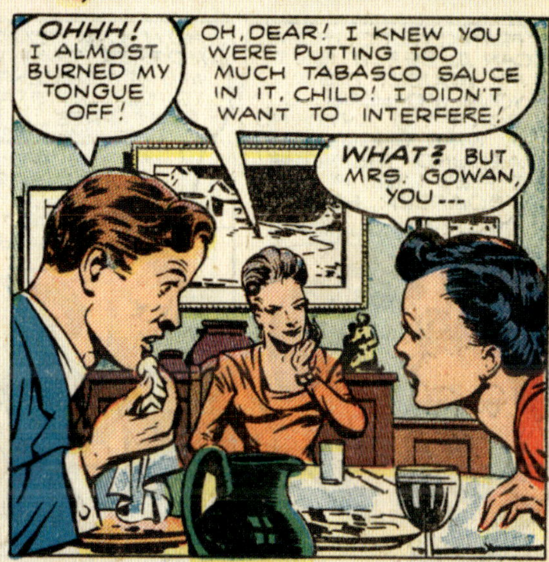
OHHH! I ALMOST BURNED MY TONGUE OFF!
OH, DEAR! I KNEW YOU WERE PUTTING TOO MUCH TABASCO SAUCE IN IT, CHILD! I DIDN'T WANT TO INTERFERE!
WHAT? BUT MRS. GOWAN, YOU...

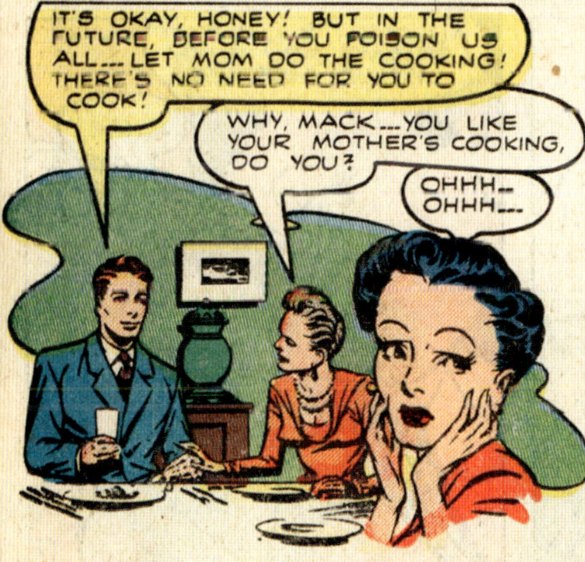
IT'S OKAY, HONEY! BUT IN THE FUTURE, BEFORE YOU POISON US ALL... LET MOM DO THE COOKING! THERE'S NO NEED FOR YOU TO COOK!
WHY, MACK... YOU LIKE YOUR MOTHER'S COOKING, DO YOU?
OHHH... OHHH...

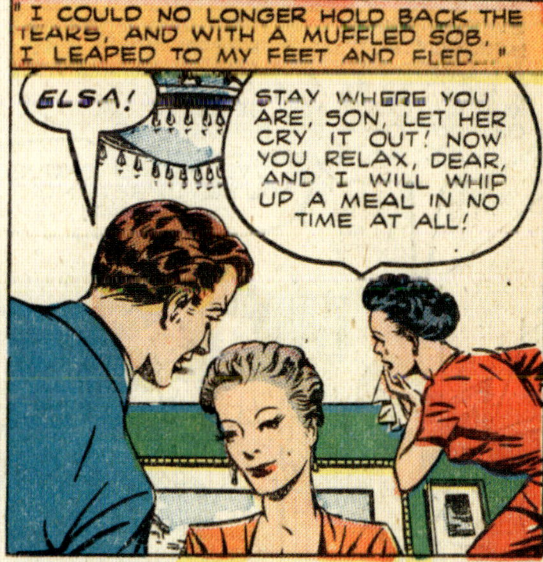
"I COULD NO LONGER HOLD BACK THE TEARS, AND WITH A MUFFLED SOB, I LEAPED TO MY FEET AND FLED..."
ELSA!
STAY WHERE YOU ARE, SON, LET HER CRY IT OUT! NOW YOU RELAX, DEAR, AND I WILL WHIP UP A MEAL IN NO TIME AT ALL!

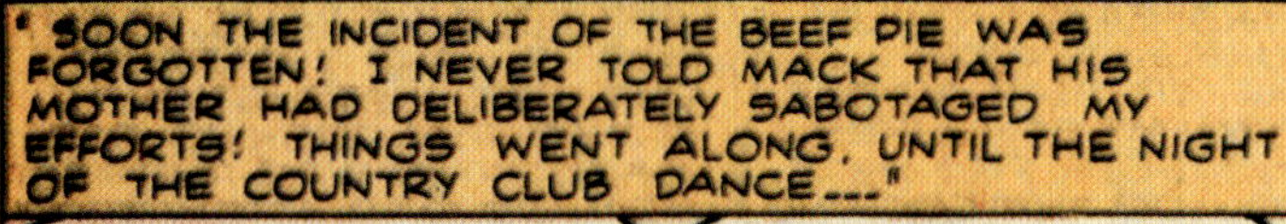
"SOON THE INCIDENT OF THE BEEF PIE WAS FORGOTTEN! I NEVER TOLD MACK THAT HIS MOTHER HAD DELIBERATELY SABOTAGED MY EFFORTS! THINGS WENT ALONG, UNTIL THE NIGHT OF THE COUNTRY CLUB DANCE..."

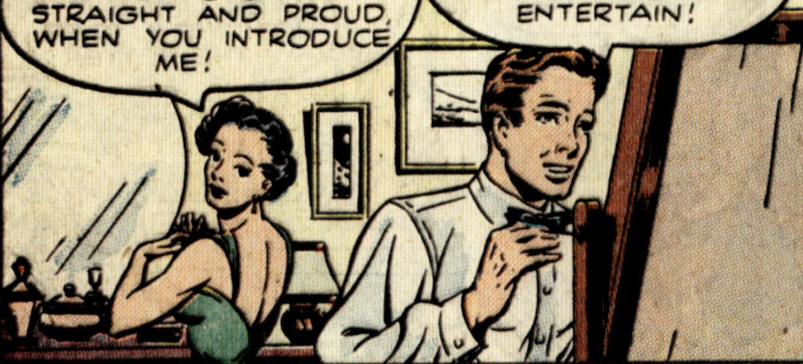
MACK, DARLING, OUR FIRST BIG DANCE TOGETHER! I'VE BEEN WAITING TO MEET YOUR FRIENDS! TO STAND STRAIGHT AND PROUD, WHEN YOU INTRODUCE ME!
THAT'S TRUE, DEAR! YOU HAVEN'T MET THE CROWD YET! IT NEVER DAWNED ON ME THAT WE NEVER ENTERTAIN!

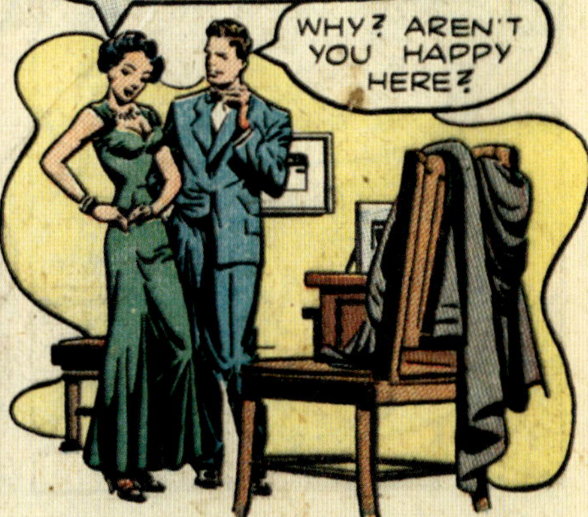
EVERYTIME I SUGGESTED HAVING PEOPLE OVER... YOUR MOTHER DIDN'T FEEL WELL, OR THERE WAS SOME OTHER EXCUSE! MACK... WHEN ARE WE GOING TO MOVE OUT?
WHY? AREN'T YOU HAPPY HERE?

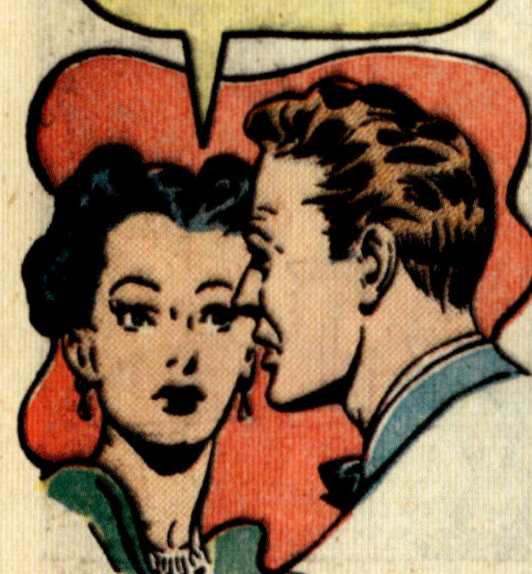
FRANKLY... NO! HOW CAN I BE? IT ISN'T MY HOUSE! IT'S YOUR MOTHERS'! I DON'T DO ANYTHING A WIFE SHOULD AROUND THE HOME! I FEEL LIKE A BOARDER HERE!

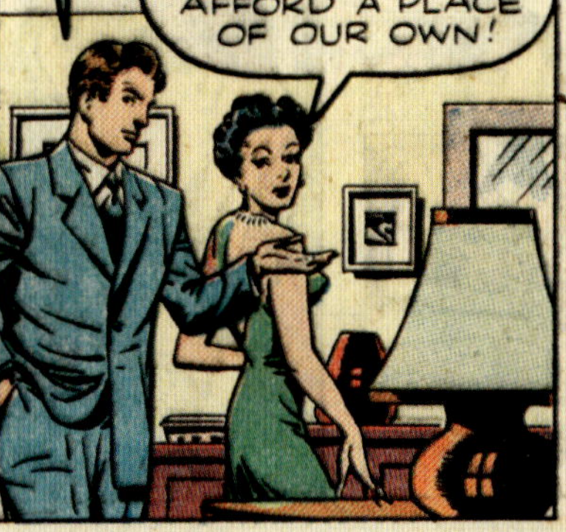
HOW CAN YOU TALK OF MOTHER THAT WAY? IT'S MIGHTY DECENT OF HER TO LET US STAY HERE, RENT FREE...
ARE WE BABIES? YOU EARN A GOOD LIVING! WE CAN AFFORD A PLACE OF OUR OWN!

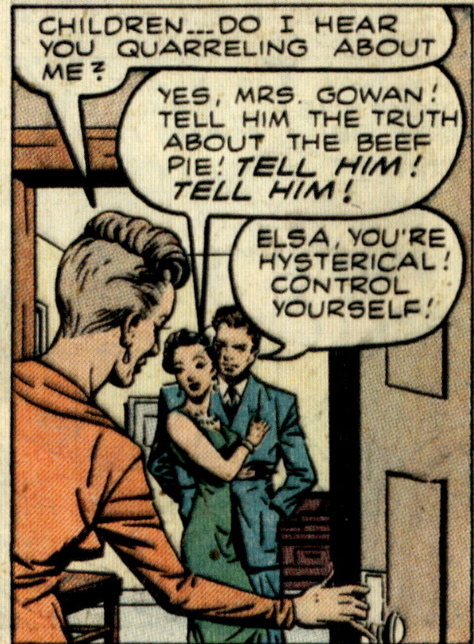
CHILDREN... DO I HEAR YOU QUARRELING ABOUT ME?
YES, MRS. GOWAN! TELL HIM THE TRUTH ABOUT THE BEEF PIE! TELL HIM! TELL HIM!
ELSA, YOU'RE HYSTERICAL! CONTROL YOURSELF!

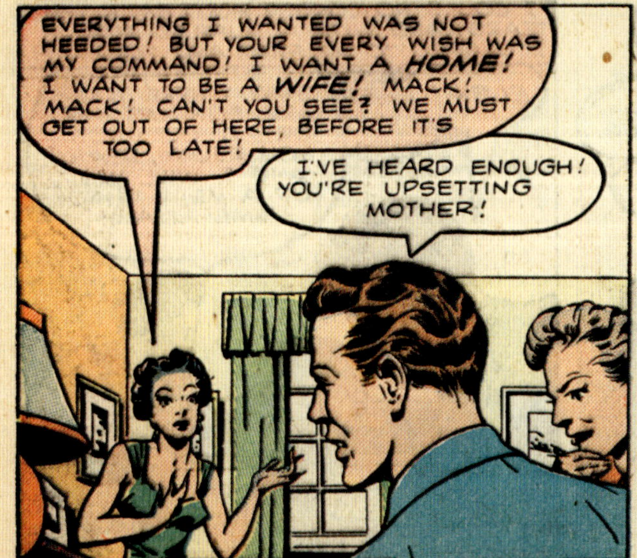
EVERYTHING I WANTED WAS NOT HEEDED! BUT YOUR EVERY WISH WAS MY COMMAND! I WANT A HOME! I WANT TO BE A WIFE! MACK! MACK! CAN'T YOU SEE? WE MUST GET OUT OF HERE, BEFORE IT'S TOO LATE!
I'VE HEARD ENOUGH! YOU'RE UPSETTING MOTHER!

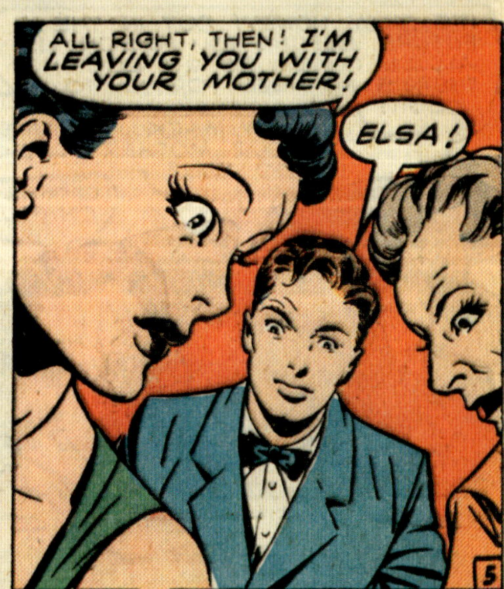
ALL RIGHT, THEN! I'M LEAVING YOU WITH YOUR MOTHER!
ELSA!
5

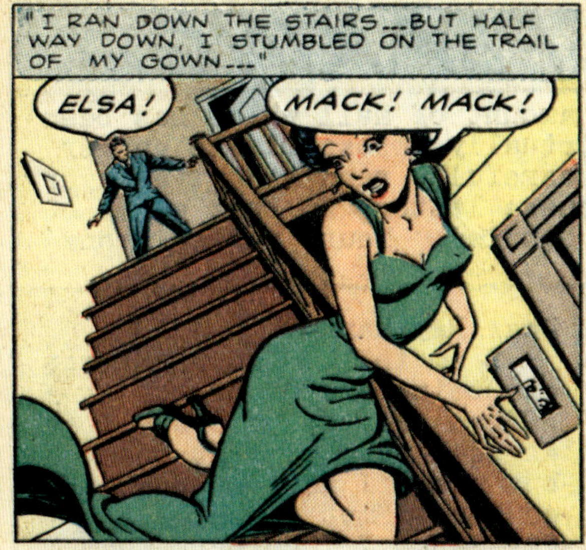
"I RAN DOWN THE STAIRS...BUT HALF WAY DOWN, I STUMBLED ON THE TRAIL OF MY GOWN..."
ELSA!
MACK! MACK!

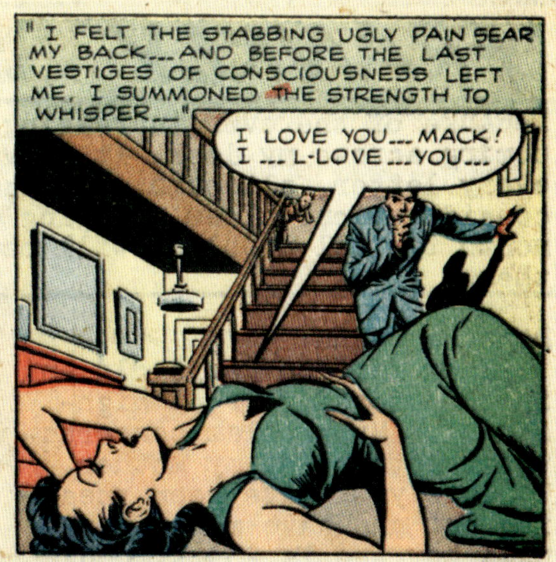
"I FELT THE STABBING UGLY PAIN SEAR MY BACK...AND BEFORE THE LAST VESTIGES OF CONSCIOUSNESS LEFT ME, I SUMMONED THE STRENGTH TO WHISPER..."
I LOVE YOU... MACK! I ... L-LOVE ... YOU...

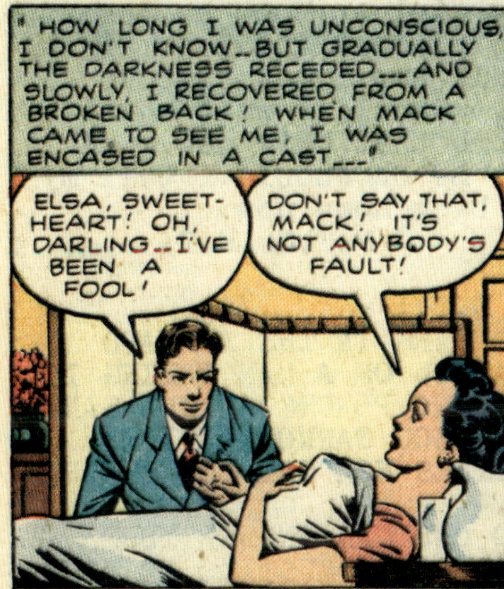
"HOW LONG I WAS UNCONSCIOUS, I DON'T KNOW...BUT GRADUALLY THE DARKNESS RECEDED...AND SLOWLY, I RECOVERED FROM A BROKEN BACK! WHEN MACK CAME TO SEE ME, I WAS ENCASED IN A CAST..."
ELSA, SWEET-HEART! OH, DARLING...I'VE BEEN A FOOL!
DON'T SAY THAT, MACK! IT'S NOT ANYBODY'S FAULT!

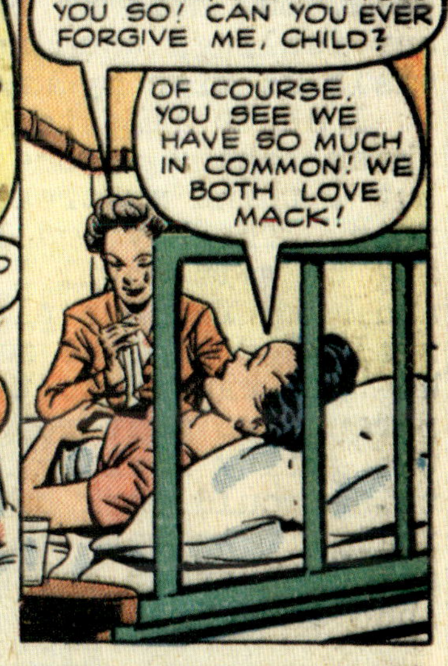
MOTHER TOLD ME EVERYTHING! EVEN ABOUT THE BEEF PIE! SHE MISTAKENLY THOUGHT SHE'D HOLD ME FOREVER, BY DISCREDITING YOU! SHE'S TERRIBLY SORRY, ELSA! SHE'S WAITING OUTSIDE!
PLEASE SEND HER IN!
OH, CHILD, I'VE WRONGED YOU SO! CAN YOU EVER FORGIVE ME, CHILD?
OF COURSE. YOU SEE WE HAVE SO MUCH IN COMMON! WE BOTH LOVE MACK!

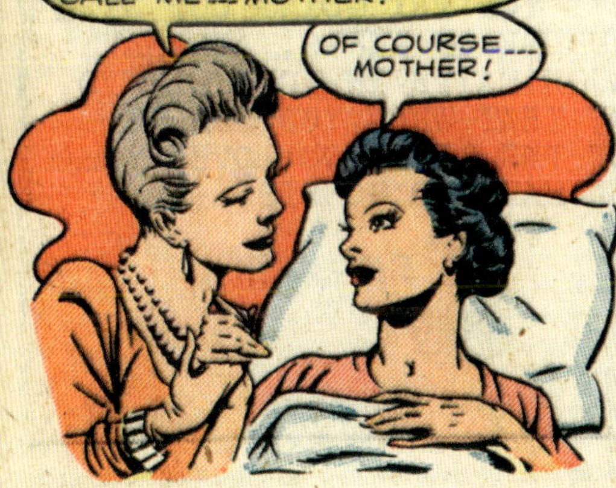
YES, CHILD! AND I HOPE YOU FORGET THAT I WAS AN OLD, SELFISH WOMAN WHO HAD FORGOTTEN THAT YOUNG FOLKS NEED A SPOT IN THE SUN...SO THEIR LOVE CAN CHERISH AND GROW! OH, CHILD...PLEASE... CALL ME...MOTHER!
OF COURSE... MOTHER!

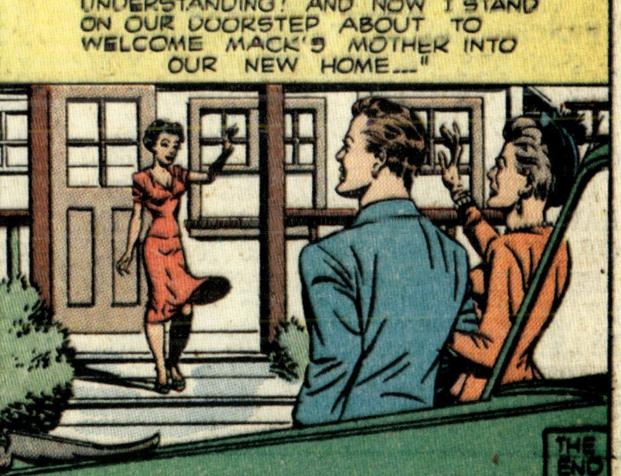
"...THUS OUR SPOT IN THE SUN WAS SECURED! THROUGH THE DEPTHS OF DESPAIR TO THE HEIGHTS OF UNDERSTANDING! AND NOW I STAND ON OUR DOORSTEP ABOUT TO WELCOME MACK'S MOTHER INTO OUR NEW HOME..."
THE END

Are you the girl he married?

DON'T NEGLECT THE MAN IN YOUR LIFE JUST BECAUSE HE'S YOUR HUSBAND!

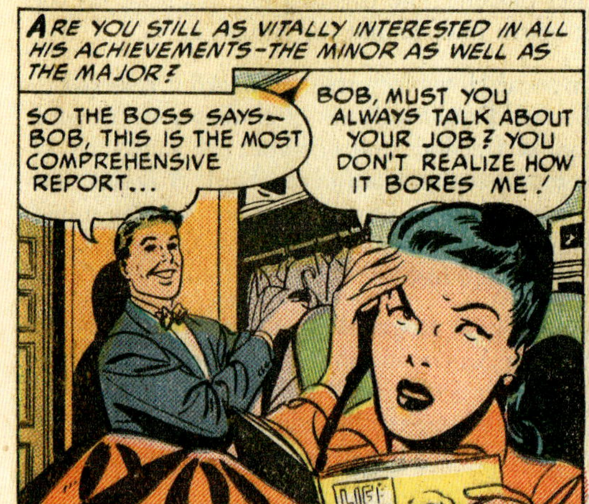

ARE YOU AS CAREFUL OF YOUR APPEARANCE AS YOU WERE WHEN HE WAS DATING YOU? REMEMBER HE LIKES YOU TO DRESS UP JUST FOR HIM!

GEE, HONEY—YOU AREN'T GOING TO WEAR THAT OLD DRESS, ARE YOU?

WHY NOT? WE'RE JUST GOING TO THE NEIGHBORHOOD MOVIE! WE WON'T RUN INTO ANYONE!

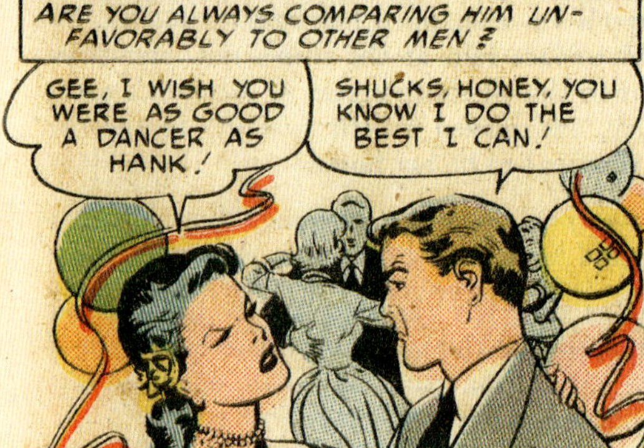

BEFORE YOUR MARRIAGE, YOU TRIED TO MAKE A GOOD IMPRESSION ON HIS FAMILY! HAVE YOU CHANGED? DO YOU ALWAYS SEEK AN OPPORTUNITY TO RUN THEM DOWN?

HOW ABOUT DROPPING OVER TO SUE'S FOR AWHILE?

OH, YOU GO AHEAD IF YOU LIKE! YOU KNOW I CAN'T STAND YOUR SISTER—SHE'S SUCH A CAT!

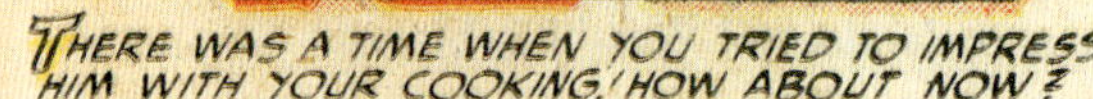

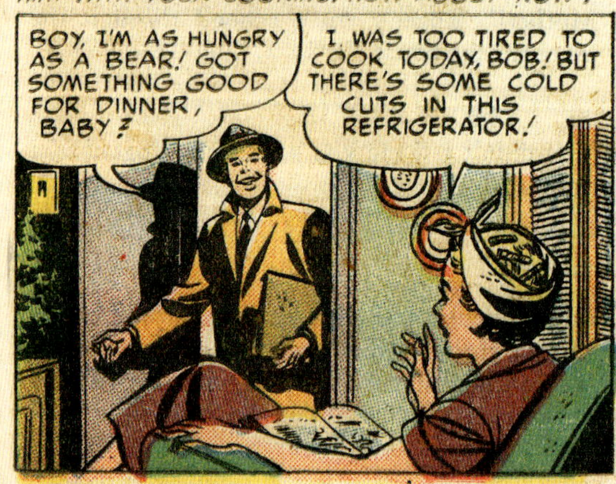

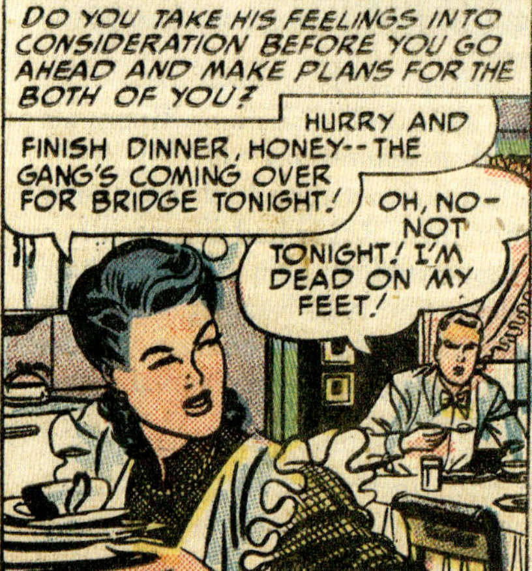

ARE YOU GUILTY OF ONE OR MORE OF THESE MARRIAGE SINS? IF SO, YOU'D BETTER TAKE STOCK OF YOURSELF! MAKE YOUR HUSBAND GLAD HE MARRIED YOU!

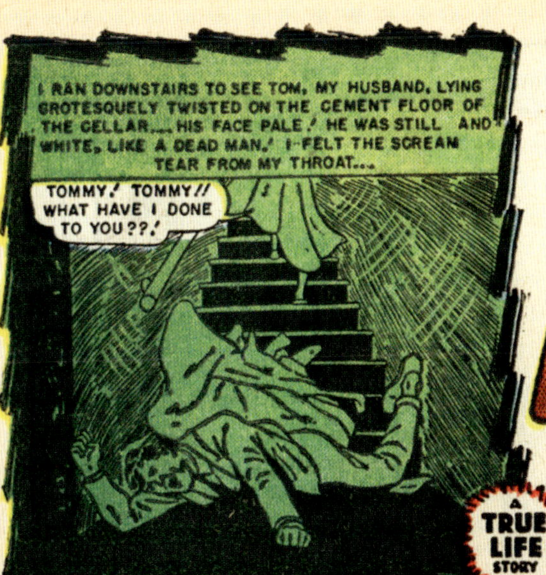

ONLY TOM COULD ANSWER THAT ONE QUESTION WHICH WAS BURNING INTO MY HEART LIKE A FIREBRAND! BUT TOM WAS HOVERING AT DEATH'S DOOR... BECAUSE OF WHAT I HAD DONE TO HIM!

"WAS I A WICKED WIFE?"

A TRUE LIFE STORY

WE HAD BEEN MARRIED EXACTLY THREE HOURS AND FORTY-TWO MINUTES... I FELT POSITIVE THAT I KNEW WHAT MARRIAGE WAS ALL ABOUT! I KNOW *NOW*, BUT I HAD TO LEARN... THE HARD WAY...

WELCOME HOME, MRS. GRAVES!

OH, TOM, IT'S BEAUTIFUL! THE MOST BEAUTIFUL COTTAGE IN THE WHOLE WORLD! IT'S A PALACE!

HARDLY A PALACE, DARLING! JUST ANOTHER FOUR-ROOM COTTAGE, BUILT IN A BIG HURRY, AND BOUGHT UNDER THE G.I. BILL! BUT IT'S OUR HOME, SWEETHEART-- AND WE'LL BE HAPPY HERE!

OH YES, TOMMY DARLING! VERY HAPPY! I'LL COOK AND CLEAN... AND WE'LL HAVE FUN ... ALWAYS!

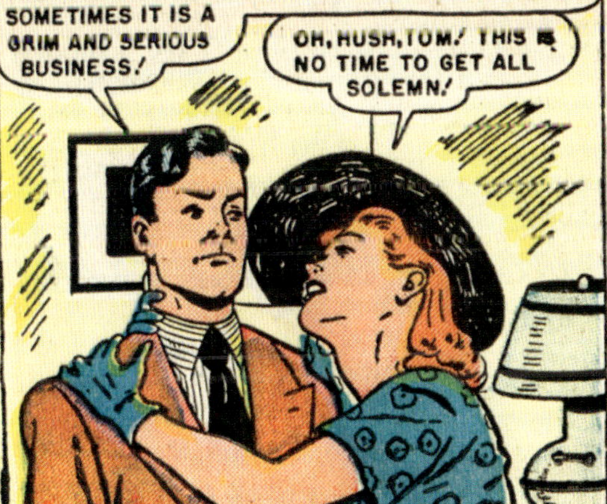

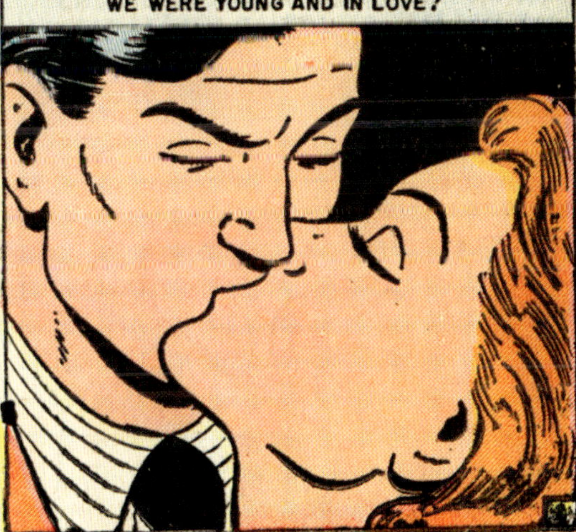

Page 106:
ROMANIC MARRIAGE
#13, May 1952

This page:
UNKNOWN ISSUE
circa 1950

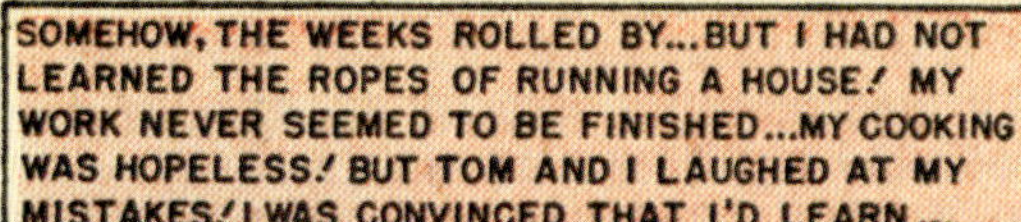

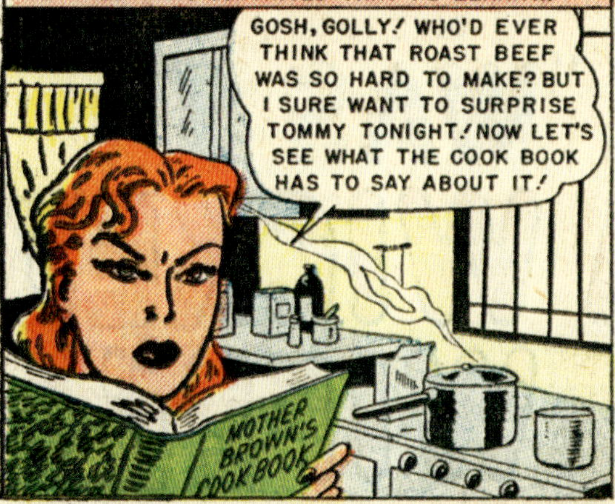

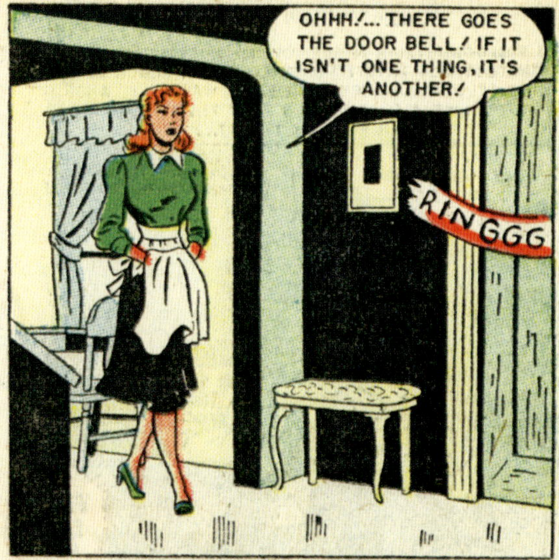

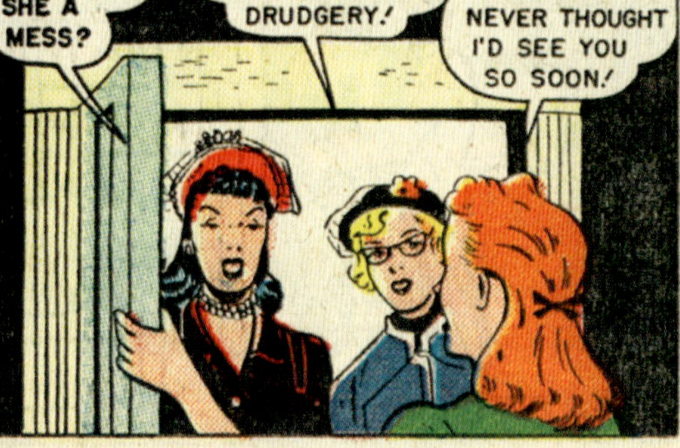

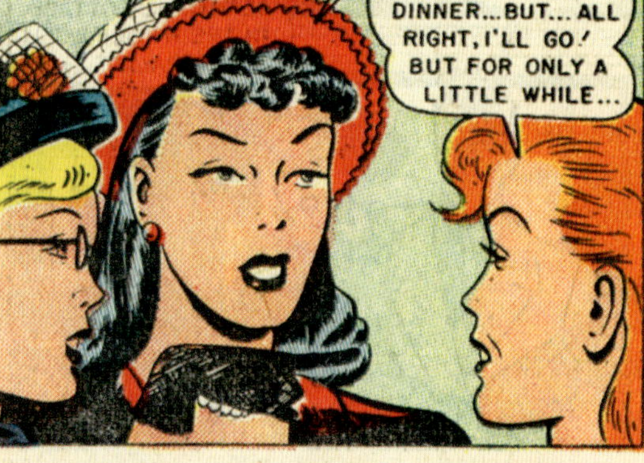

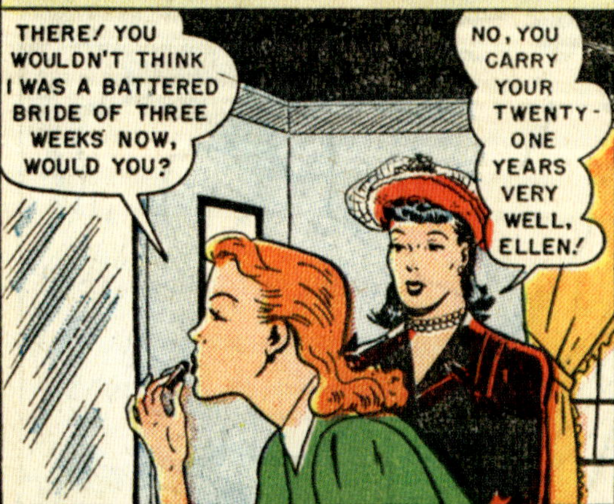

AT THE SORORITY HOUSE I HAD A FINE TIME!... AN AFTERNOON FILLED WITH JOKES AND GAY HILARITY! FOR A WHILE I WAS NOT ELLEN GRAVES AT ALL... BUT ELLEN ROSS, THE BIG WHEEL ON THE CAMPUS!

SAY, GIRLS, I DON'T LIKE TO BREAK THIS UP... BUT I HAVE AN EVENING DATE!... IT'S ALMOST SEVEN NOW!

YES... I GUESS WE'D ALL BETTER GO! COME ON, ELLEN... WE'LL DRIVE YOU HOME!

OKAY! IT'S BEEN SUCH FUN!

2

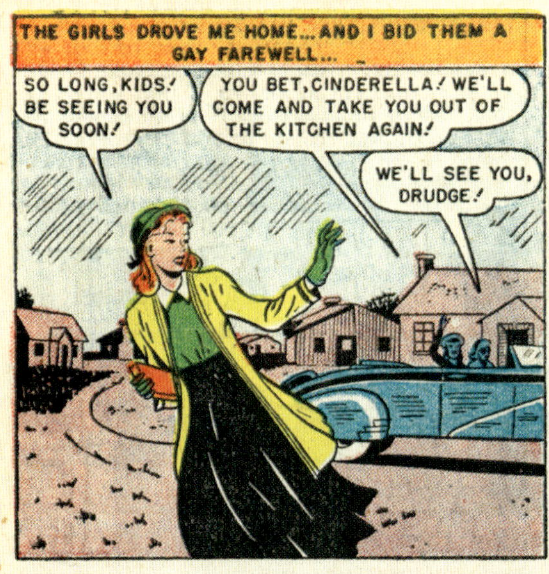
THE GIRLS DROVE ME HOME... AND I BID THEM A GAY FAREWELL...
SO LONG, KIDS! BE SEEING YOU SOON!
YOU BET, CINDERELLA! WE'LL COME AND TAKE YOU OUT OF THE KITCHEN AGAIN!
WE'LL SEE YOU, DRUDGE!

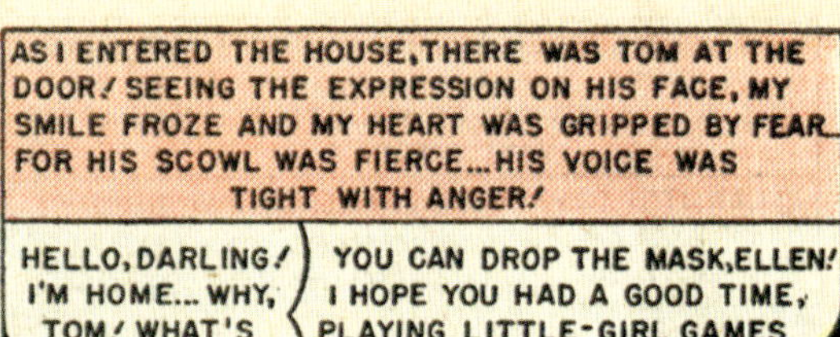
AS I ENTERED THE HOUSE, THERE WAS TOM AT THE DOOR! SEEING THE EXPRESSION ON HIS FACE, MY SMILE FROZE AND MY HEART WAS GRIPPED BY FEAR FOR HIS SCOWL WAS FIERCE... HIS VOICE WAS TIGHT WITH ANGER!
HELLO, DARLING! I'M HOME... WHY, TOM! WHAT'S THE MATTER?
YOU CAN DROP THE MASK, ELLEN! I HOPE YOU HAD A GOOD TIME, PLAYING LITTLE-GIRL GAMES WITH YOUR CRONIES, WHILE YOUR HOUSE LOOKS LIKE A PIGSTY!

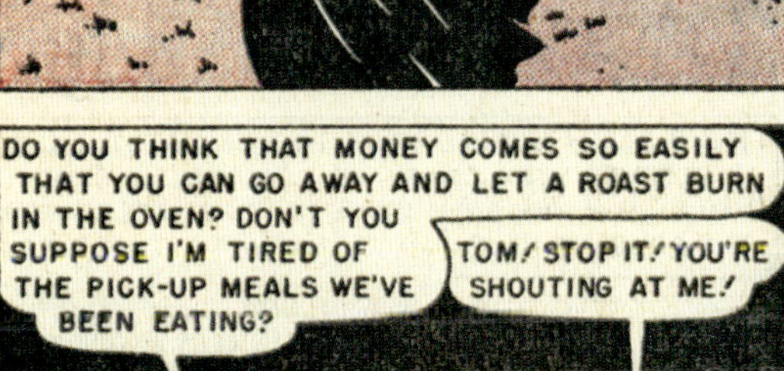
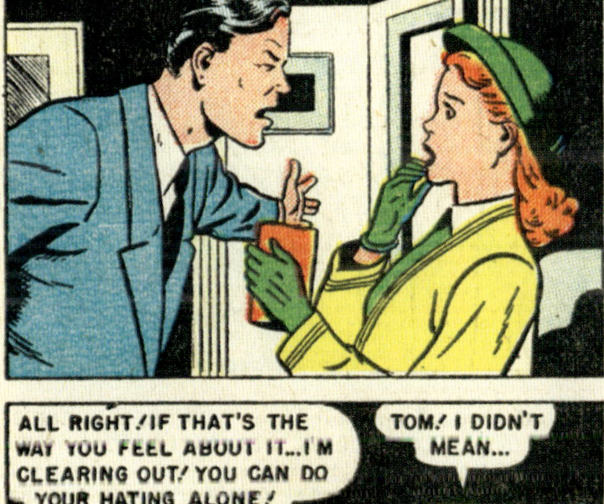
DO YOU THINK THAT MONEY COMES SO EASILY THAT YOU CAN GO AWAY AND LET A ROAST BURN IN THE OVEN? DON'T YOU SUPPOSE I'M TIRED OF THE PICK-UP MEALS WE'VE BEEN EATING?
TOM! STOP IT! YOU'RE SHOUTING AT ME!

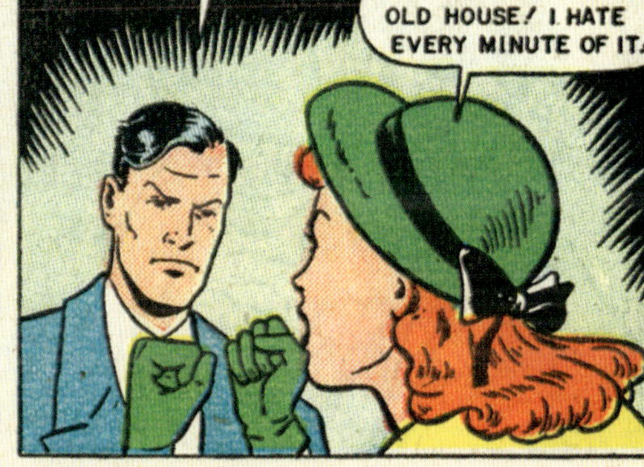
I THOUGHT I HAD MARRIED A WOMAN, ELLEN! BUT I WAS WRONG! YOU'RE STILL A LITTLE GIRL... THE QUEEN OF THE CAMPUS! WELL, YOUR COLLEGE DAYS ARE OVER! THIS IS REALITY!
HOW DARE YOU TALK TO ME LIKE THIS! JUST BECAUSE I BURNED AN OLD ROAST! I'M TIRED OF COOKING AND CLEANING AND MOPPING AROUND THIS DOPEY OLD HOUSE! I HATE EVERY MINUTE OF IT!

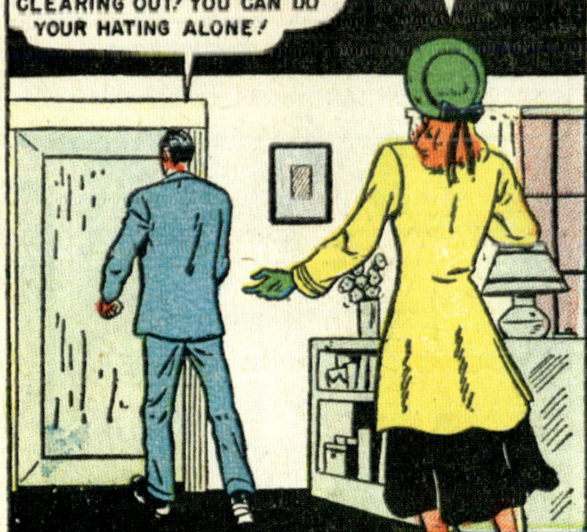
ALL RIGHT! IF THAT'S THE WAY YOU FEEL ABOUT IT... I'M CLEARING OUT! YOU CAN DO YOUR HATING ALONE!
TOM! I DIDN'T MEAN...

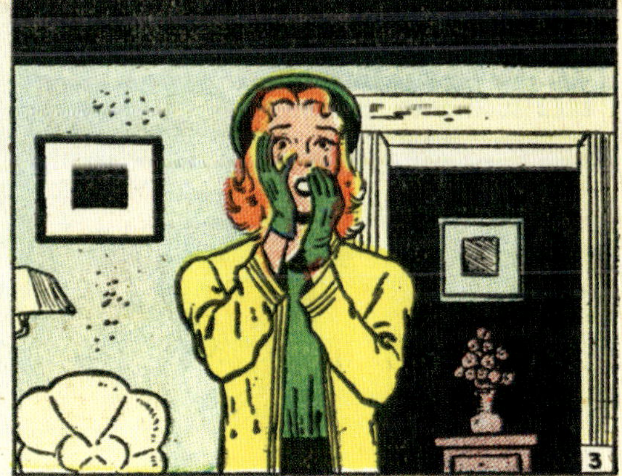
AN INSTANT LATER, THE DOOR SLAMMED BEHIND HIM... AND I WAS ALONE IN OUR LITTLE DREAM COTTAGE... ONLY NOW THE DREAM WAS DISSOLVING IN MY TEARS, AS LOUD SOBS WRACKED MY BODY!
3

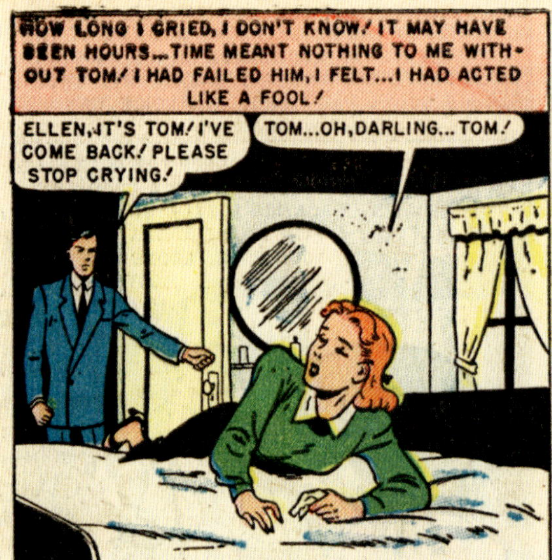
HOW LONG I CRIED, I DON'T KNOW! IT MAY HAVE BEEN HOURS...TIME MEANT NOTHING TO ME WITHOUT TOM! I HAD FAILED HIM, I FELT...I HAD ACTED LIKE A FOOL!
ELLEN, IT'S TOM! I'VE COME BACK! PLEASE STOP CRYING!
TOM...OH, DARLING...TOM!

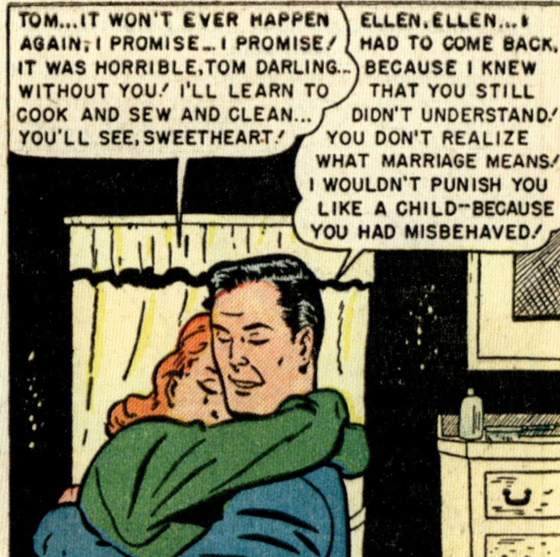
TOM...IT WON'T EVER HAPPEN AGAIN, I PROMISE...I PROMISE! IT WAS HORRIBLE, TOM DARLING... WITHOUT YOU! I'LL LEARN TO COOK AND SEW AND CLEAN... YOU'LL SEE, SWEETHEART!
ELLEN, ELLEN...I HAD TO COME BACK, BECAUSE I KNEW THAT YOU STILL DIDN'T UNDERSTAND! YOU DON'T REALIZE WHAT MARRIAGE MEANS! I WOULDN'T PUNISH YOU LIKE A CHILD--BECAUSE YOU HAD MISBEHAVED!

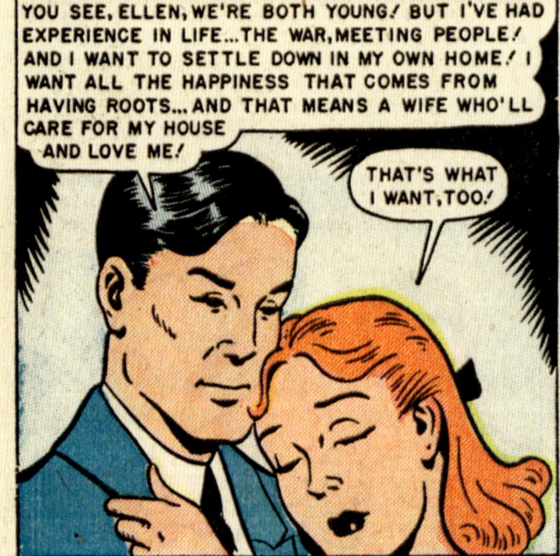
YOU SEE, ELLEN, WE'RE BOTH YOUNG! BUT I'VE HAD EXPERIENCE IN LIFE...THE WAR, MEETING PEOPLE! AND I WANT TO SETTLE DOWN IN MY OWN HOME! I WANT ALL THE HAPPINESS THAT COMES FROM HAVING ROOTS...AND THAT MEANS A WIFE WHO'LL CARE FOR MY HOUSE AND LOVE ME!
THAT'S WHAT I WANT, TOO!

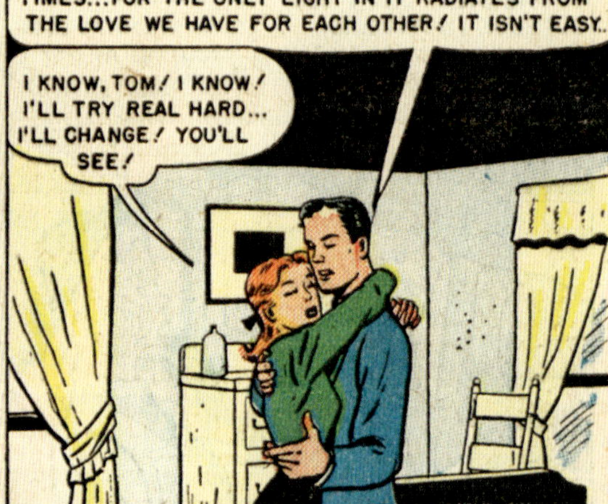
I KNOW, DEAR! BUT YOU HAVE TO WORK AT IT... AND IT BECOMES VERY DRAB AND MONOTONOUS SOMETIMES...FOR THE ONLY LIGHT IN IT RADIATES FROM THE LOVE WE HAVE FOR EACH OTHER! IT ISN'T EASY...
I KNOW, TOM! I KNOW! I'LL TRY REAL HARD... I'LL CHANGE! YOU'LL SEE!

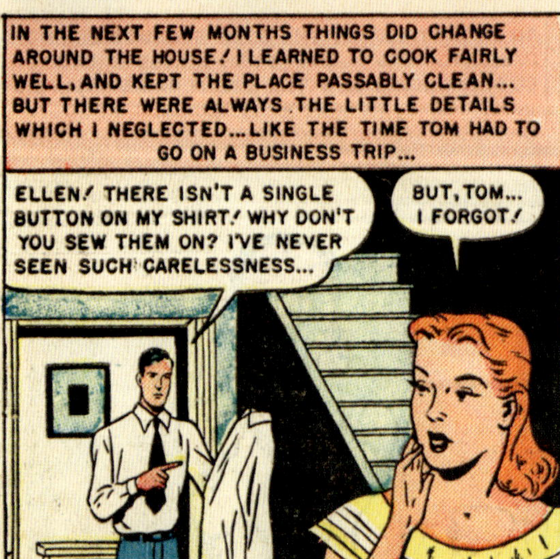
IN THE NEXT FEW MONTHS THINGS DID CHANGE AROUND THE HOUSE! I LEARNED TO COOK FAIRLY WELL, AND KEPT THE PLACE PASSABLY CLEAN... BUT THERE WERE ALWAYS THE LITTLE DETAILS WHICH I NEGLECTED...LIKE THE TIME TOM HAD TO GO ON A BUSINESS TRIP...
ELLEN! THERE ISN'T A SINGLE BUTTON ON MY SHIRT! WHY DON'T YOU SEW THEM ON? I'VE NEVER SEEN SUCH CARELESSNESS...
BUT, TOM... I FORGOT!

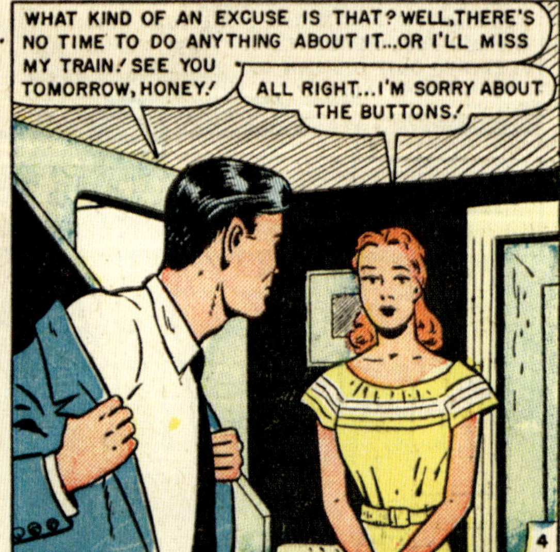
WHAT KIND OF AN EXCUSE IS THAT? WELL, THERE'S NO TIME TO DO ANYTHING ABOUT IT...OR I'LL MISS MY TRAIN! SEE YOU TOMORROW, HONEY!
ALL RIGHT...I'M SORRY ABOUT THE BUTTONS!
4

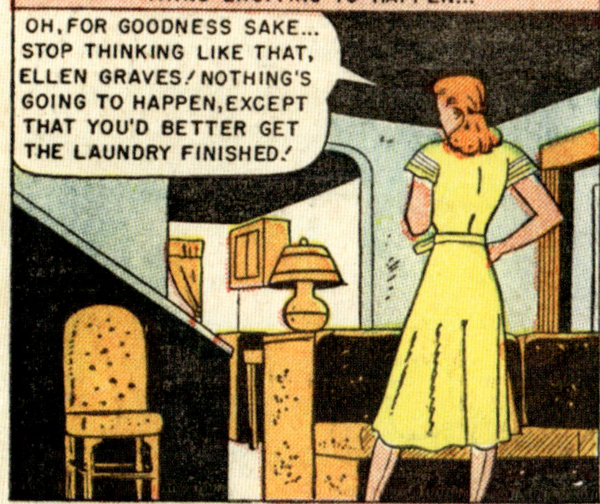
AFTER TOM HAD LEFT, THE OLD FEELING SUDDENLY CAME OVER ME/ I WAS BORED...TIRED OF DOING THE HOUSE WORK/ I WISHED FRANTICALLY FOR SOMETHING EXCITING TO HAPPEN...
OH, FOR GOODNESS SAKE... STOP THINKING LIKE THAT, ELLEN GRAVES/ NOTHING'S GOING TO HAPPEN, EXCEPT THAT YOU'D BETTER GET THE LAUNDRY FINISHED/

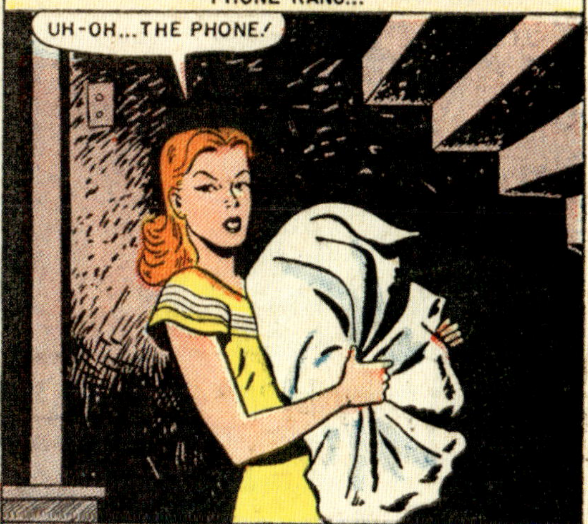
I HAD GATHERED UP THE LAUNDRY AND STARTED DOWN TO THE WASHING MACHINE WHEN THE TELEPHONE RANG...
UH-OH...THE PHONE/

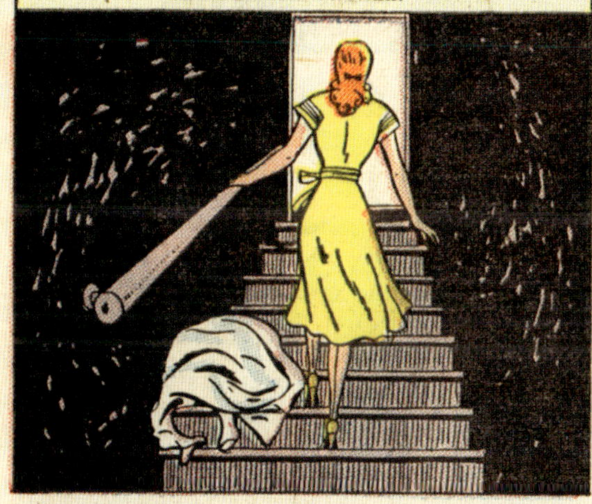
ON THE WAY UPSTAIRS, I MADE A MENTAL NOTE TO REPLACE THE LIGHT BULB AT THE FOOT OF THE CELLAR STAIRS...AS I DROPPED THE LAUNDRY TO ANSWER THE PHONE...

I ANSWERED THE PHONE...AND MY HEART FELT GAY..
MIDGE/ HELLO, DARLING/ WHAT? YOU HAVE TICKETS FOR THE FOOTBALL GAME? WONDERFUL... TOM IS AWAY UNTIL TOMORROW/ YOU BET/ I'LL BE THERE IN HALF AN HOUR/

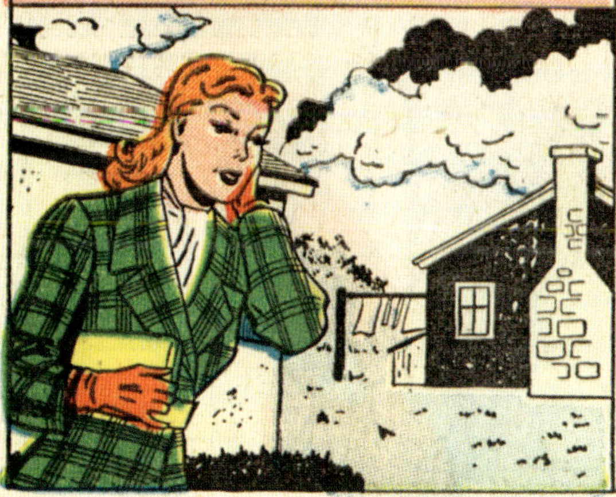
I HURRIED FROM THE HOUSE...FORGETTING ABOUT THE ELECTRIC LIGHT BULB TO BE REPLACED, OR THE LAUNDRY ON THE CELLAR STAIRS/..I ONLY KNEW THAT I WANTED TO SEE THAT FOOTBALL GAME... VERY BADLY...

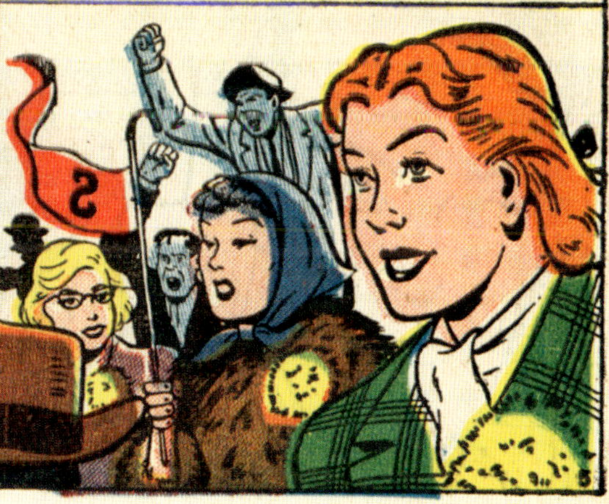
BUT PERHAPS I WOULDN'T HAVE BEEN SO CAREFREE IF I HAD KNOWN WHAT MY NEGLIGENCE WOULD RESULT IN/ IN THE BRIGHT SUNLIGHT I WAS ONCE AGAIN HAPPY AND FREE...A LITTLE CO-ED, HAVING FUN...

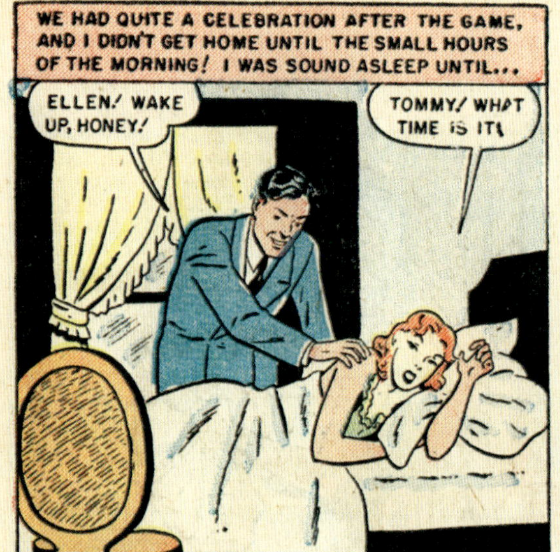
WE HAD QUITE A CELEBRATION AFTER THE GAME, AND I DIDN'T GET HOME UNTIL THE SMALL HOURS OF THE MORNING! I WAS SOUND ASLEEP UNTIL...
ELLEN! WAKE UP, HONEY!
TOMMY! WHAT TIME IS IT!

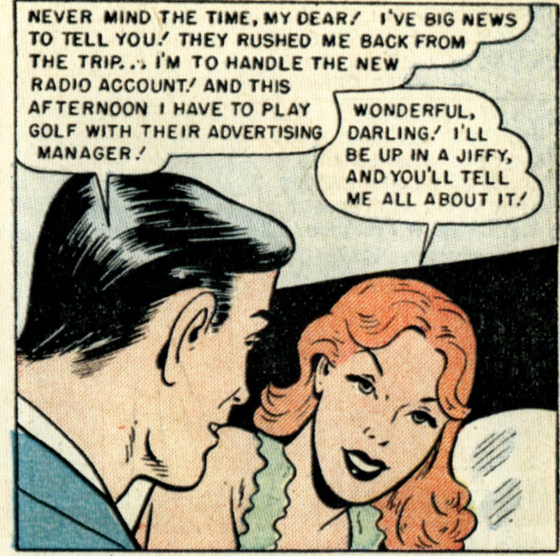
NEVER MIND THE TIME, MY DEAR! I'VE BIG NEWS TO TELL YOU! THEY RUSHED ME BACK FROM THE TRIP... I'M TO HANDLE THE NEW RADIO ACCOUNT! AND THIS AFTERNOON I HAVE TO PLAY GOLF WITH THEIR ADVERTISING MANAGER!
WONDERFUL, DARLING! I'LL BE UP IN A JIFFY, AND YOU'LL TELL ME ALL ABOUT IT!

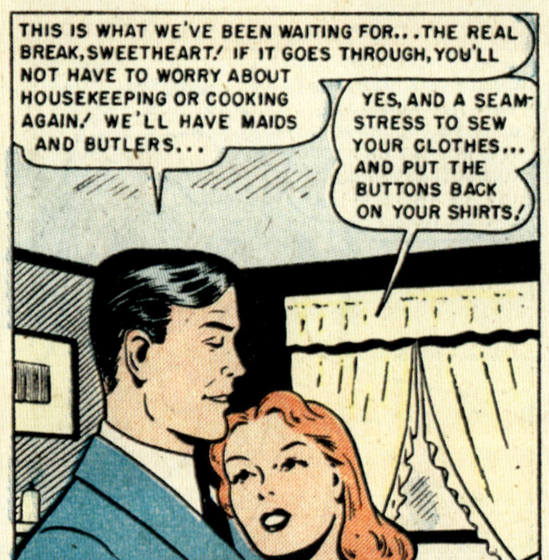
THIS IS WHAT WE'VE BEEN WAITING FOR...THE REAL BREAK, SWEETHEART! IF IT GOES THROUGH, YOU'LL NOT HAVE TO WORRY ABOUT HOUSEKEEPING OR COOKING AGAIN! WE'LL HAVE MAIDS AND BUTLERS...
YES, AND A SEAMSTRESS TO SEW YOUR CLOTHES... AND PUT THE BUTTONS BACK ON YOUR SHIRTS!

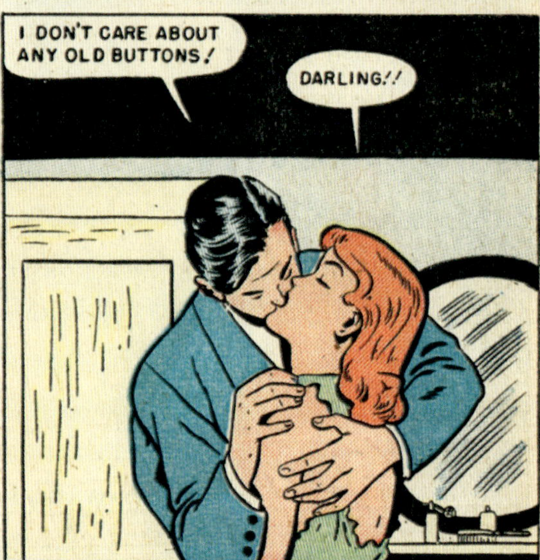
I DON'T CARE ABOUT ANY OLD BUTTONS!
DARLING!!

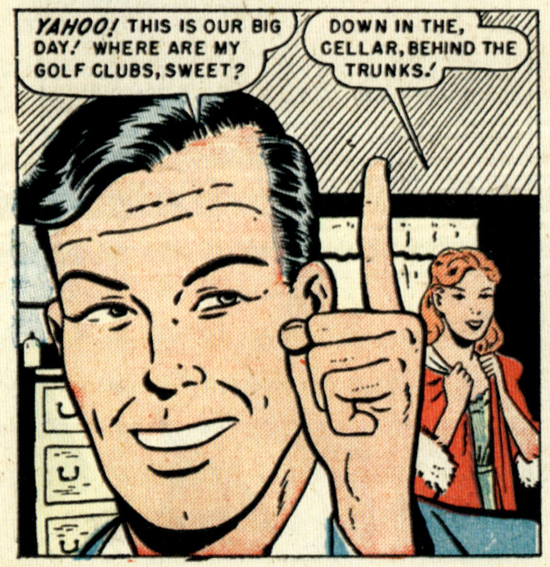
YAHOO! THIS IS OUR BIG DAY! WHERE ARE MY GOLF CLUBS, SWEET?
DOWN IN THE CELLAR, BEHIND THE TRUNKS!

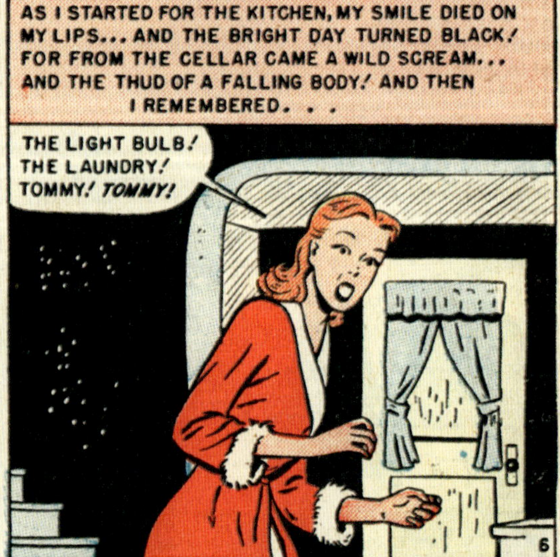
AS I STARTED FOR THE KITCHEN, MY SMILE DIED ON MY LIPS... AND THE BRIGHT DAY TURNED BLACK! FOR FROM THE CELLAR CAME A WILD SCREAM... AND THE THUD OF A FALLING BODY! AND THEN I REMEMBERED...
THE LIGHT BULB! THE LAUNDRY! TOMMY! TOMMY!
6

I RAN DOWNSTAIRS TO SEE TOM, MY HUSBAND, LYING GROTESQUELY TWISTED ON THE CEMENT FLOOR OF THE CELLAR... HIS FACE PALE! HE WAS STILL AND WHITE, LIKE A DEAD MAN! I FELT THE SCREAM TEAR FROM MY THROAT...

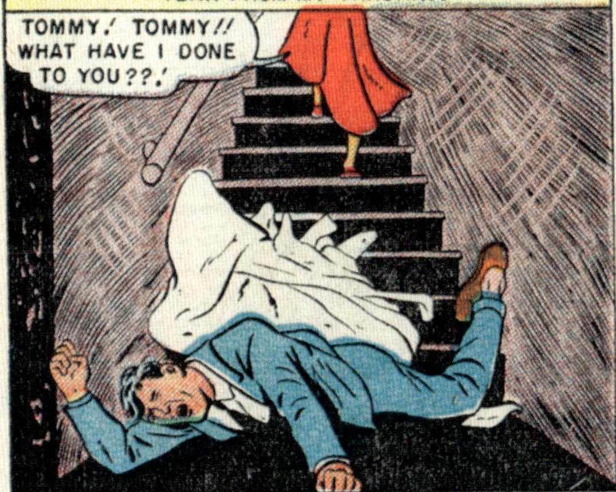

SOMEHOW I MANAGED TO GET HELP... BUT EVEN IN MY CONFUSION I KNEW THE TERRIBLE STABS OF GUILT! IT WAS I WHO HAD INJURED TOMMY, AS SURELY AS IF I HAD PUSHED HIM DOWN THOSE STAIRS!

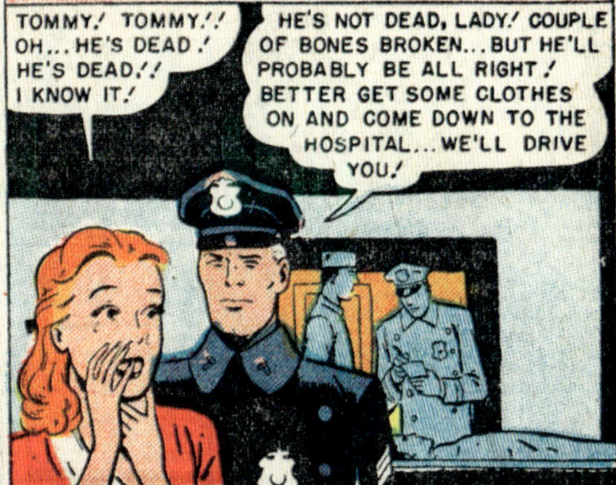

AT THE HOSPITAL I LEARNED THAT TOM HAD BEEN RUSHED TO SURGERY... AND FOR AN ENDLESS ETERNITY I PACED THE TILED FLOORS... RESTLESSLY... BACK AND FORTH... BACK AND FORTH... BERATING MYSELF BITTERLY!

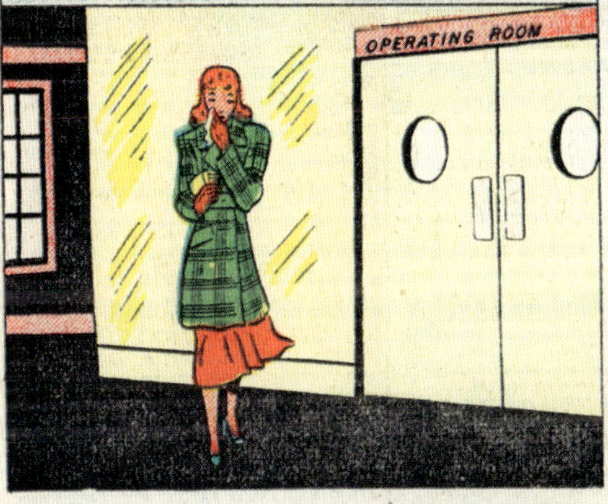

FINALLY THE OPERATION WAS OVER! I RUSHED TO MEET THE DOCTOR...

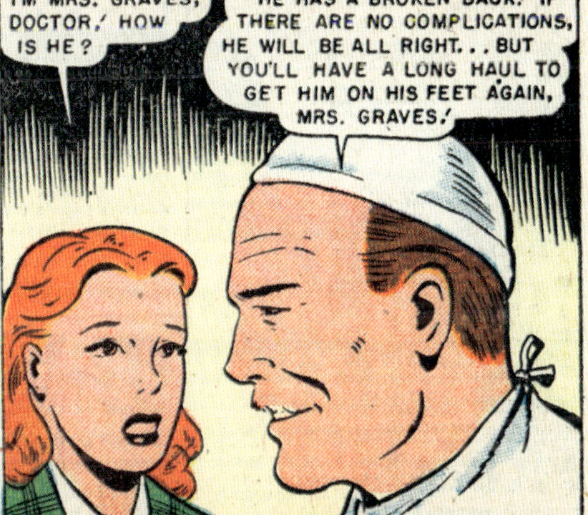

IT DOESN'T MATTER, DOCTOR! I'LL DO ANYTHING! FOR TOM IS THE ONLY THING IN THIS WORLD THAT I CARE ABOUT! I LOVE HIM! I NEVER KNEW HOW MUCH TILL NOW!

GOOD! GO TO IT, MRS. GRAVES... HE'LL NEED YOU!

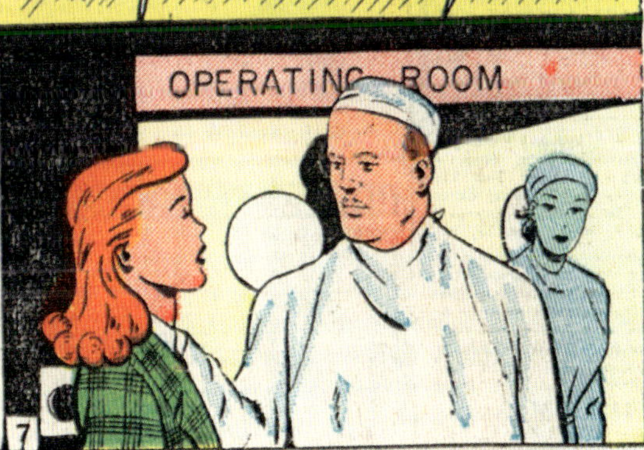

SO AT LAST I KNOW THAT MARRIAGE IS NO GAME... THAT YOU CAN'T WORK AT IT HALF-HEARTEDLY! TRUE, I LEARNED MY LESSON THE BITTER WAY... BUT THESE ARE THE LESSONS THAT STICK! AND WHEN TOM RECOVERS, AS HE MUST... I WILL SHOW HIM THAT MY LIFE BELONGS TO HIM AND HIM ALONE... HE MARRIED AN IRRESPONSIBLE BRIDE... BUT I'LL PROVE HE NOW HAS A WIFE WHO IS A PARTNER IN LOVE... AND LIFE!

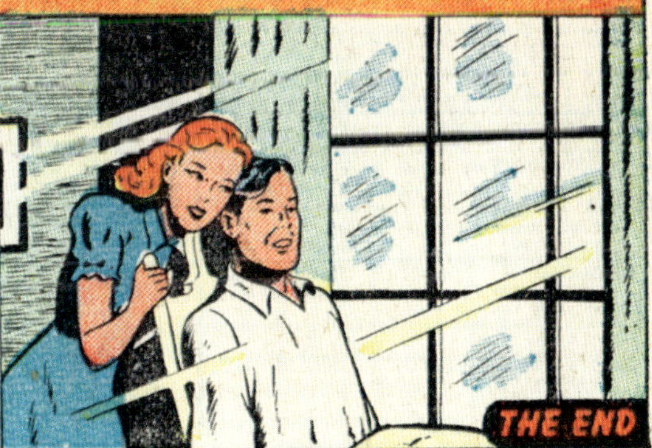

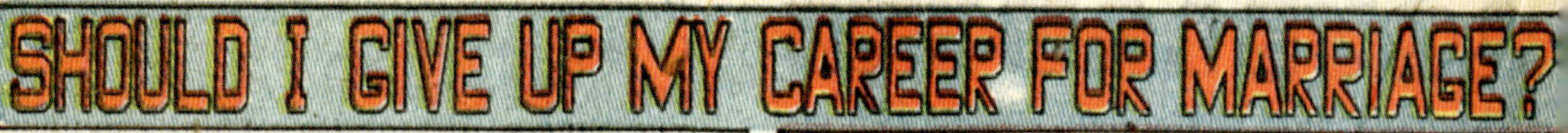

SHOULD I GIVE UP MY CAREER FOR MARRIAGE?

IT ALL STARTED ABOUT A YEAR AGO WHEN MR. JOHNSON PROMOTED ME FROM A SECRETARY TO THIS VERY IMPORTANT POSITION...

AND MISS BENSON, DUE TO YOUR EFFORTS AND ABILITY, WE FEEL THAT YOUR IN LINE FOR THIS VERY WONDERFUL JOB WITH OUR FIRM...I KNOW YOU'LL DO WELL... GOOD LUCK!..

THANK YOU... THANK YOU, MR. JOHNSON...

GOLLY, THIS IS WHAT I'VE DREAMED OF...NOW I'M HEAD OF THE DEPARTMENT...

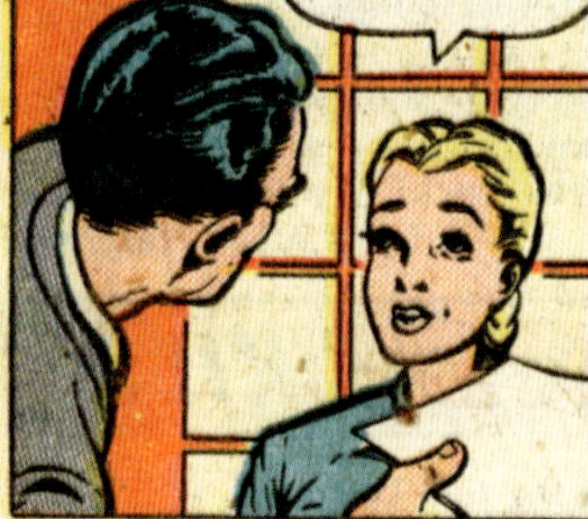

ISN'T THIS SWELL, DARLING?..LUIGI PROVIDES ATMOSPHERE...AND GOOD FOOD...JUST RIGHT FOR PROPOSING...

OH, PAUL... I LOVE YOU SO...

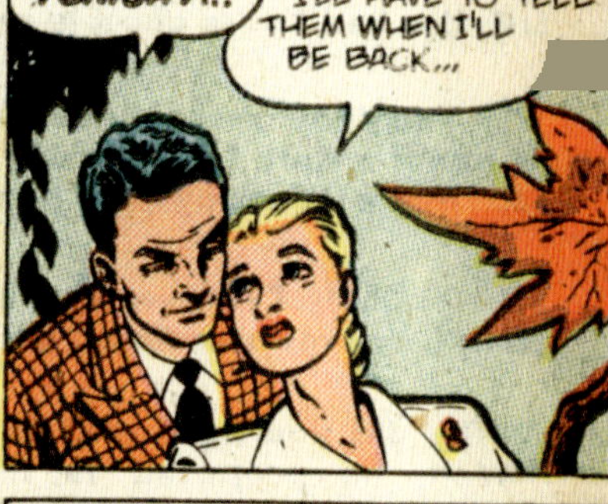

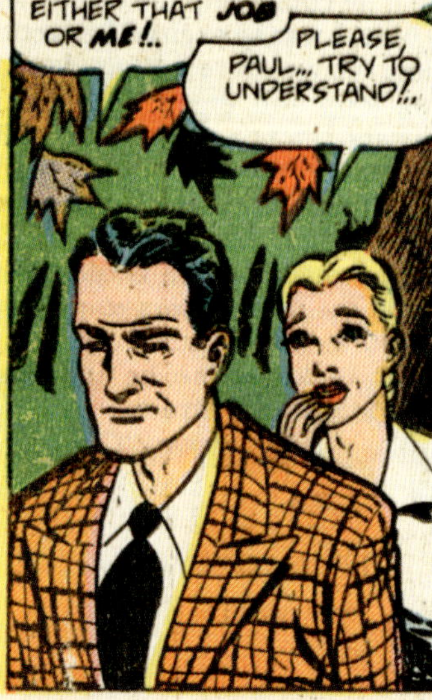

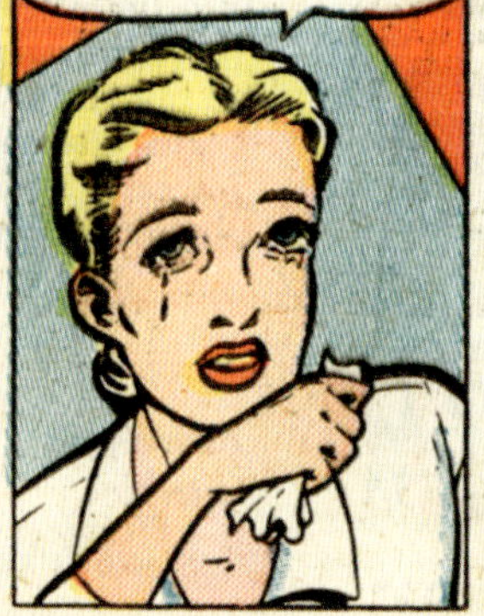

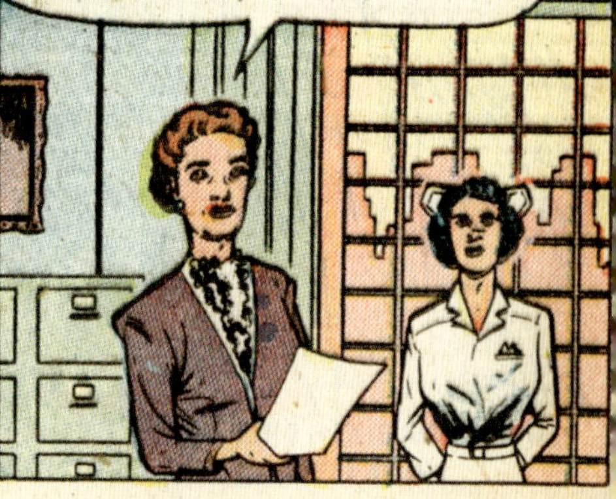

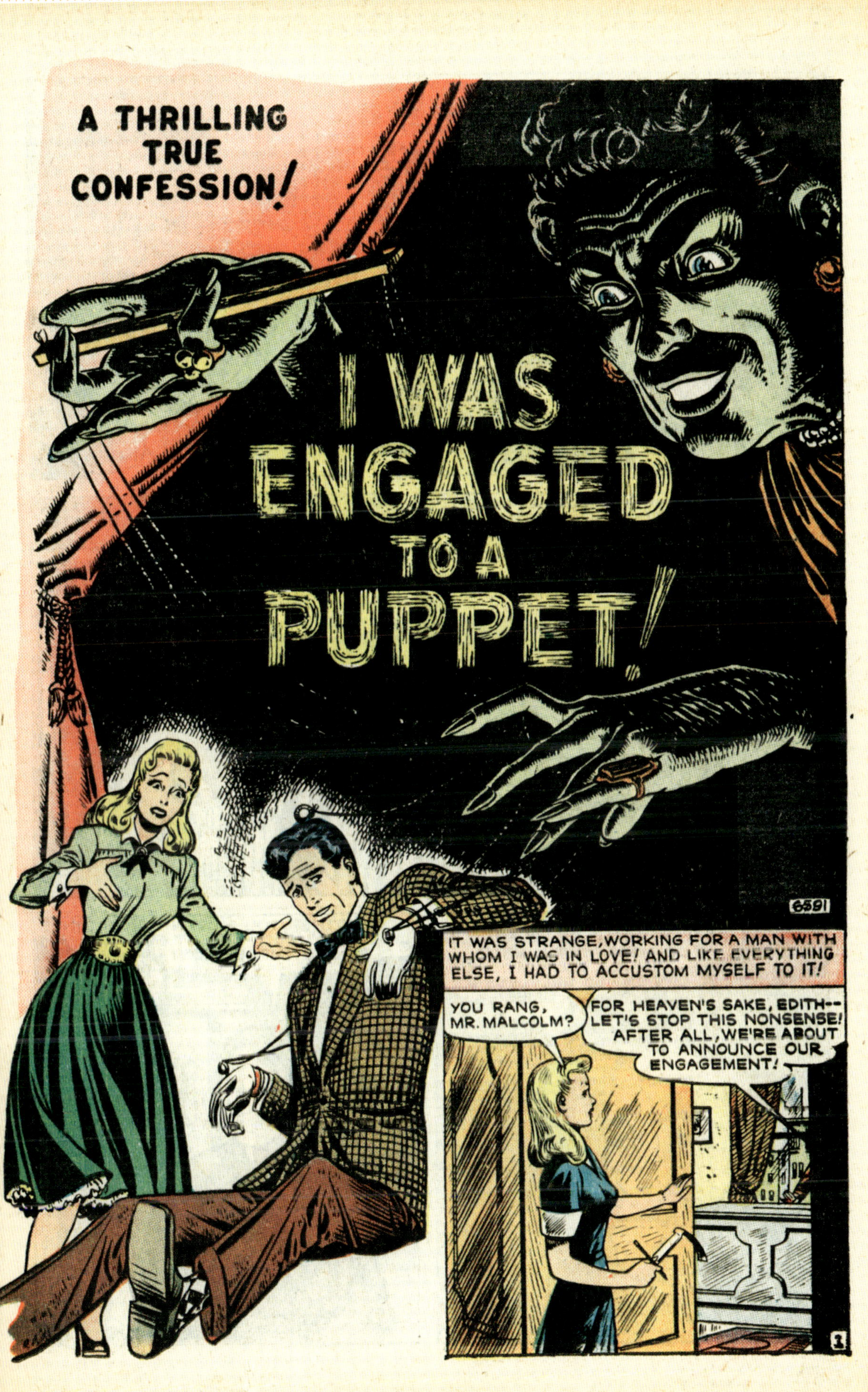

Page 114:
FIRST LOVE
Unknown issue, circa 1951

This page:
MY LOVE
#4, April 1950

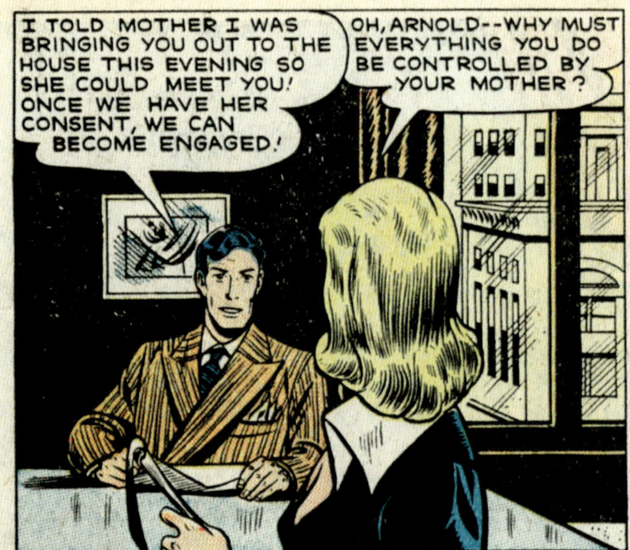

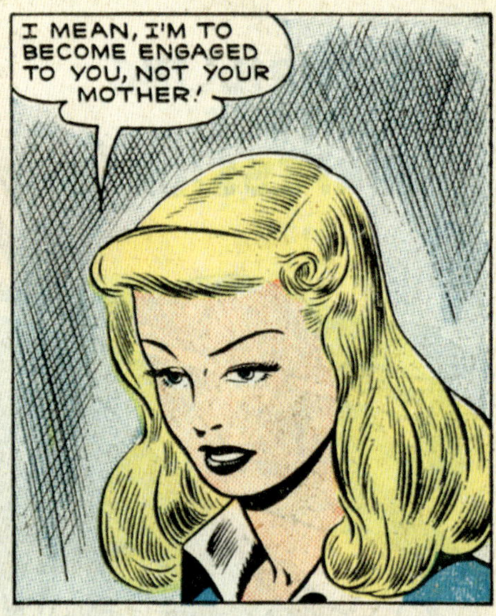

NOW THAT'S NOT THE WAY TO LOOK AT IT! AFTER ALL, SHE IS MY MOTHER! YOU'LL LIKE HER, EDITH--SHE'S A WONDERFUL PERSON!

WELL, I SUPPOSE IT'S ONLY RIGHT THAT SHE SHOULD HAVE SOMETHING TO SAY ABOUT IT!...I'M LOOKING FORWARD TO MEETING HER!

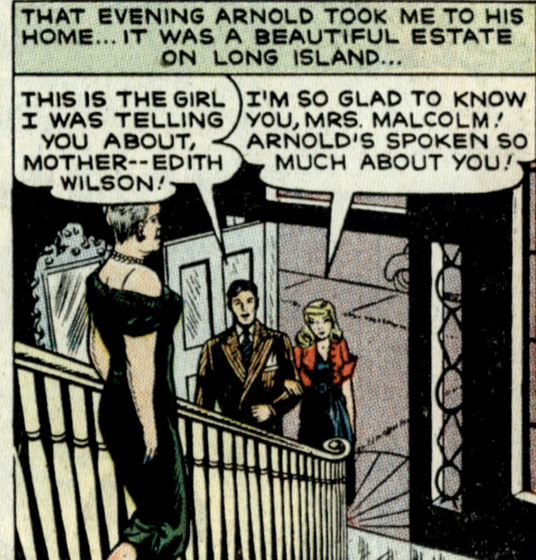

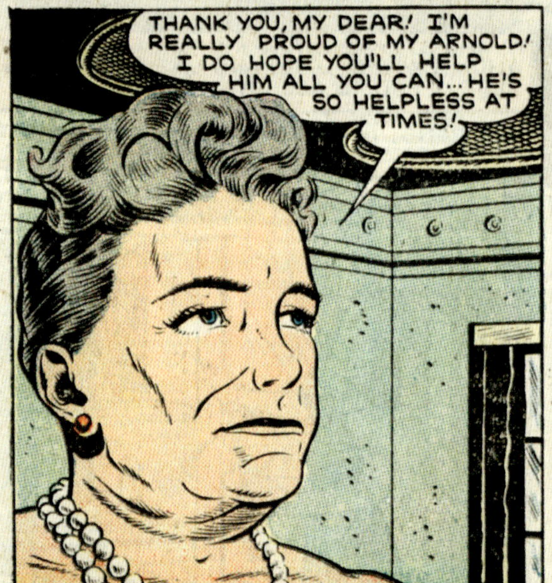

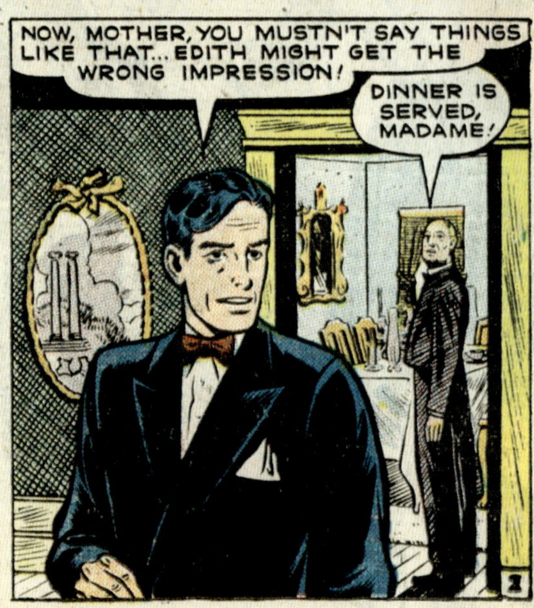

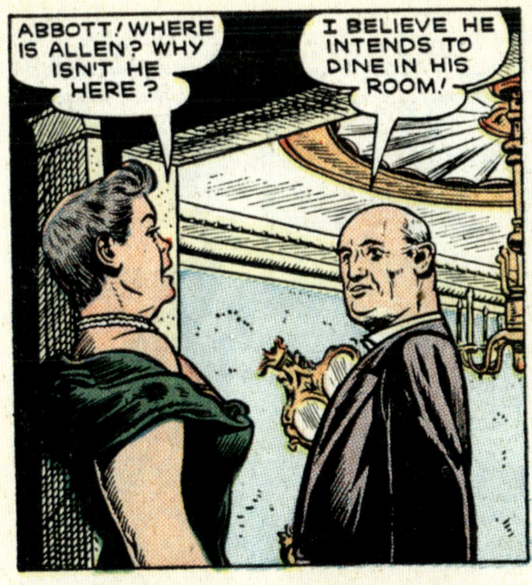
ABBOTT! WHERE IS ALLEN? WHY ISN'T HE HERE?
I BELIEVE HE INTENDS TO DINE IN HIS ROOM!

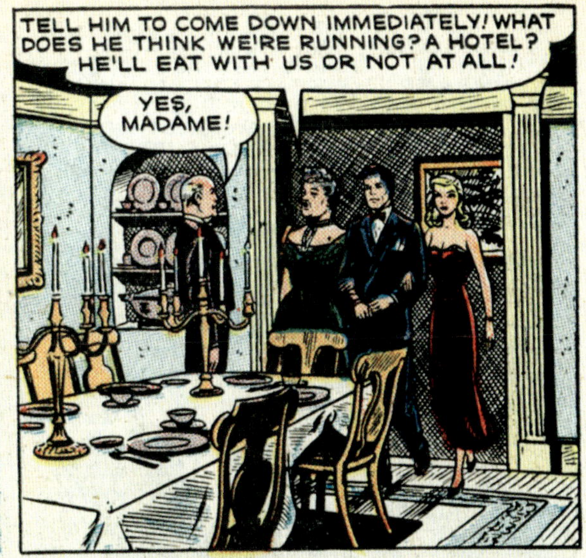
TELL HIM TO COME DOWN IMMEDIATELY! WHAT DOES HE THINK WE'RE RUNNING? A HOTEL? HE'LL EAT WITH US OR NOT AT ALL!
YES, MADAME!

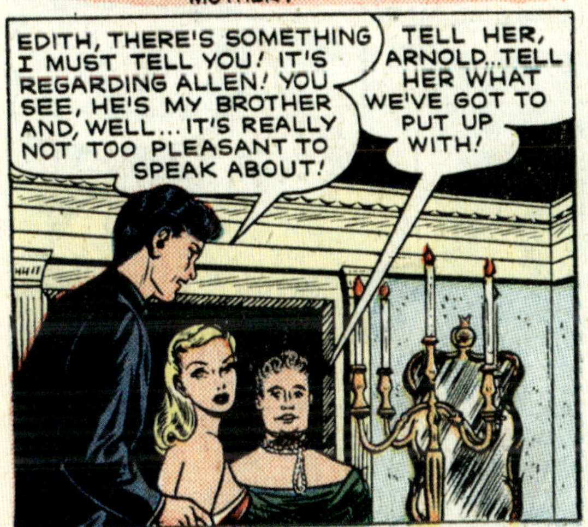
I WAS SHOCKED AT WHAT I'D HEARD! I'D NEVER DREAMED THAT ARNOLD WAS CONFRONTED BY SUCH A DOMINEERING MOTHER!
EDITH, THERE'S SOMETHING I MUST TELL YOU! IT'S REGARDING ALLEN! YOU SEE, HE'S MY BROTHER AND, WELL... IT'S REALLY NOT TOO PLEASANT TO SPEAK ABOUT!
TELL HER, ARNOLD...TELL HER WHAT WE'VE GOT TO PUT UP WITH!

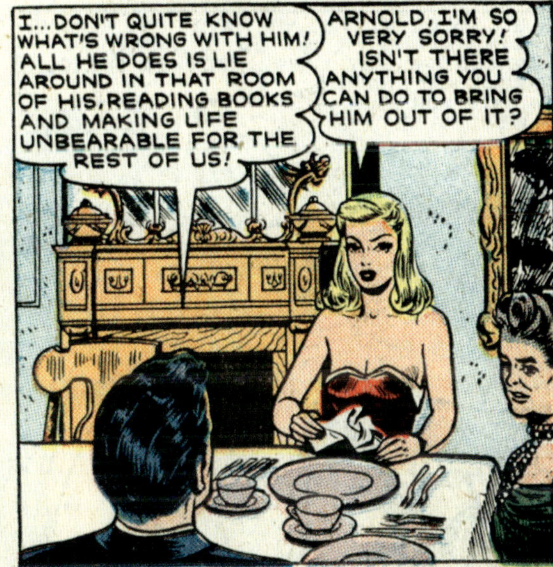
I...DON'T QUITE KNOW WHAT'S WRONG WITH HIM! ALL HE DOES IS LIE AROUND IN THAT ROOM OF HIS, READING BOOKS AND MAKING LIFE UNBEARABLE FOR THE REST OF US!
ARNOLD, I'M SO VERY SORRY! ISN'T THERE ANYTHING YOU CAN DO TO BRING HIM OUT OF IT?

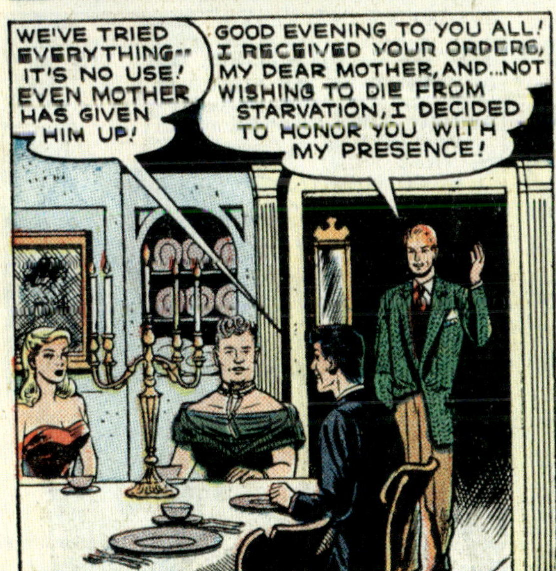
WE'VE TRIED EVERYTHING-- IT'S NO USE! EVEN MOTHER HAS GIVEN HIM UP!
GOOD EVENING TO YOU ALL! I RECEIVED YOUR ORDERS, MY DEAR MOTHER, AND...NOT WISHING TO DIE FROM STARVATION, I DECIDED TO HONOR YOU WITH MY PRESENCE!

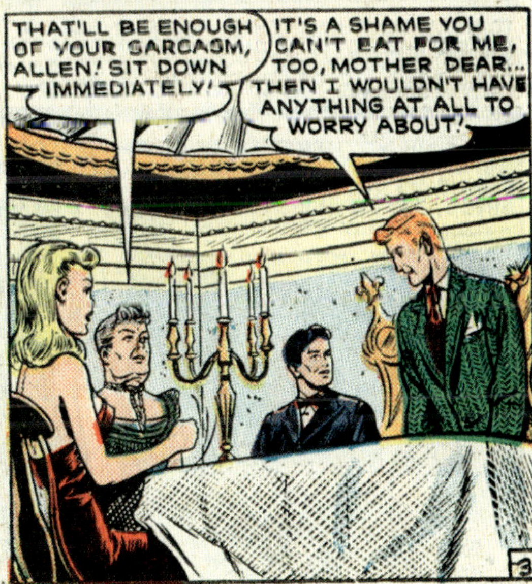
THAT'LL BE ENOUGH OF YOUR SARCASM, ALLEN! SIT DOWN IMMEDIATELY!
IT'S A SHAME YOU CAN'T EAT FOR ME, TOO, MOTHER DEAR... THEN I WOULDN'T HAVE ANYTHING AT ALL TO WORRY ABOUT!

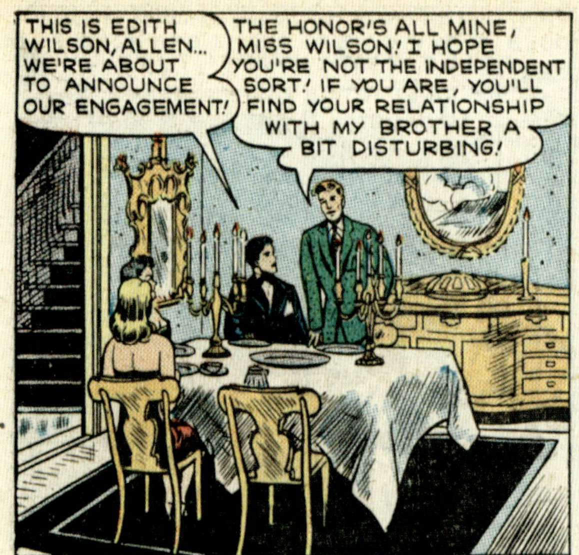
THIS IS EDITH WILSON, ALLEN... WE'RE ABOUT TO ANNOUNCE OUR ENGAGEMENT!
THE HONOR'S ALL MINE, MISS WILSON! I HOPE YOU'RE NOT THE INDEPENDENT SORT! IF YOU ARE, YOU'LL FIND YOUR RELATIONSHIP WITH MY BROTHER A BIT DISTURBING!

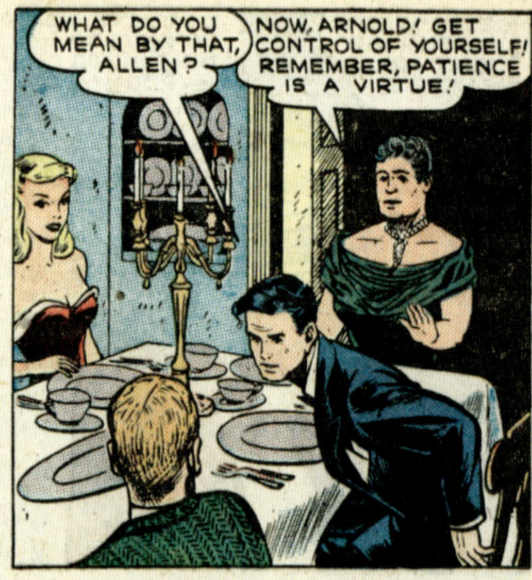
WHAT DO YOU MEAN BY THAT, ALLEN?
NOW, ARNOLD! GET CONTROL OF YOURSELF! REMEMBER, PATIENCE IS A VIRTUE!

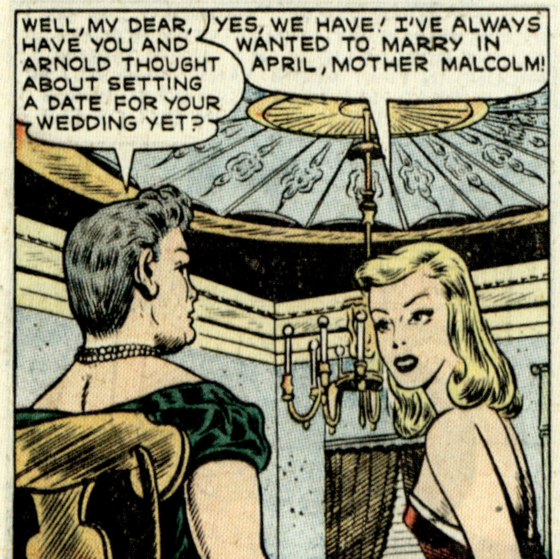
WELL, MY DEAR, HAVE YOU AND ARNOLD THOUGHT ABOUT SETTING A DATE FOR YOUR WEDDING YET?
YES, WE HAVE! I'VE ALWAYS WANTED TO MARRY IN APRIL, MOTHER MALCOLM!

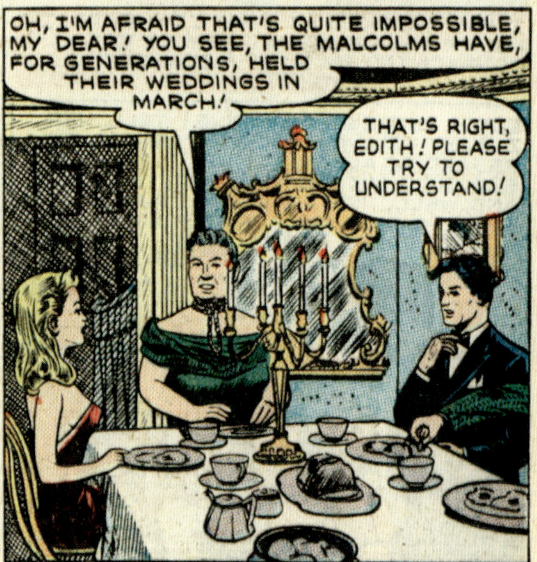
OH, I'M AFRAID THAT'S QUITE IMPOSSIBLE, MY DEAR! YOU SEE, THE MALCOLMS HAVE, FOR GENERATIONS, HELD THEIR WEDDINGS IN MARCH!
THAT'S RIGHT, EDITH! PLEASE TRY TO UNDERSTAND!

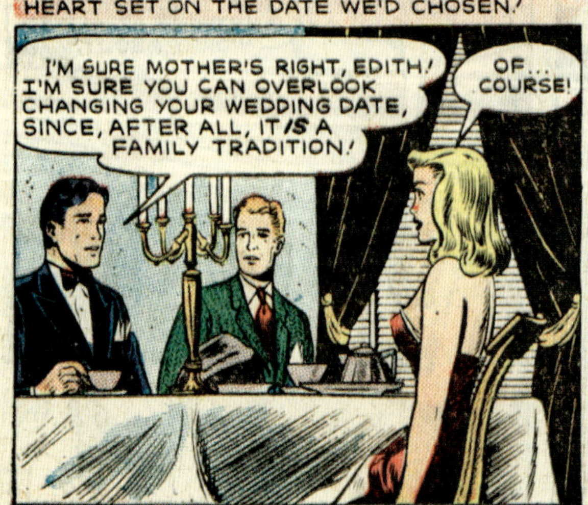
IT HURT TO THINK THAT ARNOLD WOULD TAKE HIS MOTHER'S SIDE ON THIS POINT! AFTER ALL, A GIRL MARRIES ONLY ONCE, AND I HAD MY HEART SET ON THE DATE WE'D CHOSEN!
I'M SURE MOTHER'S RIGHT, EDITH! I'M SURE YOU CAN OVERLOOK CHANGING YOUR WEDDING DATE, SINCE, AFTER ALL, IT IS A FAMILY TRADITION!
OF... COURSE!

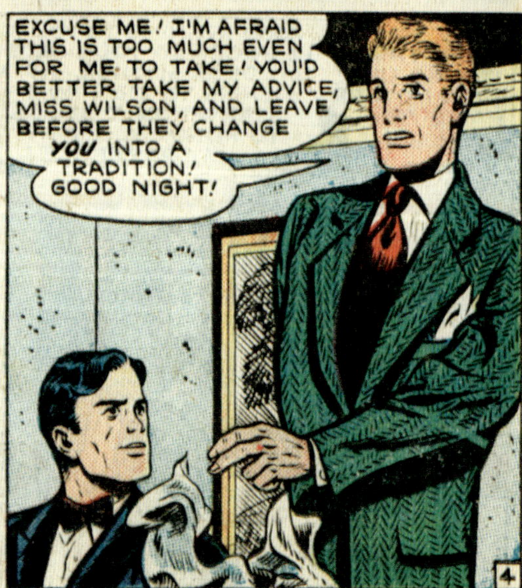
EXCUSE ME! I'M AFRAID THIS IS TOO MUCH EVEN FOR ME TO TAKE! YOU'D BETTER TAKE MY ADVICE, MISS WILSON, AND LEAVE BEFORE THEY CHANGE YOU INTO A TRADITION! GOOD NIGHT!
4

I WAS STRANGELY MOVED BY ALLEN'S OUTBURST THAT EVENING, AND FELT SYMPATHY IN MY HEART FOR HIM! I SIMPLY HAD TO SPEAK TO HIM...

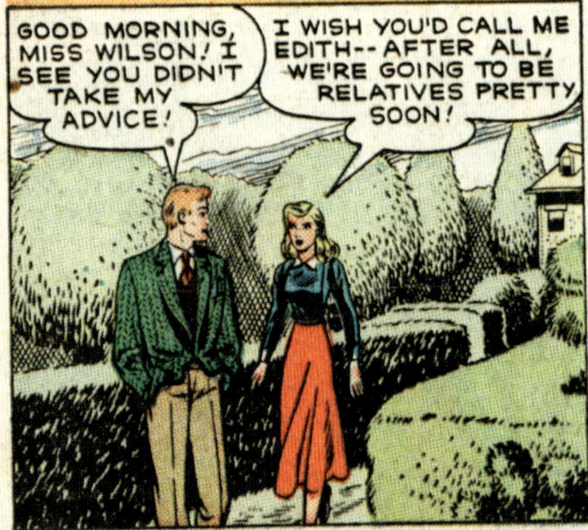

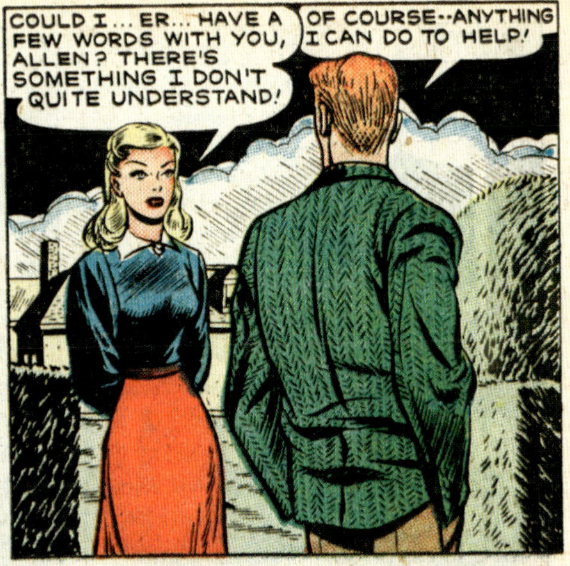

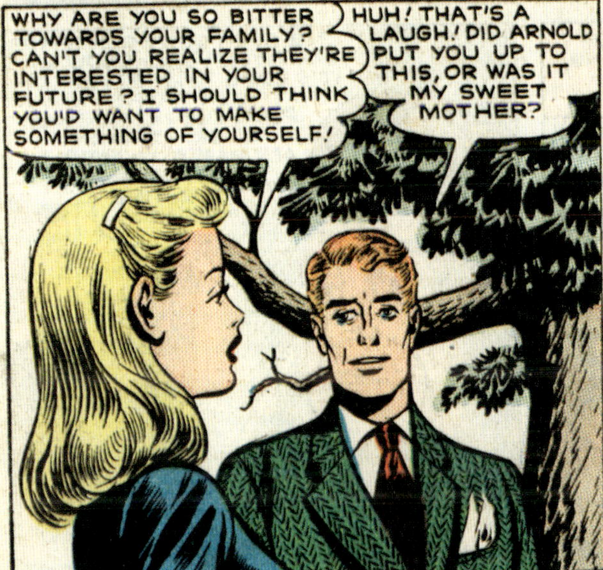

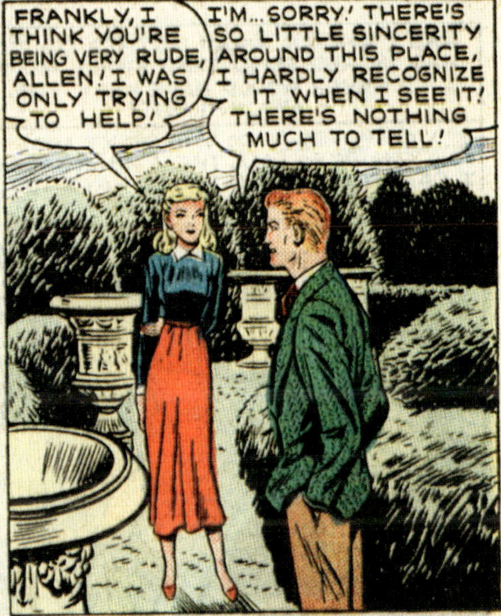

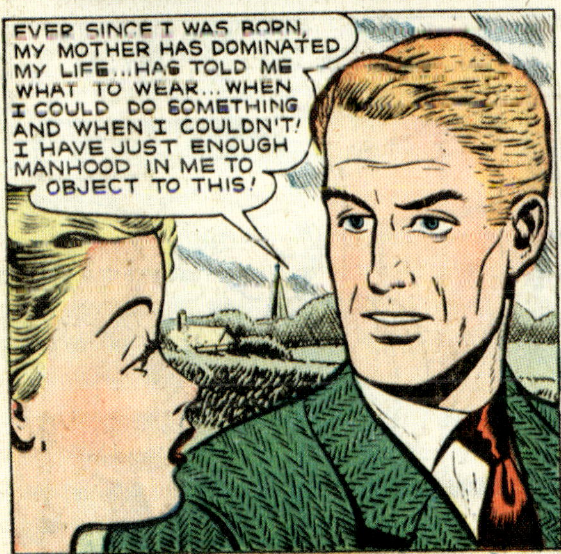

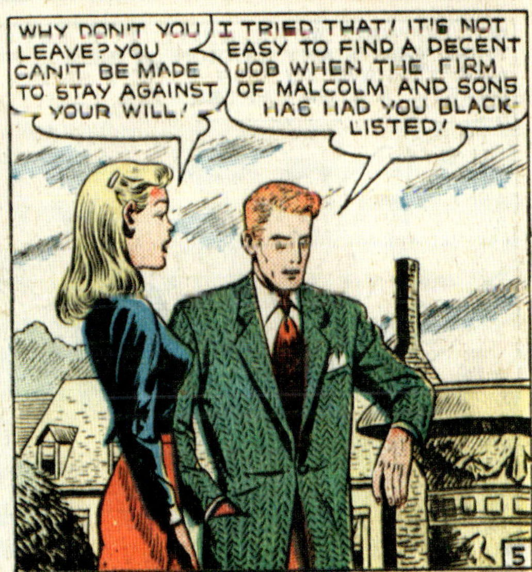

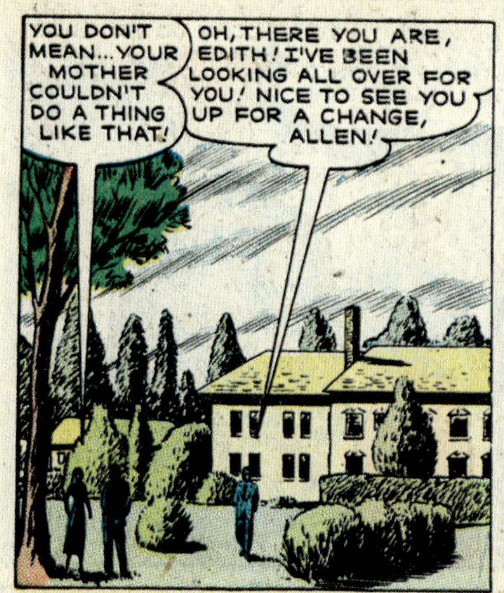
YOU DON'T MEAN...YOUR MOTHER COULDN'T DO A THING LIKE THAT!
OH, THERE YOU ARE, EDITH! I'VE BEEN LOOKING ALL OVER FOR YOU! NICE TO SEE YOU UP FOR A CHANGE, ALLEN!

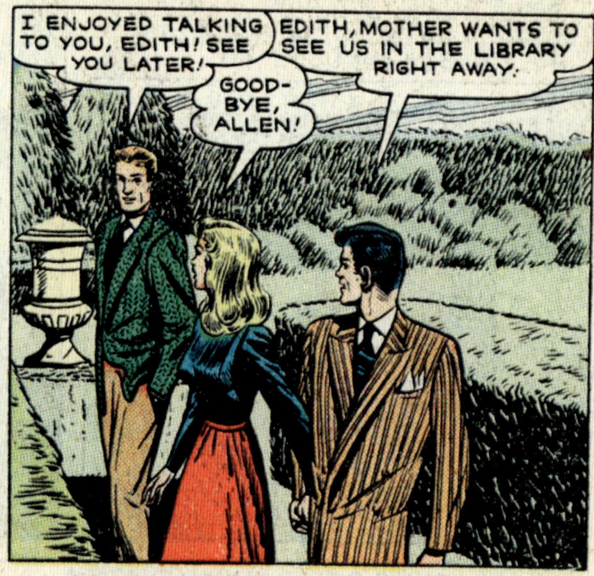
I ENJOYED TALKING TO YOU, EDITH! SEE YOU LATER!
GOOD-BYE, ALLEN!
EDITH, MOTHER WANTS TO SEE US IN THE LIBRARY RIGHT AWAY.

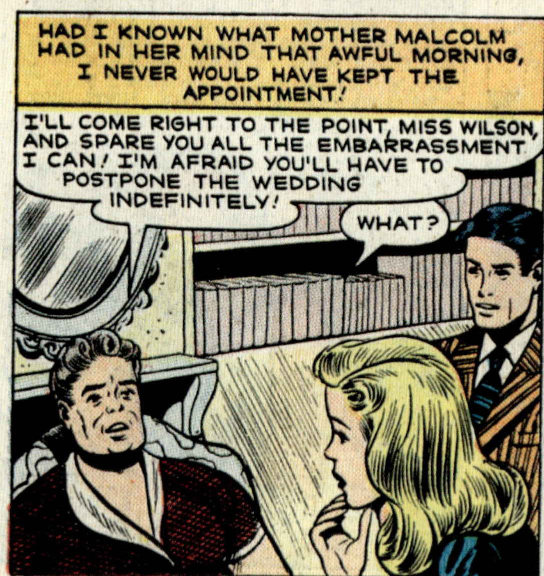
HAD I KNOWN WHAT MOTHER MALCOLM HAD IN HER MIND THAT AWFUL MORNING, I NEVER WOULD HAVE KEPT THE APPOINTMENT!
I'LL COME RIGHT TO THE POINT, MISS WILSON, AND SPARE YOU ALL THE EMBARRASSMENT I CAN! I'M AFRAID YOU'LL HAVE TO POSTPONE THE WEDDING INDEFINITELY!
WHAT?

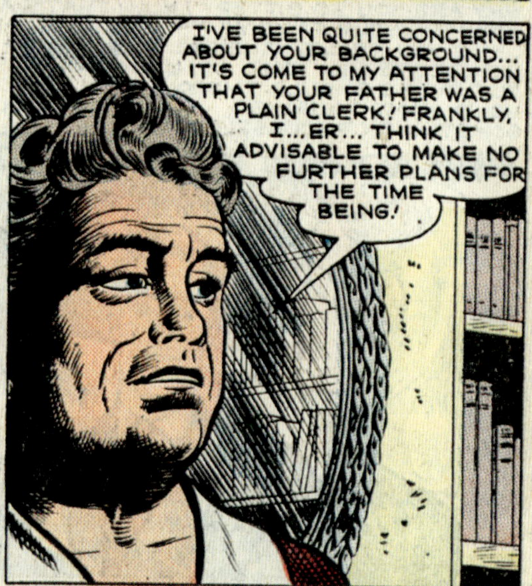
I'VE BEEN QUITE CONCERNED ABOUT YOUR BACKGROUND... IT'S COME TO MY ATTENTION THAT YOUR FATHER WAS A PLAIN CLERK! FRANKLY, I...ER... THINK IT ADVISABLE TO MAKE NO FURTHER PLANS FOR THE TIME BEING!

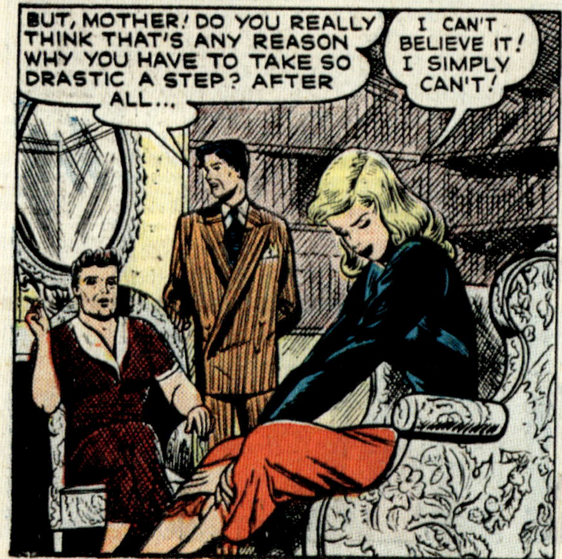
BUT, MOTHER! DO YOU REALLY THINK THAT'S ANY REASON WHY YOU HAVE TO TAKE SO DRASTIC A STEP? AFTER ALL...
I CAN'T BELIEVE IT! I SIMPLY CAN'T!

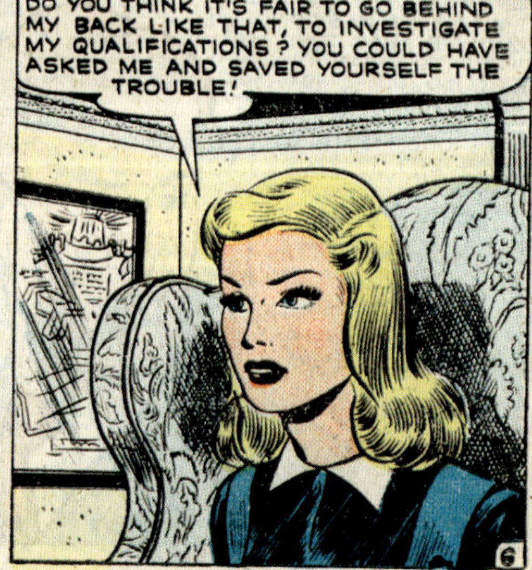
DO YOU THINK IT'S FAIR TO GO BEHIND MY BACK LIKE THAT, TO INVESTIGATE MY QUALIFICATIONS? YOU COULD HAVE ASKED ME AND SAVED YOURSELF THE TROUBLE!
6

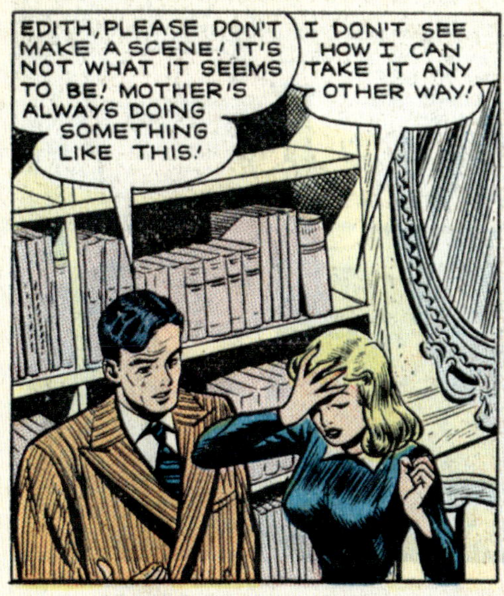
EDITH, PLEASE DON'T MAKE A SCENE! IT'S NOT WHAT IT SEEMS TO BE! MOTHER'S ALWAYS DOING SOMETHING LIKE THIS!
I DON'T SEE HOW I CAN TAKE IT ANY OTHER WAY!

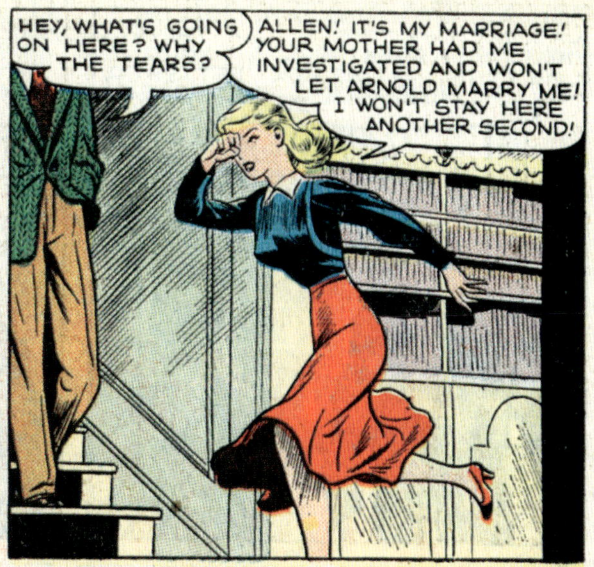
HEY, WHAT'S GOING ON HERE? WHY THE TEARS?
ALLEN! IT'S MY MARRIAGE! YOUR MOTHER HAD ME INVESTIGATED AND WON'T LET ARNOLD MARRY ME! I WON'T STAY HERE ANOTHER SECOND!

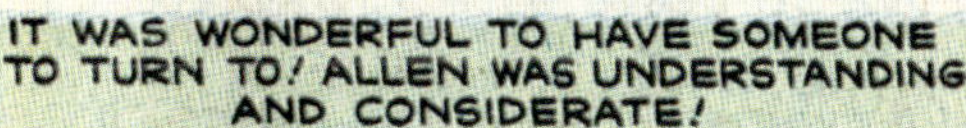
IT WAS WONDERFUL TO HAVE SOMEONE TO TURN TO! ALLEN WAS UNDERSTANDING AND CONSIDERATE!

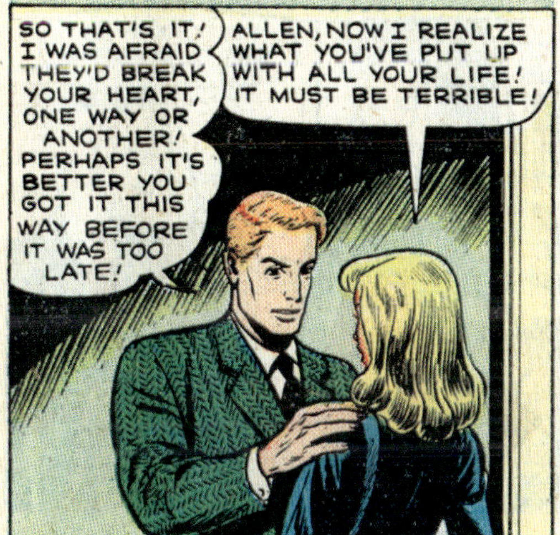
SO THAT'S IT! I WAS AFRAID THEY'D BREAK YOUR HEART, ONE WAY OR ANOTHER! PERHAPS IT'S BETTER YOU GOT IT THIS WAY BEFORE IT WAS TOO LATE!
ALLEN, NOW I REALIZE WHAT YOU'VE PUT UP WITH ALL YOUR LIFE! IT MUST BE TERRIBLE!

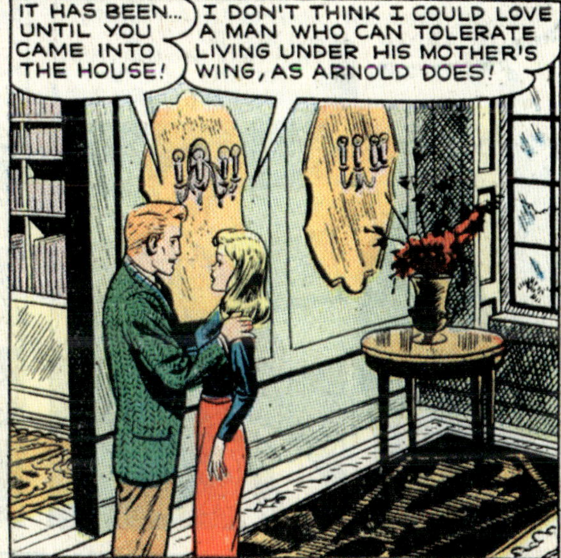
IT HAS BEEN... UNTIL YOU CAME INTO THE HOUSE!
I DON'T THINK I COULD LOVE A MAN WHO CAN TOLERATE LIVING UNDER HIS MOTHER'S WING, AS ARNOLD DOES!

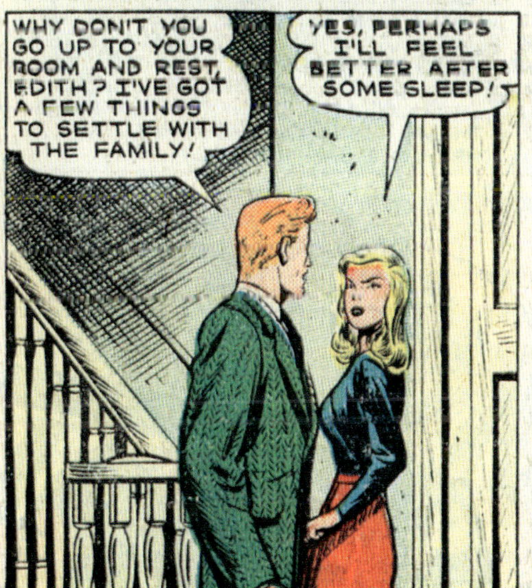
WHY DON'T YOU GO UP TO YOUR ROOM AND REST, EDITH? I'VE GOT A FEW THINGS TO SETTLE WITH THE FAMILY!
YES, PERHAPS I'LL FEEL BETTER AFTER SOME SLEEP!

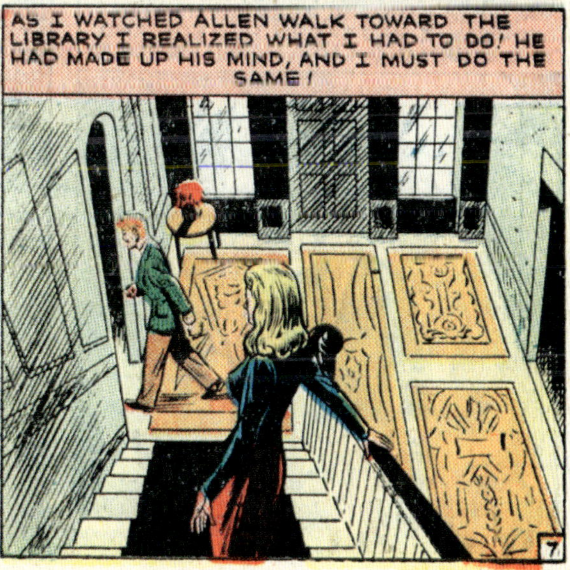
AS I WATCHED ALLEN WALK TOWARD THE LIBRARY I REALIZED WHAT I HAD TO DO! HE HAD MADE UP HIS MIND, AND I MUST DO THE SAME!
7

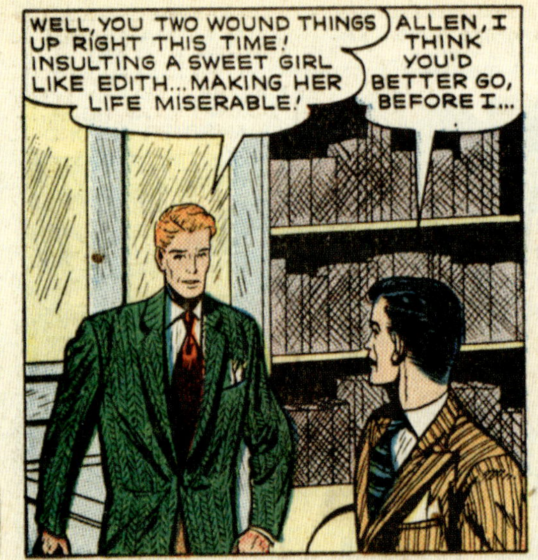
WELL, YOU TWO WOUND THINGS UP RIGHT THIS TIME! INSULTING A SWEET GIRL LIKE EDITH...MAKING HER LIFE MISERABLE!
ALLEN, I THINK YOU'D BETTER GO, BEFORE I...

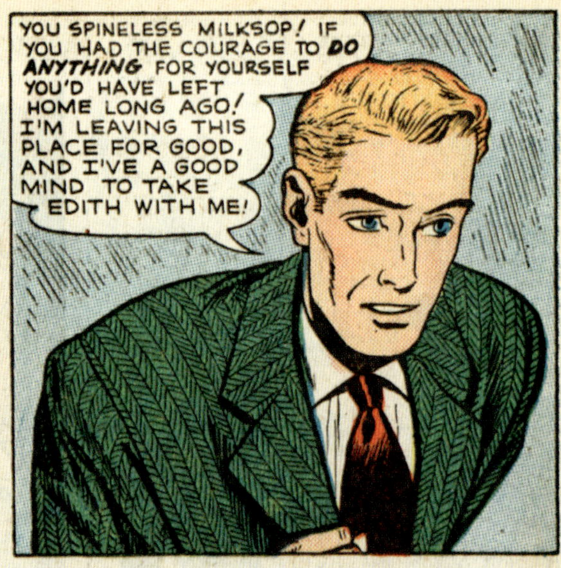
YOU SPINELESS MILKSOP! IF YOU HAD THE COURAGE TO DO ANYTHING FOR YOURSELF YOU'D HAVE LEFT HOME LONG AGO! I'M LEAVING THIS PLACE FOR GOOD, AND I'VE A GOOD MIND TO TAKE EDITH WITH ME!

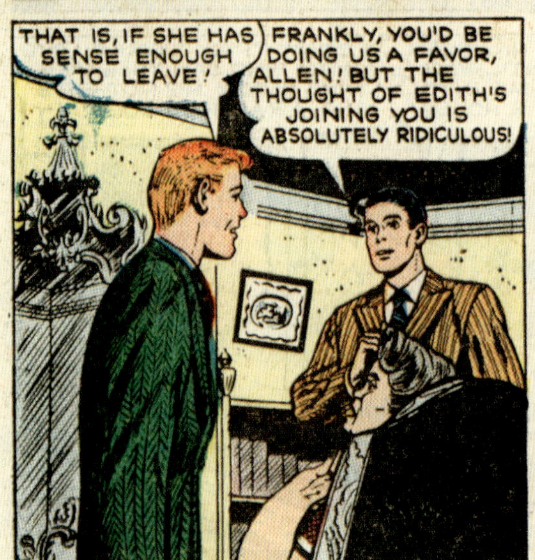
THAT IS, IF SHE HAS SENSE ENOUGH TO LEAVE!
FRANKLY, YOU'D BE DOING US A FAVOR, ALLEN! BUT THE THOUGHT OF EDITH'S JOINING YOU IS ABSOLUTELY RIDICULOUS!

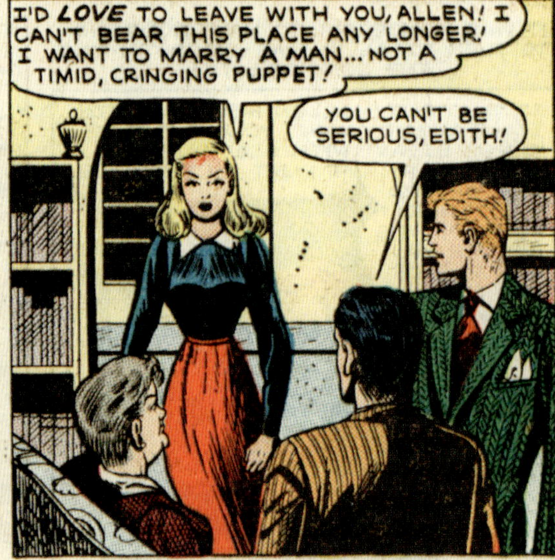
I'D LOVE TO LEAVE WITH YOU, ALLEN! I CAN'T BEAR THIS PLACE ANY LONGER! I WANT TO MARRY A MAN... NOT A TIMID, CRINGING PUPPET!
YOU CAN'T BE SERIOUS, EDITH!

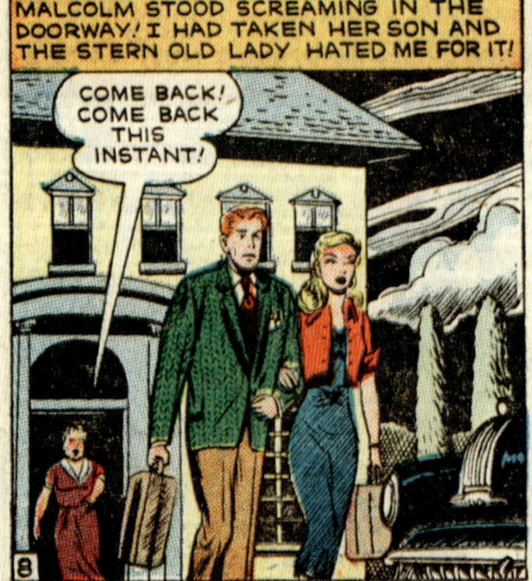
AS WE LEFT THEIR HOME, MOTHER MALCOLM STOOD SCREAMING IN THE DOORWAY! I HAD TAKEN HER SON AND THE STERN OLD LADY HATED ME FOR IT!
COME BACK! COME BACK THIS INSTANT!
8

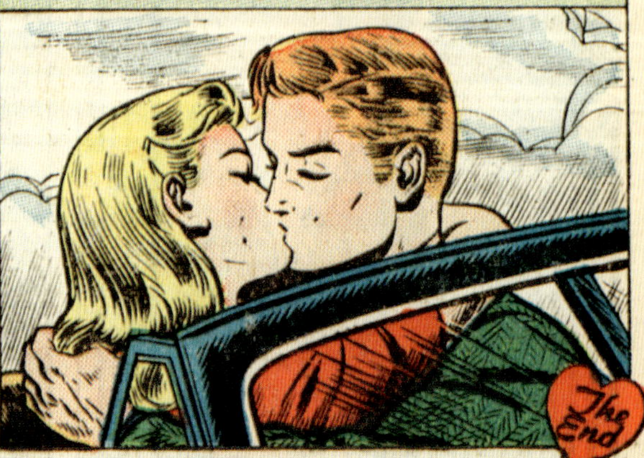
ALONE AT LAST IN THE CAR, WE DROVE TO THE EDGE OF THE ESTATE! THEN, AFTER TAKING A LAST LOOK AT THE PLACE ALLEN HAD CALLED "HOME," HE TURNED AND KISSED ME! I DON'T CARE WHERE THE ROAD LEADS TO NOW... AS LONG AS I BECOME MRS. ALLEN MALCOLM, I KNOW I'LL FIND HAPPINESS WITH MY HUSBAND--THE MAN I LOVE ... THE MAN I CAN RESPECT!
The End

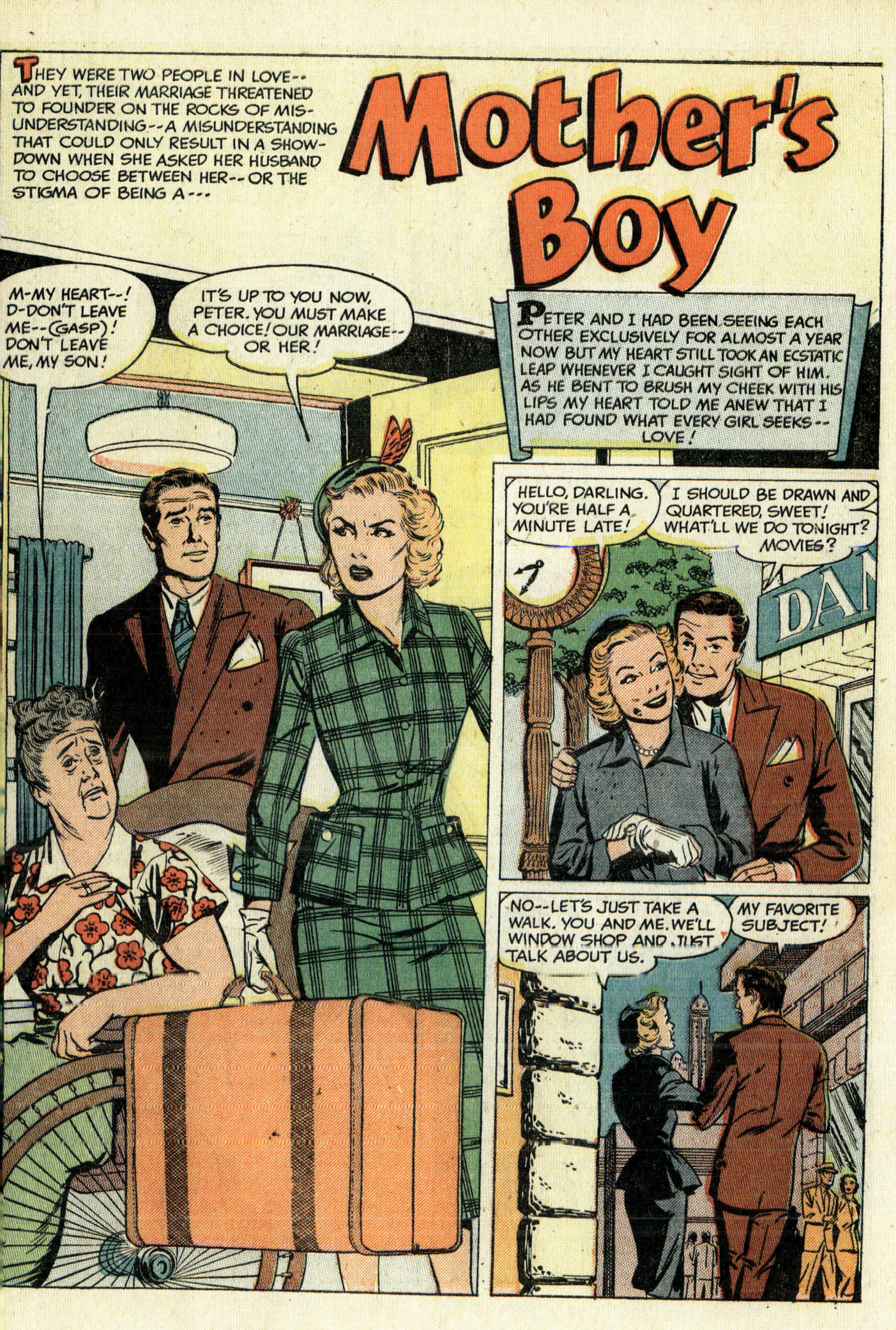

ROMANTIC MARRIAGE
#2, 1950

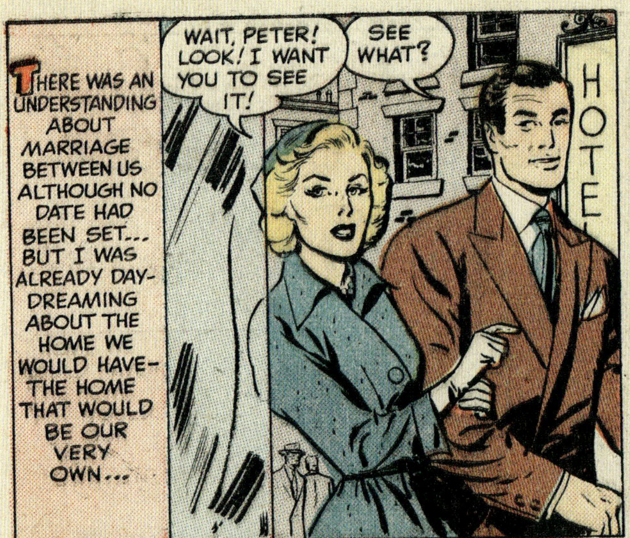
THERE WAS AN UNDERSTANDING ABOUT MARRIAGE BETWEEN US ALTHOUGH NO DATE HAD BEEN SET... BUT I WAS ALREADY DAY-DREAMING ABOUT THE HOME WE WOULD HAVE-THE HOME THAT WOULD BE OUR VERY OWN...
WAIT, PETER! LOOK! I WANT YOU TO SEE IT!
SEE WHAT?
HOTE

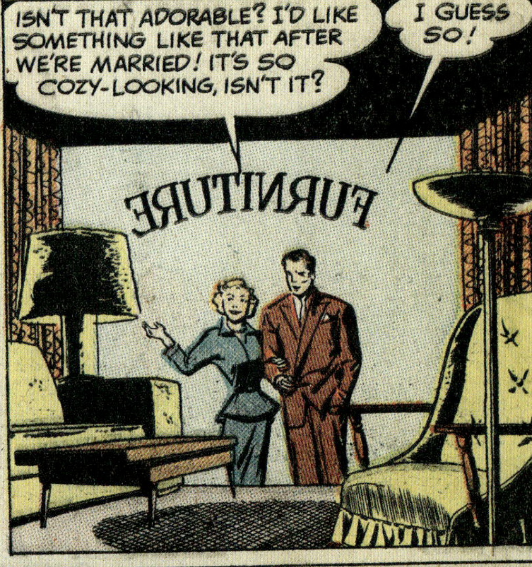
ISN'T THAT ADORABLE? I'D LIKE SOMETHING LIKE THAT AFTER WE'RE MARRIED! IT'S SO COZY-LOOKING, ISN'T IT?
I GUESS SO!
FURNITURE

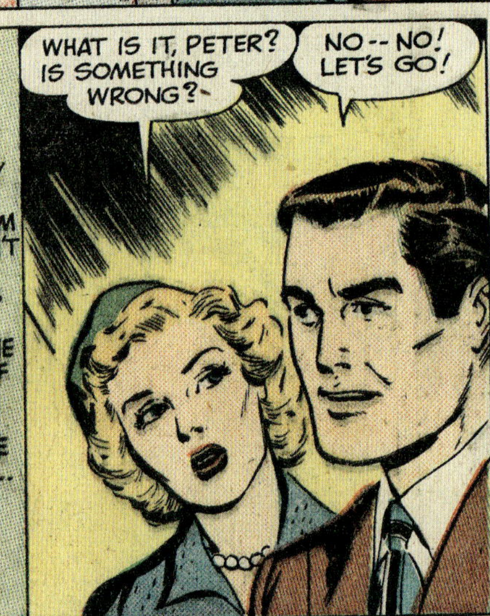
HIS NON-COMMITTAL ANSWER IMMEDIATELY DAMPENED MY ENTHUSIASM AND I COULDN'T HELP RECALL OTHER TIMES WHEN I BROACHED THE SUBJECT OF OUR OWN HOME... OF OUR FUTURE MARRIAGE...
WHAT IS IT, PETER? IS SOMETHING WRONG?
NO--NO! LET'S GO!

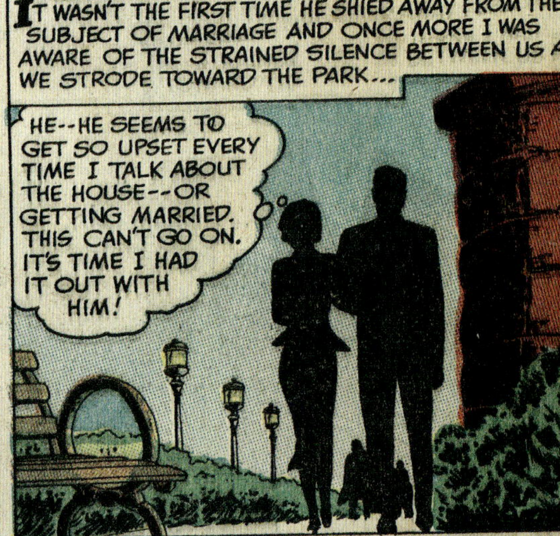
IT WASN'T THE FIRST TIME HE SHIED AWAY FROM THE SUBJECT OF MARRIAGE AND ONCE MORE I WAS AWARE OF THE STRAINED SILENCE BETWEEN US AS WE STRODE TOWARD THE PARK...
HE--HE SEEMS TO GET SO UPSET EVERY TIME I TALK ABOUT THE HOUSE--OR GETTING MARRIED. THIS CAN'T GO ON. IT'S TIME I HAD IT OUT WITH HIM!

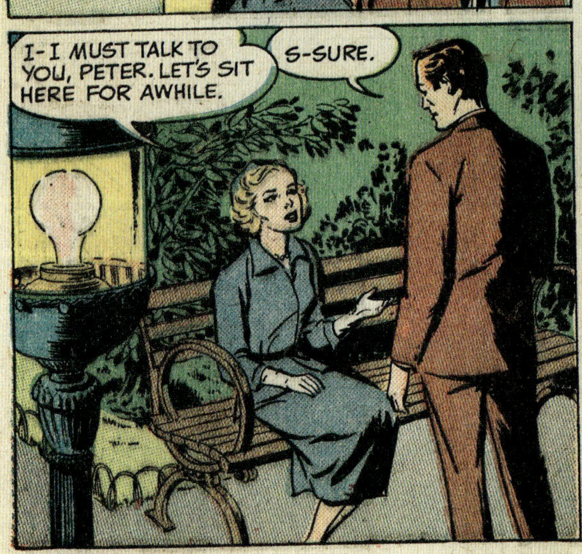
I-I MUST TALK TO YOU, PETER. LET'S SIT HERE FOR AWHILE.
S-SURE.

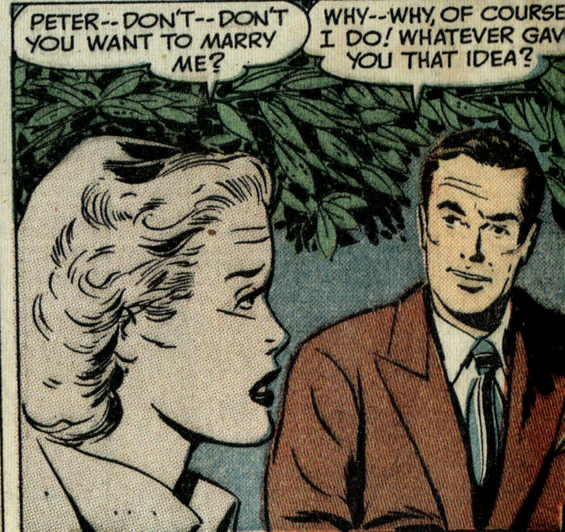
PETER--DON'T--DON'T YOU WANT TO MARRY ME?
WHY--WHY, OF COURSE I DO! WHATEVER GAV YOU THAT IDEA?

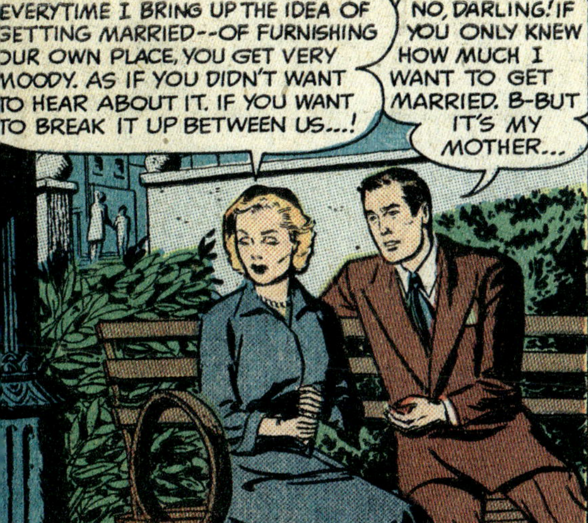

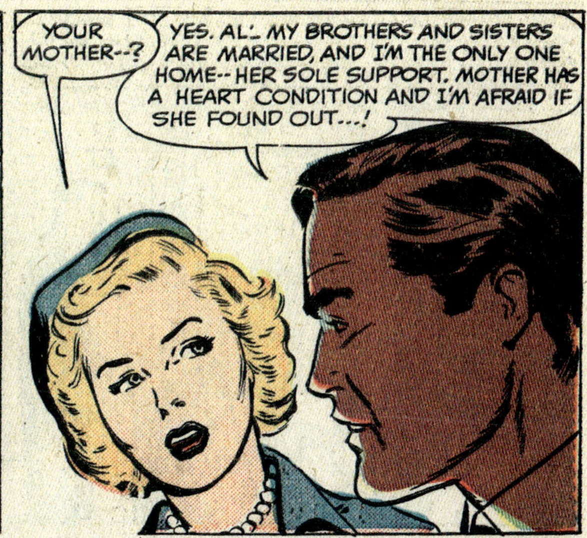

HIS FACE SUDDENLY BECAME STRAINED AND DISTRAUGHT AND I SENSED HIS DIFFICULTY IN WRESTLING WITH THE DILEMMA. HE WAS SADDLED WITH. MY HEART WENT OUT TO HIM IN SYMPATHY AS PUT A CONSOLING HAND ON HIS ARM...

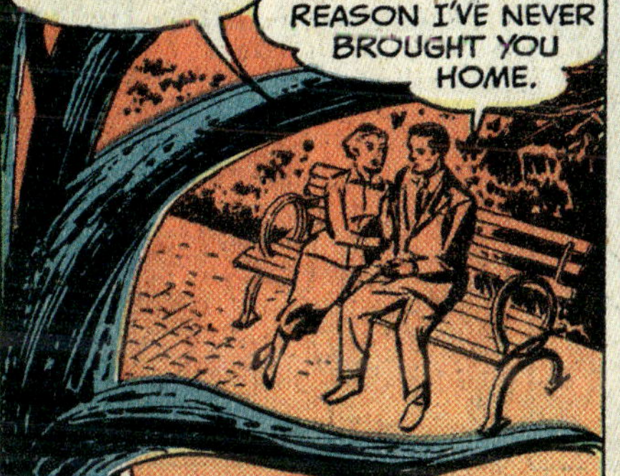

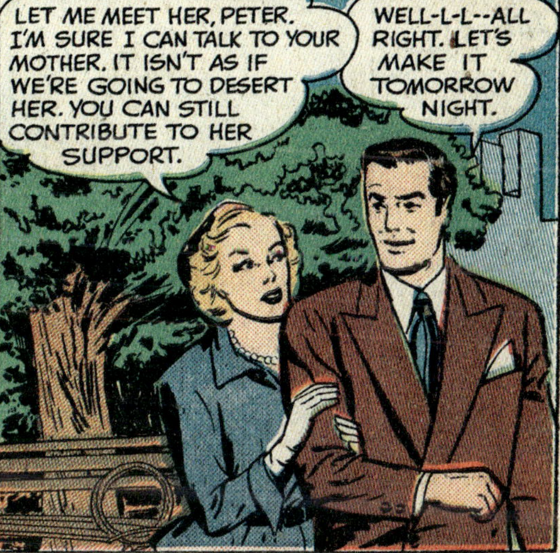

I WENT TO PETER'S HOME THE FOLLOWING DAY, AND AS SOON AS I MET HIS MOTHER, I SENSED HER HOSTILITY TO ME. SHE MADE ME FEEL AS IF I WERE AN INTRUDER IN HER HOME WHILE PETER NERVOUSLY HOVERED OVER US...

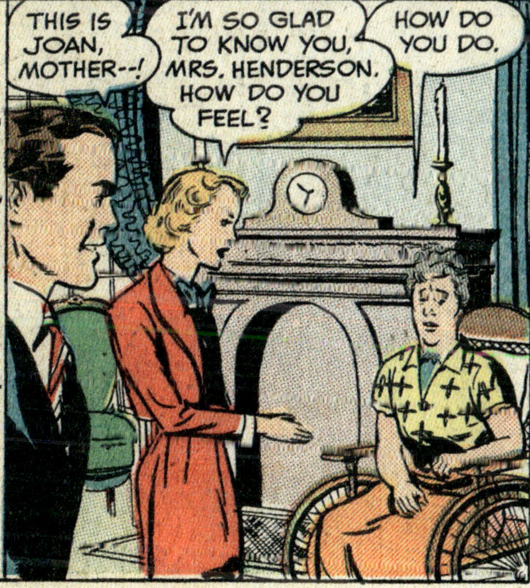

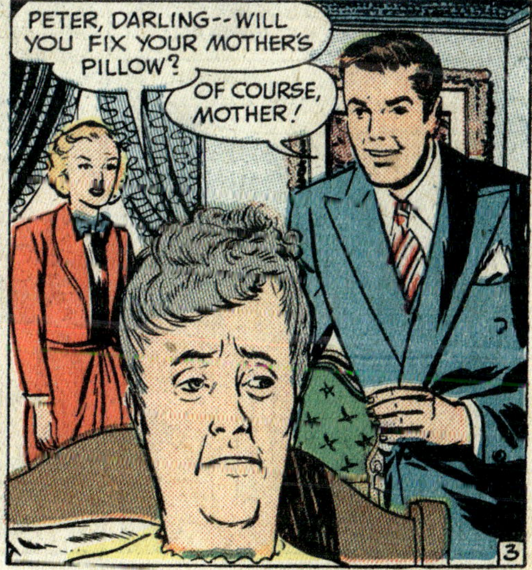

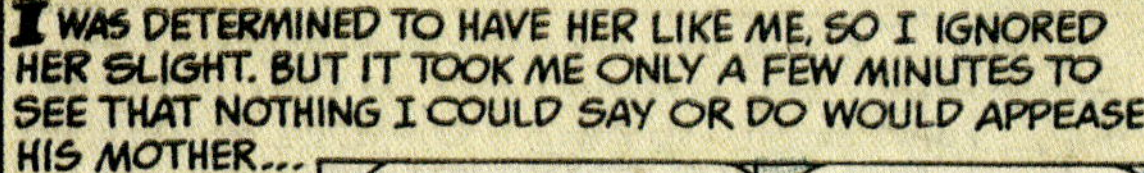

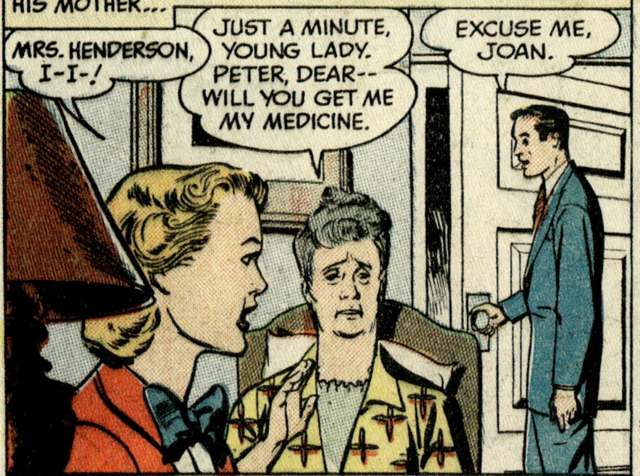

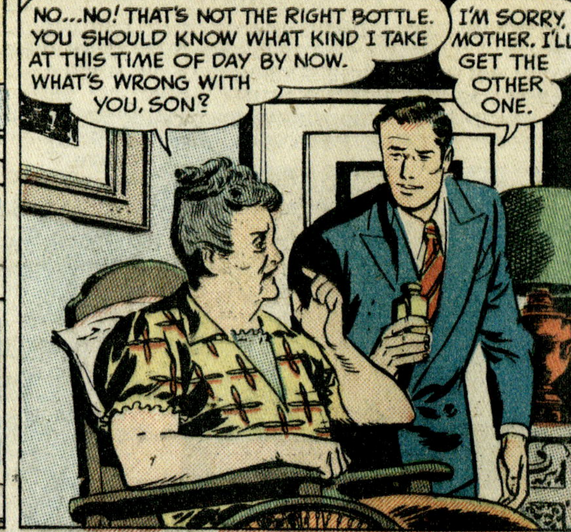

AND SO IT WENT THROUGHOUT THE EVENING. THE WOMAN WAS A TYRANT, DEMANDING AND PLEADING IN TURN. I BEGAN TO SENSE THAT SHE WAS USING HER ILLNESS AS A PROP TO HOLD PETER IN LINE. EVERYTIME I STARTED TO BRING UP THE RELATIONSHIP BETWEEN PETER AND MYSELF, SHE CURTLY CUT ME SHORT...

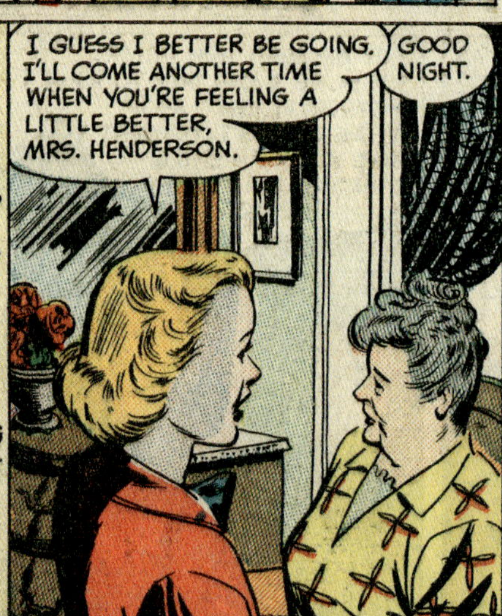

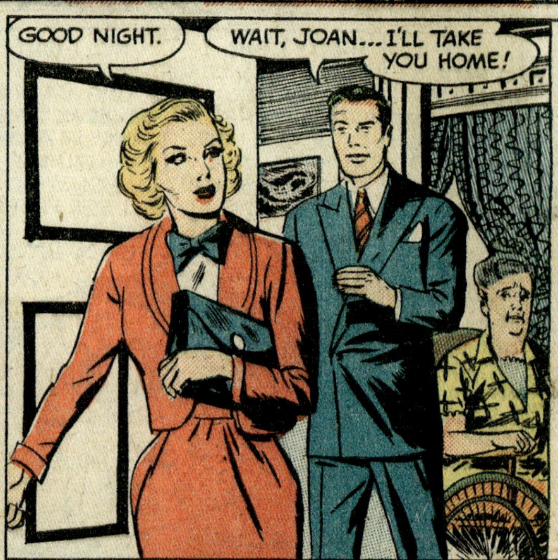

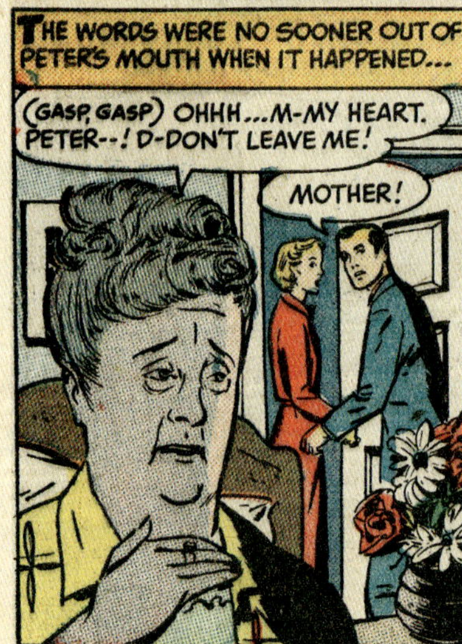

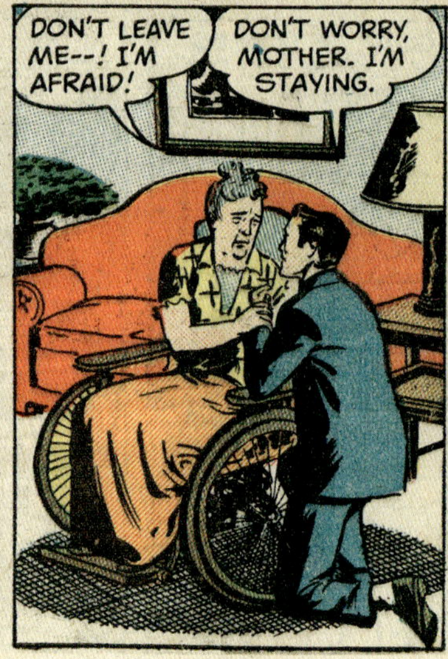

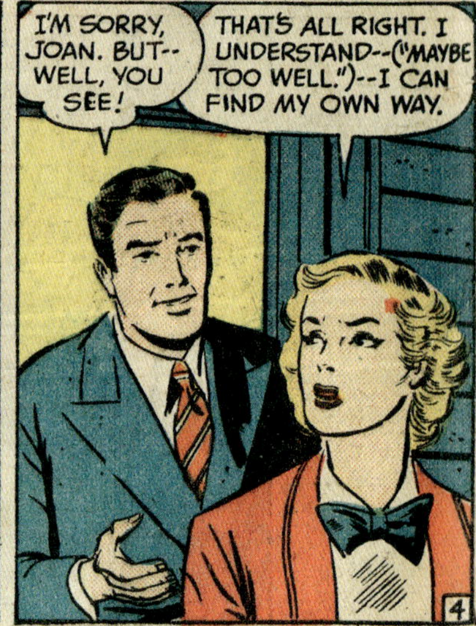

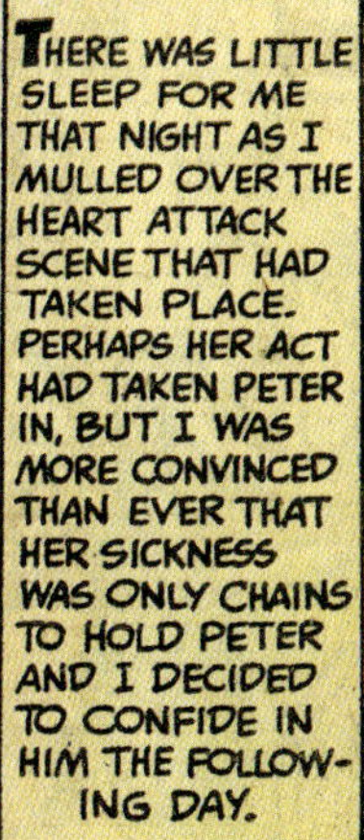

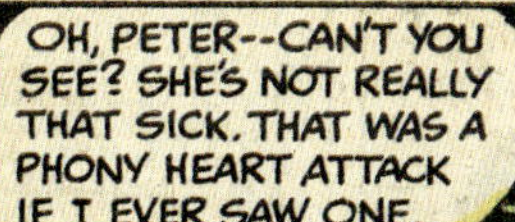

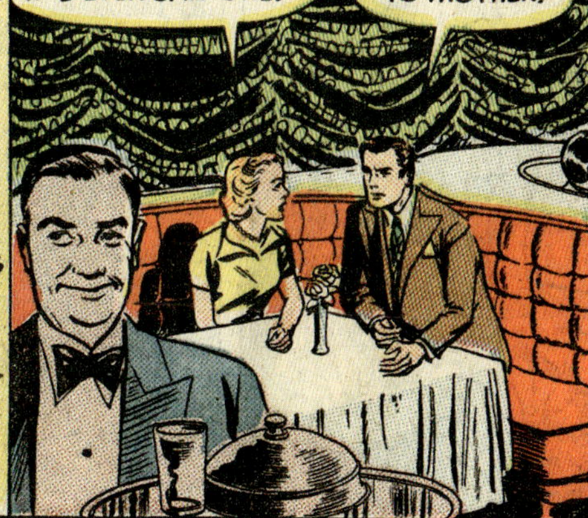

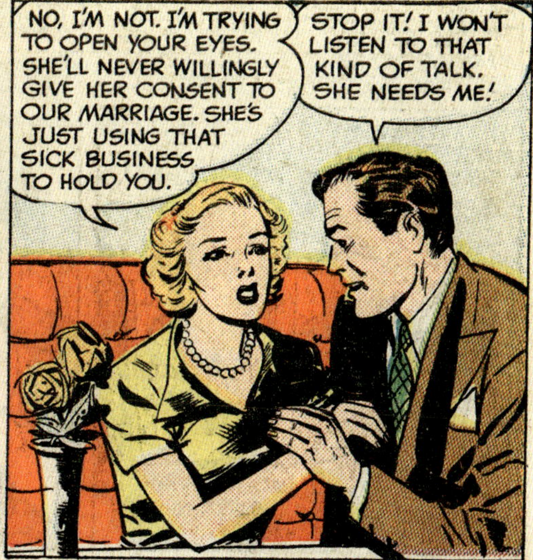

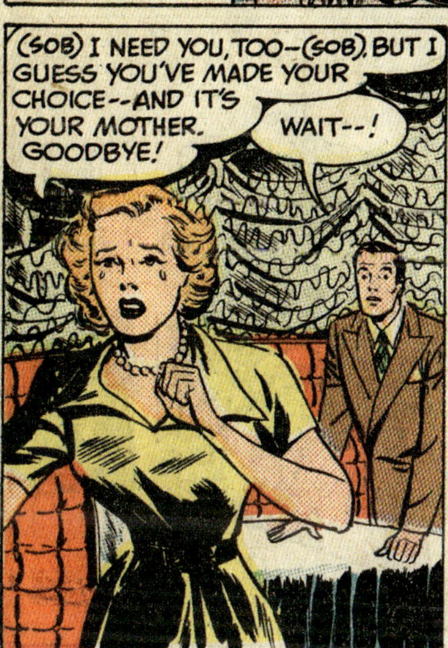

THERE WAS NO WORD FROM PETER THE NEXT FEW DAYS AND NOT EVEN THE TEARS OF HEART-BREAK COULD EASE THE DISMAL LONELY HOURS. THEN--WHEN IT SEEMED AS IF THERE WERE NO MORE TEARS TO SHED--- WHEN IT SEEMED AS IF THE HOLLOW ACHE IN MY HEART WAS NO LONGER ENDURABLE...

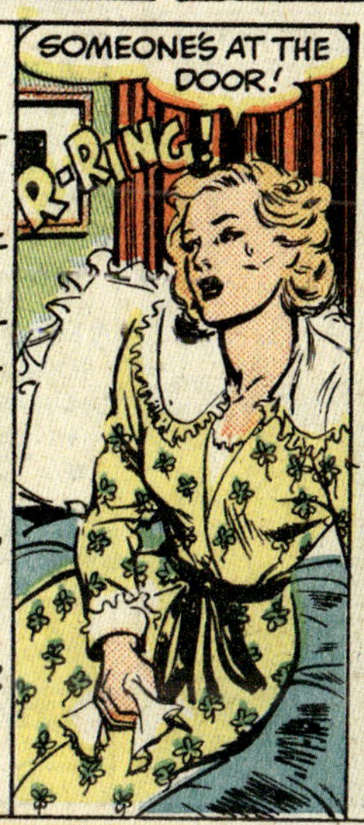

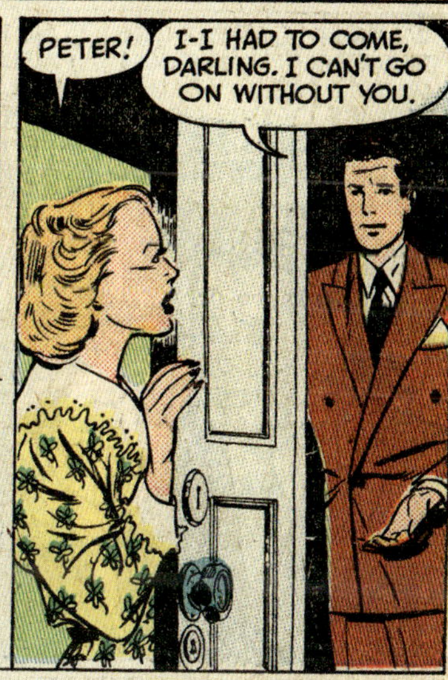

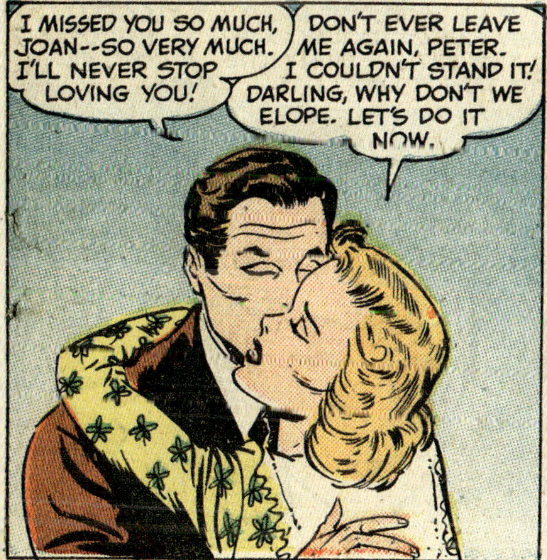

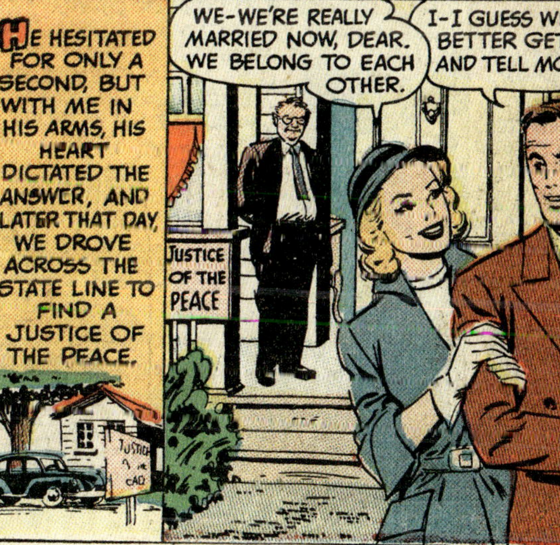

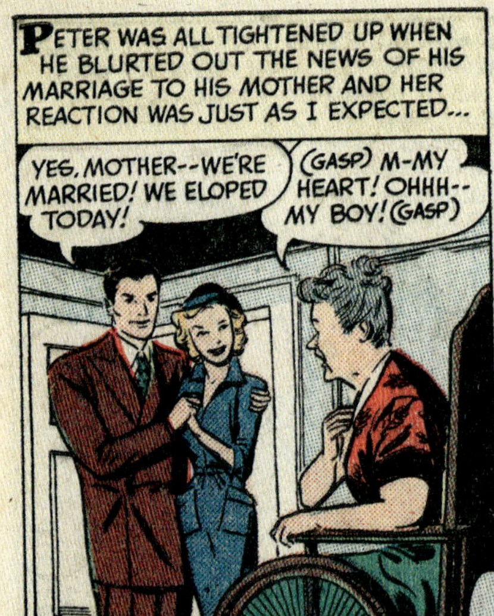

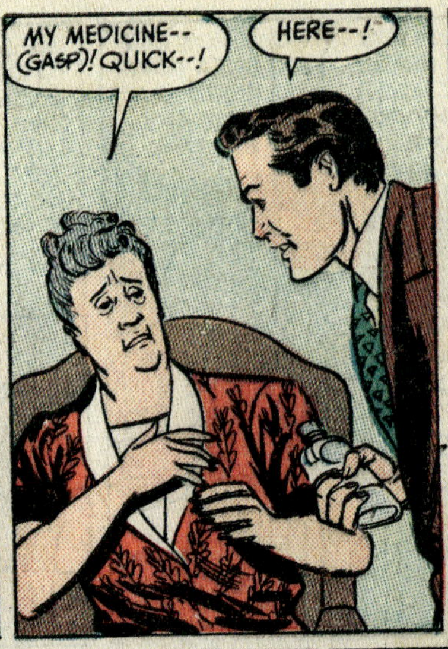

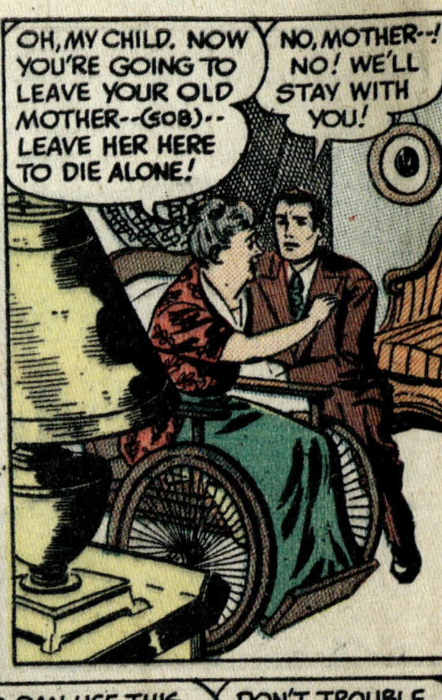

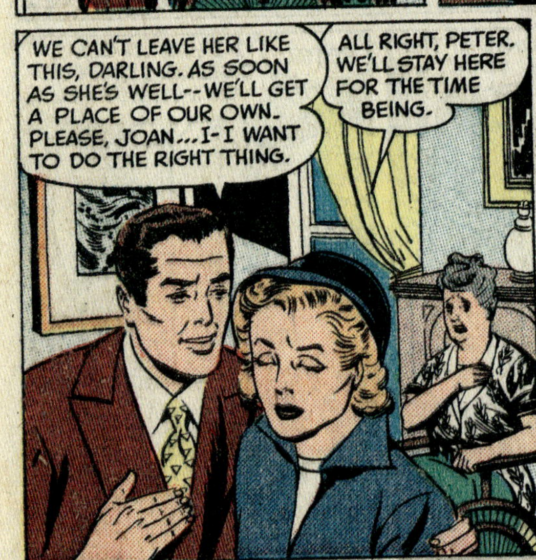

BUT ALMOST IMMEDIATELY, I HAD CAUSE TO REGRET MY DECISION, FROM THE VERY BEGINNING, HIS MOTHER STARTED OUT TO IMPRESS UPON ME WHOSE HOUSE I WAS TO LIVE IN...

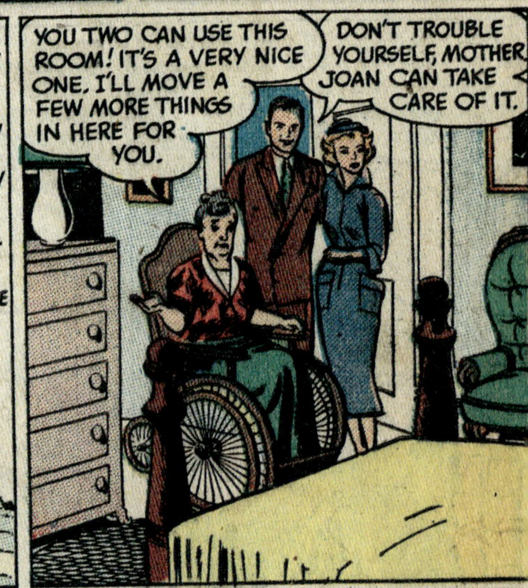

AFTER THAT, LIFE BECAME A TORMENT FOR ME. PETER'S MOTHER SEEMED QUITE VIGOROUS AND WELL WHEN PETER WASN'T IN THE HOUSE. BUT HE NO SOONER CAME THROUGH THE DOOR WHEN SHE STARTED HER WHINING SICK ACT...

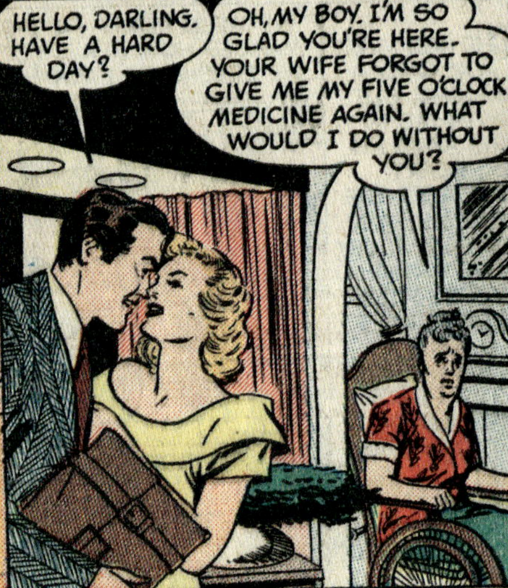

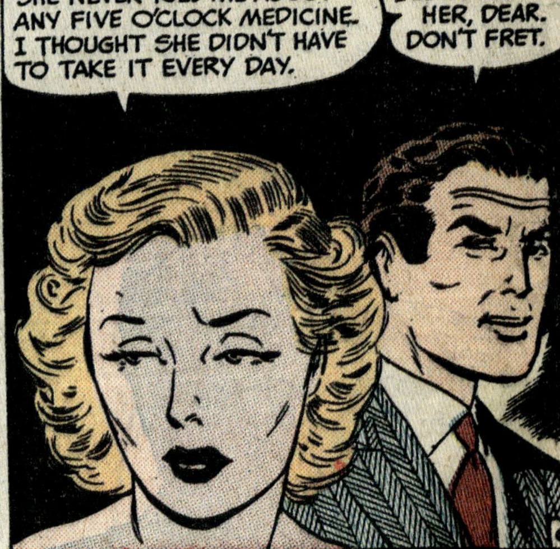

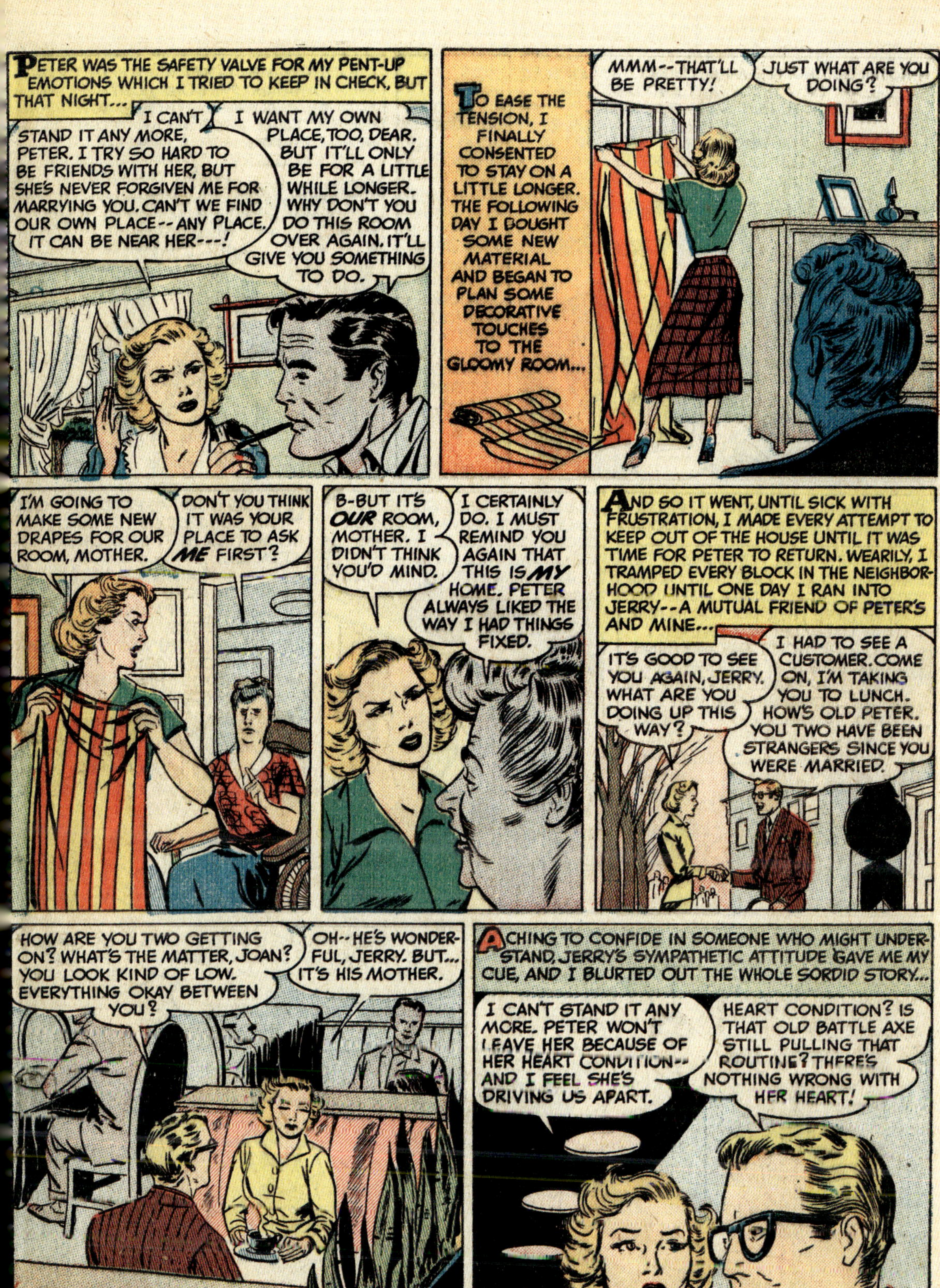
PETER WAS THE SAFETY VALVE FOR MY PENT-UP EMOTIONS WHICH I TRIED TO KEEP IN CHECK, BUT THAT NIGHT...
I CAN'T STAND IT ANY MORE, PETER. I TRY SO HARD TO BE FRIENDS WITH HER, BUT SHE'S NEVER FORGIVEN ME FOR MARRYING YOU. CAN'T WE FIND OUR OWN PLACE--ANY PLACE. IT CAN BE NEAR HER---!
I WANT MY OWN PLACE, TOO, DEAR. BUT IT'LL ONLY BE FOR A LITTLE WHILE LONGER. WHY DON'T YOU DO THIS ROOM OVER AGAIN. IT'LL GIVE YOU SOMETHING TO DO.
TO EASE THE TENSION, I FINALLY CONSENTED TO STAY ON A LITTLE LONGER. THE FOLLOWING DAY I BOUGHT SOME NEW MATERIAL AND BEGAN TO PLAN SOME DECORATIVE TOUCHES TO THE GLOOMY ROOM...
MMM--THAT'LL BE PRETTY!
JUST WHAT ARE YOU DOING?
I'M GOING TO MAKE SOME NEW DRAPES FOR OUR ROOM, MOTHER.
DON'T YOU THINK IT WAS YOUR PLACE TO ASK ME FIRST?
B-BUT IT'S OUR ROOM, MOTHER. I DIDN'T THINK YOU'D MIND.
I CERTAINLY DO. I MUST REMIND YOU AGAIN THAT THIS IS MY HOME. PETER ALWAYS LIKED THE WAY I HAD THINGS FIXED.
AND SO IT WENT, UNTIL SICK WITH FRUSTRATION, I MADE EVERY ATTEMPT TO KEEP OUT OF THE HOUSE UNTIL IT WAS TIME FOR PETER TO RETURN. WEARILY, I TRAMPED EVERY BLOCK IN THE NEIGHBORHOOD UNTIL ONE DAY I RAN INTO JERRY--A MUTUAL FRIEND OF PETER'S AND MINE...
IT'S GOOD TO SEE YOU AGAIN, JERRY. WHAT ARE YOU DOING UP THIS WAY?
I HAD TO SEE A CUSTOMER. COME ON, I'M TAKING YOU TO LUNCH. HOW'S OLD PETER. YOU TWO HAVE BEEN STRANGERS SINCE YOU WERE MARRIED.
HOW ARE YOU TWO GETTING ON? WHAT'S THE MATTER, JOAN? YOU LOOK KIND OF LOW. EVERYTHING OKAY BETWEEN YOU?
OH--HE'S WONDERFUL, JERRY. BUT... IT'S HIS MOTHER.
ACHING TO CONFIDE IN SOMEONE WHO MIGHT UNDERSTAND, JERRY'S SYMPATHETIC ATTITUDE GAVE ME MY CUE, AND I BLURTED OUT THE WHOLE SORDID STORY...
I CAN'T STAND IT ANY MORE. PETER WON'T LEAVE HER BECAUSE OF HER HEART CONDITION--AND I FEEL SHE'S DRIVING US APART.
HEART CONDITION? IS THAT OLD BATTLE AXE STILL PULLING THAT ROUTINE? THERE'S NOTHING WRONG WITH HER HEART!
7

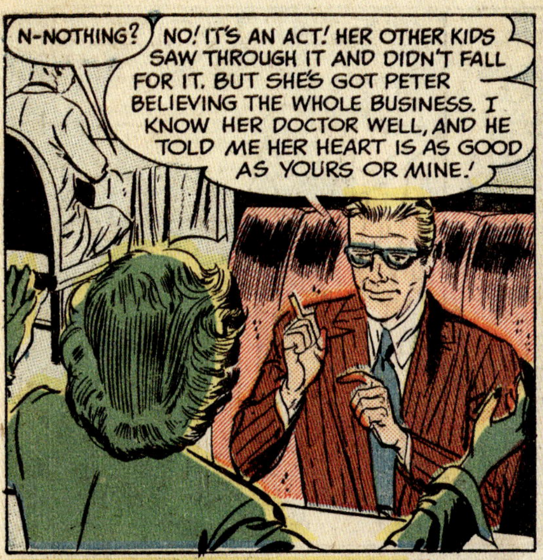

MY LONG DORMANT SUSPICIONS WERE FINALLY CONFIRMED. ALL THESE YEARS SHE HAD BEEN HOLDING PETER IN BONDAGE WITH HER SIMULATED ILLNESS FOR FEAR OF LOSING HIM...

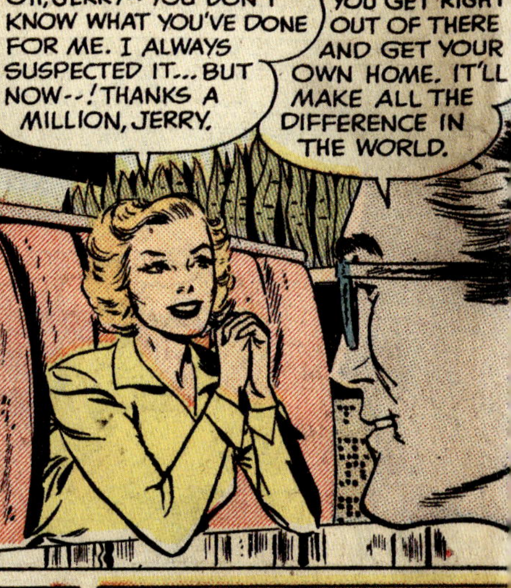

THAT EVENING, I CONFIDED IN PETER WHAT I HAD LEARNED FROM JERRY...

NO--YOU'RE WRONG. JERRY'S WRONG, TOO--SHE WOULDN'T DO A THING LIKE THAT!

LET'S PROVE IT... ONE WAY OR THE OTHER. WE'LL CALL HER DOCTOR IN AND LET HIM TELL US. I WON'T SAY ANYTHING ELSE IF HE SAYS SHE HAS A BAD HEART. THERE MUST BE SOME REASON WHY SHE ALWAYS HAS THE DOCTOR WHEN SHE'S ALONE.

ALL RIGHT, JOAN. I GUESS IT'S ONLY FAIR TO HAVE THE DOCTOR DECIDE. I'LL TELL MOTHER AND WE'LL SCHEDULE AN APPOINTMENT.

GOOD...!

BUT AS SOON AS PETER BROACHED THE SUBJECT OF THE DOCTOR, HIS MOTHER WENT INTO ONE OF HER ATTACKS...

A DOCTOR. (GASP)! OH, NO--! I COULDN'T! (GASP) YOU KNOW HOW THEY UPSET ME! (SOB) TO THINK MY OWN SON WOULD DOUBT HIS MOTHER (GASP)!

ALL RIGHT, MOTHER--WE WON'T HAVE HIM IF YOU FEEL SO STRONGLY ABOUT IT.

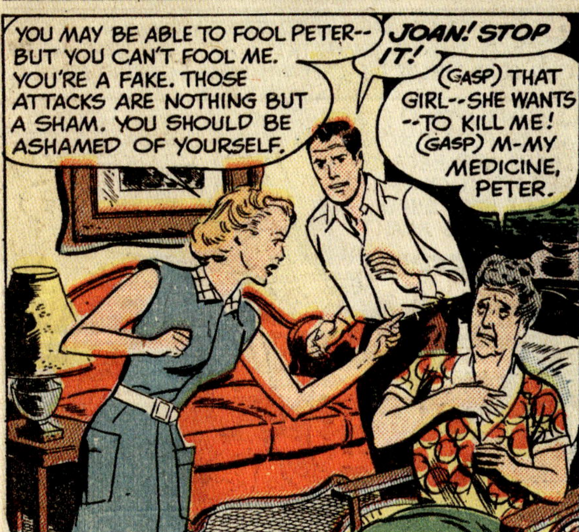

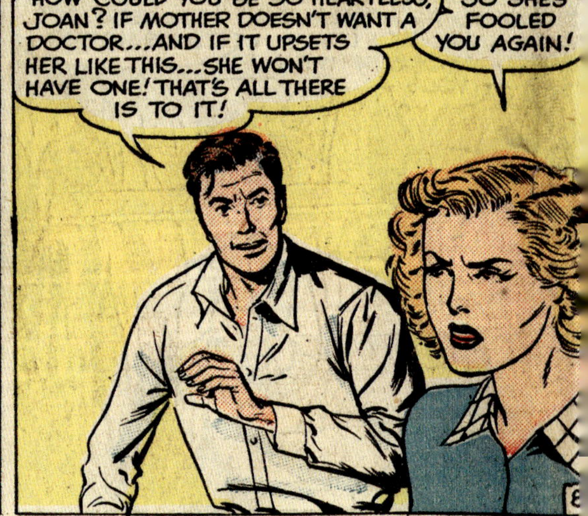

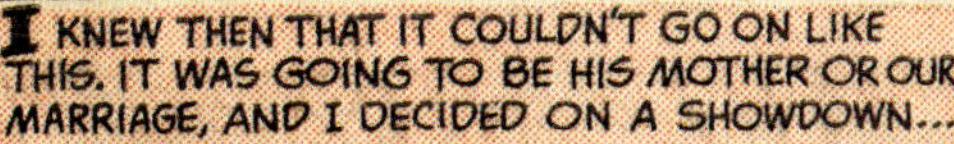
I KNEW THEN THAT IT COULDN'T GO ON LIKE THIS. IT WAS GOING TO BE HIS MOTHER OR OUR MARRIAGE, AND I DECIDED ON A SHOWDOWN...

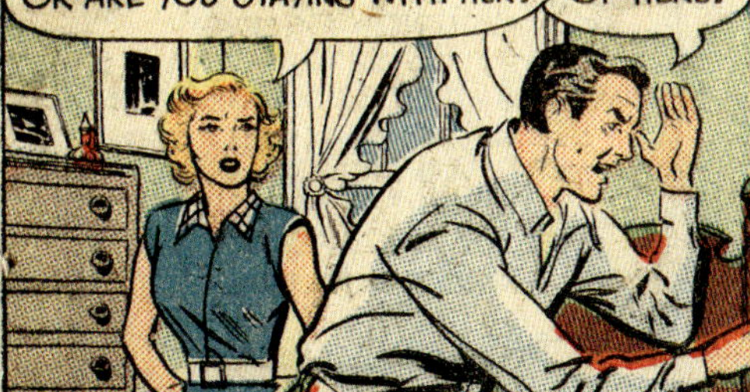
ONCE BEFORE I ASKED YOU TO MAKE A CHOICE, PETER. I'M ASKING YOU AGAIN. YOUR MOTHER'S POSSESSIVENESS IS KILLING OUR MARRIAGE-- KILLING OUR LOVE. I'M NOT STAYING HERE ANOTHER NIGHT. ARE YOU COMING WITH ME-- OR ARE YOU STAYING WITH HER?
I CAN'T TAKE ANY MORE OF THIS QUARRELLING! LET ME OUT OF HERE.
THE SLAMMING OF THE DOOR BEHIND HIM SOUNDED LIKE THE DEATH KNELL TO MY MARRIAGE, AND FIGHTING TO CHOKE BACK MY TEARS, I BEGAN TO PACK. HIS MOTHER HAD WON. WHEN I LOOKED UP AND SAW HER STANDING IN THE DOORWAY GLOATING, I WASN'T TOO SURPRISED...

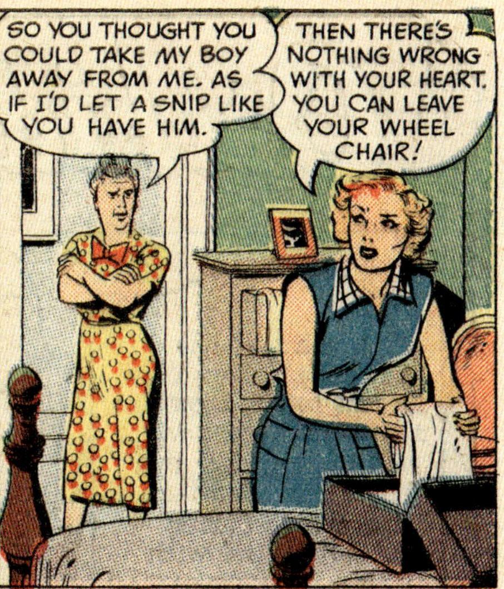
SO YOU THOUGHT YOU COULD TAKE MY BOY AWAY FROM ME. AS IF I'D LET A SNIP LIKE YOU HAVE HIM.
THEN THERE'S NOTHING WRONG WITH YOUR HEART. YOU CAN LEAVE YOUR WHEEL CHAIR!

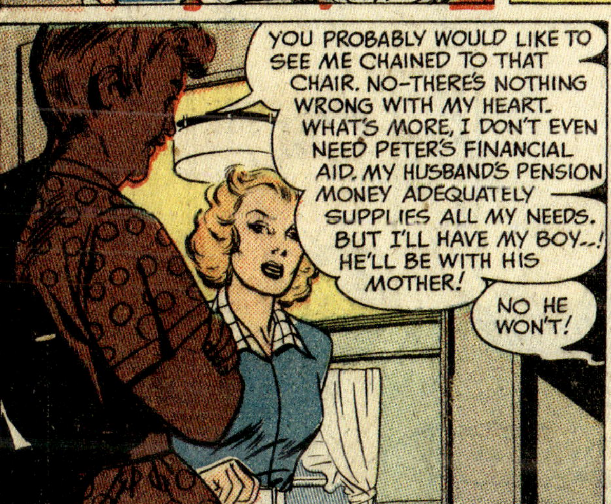
YOU PROBABLY WOULD LIKE TO SEE ME CHAINED TO THAT CHAIR. NO-THERE'S NOTHING WRONG WITH MY HEART. WHAT'S MORE, I DON'T EVEN NEED PETER'S FINANCIAL AID. MY HUSBAND'S PENSION MONEY ADEQUATELY SUPPLIES ALL MY NEEDS. BUT I'LL HAVE MY BOY--! HE'LL BE WITH HIS MOTHER!
NO HE WON'T!

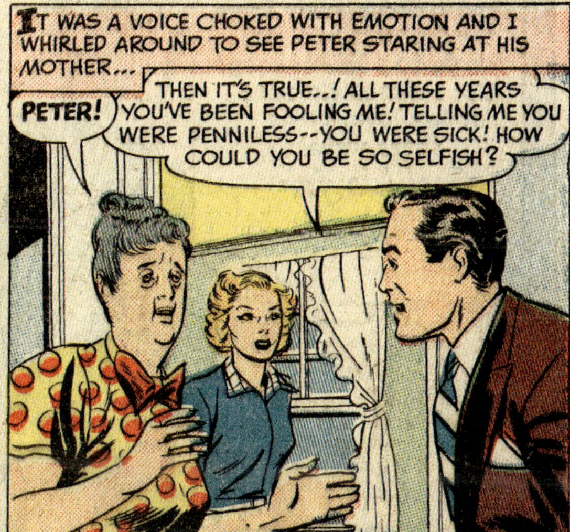
IT WAS A VOICE CHOKED WITH EMOTION AND I WHIRLED AROUND TO SEE PETER STARING AT HIS MOTHER...
PETER!
THEN IT'S TRUE--! ALL THESE YEARS YOU'VE BEEN FOOLING ME! TELLING ME YOU WERE PENNILESS--YOU WERE SICK! HOW COULD YOU BE SO SELFISH?

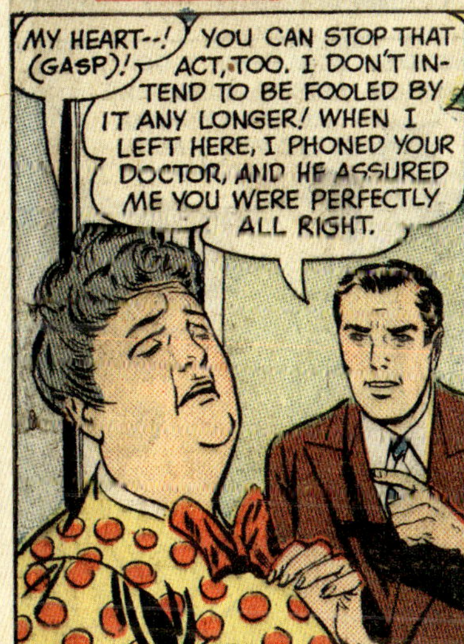
MY HEART--! (GASP)!
YOU CAN STOP THAT ACT, TOO. I DON'T INTEND TO BE FOOLED BY IT ANY LONGER! WHEN I LEFT HERE, I PHONED YOUR DOCTOR, AND HE ASSURED ME YOU WERE PERFECTLY ALL RIGHT.

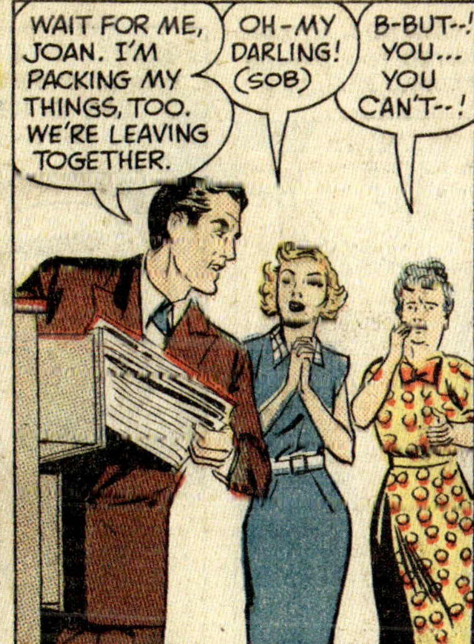
WAIT FOR ME, JOAN. I'M PACKING MY THINGS, TOO. WE'RE LEAVING TOGETHER.
OH-MY DARLING! (SOB)
B-BUT--! YOU... YOU CAN'T--!

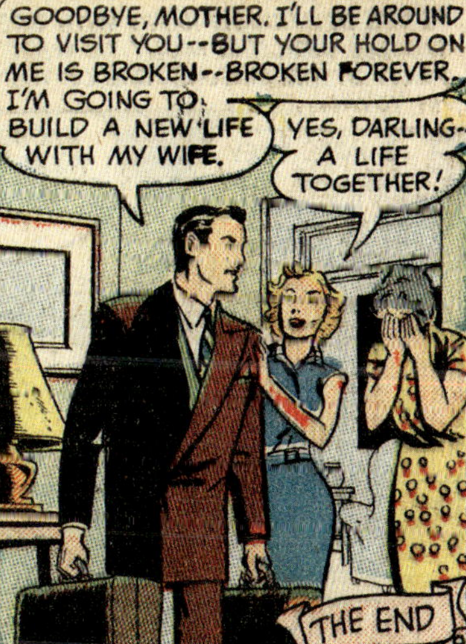
GOODBYE, MOTHER. I'LL BE AROUND TO VISIT YOU--BUT YOUR HOLD ON ME IS BROKEN--BROKEN FOREVER. I'M GOING TO BUILD A NEW LIFE WITH MY WIFE.
YES, DARLING-- A LIFE TOGETHER!
THE END
9

LOVE ITSELF WASN'T ENOUGH FOR ME! AS SOON AS GARY RUSSELL AND I, JILL SAGER, HAD SET OUR WEDDING DATE, I PLUNGED INTO AN EXCITING PROGRAM OF SHALLOW ACTIVITIES THAT LEFT ME NO TIME OR ENERGY TO SATISFY THE HUNGER OF GARY'S LIPS! THEN I LEARNED THAT A MAN CRAVES MORE FROM THE WOMAN HE IS GOING TO MARRY... MORE THAN I WAS WILLING TO GIVE! FOR TO ME,

KISSES came SECOND

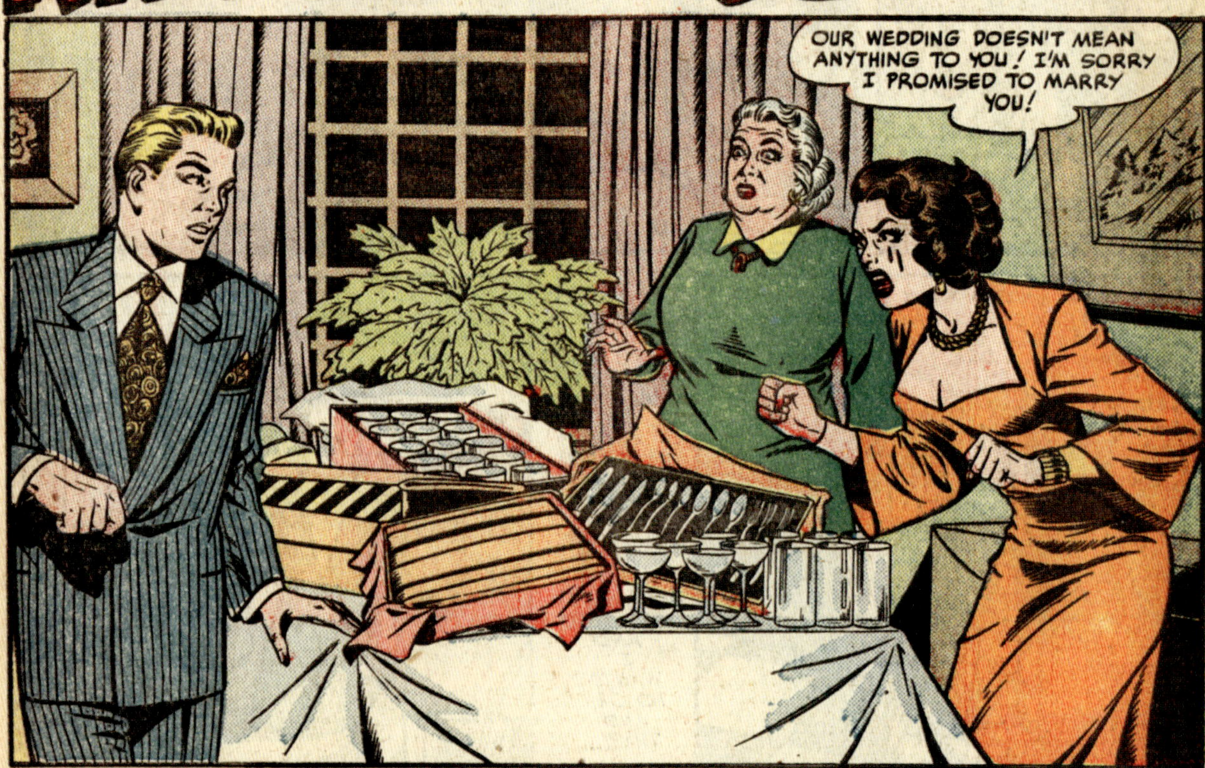

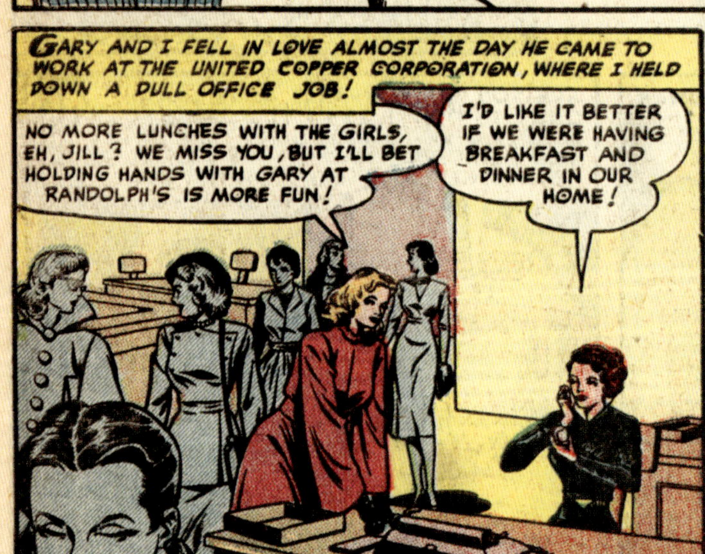

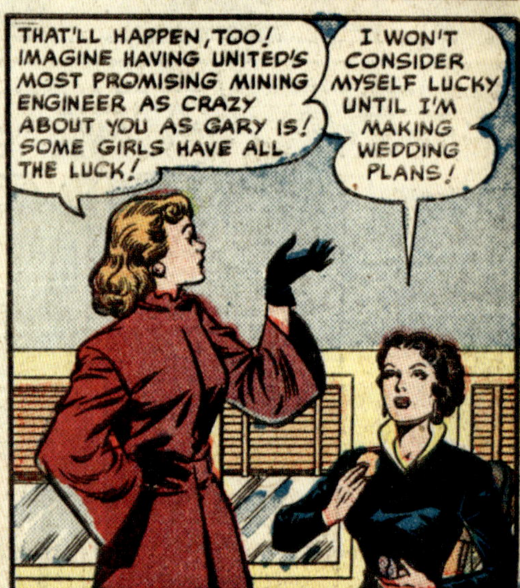

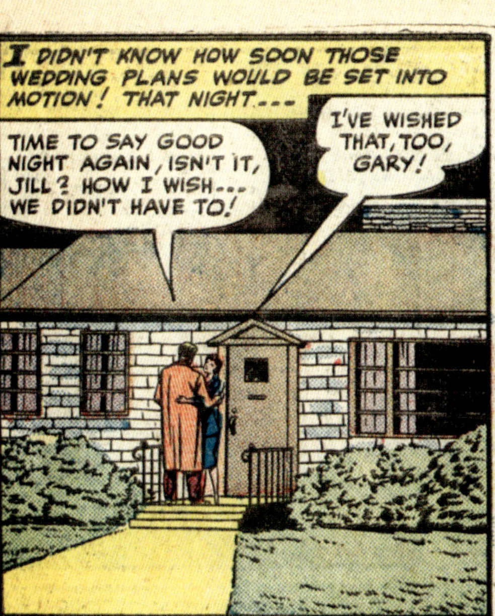

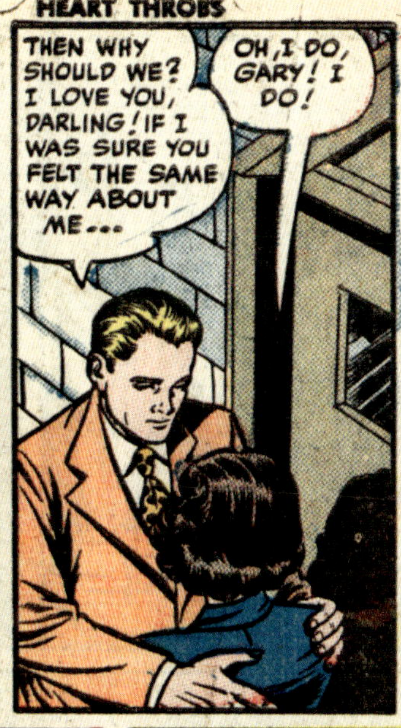

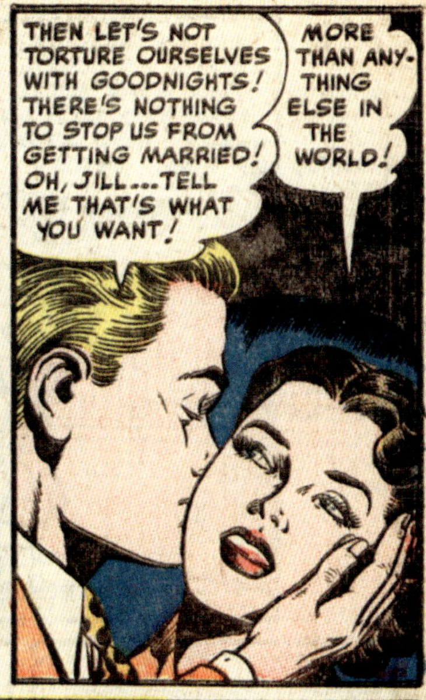

That SEALED AN UNSPOKEN PROMISE! BUT EVEN AS I FELT THE PASSIONATE TREMOR OF HIS LIPS ON MINE, I STARTED WEAVING THE THE WEB THAT WAS TO TRAP US BOTH!

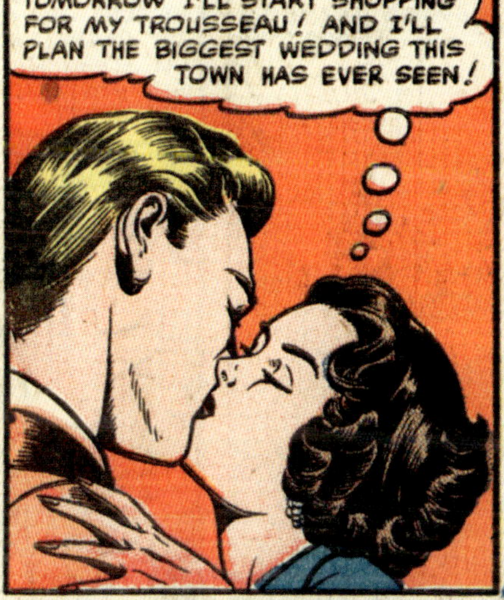

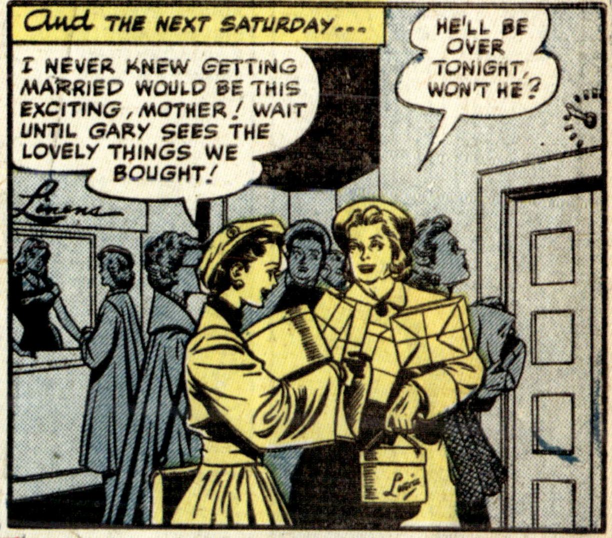

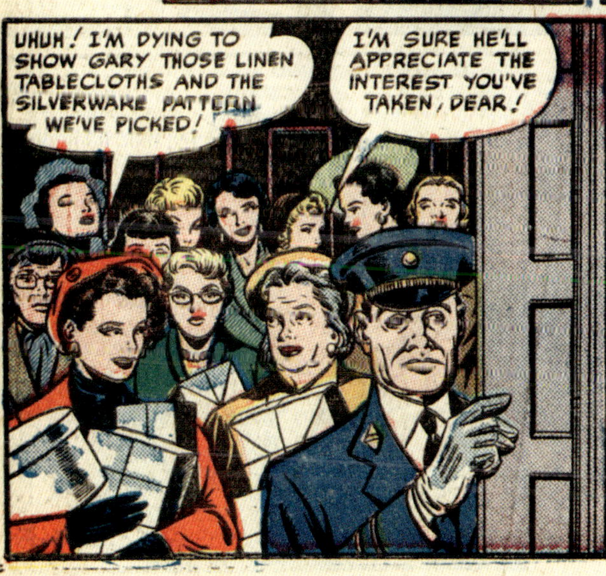

How COULD I HAVE BEEN SO BLIND? THAT WAS WHAT MARRIAGE MEANT TO ME...A CHANCE TO PLAY HOUSE, TO ACCUMULATE MATERIAL THINGS THAT WOULD IMPRESS MY FRIENDS AND PLEASE MY VANITY!

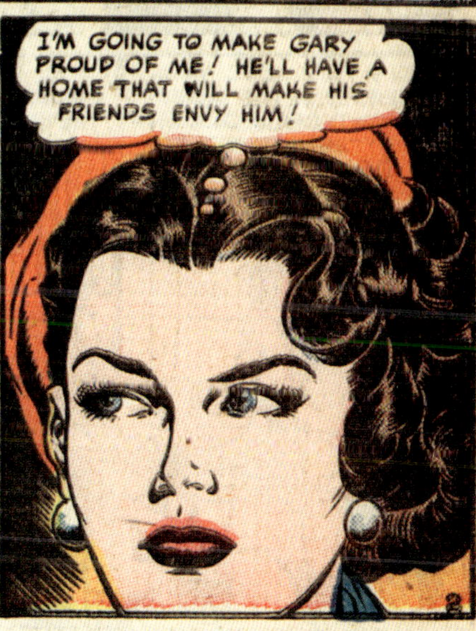

HEART THROBS
#11, June 1952

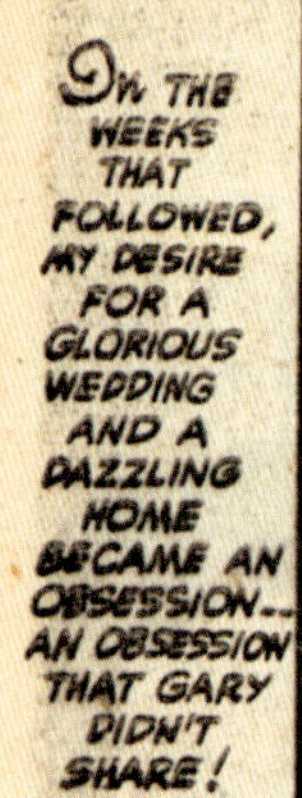
In the weeks that followed, my desire for a glorious wedding and a dazzling home became an obsession... an obsession that Gary didn't share!

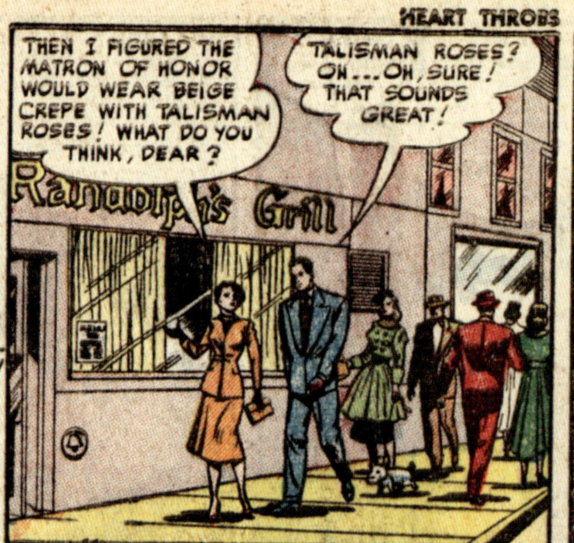
THEN I FIGURED THE MATRON OF HONOR WOULD WEAR BEIGE CREPE WITH TALISMAN ROSES! WHAT DO YOU THINK, DEAR?
TALISMAN ROSES? OH... OH, SURE! THAT SOUNDS GREAT!

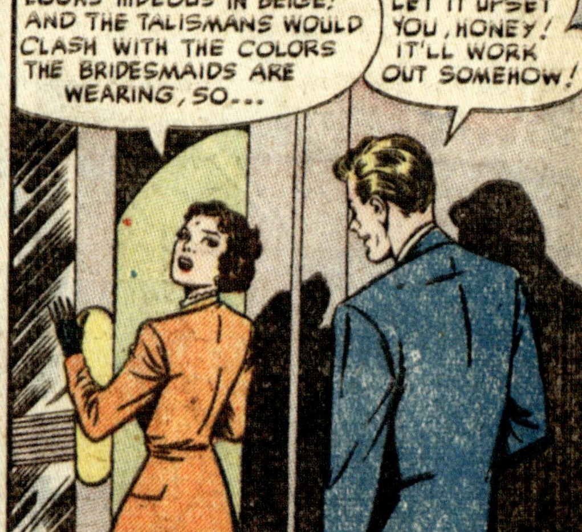
BUT DOROTHY SAYS SHE LOOKS HIDEOUS IN BEIGE! AND THE TALISMANS WOULD CLASH WITH THE COLORS THE BRIDESMAIDS ARE WEARING, SO...
WELL, DON'T LET IT UPSET YOU, HONEY! IT'LL WORK OUT SOMEHOW!

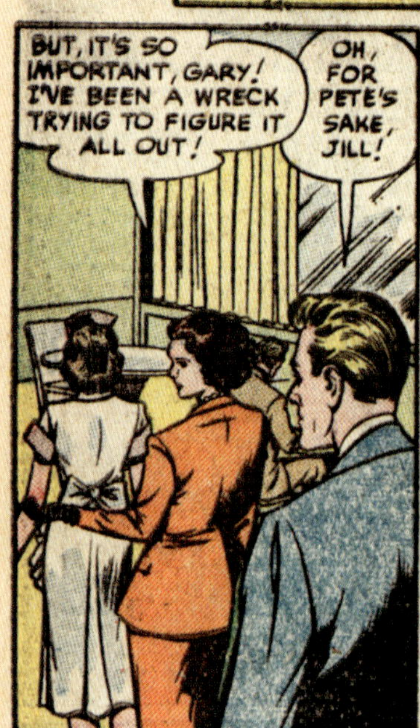
BUT, IT'S SO IMPORTANT, GARY! I'VE BEEN A WRECK TRYING TO FIGURE IT ALL OUT!
OH, FOR PETE'S SAKE, JILL!

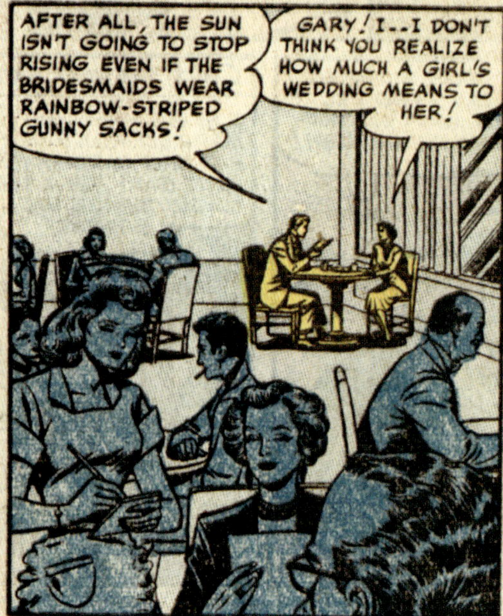
AFTER ALL, THE SUN ISN'T GOING TO STOP RISING EVEN IF THE BRIDESMAIDS WEAR RAINBOW-STRIPED GUNNY SACKS!
GARY! I--I DON'T THINK YOU REALIZE HOW MUCH A GIRL'S WEDDING MEANS TO HER!

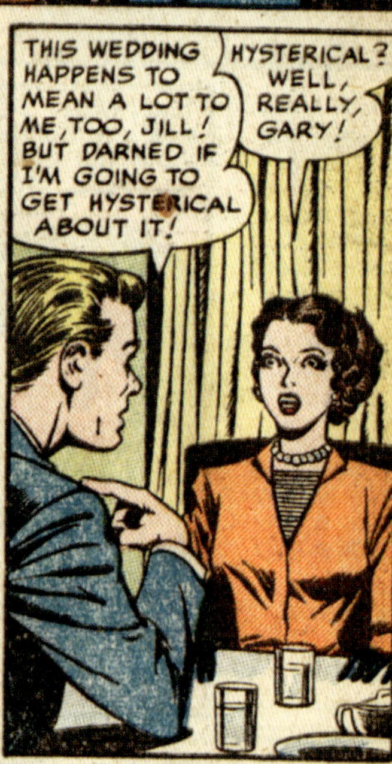
THIS WEDDING HAPPENS TO MEAN A LOT TO ME, TOO, JILL! BUT DARNED IF I'M GOING TO GET HYSTERICAL ABOUT IT!
HYSTERICAL? WELL, REALLY, GARY!

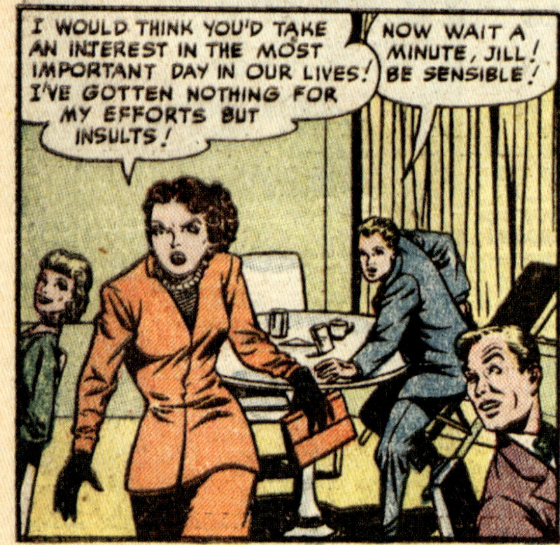
I WOULD THINK YOU'D TAKE AN INTEREST IN THE MOST IMPORTANT DAY IN OUR LIVES! I'VE GOTTEN NOTHING FOR MY EFFORTS BUT INSULTS!
NOW WAIT A MINUTE, JILL! BE SENSIBLE!

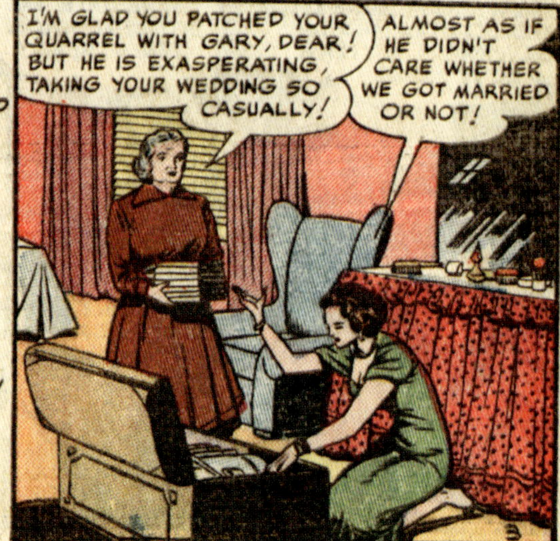
Later THAT DAY I APOLOGIZED TO GARY FOR THAT SCENE AND WE MADE UP! BUT THE DAMAGE HAD BEEN DONE... AND THAT WAS ONLY THE BEGINNING!
I'M GLAD YOU PATCHED YOUR QUARREL WITH GARY, DEAR! BUT HE IS EXASPERATING, TAKING YOUR WEDDING SO CASUALLY!
ALMOST AS IF HE DIDN'T CARE WHETHER WE GOT MARRIED OR NOT!

BUT MY ANNOYANCE WITH GARY WAS ONLY A MINOR FLAW IN OUR HAPPY RELATIONSHIP! AS MY MANIA FOR A CRAMMED HOPE CHEST GREW, I FOUND LESS AND LESS TIME FOR GARY!

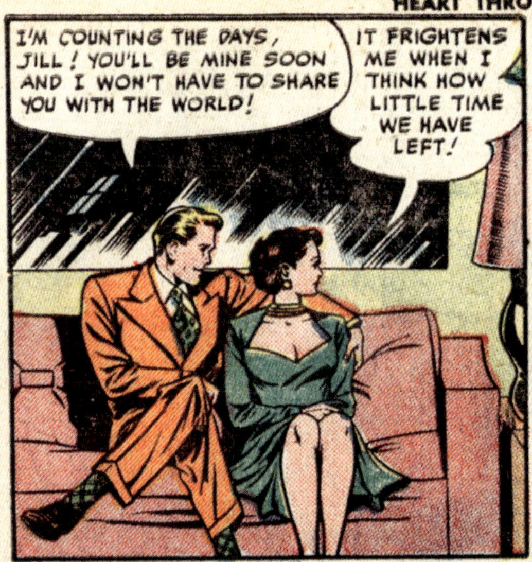

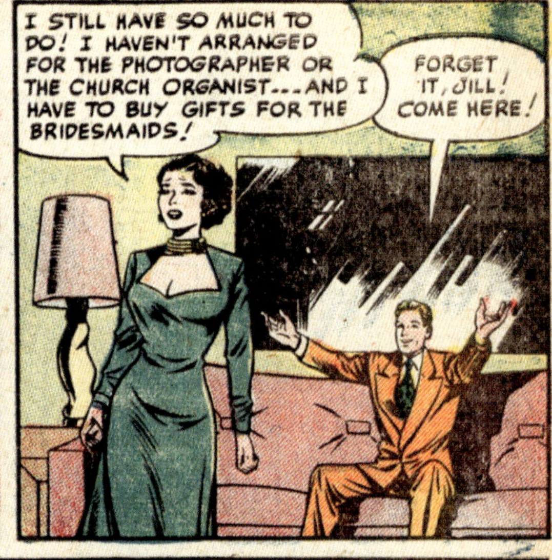

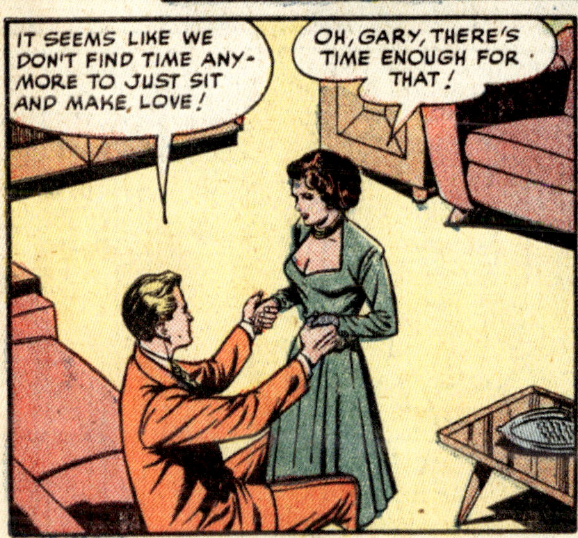

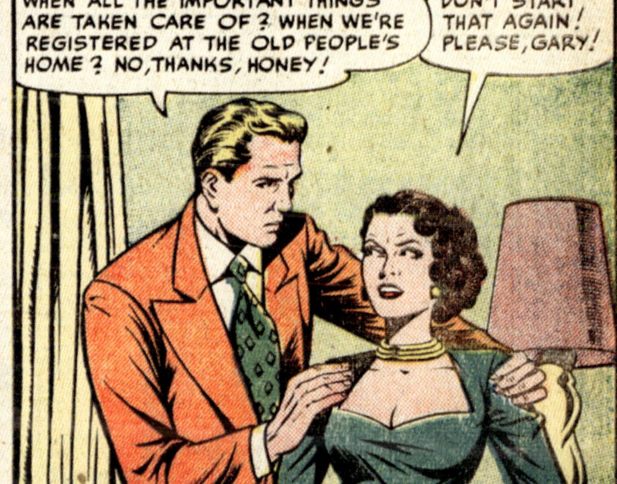

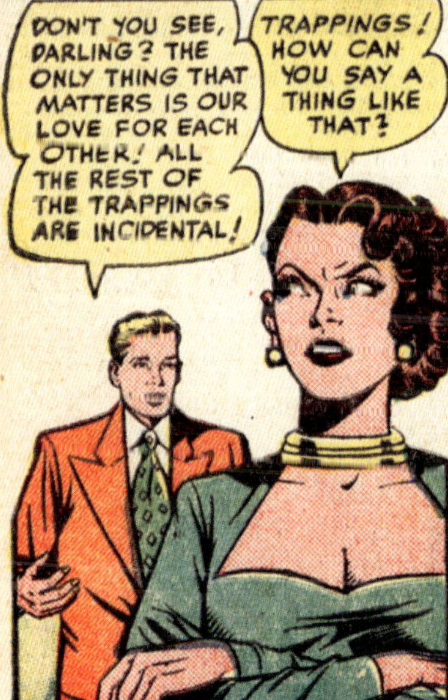

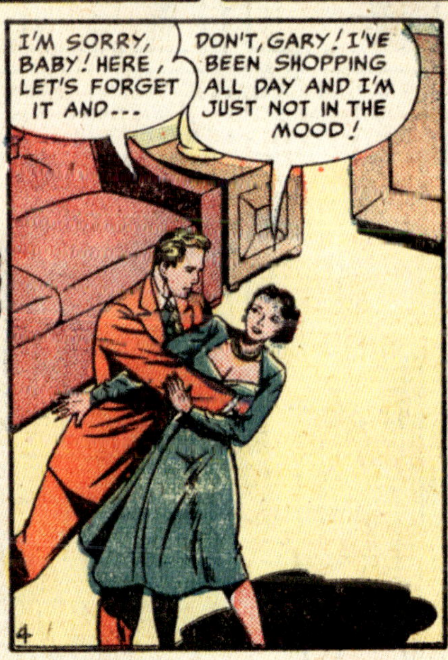

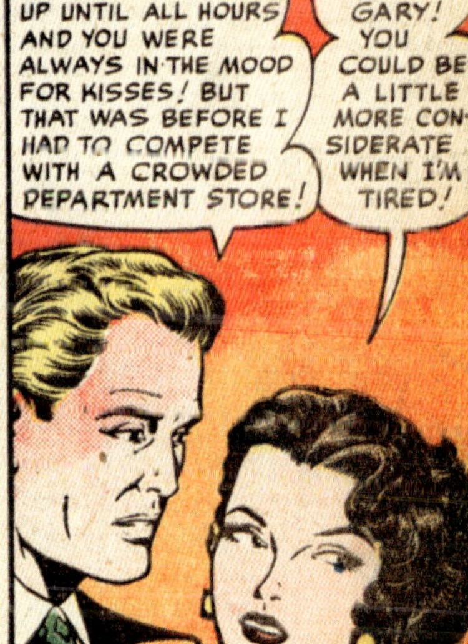

OH, I SHOULD HAVE TAKEN WARNING THEN! I SHOULD HAVE REALIZED THAT GARY'S CONSUMING LOVE FOR ME HAD TO FIND EXPRESSION IN MY ARMS.. IN THE IMPASSIONED MEETING OF OUR LIPS! BUT INSTEAD A FEW NIGHTS LATER.

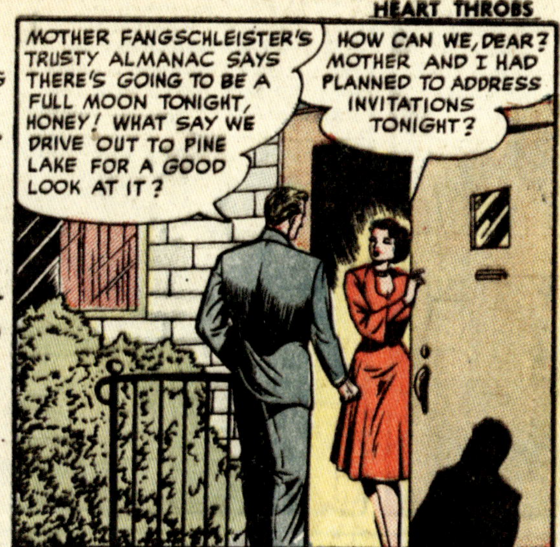

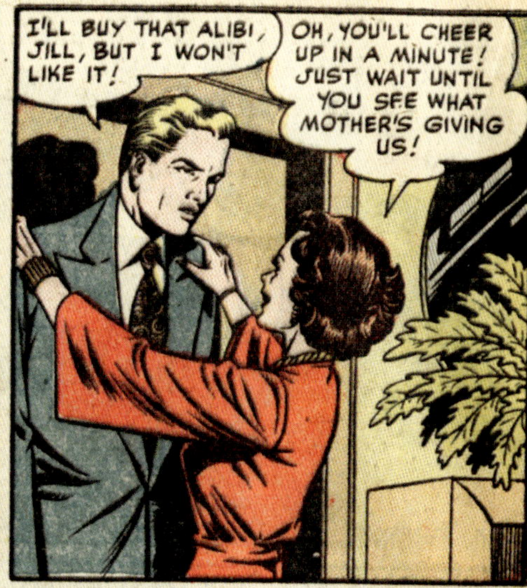

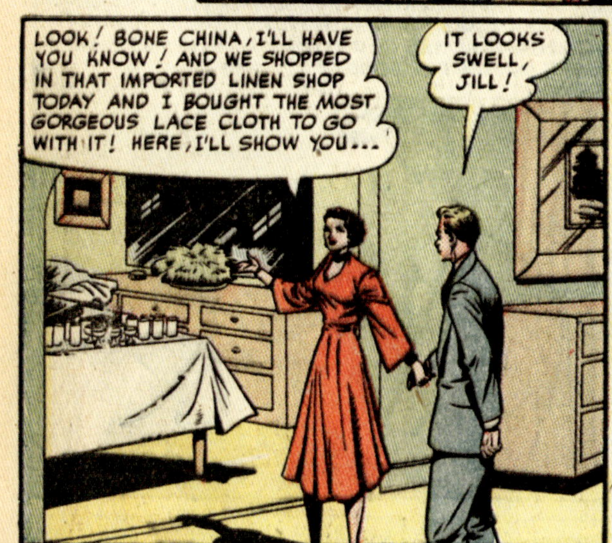

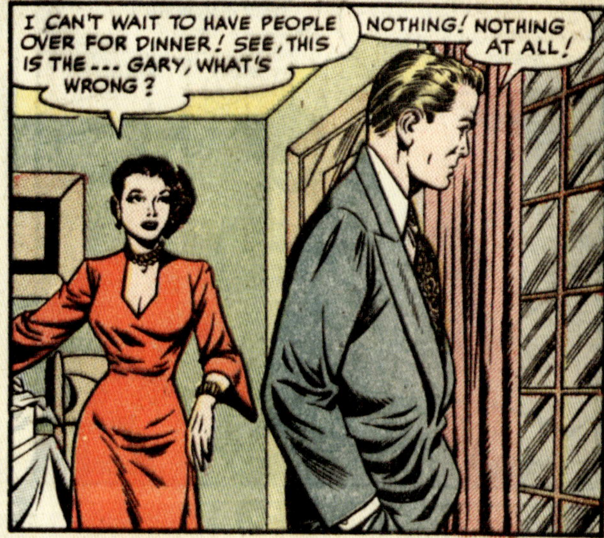

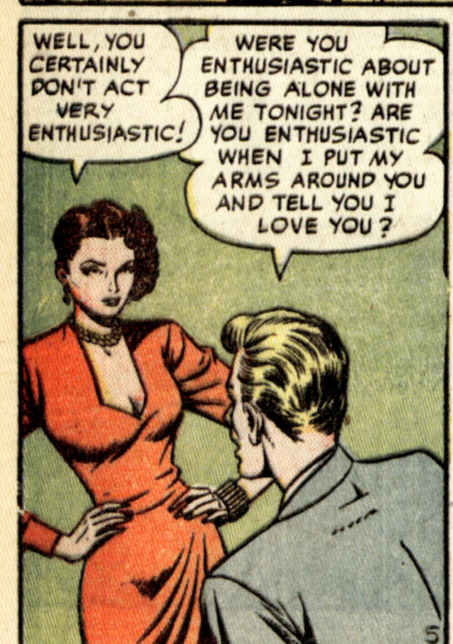

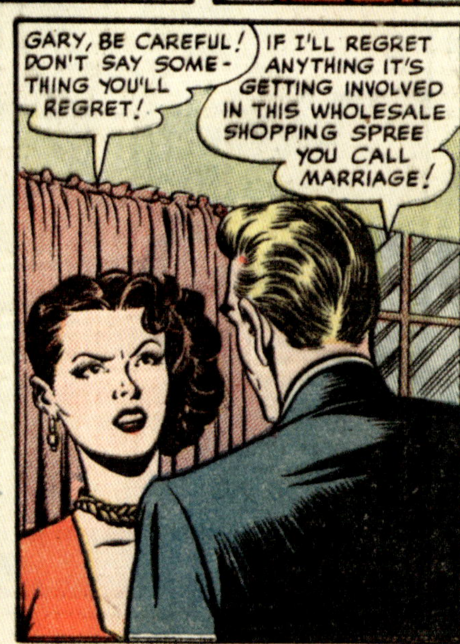

I POUR OUT MY HEART TO YOU AND YOU TELL ME ABOUT THE DAY'S PURCHASES! I KISS YOU AND IT'S LIKE KISSING A STONE STATUE BECAUSE YOU'RE THINKING ABOUT HOW IMPRESSED YOUR FRIENDS WILL BE WITH ITALIAN DOILIES!

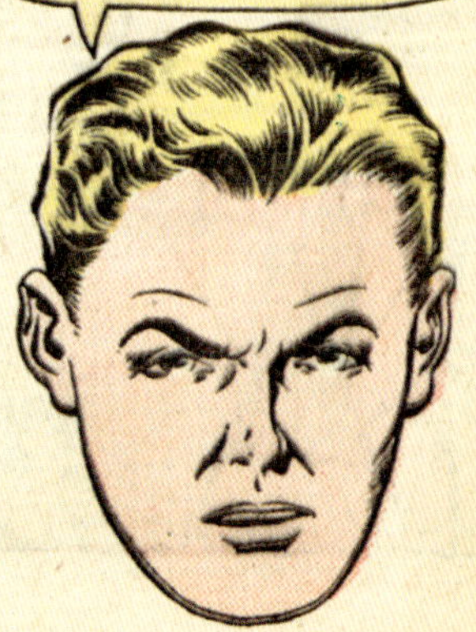

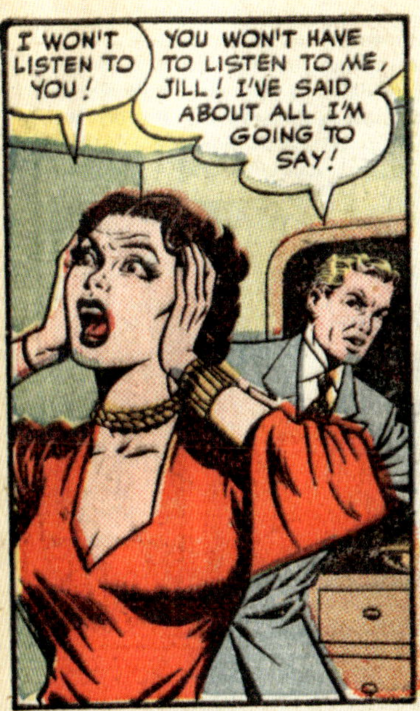

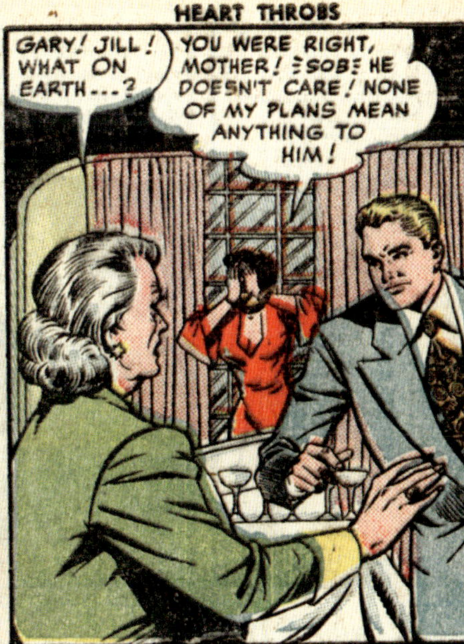

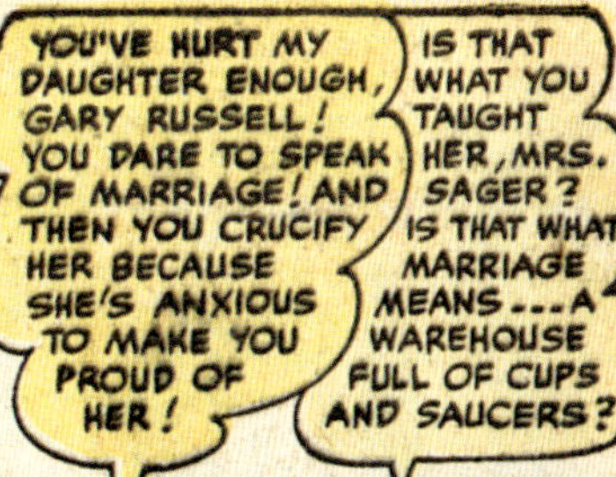

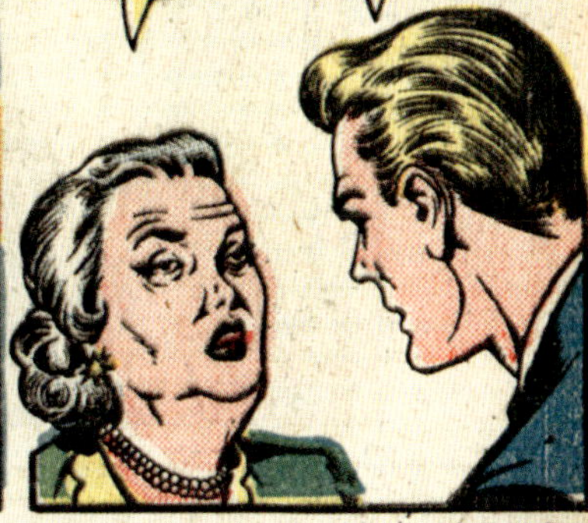

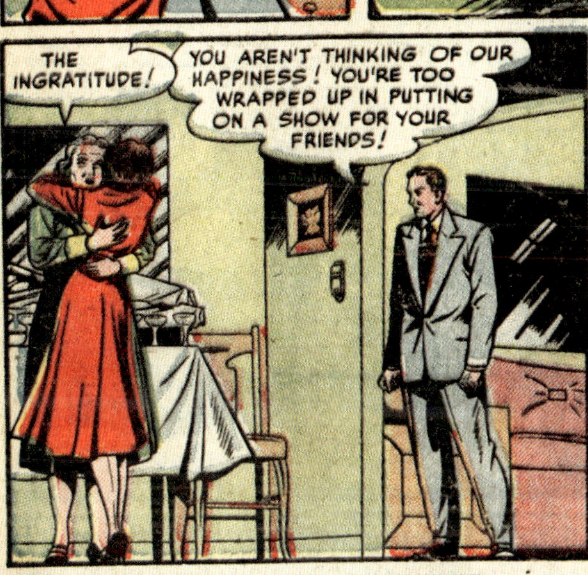

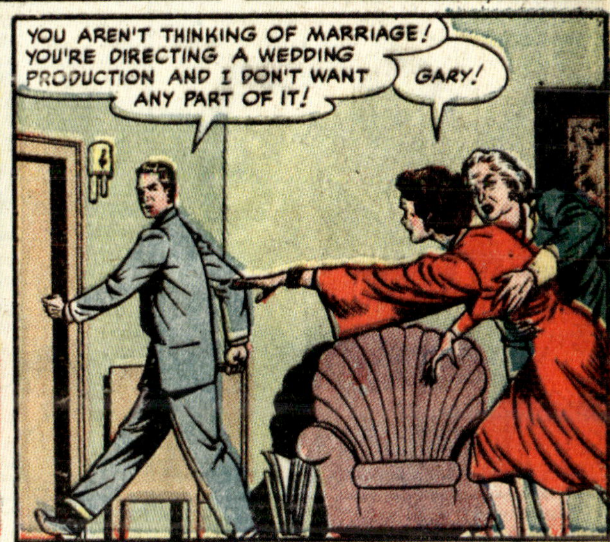

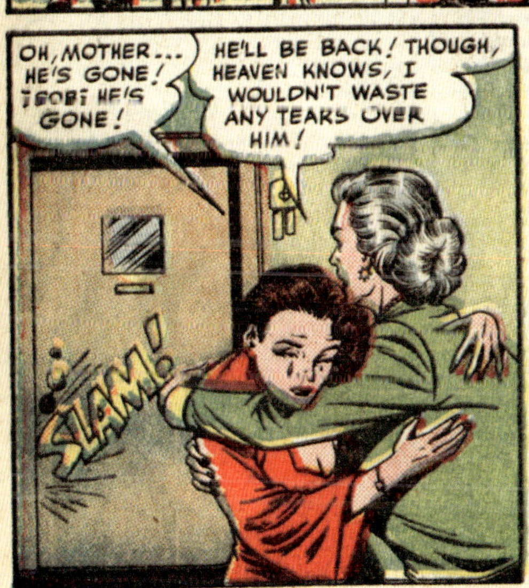

Fury is a fleeting emotion! When mine subsided, there was nothing left but the hollow ache in my heart that told me I had thrown away my chance for happiness!

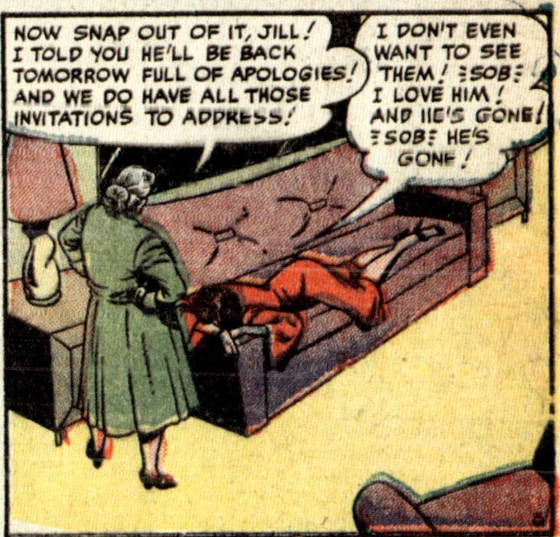

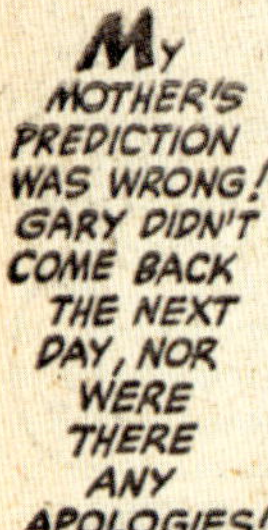
MY MOTHER'S PREDICTION WAS WRONG! GARY DIDN'T COME BACK THE NEXT DAY, NOR WERE THERE ANY APOLOGIES! AND WHEN I SAW HIM AT THE OFFICE!

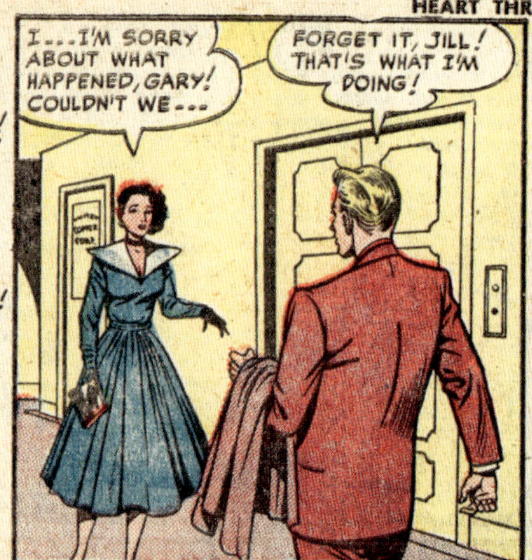
I...I'M SORRY ABOUT WHAT HAPPENED, GARY! COULDN'T WE...
FORGET IT, JILL! THAT'S WHAT I'M DOING!

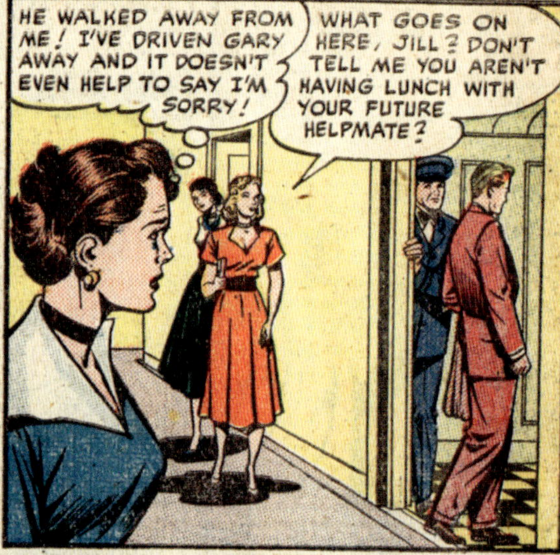
HE WALKED AWAY FROM ME! I'VE DRIVEN GARY AWAY AND IT DOESN'T EVEN HELP TO SAY I'M SORRY!
WHAT GOES ON HERE, JILL? DON'T TELL ME YOU AREN'T HAVING LUNCH WITH YOUR FUTURE HELPMATE?

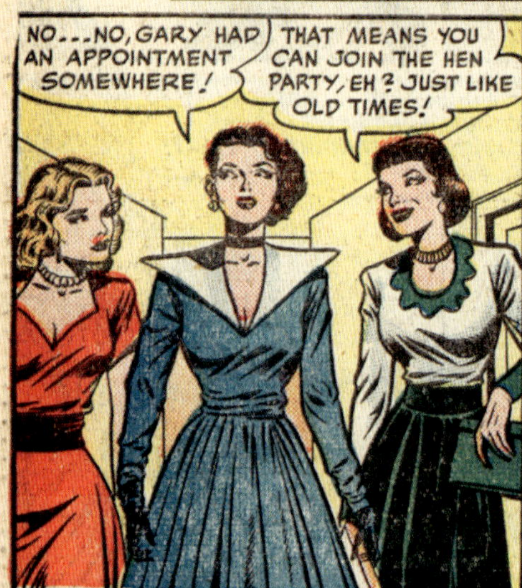
NO...NO, GARY HAD AN APPOINTMENT SOMEWHERE!
THAT MEANS YOU CAN JOIN THE HEN PARTY, EH? JUST LIKE OLD TIMES!
MY MISERY WAS ONLY HEIGHTENED BY THE HUMILIATION OF SEEING GARY AT OUR FAVORITE RENDEZVOUS ...ALONE AND OBVIOUSLY DEJECTED!

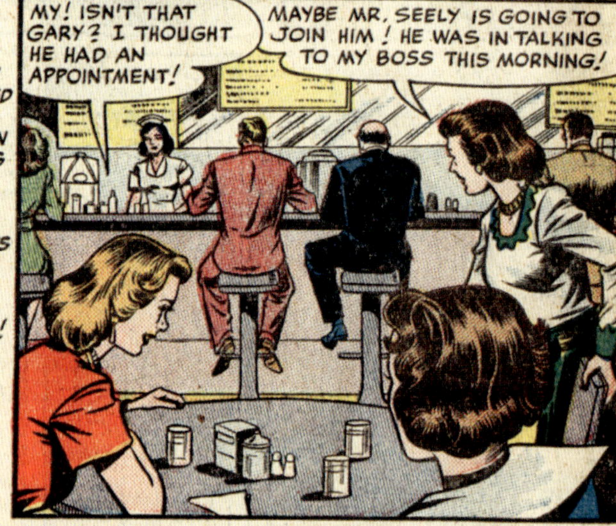
MY! ISN'T THAT GARY? I THOUGHT HE HAD AN APPOINTMENT!
MAYBE MR. SEELY IS GOING TO JOIN HIM! HE WAS IN TALKING TO MY BOSS THIS MORNING!

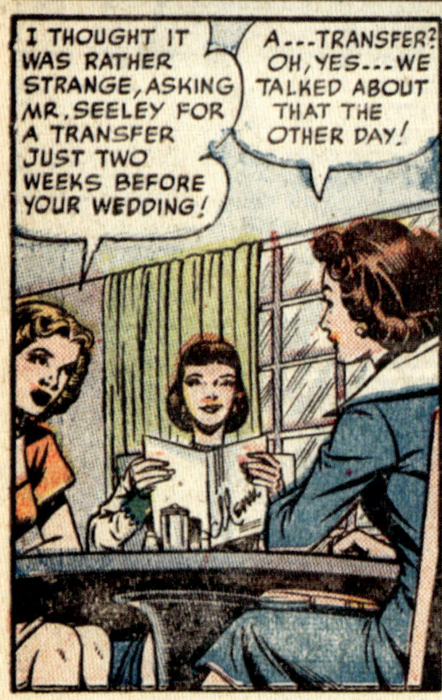
I THOUGHT IT WAS RATHER STRANGE, ASKING MR. SEELEY FOR A TRANSFER JUST TWO WEEKS BEFORE YOUR WEDDING!
A...TRANSFER? OH, YES...WE TALKED ABOUT THAT THE OTHER DAY!

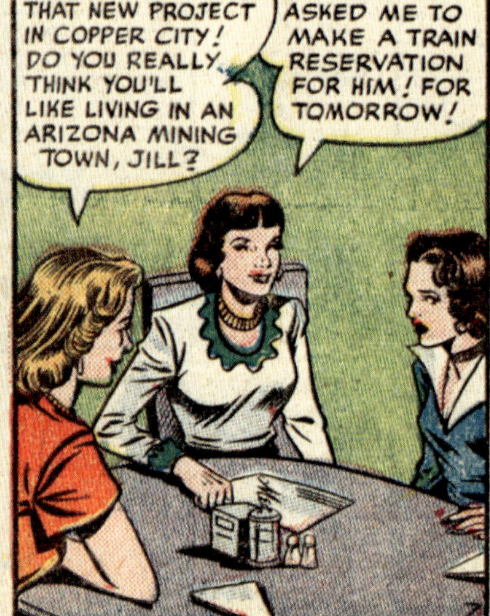
HMM! HE SAID HE'D LIKE TO WORK ON THAT NEW PROJECT IN COPPER CITY! DO YOU REALLY THINK YOU'LL LIKE LIVING IN AN ARIZONA MINING TOWN, JILL?
COME TO THINK, OF IT, GARY ASKED ME TO MAKE A TRAIN RESERVATION FOR HIM! FOR TOMORROW!

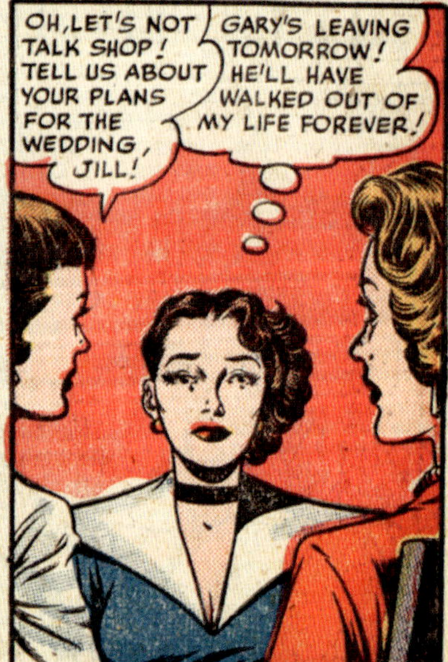
OH, LET'S NOT TALK SHOP! TELL US ABOUT YOUR PLANS FOR THE WEDDING, JILL!
GARY'S LEAVING TOMORROW! HE'LL HAVE WALKED OUT OF MY LIFE FOREVER!

SOMEHOW I CHOKED BACK THE BLISTERING TEARS AND STRUGGLED THROUGH THE ORDEAL OF PRETENDING I KNEW GARY WAS LEAVING! BUT ALONE AT MY DESK!

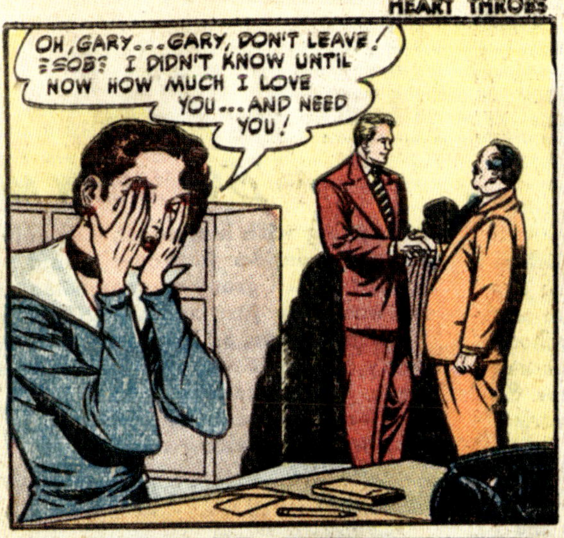

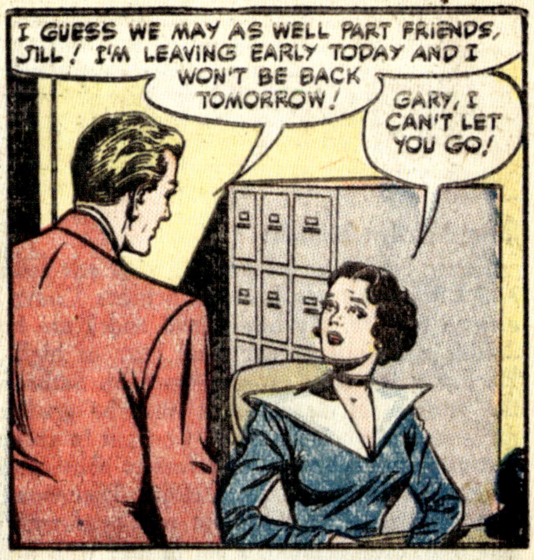

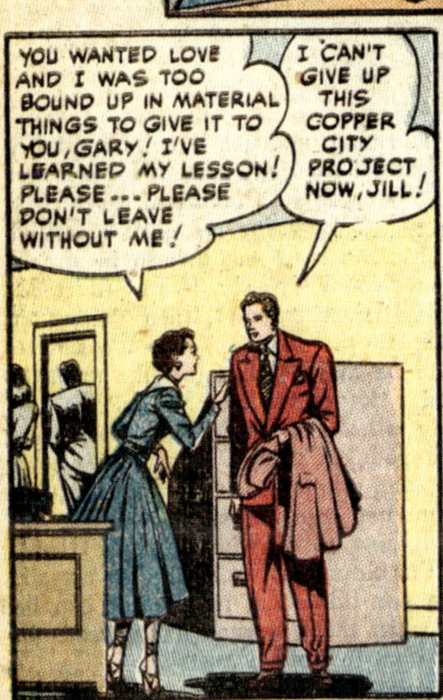

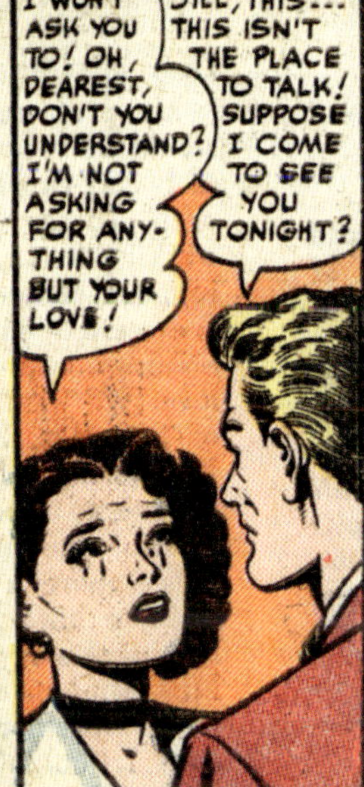

WAS GARY'S EXCUSE SINCERE, OR DID HE WANT TO AVOID AN UNPLEASANT SCENE? WHAT IF HE LEFT TOWN WITHOUT KEEPING HIS DATE WITH ME? MY AFTERNOON WAS SPENT IN AN AGONY OF SUSPENSE! BUT THAT EVENING...

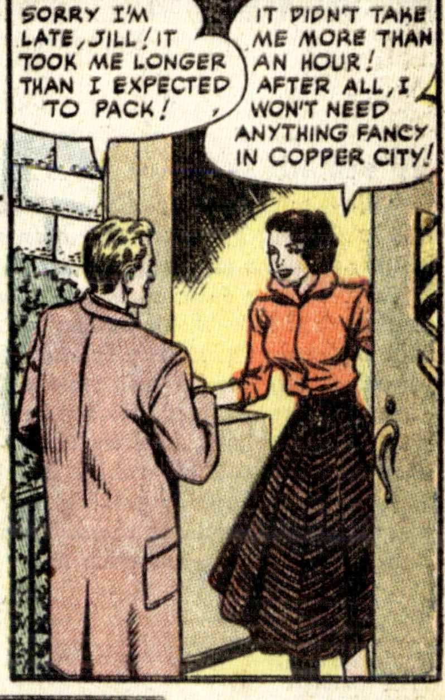

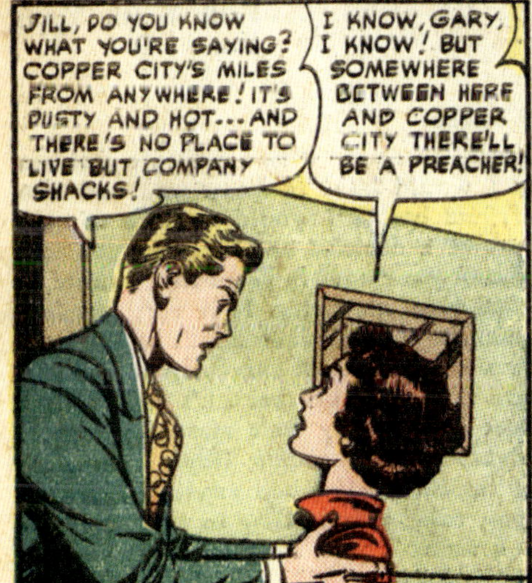

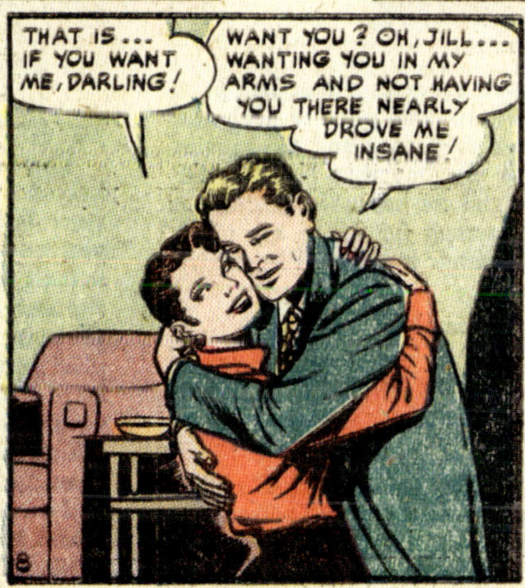

IT WOULD BE A YEAR OR MORE BEFORE GARY AND I RETURNED... AND OUR "NEW HOME" WOULD HARDLY BE THE PLACE FOR BONE CHINA AND IRISH LINENS! PERHAPS THE HOPE CHEST WOULD NEVER BE UNPACKED! BUT WITH GARY'S ARMS AROUND ME, EVEN A DUSTY COPPER CITY SHACK WOULD BE HEAVEN, FOR I HAD LEARNED THE REAL MEANING OF MARRIAGE!

Here are six different species of the Male--

WHICH IS YOUR DREAM MAN?

"I LIKE THE OUT-DOOR TYPE OF MAN, BECAUSE YOU ARE NEVER BORED WHEN YOU'RE WITH HIM. HE ALWAYS KNOWS SO MANY THINGS TO DO! BEING A MAN WHO LOVES NATURE HE IS INVARIABLY CLEAN AND WHOLESOME... SOMEONE YOU'RE REALLY PROUD TO KNOW!

Judith R.

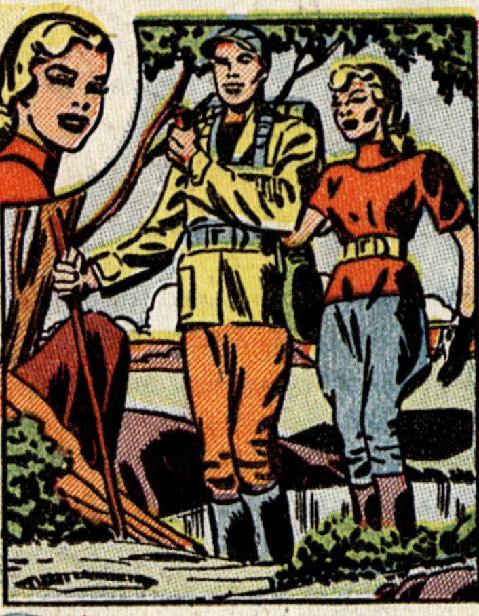

"I LIKE A POSSESSIVE MAN, BECAUSE HE MAKES ME FEEL REALLY WANTED! I LIKE THE WAY HE TAKES HOLD OF ME WHEN ANOTHER MAN LOOKS IN MY DIRECTION! WHEN I LIKE SOMEONE, I WANT TO SPEND ALL MY TIME WITH HIM, AND A POSSESSIVE MAN **WANTS** ALL OF YOUR TIME TOO! I'M NEVER IN DOUBT HOW I STAND HERE!

Susan M.

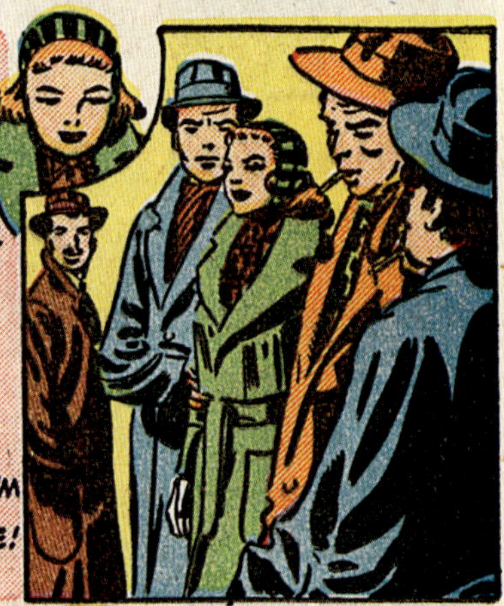

"I LIKE A MAN WHO SHOWS ME WHO'S BOSS! LIKE MOST GIRLS I'M INCLINED TO WANT MY OWN WAY REGARDLESS OF THE FEELINGS OF MY DATE! BUT WITH THE MASTERFUL TYPE, I HAVE TO TOE THE LINE! THIS IS A MAN I REALLY CAN RESPECT!

Joyce L.

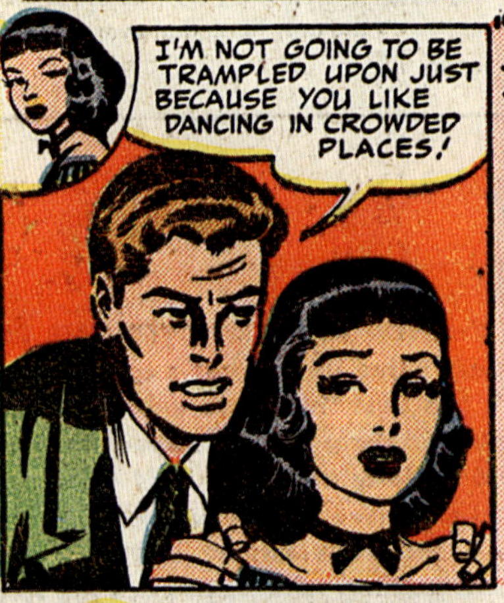

"I LIKE A SMOOTH SOPHISTICATED MAN, WHO TAKES YOU TO NICE PLACES! HE DANCES BEAUTIFULLY, KNOWS A VARIETY OF SPORTS! HE ALWAYS KNOWS HOW TO ENTERTAIN YOU, AND ESPECIALLY IMPORTANT, THE RIGHT THING TO SAY...MAKING A GIRL FEEL WONDERFUL!

Edith D.

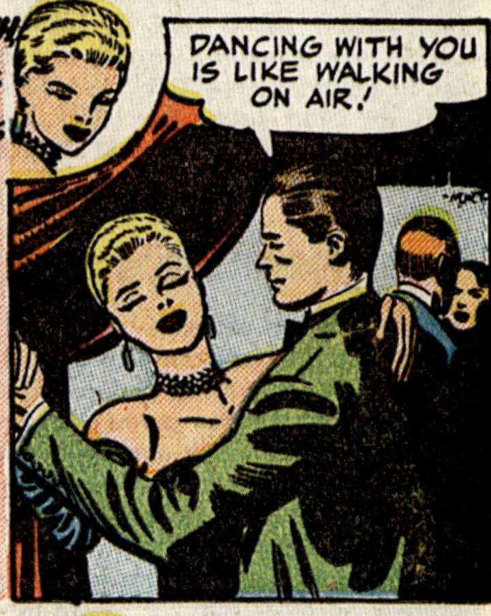

"I LIKE THE HOME-LOVING TYPE OF MAN... ONE WHO DOESN'T WANT TO CHASE AROUND ALL THE TIME. HE'S THE FELLOW WHO LIKES TO SIT IN FRONT OF MY FIREPLACE AND JUST TALK! HE'S EVEN WILLING TO SAMPLE MY AMATEUR ATTEMPTS AT COOKING! THIS IS THE MAN I CAN REALLY RELAX WITH AND JUST BE MYSELF! IN SHORT, HE'S THE GUY FOR ME!

Della S.

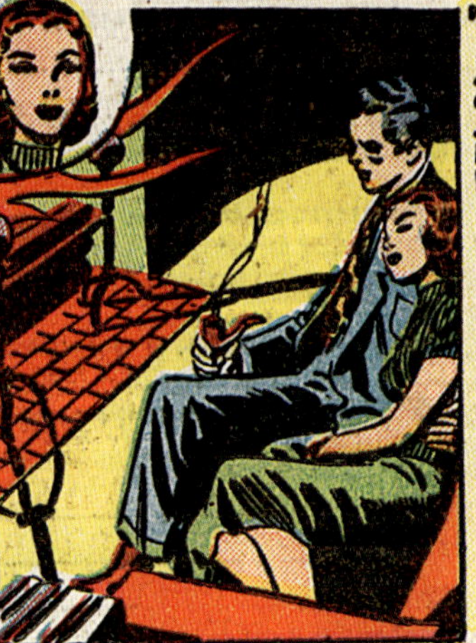

"I LIKE A MAN WHO TRUSTS ME IMPLICITLY... ONE WHO IS NEVER JEALOUS BECAUSE I HAVE A GOOD TIME WITH SOMEONE ELSE AND WHO KNOWS A LITTLE FLIRTING DOES NO HARM! HE KNOWS I'M HIS GIRL BECAUSE I TOLD HIM I WAS, JUST LIKE I KNOW HE'S MY GUY! HE REALIZES I WOULD NEVER DO ANYTHING TO HURT OUR ROMANCE ANY MORE THAN HE WOULD!

Kathleen R.

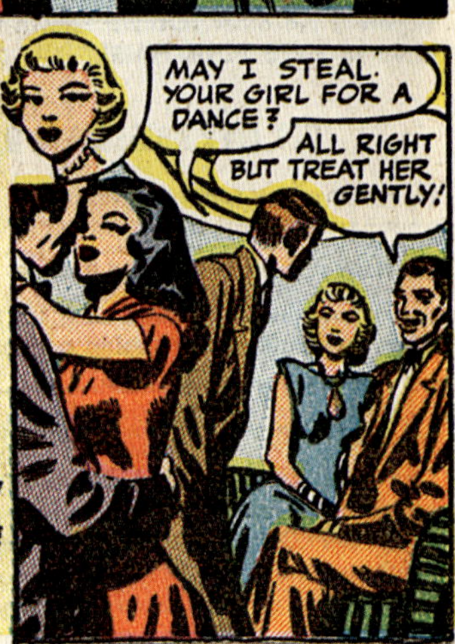

Harry could never understand how I felt. I didn't want mere acquaintances to intrude on the orderly existence I had planned for us. My whole life was wrapped up in trying to make a real home, but Harry was...

Married to His Work

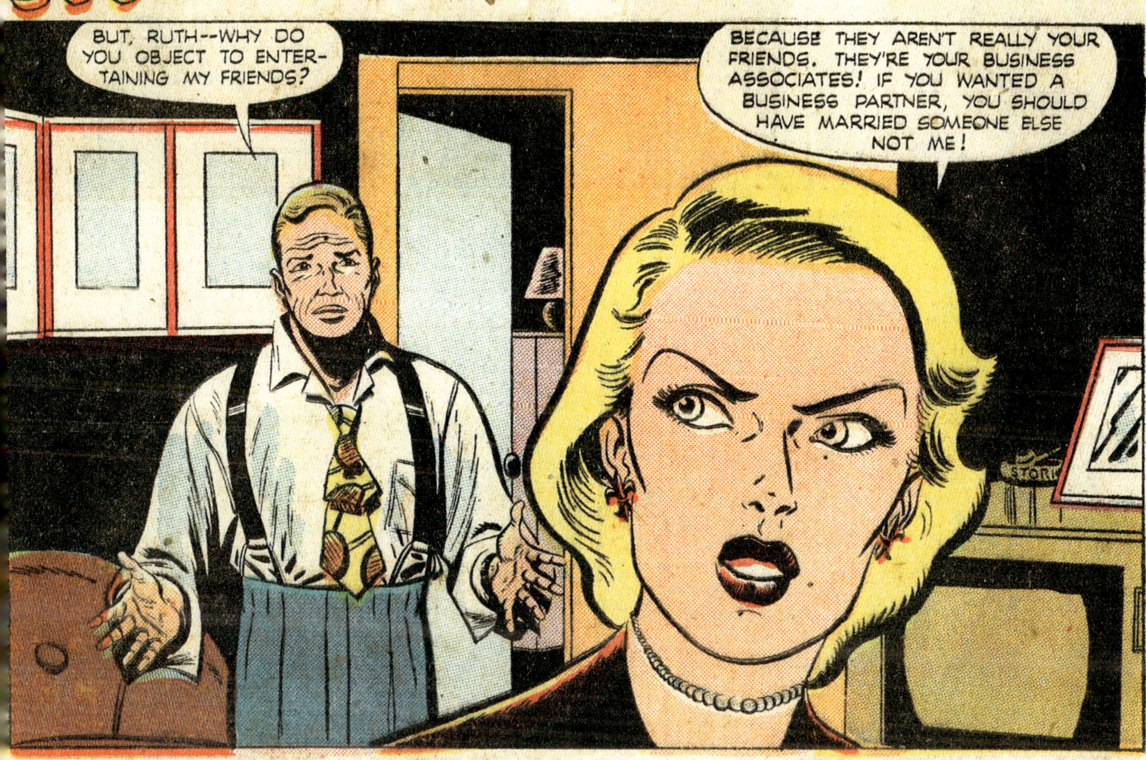

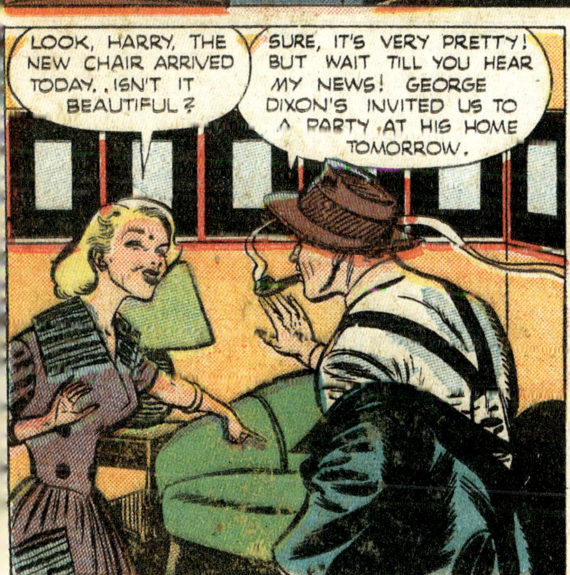

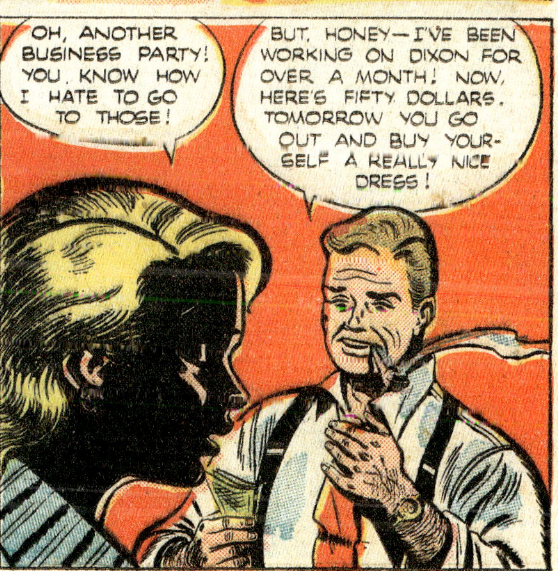

Page 140:
YOUNG LOVE
Volume 2, #2
April 1950

This page:
ROMANTIC MARRIAGE
#13, May 1952

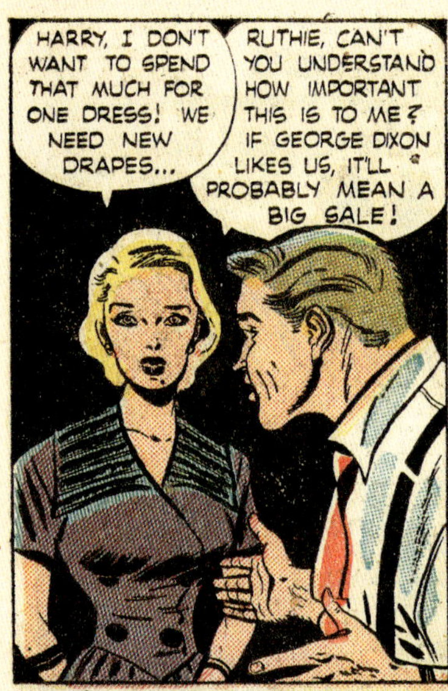

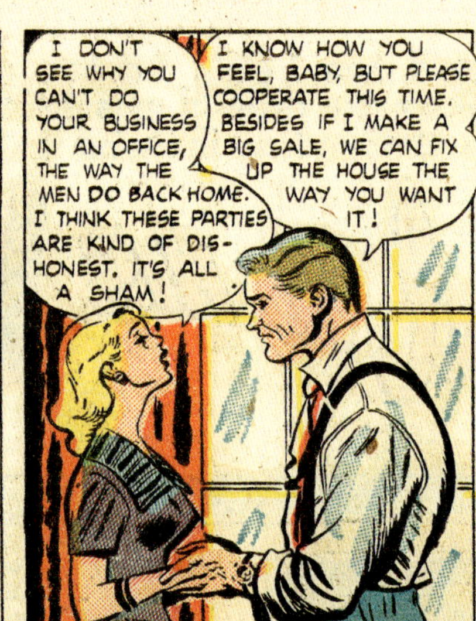

I DIDN'T PRETEND TO UNDERSTAND OR LIKE THE INTRICACIES OF CITY BUSINESS. IN MY HOME TOWN, YOU MIXED SOCIALLY ONLY WITH YOUR PERSONAL FRIENDS. THE NEXT DAY...

THAT'S JUST THE MATERIAL I WANT FOR THE DRAPES. IF ONLY I DARED ...OH, I DON'T NEED A NEW DRESS! I CAN FIX UP MY OLD ONE!

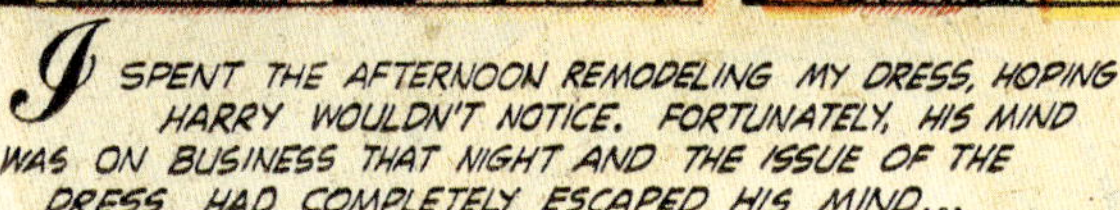

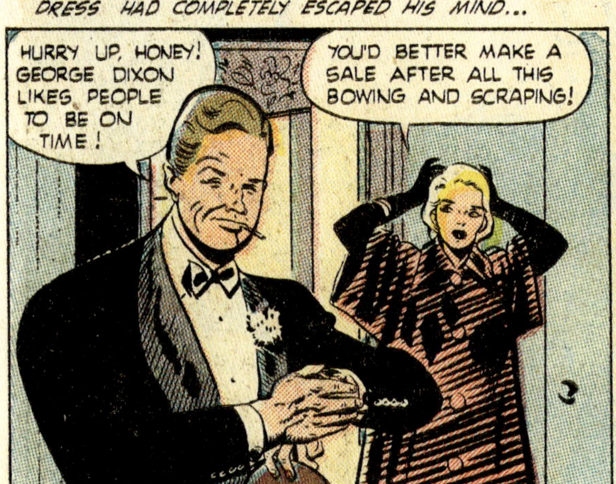

I WAS HARDLY PREPARED FOR THE LAVISHNESS OF THE DIXON PARTY. MOST OF THE WOMEN LOOKED AS THOUGH THEY HAD JUST STEPPED OUT OF A FASHION MAGAZINE. I KNEW I WOULDN'T LIKE ANY OF THEM. THAT TYPE OF WOMAN WAS ALMOST ALWAYS VAIN AND SELF-CENTERED...

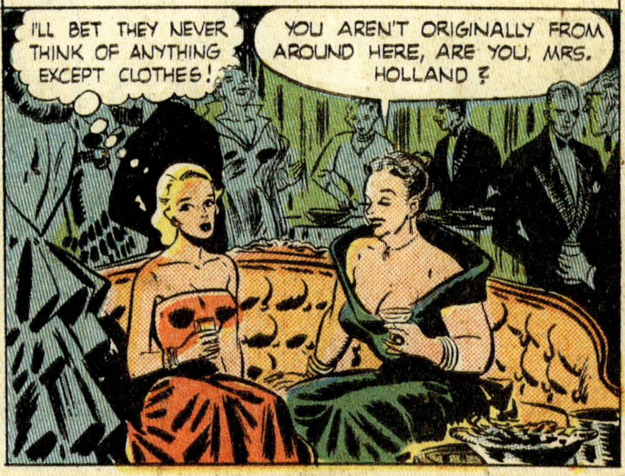

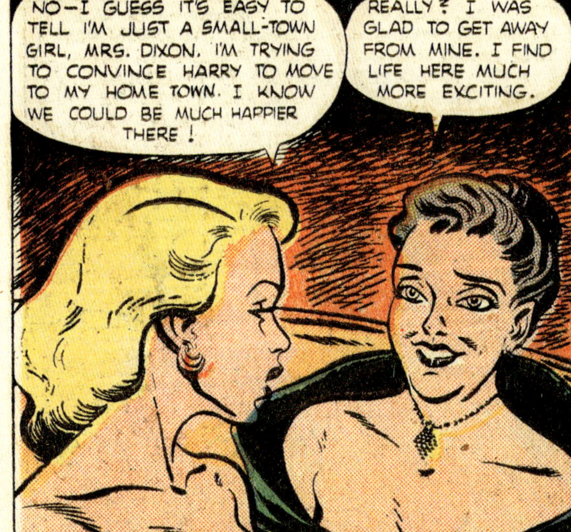

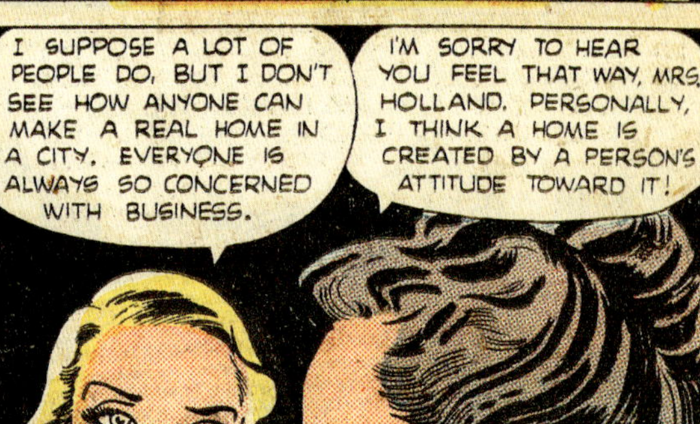

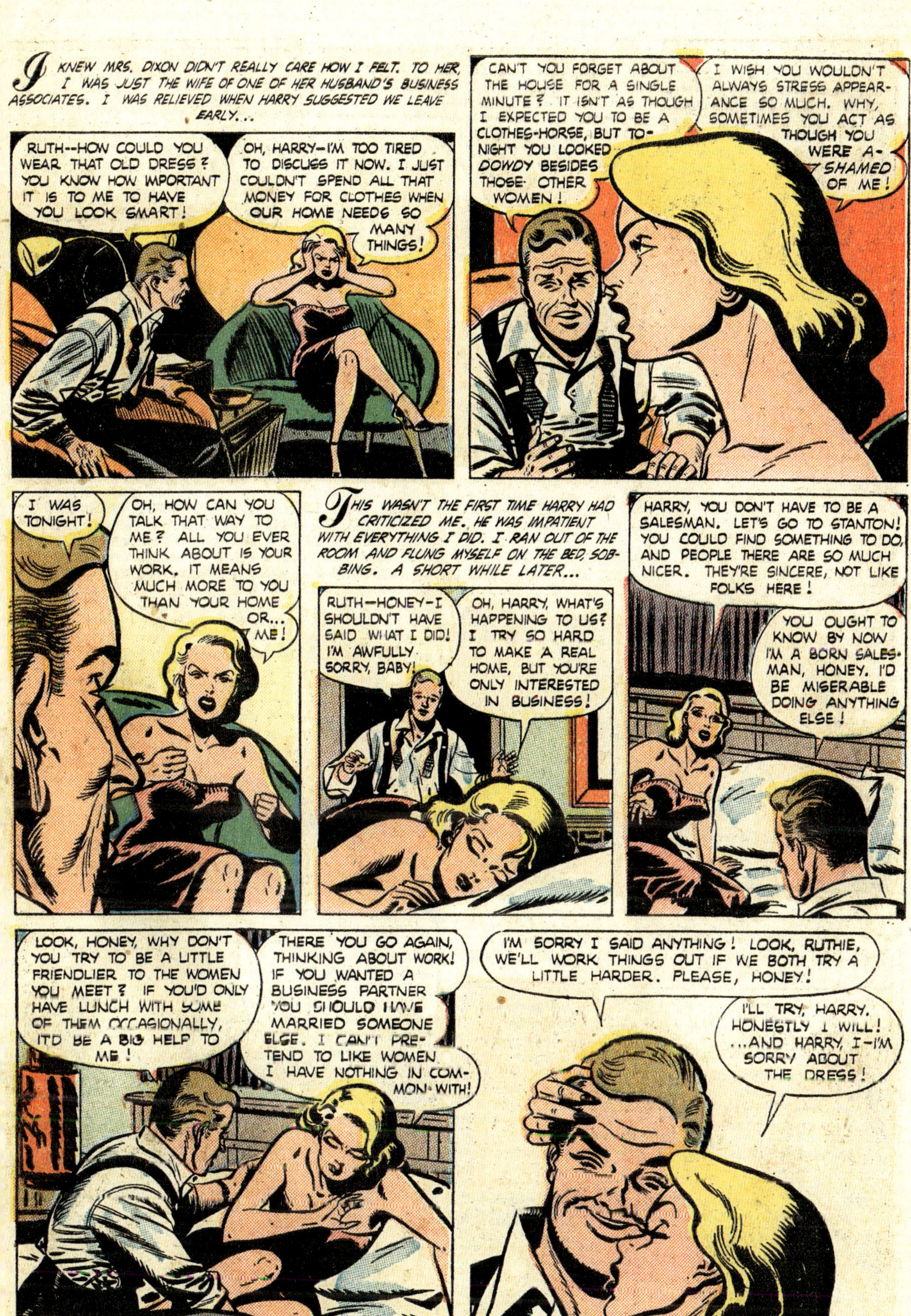
I KNEW MRS. DIXON DIDN'T REALLY CARE HOW I FELT. TO HER, I WAS JUST THE WIFE OF ONE OF HER HUSBAND'S BUSINESS ASSOCIATES. I WAS RELIEVED WHEN HARRY SUGGESTED WE LEAVE EARLY...
RUTH--HOW COULD YOU WEAR THAT OLD DRESS? YOU KNOW HOW IMPORTANT IT IS TO ME TO HAVE YOU LOOK SMART!
OH, HARRY--I'M TOO TIRED TO DISCUSS IT NOW. I JUST COULDN'T SPEND ALL THAT MONEY FOR CLOTHES WHEN OUR HOME NEEDS SO MANY THINGS!
CAN'T YOU FORGET ABOUT THE HOUSE FOR A SINGLE MINUTE? IT ISN'T AS THOUGH I EXPECTED YOU TO BE A CLOTHES-HORSE, BUT TO-NIGHT YOU LOOKED DOWDY BESIDES THOSE OTHER WOMEN!
I WISH YOU WOULDN'T ALWAYS STRESS APPEAR-ANCE SO MUCH. WHY, SOMETIMES YOU ACT AS THOUGH YOU WERE A-SHAMED OF ME!
I WAS TONIGHT!
OH, HOW CAN YOU TALK THAT WAY TO ME? ALL YOU EVER THINK ABOUT IS YOUR WORK. IT MEANS MUCH MORE TO YOU THAN YOUR HOME OR... ME!
THIS WASN'T THE FIRST TIME HARRY HAD CRITICIZED ME. HE WAS IMPATIENT WITH EVERYTHING I DID. I RAN OUT OF THE ROOM AND FLUNG MYSELF ON THE BED, SOB-BING. A SHORT WHILE LATER...
RUTH--HONEY--I SHOULDN'T HAVE SAID WHAT I DID! I'M AWFULLY SORRY, BABY!
OH, HARRY, WHAT'S HAPPENING TO US? I TRY SO HARD TO MAKE A REAL HOME, BUT YOU'RE ONLY INTERESTED IN BUSINESS!
HARRY, YOU DON'T HAVE TO BE A SALESMAN. LET'S GO TO STANTON! YOU COULD FIND SOMETHING TO DO, AND PEOPLE THERE ARE SO MUCH NICER. THEY'RE SINCERE, NOT LIKE FOLKS HERE!
YOU OUGHT TO KNOW BY NOW I'M A BORN SALES-MAN, HONEY. I'D BE MISERABLE DOING ANYTHING ELSE!
LOOK, HONEY, WHY DON'T YOU TRY TO BE A LITTLE FRIENDLIER TO THE WOMEN YOU MEET? IF YOU'D ONLY HAVE LUNCH WITH SOME OF THEM OCCASIONALLY, IT'D BE A BIG HELP TO ME!
THERE YOU GO AGAIN, THINKING ABOUT WORK! IF YOU WANTED A BUSINESS PARTNER YOU SHOULD HAVE MARRIED SOMEONE ELSE. I CAN'T PRE-TEND TO LIKE WOMEN I HAVE NOTHING IN COM-MON WITH!
I'M SORRY I SAID ANYTHING! LOOK, RUTHIE, WE'LL WORK THINGS OUT IF WE BOTH TRY A LITTLE HARDER. PLEASE, HONEY!
I'LL TRY, HARRY. HONESTLY I WILL! ...AND HARRY, I--I'M SORRY ABOUT THE DRESS!
3

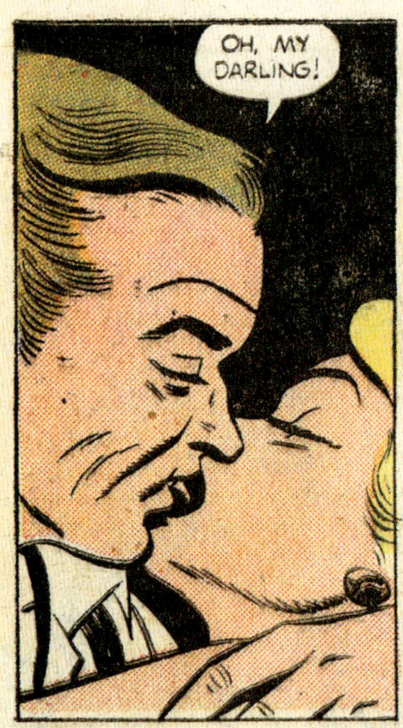
OH, MY DARLING!

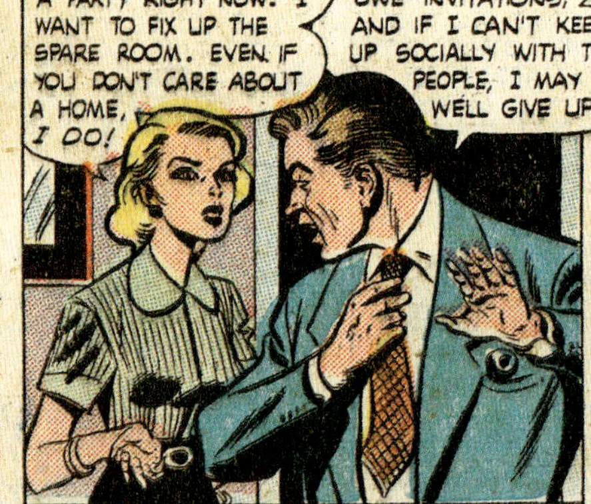
I DID TRY TO COOPERATE IN THE WEEKS THAT FOLLOWED BECAUSE OF MY LOVE FOR HARRY. BUT WHEN HE SUGGESTED GIVING A PARTY, IT WAS JUST TOO MUCH...
HARRY, IN THE FIRST PLACE WE CAN'T AFFORD TO HAVE A PARTY RIGHT NOW! I WANT TO FIX UP THE SPARE ROOM. EVEN IF YOU DON'T CARE ABOUT A HOME, I DO!
RUTH, PLEASE BE REASONABLE! WE OWE INVITATIONS, AND IF I CAN'T KEEP UP SOCIALLY WITH THOSE PEOPLE, I MAY AS WELL GIVE UP!

WELL, I'M NOT GOING TO CHANGE MY FEELINGS! I'M NOT TURNING MY HOME INTO A BUSINESS OFFICE TO PRETEND TO ENJOY THE COMPANY OF A LOT OF STRANGERS; IT'S—IT'S CHEAP AND I WON'T BE PARTY TO IT!
I'M SORRY YOU FEEL THE WAY YOU DO, RUTH, BUT MY BUSINESS DEPENDS ON IT. I HAVE TO GIVE A PARTY WITH OR WITHOUT YOUR CONSENT!

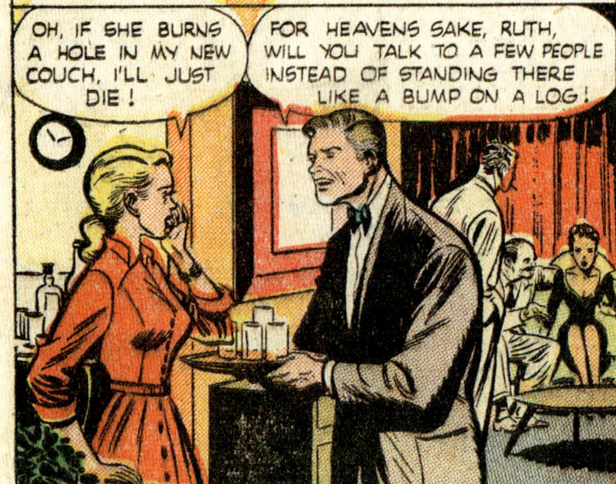
RELUCTANTLY, I HELPED HARRY MAKE HIS PLANS, THOUGH I FELT DISHONEST AND ASHAMED. THE NIGHT OF THE PARTY, I WAS TENSE AND NERVOUS...
OH, IF SHE BURNS A HOLE IN MY NEW COUCH, I'LL JUST DIE!
FOR HEAVENS SAKE, RUTH, WILL YOU TALK TO A FEW PEOPLE INSTEAD OF STANDING THERE LIKE A BUMP ON A LOG!

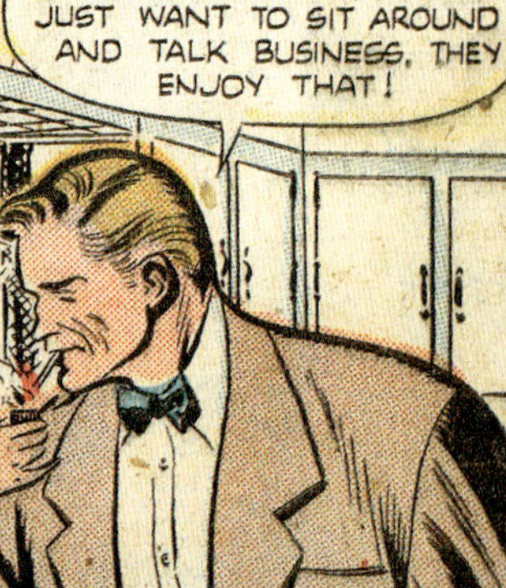
WELL, I HOPE THEY DON'T STAY TOO LATE. DO YOU THINK ANYONE WOULD LIKE TO PLAY A LITTLE BRIDGE?
HONEY, IT ISN'T THAT KIND OF A PARTY! THESE PEOPLE JUST WANT TO SIT AROUND AND TALK BUSINESS. THEY ENJOY THAT!

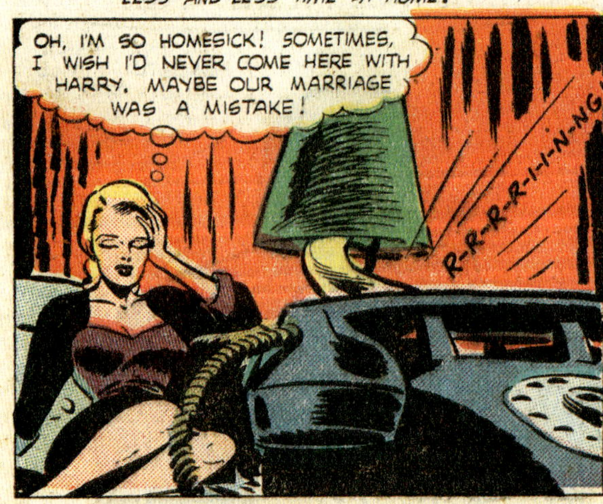
ALTOGETHER, IT WAS A MISERABLE EVENING FOR ME... IN THE WEEKS THAT FOLLOWED, BUSINESS SEEMED TO TAKE MORE OF HARRY'S TIME THAN EVER. HE WAS SPENDING LESS AND LESS TIME AT HOME.
OH, I'M SO HOMESICK! SOMETIMES, I WISH I'D NEVER COME HERE WITH HARRY. MAYBE OUR MARRIAGE WAS A MISTAKE!
R-R-R-R-I-I-N-N-NG!

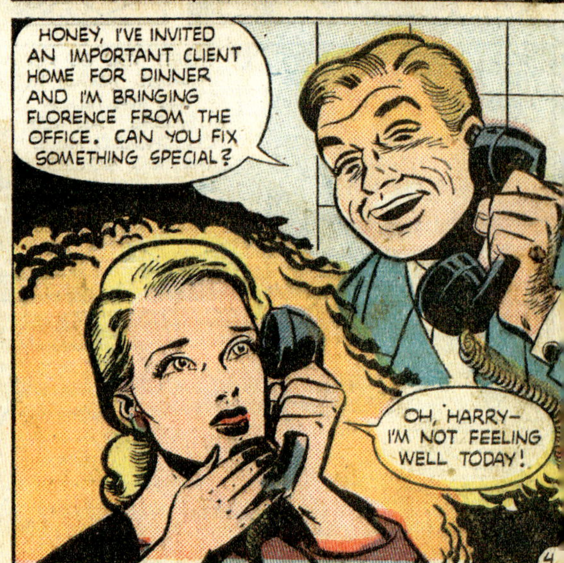
HONEY, I'VE INVITED AN IMPORTANT CLIENT HOME FOR DINNER AND I'M BRINGING FLORENCE FROM THE OFFICE. CAN YOU FIX SOMETHING SPECIAL?
OH, HARRY—I'M NOT FEELING WELL TODAY!
4

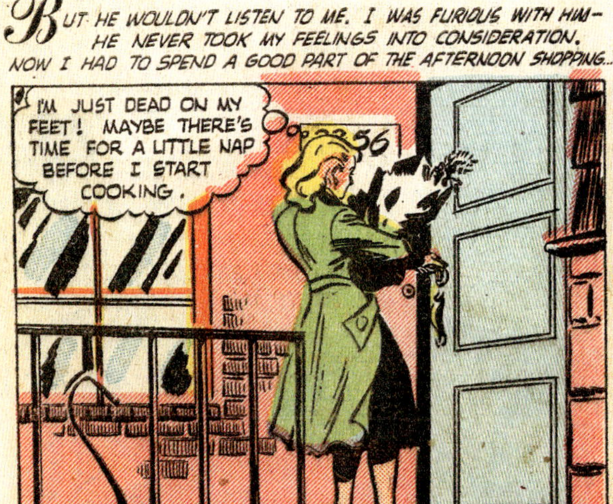
BUT HE WOULDN'T LISTEN TO ME. I WAS FURIOUS WITH HIM—HE NEVER TOOK MY FEELINGS INTO CONSIDERATION. NOW I HAD TO SPEND A GOOD PART OF THE AFTERNOON SHOPPING...
I'M JUST DEAD ON MY FEET! MAYBE THERE'S TIME FOR A LITTLE NAP BEFORE I START COOKING.
56

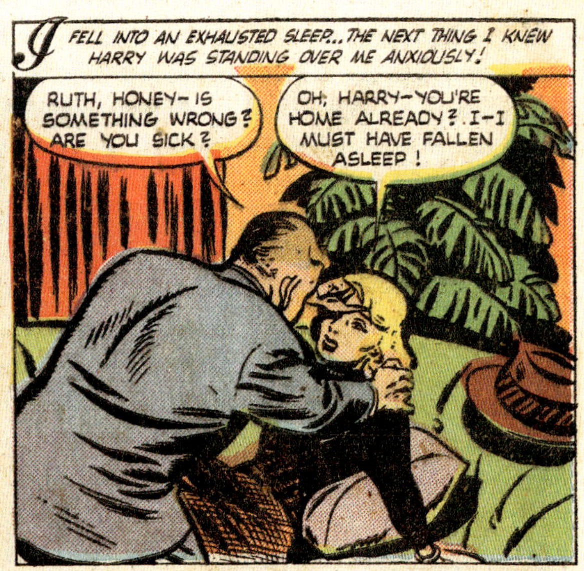
I FELL INTO AN EXHAUSTED SLEEP... THE NEXT THING I KNEW HARRY WAS STANDING OVER ME ANXIOUSLY!
RUTH, HONEY—IS SOMETHING WRONG? ARE YOU SICK?
OH, HARRY—YOU'RE HOME ALREADY? I—I MUST HAVE FALLEN ASLEEP!

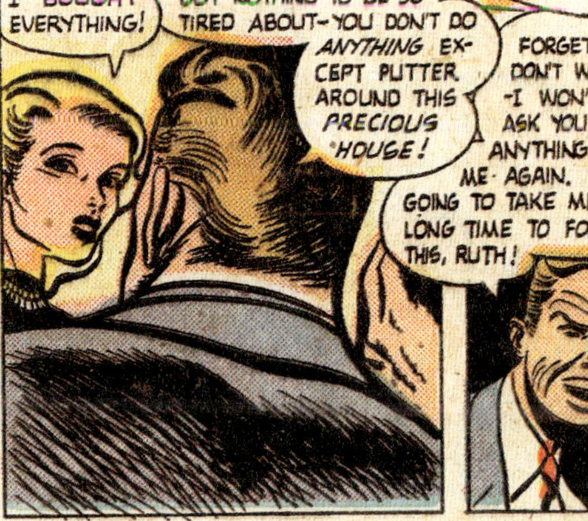
I SAW DARK ANGER IN HARRY'S FACE AS HE TURNED AWAY FROM ME. IN THE OTHER ROOM I HEARD HIM MAKING EMBARRASSED APOLOGIES...
I—I GUESS WE'LL HAVE TO GO OUT, JOHN! ...RUTH ISN'T WELL!
THAT'S FINE WITH ME, HARRY! WE CAN PROBABLY GET MORE BUSINESS DONE IN A RESTAURANT, ANYWAY!
YOU DON'T HAVE TO GO OUT HARRY! I CAN STILL FIX DINNER—I BOUGHT EVERYTHING!
NO, THANKS—I WOULDN'T WANT TO TROUBLE YOU! BUT I THINK THIS IS A PRETTY LOUSY TRICK! YOU'VE GOT NOTHING TO BE SO TIRED ABOUT—YOU DON'T DO ANYTHING EXCEPT PUTTER AROUND THIS PRECIOUS HOUSE!

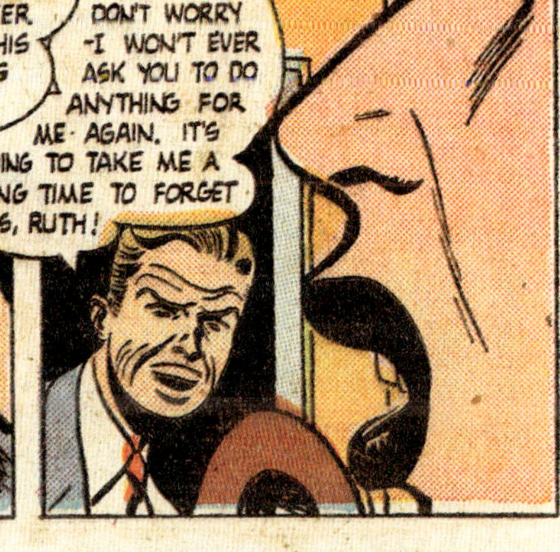
ALL RIGHT, I DIDN'T WANT TO FIX DINNER ANYWAY. I'VE TOLD YOU OFTEN ENOUGH I WON'T HAVE MY HOUSE USED FOR BUSINESS. I'M SICK OF ALL THE SHAM AND PRETENSE OF YOUR BUSINESS METHODS!
FORGET IT! DON'T WORRY—I WON'T EVER ASK YOU TO DO ANYTHING FOR ME AGAIN. IT'S GOING TO TAKE ME A LONG TIME TO FORGET THIS, RUTH!

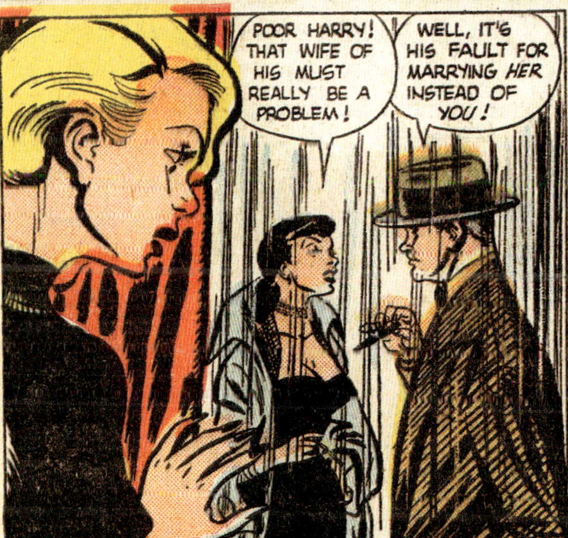
POOR HARRY! THAT WIFE OF HIS MUST REALLY BE A PROBLEM!
WELL, IT'S HIS FAULT FOR MARRYING HER INSTEAD OF YOU!

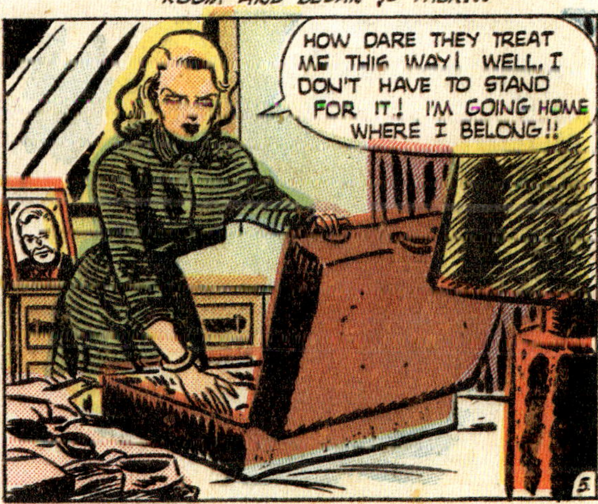
FLORENCE WAS A GIRL HARRY HAD DATED BEFORE HE MARRIED ME. I HAD NEVER LIKED HER, AND NOW HER REMARK WAS THE FINAL BLOW. I RAN INTO THE BEDROOM AND BEGAN TO PACK...
HOW DARE THEY TREAT ME THIS WAY! WELL, I DON'T HAVE TO STAND FOR IT! I'M GOING HOME WHERE I BELONG!!

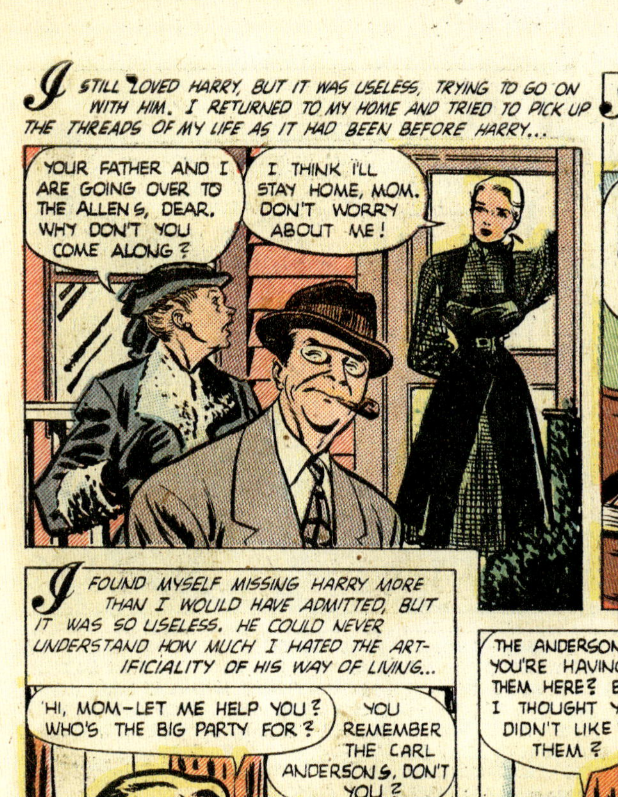
I STILL LOVED HARRY, BUT IT WAS USELESS, TRYING TO GO ON WITH HIM. I RETURNED TO MY HOME AND TRIED TO PICK UP THE THREADS OF MY LIFE AS IT HAD BEEN BEFORE HARRY...
YOUR FATHER AND I ARE GOING OVER TO THE ALLENS, DEAR. WHY DON'T YOU COME ALONG?
I THINK I'LL STAY HOME, MOM. DON'T WORRY ABOUT ME!

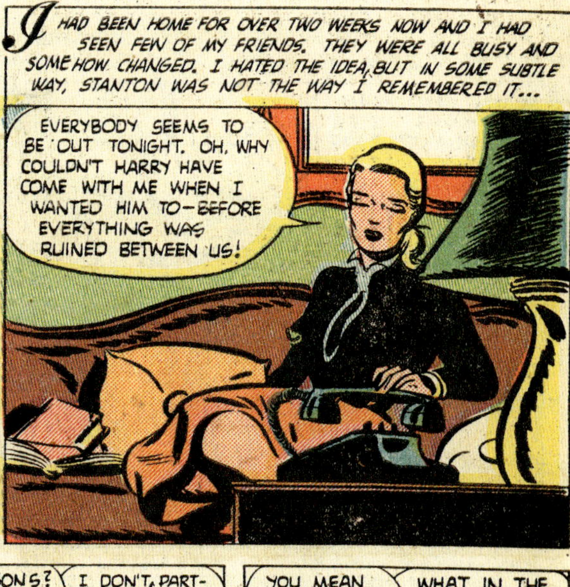
I HAD BEEN HOME FOR OVER TWO WEEKS NOW AND I HAD SEEN FEW OF MY FRIENDS. THEY WERE ALL BUSY AND SOMEHOW CHANGED. I HATED THE IDEA, BUT IN SOME SUBTLE WAY, STANTON WAS NOT THE WAY I REMEMBERED IT...
EVERYBODY SEEMS TO BE OUT TONIGHT. OH, WHY COULDN'T HARRY HAVE COME WITH ME WHEN I WANTED HIM TO--BEFORE EVERYTHING WAS RUINED BETWEEN US!

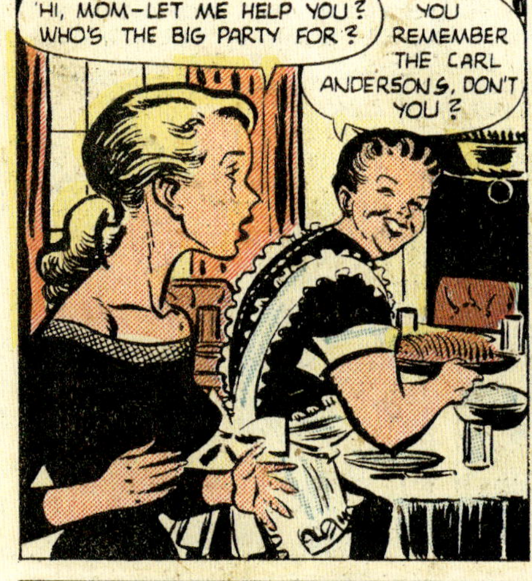
I FOUND MYSELF MISSING HARRY MORE THAN I WOULD HAVE ADMITTED, BUT IT WAS SO USELESS. HE COULD NEVER UNDERSTAND HOW MUCH I HATED THE ARTIFICIALITY OF HIS WAY OF LIVING...
HI, MOM--LET ME HELP YOU? WHO'S THE BIG PARTY FOR?
YOU REMEMBER THE CARL ANDERSONS, DON'T YOU?

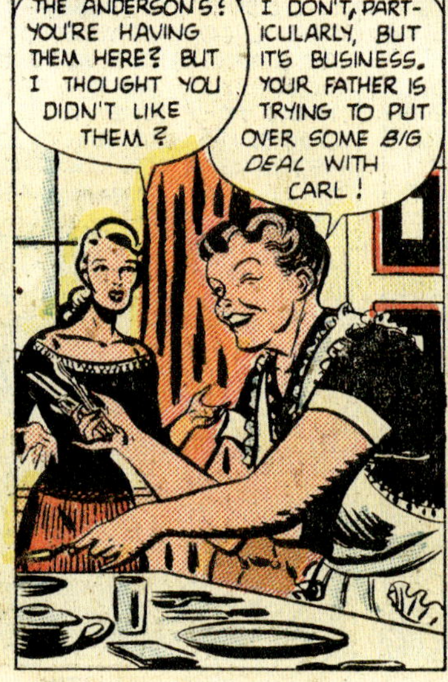
THE ANDERSONS? YOU'RE HAVING THEM HERE? BUT I THOUGHT YOU DIDN'T LIKE THEM?
I DON'T, PARTICULARLY, BUT IT'S BUSINESS. YOUR FATHER IS TRYING TO PUT OVER SOME BIG DEAL WITH CARL!

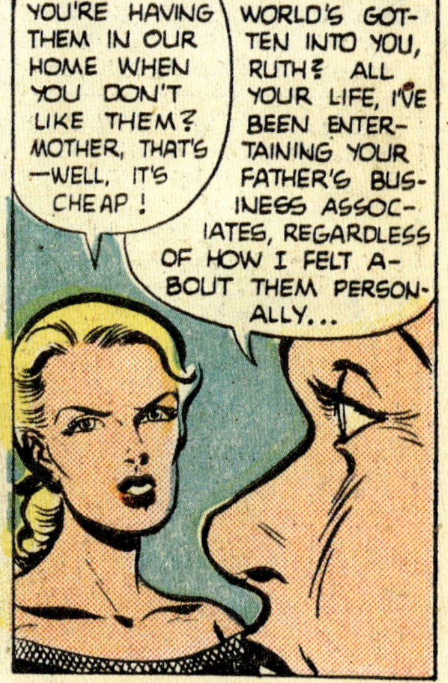
YOU MEAN YOU'RE HAVING THEM IN OUR HOME WHEN YOU DON'T LIKE THEM? MOTHER, THAT'S --WELL, IT'S CHEAP!
WHAT IN THE WORLD'S GOTTEN INTO YOU, RUTH? ALL YOUR LIFE, I'VE BEEN ENTERTAINING YOUR FATHER'S BUSINESS ASSOCIATES, REGARDLESS OF HOW I FELT ABOUT THEM PERSONALLY...

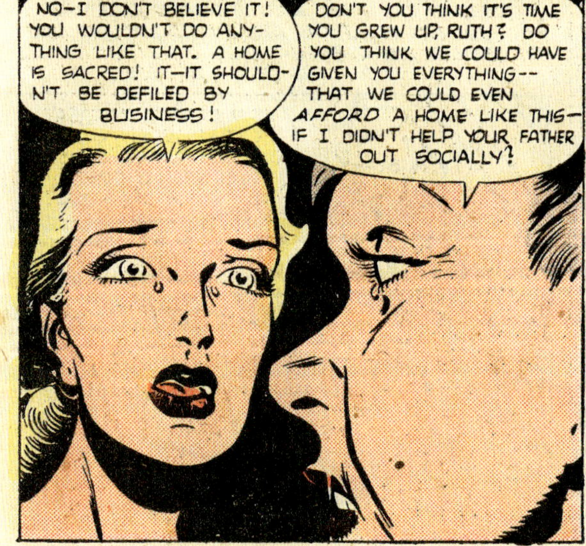
NO--I DON'T BELIEVE IT! YOU WOULDN'T DO ANYTHING LIKE THAT. A HOME IS SACRED! IT--IT SHOULDN'T BE DEFILED BY BUSINESS!
DON'T YOU THINK IT'S TIME YOU GREW UP, RUTH? DO YOU THINK WE COULD HAVE GIVEN YOU EVERYTHING-- THAT WE COULD EVEN AFFORD A HOME LIKE THIS-- IF I DIDN'T HELP YOUR FATHER OUT SOCIALLY?

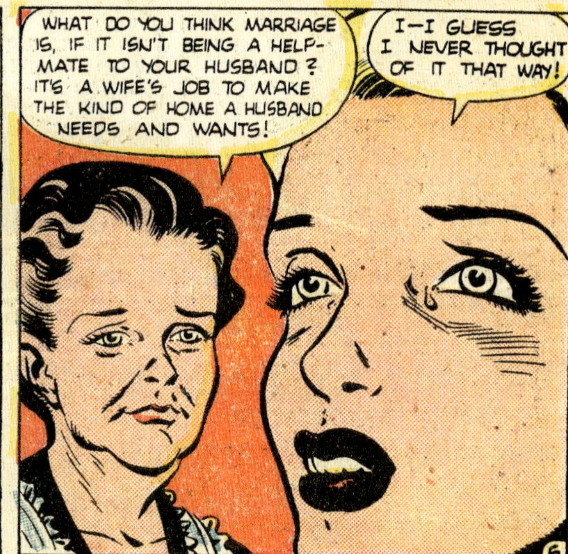
WHAT DO YOU THINK MARRIAGE IS, IF IT ISN'T BEING A HELPMATE TO YOUR HUSBAND? IT'S A WIFE'S JOB TO MAKE THE KIND OF HOME A HUSBAND NEEDS AND WANTS!
I--I GUESS I NEVER THOUGHT OF IT THAT WAY!
6

I STOOD THERE IN AMAZEMENT, A THOUSAND CONFUSED IDEAS GOING THROUGH MY MIND AS I REMEMBERED THE COUNTLESS DINNERS AND PARTIES MOTHER HAD GIVEN. I HAD ALWAYS THOUGHT SHE HAD BEEN ENTERTAINING FRIENDS. THAT NIGHT, AFTER THE ANDERSONS WERE GONE...

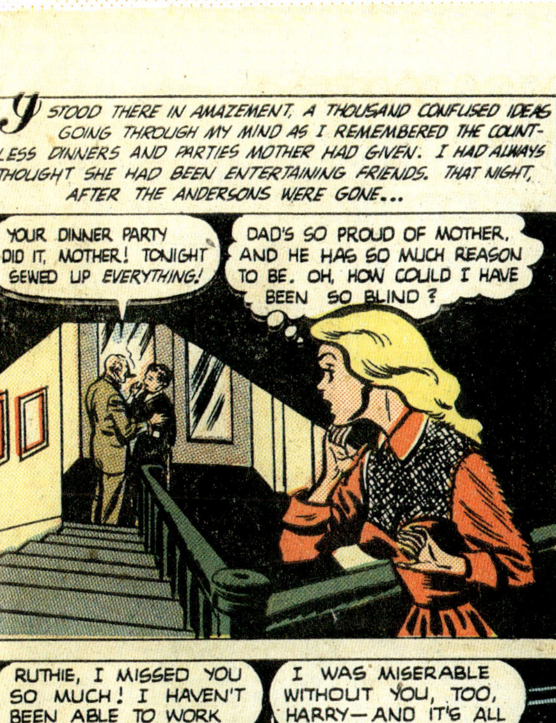

I COULDN'T STAND SEEING THE PRIDE IN DAD'S EYES. I HAD NEVER GIVEN HARRY A CHANCE TO LOOK AT ME IN THAT WAY. I HAD ALWAYS THOUGHT ONLY OF MY OWN SELFISH DESIRES. BUT MAYBE IT WASN'T TOO LATE TO CHANGE ALL THAT.

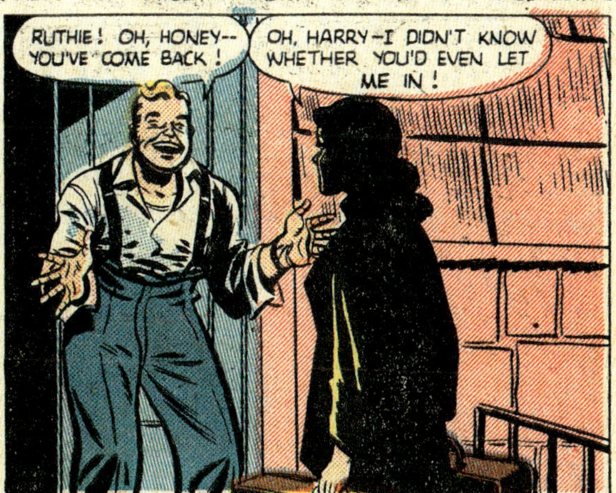

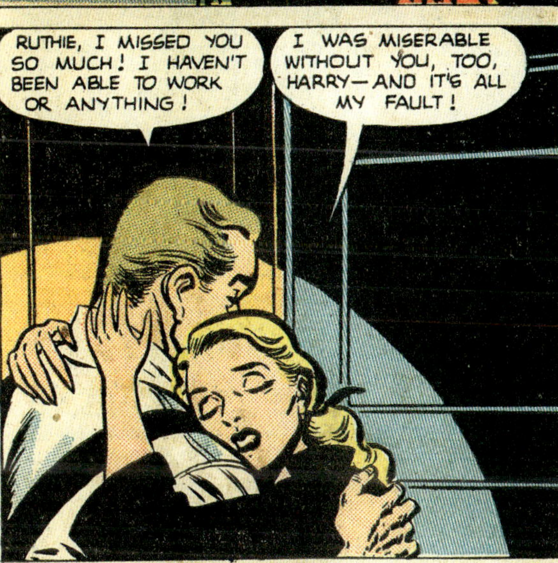

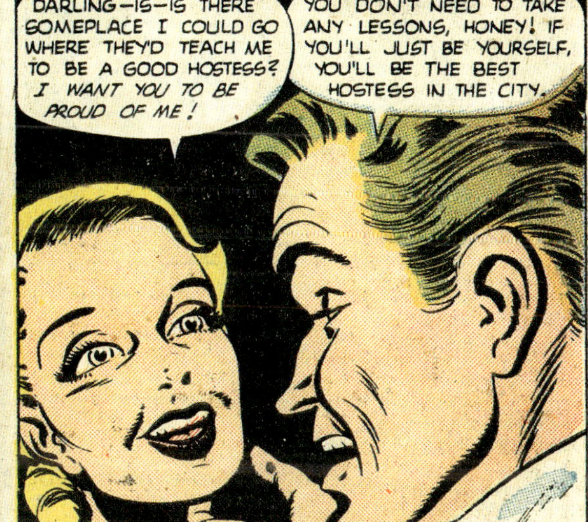

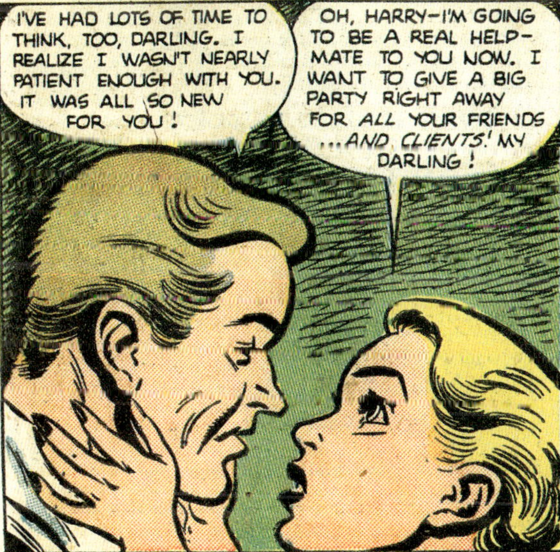

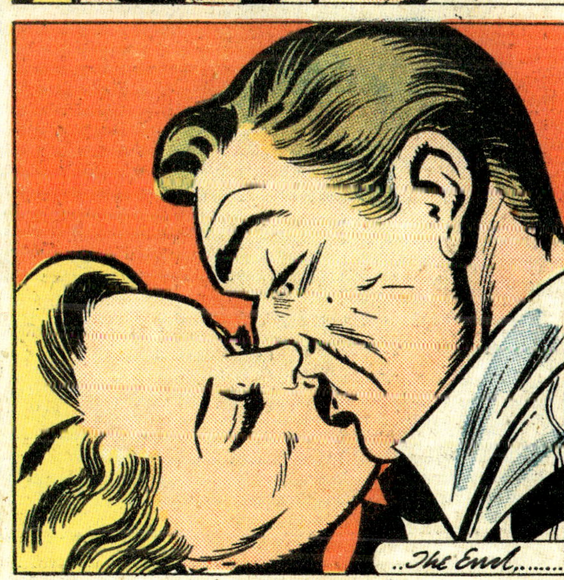

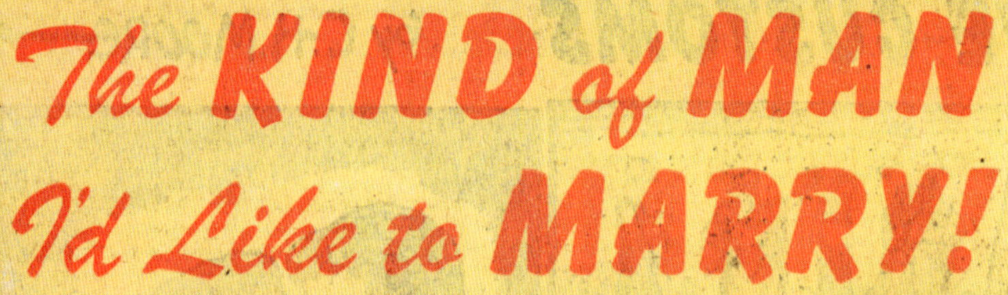

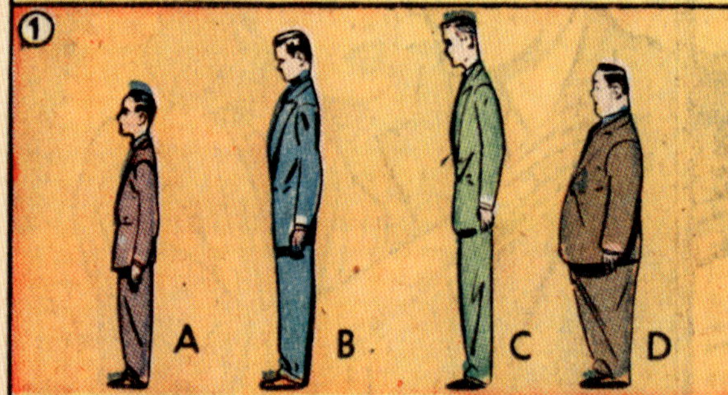

Shall he be short or tall . . . slender or plump? Got any preferences?

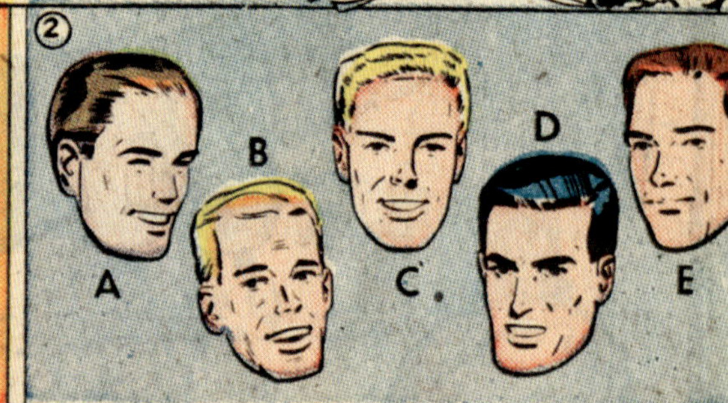

Some like 'em red . . . some like 'em dark. Curly straight . . . which do YOU like?

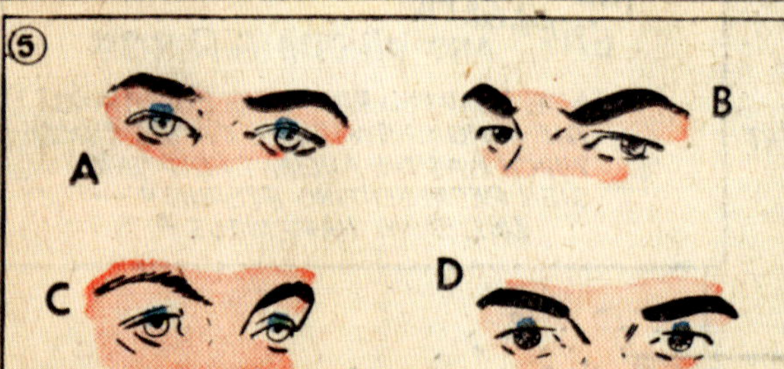

Eyes—a bold laughing blue or a mysterious black? Dreamy gray or warm, deep brown? Which eyes have IT . . . for you?

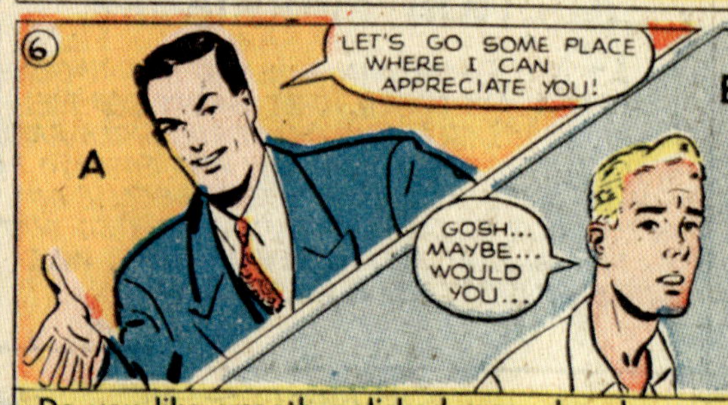

Do you like smooth, polished men who always sa the right thing . . . or the shy, boyish type who overcome at the sight of you?

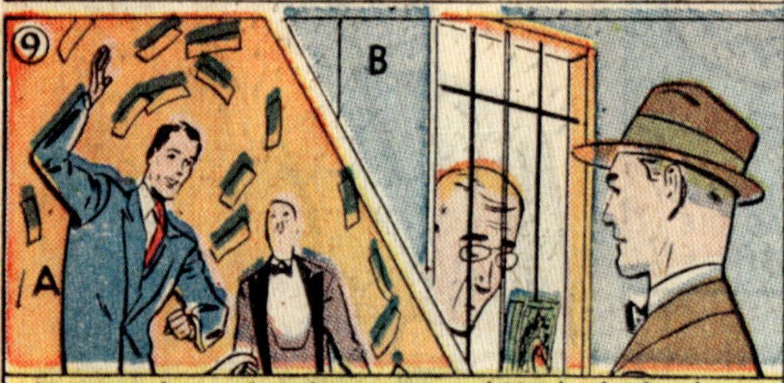

Here we have Kip, the tip-er, and Hank, the bank-er. Would you rather have a man who spends lavishly or one who has a nest-egg for that dream house?

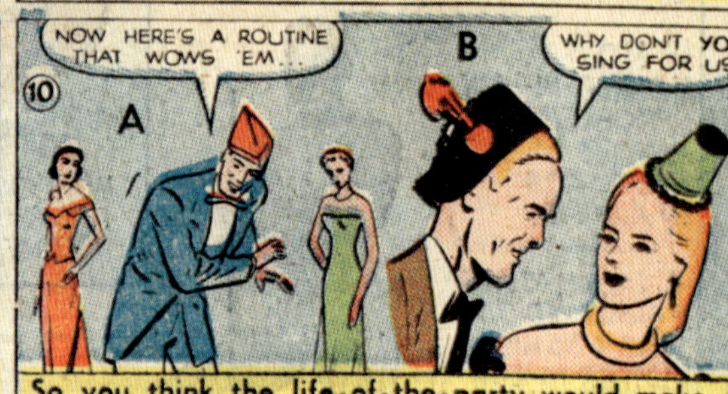

So you think the life-of-the-party would make good husband? But how about the chap who think *everyone* should have a chance?

TELL US WHAT KIND OF MAN YOU'D LIKE TO MARRY! FIRST, USING THE CHECK LIST ON THE RIGHT (OR A COPY OF THE LIST), MAKE YOUR CHOICE ACCORDING TO LETTERED FIGURES IN EACH PANEL, ONE LETTER TO A NUMBER. THEN, IN NO MORE THAN 250 WORDS, WRITE WHY YOU'VE MADE THESE PARTICULAR SELECTIONS. SEND LETTER AND CHECK LIST TO: CONTEST EDITOR, BOY MEETS GIRL, 114 E. 32nd ST., NEW YORK 16, N. Y.

CHECK LIST

1 ________	7 ________
2 ________	8 ________
3 ________	9 ________
4 ________	10 ________
5 ________	11 ________
6 ________	12 ________

OF COURSE you've often thought about the kind of man you'd like to marry. You should – he's the most important man in your life, even if you haven't met him yet. Herewith we submit samples – do any of them meet your dream-beam specifications?

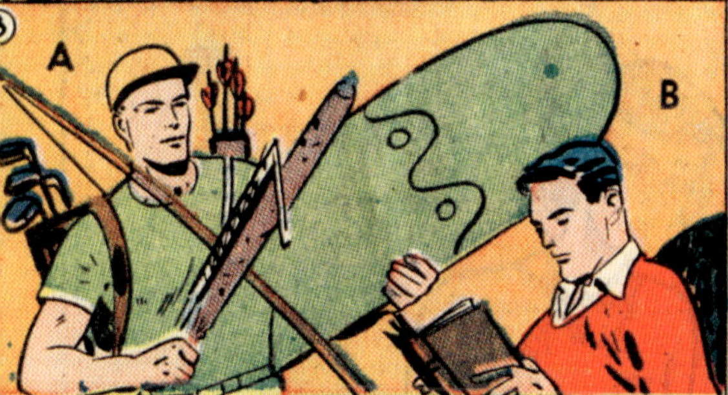

Does the strictly athletic type send you . . . or the man that enjoys reading a book now and then?

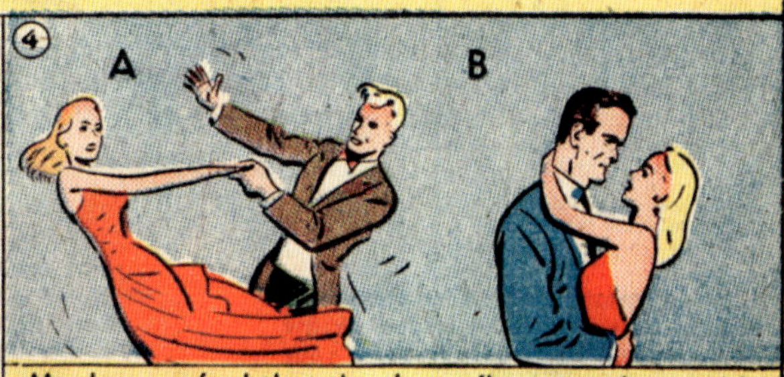

Maybe you feel that the dance floor wrestler would make an exciting companion for life. Or do you prefer the man who takes his dancing with more dignity and less violence?

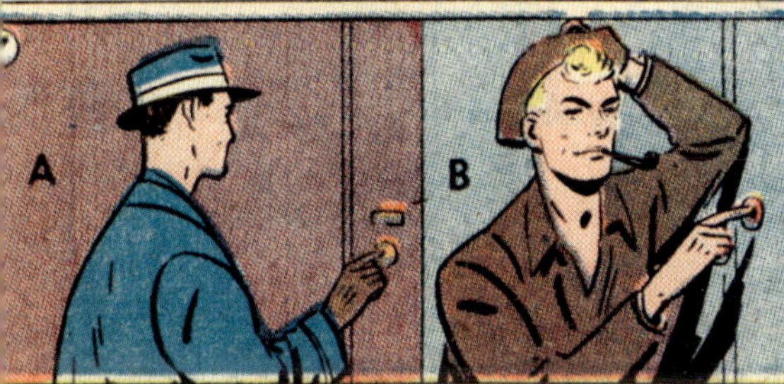

Are you attracted by the man who is conventionally dressed and neatly groomed when he comes calling? Or is your ideal the man who "won't dress up for anybody"?

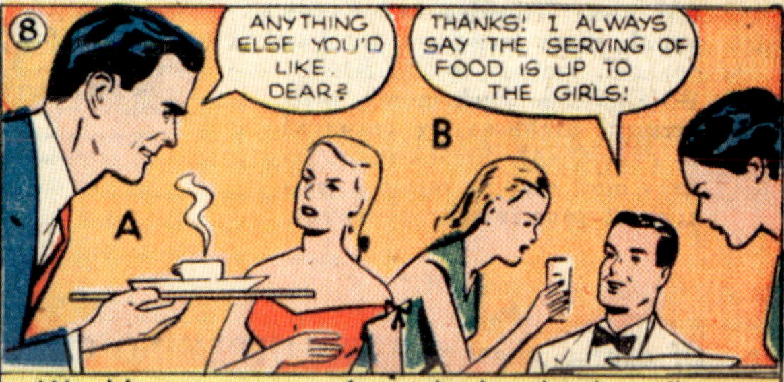

Would you want your future husband to be willing to wait on you when the occasion demands? Or do you believe a man should be waited on?

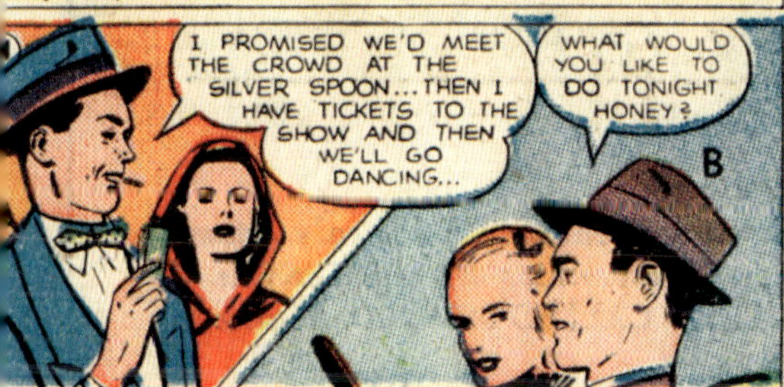

Do you thrill to the wasteful man who makes plans for you? Or do you want a man who consults you about the evening's doings?

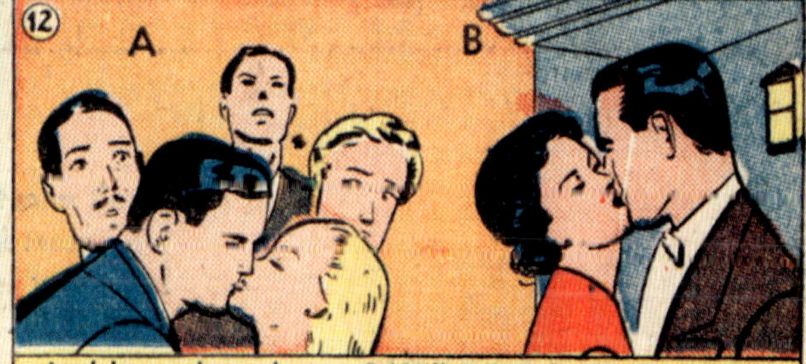

And how about kissing? Will it be the kiss-in-public man who wants the whole town to see . . . or the one who thinks kissing is a private affair?

or the best letter explaining your choice, The Editors f BOY MEETS GIRL will pay:

1st Prize . . $10
2nd Prize $5
3rd Prize $2

Contest for this issue closes on JANUARY 31st, 1950. Your letter should be postmarked on or before that date. Letters and check lists will not be returned, and the decision of the Editors is final.

MORE DREAM-BEAM SAMPLES IN NEXT ISSUE

DON'T MISS THEM!

BOY MEETS GIRL
#2, April 1950

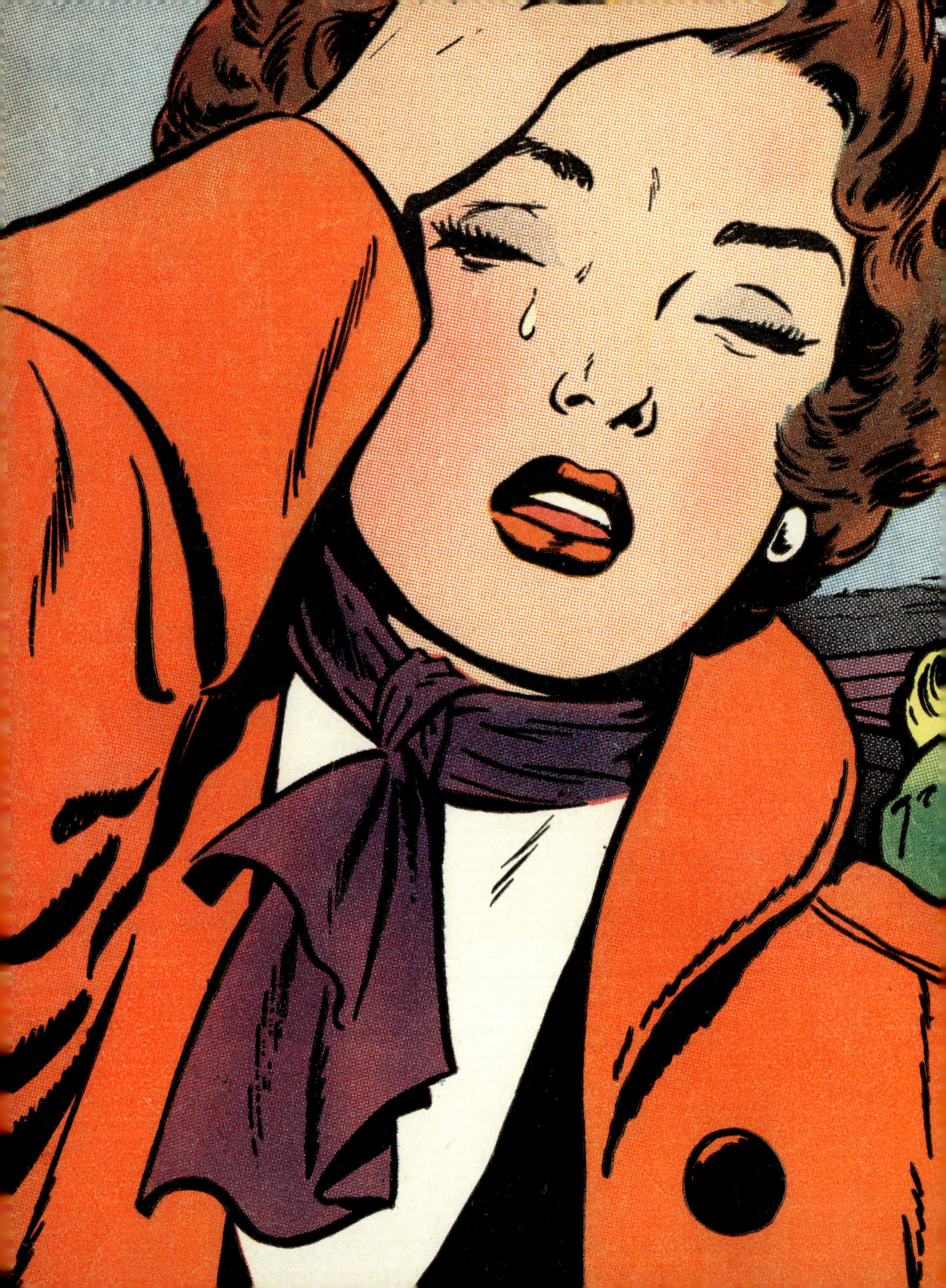

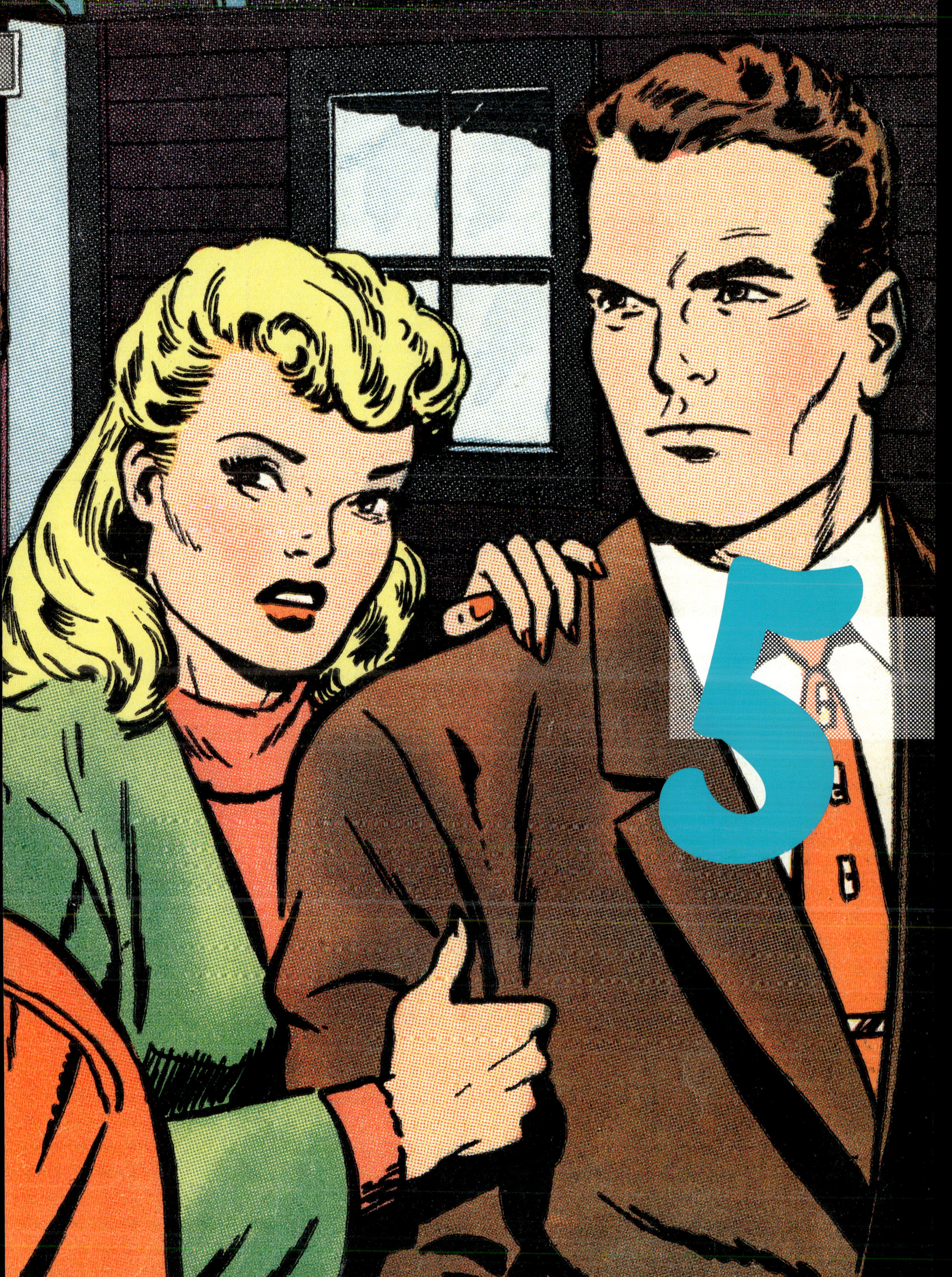
5

Gang Sweetheart

CLASS STRUGGLES

One of the peculiarities of classic love comics is that every now and again they aspired to take on themes quite a bit weightier than the standard two-timing boyfriend or status-obsessed wife. Maybe it was the social consciousness of the time seeping into these ten-cent entertainments — call it the *Gentleman's Agreement* factor, after Laura Z. Hobson's hugely popular bestseller about anti-Semitism, the film version of which won the Oscar for best picture in 1947 — or maybe it provided a blessed relief to artists and writers who relished the chance to express their inner Paddy Chayefsky in between extended bouts of serving up boilerplate soap-opera melodrama. Genre pioneers Joe Simon and Jack Kirby broke the mold set by the confession magazines in their trailblazing comic book *Young Romance* by including stories on everything from religious and ethnic prejudice to class distinctions, from financial pressures to family obligations — not to mention the thousand and one mundane yarns about thwarted love. While the rest of the industry that followed in the wake of the Simon and Kirby books was less likely to veer off the path established over the years by the confession magazines, every now and then they, too, would take up the cudgel of social justice and pummel their readers with it.

So in this section, we proudly present a stirring array of covers and stories from the romance comics that dealt with the decidedly untidy issue of class struggles. From the wonderful Simon and Kirby cover of *Young Romance* #5 — "I may lose Ted if he ever discovers that my mother is the office scrubwoman!" — to the profound question posed on the cover of *My Own Romance* #63—"Can romance really come to a girl who lives 'on the wrong side of the tracks?'" — to the story "Love Conquers Bigotry" from *Love Confessions* #9 — there are trials aplenty here to test those sweethearts separated by the gulf between their breeding, their bank accounts, and their relative ability to join a country club.

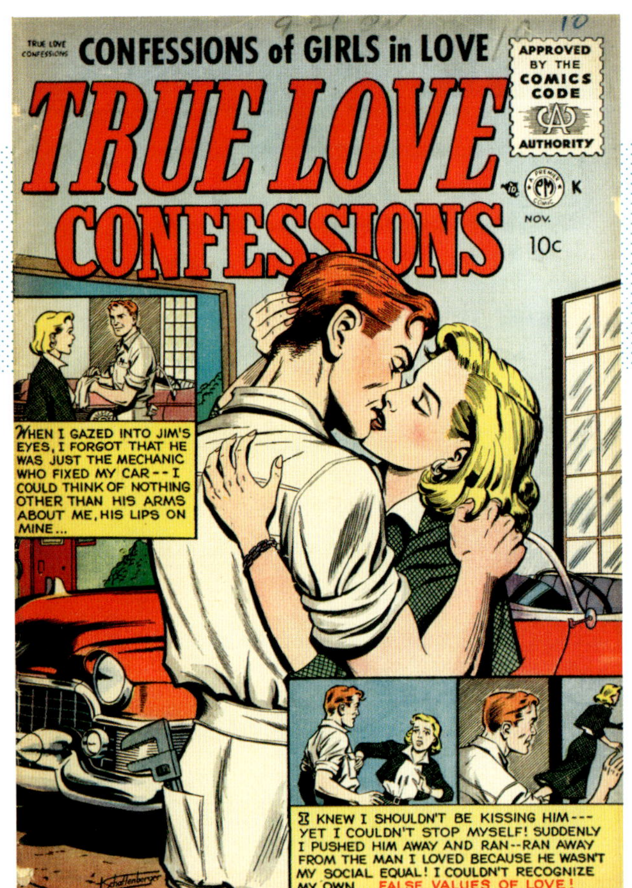
TRUE LOVE CONFESSIONS
CONFESSIONS of GIRLS in LOVE
APPROVED BY THE COMICS CODE AUTHORITY
TRUE LOVE CONFESSIONS
NOV.
10c
WHEN I GAZED INTO JIM'S EYES, I FORGOT THAT HE WAS JUST THE MECHANIC WHO FIXED MY CAR-- I COULD THINK OF NOTHING OTHER THAN HIS ARMS ABOUT ME, HIS LIPS ON MINE...
I KNEW I SHOULDN'T BE KISSING HIM--- YET I COULDN'T STOP MYSELF! SUDDENLY I PUSHED HIM AWAY AND RAN--RAN AWAY FROM THE MAN I LOVED BECAUSE HE WASN'T MY SOCIAL EQUAL! I COULDN'T RECOGNIZE MY OWN... FALSE VALUES OF LOVE!

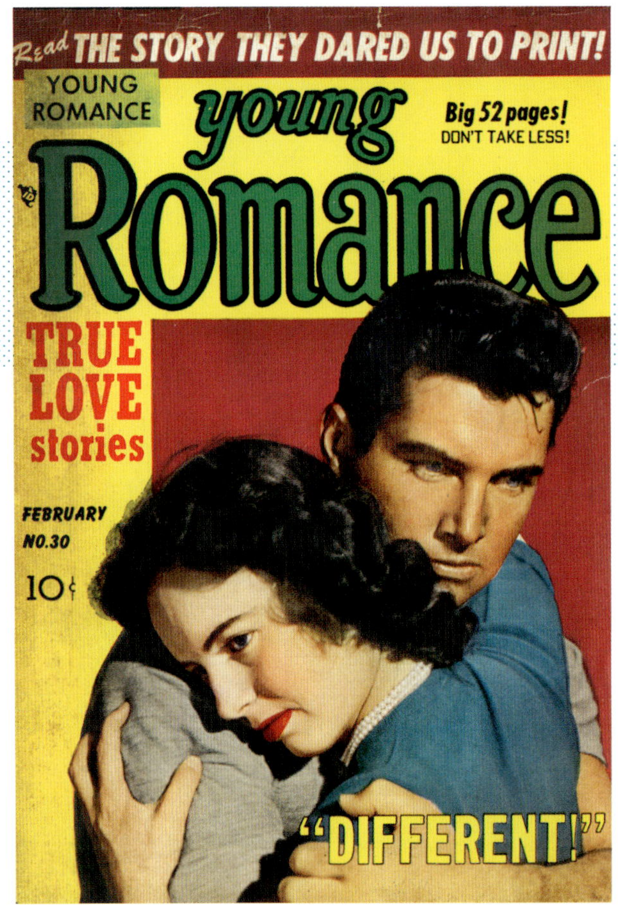
Read THE STORY THEY DARED US TO PRINT!
YOUNG ROMANCE
young Romance
Big 52 pages!
DON'T TAKE LESS!
TRUE LOVE stories
FEBRUARY
NO.30
10¢
"DIFFERENT!"

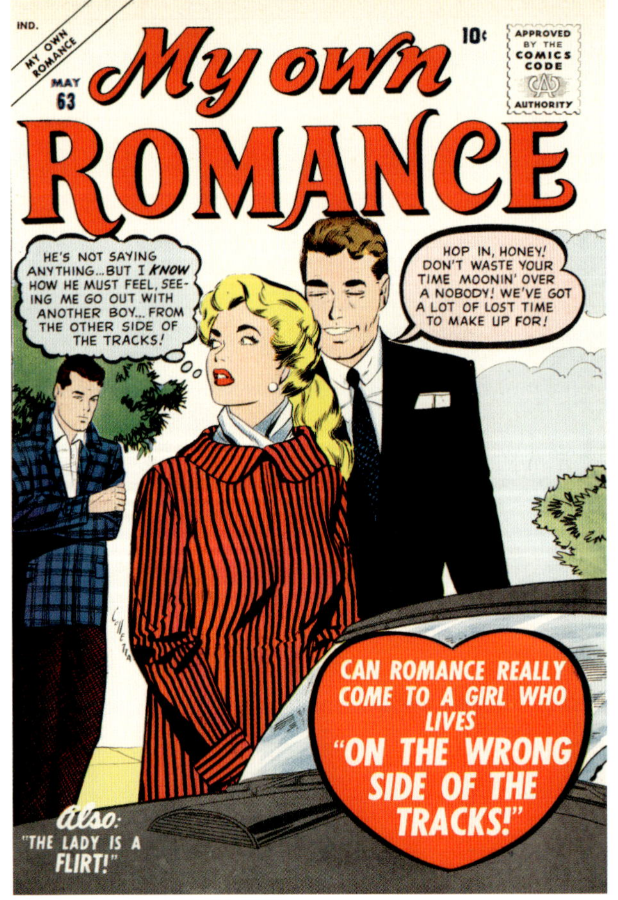
IND.
MY OWN ROMANCE
MAY
63
10¢
APPROVED BY THE COMICS CODE AUTHORITY
My own ROMANCE
HE'S NOT SAYING ANYTHING...BUT I KNOW HOW HE MUST FEEL, SEEING ME GO OUT WITH ANOTHER BOY... FROM THE OTHER SIDE OF THE TRACKS!
HOP IN, HONEY! DON'T WASTE YOUR TIME MOONIN' OVER A NOBODY! WE'VE GOT A LOT OF LOST TIME TO MAKE UP FOR!
CAN ROMANCE REALLY COME TO A GIRL WHO LIVES "ON THE WRONG SIDE OF THE TRACKS!"
Also: "THE LADY IS A FLIRT!"

"LOVE CONQUERS ALL THINGS—EXCEPT POVERTY AND TOOTHACHE."
— MAE WEST

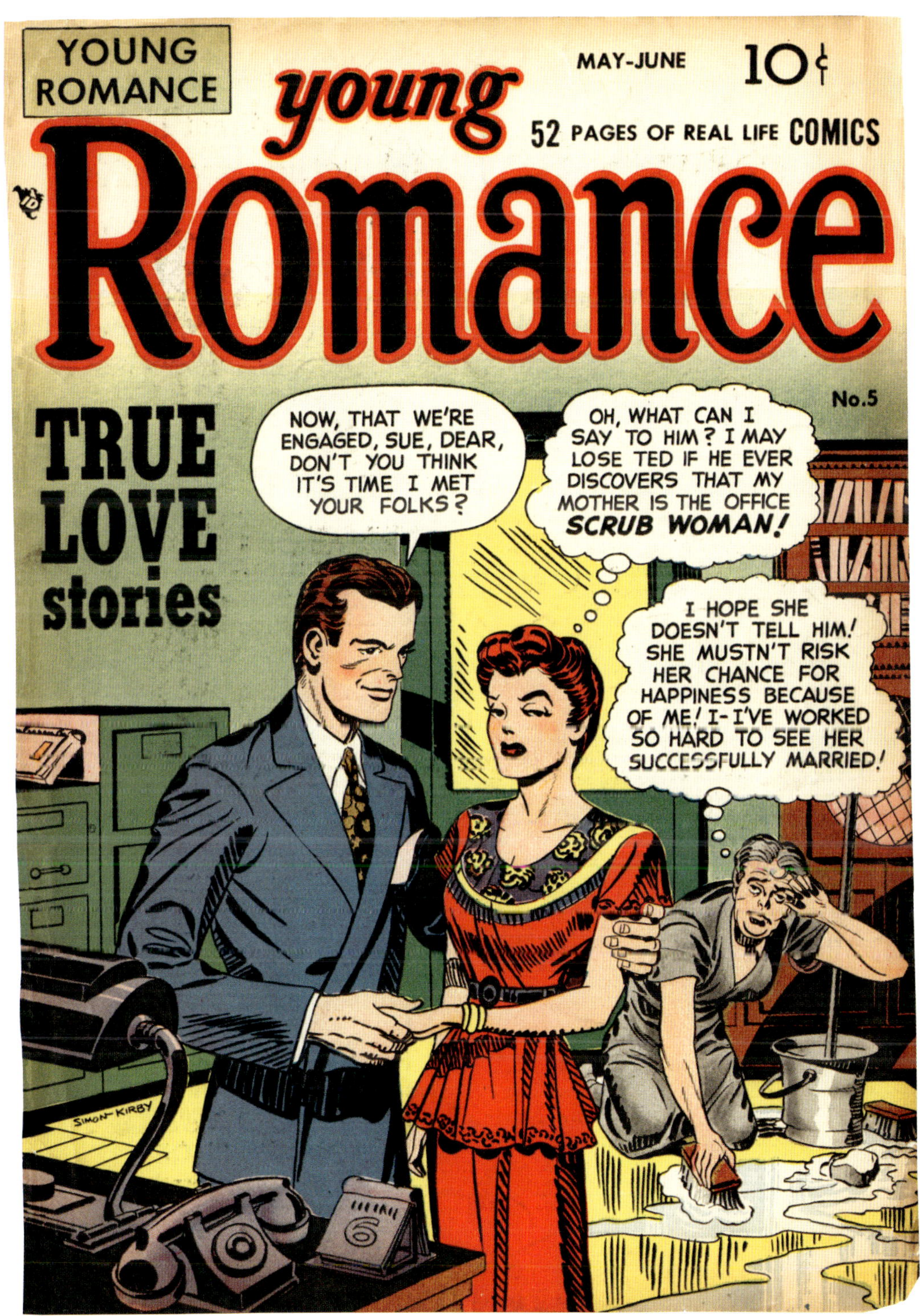

Pages 150–151:
BRIDES ROMANCES
#7, September 1954, cover detail

Page 154, clockwise from top left:
TRUE LOVE CONFESSIONS
#10, November 1955

YOUNG ROMANCE
#30, February 1951

MY OWN ROMANCE
#63, May 1958

This page:
YOUNG ROMANCE
#5, May–June 1948

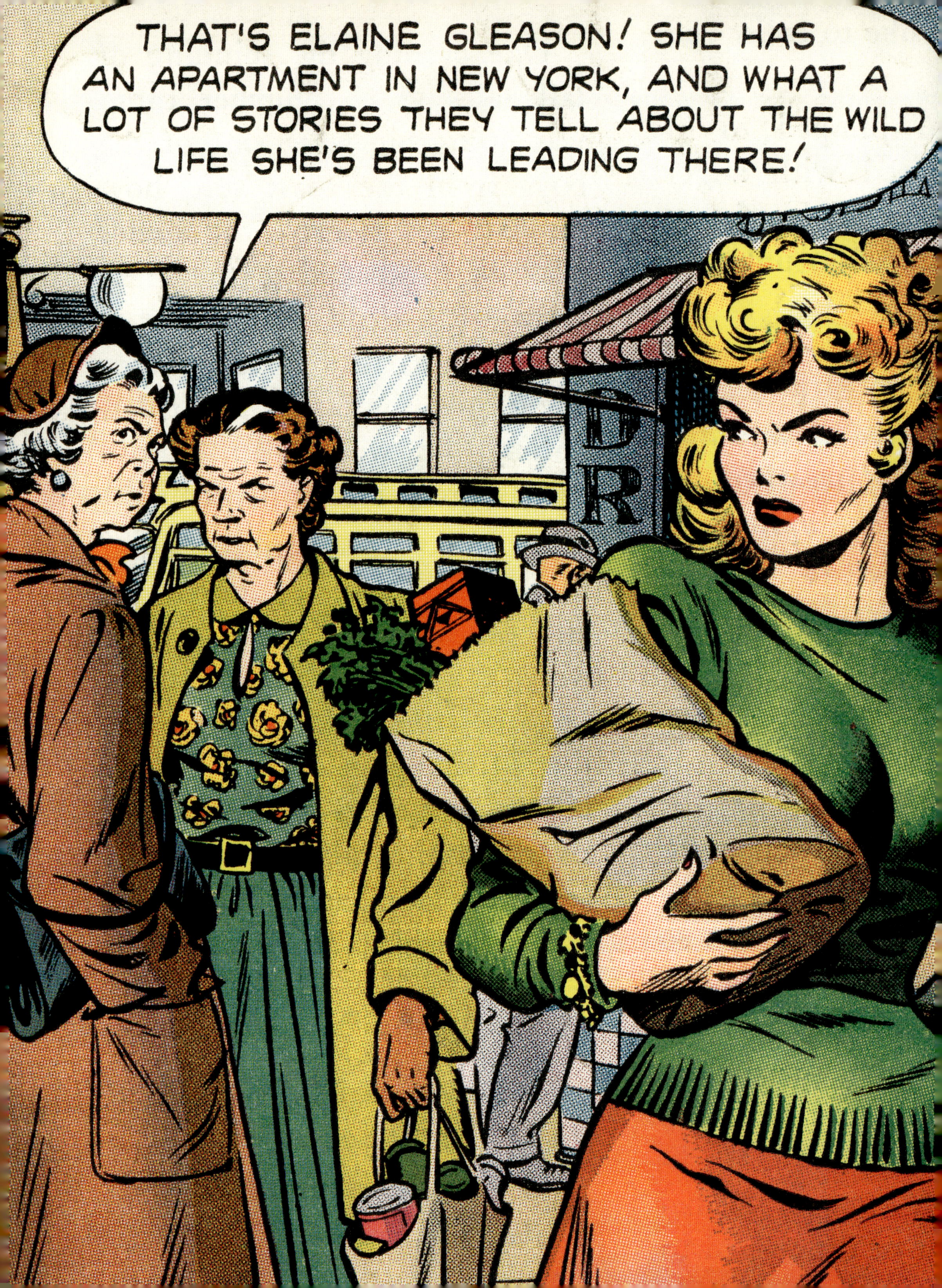
THAT'S ELAINE GLEASON! SHE HAS AN APARTMENT IN NEW YORK, AND WHAT A LOT OF STORIES THEY TELL ABOUT THE WILD LIFE SHE'S BEEN LEADING THERE!

Page 156:
DIARY SECRETS
#14, October 1952, cover detail

Below, from left to right:
LOVE DIARY
#14, March 1951

YOUNG ROMANCE
#8, November–December 1948, splash page

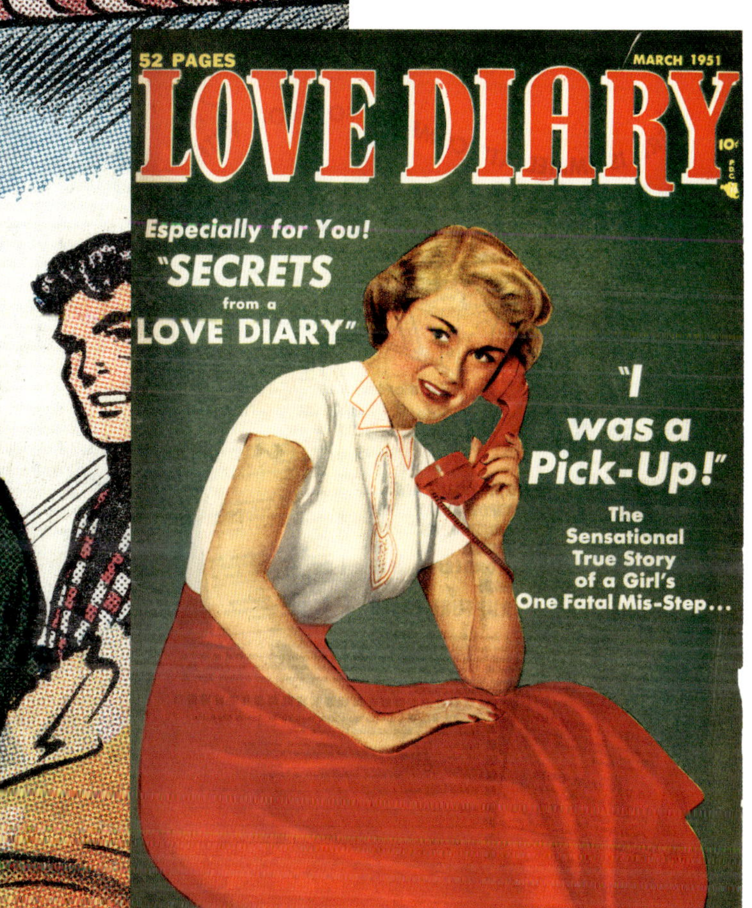

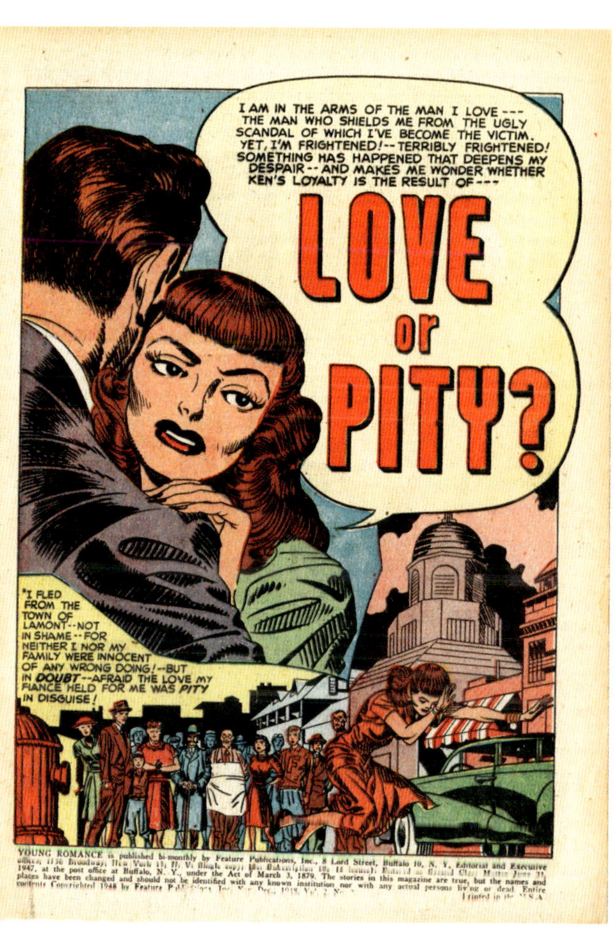

"I'VE NEVER YET MET A MAN WHO COULD LOOK AFTER ME. I DON'T NEED A HUSBAND. WHAT I NEED IS A WIFE."
—— JOAN COLLINS

OF ALL THE MEN IN THE WORLD, WHY, OH WHY, DID THE ONE MAN IN MY LIFE HAVE TO BE...

"THE MAN I COULDN'T LOVE!"

A TRUE LIFE STORY

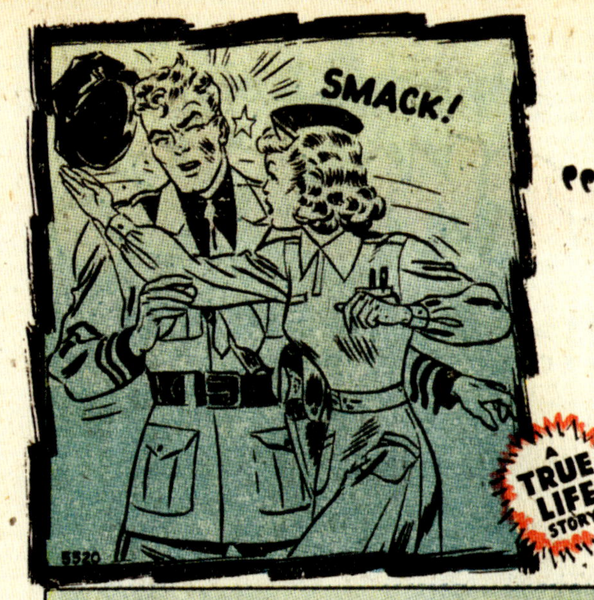

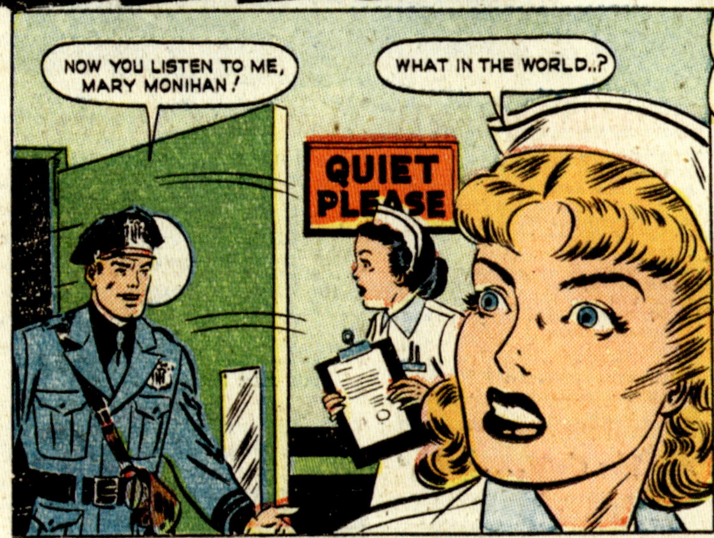

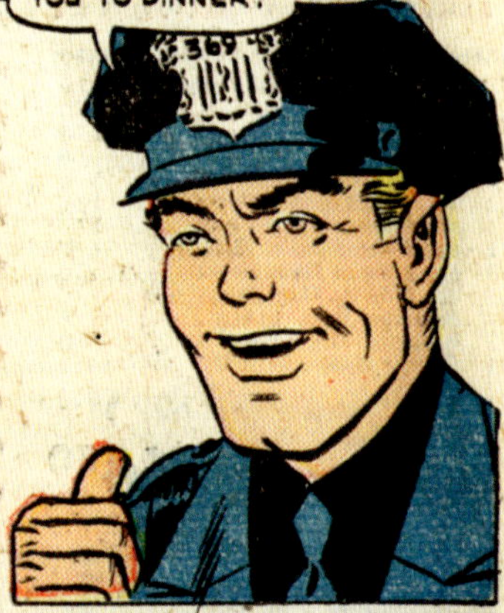

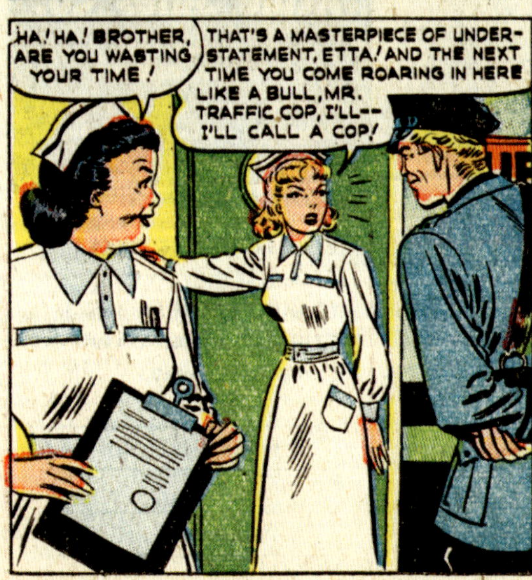

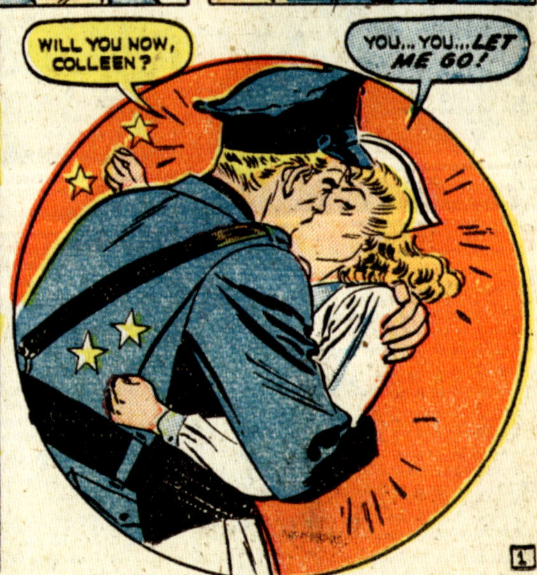

1

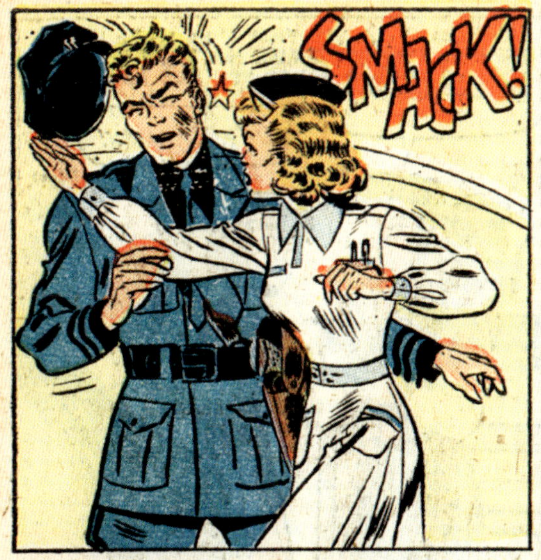

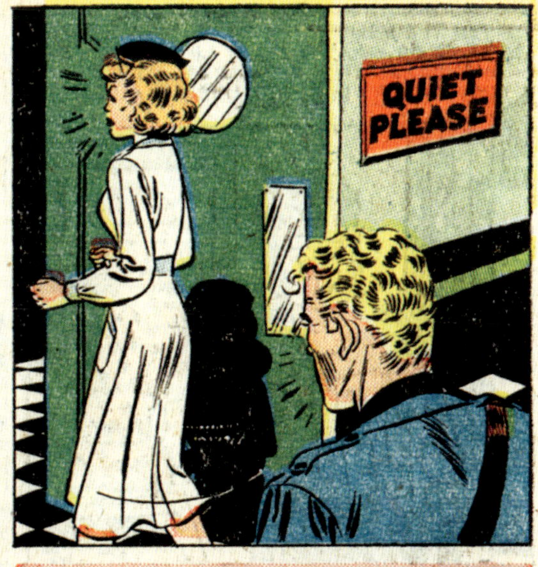

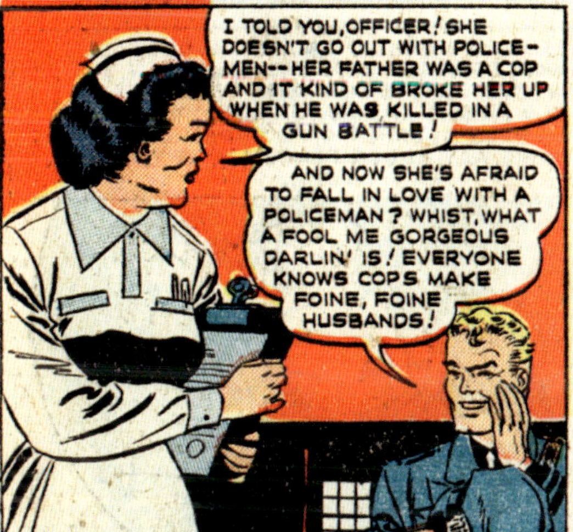

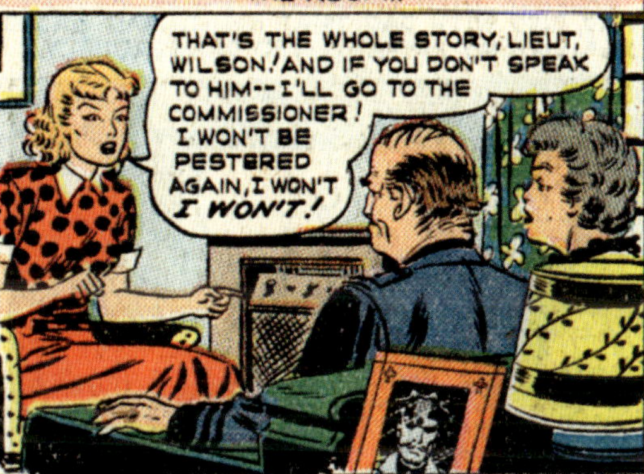

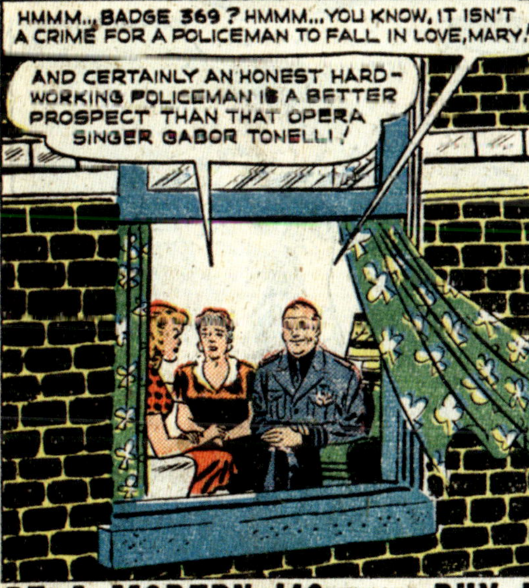

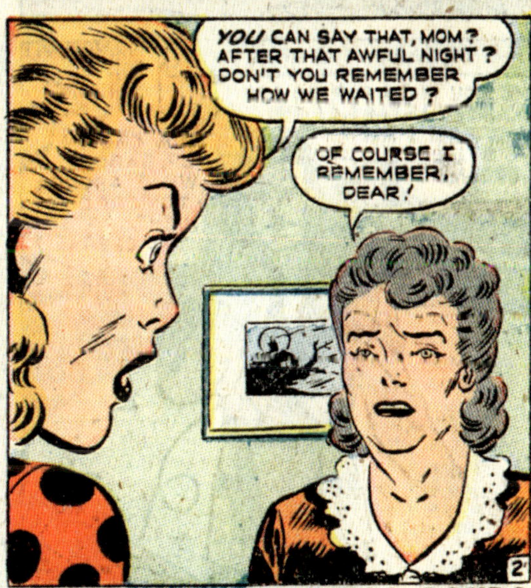

BEST LOVE
#33 (or #34),
August 1949
Art by Joe Kubert

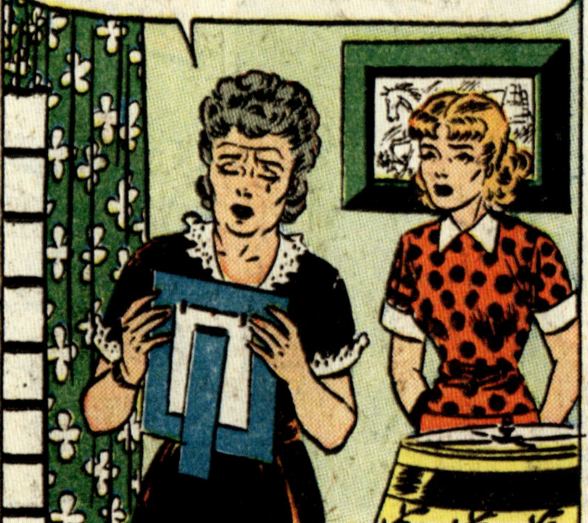

DAD WOULD TELL YOU THAT IF HE WERE HERE! PERHAPS THIS POLICEMAN ISN'T THE MAN FOR YOU--BUT LOVE IS FOR YOU AND FOR EVERY WOMAN!

SHE'S RIGHT, MARY!

I COULDN'T SLEEP THAT NIGHT! TERRY'S FIERY KISS BURNED ON MY LIPS... MOTHER'S WORDS HAUNTED ME! *WAS* I BEHAVING LIKE A CHILD? THEN A MEMORY INTRUDED, MAKING ME SHUDDER WITH TERROR! PART OF MOTHER HAD DIED WITH DAD, THAT NIGHT... AND BADGE 369, LIKE MY FATHER, LIVED DANGEROUSLY...

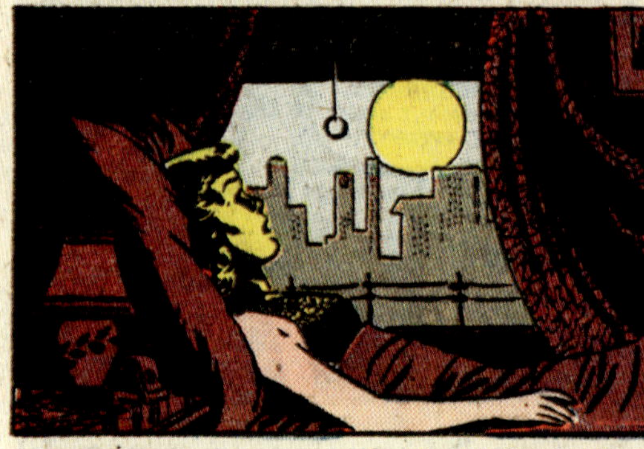

TOWARD MORNING I MADE MY DECISION! I WOULD *NEVER* DATE THE POLICEMAN, BUT I *WOULD* DATE OTHER MEN, FINE MEN LIKE OUR OLD FRIEND GABOR TONELLI! OPERA SINGERS I THOUGHT, DIDN'T LIVE DANGEROUSLY--AND IN HIS WAY GABOR TONELLI WAS EXCITING TOO...

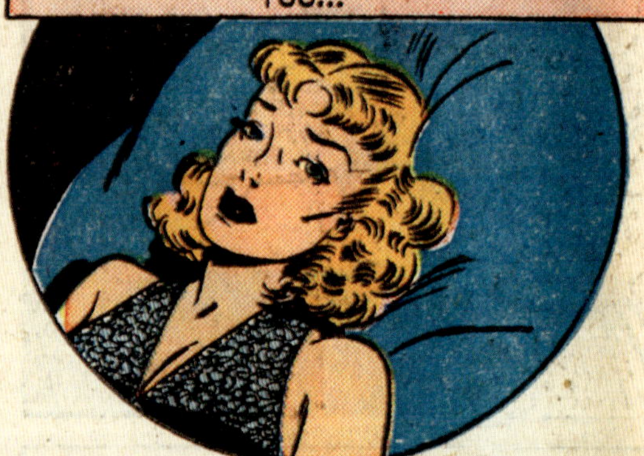

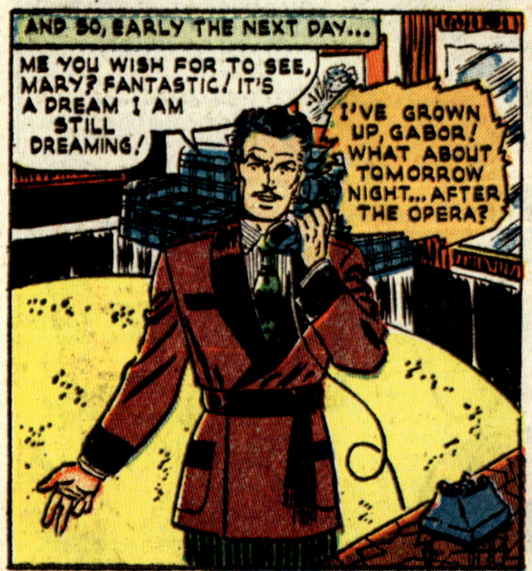

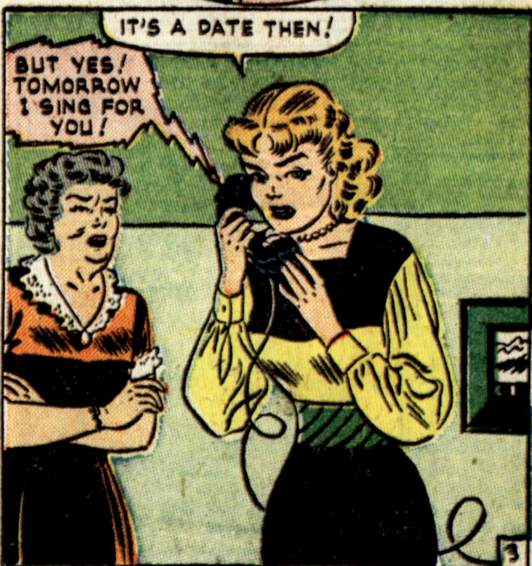

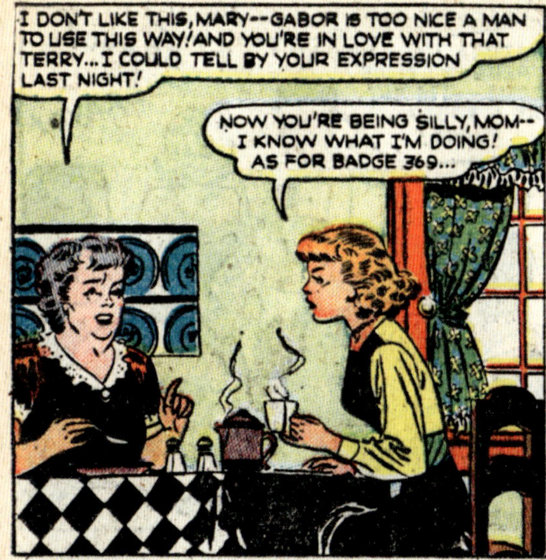
I DON'T LIKE THIS, MARY--GABOR IS TOO NICE A MAN TO USE THIS WAY! AND YOU'RE IN LOVE WITH THAT TERRY... I COULD TELL BY YOUR EXPRESSION LAST NIGHT!
NOW YOU'RE BEING SILLY, MOM-- I KNOW WHAT I'M DOING! AS FOR BADGE 369...

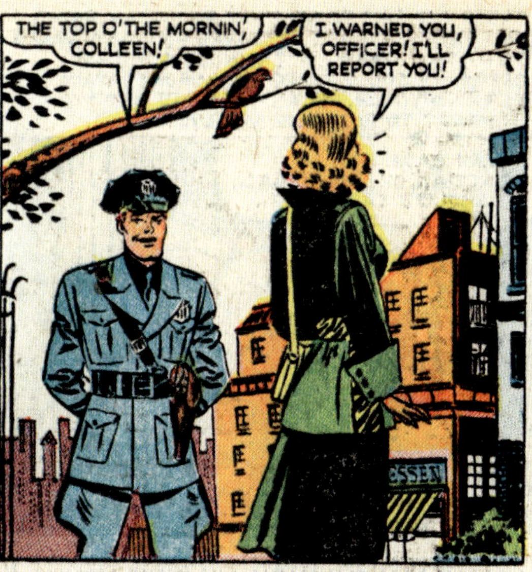
THE TOP O' THE MORNIN', COLLEEN!
I WARNED YOU, OFFICER! I'LL REPORT YOU!

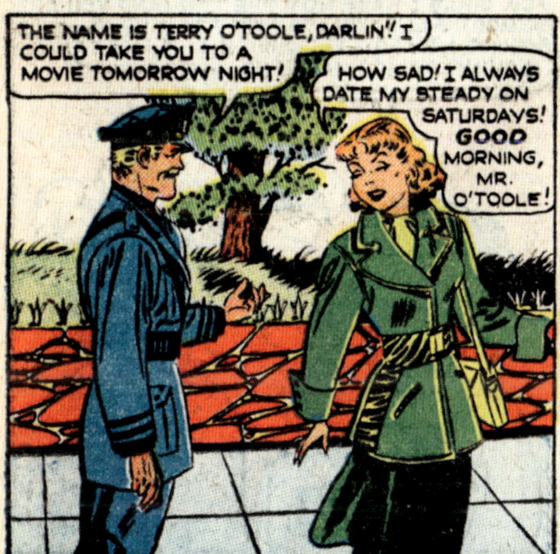
THE NAME IS TERRY O'TOOLE, DARLIN'! I COULD TAKE YOU TO A MOVIE TOMORROW NIGHT!
HOW SAD! I ALWAYS DATE MY STEADY ON SATURDAYS! GOOD MORNING, MR. O'TOOLE!

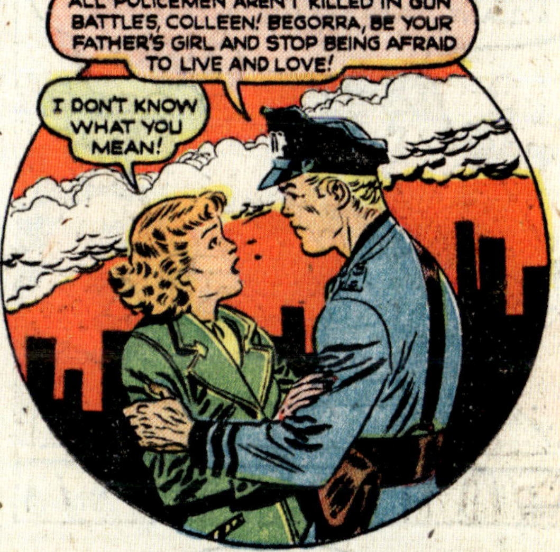
ALL POLICEMEN AREN'T KILLED IN GUN BATTLES, COLLEEN! BEGORRA, BE YOUR FATHER'S GIRL AND STOP BEING AFRAID TO LIVE AND LOVE!
I DON'T KNOW WHAT YOU MEAN!

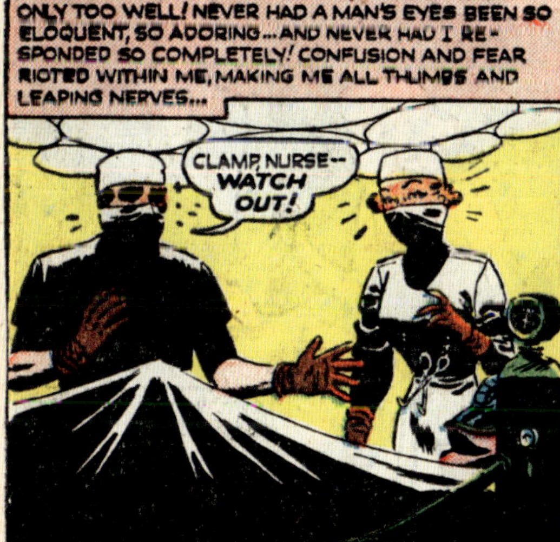
I DID KNOW WHAT TERRY MEANT, THOUGH... KNEW ONLY TOO WELL! NEVER HAD A MAN'S EYES BEEN SO ELOQUENT, SO ADORING... AND NEVER HAD I RE-SPONDED SO COMPLETELY! CONFUSION AND FEAR RIOTED WITHIN ME, MAKING ME ALL THUMBS AND LEAPING NERVES...
CLAMP, NURSE-- WATCH OUT!

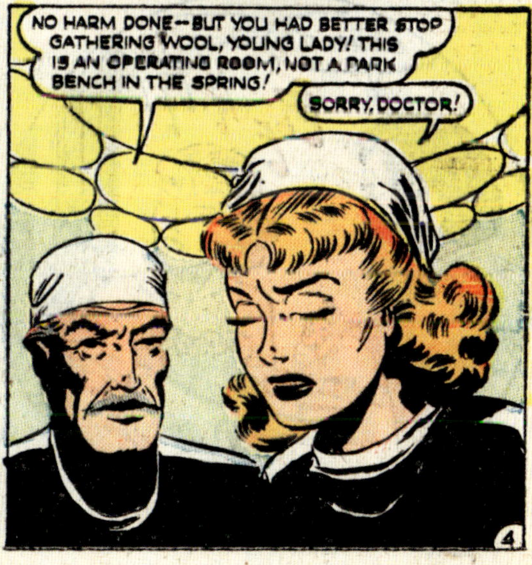
NO HARM DONE-- BUT YOU HAD BETTER STOP GATHERING WOOL, YOUNG LADY! THIS IS AN OPERATING ROOM, NOT A PARK BENCH IN THE SPRING!
SORRY, DOCTOR!
4

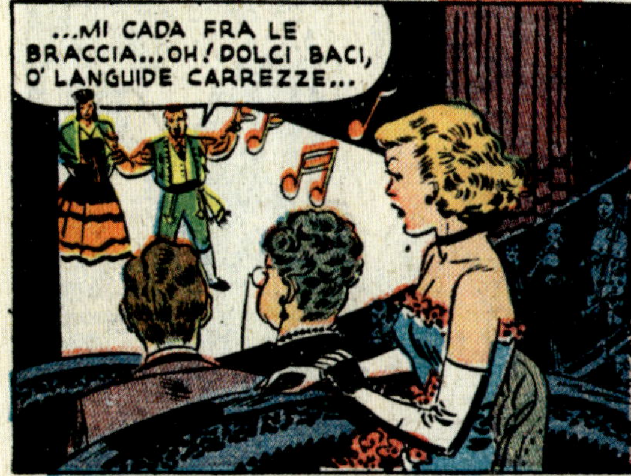
GABOR DID SING TO ME THAT SATURDAY NIGHT, AND HIS FINE TENOR VOICE WAS RICH AND WARM! BUT NOW I WASN'T IN THE MOOD FOR THE OPERA--I COULD THINK ONLY OF A CERTAIN TERRY O'TOOLE, A MAN WHO HAD SET MY HEART TO POUNDING MADLY!
...MI CADA FRA LE BRACCIA...OH! DOLCI BACI, O' LANGUIDE CARREZZE...

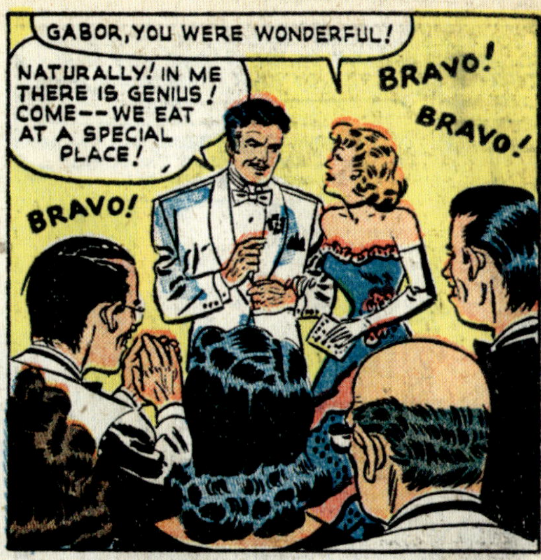
GABOR, YOU WERE WONDERFUL!
NATURALLY! IN ME THERE IS GENIUS! COME--WE EAT AT A SPECIAL PLACE!
BRAVO!
BRAVO!
BRAVO!

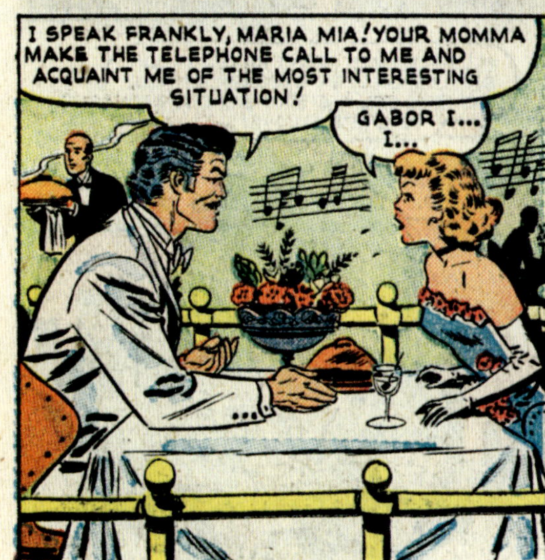
I SPEAK FRANKLY, MARIA MIA! YOUR MOMMA MAKE THE TELEPHONE CALL TO ME AND ACQUAINT ME OF THE MOST INTERESTING SITUATION!
GABOR I... I...

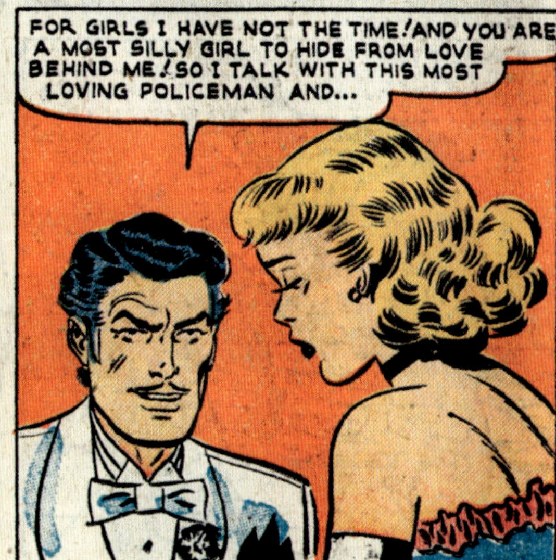
FOR GIRLS I HAVE NOT THE TIME! AND YOU ARE A MOST SILLY GIRL TO HIDE FROM LOVE BEHIND ME! SO I TALK WITH THIS MOST LOVING POLICEMAN AND...

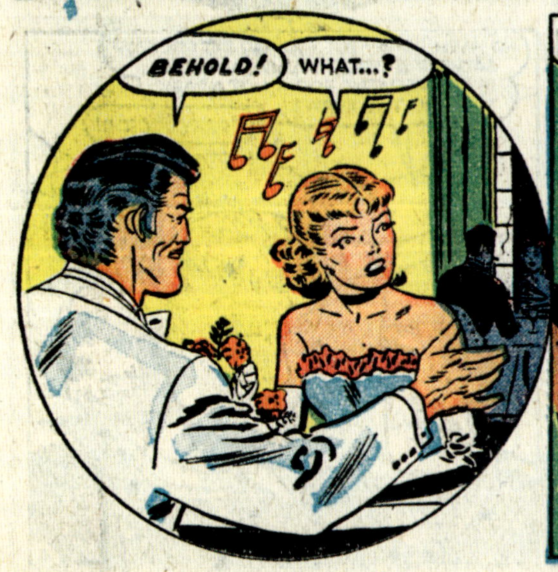
BEHOLD!
WHAT...?

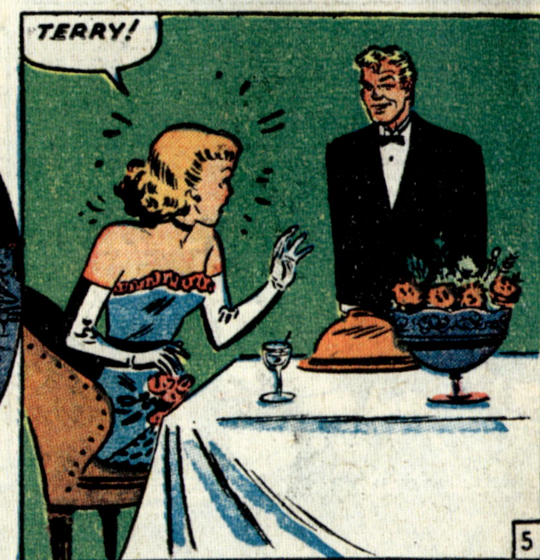
TERRY!
5

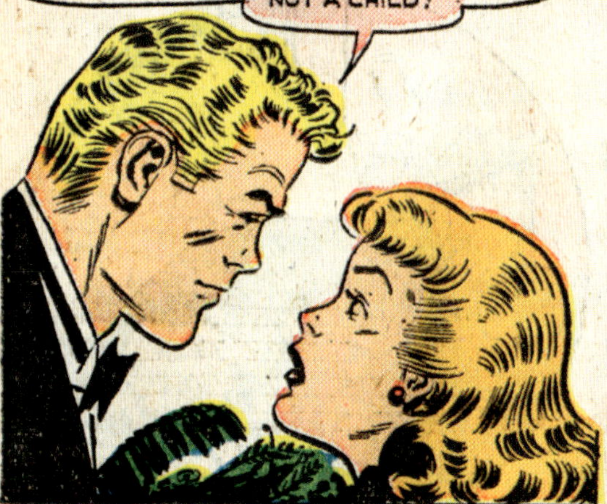
YOU'LL STAND UP TO YOUR FEARS, BEGORRA, THE WAY YOUR FOINE FATHER STOOD UP TO THEM CROOKS! YOU'LL MARRY ME AS I ALWAYS KNEW YOU WOULD, FROM THE DAY I FIRST SAW YOU ON MY BEAT! YOU'RE A WOMAN, COLLEEN, NOT A CHILD!

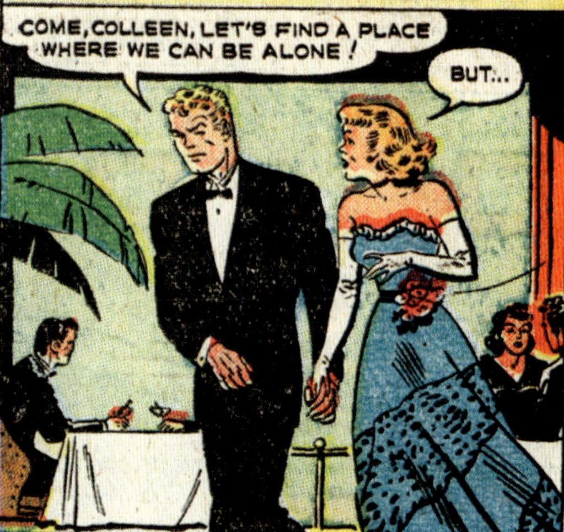
THERE WAS NO RESISTING HIM NOW! HE WAS STRONG AND DETERMINED... AND WHEN AN IRISH COP HAS HIS MIND MADE UP...
COME, COLLEEN, LET'S FIND A PLACE WHERE WE CAN BE ALONE!
BUT...

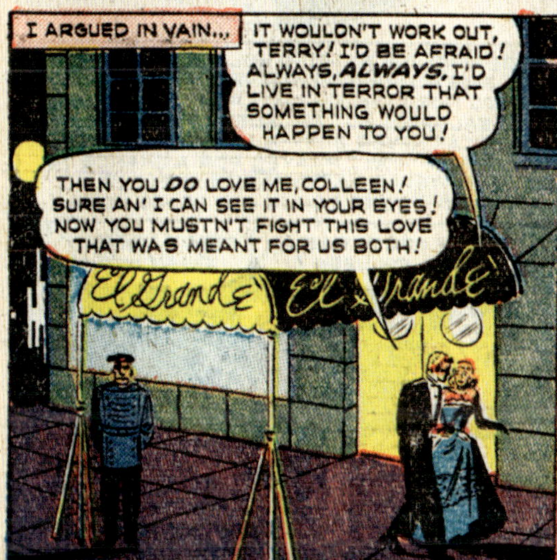
I ARGUED IN VAIN...
IT WOULDN'T WORK OUT, TERRY! I'D BE AFRAID! ALWAYS, ALWAYS, I'D LIVE IN TERROR THAT SOMETHING WOULD HAPPEN TO YOU!
THEN YOU DO LOVE ME, COLLEEN! SURE AN' I CAN SEE IT IN YOUR EYES! NOW YOU MUSTN'T FIGHT THIS LOVE THAT WAS MEANT FOR US BOTH!
El Grande
El Grande

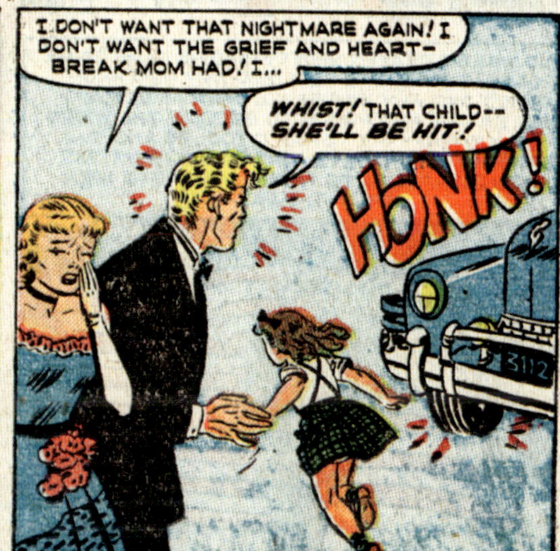
I DON'T WANT THAT NIGHTMARE AGAIN! I DON'T WANT THE GRIEF AND HEART-BREAK MOM HAD! I...
WHIST! THAT CHILD-- SHE'LL BE HIT!
HONK!

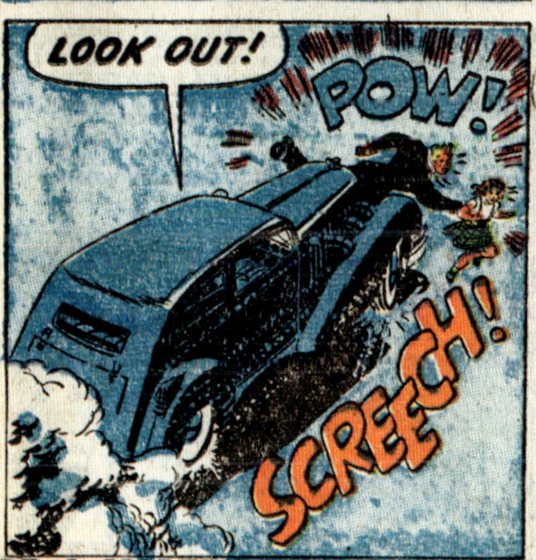
LOOK OUT!
POW!
SCREECH!

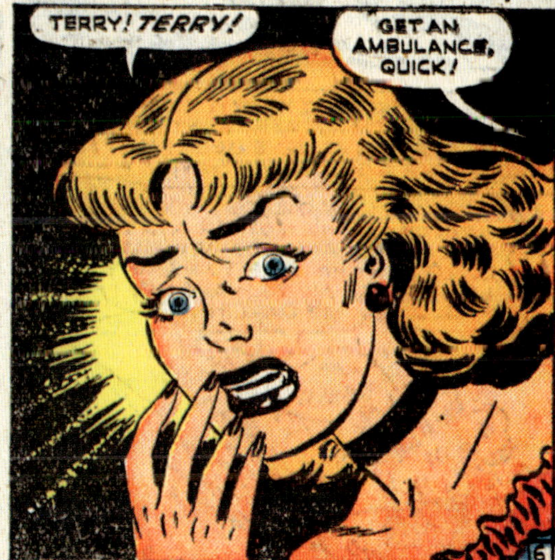
TERRY! TERRY!
GET AN AMBULANCE, QUICK!

BUT MY DARLING COULDN'T ANSWER! FOR SEVERAL DAYS HE COULDN'T SPEAK COHERENTLY! CONCUSSION WAS THE VERDICT OF THE ALL-CREEDS HOSPITAL DOCTORS! HIS CONDITION WAS GRAVE, ALMOST HELPLESS! AGAIN THE DARK SHADOWS OF DEATH WERE ROLLING IN TO ENFOLD A POLICEMAN I LOVED...

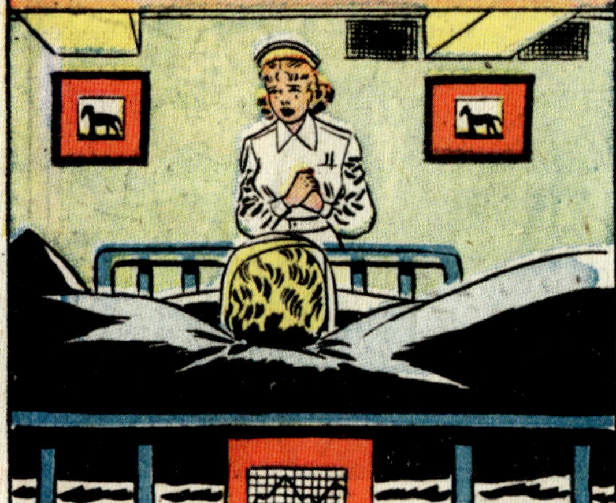

I PRAYED... I PRAYED AS I HAD NEVER PRAYED BEFORE! I ASKED GOD TO GIVE MY LOVE BACK TO ME...MY BRAVE POLICEMAN WHO HAD RISKED DEATH SO A CHILD MIGHT LIVE...

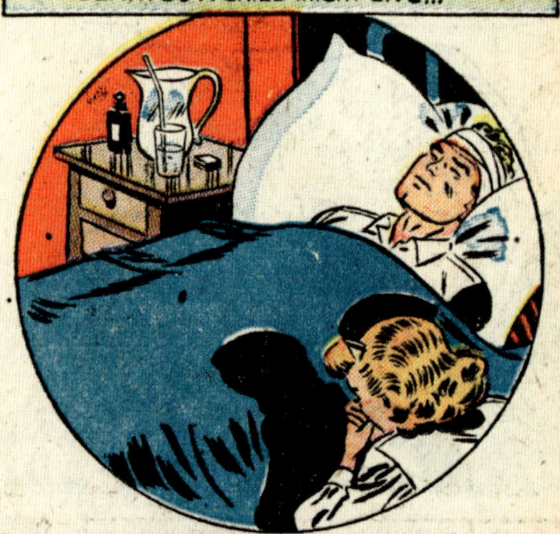

AND WHILE I PRAYED, UNDERSTANDING CAME TO ME AT LAST! SUDDENLY I REALIZED WHY MOM HAD MARRIED DAD, WHY WOMEN ALL OVER AMERICA WERE EAGER AND PROUD TO BECOME THE WIVES OF POLICEMEN--THE TERRY O'TOOLES AND TIM MONIHANS AND LIEUTENANT WILSONS OF THE POLICE DEPARTMENTS WERE THE GREAT MEN OF THE EARTH...

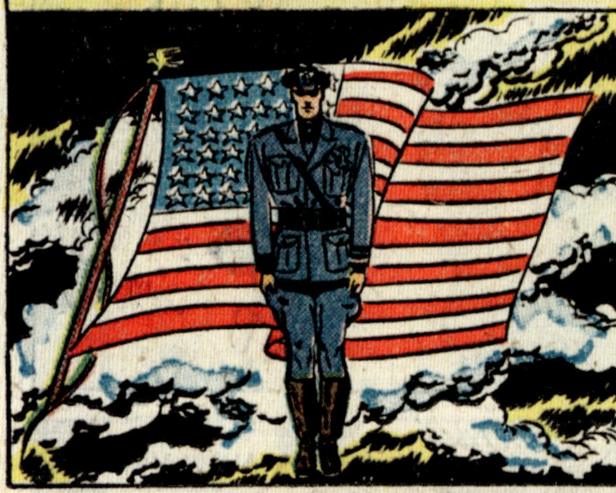

TO DEFEND THE RIGHT, TO HELP ALL IN NEED, THEY GIVE ALL--EVEN THEIR VERY LIVES! AND THEY DO THIS, I THOUGHT, NOT FOR THEIR MISERABLE SALARIES, BUT BECAUSE OF SOMETHING MONEY CAN NEVER BUY--A LOVE FOR THEIR FELLOW MEN! HOW I PRAYED FOR A CHANCE TO MAKE MY TERRY HAPPY! AND A MIRACLE HAPPENED--TERRY CAME OUT OF HIS COMA!

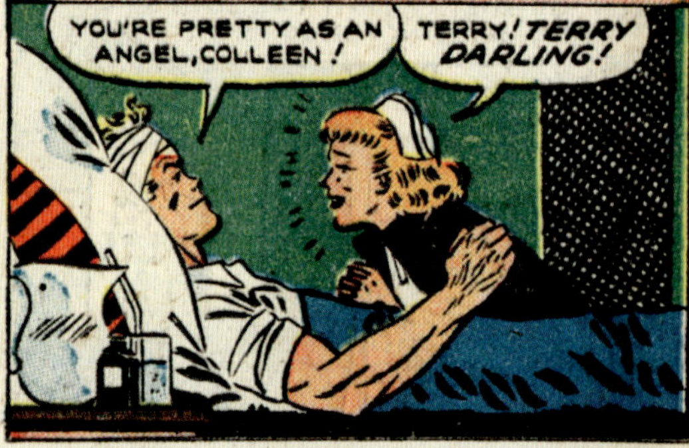

I DO LOVE YOU, TERRY--I KNEW IT WHEN YOU KISSED ME! AND I'M NOT AFRAID ANY MORE! MOM IS RIGHT...SHE HAS ALWAYS BEEN RIGHT! WITHOUT LOVE A GIRL IS *NOTHING!*

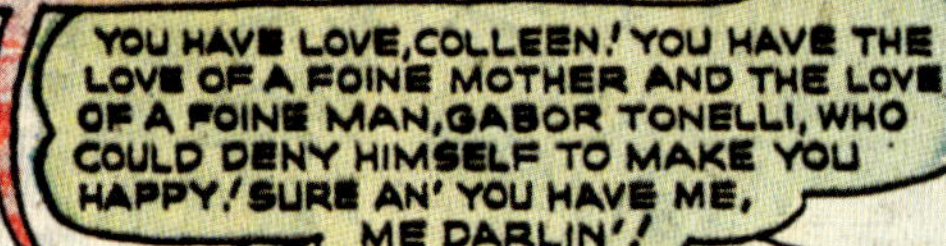

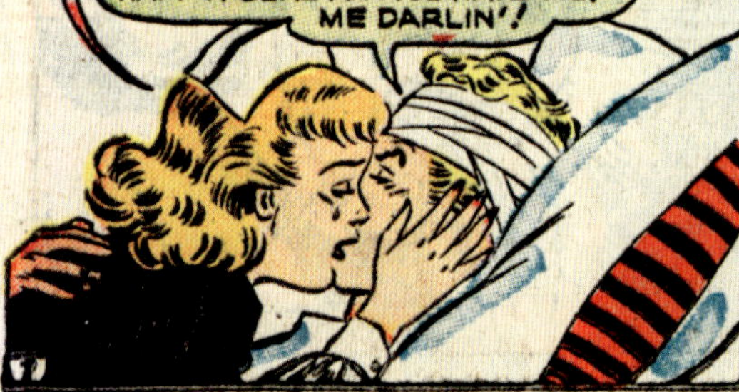

HIS KISSES ON OUR WEDDING DAY RELEASED ME FROM FEAR FOREVER! I HAD GROWN UP AT LAST! I KNEW THERE WOULD BE TIMES WHEN TERRY WOULD FACE GRAVE DANGER, BUT I COULD FACE THAT NOW AS MOTHER HAD FACED IT! INSPIRED BY TERRY'S LOVE, I WAS STRONG ENOUGH TO FACE WHATEVER THE FUTURE MIGHT BRING--YES, EVEN STRONG ENOUGH TO RETURN HIS LOVE AND MAKE MY WONDERFUL POLICEMAN HAPPY!

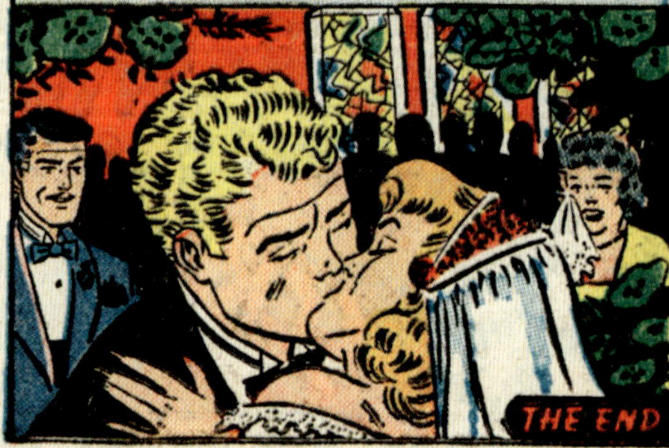

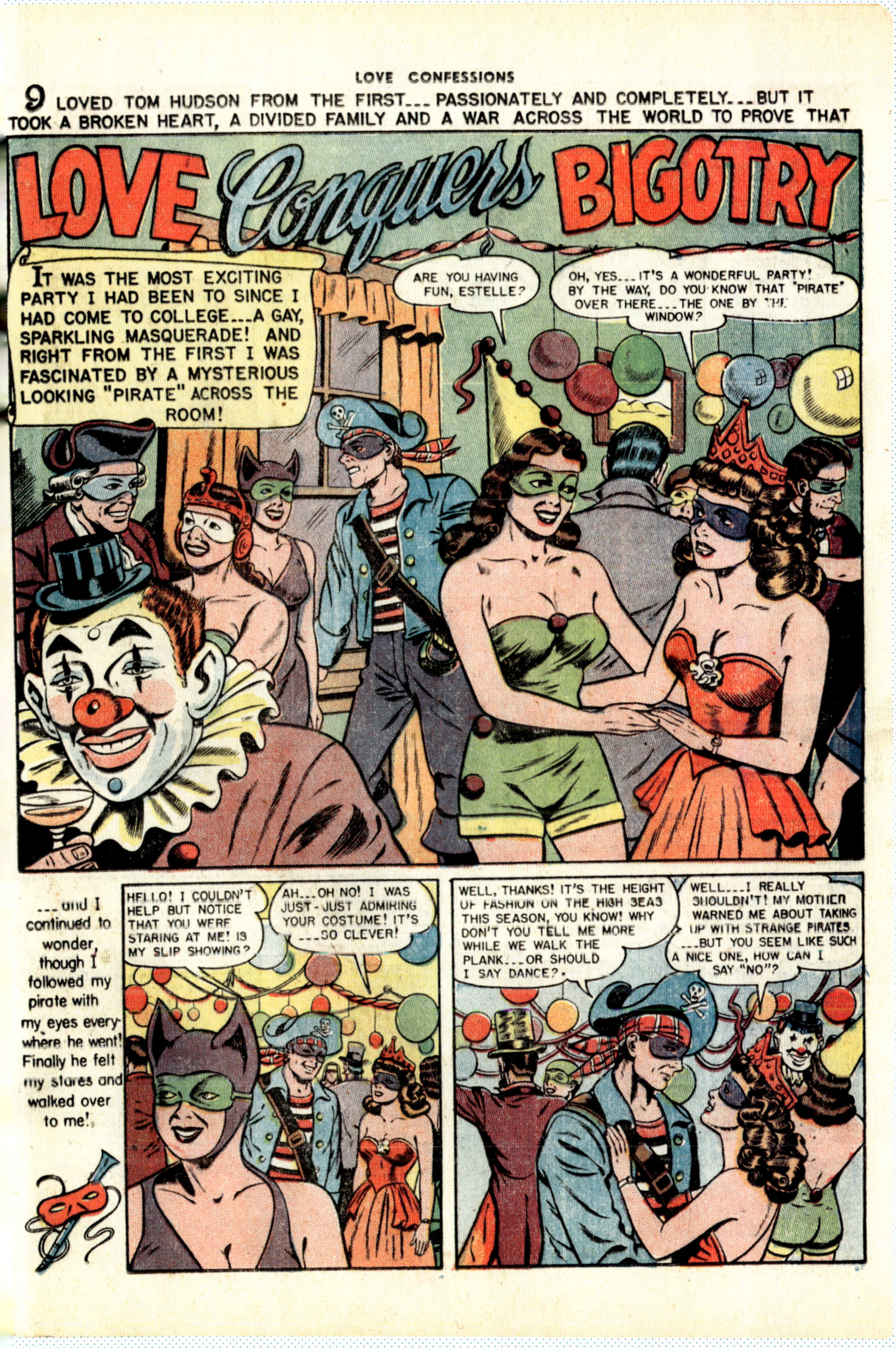

I LOVED TOM HUDSON FROM THE FIRST... PASSIONATELY AND COMPLETELY... BUT IT TOOK A BROKEN HEART, A DIVIDED FAMILY AND A WAR ACROSS THE WORLD TO PROVE THAT

LOVE Conquers BIGOTRY

IT WAS THE MOST EXCITING PARTY I HAD BEEN TO SINCE I HAD COME TO COLLEGE... A GAY, SPARKLING MASQUERADE! AND RIGHT FROM THE FIRST I WAS FASCINATED BY A MYSTERIOUS LOOKING "PIRATE" ACROSS THE ROOM!

ARE YOU HAVING FUN, ESTELLE?

OH, YES... IT'S A WONDERFUL PARTY! BY THE WAY, DO YOU KNOW THAT "PIRATE" OVER THERE... THE ONE BY THE WINDOW?

... and I continued to wonder, though I followed my pirate with my eyes everywhere he went! Finally he felt my stares and walked over to me!

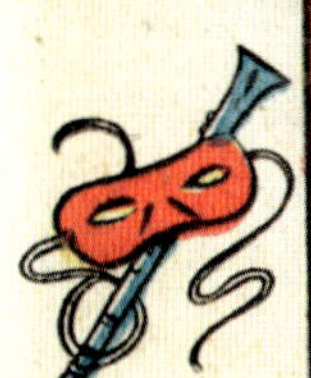

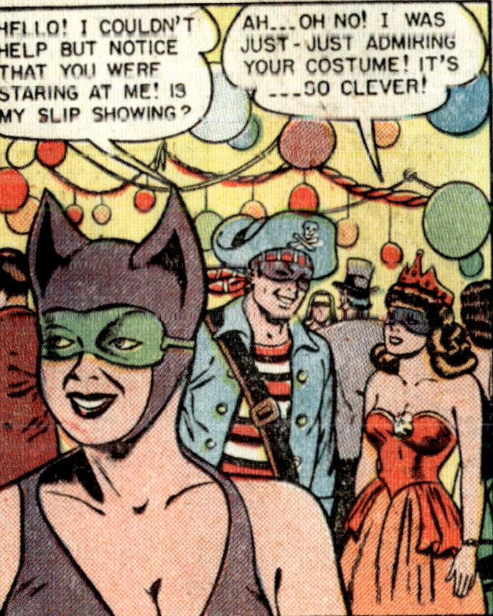

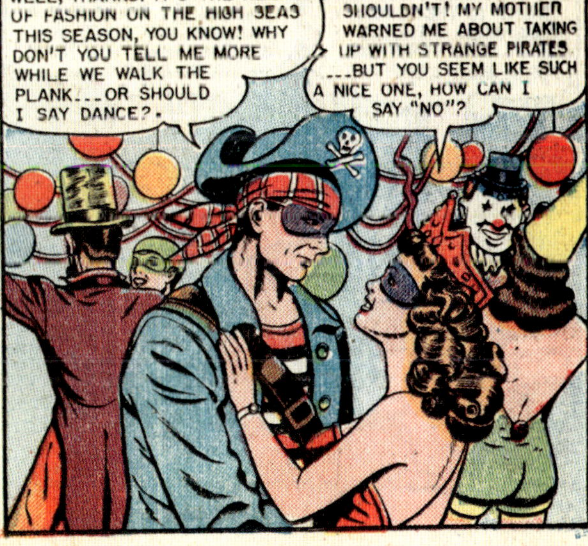

LOVE CONFESSIONS
#9, June 1951

Dancing close to Tom, with his arms around me, everyone else in the room seemed to vanish! Suddenly I hated all clocks, with their relentless tick-tocking ... for I knew that all too soon it would be the invisible hand of time that would tear me from my pirate's embrace ... and finally midnight came!

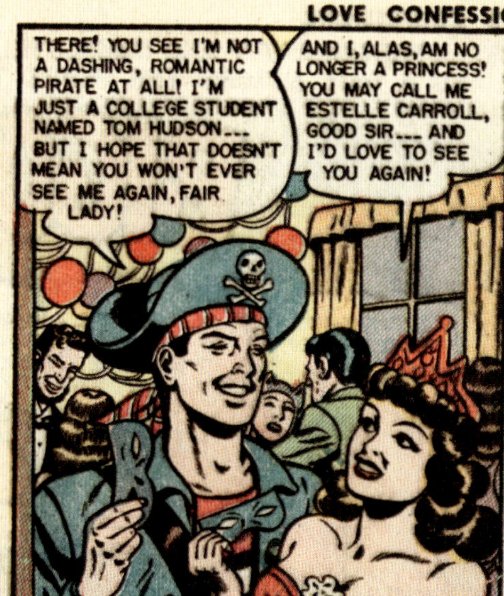

And Tom and I did see each other after that... often! The attraction I had felt for my mysterious "pirate" blossomed gradually into a deep, enduring love... a love built on a kinship of interests, aspirations and tastes!

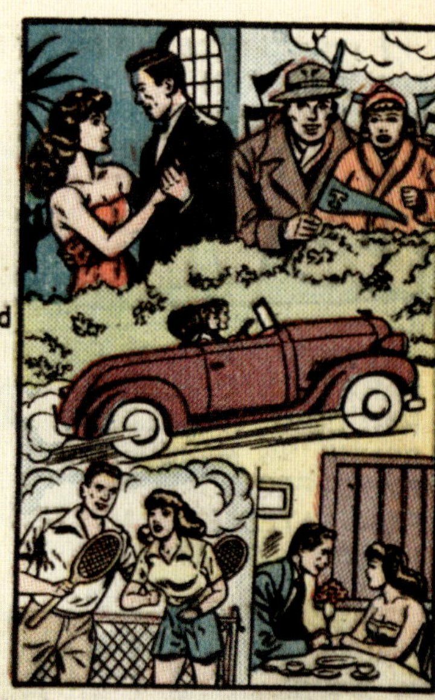

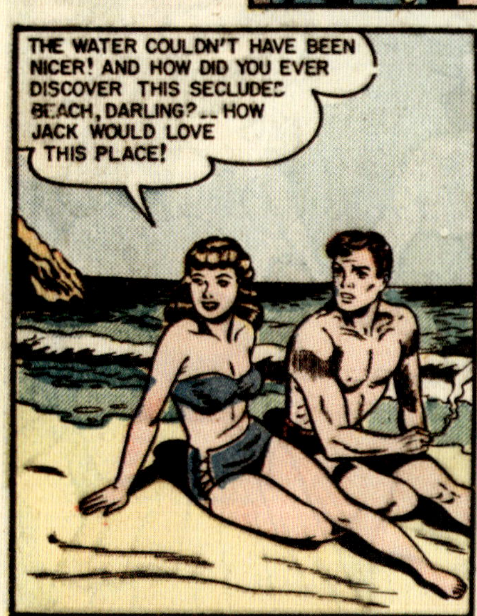

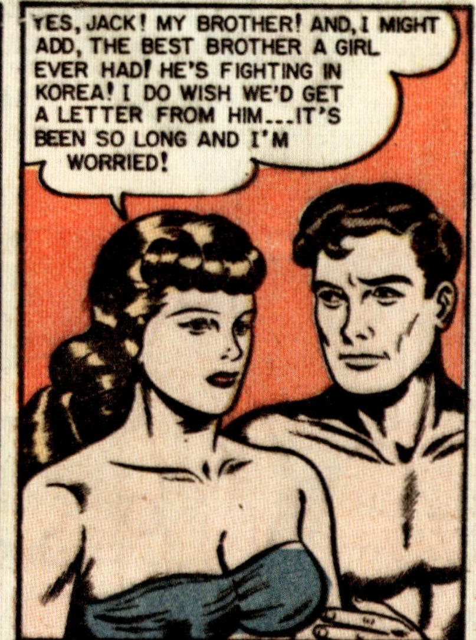

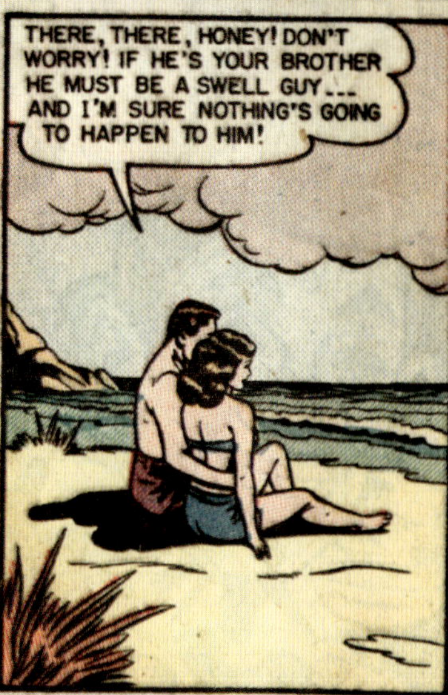

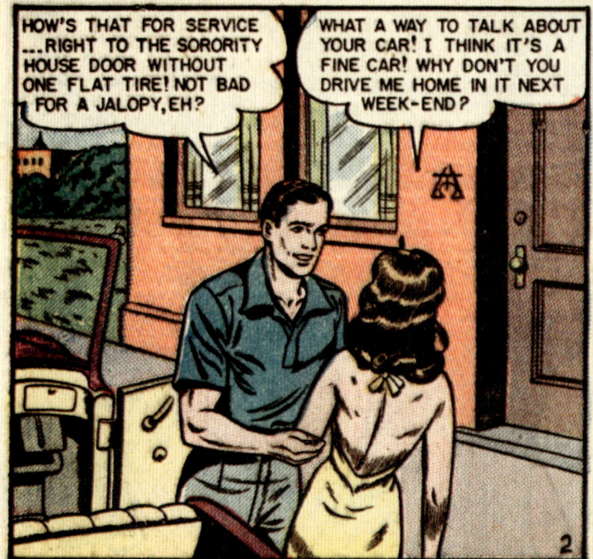

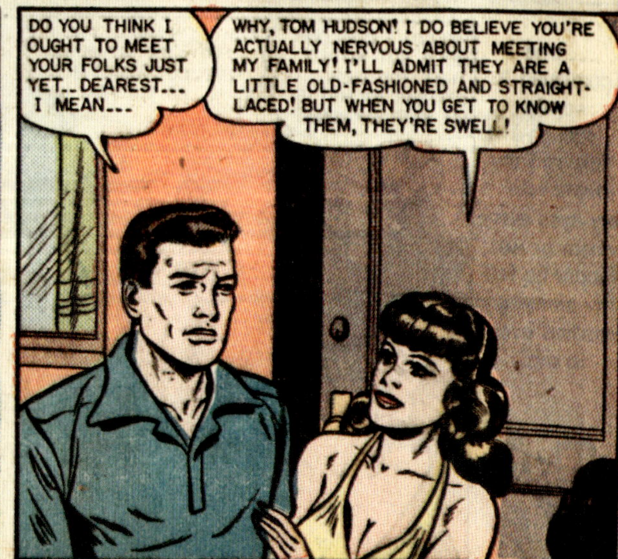

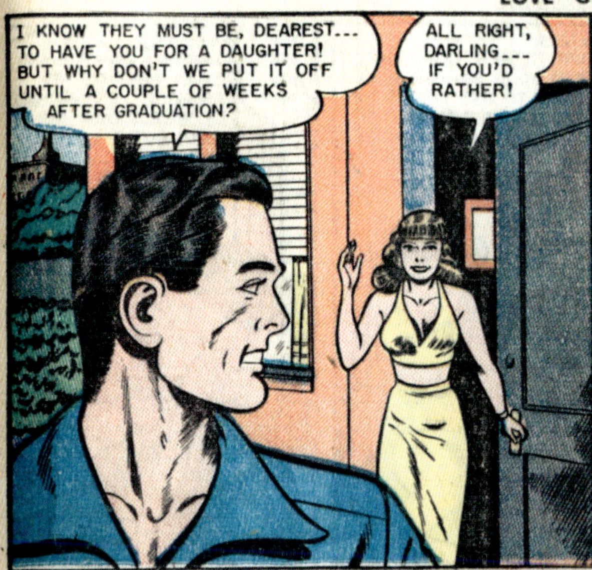

After graduation, Tom took a job in my home town and the first Sunday after he was settled he came over to meet my parents!

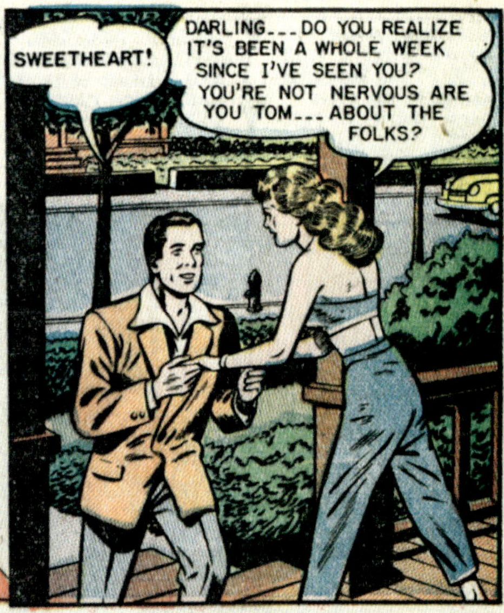

I'll admit that Mom and Dad did give Tom a pretty good going-over, and I did so want them to like him! I knew they did shortly after supper when Mom said...

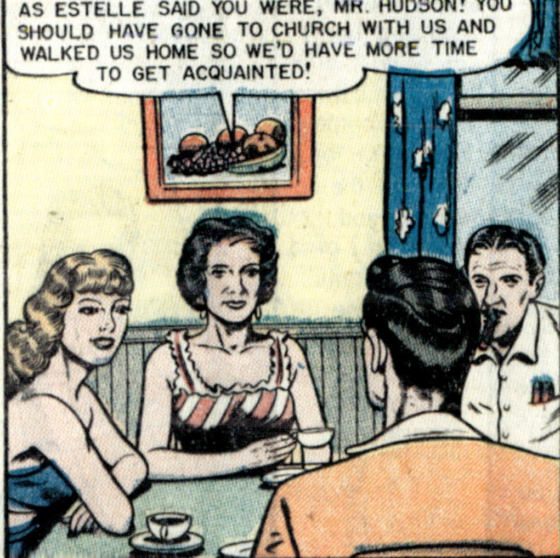

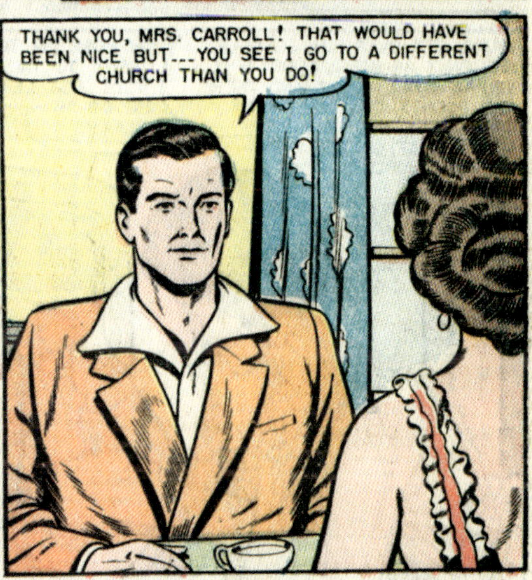

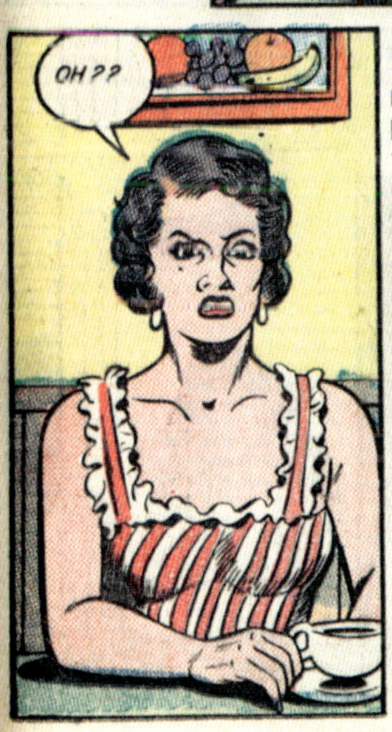

From the moment Mom and Dad found out Tom belonged to a different church, their attitude changed! They became cold and aloof ...almost rude! But it wasn't until after he had left that I discovered the reason!

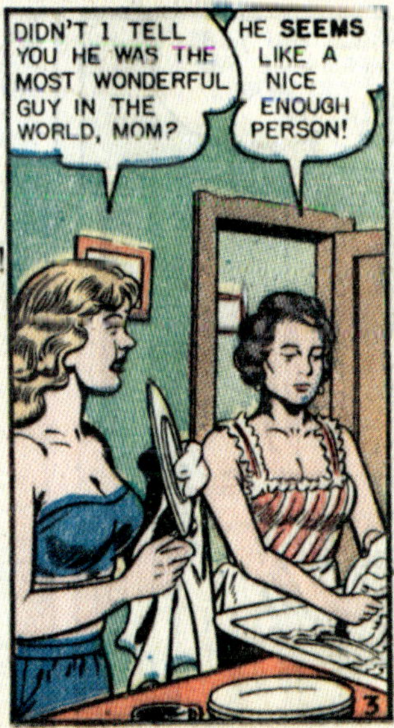

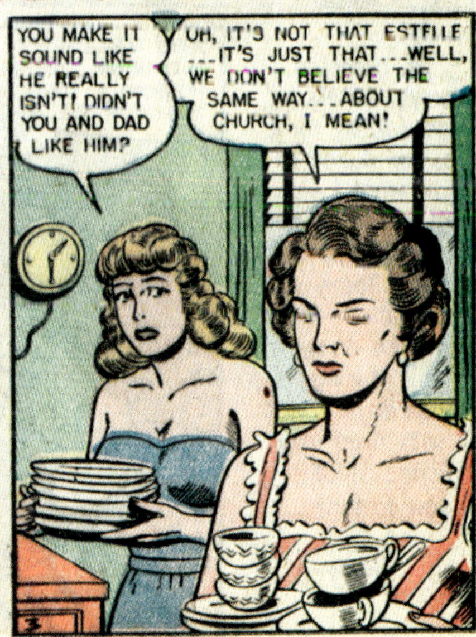

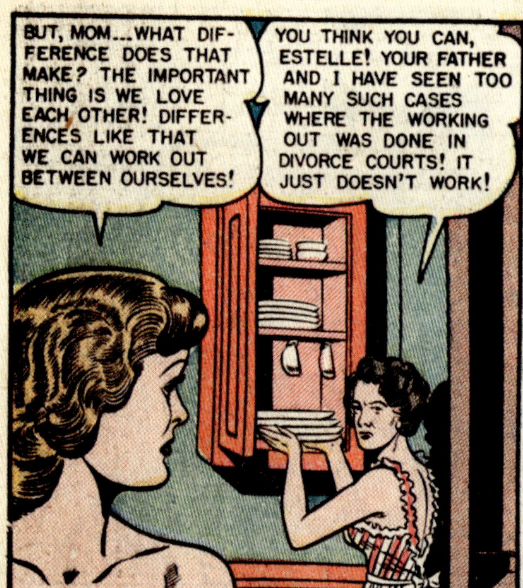

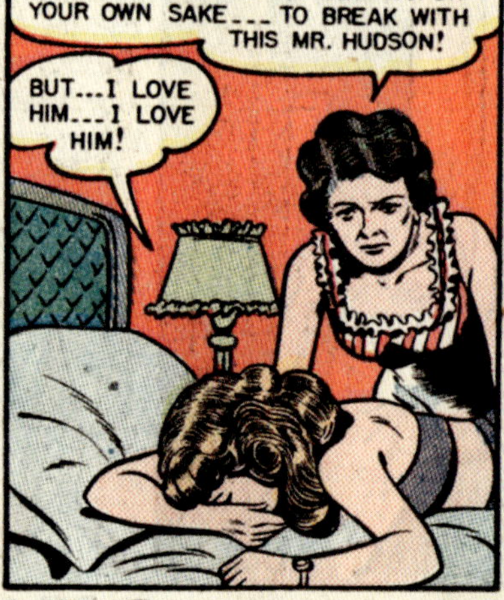

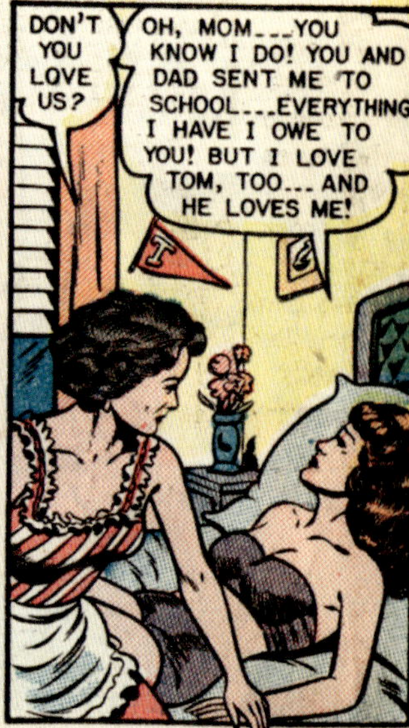

YOU'LL GET OVER HIM, ESTELLE... IT'S ONLY AN INFATUATION! WHY YOU'RE STILL YOUNG AND THERE ARE PLENTY OF YOUNG MEN! TAKE THAT NICE HARRY MILLS THAT GOES TO OUR CHURCH!

OH MOM, I'M TOO UPSET TO TALK NOW! JUST LET ME GO TO SLEEP!

But I couldn't sleep...my heart was being torn in two! Torn between the passionate love I felt for Tom and the devotion and obligation I owed to my parents! To please them I began dating Harry Mills occasionally!

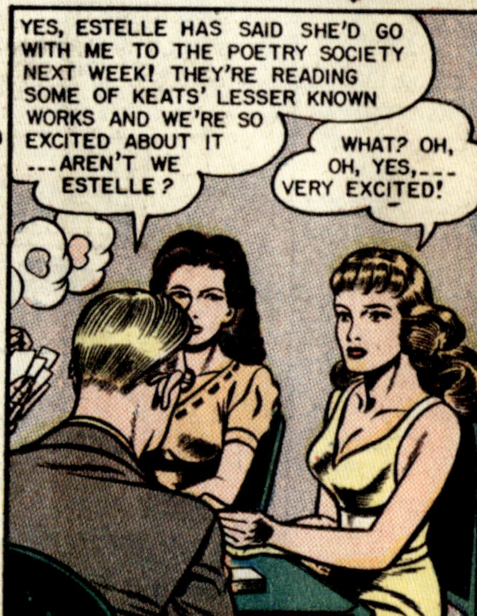

I accepted Harry's invitations mechanically for I was too dazed to know what I was doing! But in my heart I longed to be crushed again in Tom's virile embrace...to feel his warm lips on mine! But during those days I was with Tom very little...Mother saw to that...!

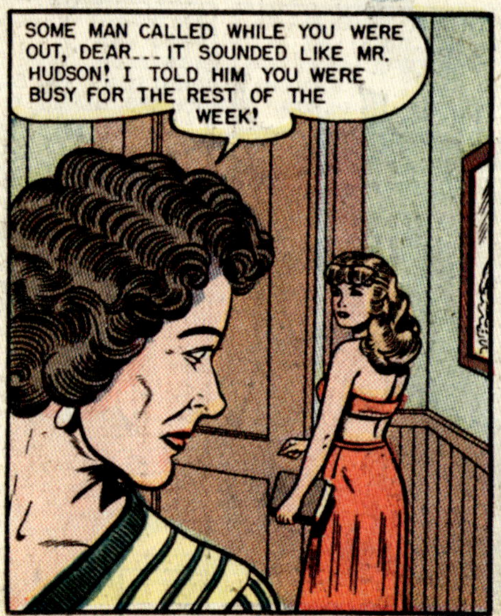

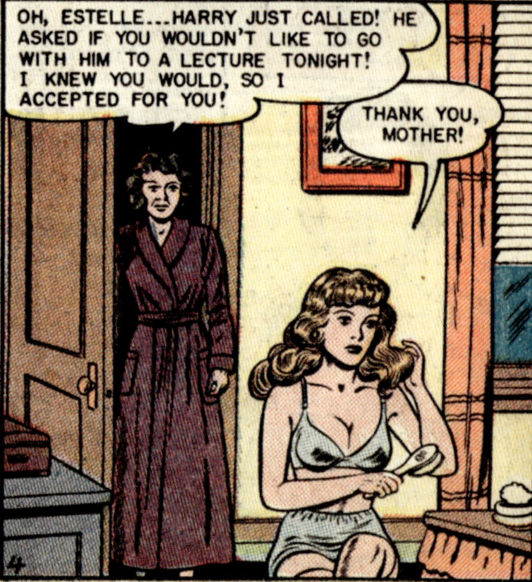

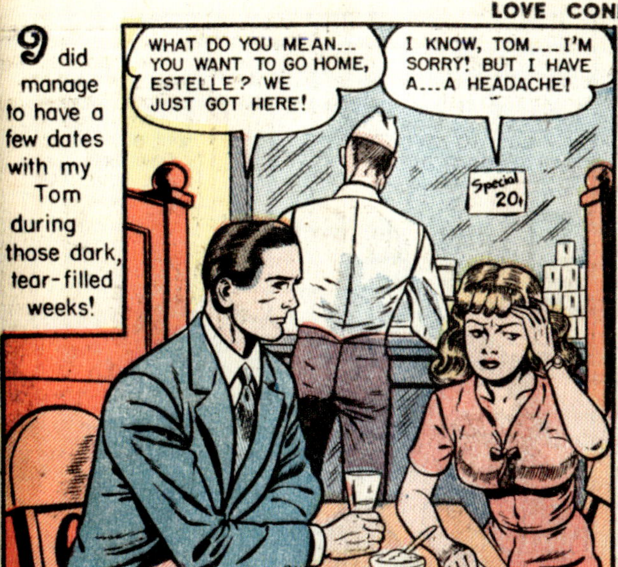

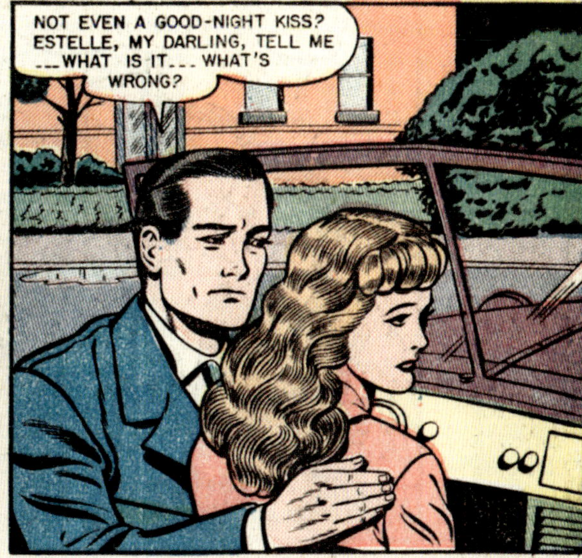

How my whole being throbbed and cried out for the very kiss I was refusing! For an instant my heart told me to throw myself into Tom's arms... to again experience the ecstacy of his white-hot kisses, the security of his strong masculine arms! Then ...

ESTELLE! IT'S TIME YOU CAME IN!

Dad's voice brought me back to cruel reality! I knew I couldn't go on like this and in that quick, mad moment I decided to break with the man I loved!

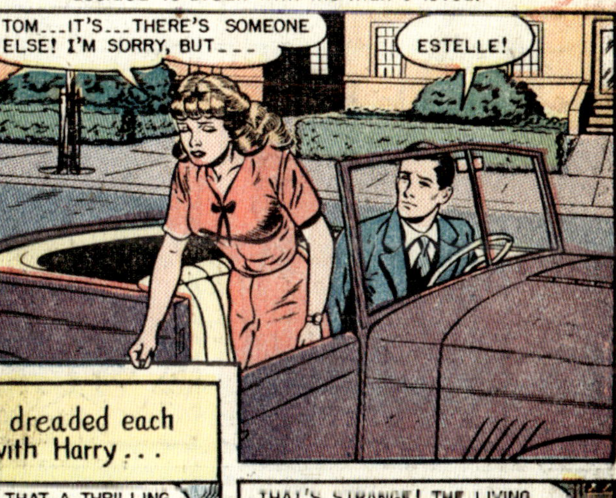

And I dreaded each date with Harry...

The lie I had told made me feel sick! I ran from the car into the house ...I didn't want to look back, I couldn't have stood it! That night... and for many nights to come ... I cried myself to sleep!

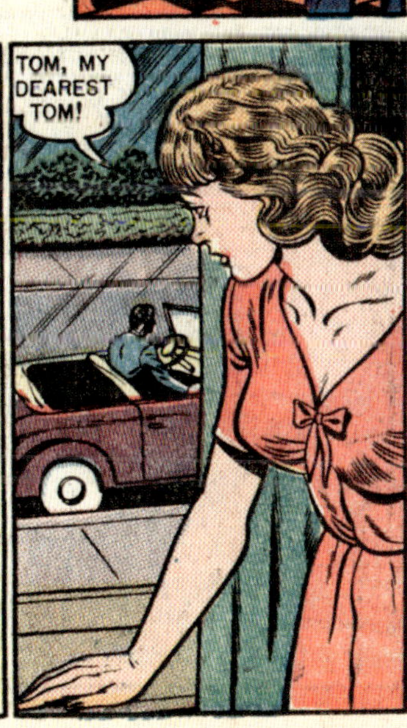

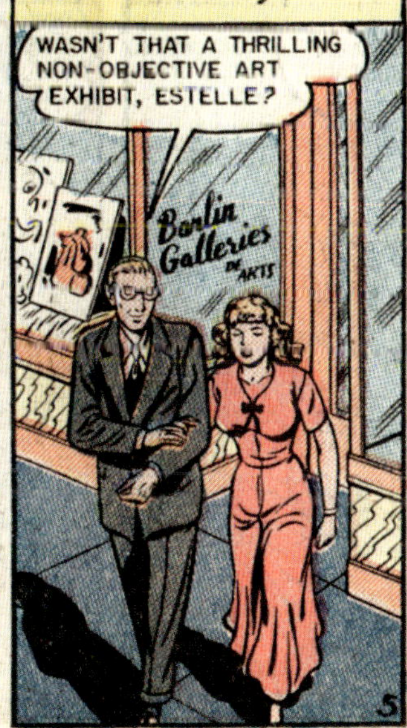

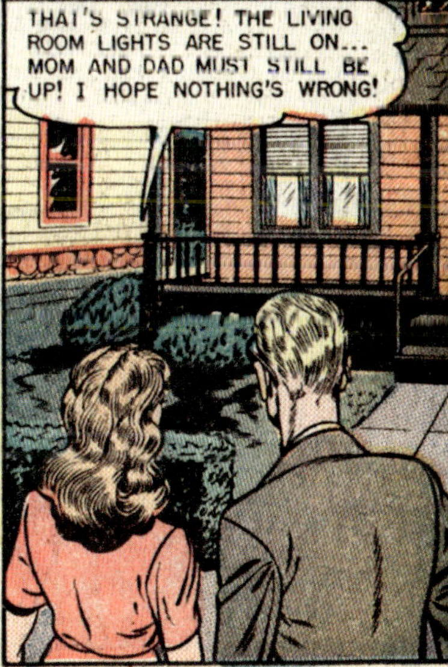

Something had happened to my brother Jack! I sensed it the moment I walked in the house! Cold horror ran through my body! Fate seemed determined to strike me one cruel blow after the other!

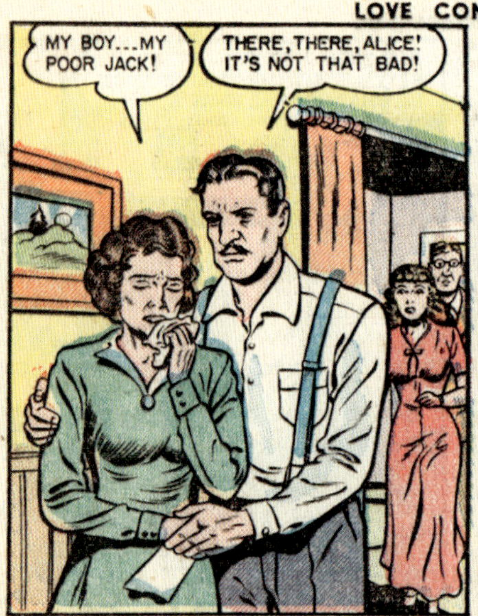

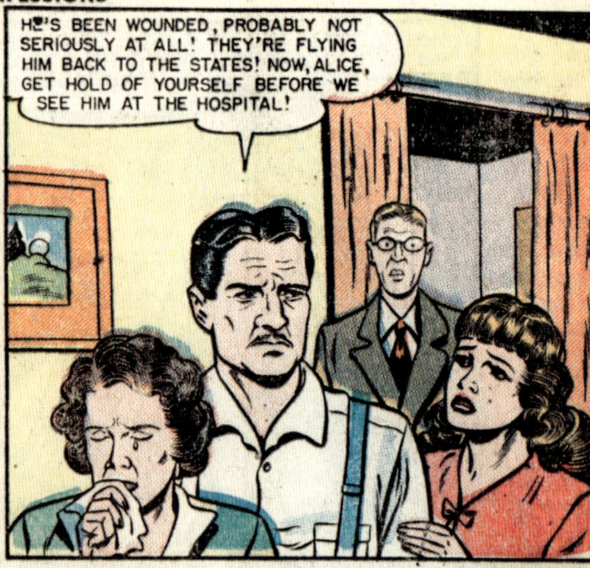

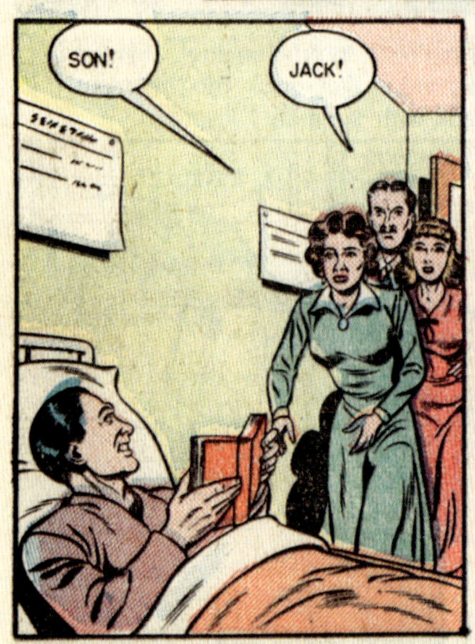

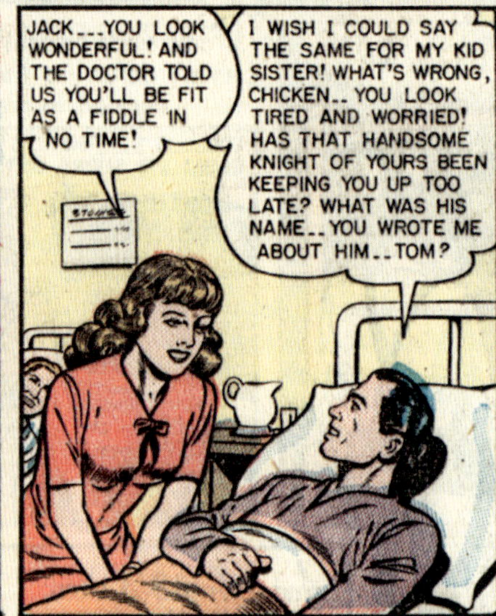

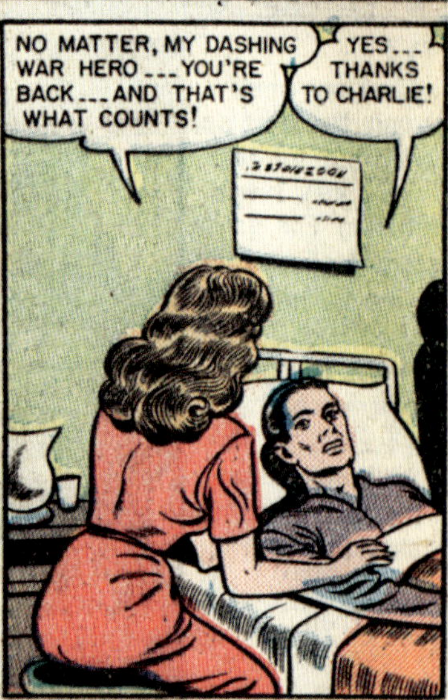

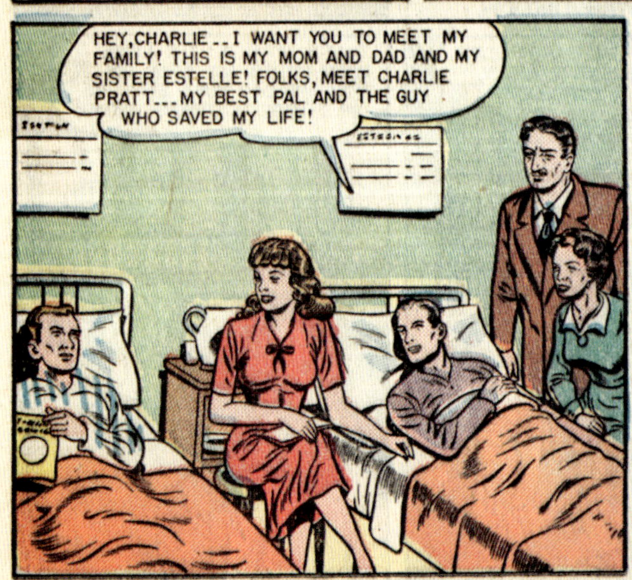

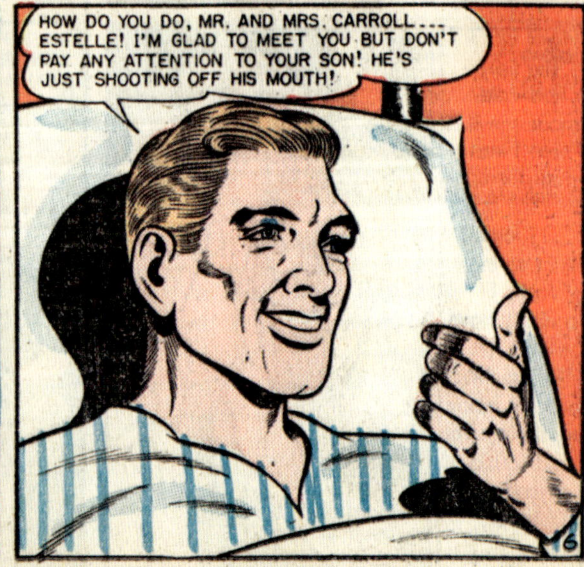

HE'LL NEVER TELL YOU HOW IT ALL HAPPENED.. TOO MODEST! SO I GUESS I'LL HAVE TO TELL YOU!

"IT WAS OUTSIDE OF SEOUL..AND OUR SQUAD HAD BEEN CUT OFF FROM THE OUTFIT! BUT WE KEPT ON FIGHTING..FIGHTING THE REDS, AND THE COLD AND THE HUNGER!"

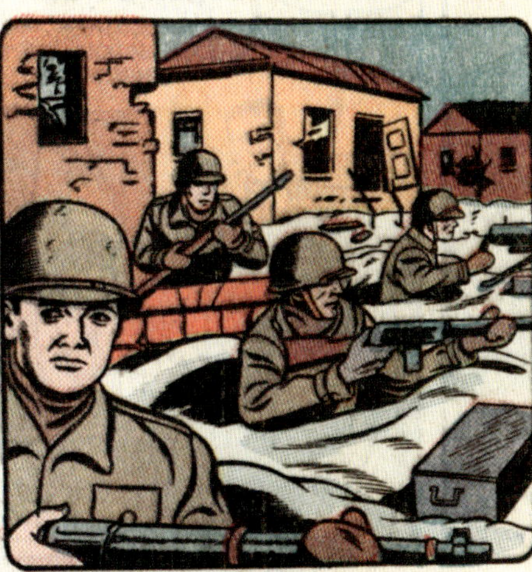

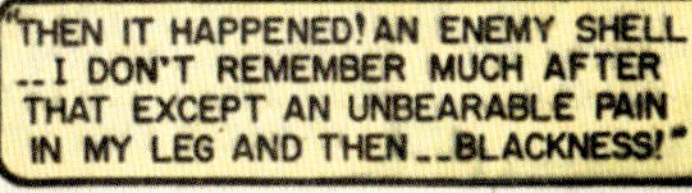

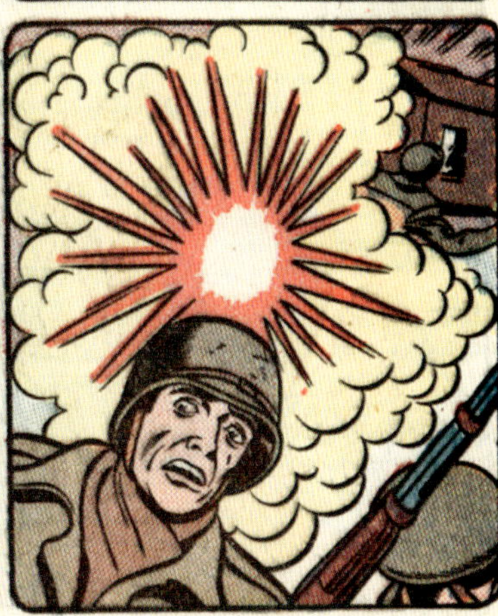

"THE OTHERS TRIED TO CARRY THE WOUNDED, BUT I HAD FALLEN BEHIND A SMALL RIDGE AND THEY DIDN'T SEE ME! IT WASN'T UNTIL THEY HAD MADE CONTACT WITH THE COMPANY THAT CHARLIE HERE NOTICED I WASN'T AMONG THE WOUNDED!"

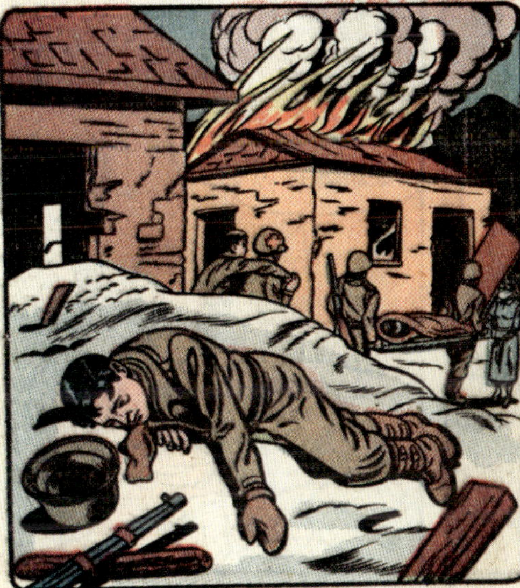

"HE CAME BACK FOR ME AND FOUND ME..I DON'T KNOW HOW! HE CARRIED ME ON HIS BACK AND THE DANGEROUS TRIP BEGAN! WE HAD ALMOST REACHED OUR LINES WHEN A SHOT RANG OUT..A SNIPER'S BULLET! IT GOT CHARLIE IN THE SHOULDER!"

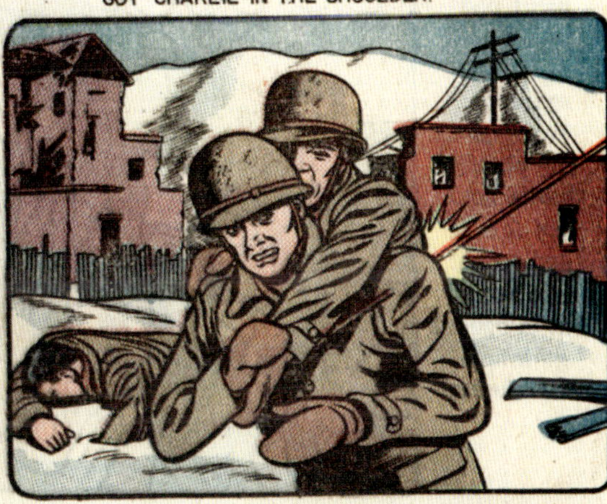

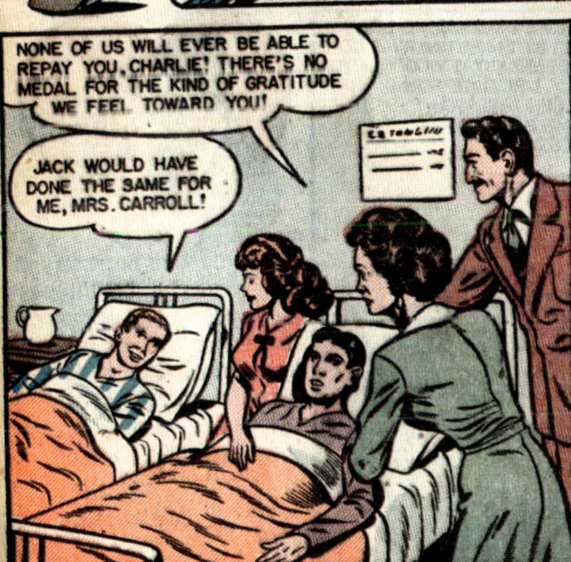

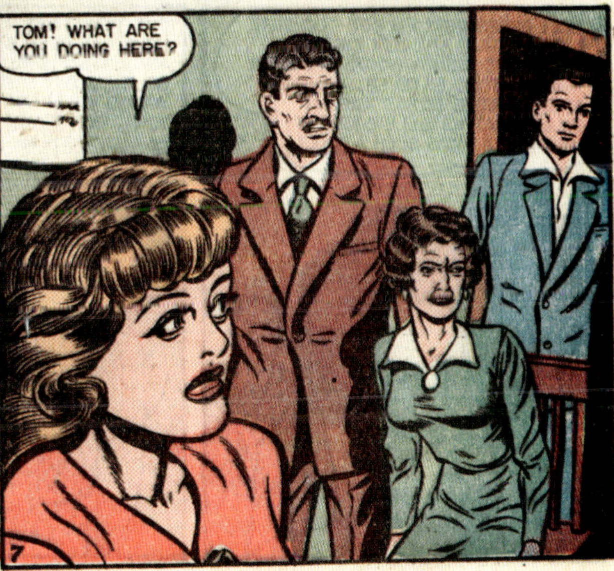

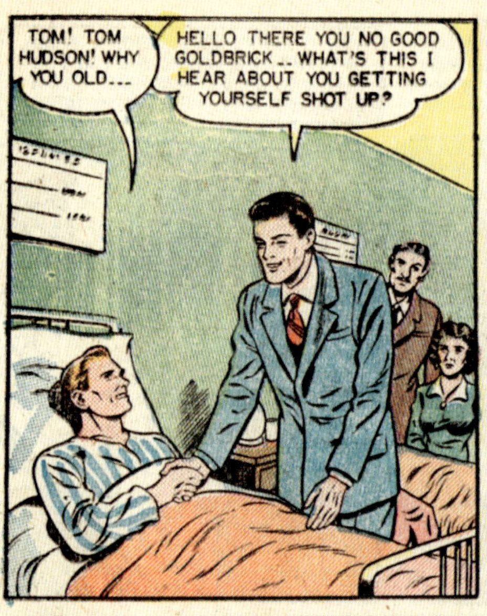

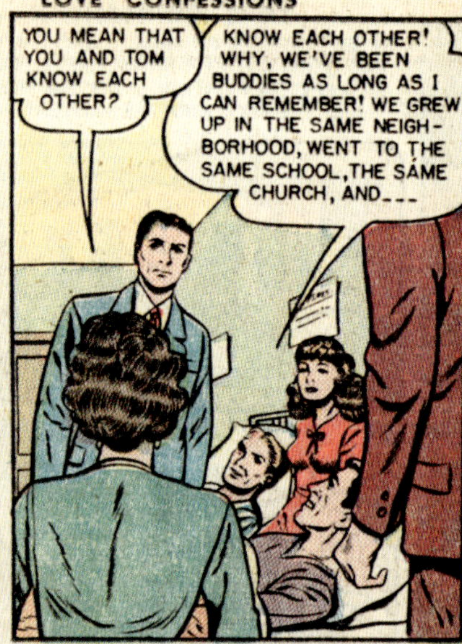

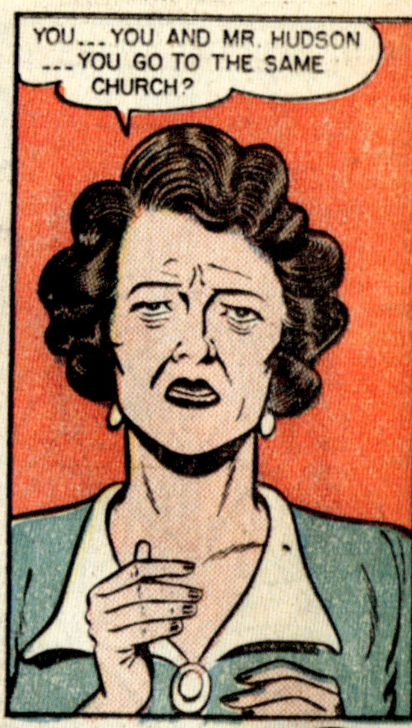

I could tell that within Mom's heart and mind a battle was raging as fierce as any physical battle Jack and Charlie had fought ---it was a battle against a lifetime of prejudice!

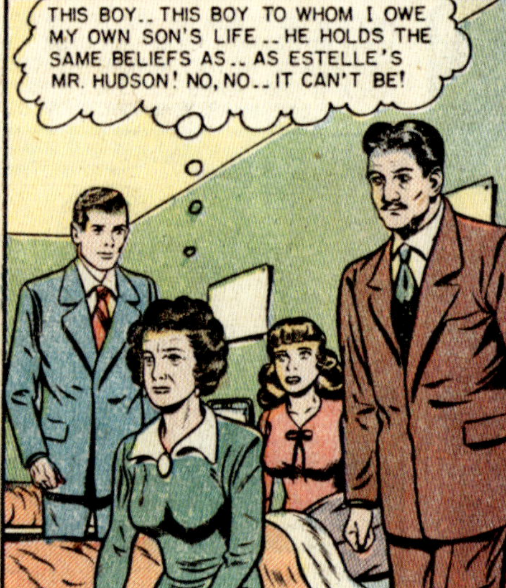

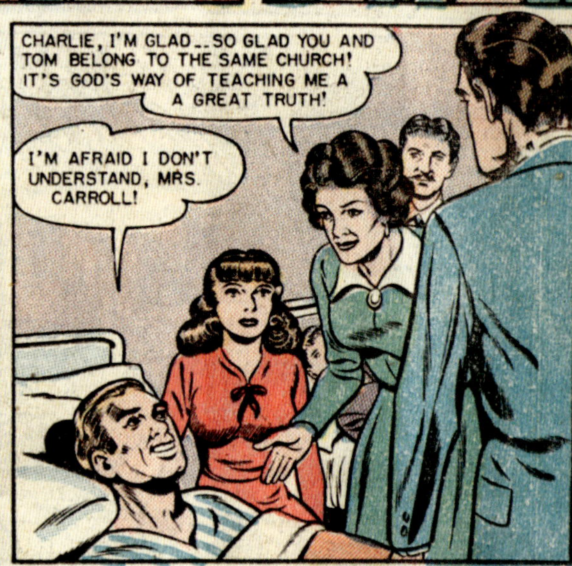

NO, I GUESS NOT! I'M NOT TOO SURE I UNDERSTAND, MYSELF! EXCEPT I KNOW I'VE BEEN A BIGOTED, FOOLISH WOMAN! TOM -- ESTELLE -- CAN YOU EVER FORGIVE ME? IT WAS MY FAULT THAT ESTELLE BROKE UP WITH YOU! I WAS SUCH A FOOL!

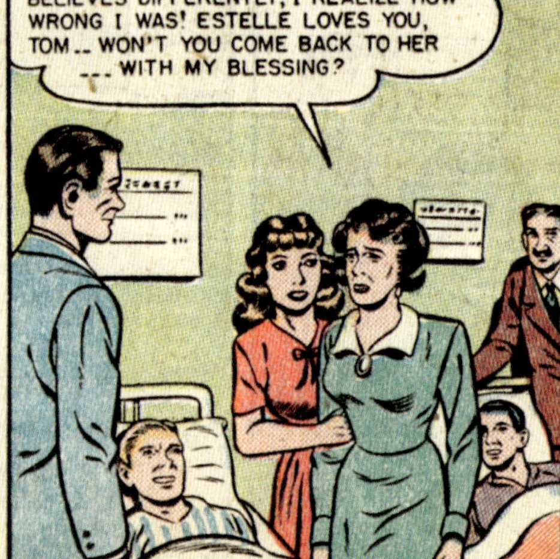

No words were necessary in that wonderful, breathless moment -- our kiss said more than a thousand words! Tom's lips pressed close to mine, his arm's so tight around me told me that love --- deep, meaningful love --- was ours forever! I had learned that

LOVE CONQUERS BIGOTRY!

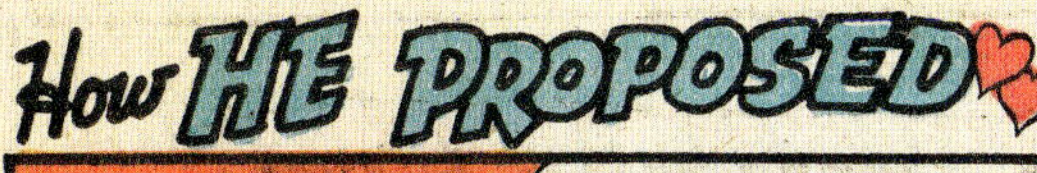

I'M *BETTY HAMPTON*, OF DURHAM, NORTH CAROLINA--- AND I MET THE LOVE OF MY LIFE WHILE I WAS ATTENDING DUKE UNIVERSITY IN MY HOME TOWN! MY DREAM MAN'S NAME WAS *ROY ANDERSON*--- BUT ALL HE SEEMED TO BE INTERESTED IN WAS THE SCIENCE OF TELEPATHY, OR THOUGHT-TRANSFERENCE! AND ALL *I* WAS INTERESTED IN, OF COURSE, WAS GETTING HIM TO *PROPOSE!*

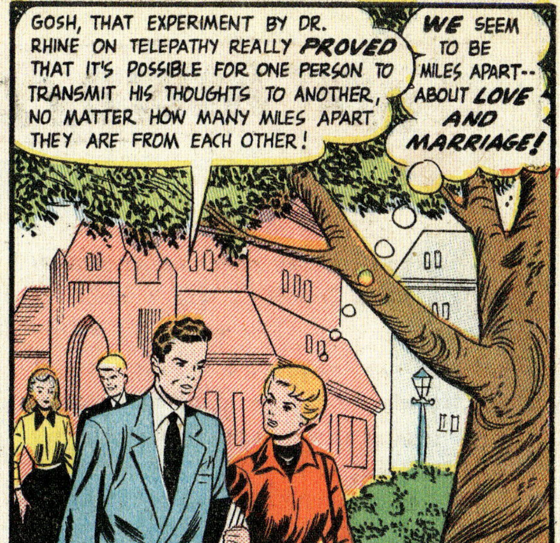

"THEN, ONE DAY, I GOT THE BRIGHT IDEA OF HOW TO USE HIS INTEREST IN TELEPATHY TO HINT ABOUT MARRIAGE..."

BY THE WAY, ROY, I'M VISITING MY AUNT'S HOUSE IN RALEIGH THIS WEEK-END--AND I THOUGHT WE MIGHT TRY A TELEPATHY EXPERIMENT THEN! AT NOON ON SUNDAY, YOU CONCENTRATE AS HARD AS YOU CAN AND TRY TO TRANSMIT A THOUGHT TO ME--AND I'LL ALSO CONCENTRATE AND TRY TO RECEIVE YOUR THOUGHT! THEN, WHEN I RETURN, WE'LL COMPARE NOTES!

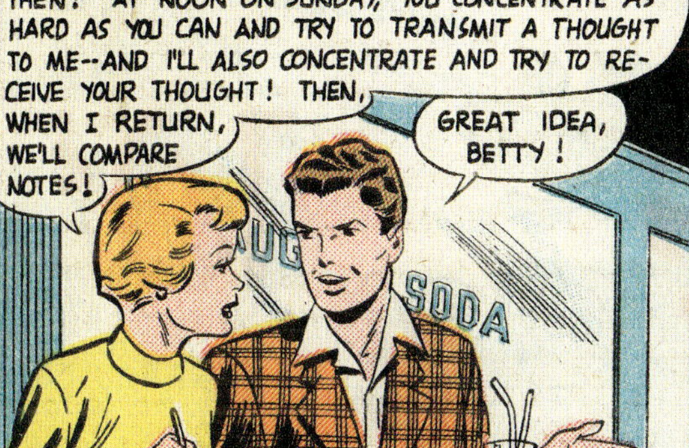

"THAT SUNDAY EVENING, TRAVELING BACK TO DURHAM..."

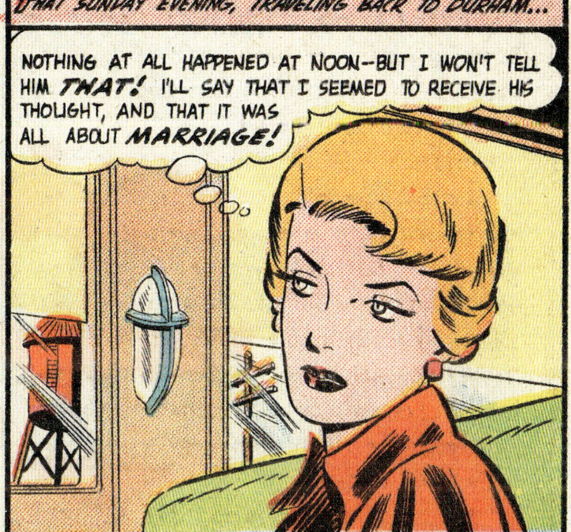

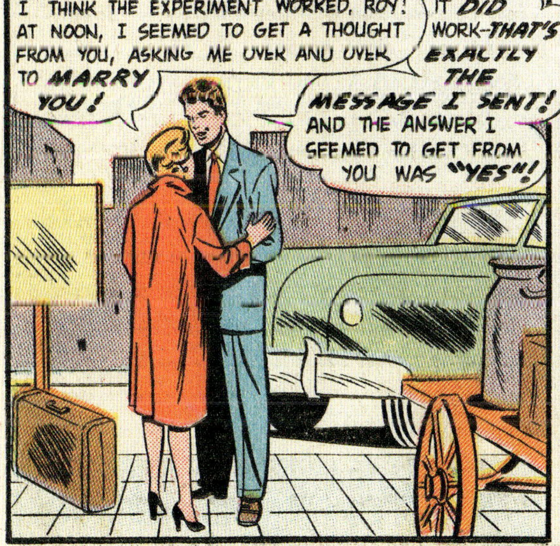

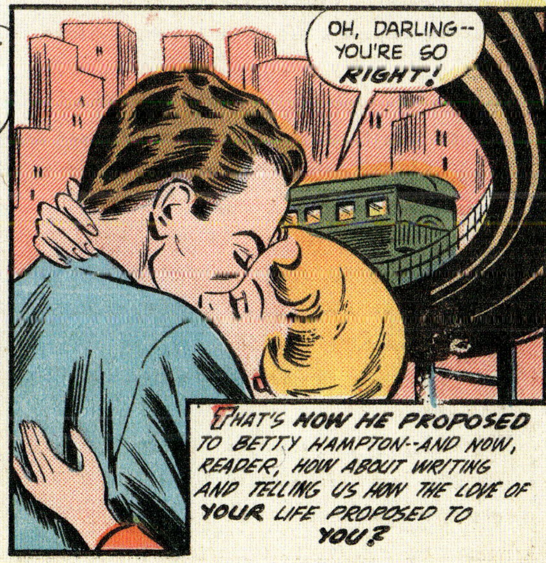

LOVELORN
#23, March 1952

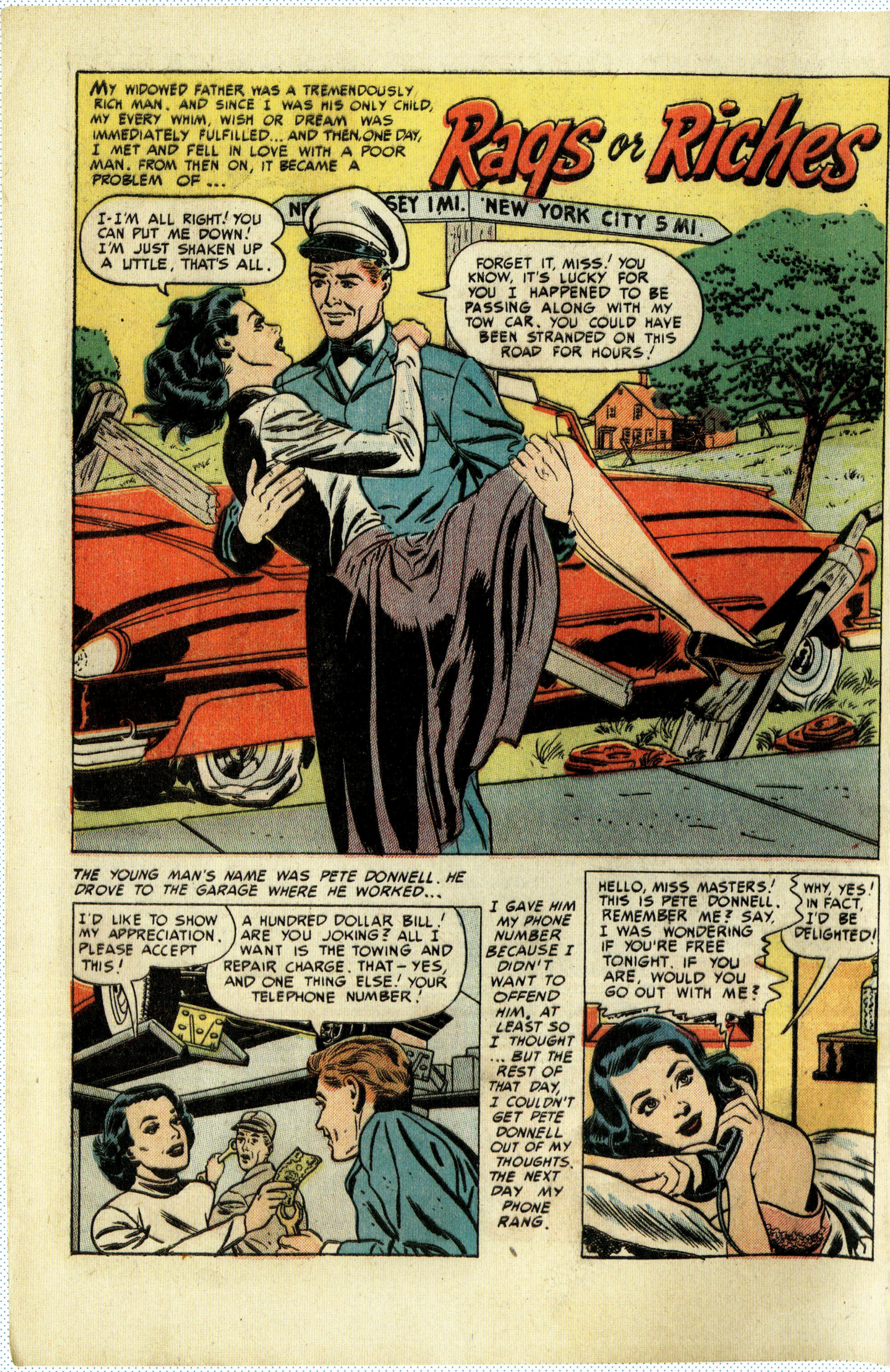

MY WIDOWED FATHER WAS A TREMENDOUSLY RICH MAN. AND SINCE I WAS HIS ONLY CHILD, MY EVERY WHIM, WISH OR DREAM WAS IMMEDIATELY FULFILLED... AND THEN, ONE DAY, I MET AND FELL IN LOVE WITH A POOR MAN. FROM THEN ON, IT BECAME A PROBLEM OF ...

Rags or Riches

I-I'M ALL RIGHT! YOU CAN PUT ME DOWN! I'M JUST SHAKEN UP A LITTLE, THAT'S ALL.

FORGET IT, MISS! YOU KNOW, IT'S LUCKY FOR YOU I HAPPENED TO BE PASSING ALONG WITH MY TOW CAR. YOU COULD HAVE BEEN STRANDED ON THIS ROAD FOR HOURS!

THE YOUNG MAN'S NAME WAS PETE DONNELL. HE DROVE TO THE GARAGE WHERE HE WORKED...

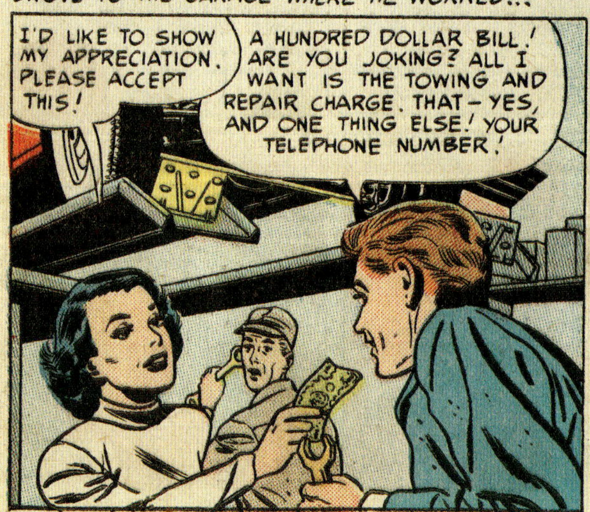

I GAVE HIM MY PHONE NUMBER BECAUSE I DIDN'T WANT TO OFFEND HIM. AT LEAST SO I THOUGHT ... BUT THE REST OF THAT DAY, I COULDN'T GET PETE DONNELL OUT OF MY THOUGHTS. THE NEXT DAY MY PHONE RANG.

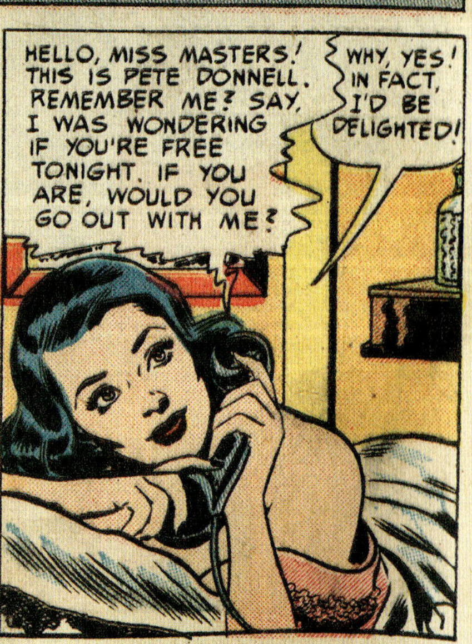

PETE CAME TO PICK ME UP AT 8:30! YOU SHOULD HAVE SEEN THE LOOK ON HIS FACE WHEN HE ENTERED OUR HOUSE...

HOLY SMOKES! IF I HAD KNOWN YOU LIVED IN A JOINT LIKE THIS, I NEVER WOULD HAVE HAD THE NERVE TO CALL YOU!

THEN I'M GLAD YOU DIDN'T KNOW! OH, BY THE WAY, PETE, I WANT YOU TO MEET MY FATHER!

HARUMPH!

Wall St. Journal

PETE TOOK ME TO A QUIET INN IN TUCKAHOE! THERE HE BEGAN TO TELL ME ABOUT HIMSELF. HE HAD LIVED A HECTIC LIFE! AN ORPHAN AT AN EARLY AGE... A VETERAN OF THE PACIFIC CAMPAIGN!

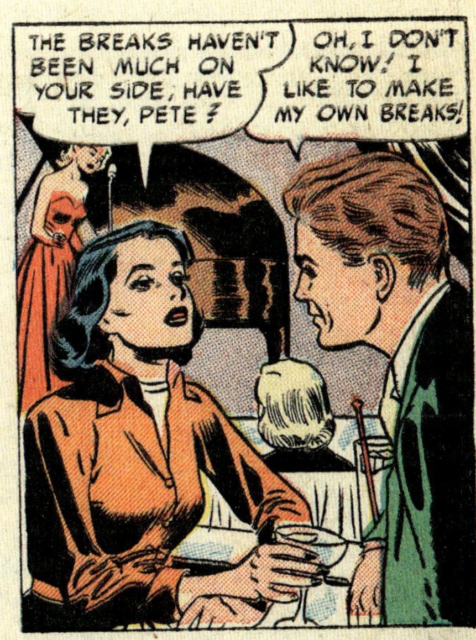

HIS GREAT AMBITION WAS TO BE HIS OWN BOSS, TO OWN HIS OWN GARAGE! TO FULFILL HIS AMBITION, HE WAS SCRIMPING AND SAVING EVERY PENNY!

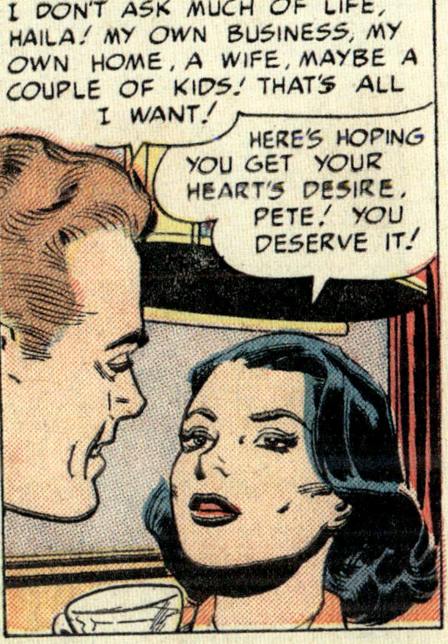

AS THE EVENING WORE ON, PETE GREW ON ME. HIS SIMPLICITY, HIS STRAIGHT-FORWARDNESS, HIS WARMTH MADE HIM DIFFERENT FROM ANY OTHER MAN I HAD EVER KNOWN!

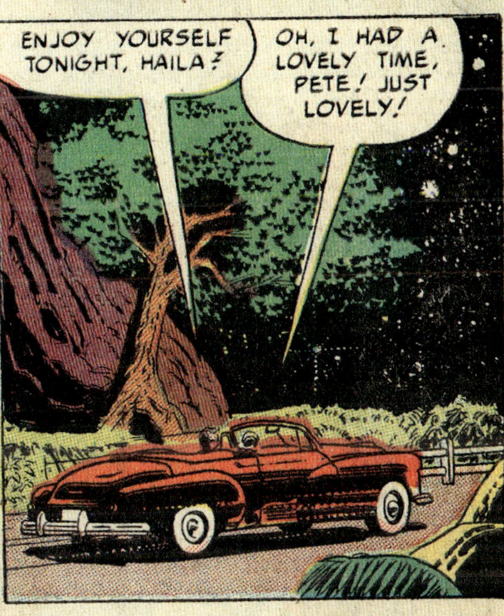

THE NEXT NIGHT I WENT OUT WITH PETE AGAIN AND THE NIGHT AFTER THAT... BEFORE THE WEEK WAS OUT I WAS MADLY IN LOVE WITH HIM... AND HE WITH ME!

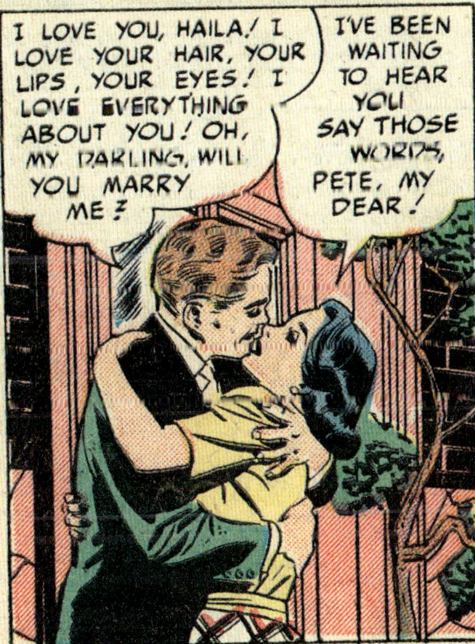

THAT SAME NIGHT I TOLD MY FATHER ABOUT PETE AND MYSELF. HE NEARLY HAD A STROKE HE WAS SO ANGRY...

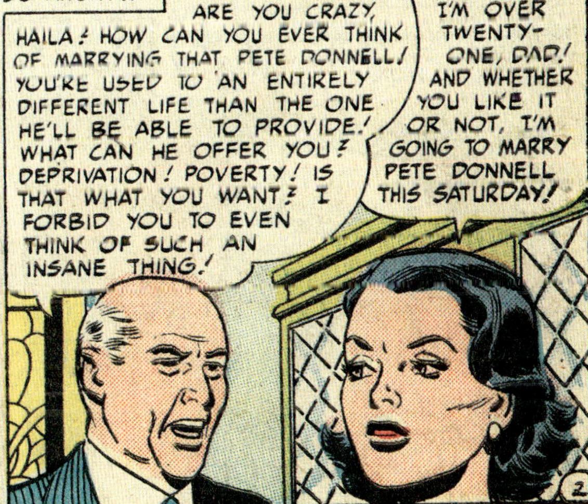

ROMANTIC MARRIAGE
#7, November 1951

THAT SATURDAY AT CITY HALL..

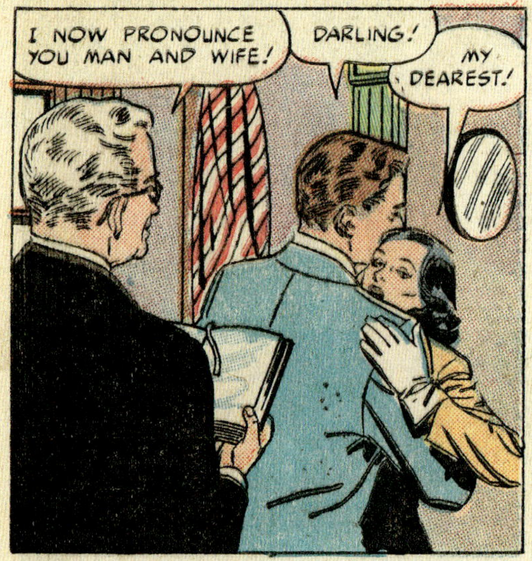

AFTER THE CEREMONY PETE TOOK ME TO OUR NEW HOME! A THREE-ROOM FURNISHED FLAT IN ONE OF THE POORER SECTIONS OF TOWN...

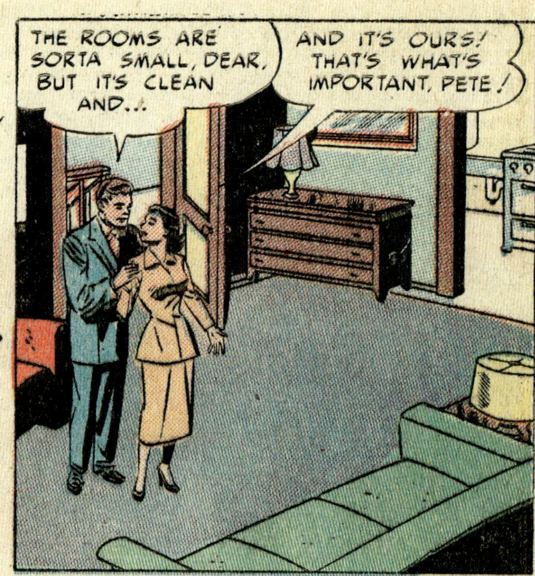

IN THE FOLLOWING WEEKS AND MONTHS I SET ABOUT LEARNING THE CHORES OF A HOUSE-WIFE! I CLEANED, COOKED, SHOPPED...

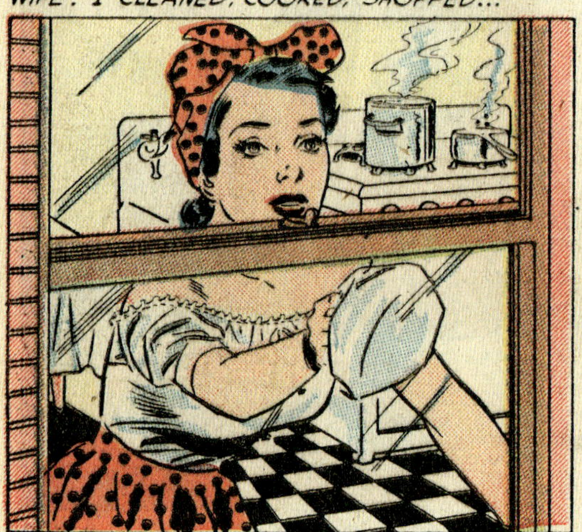

I DID MY BEST TO REDECORATE THE APARTMENT. I EVEN RE-UPHOLSTERED THE FURNITURE AND REPAINTED THE WALLS! I DID EVERY-THING I COULD TO MAKE IT A REAL HOME!

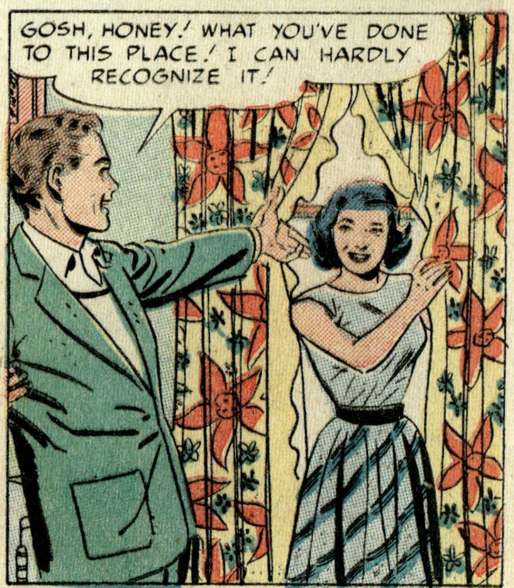

AND I SCRIMPED ON THE PENNIES, TOO! I WANTED TO HELP PETE BUY HIS OWN GARAGE...

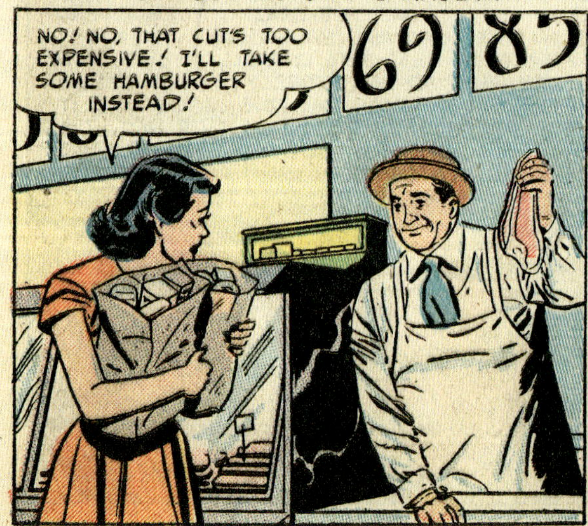

AND THEN, ONE EVENING, MY FATHER APPEARED! IT WAS THE FIRST TIME I HAD SEEN HIM SINCE MY MARRIAGE...

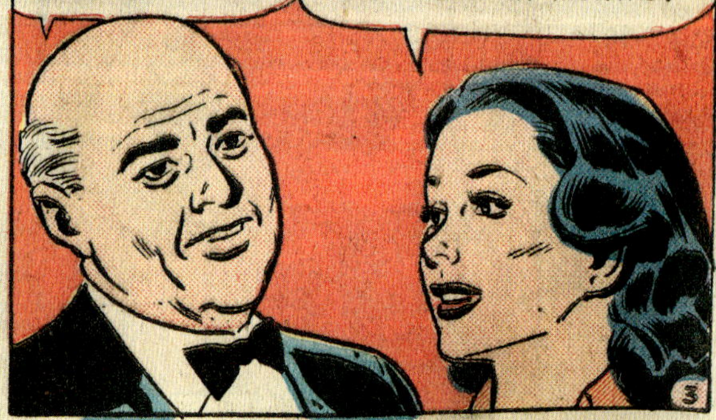

AT THE SHOW I MET A LOT OF OLD FRIENDS...

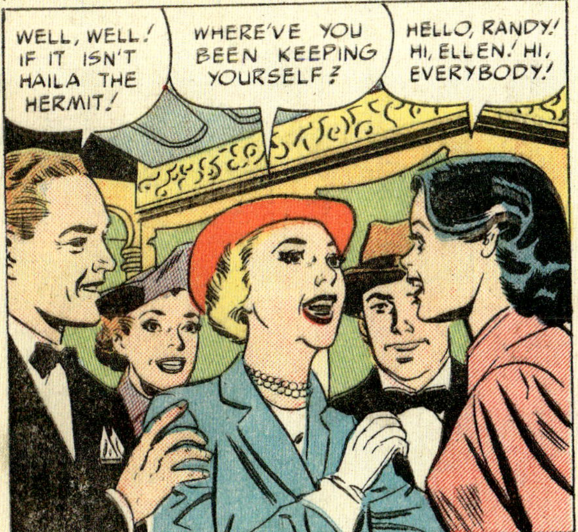

AFTER THE SHOW MY FATHER SUGGESTED WE GO TO THE SWANK PENGUIN CLUB! I KNEW WHAT HE WAS SCHEMING! HE WAS TRYING TO REMIND ME OF MY OLD GLAMOROUS LIFE! NEVERTHELESS, I AGREED TO GO!

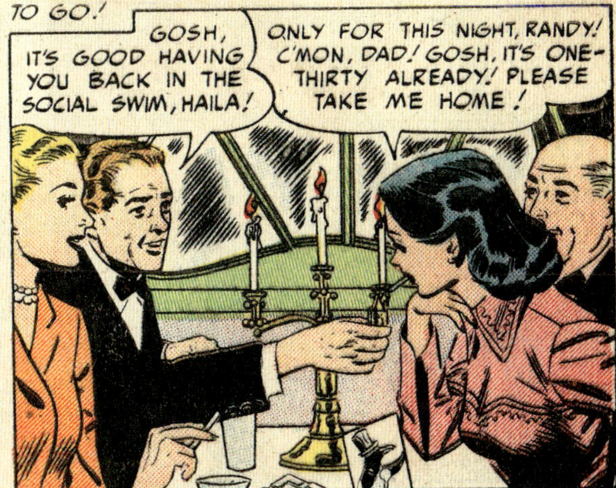

WHEN DAD LEFT ME AT MY HOUSE, I TOOK A SWIFT LOOK AT OUR BLOCK! IT SUDDENLY SEEMED SHABBIER THAN EVER...

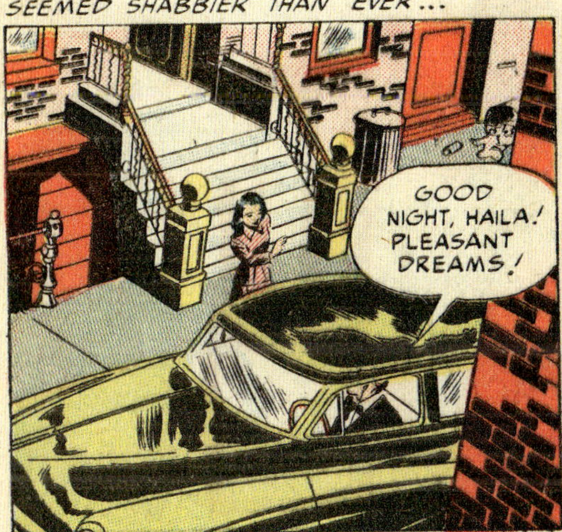

I COULDN'T SLEEP THAT NIGHT! I KEPT COMPARING MY OLD LIFE WITH THE DRAB ONE I WAS LIVING NOW...

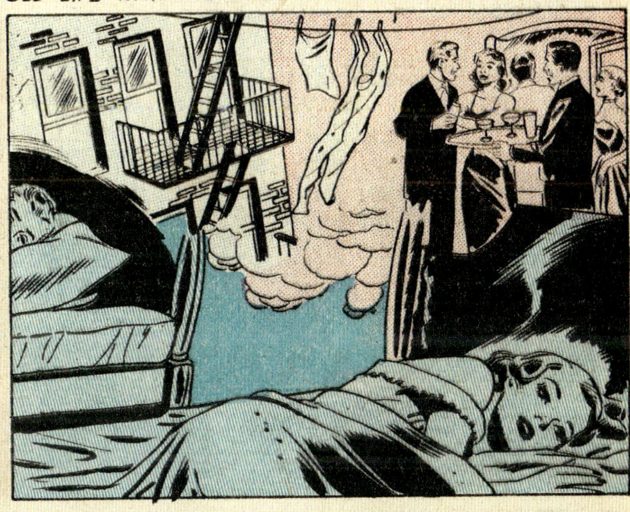

THE NEXT DAY I JUST COULDN'T DO ANYTHING! I LET THE HOUSE GO COMPLETELY; WHEN PETE CAME HOME FROM WORK, I ASKED HIM WHETHER WE COULD EAT OUT FOR A CHANGE! HE WAS SURPRISED, BUT SAID, "OF COURSE!"

I KNOW I'VE NO RIGHT TO ASK THIS, PETE, BUT COULD WE REALLY STEP OUT TONIGHT? MAYBE GO TO A NIGHTCLUB OR...

YOU HAVE A NIGHT OFF COMING TO YOU, DARLING! I KNOW HOW HARD IT'S BEEN ON YOU! SURE, WE CAN STEP OUT THIS ONCE...

WE STEPPED OUT NOT ONE NIGHT BUT THREE NIGHTS THAT WEEK!

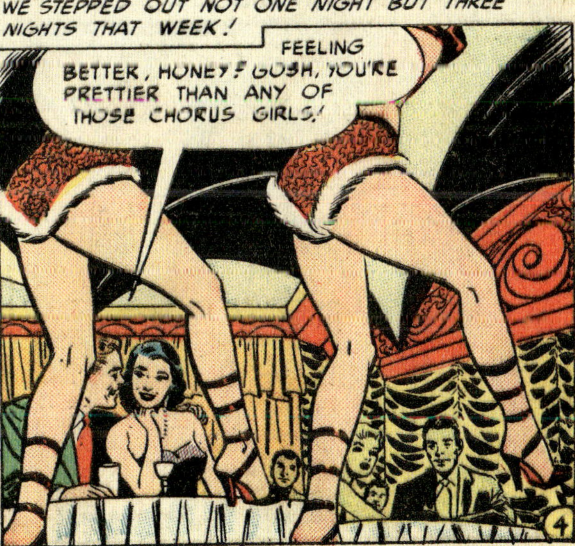

AND THE NEXT WEEK WE WENT OUT FOUR TIMES!

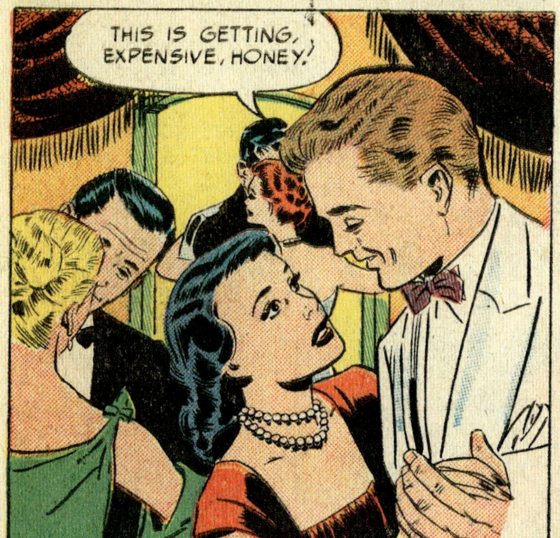

OH, MY FATHER'S PLAN WORKED BEAUTIFULLY! I COULDN'T STOP ANYMORE! I WAS LIKE A DRUNKARD.. ALWAYS ASKING FOR ONE MORE! I KNEW THAT PETE WAS GETTING HIS FILL OF THIS AND FINALLY...

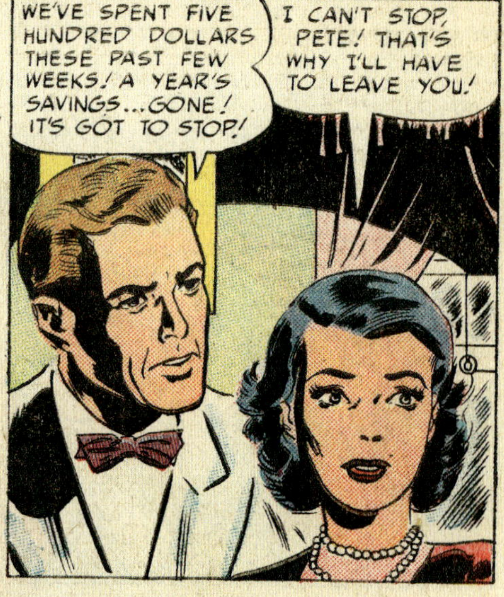

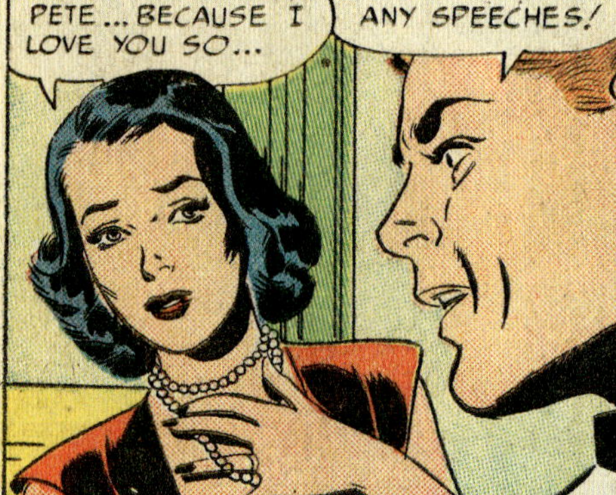

I RETURNED TO MY FATHER'S MANSION THAT AFTERNOON! AS I OPENED THE DOOR TO THE BEAUTIFUL FOYER, A CHILL SWEPT OVER ME! IT SEEMED SO LONELY, SO EMPTY...

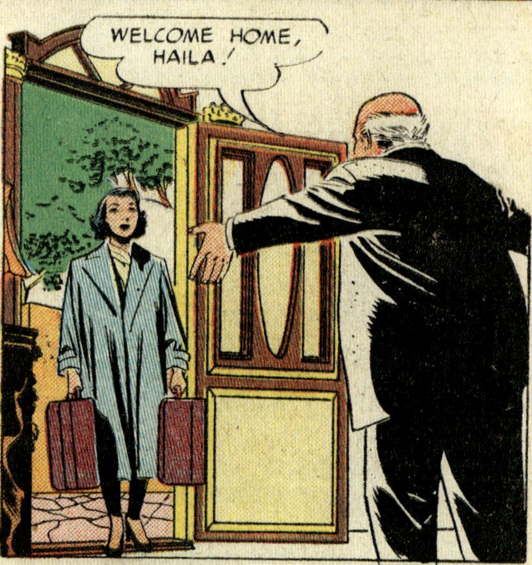

THE NEXT NIGHT I STARTED THE MERRY OLD LIFE AGAIN!

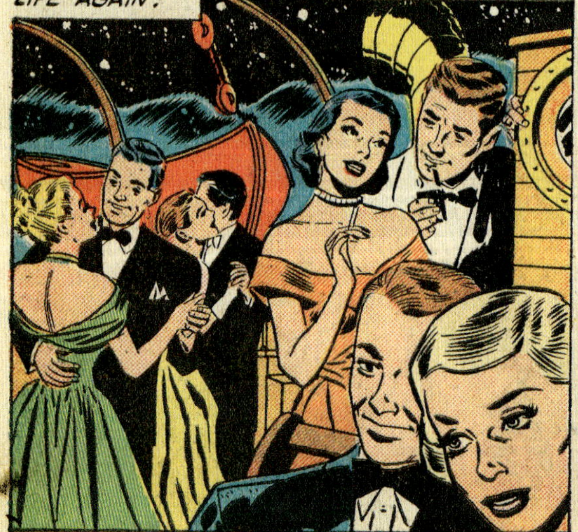

BUT SOMETHING WAS WRONG WITH THE MERRY, OLD LIFE! SUDDENLY, IT SEEMED TASTELESS, ROOTLESS, IRRESPONSIBLE...

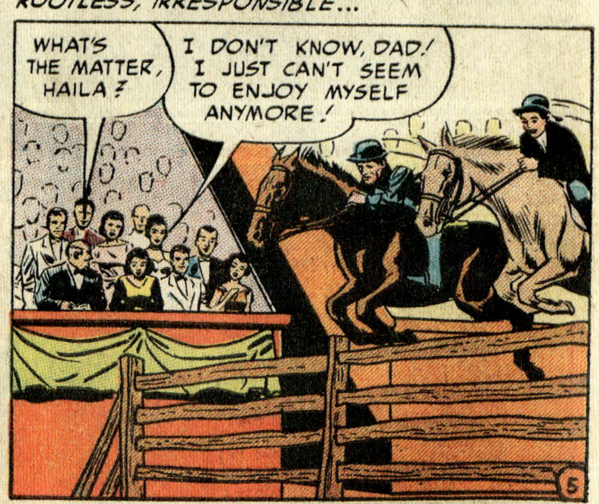

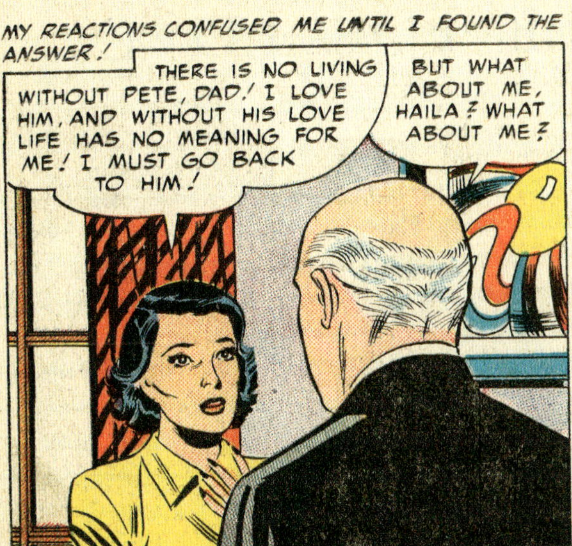
MY REACTIONS CONFUSED ME UNTIL I FOUND THE ANSWER!
THERE IS NO LIVING WITHOUT PETE, DAD! I LOVE HIM, AND WITHOUT HIS LOVE LIFE HAS NO MEANING FOR ME! I MUST GO BACK TO HIM!
BUT WHAT ABOUT ME, HAILA? WHAT ABOUT ME?

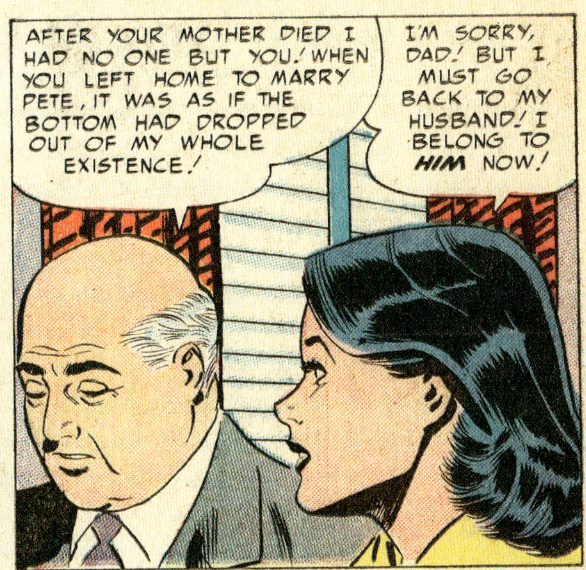
AFTER YOUR MOTHER DIED I HAD NO ONE BUT YOU! WHEN YOU LEFT HOME TO MARRY PETE, IT WAS AS IF THE BOTTOM HAD DROPPED OUT OF MY WHOLE EXISTENCE!
I'M SORRY, DAD! BUT I MUST GO BACK TO MY HUSBAND! I BELONG TO HIM NOW!

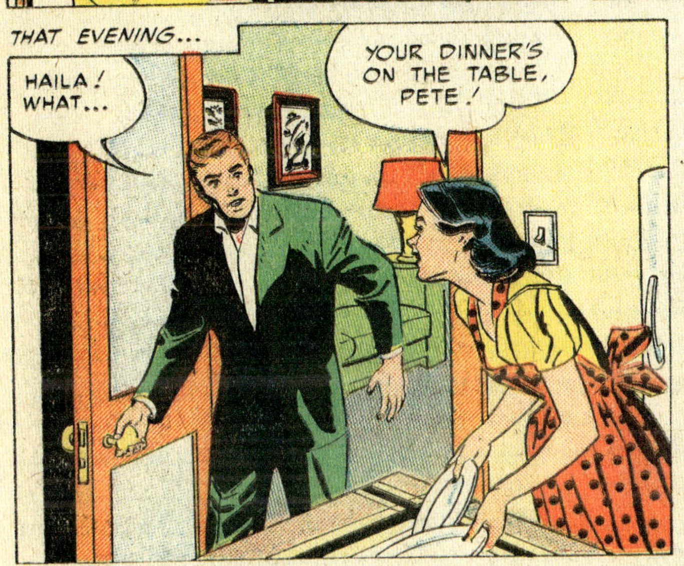
THAT EVENING...
HAILA! WHAT...
YOUR DINNER'S ON THE TABLE, PETE!

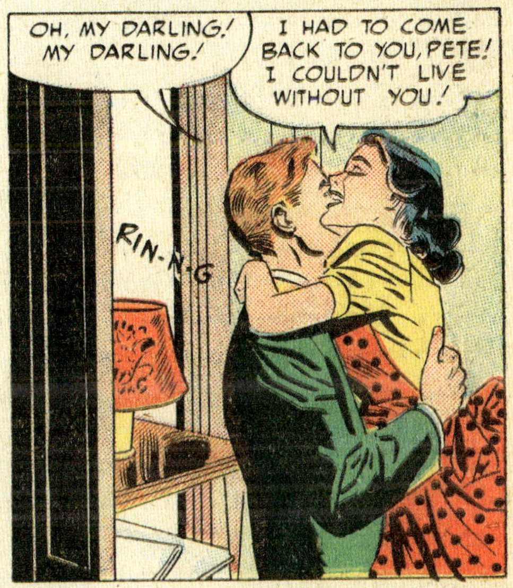
OH, MY DARLING! MY DARLING!
I HAD TO COME BACK TO YOU, PETE! I COULDN'T LIVE WITHOUT YOU!
RIN-N-G

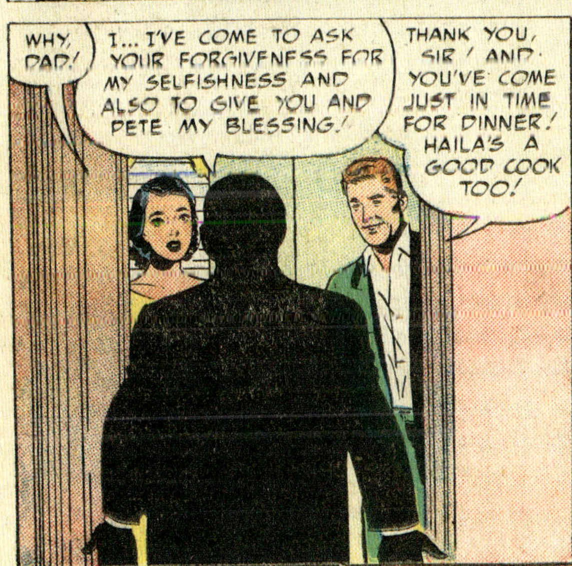
WHY, DAD!
I... I'VE COME TO ASK YOUR FORGIVENESS FOR MY SELFISHNESS AND ALSO TO GIVE YOU AND PETE MY BLESSING!
THANK YOU, SIR! AND YOU'VE COME JUST IN TIME FOR DINNER! HAILA'S A GOOD COOK TOO!

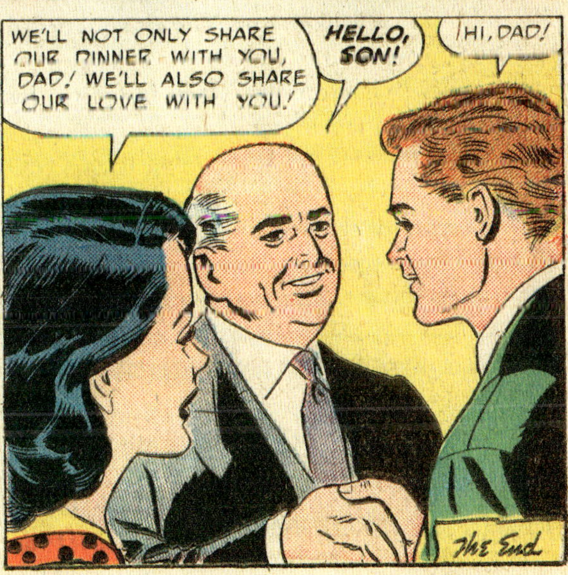
WE'LL NOT ONLY SHARE OUR DINNER WITH YOU, DAD! WE'LL ALSO SHARE OUR LOVE WITH YOU!
HELLO, SON!
HI, DAD!
The End

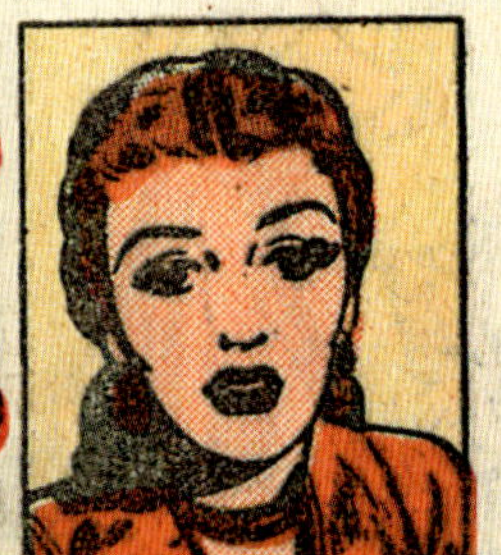

Are You Fickle?

by Nancy Hale

"I THINK there must be something wrong with me!" one Problem Clinic reader recently wrote in anxiously. "I like a boy until he falls for me, then I get bored with him and go on to someone new. The same thing happens over and over again!" Her problem is, surprisingly enough, not an unusual one. Many girls and boys—for that matter, many men and women—enjoy the thrill of making a conquest, and then discover it turns to ashes in their hands. Once they have gained their goal, they no longer want it!

Fickleness, as defined by Webster's Collegiate, means "liable to change; unstable; capricious." It denotes an incapacity to remain mentally and emotionally stable. More often than not it is an inherent tendency toward change rather than an intentional desire to reap conquests for purely selfish satisfaction. In the end it is the fickle individual who pays for he discovers that he is always restless, never content for long. He is always seeking new joys, new victories.

A Curse

If not curbed soon enough, fickleness can become a curse. It can disrupt the lives of those directly affected and in many instances leaves heartbreak and painful scars in its wake. Ironically, the heartbreak may boomerang on its inflicter, as happened in the case of a handsome young man by the name of Bill S.

Bill was tall, dark and extremely appealing to the feminine sex. Women fell for his charms with amazing rapidity, and Bill reveled in his role of Casanova. As soon as he tired of one girl, he threw her over for another. Then, one day, something went wrong. Bill discovered that his newest flame was suddenly casting him aside for another man! More than Bill's pride was hurt. To his grief he learned that life without Ellen was empty, that it was like living in a vacuum. He tasted the bitter fruit fickleness can reap and learned first hand what heartbreak was really like.

Test Yourself

To determine whether or not YOU are fickle, answer the following questions YES or NO. Be truthful with yourself.

1. Do you tire easily of your boy friend (girl friend) or marriage partner?

2. Do you like to have one person always at your beck and call, and still play around on the side?

3. Does your heart beat faster every time you see a handsome man (attractive girl) pass by?

4. Does a come-hither glance tempt you even though you are happy with another?

5. Do you delight in keeping several romances going at the same time?

6. Are you constantly swept off your feet by good looks, a beckoning glance, a kiss?

Combat It

If you have answered YES to three or more of these questions, *watch out!* You are on the brink of heartaches and a life of doubt and insecurity. Try to take new hold of yourself and learn to control the impulses which endanger your happiness and the happiness of those close to you.

Evaluate your present boy or girl friend's good qualities and then learn to appreciate them anew. Remember that no one is perfect, not even YOU! Do not let good looks alone sway you or cause you to do anything you will later regret. A kind heart and a helpful hand mean more than a handsome exterior, shallow flattery or tempestuous romances that soon fizzle. Don't run the risk of losing a worthwhile love for the sake of glamor or momentary thrills.

Be grateful for the love you have and, instead of looking around for someone new, someone more exciting, try improving your own shortcomings so that the one who loves you now will love you even more!

HOW TO INCREASE YOUR DATEABILITY!

Some tips on how to up your popularity quotient.

IF YOU FEEL YOU'RE NOT AS POPULAR AS YOU ***MIGHT BE,*** ARE YOU SURE YOU'RE AS ***ALERT*** AS YOU COULD BE? PERHAPS THE FELLOW WHO WORKS AT THE NEXT DESK IS A LITTLE SHY-- MAYBE HE'S BEEN THROWING HINTS YOUR WAY AND ***YOU HAVEN'T BEEN CATCHING THEM!***

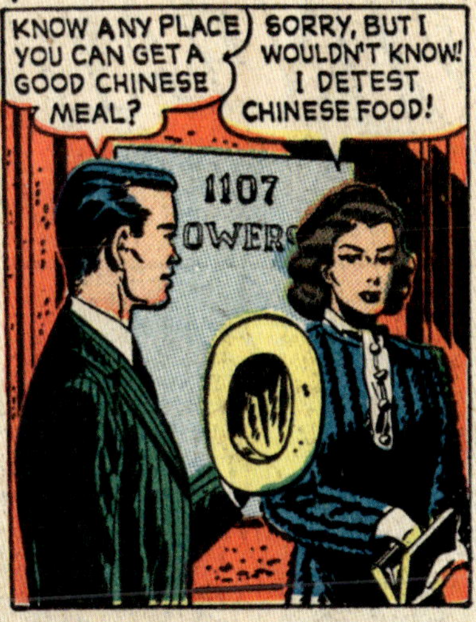

ARE YOU MAKING THE ***MOST*** OF AVAILABLE OPPORTUNITIES TO MEET YOUNG MEN YOUR AGE? IN SHORT, DO YOU GO PLACES WHERE THE YOUNG MEN ARE? JOIN A SOCIAL CLUB OR TRY THE SWIMMING POOL AT THE LOCAL "Y"! YOU MIGHT BE SURPRISED AT THE RESULTS!

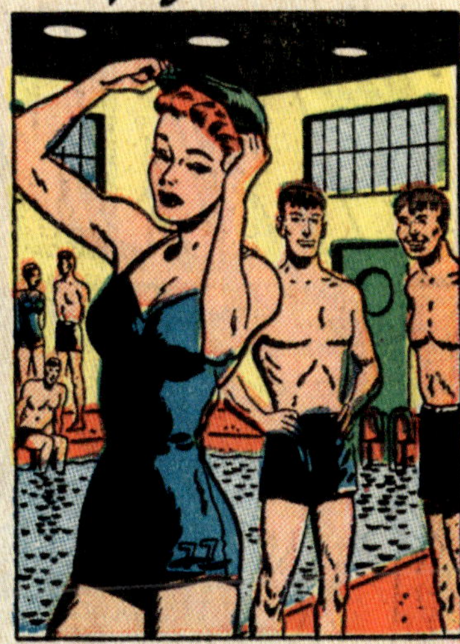

THIS IS NO TIME TO BE TOO PROUD! LET YOUR FRIENDS ***KNOW*** YOU'D LIKE TO MEET SOME ELIGIBLE YOUNG MEN! THEY'RE USUALLY VERY GLAD TO COOPERATE!

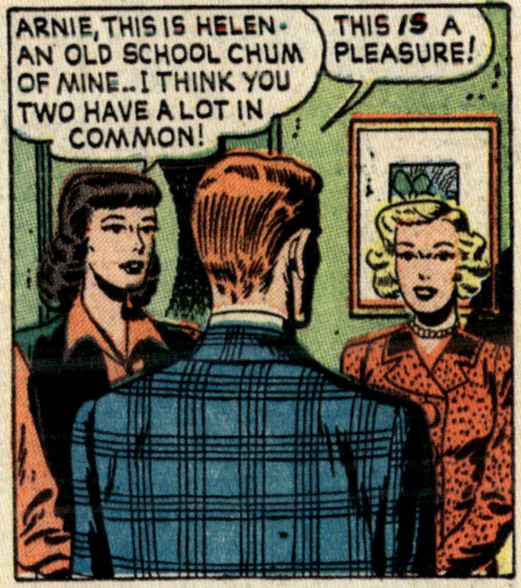

ARE YOU TOO ANXIOUS? DOES YOUR WHOLE ATTITUDE ADVERTISE THE FACT THAT ***YOU'RE MAN HUNGRY?*** BE CAREFUL NOT TO SCARE POTENTIAL DATES AWAY WITH OVER EAGERNESS!

WHY DON'T YOU COME OVER FOR A REAL HOME COOKED MEAL! I'D LIKE YOU TO MEET MOTHER AND DAD!

OH, THANKS, BUT I CAN'T MAKE IT TONIGHT!

PERHAPS YOU'RE SO BUSY WAITING FOR YOUR ***DREAM MAN*** TO COME ALONG YOU'RE OVERLOOKING SOME VERY GOOD BETS! SOMETIMES A GIRL HAS SUCH A DETAILED PICTURE OF HER "HERO" IN MIND THAT SHE OVERLOOKS HIM IF HE SHOULD SHOW UP IN SLIGHTLY DIFFERENT GARB!

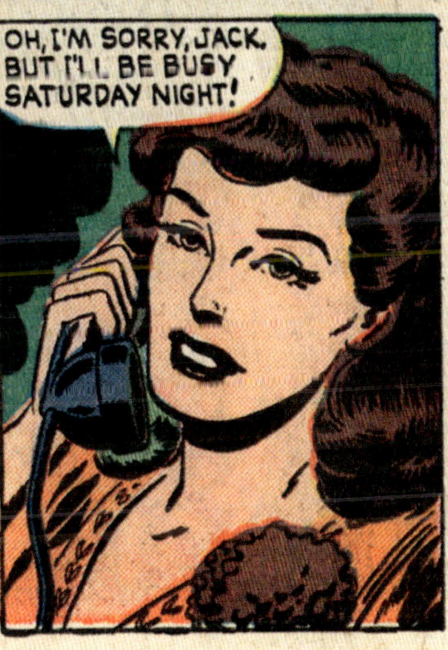

ARE YOU ***FRIENDLY AND SWEET*** TO EVERYONE-NOT JUST THE MEN ON WHOM YOU WANT TO MAKE AN IMPRESSION! PERHAPS-JUST PERHAPS THE NICE OLD COUPLE DOWN THE STREET MAY BE THE ONES TO INTRODUCE YOU TO ***HIM*** IF THEY LIKE YOU!

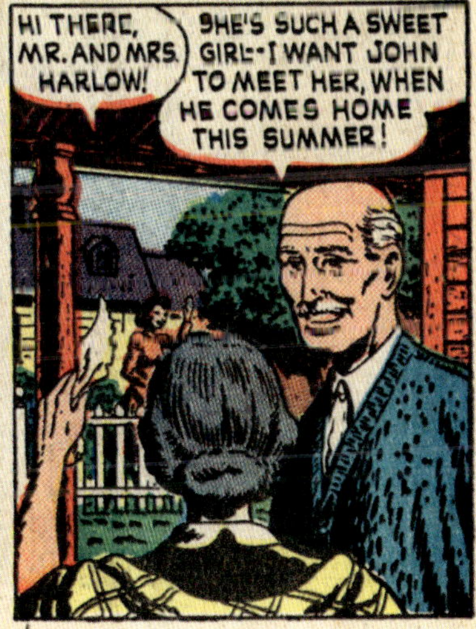

Page 180: **YOUNG ROMANCE** Volume 3, #11, July 1950

This page: **YOUNG LOVE** Volume 2, #2, April 1950

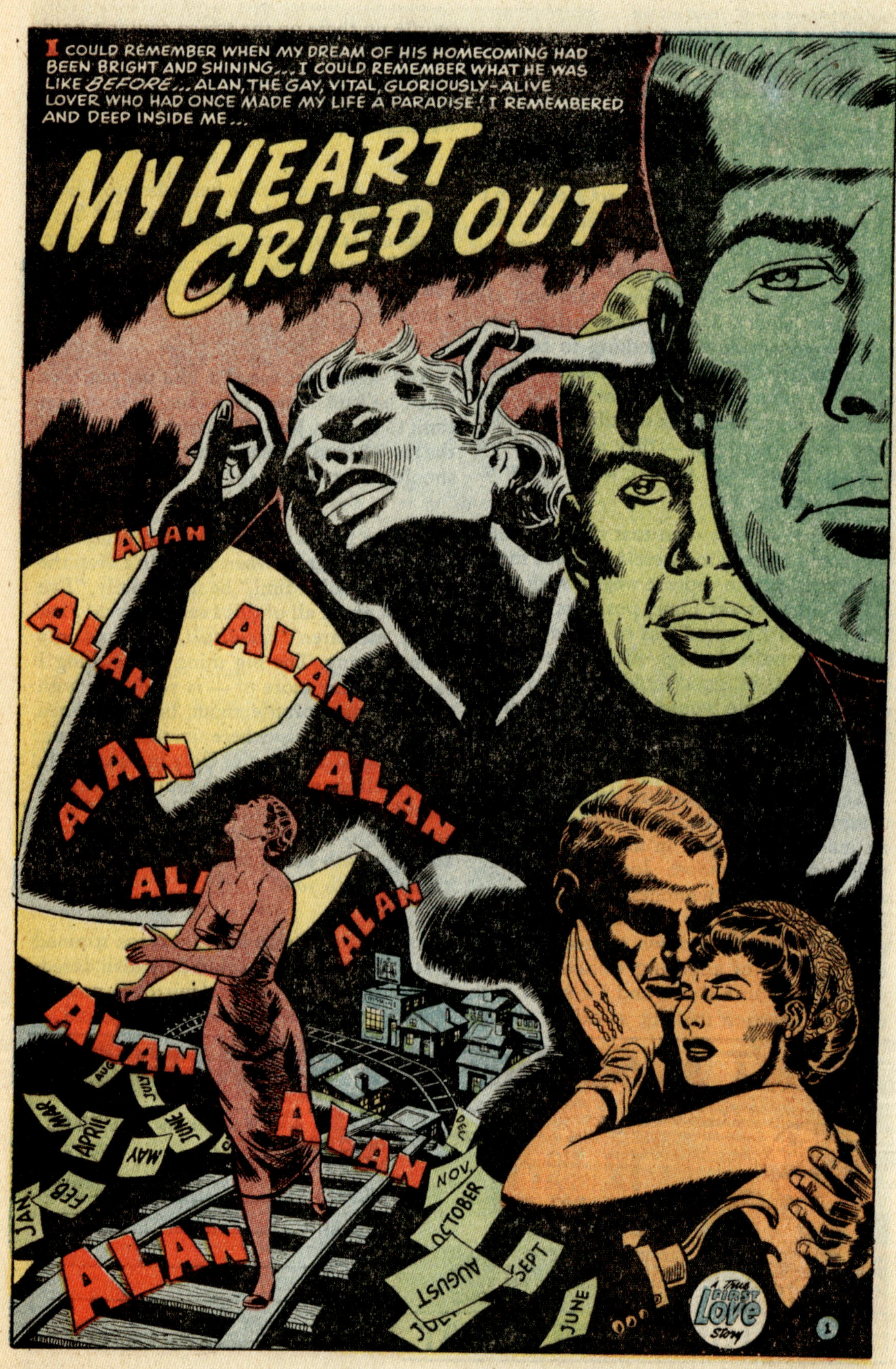
I COULD REMEMBER WHEN MY DREAM OF HIS HOMECOMING HAD BEEN BRIGHT AND SHINING... I COULD REMEMBER WHAT HE WAS LIKE BEFORE... ALAN, THE GAY, VITAL, GLORIOUSLY-ALIVE LOVER WHO HAD ONCE MADE MY LIFE A PARADISE! I REMEMBERED, AND DEEP INSIDE ME...
MY HEART CRIED OUT
ALAN
ALAN
ALAN
ALAN
ALAN
ALAN
ALAN
ALAN
ALAN
ALAN
JAN.
FEB.
MAR
APRIL
MAY
JUNE
JULY
AUG
AUGUST
SEPT
OCTOBER
NOV.
JUNE
A TRUE FIRST LOVE STORY
1

BUT NOW THAT DREAM HAD BECOME A NIGHTMARE. NOW THAT PARADISE WAS LOST--LOST ALONG WITH ALAN'S LEG AND PART OF HIS ARM SOMEWHERE IN KOREA. NOW I STOOD ON THE PLATFORM WITH HIS MOTHER, WAITING FOR THE TRAIN THAT WAS BRINGING HIM BACK TO ME, AND MY SOUL WAS SICK WITH DREAD...

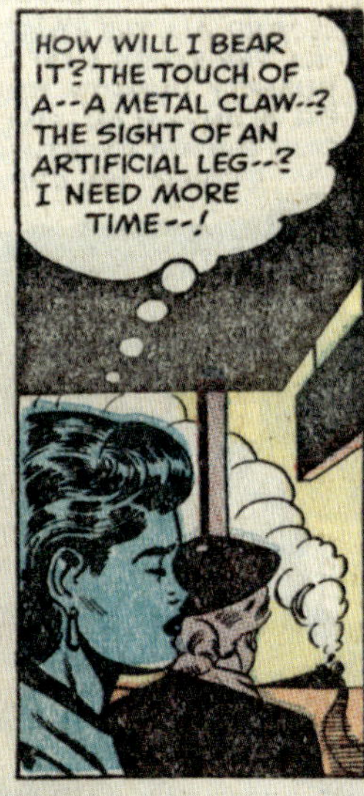

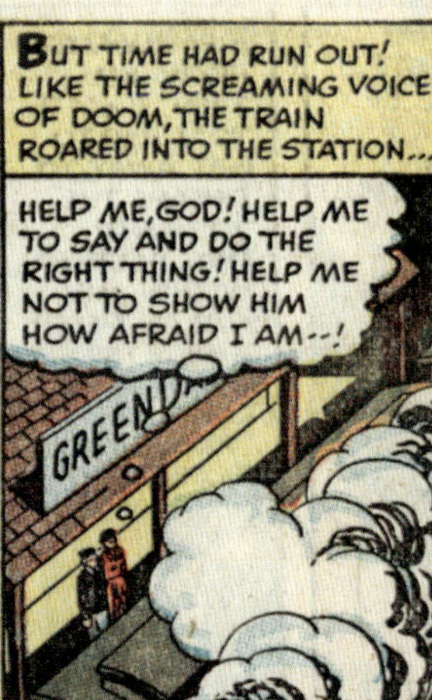

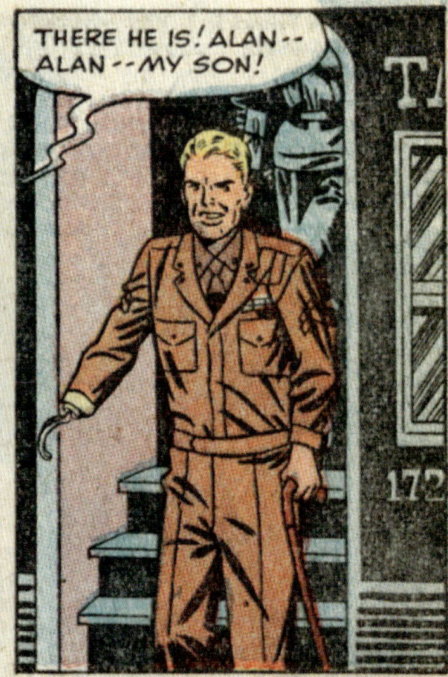

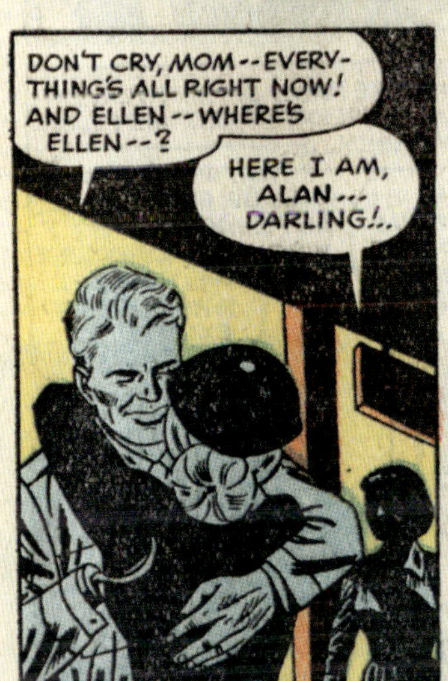

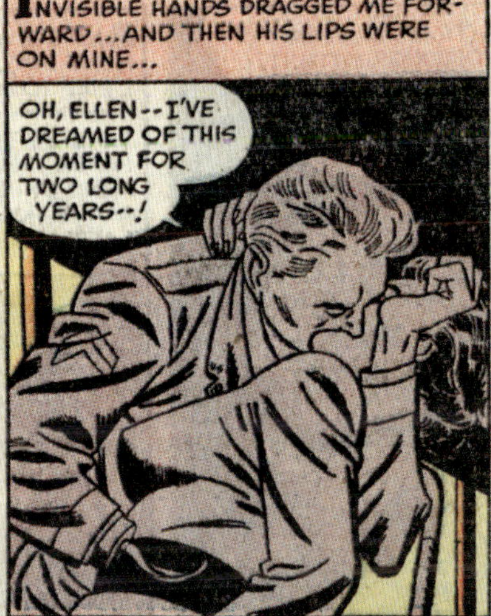

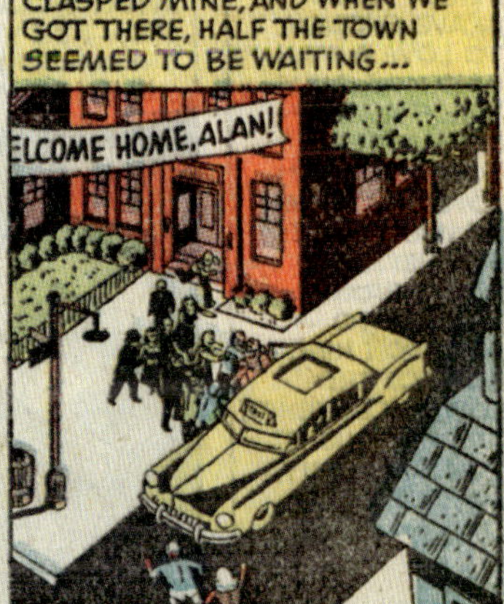

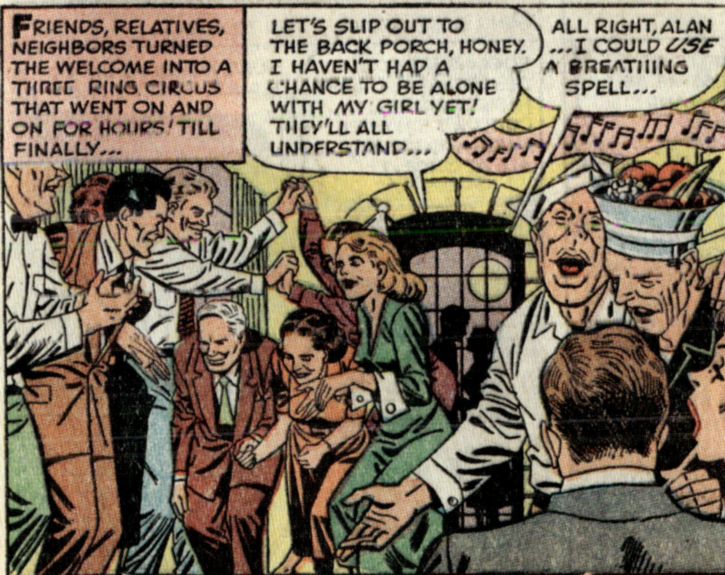

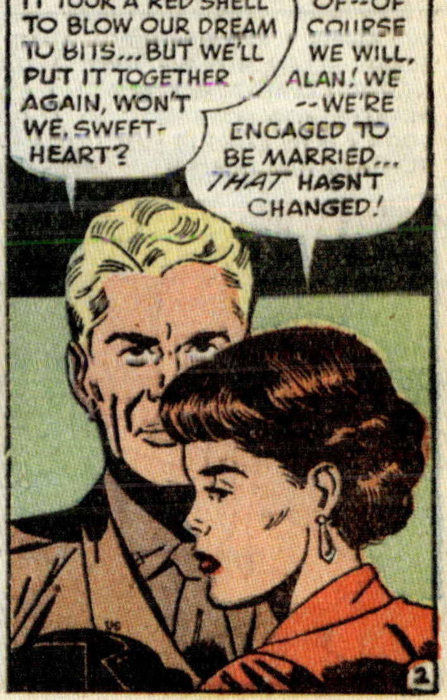

FIRST LOVE
#34, November 1953

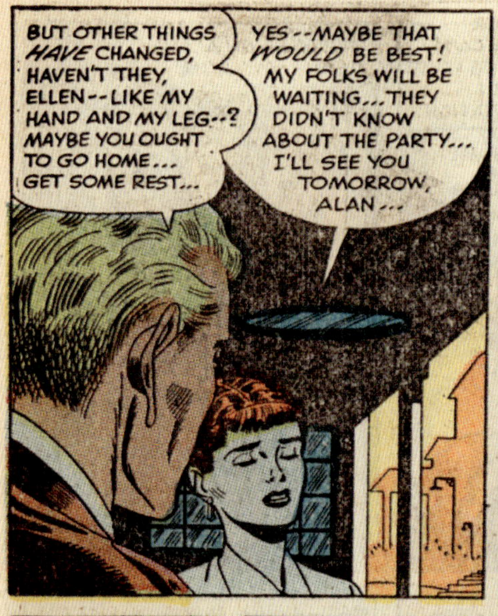

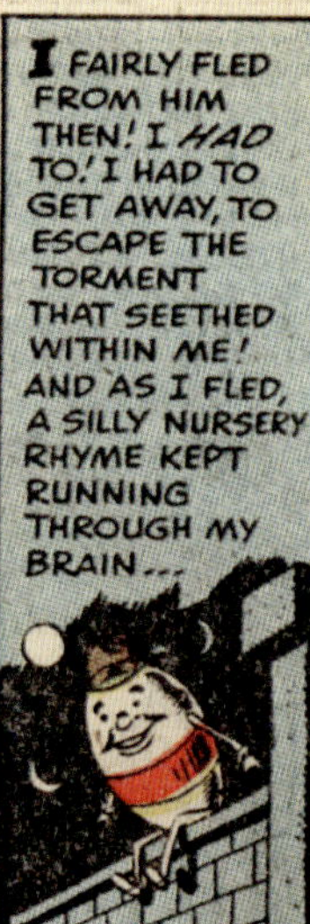

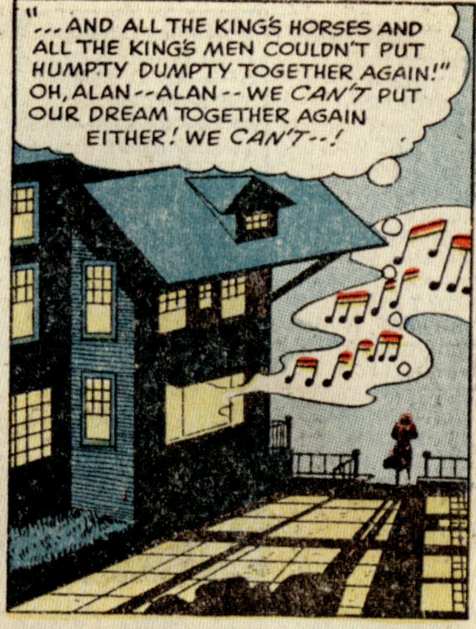

IT WAS SMASHED BEYOND REPAIR! I JUST WASN'T BRAVE ENOUGH TO LOVE A MAN WHO WAS ONLY *HALF* A MAN--NO MATTER HOW MUCH I'D LOVED HIM WHEN HE WAS WHOLE! YET NEITHER WAS I BRAVE ENOUGH TO ABANDON HIM, TO FACE THE TOWN'S CONTEMPT! ALL THAT NIGHT, I SOBBED OUT MY DESPAIR...

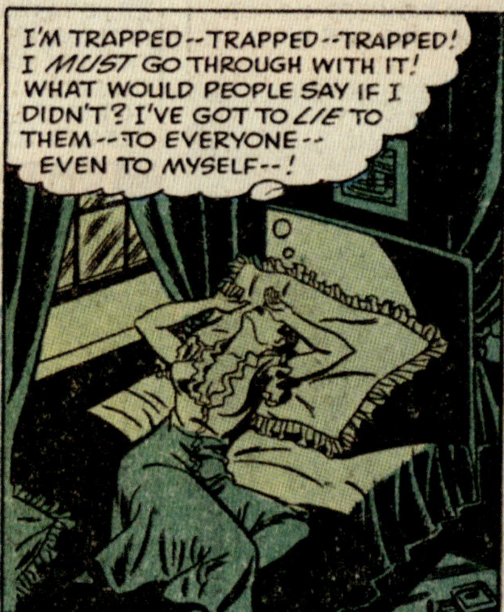

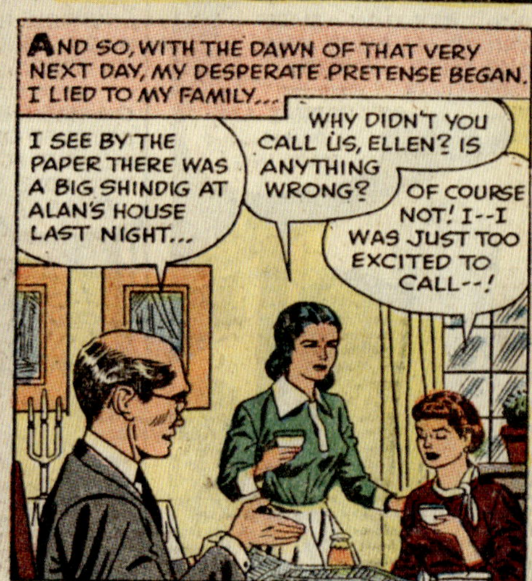

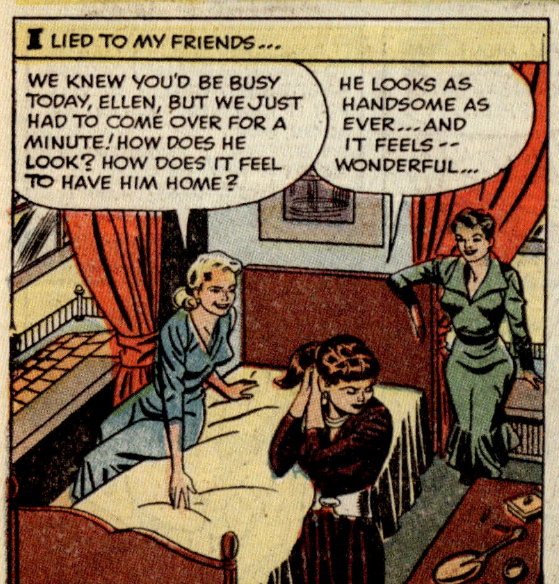

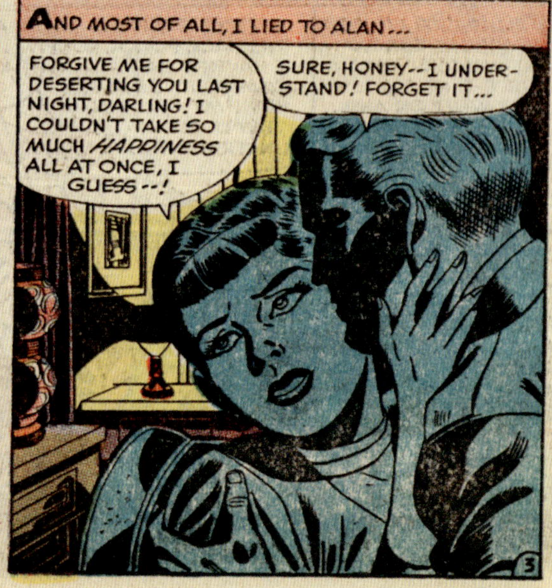

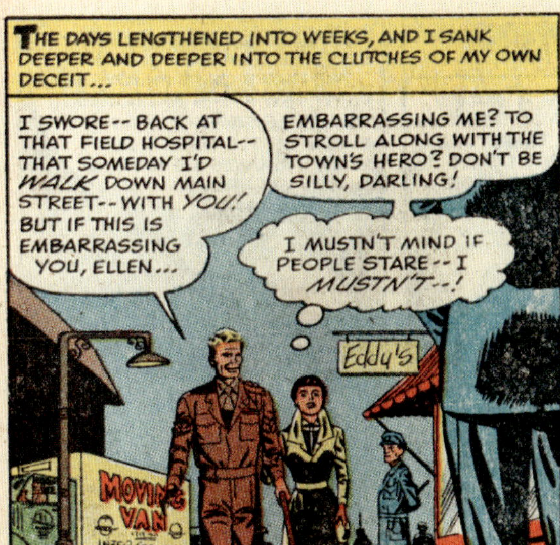

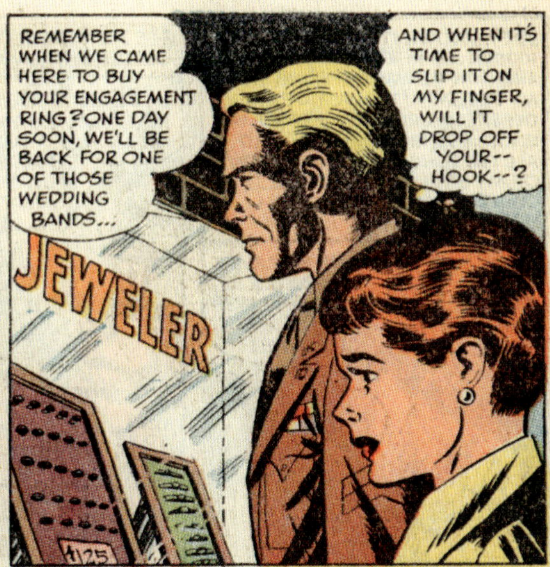

I TRIED TO MAKE OUR LOVE COME ALIVE AGAIN. WE WENT TO THE SAME PLACES, DID THE SAME THINGS-- BUT IT *WASN'T* THE SAME! NOTHING WOULD EVER BE THE SAME AGAIN...

OH, ELLEN, ELLEN-- WHEN DEATH WAS STARING ME IN THE FACE, IT WAS THE MEMORY OF KISSES LIKE THIS THAT GAVE ME COURAGE!

I WISH *I* HAD SOME OF THAT COURAGE-- ENOUGH TO TELL YOU THE TRUTH--!

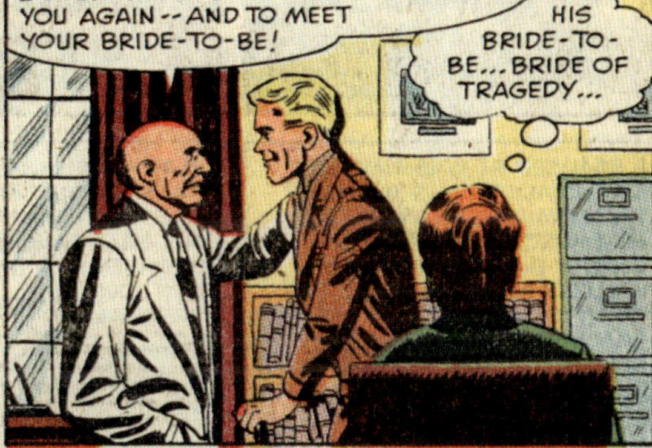

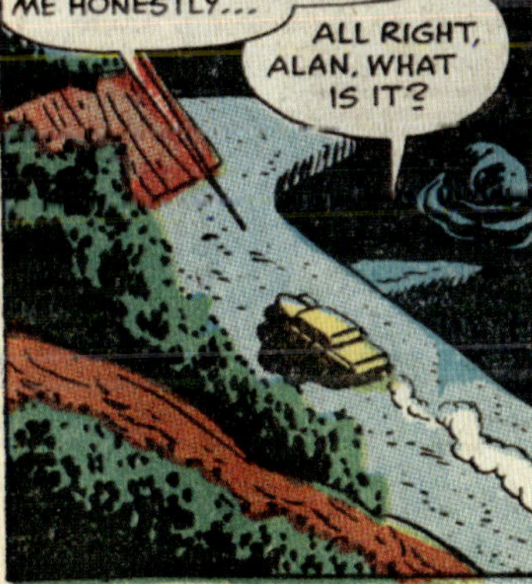

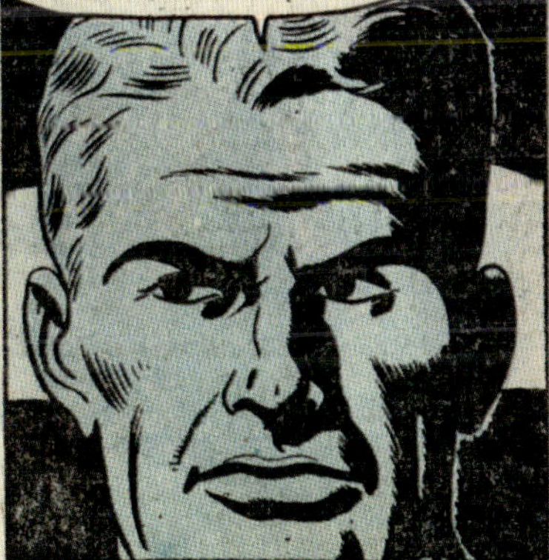

OH, ALAN, ALAN-- FORGIVE ME! I KNOW I'M WEAK AND COWARDLY, BUT I-- (SOB-SOB) --I CAN'T HELP IT! IT'S TRUE--! EVERYTHING YOU SAID IS-- TRUE--!

4

HE'D KNOWN IT ALL ALONG--AND HIDDEN HIS HURT FROM MY EYES! AND NOW HE WAS OFFERING ME MY FREEDOM! THE LAST OF MY DEFENSES CRUMBLED BEFORE HIS GOODNESS, HIS COURAGE--AND ALL THE LONG-REPRESSED AGONY OF MY SOUL SPILLED OVER! I COULDN'T STOP CRYING! TILL SUDDENLY...

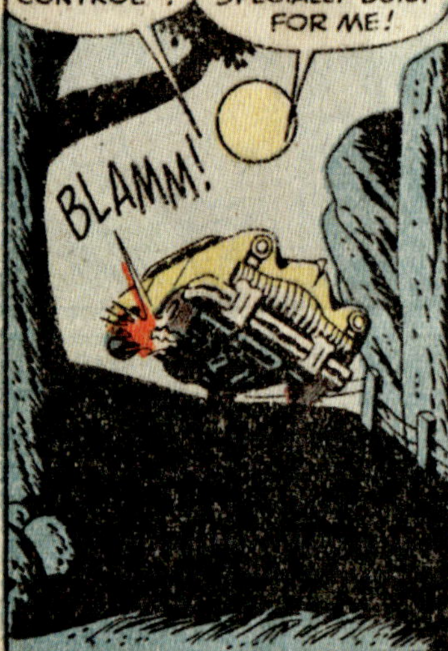

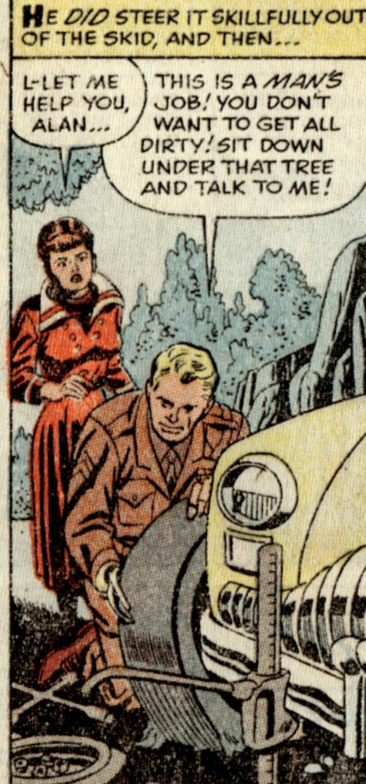

IT'S FUNNY...I ALMOST ENJOY USING THIS DARNED CLAW NOW ...THE WAY A CHILD ENJOYS HIS FIRST FEW STEPS AFTER HE'S REALLY LEARNED TO WALK! EVERY LITTLE THING I DO WITH IT MAKES ME KIND OF PROUD!

I REALIZED HE WAS MAKING SMALL TALK, TRYING TO EASE THE STRAIN BETWEEN US. BUT AS I WATCHED HIM WORK--SLOWLY BUT CONFIDENTLY--I REALIZED SOMETHING ELSE TOO...

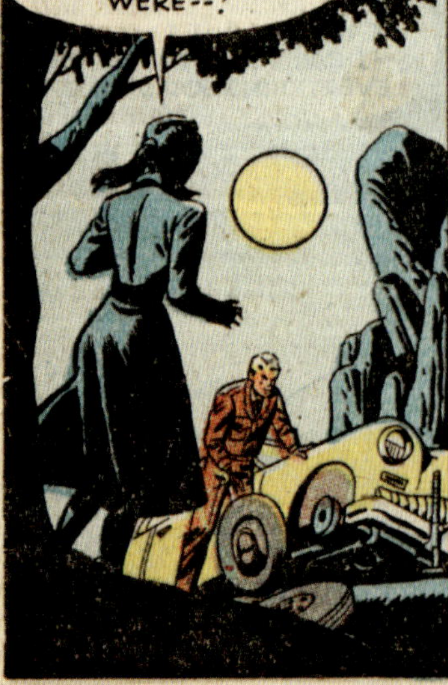

ALAN--DARLING--I'VE BEEN A FOOL! IT ISN'T ARMS OR LEGS THAT MAKE A MAN! IT'S THE HEART INSIDE HIM--THE COURAGE AND THE STRENGTH! AND YOU HAVE THEM ALL--!

ELLEN! DO YOU MEAN--?

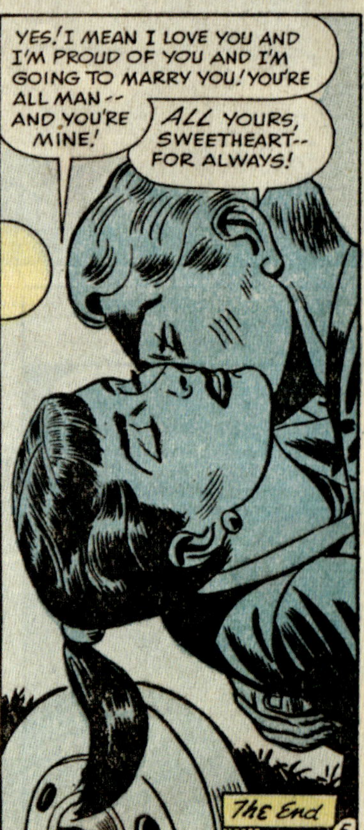

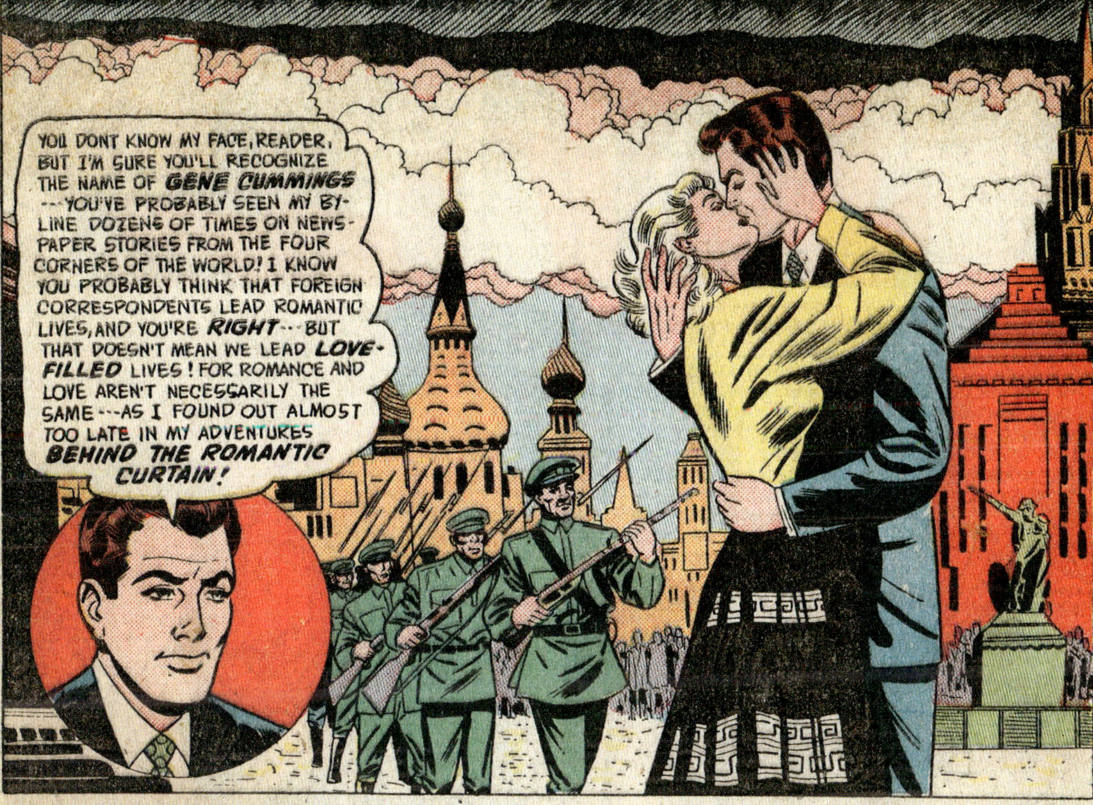

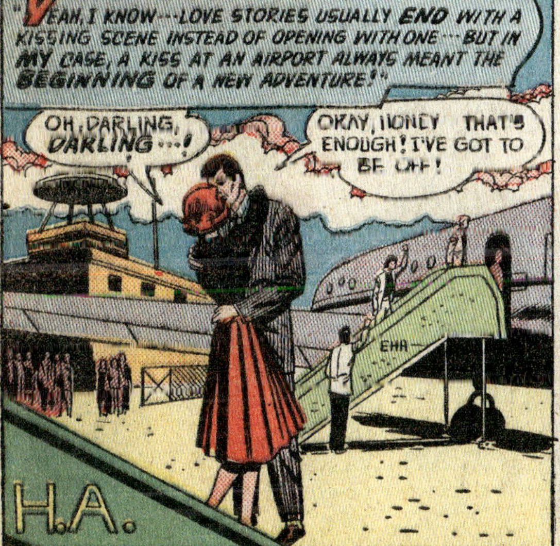

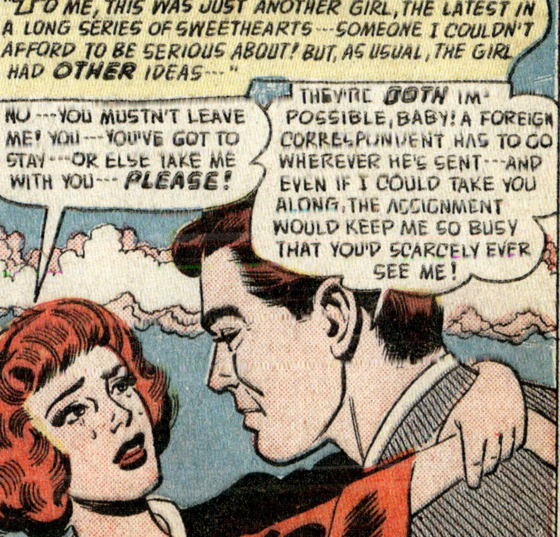

LOVELORN, publishedmonthly and copyright, 1952, by Michel Publications, Inc., Sparta, Ill. Editorial offices, 45 West 45 St., New York 19, N. Y. Richard E. Hughes, Editor; Frederick H. Iger, Business Manager. Subscription (12 issues), $1.20; single copies, $0.10; foreign postage extra. All characters are fictitious and use of any real names is coincidental. For advertising information, address American Comics Group, 45 West 45 St., New York 19, N. Y. Entered as second class matter at the Post Office at Sparta, Ill. No. 23, March, 1952. Printed in U.S.A.

LOVELORN
#23, March 1952

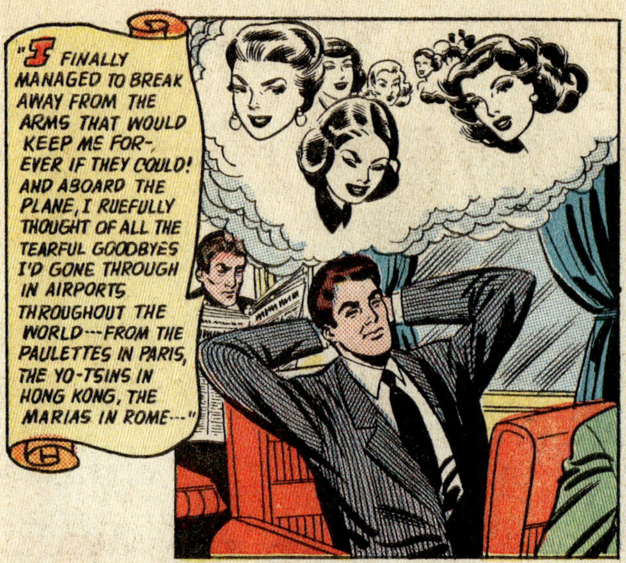
"I FINALLY MANAGED TO BREAK AWAY FROM THE ARMS THAT WOULD KEEP ME FOR-EVER IF THEY COULD! AND ABOARD THE PLANE, I RUEFULLY THOUGHT OF ALL THE TEARFUL GOODBYES I'D GONE THROUGH IN AIRPORTS THROUGHOUT THE WORLD---FROM THE PAULETTES IN PARIS, THE YO-TSINS IN HONG KONG, THE MARIAS IN ROME---"
I'M LUCKY I NEVER LET MYSELF FORM ANY PERMANENT ATTACHMENTS TO ANY OF THEM, NO MATTER HOW BEAUTIFUL AND WONDERFUL THEY WERE---BECAUSE A FOREIGN CORRESPONDENT CAN'T AFFORD TO BE TIED DOWN---HE'S GOT TO BE FOOTLOOSE AND FREE TO ROAM THE WORLD! BUT AT LEAST I'M HEADING NOW FOR THE ONE PLACE WHERE I'M SURE THE GIRLS WON'T FALL FOR ME---BECAUSE AMERICANS ARE SHUNNED LIKE THE PLAGUE IN MOSCOW!

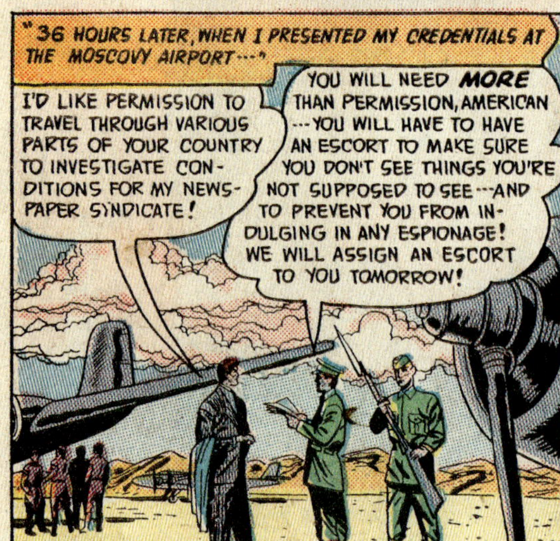
"36 HOURS LATER, WHEN I PRESENTED MY CREDENTIALS AT THE MOSCOVY AIRPORT---"
I'D LIKE PERMISSION TO TRAVEL THROUGH VARIOUS PARTS OF YOUR COUNTRY TO INVESTIGATE CONDITIONS FOR MY NEWSPAPER SYNDICATE!
YOU WILL NEED MORE THAN PERMISSION, AMERICAN---YOU WILL HAVE TO HAVE AN ESCORT TO MAKE SURE YOU DON'T SEE THINGS YOU'RE NOT SUPPOSED TO SEE---AND TO PREVENT YOU FROM INDULGING IN ANY ESPIONAGE! WE WILL ASSIGN AN ESCORT TO YOU TOMORROW!

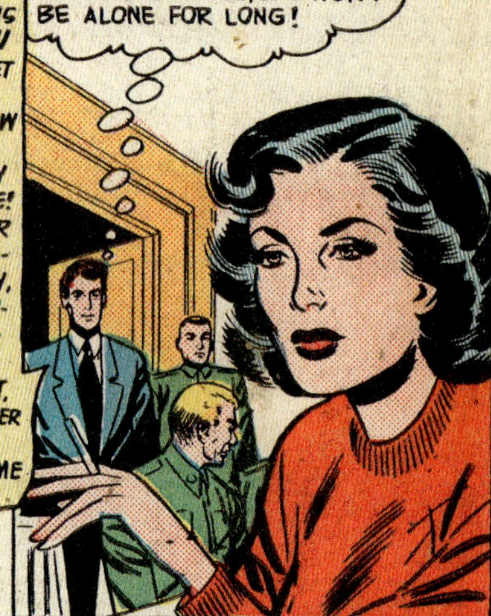
"I KNEW THAT A COUPLE OF GOONS FROM THE OGPU---THE RED SECRET SERVICE---TAILED ME TO MY MOSCOW HOTEL FROM THE AIRPORT, BUT THEY DIDN'T BOTHER ME! WHAT DID BOTHER ME WAS THE PROSPECT OF A LONELY, WOMANLESS EVENING---AND I WANDERED INTO THE HOTEL RESTAURANT, WONDERING WHETHER I COULD TRY MY CHARM OUT ON SOME RUSSIAN GIRLS!"
AH, THERE'S A LOVELY ONE---AND ALONE! WELL, SHE WON'T BE ALONE FOR LONG!

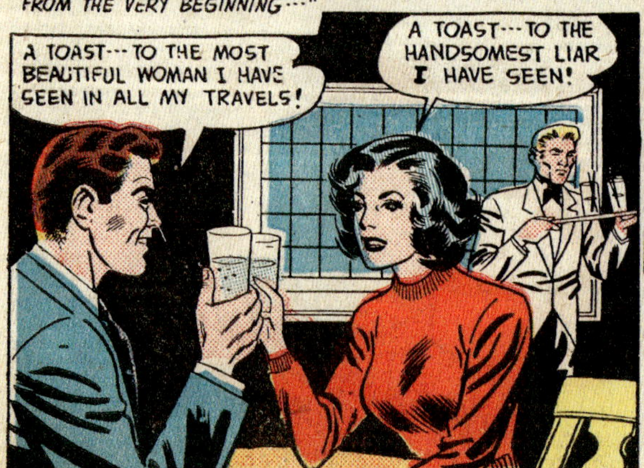
"I SPOKE RUSSIAN FLUENTLY, OF COURSE---AND SINCE I REALIZED THAT THE GIRL WOULD HAVE NOTHING TO DO WITH ME IF SHE KNEW I WERE AN AMERICAN, I STRUCK UP A CONVERSATION WITH HER BY PRETENDING TO BE A RED NEWSPAPER-MAN, JUST RETURNED FROM THE U.S.A! WE GOT ALONG FAMOUSLY FROM THE VERY BEGINNING---"
A TOAST---TO THE MOST BEAUTIFUL WOMAN I HAVE SEEN IN ALL MY TRAVELS!
A TOAST---TO THE HANDSOMEST LIAR I HAVE SEEN!

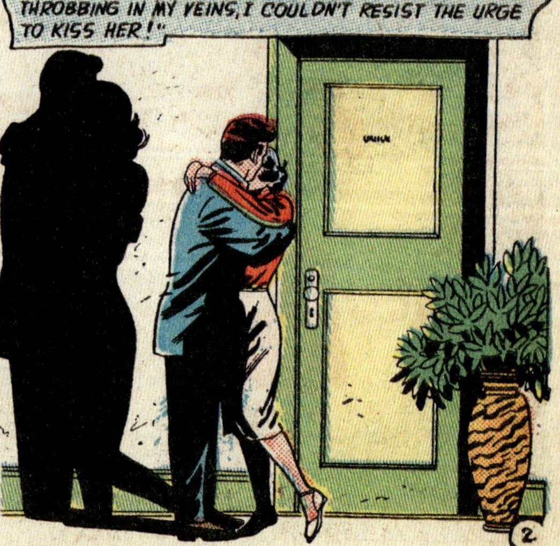
"LATER, IN FRONT OF HER HOTEL ROOM, WITH THE VODKA THROBBING IN MY VEINS, I COULDN'T RESIST THE URGE TO KISS HER!"
2

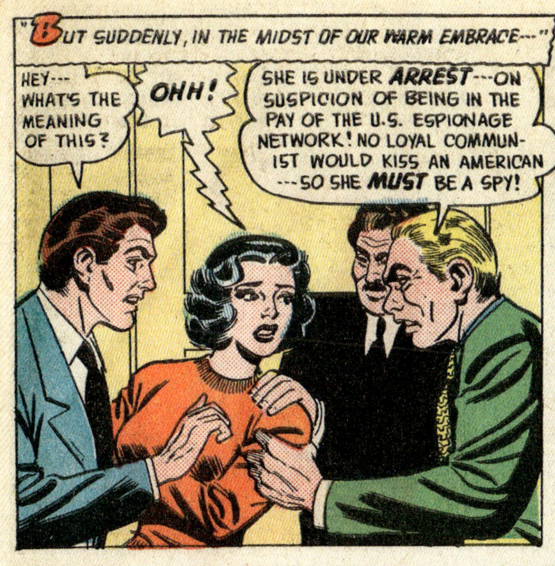

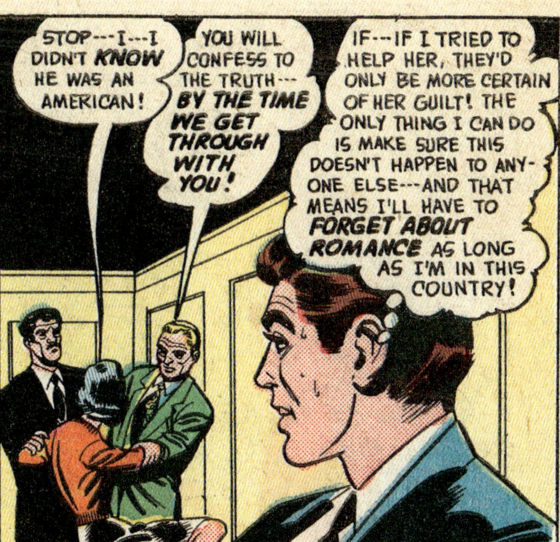

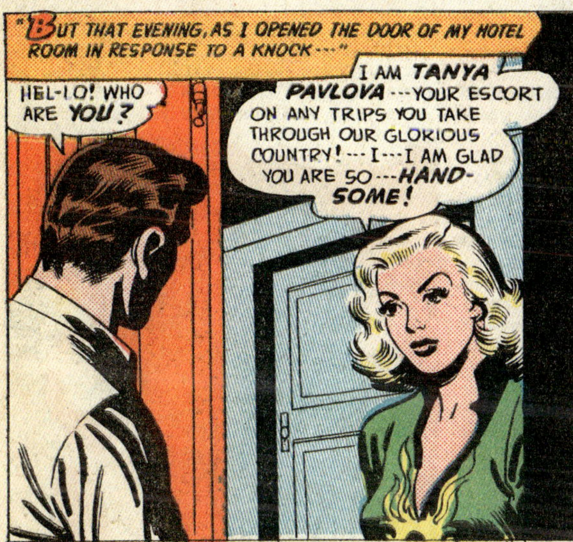

"HER EXOTIC LOVELINESS DAZZLED ME, MADE ME ACHE TO TAKE HER IN MY ARMS---BUT I WAS STOPPED BY THE GRIM REALIZATION THAT THERE COULD ONLY BE ONE REASON WHY THE REDS ASSIGNED A BEAUTY LIKE TANYA TO BE MY ESCORT!"

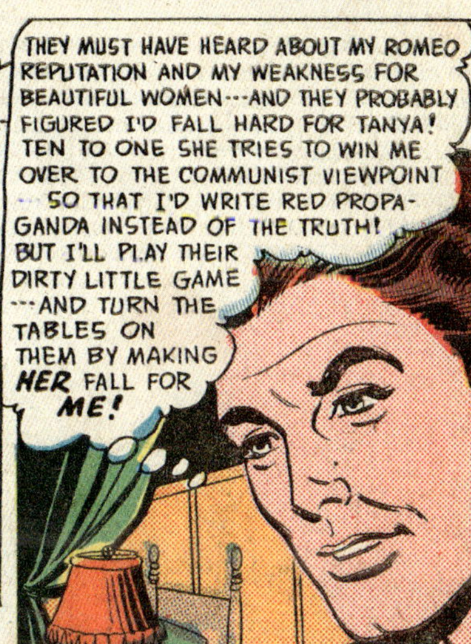

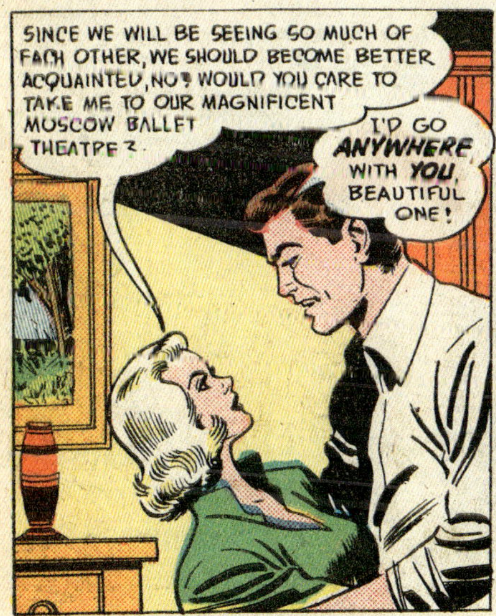

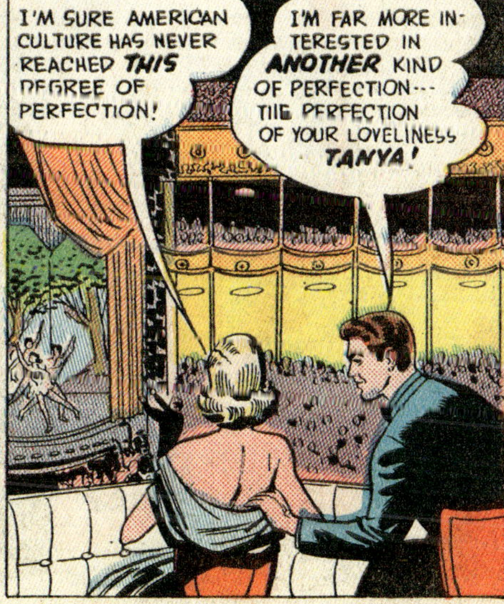

*"THE FUNNY THING WAS, IT WASN'T JUST A LINE---I WAS ABLE TO PUT REAL FEELING INTO MY FLATTERIES ALL THROUGH THAT EVENING---BECAUSE I **MEANT** WHAT I SAID! BUT AS LONG AS I KEPT REMEMBERING THAT SHE WAS A COMMUNIST FANATIC, I KNEW I WOULD NEVER REALLY FALL FOR HER!"*

3.

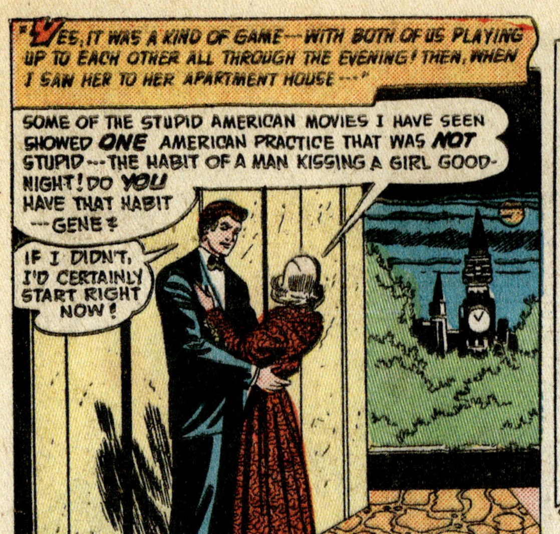

"HER LIPS WERE THRILLINGLY SOFT AND YIELDING, MAKING MY PULSES RACE WITH AN ARDOR I HAD NEVER KNOWN BEFORE---AND I SUDDENLY FOUND I DIDN'T HAVE TO PRETEND I'D FALLEN FOR HER---FOR I ACTUALLY HAD! OVER AND OVER AGAIN I KISSED HER FACE, HER THROAT, HER MOUTH---TENDERLY, CARESSINGLY, LOVINGLY!"

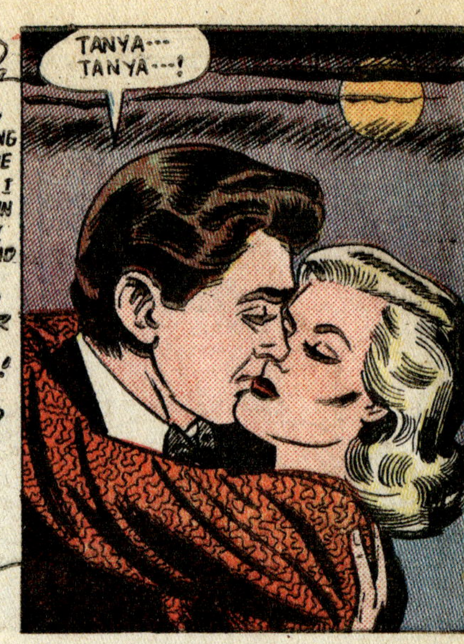

"FINALLY, FRIGHTENED AT THE DEPTH AND INTENSITY OF MY EMOTIONS, I BROKE AWAY---AND SAW THE LOOK OF STARRY-EYED WONDER AND UNABASHED LOVE IN TANYA'S EYES!"

NEVER HAVE I BEEN KISSED LIKE THAT! RUSSIAN MEN KISS CRUDELY, ROUGHLY---LIKE---LIKE BEARS! I NEVER DREAMED A KISS COULD BE SO SWEET, SO TENDER, SO LOVING!

I KNOW ENOUGH ABOUT WOMEN TO KNOW THAT THAT LOOK IN HER EYES IS GENUINE! SHE'S FALLEN FOR ME---JUST AS I HAVE FOR HER!

"WE FELL INTO EACH OTHER'S ARMS AGAIN, CLUNG TIGHTLY TOGETHER---AND IT WAS THEN THAT I FIRST NOTICED MY TWO OGPU SHADOWS GRINNING EVILLY AT US FROM THE NEXT DOORWAY! SEEING THEM WAS LIKE POURING A BUCKET OF ICE WATER OVER THE FLAMES OF MY LOVE!"

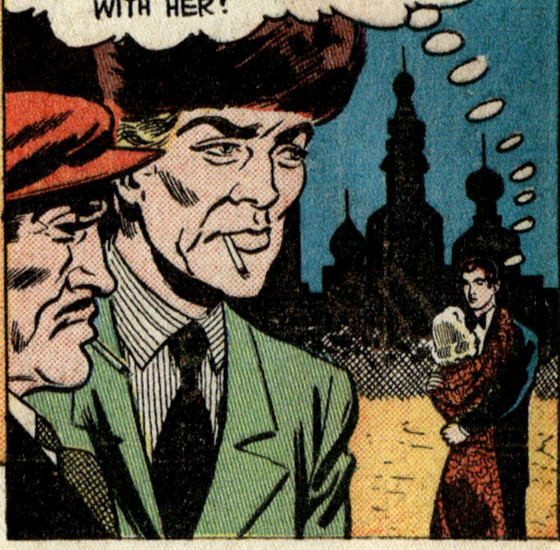

"GONE WERE ALL MY TENDER FEELINGS TOWARD TANYA---AND IN THEIR PLACE THERE WAS ONLY A CONTEMPT AND HATRED FOR ALL SHE STOOD FOR! BUT OUTWARDLY I STILL PLAYED THE PART OF THE SMILING, GALLANT LOVER!"

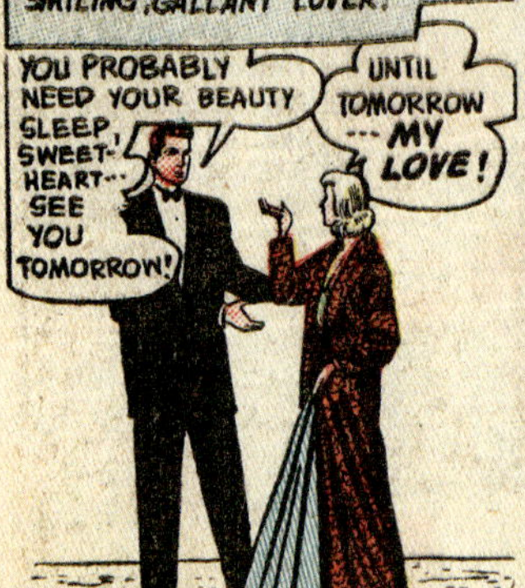

"BUT I COULDN'T SEEM TO RID MY MIND THAT NIGHT OF VISIONS OF TANYA'S LOVELINESS!"

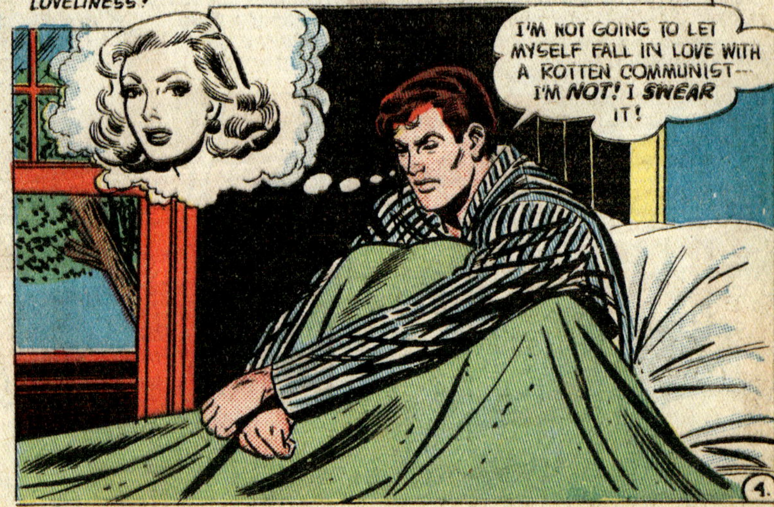

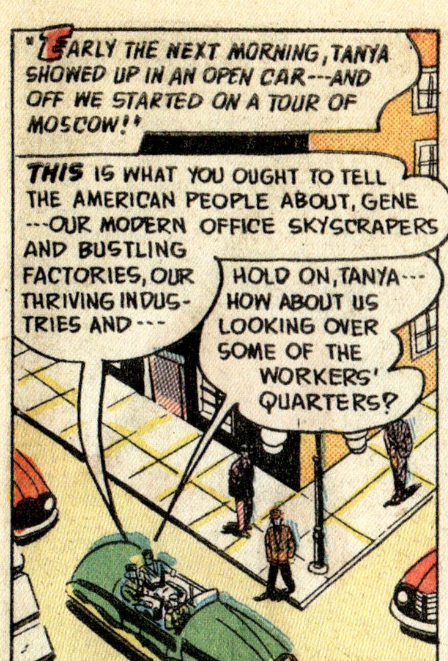
"EARLY THE NEXT MORNING, TANYA SHOWED UP IN AN OPEN CAR---AND OFF WE STARTED ON A TOUR OF MOSCOW!"
THIS IS WHAT YOU OUGHT TO TELL THE AMERICAN PEOPLE ABOUT, GENE ---OUR MODERN OFFICE SKYSCRAPERS AND BUSTLING FACTORIES, OUR THRIVING INDUSTRIES AND ---
HOLD ON, TANYA--- HOW ABOUT US LOOKING OVER SOME OF THE WORKERS' QUARTERS?

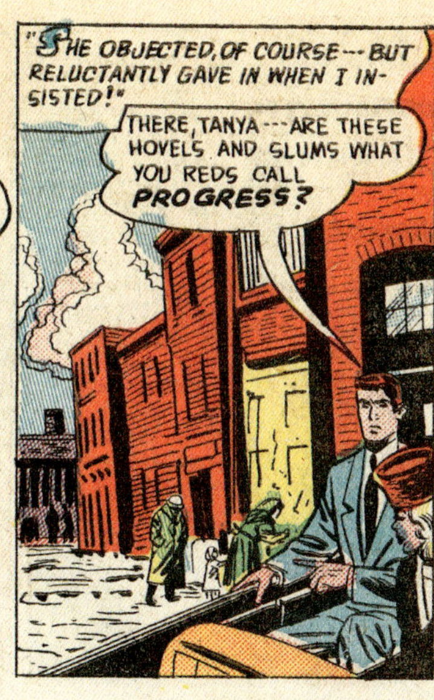
"SHE OBJECTED, OF COURSE --- BUT RELUCTANTLY GAVE IN WHEN I INSISTED!"
THERE, TANYA --- ARE THESE HOVELS AND SLUMS WHAT YOU REDS CALL PROGRESS?

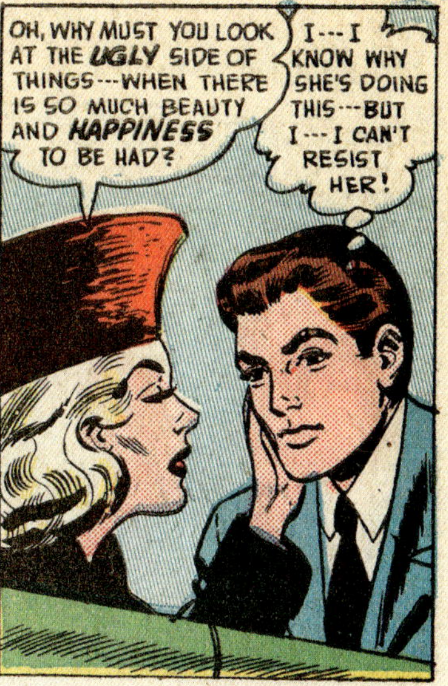
OH, WHY MUST YOU LOOK AT THE UGLY SIDE OF THINGS---WHEN THERE IS SO MUCH BEAUTY AND HAPPINESS TO BE HAD?
I---I KNOW WHY SHE'S DOING THIS---BUT I---I CAN'T RESIST HER!

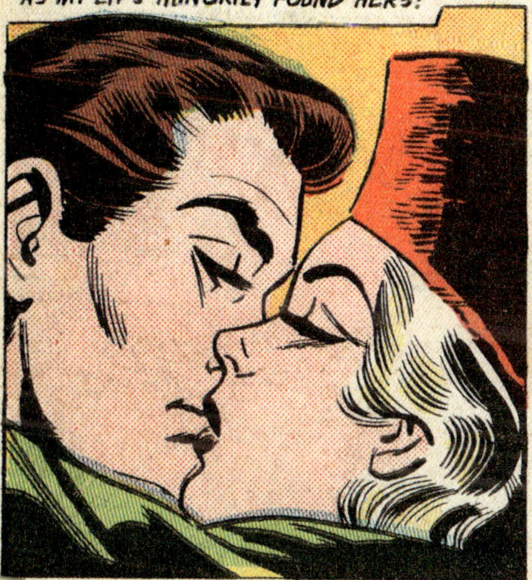
"SHE MELTED INTO MY ARMS---AND MY BLOOD RAN LIKE LIQUID FIRE IN MY VEINS ONCE MORE AS MY LIPS HUNGRILY FOUND HERS!"

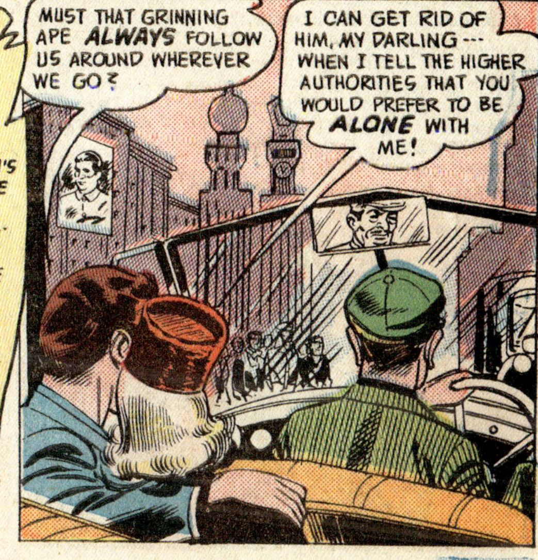
"BUT WHEN WE PARTED TO CATCH OUR BREATHS, I CAUGHT A GLIMPSE OF THE OGPU MAN'S GRINNING FACE IN THE REAR-VIEW MIRROR--- AND ONCE MORE THE LOVE TURNED TO ASHES IN MY THROAT AS I REMEMBERED THAT HE AND TANYA BOTH STOOD FOR RED TYRANNY!"
MUST THAT GRINNING APE ALWAYS FOLLOW US AROUND WHEREVER WE GO?
I CAN GET RID OF HIM, MY DARLING --- WHEN I TELL THE HIGHER AUTHORITIES THAT YOU WOULD PREFER TO BE ALONE WITH ME!

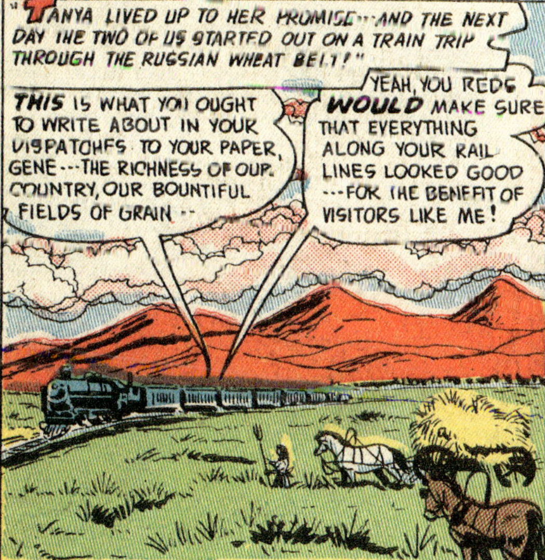
"TANYA LIVED UP TO HER PROMISE---AND THE NEXT DAY THE TWO OF US STARTED OUT ON A TRAIN TRIP THROUGH THE RUSSIAN WHEAT BELT!"
THIS IS WHAT YOU OUGHT TO WRITE ABOUT IN YOUR DISPATCHES TO YOUR PAPER, GENE---THE RICHNESS OF OUR COUNTRY, OUR BOUNTIFUL FIELDS OF GRAIN--
YEAH, YOU REDS WOULD MAKE SURE THAT EVERYTHING ALONG YOUR RAIL LINES LOOKED GOOD ---FOR THE BENEFIT OF VISITORS LIKE ME!

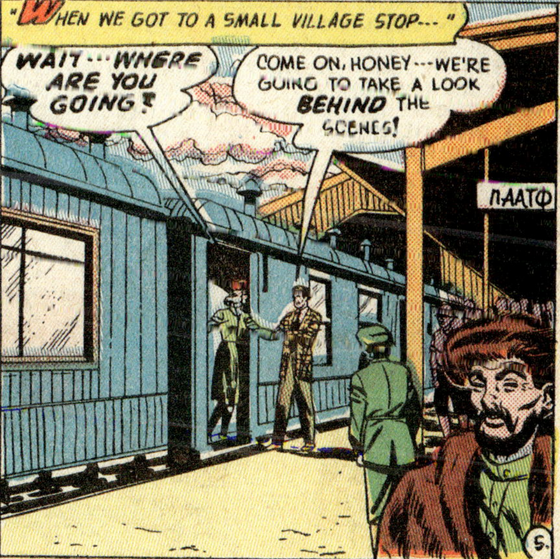
"WHEN WE GOT TO A SMALL VILLAGE STOP---"
WAIT---WHERE ARE YOU GOING?
COME ON, HONEY---WE'RE GOING TO TAKE A LOOK BEHIND THE SCENES!
ПЛАТФ
5.

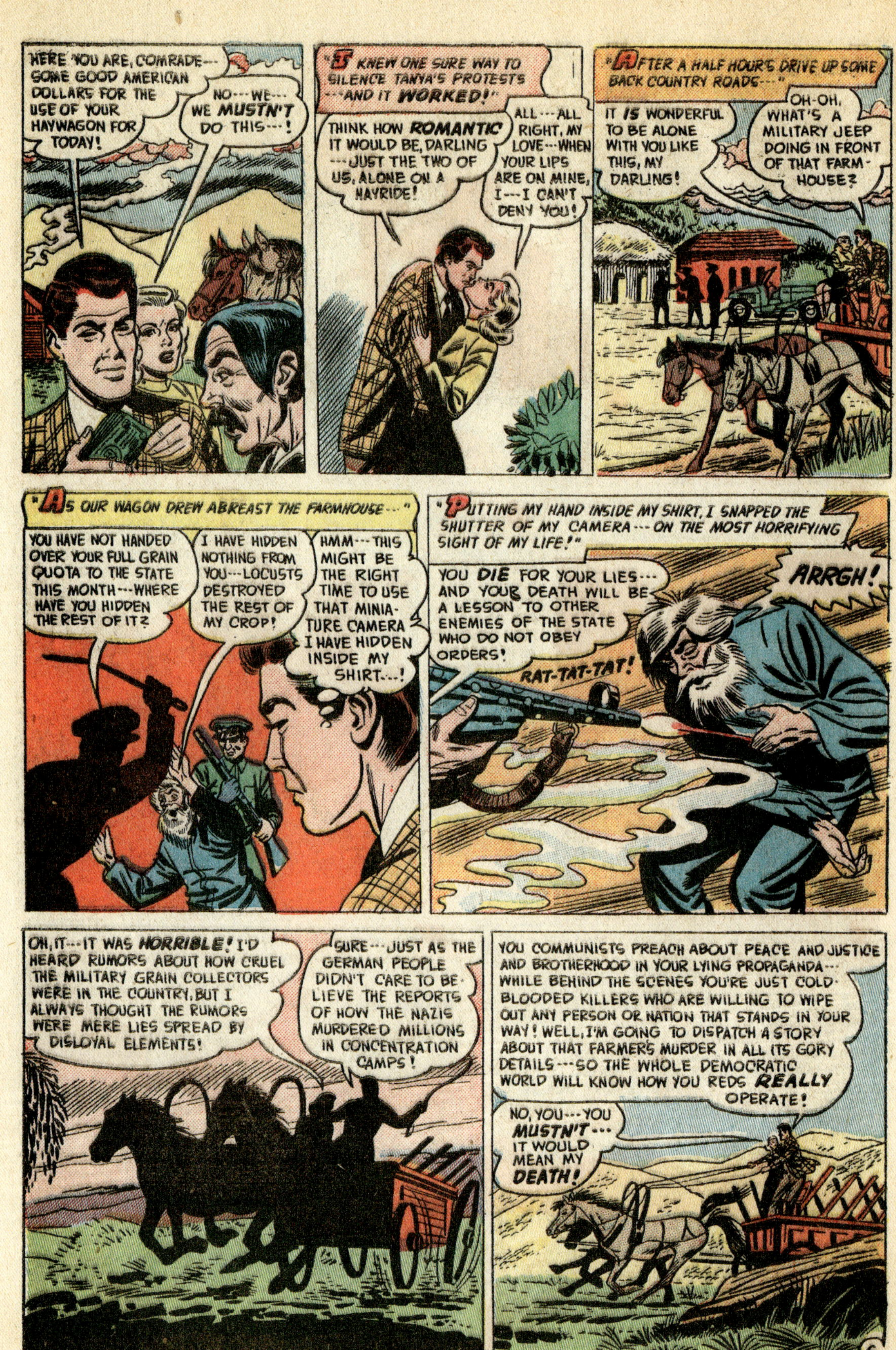
HERE YOU ARE, COMRADE--- SOME GOOD AMERICAN DOLLARS FOR THE USE OF YOUR HAYWAGON FOR TODAY!
NO---WE--- WE MUSTN'T DO THIS---!
"I KNEW ONE SURE WAY TO SILENCE TANYA'S PROTESTS ---AND IT WORKED!"
THINK HOW ROMANTIC IT WOULD BE, DARLING ---JUST THE TWO OF US, ALONE ON A HAYRIDE!
ALL---ALL RIGHT, MY LOVE---WHEN YOUR LIPS ARE ON MINE, I---I CAN'T DENY YOU!
"AFTER A HALF HOUR'S DRIVE UP SOME BACK COUNTRY ROADS---"
IT IS WONDERFUL TO BE ALONE WITH YOU LIKE THIS, MY DARLING!
OH-OH. WHAT'S A MILITARY JEEP DOING IN FRONT OF THAT FARM-HOUSE?
"AS OUR WAGON DREW ABREAST THE FARMHOUSE---"
YOU HAVE NOT HANDED OVER YOUR FULL GRAIN QUOTA TO THE STATE THIS MONTH---WHERE HAVE YOU HIDDEN THE REST OF IT?
I HAVE HIDDEN NOTHING FROM YOU---LOCUSTS DESTROYED THE REST OF MY CROP!
HMM---THIS MIGHT BE THE RIGHT TIME TO USE THAT MINIA-TURE CAMERA I HAVE HIDDEN INSIDE MY SHIRT---!
"PUTTING MY HAND INSIDE MY SHIRT, I SNAPPED THE SHUTTER OF MY CAMERA---ON THE MOST HORRIFYING SIGHT OF MY LIFE!"
YOU DIE FOR YOUR LIES--- AND YOUR DEATH WILL BE A LESSON TO OTHER ENEMIES OF THE STATE WHO DO NOT OBEY ORDERS!
ARRGH!
RAT-TAT-TAT!
OH, IT---IT WAS HORRIBLE! I'D HEARD RUMORS ABOUT HOW CRUEL THE MILITARY GRAIN COLLECTORS WERE IN THE COUNTRY, BUT I ALWAYS THOUGHT THE RUMORS WERE MERE LIES SPREAD BY DISLOYAL ELEMENTS!
SURE---JUST AS THE GERMAN PEOPLE DIDN'T CARE TO BE-LIEVE THE REPORTS OF HOW THE NAZIS MURDERED MILLIONS IN CONCENTRATION CAMPS!
YOU COMMUNISTS PREACH ABOUT PEACE AND JUSTICE AND BROTHERHOOD IN YOUR LYING PROPAGANDA--- WHILE BEHIND THE SCENES YOU'RE JUST COLD-BLOODED KILLERS WHO ARE WILLING TO WIPE OUT ANY PERSON OR NATION THAT STANDS IN YOUR WAY! WELL, I'M GOING TO DISPATCH A STORY ABOUT THAT FARMER'S MURDER IN ALL ITS GORY DETAILS---SO THE WHOLE DEMOCRATIC WORLD WILL KNOW HOW YOU REDS REALLY OPERATE!
NO, YOU---YOU MUSTN'T--- IT WOULD MEAN MY DEATH!
6

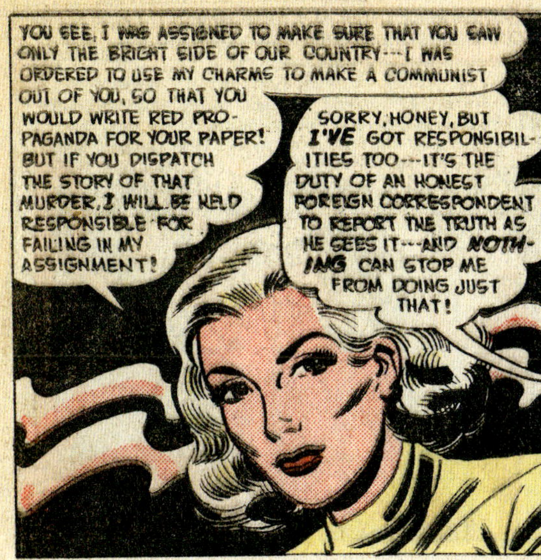
YOU SEE, I WAS ASSIGNED TO MAKE SURE THAT YOU SAW ONLY THE BRIGHT SIDE OF OUR COUNTRY---I WAS ORDERED TO USE MY CHARMS TO MAKE A COMMUNIST OUT OF YOU, SO THAT YOU WOULD WRITE RED PROPAGANDA FOR YOUR PAPER! BUT IF YOU DISPATCH THE STORY OF THAT MURDER, I WILL BE HELD RESPONSIBLE FOR FAILING IN MY ASSIGNMENT!
SORRY, HONEY, BUT I'VE GOT RESPONSIBILITIES TOO---IT'S THE DUTY OF AN HONEST FOREIGN CORRESPONDENT TO REPORT THE TRUTH AS HE SEES IT---AND NOTHING CAN STOP ME FROM DOING JUST THAT!

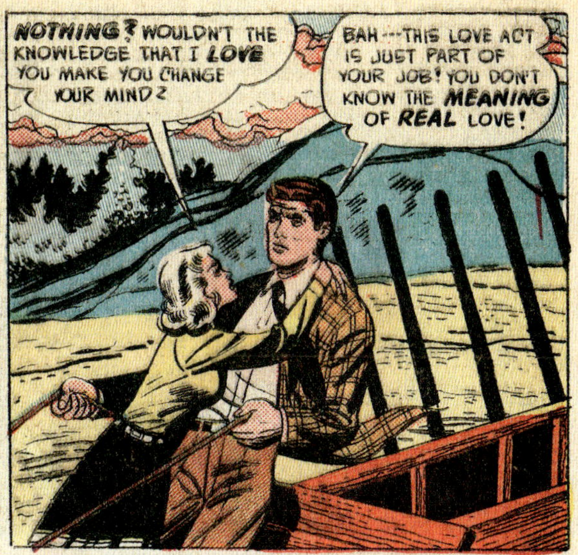
NOTHING? WOULDN'T THE KNOWLEDGE THAT I LOVE YOU MAKE YOU CHANGE YOUR MIND?
BAH---THIS LOVE ACT IS JUST PART OF YOUR JOB! YOU DON'T KNOW THE MEANING OF REAL LOVE!

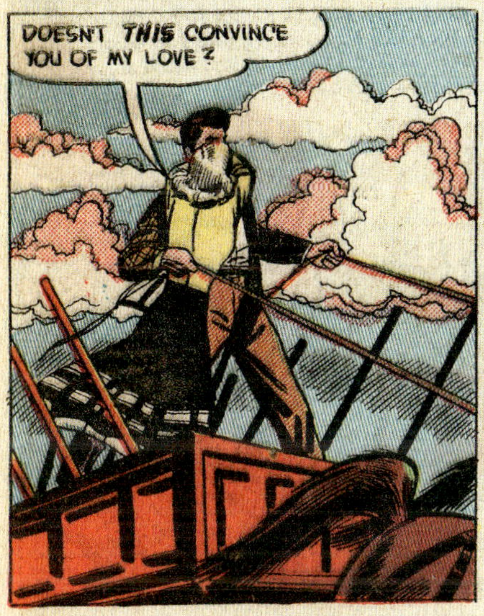
DOESN'T THIS CONVINCE YOU OF MY LOVE?
"HER KISS FIRED MY BLOOD, MADE MY SENSES REEL WITH A WILD, INTOXICATING DELIGHT! UNABLE TO RESTRAIN MYSELF, OBLIVIOUS TO WARNINGS OF MY MIND, I COULD ONLY WRAP HER IN MY ARMS AND KISS HER BACK AS IF NOTHING ELSE MATTERED IN ALL THE WORLD EXCEPT THE ECSTASY I FOUND IN HER LIPS!"

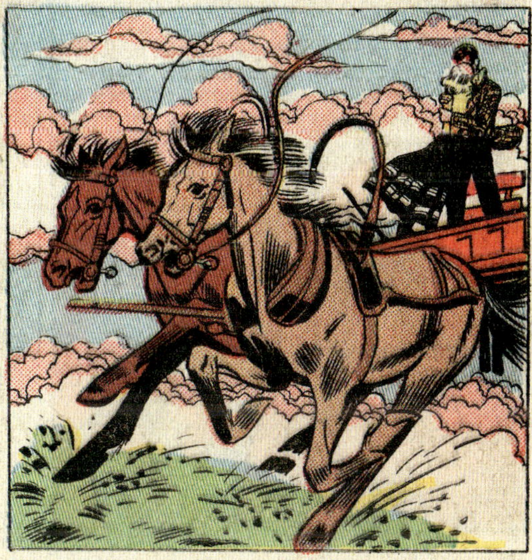

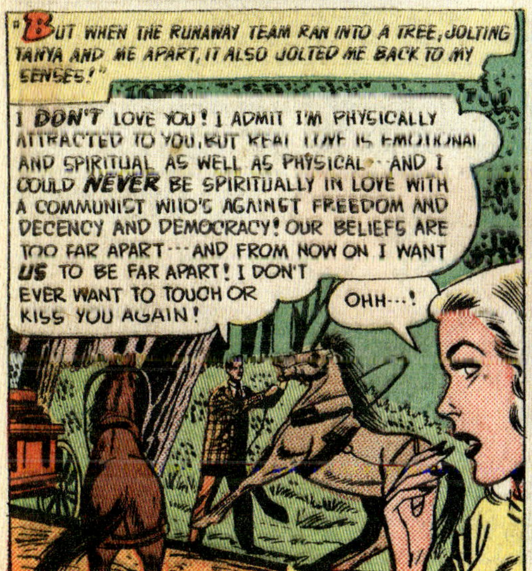
"BUT WHEN THE RUNAWAY TEAM RAN INTO A TREE, JOLTING TANYA AND ME APART, IT ALSO JOLTED ME BACK TO MY SENSES!"
I DON'T LOVE YOU! I ADMIT I'M PHYSICALLY ATTRACTED TO YOU, BUT REAL LOVE IS EMOTIONAL AND SPIRITUAL AS WELL AS PHYSICAL---AND I COULD NEVER BE SPIRITUALLY IN LOVE WITH A COMMUNIST WHO'S AGAINST FREEDOM AND DECENCY AND DEMOCRACY! OUR BELIEFS ARE TOO FAR APART---AND FROM NOW ON I WANT US TO BE FAR APART! I DON'T EVER WANT TO TOUCH OR KISS YOU AGAIN!
OHH---!

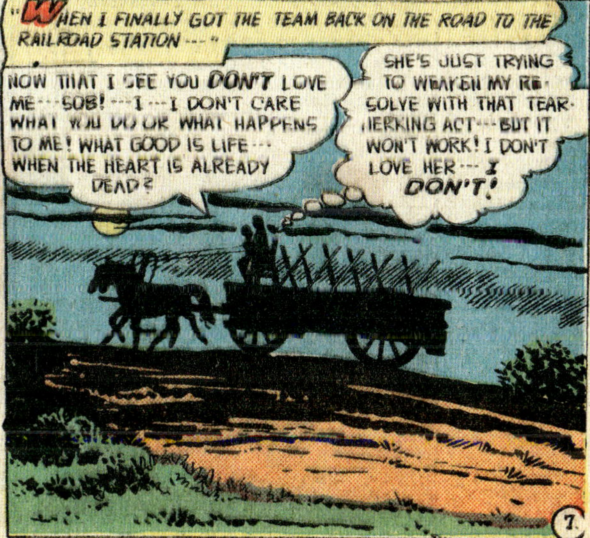
"WHEN I FINALLY GOT THE TEAM BACK ON THE ROAD TO THE RAILROAD STATION---"
NOW THAT I SEE YOU DON'T LOVE ME---SOB!---I---I DON'T CARE WHAT YOU DO OR WHAT HAPPENS TO ME! WHAT GOOD IS LIFE---WHEN THE HEART IS ALREADY DEAD?
SHE'S JUST TRYING TO WEAKEN MY RESOLVE WITH THAT TEARJERKING ACT---BUT IT WON'T WORK! I DON'T LOVE HER---I DON'T!
7

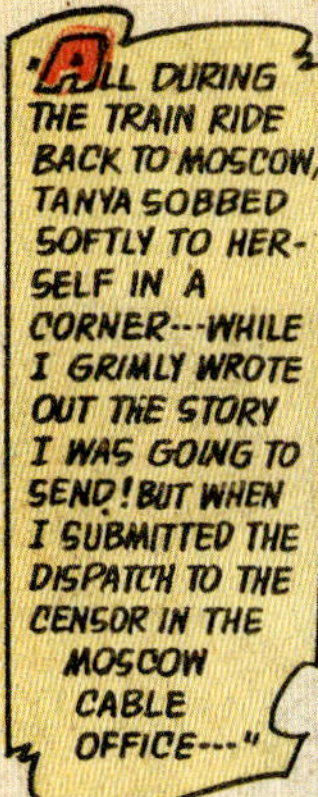

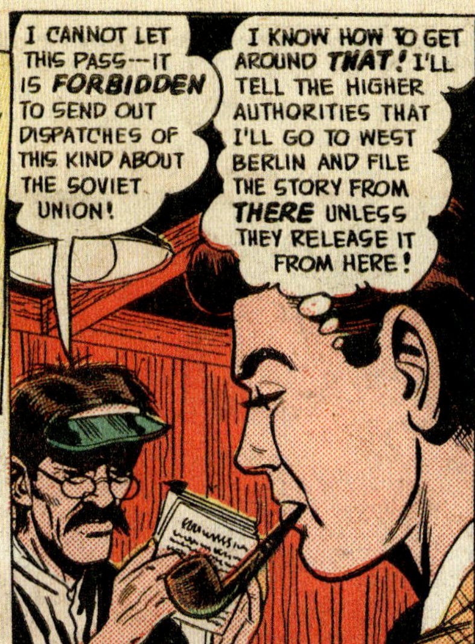

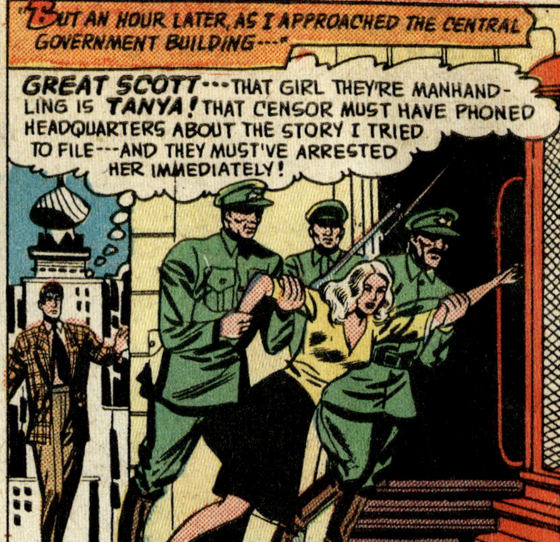

"Tanya cast one desperate, pleading look at me as they dragged her past---and I was horrified to see the dark bruises on her face and arms that indicated she had been beaten and probably tortured! Instinctively, I tried to help her---but---"

STOP---LET HER GO!

BACK, SWINE---UNLESS **YOU** WANT TO JOIN HER IN THE GAS CHAMBER!

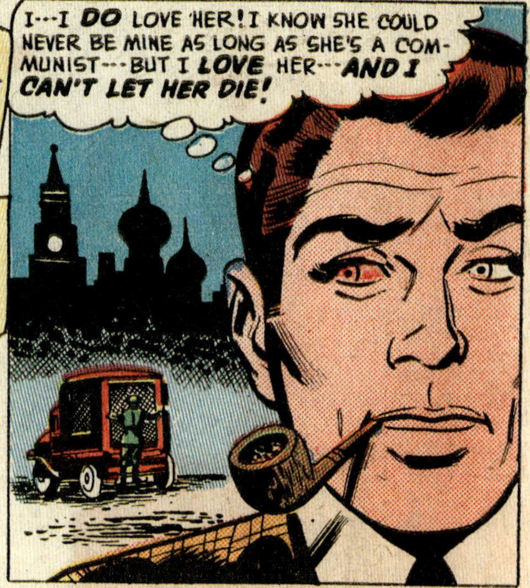

"There was only one way to save the life of the girl I loved! After making the necessary preparations, I demanded and secured an interview with a high Red Army colonel---and showed him a print of the photograph I had taken of the farmer's murder---"

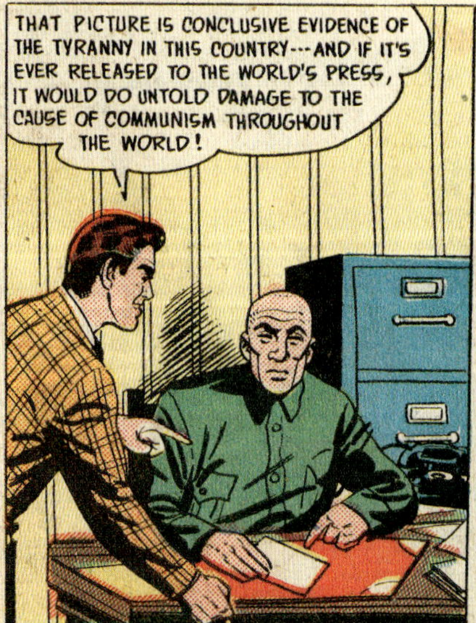

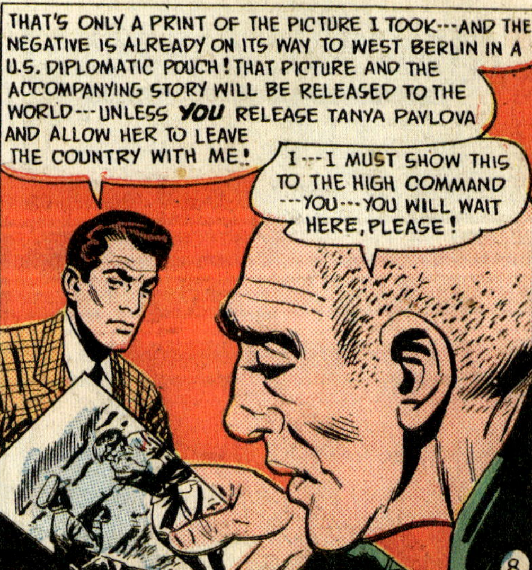

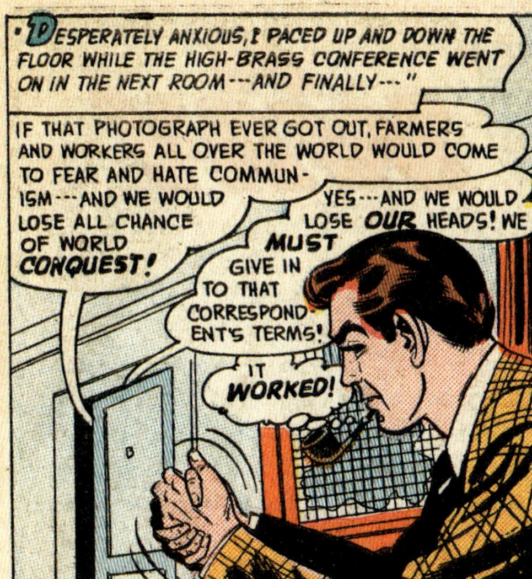
"DESPERATELY ANXIOUS, I PACED UP AND DOWN THE FLOOR WHILE THE HIGH-BRASS CONFERENCE WENT ON IN THE NEXT ROOM---AND FINALLY---"
IF THAT PHOTOGRAPH EVER GOT OUT, FARMERS AND WORKERS ALL OVER THE WORLD WOULD COME TO FEAR AND HATE COMMUNISM---AND WE WOULD LOSE ALL CHANCE OF WORLD CONQUEST!
YES---AND WE WOULD LOSE OUR HEADS! WE MUST GIVE IN TO THAT CORRESPONDENT'S TERMS!
IT WORKED!

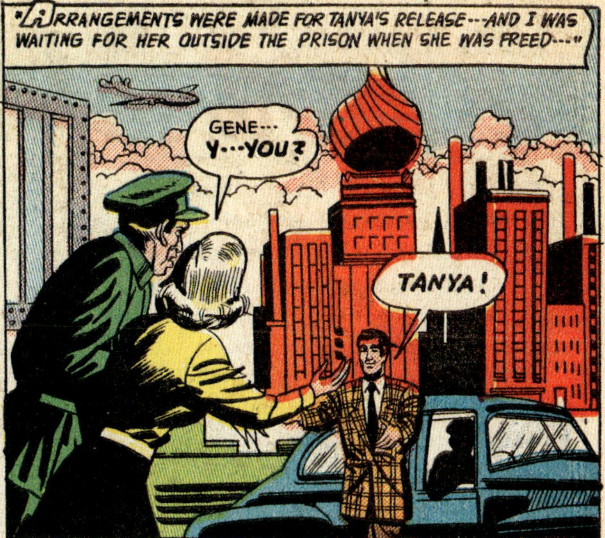
"ARRANGEMENTS WERE MADE FOR TANYA'S RELEASE---AND I WAS WAITING FOR HER OUTSIDE THE PRISON WHEN SHE WAS FREED---"
GENE--- Y---YOU?
TANYA!

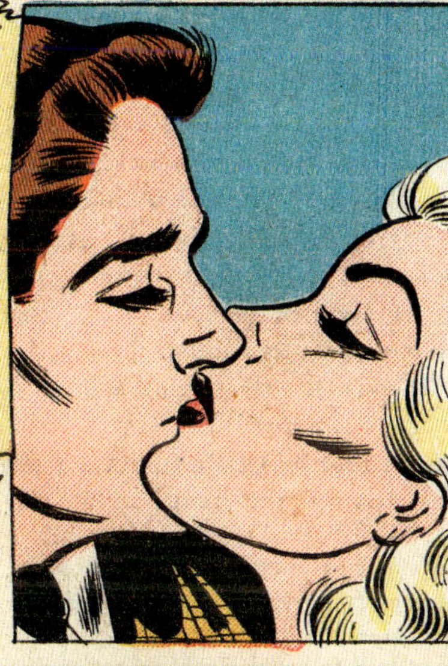
"A MOMENT LATER SHE WAS IN MY ARMS! I KISSED HER WILDLY, DESPERATELY, AS IF THIS WERE TO BE THE LAST TIME MY LIPS WOULD EVER TASTE HERS---FOR I KNEW THAT OURS WAS A LOVE THAT COULD NEVER BE!"

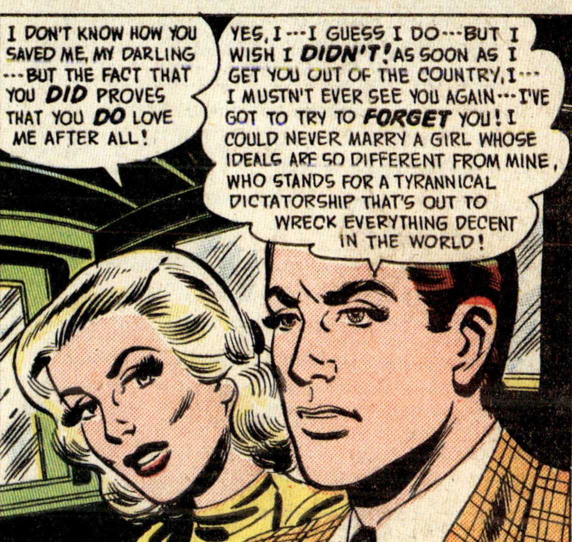
I DON'T KNOW HOW YOU SAVED ME, MY DARLING---BUT THE FACT THAT YOU DID PROVES THAT YOU DO LOVE ME AFTER ALL!
YES, I---I GUESS I DO---BUT I WISH I DIDN'T! AS SOON AS I GET YOU OUT OF THE COUNTRY, I---I MUSTN'T EVER SEE YOU AGAIN---I'VE GOT TO TRY TO FORGET YOU! I COULD NEVER MARRY A GIRL WHOSE IDEALS ARE SO DIFFERENT FROM MINE, WHO STANDS FOR A TYRANNICAL DICTATORSHIP THAT'S OUT TO WRECK EVERYTHING DECENT IN THE WORLD!

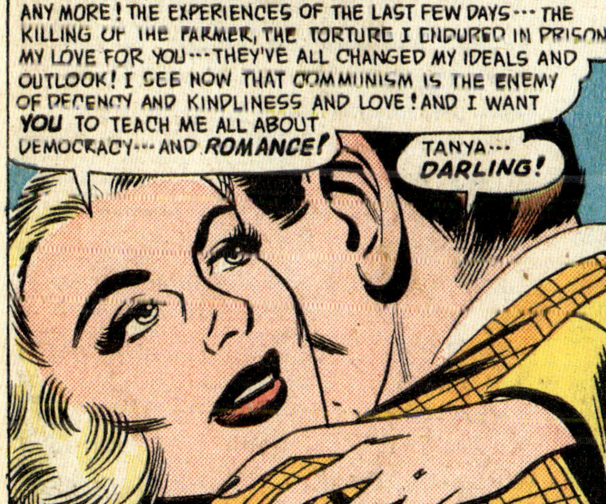
BUT DEAREST, I DON'T STAND FOR THOSE TERRIBLE THINGS ANY MORE! THE EXPERIENCES OF THE LAST FEW DAYS---THE KILLING OF THE FARMER, THE TORTURE I ENDURED IN PRISON, MY LOVE FOR YOU---THEY'VE ALL CHANGED MY IDEALS AND OUTLOOK! I SEE NOW THAT COMMUNISM IS THE ENEMY OF DECENCY AND KINDLINESS AND LOVE! AND I WANT YOU TO TEACH ME ALL ABOUT DEMOCRACY---AND ROMANCE!
TANYA--- DARLING!

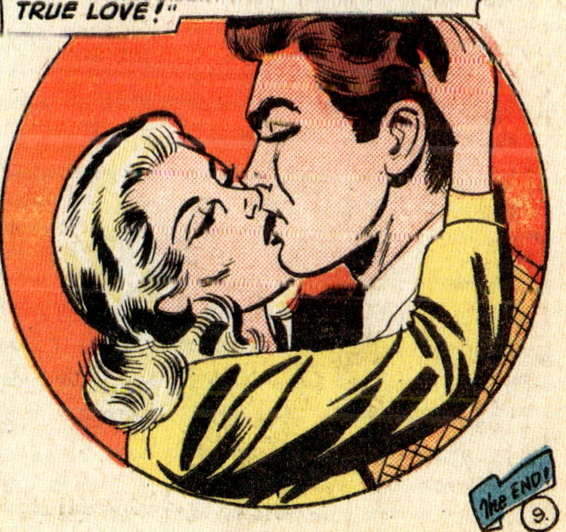
"YES, THERE WAS PLENTY TO TEACH MY FUTURE BRIDE ABOUT DEMOCRACY---BUT SHE WAS THE ONE WHO HAD TAUGHT ME THE MEANING OF TRUE LOVE!"
THE END!
9

LOVE IS WHERE YOU FIND IT!

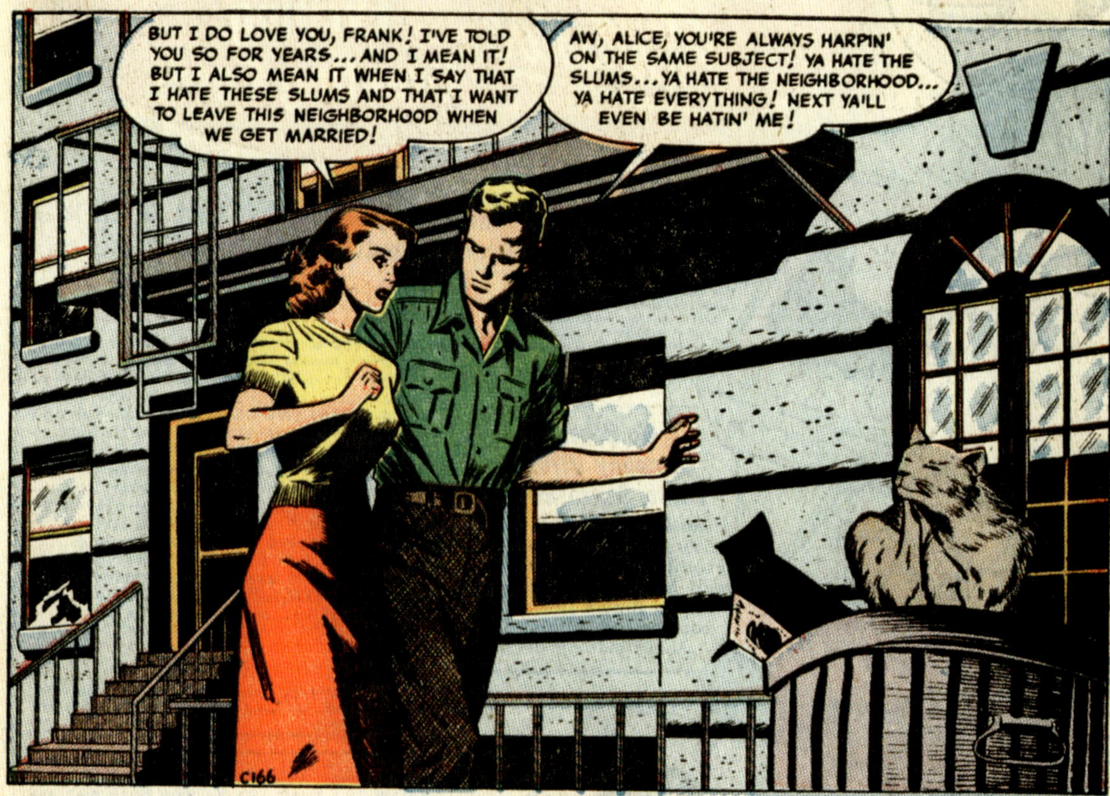

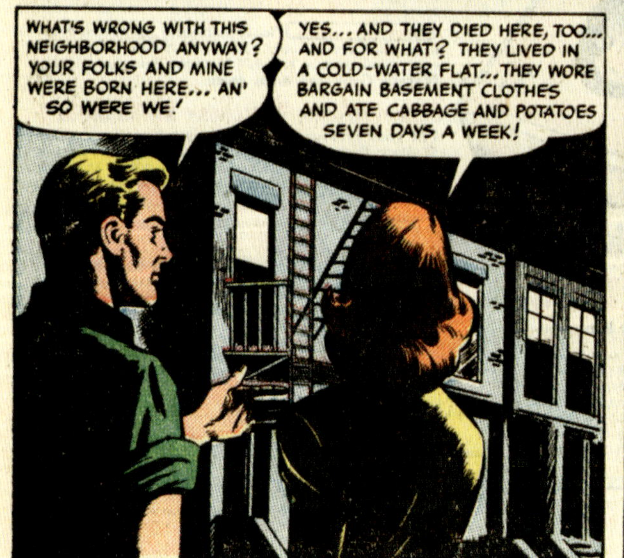

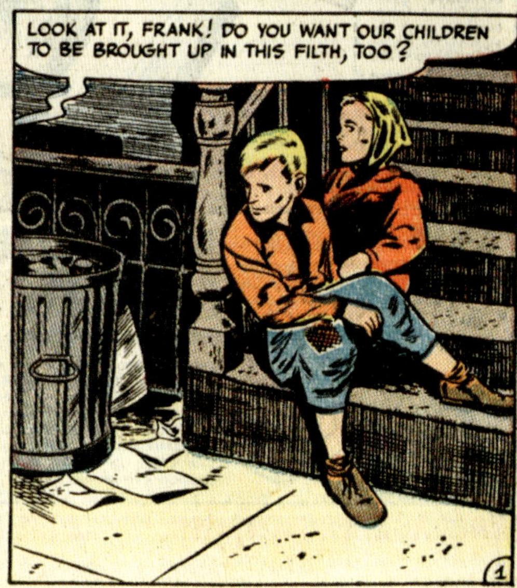

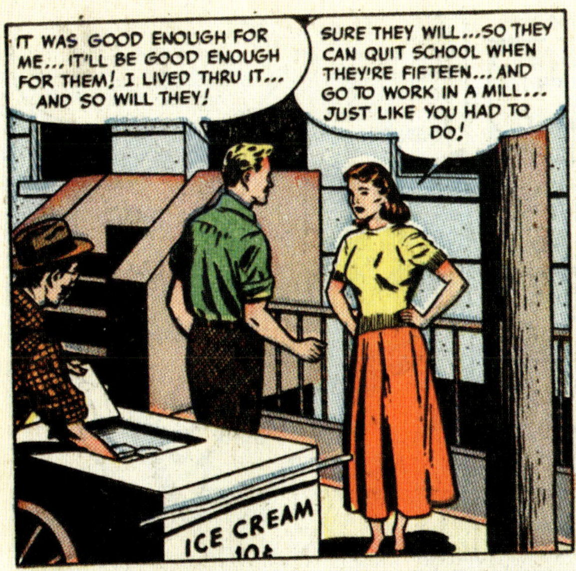

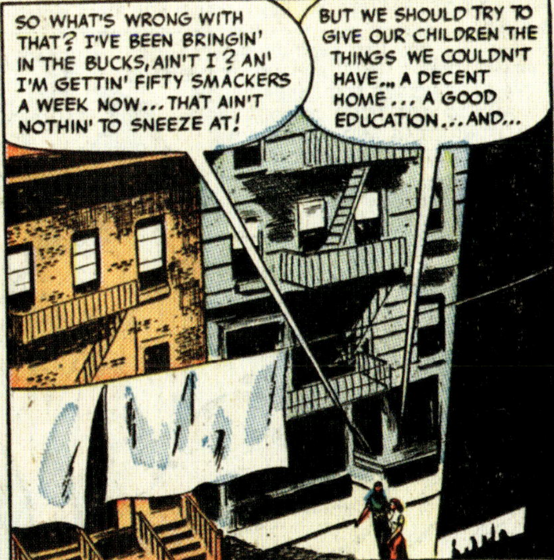

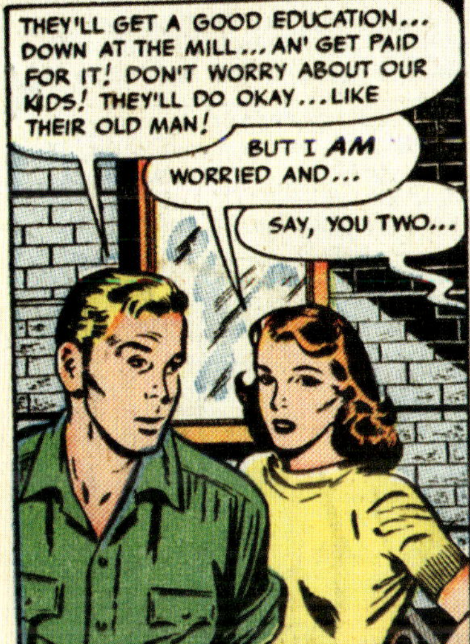

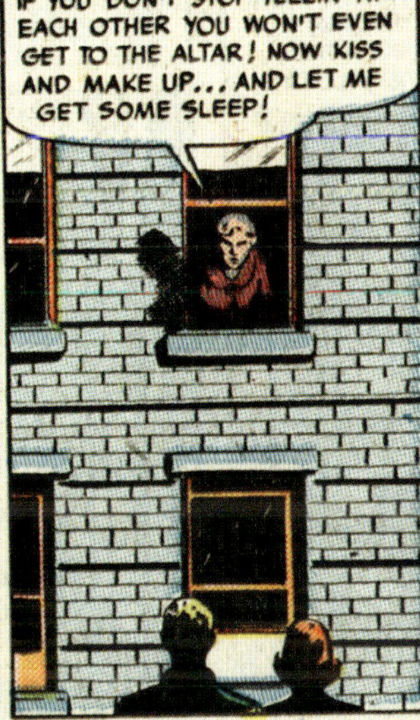

WE TOOK THE NEIGHBOR'S ADVICE... WE KISSED...

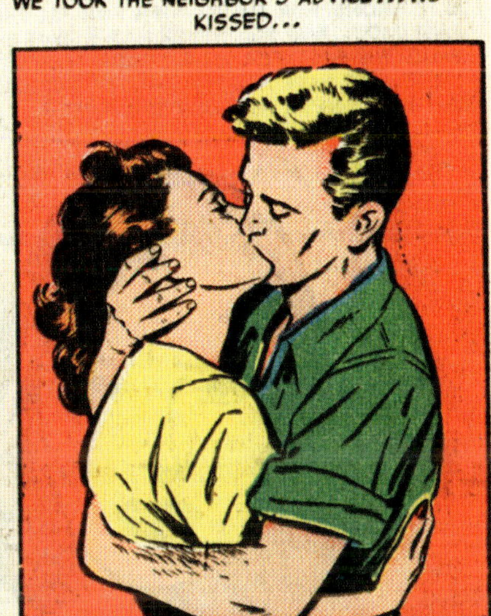

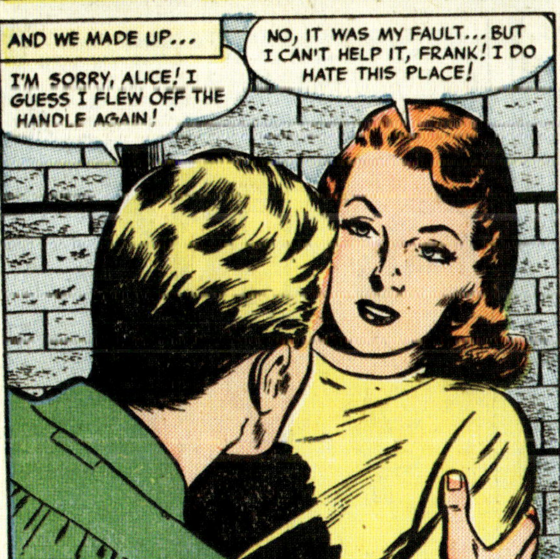

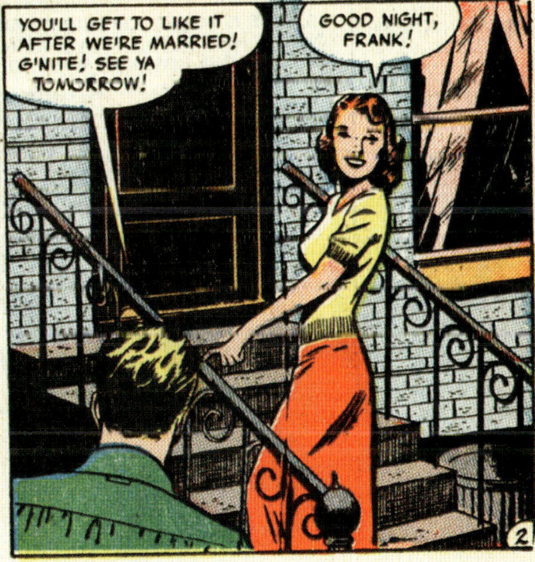

UNKNOWN TITLE
circa 1954

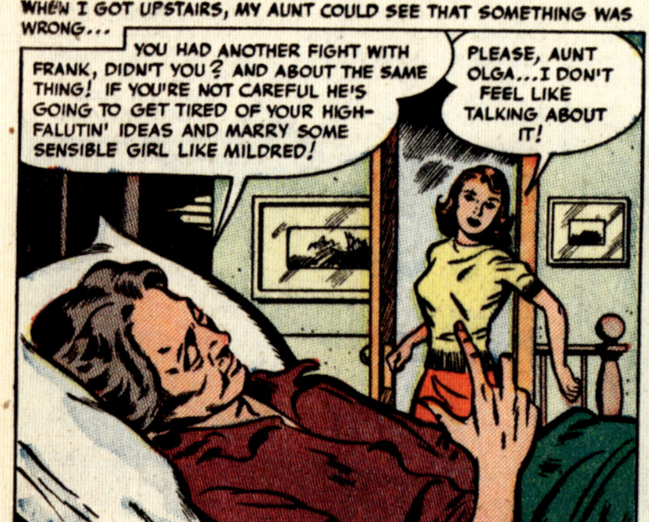

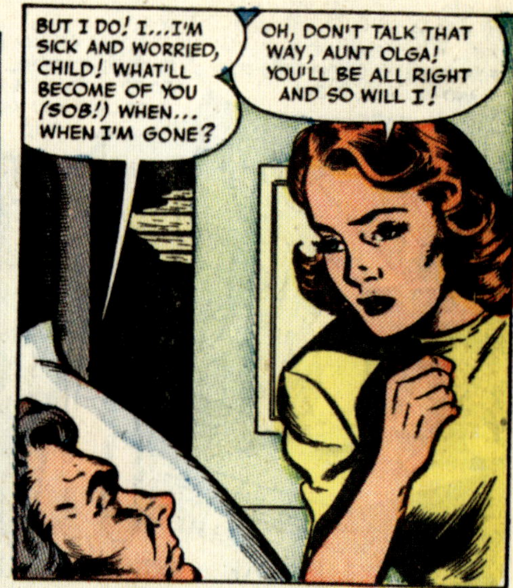

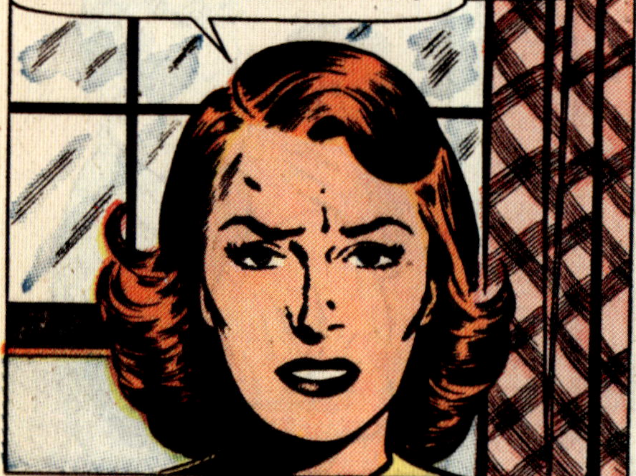

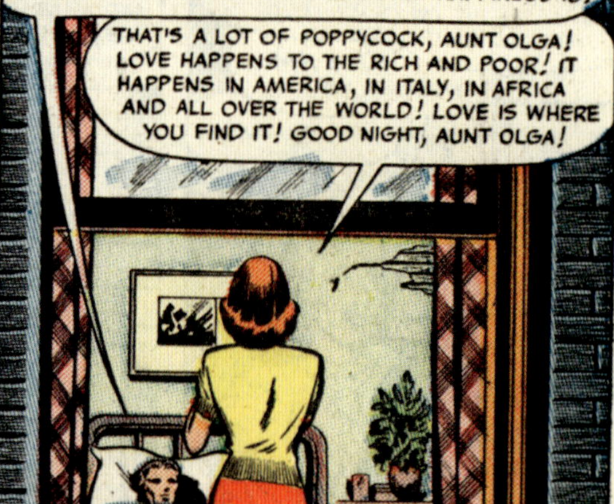

I DIDN'T TURN ON THE LIGHTS WHEN I WENT INTO MY ROOM! I JUST STOOD THERE IN THE DARK AND LOOKED BEYOND THE SLUMS... AT THE CANYON OF CITY LIGHTS IN THE DISTANCE...

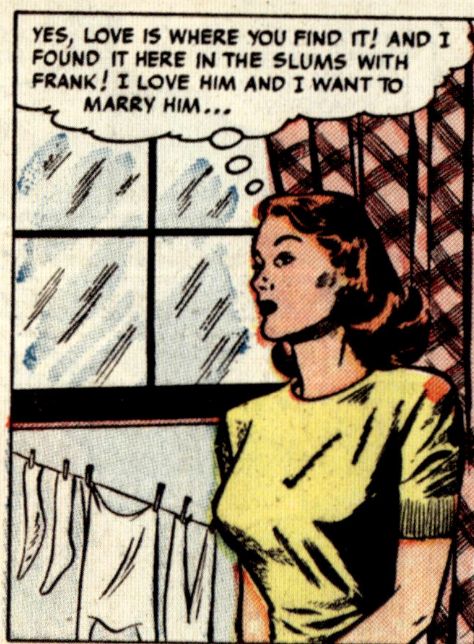

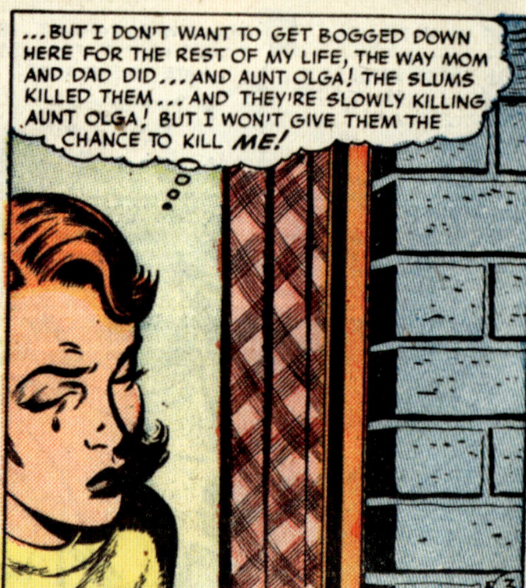

IN THE DAYS THAT FOLLOWED, FRANK AND I HAD OUR USUAL DATES...

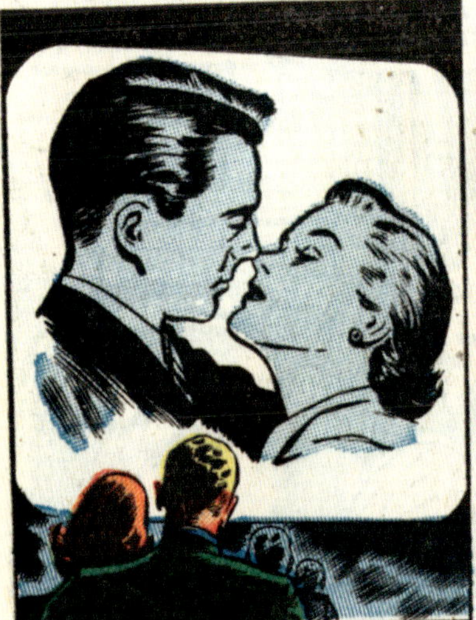

AND WE HAD OUR USUAL ARGUMENTS...

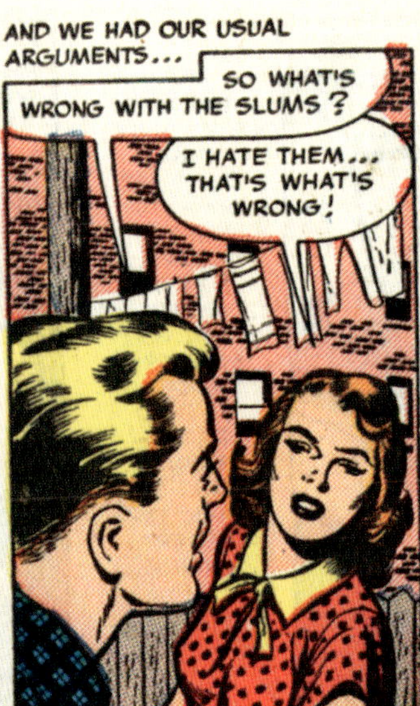

AND I GOT THE USUAL ADVICE...

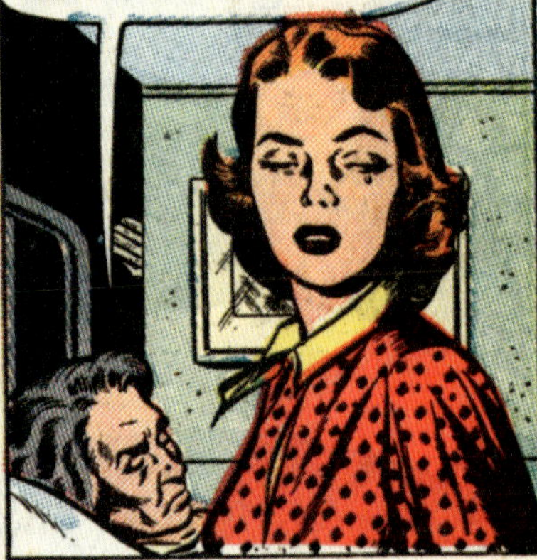

AND THE GIRLS AT THE MILL WHERE I WORKED ALWAYS TOLD ME WHAT THEY'D DO IF THEY WERE ME... ESPECIALLY MILDRED...

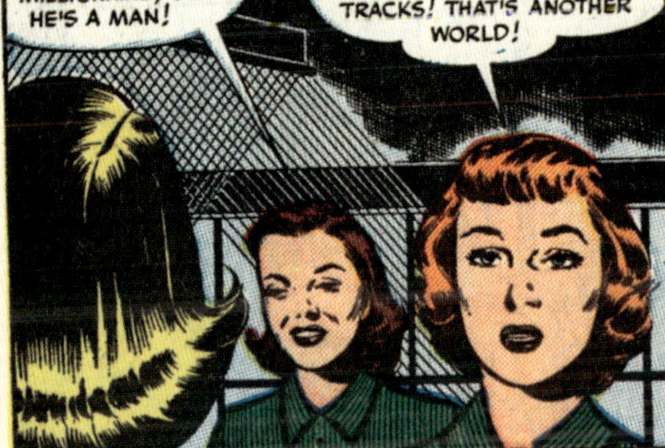

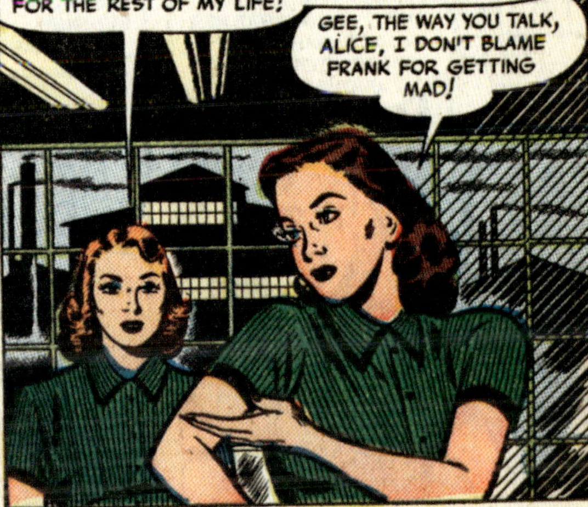

THAT NIGHT, COMING HOME FROM THE MILL, I DID A GREAT DEAL OF THINKING...

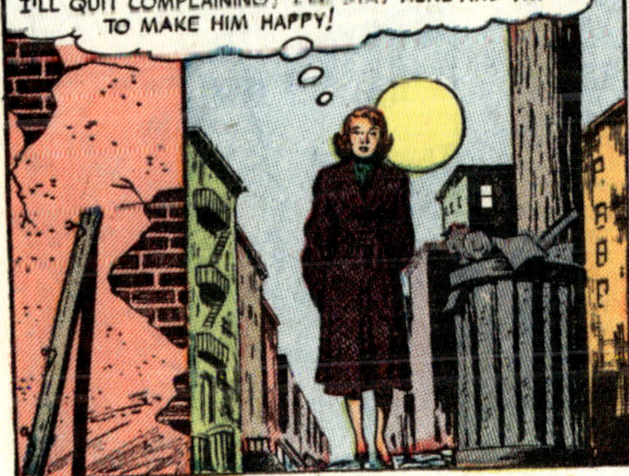

BUT ALL MY THOUGHTS AND DECISIONS ABOUT HAPPINESS WENT SMASHING INTO THE DARK OBLIVION OF SORROW THAT SAME NIGHT! WHEN I GOT HOME...!

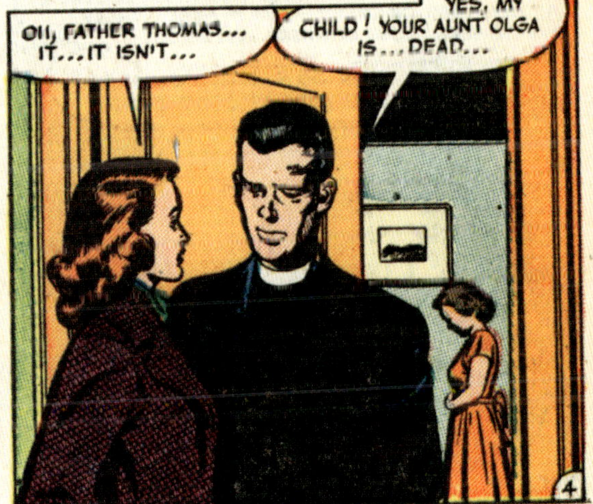

YOU WHO HAVE LOST A LOVED ONE KNOW HOW I FELT... AND THOSE OF YOU WHO HAVEN'T... WELL, I HOPE YOU NEVER HAVE TO GO THRU IT...

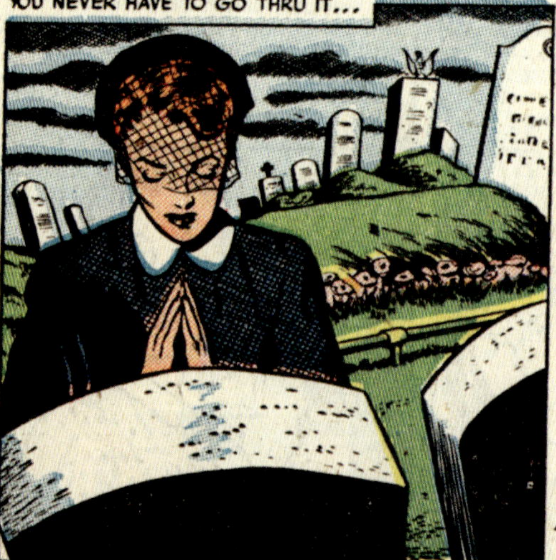

BUT THE DEATH OF MY AUNT OLGA DEEPENED MY HATE FOR THE SLUMS... FOR ITS MISERY... FOR ITS MURDERS! I MADE UP MY MIND TO TELL FRANK THAT I WOULD NEVER CHANGE...

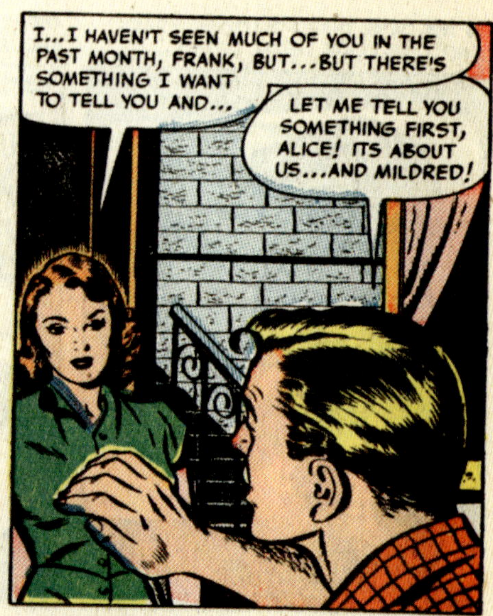

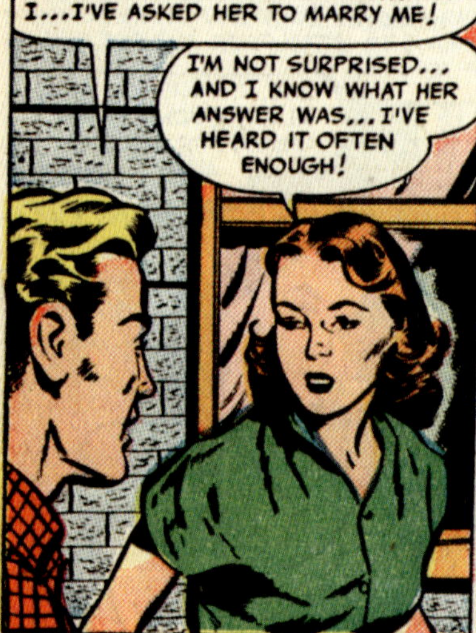

SO WHAT? SHE'S A SENSIBLE GIRL! SHE AIN'T GOT NO GOOFY HIGH-CLASS IDEAS! SHE'S WILLING TO STAY WHERE SHE BELONGS... AN' THAT'S WHAT YOU OUGHT TO DO!

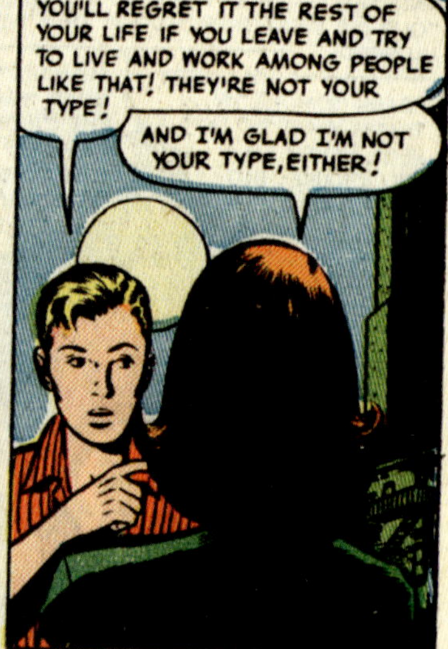

IT'S YOUR KIND OF NARROW-MINDEDNESS THAT MAKE THE DIFFERENT KINDS OF PEOPLE HATE EACH OTHER! LOVE ISN'T RESTRICTED TO THE POOR PEOPLE... NOR TO ANY CLASS OR CREED! LOVE IS HERE...THERE... EVERYWHERE! LOVE IS WHERE YOU FIND IT!

THEN GO FIND IT... 'CAUSE YOU JUST LOST IT! GOOD-BYE!

AFTER THAT, THERE WAS ABSOLUTELY NOTHING TO KEEP ME IN THE SLUMS! I PACKED THE FEW THINGS I HAD THAT NIGHT AND SAID GOOD-BYE TO THE PLACE THAT MURDERED MY FAMILY AND MY LOVE...

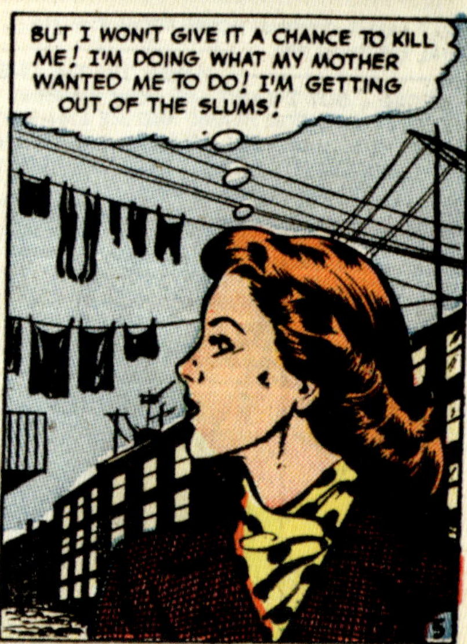

IT WASN'T EASY TO START A NEW LIFE... BUT PEOPLE WERE GOOD TO ME! I FOUND A ROOM TO SHARE WITH ANOTHER GIRL...

AND I'LL SPEAK TO MY BOSS ABOUT YOU! YOU'RE PRETTY... NICE SMILE... NICE FIGURE! THAT'S ALL THE EQUIPMENT A RECEPTIONIST NEEDS!

OH, THANK YOU, HELEN! I... I DON'T KNOW WHAT TO SAY!

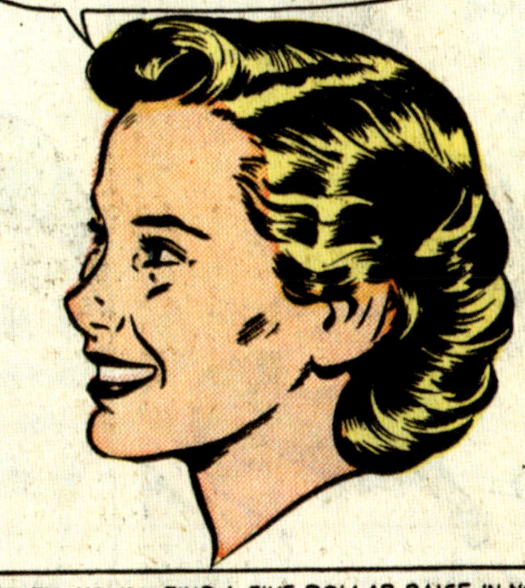

I PUT OUT THE LIGHTS AND GOT DOWN ON MY KNEES... AND I DID SAY THANKS TO SOMEBODY...

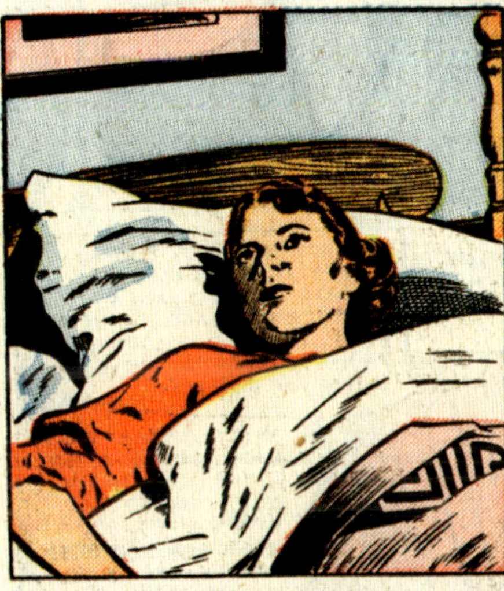

MONDAY MORNING I NOT ONLY FELT LIKE A NEW PERSON... BUT I ACTUALLY LOOKED LIKE ONE... THANKS TO HELEN AND OUR SATURDAY SHOPPING TRIP! AND WHEN HER BOSS LOOKED ME OVER...

HELEN, YOU'LL FIND A FIVE DOLLAR RAISE IN YOUR PAY ENVELOPE THIS WEEK FOR FINDING THIS LOVELY DECORATION FOR THE RECEPTION ROOM!

YOU... YOU MEAN THE JOB IS MINE, MR. BRANTON!

THAT'S WHAT HE MEANT... AND I LIKED THAT JOB! THE FIRST WEEK WENT BY TOO FAST... AND WHEN PAYDAY CAME, I WAS ALMOST THRILLED TO TEARS WITH MY FIRST SALARY...

HERE'S TWENTY OF WHAT I OWE YOU, HELEN! TEN TOWARD THE RENT... AND THAT LEAVES ME ENOUGH FOR THE WEEK! AND TONIGHT THE SPAGHETTI DINNER IS ON ME! I'M TREATING!

SOUNDS TERRIFIC! I HOPE THAT INCLUDES ME, TOO! I'M STARVED!

OH, MR. BRANTON! YES... YOU... YOU'RE WELCOME TO COME IF YOU LIKE!

HE LIKED... AND SO DID I! WE HAD DINNER... AND IT WAS A DOUBLE TREAT! MR. BRANTON TOOK US TO A FRENCH PLACE... WITH SOFT LIGHTS AND SWEET MUSIC...

THAT WINE HAS GONE TO MY HEAD, STEVE... I... I FEEL SO LIGHT... SO HAPPY!

IT ALSO MADE A TRIP TO YOUR EYES... THEY SPARKLE!

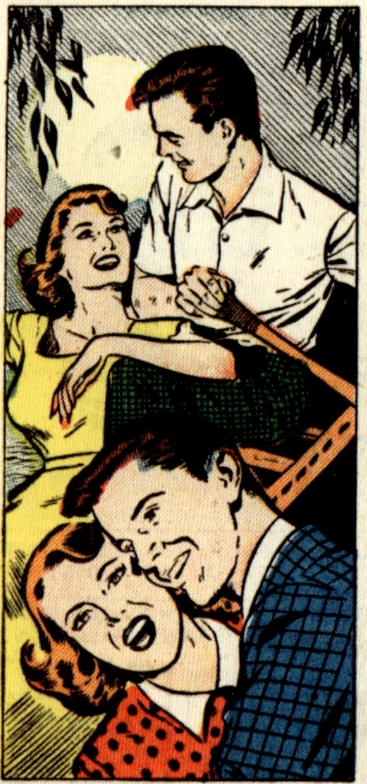
IF YOU THINK THAT WAS THE BEGINNING OF A BEAUTIFUL ROMANCE... YOU'RE RIGHT!

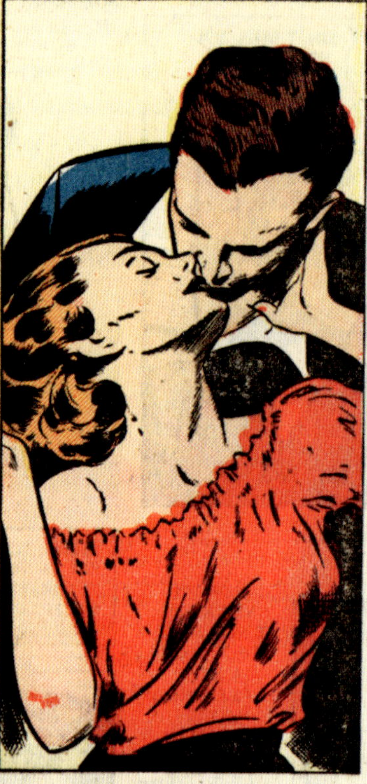
AND IF YOU THINK I LET HIM KISS ME... YOU'RE RIGHT AGAIN...

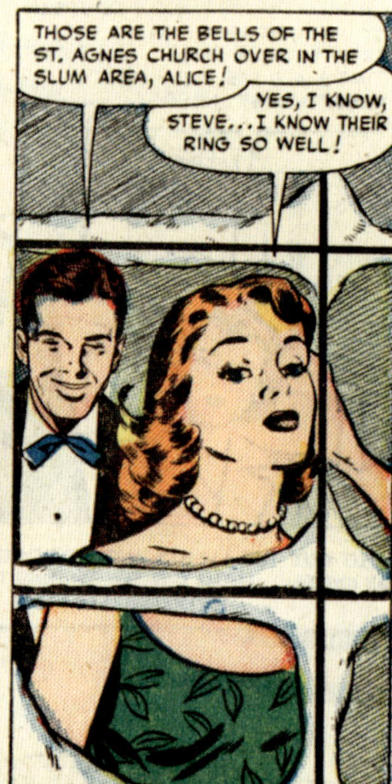
AND THEN, MONTHS LATER, ON CHRISTMAS EVE, JUST AS THE CHURCH BELLS WERE RINGING FOR THE MIDNIGHT MASS...
THOSE ARE THE BELLS OF THE ST. AGNES CHURCH OVER IN THE SLUM AREA, ALICE!
YES, I KNOW, STEVE... I KNOW THEIR RING SO WELL!

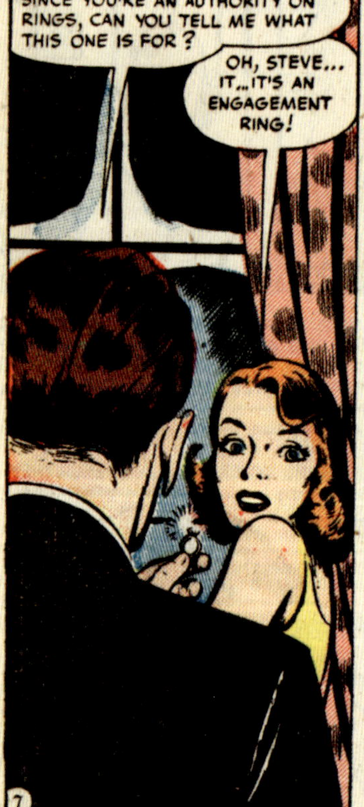
SINCE YOU'RE AN AUTHORITY ON RINGS, CAN YOU TELL ME WHAT THIS ONE IS FOR?
OH, STEVE... IT... IT'S AN ENGAGEMENT RING!

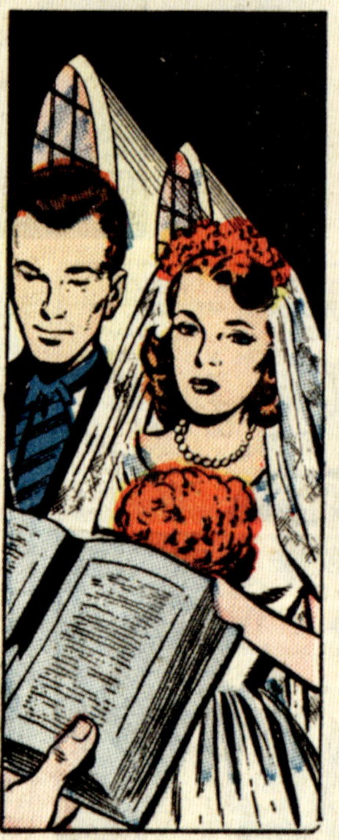
A WEDDING RING FOLLOWED SIX MONTHS AFTER THAT... AND I HAD MY WEDDING IN THE ST. AGNES CHURCH... JUST THE WAY MY MOTHER PRAYED IT WOULD BE FOR ME...

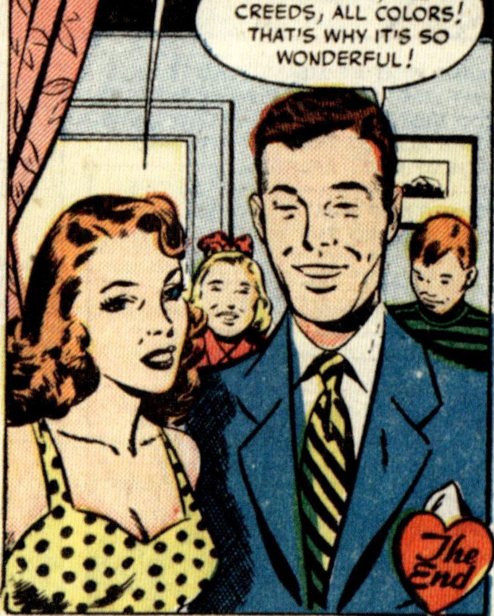
THAT WAS EXACTLY FIVE YEARS AGO TODAY... AND I HAVE NO REGRETS! BUT I DO HAVE A WONDERFUL HUSBAND... A HAPPY HOME... AND TWO CHILDREN! WHAT MORE PROOF IS THERE THAT LOVE IS WHERE YOU FIND IT?
AS YOU ALWAYS SAY, ALICE... LOVE HAPPENS TO THE POOR, TO THE RICH... AND TO ALL NATIONALITIES, ALL CREEDS, ALL COLORS! THAT'S WHY IT'S SO WONDERFUL!
The End

"SECRETS" from a LOVE DIARY

HELLO, ALL YOU GALS

This month we take up that burning question so dear to the heart of every *single* girl — "WHEN Will I Marry?" We know you're anxious to get the lowdown on this all-important subject, but before we tell you about it . . .

WE HEREWITH ANNOUNCE THE WINNERS of the February LOVE DIARY Prescription for Happiness Contest. In the opinion of ye olde editors of this magazine, the eight best letters of advice were sent in by.

1st Prize, $10.00: Judy Neff, Chester, W. Va. 2nd & 3rd Prizes, $5.00 each: Effie Lee Clewis, Palestine, Tex., Alice Anderson, Omaha, Neb. 4th to 8th Prizes, $1.00 each: Maybelle Bailey, Turlock, Calif., Maureen Finn, St. Johnsbury, Vt., Betty Joseph, Fall River, Mass., Eleanor Simpkins, West Palm Beach, Fla., and Virginia Hopkins, Chicago, Ill.

Gertrude L. and Ray Mann want to thank all of you who sent in such wonderful letters. And if you didn't win a prize this time, be sure to read the current Prescription for Happiness Contest. Then write a short, sweet letter, and win a big, sweet cash prize for yourself! Good luck!

And now, hold on to your seats, for we're going to answer that all-important question

WHEN WILL I MARRY?

No matter what your age, appearance of background, the chances are around 1000 to 1 that you WILL marry! You may feel that you are unattractive, perhaps even definitely homely, but statistics show that the plain or unattractive girls marry, if anything, faster than the glamor gals. The howling beauties have a tendency to flit like busy bees from one man to another, instead of concentrating on the ONE GUY, which is by far the wiser course. Also, glamor and beauty usually tend to scare off the average male. He may admire her from afar, but he's afraid of being rebuffed by a beautiful girl who is able to pick and choose among men.

Here at LOVE DIARY, we interviewed 100 married women, to learn how, when and where they met the men they married. And here's an interesting point. Some came from farms, some from small towns, some from big cities . . . and one even came from a desolate outpost in Alaska, where she didn't see an eligible man from one year to the next! Then, one day, a government man stopped by for a survey . . . and that was that!

So it doesn't matter where you live. Sooner or later, THE MAN will show up!

How about what you *do?* Our interview among the 100 married women showed their occupations varied from factory worker, to office worker, to nurse, to career girl, to farm girl! The few *home* girls had a rougher time finding a husband than the girls who worked. But even they found their men in time.

So your job doesn't matter, either — when it comes to meeting up with the man you will marry!

Of the 100 women interviewed, only 5 married before the age of 18. (They wish now they'd waited a little longer and had a little more fun and freedom before they entered into matrimony.) 17 girls married before 20. The large majority of them married between 20 and 25. But the girls who married between 25 and 30 usually made outstandingly fine marriages. These 25 to 30 year olds had just about resigned themselves to being old maids, when along came that extra special man!

Now for an interesting point: Only *2* out of the 100 women *knew* it would be serious when they first met the men they later married. The others met their husbands casually — either on a double date, or at a party, or on the jobs, never dreaming that HERE was the husband for them! They just let time take its course, friendship ripened into love, and love led to marriage.

93 OUT OF THE 100 WOMEN INTERVIEWED TOLD US THE MOST IMPORTANT MAN IN THEIR LIVES CAME ALONG WHEN THEY LEAST EXPECTED IT! That's one to chalk up for your diary! A few of the girls had broken off with boys they'd been going out with . . . and thought their hearts were broken forever . . . until THE GUY suddenly came along! Many of the women met their special romances at a low point emotionally in their lives.

WHAT ARE OUR CONCLUSIONS ABOUT MARRIAGE FOR YOU?

1. *The man you will marry will most likely find you when you least expect it.*
2. *When you meet him, you probably won't even know that he's the man you're going to marry.*
3. *When things are at their lowest point for you, socially, financially, or emotionally, you stand your very best chance of meeting HIM! So take heart, and don't feel bad if life seems dull now.*
4. *Most of you will be between 18 and 25 when you marry. A few will marry before 18, but women who married so young don't endorse the idea. A few of you will wait until after 25 to marry. But when you do . . . you'll almost always make a splendid marriage.*

Goodbye for now . . . and happy husband-hunting! *Ray Mann*

This page:
LOVE DIARY
#37, October 1953

Pages 204–205, from left to right:
DARLING LOVE
#4, April–May 1950, house ad

LOVE ROMANCES
Issue unknown, early 1950s, house ad

YOUNG ROMANCE
#13, September 1949, house ad

FIRST LOVE
#12, May 1951, house ad

That's Amore!

THE TOP POP SONG HITS OF 1950–1955

What better way to lie around reading the latest issues of *True Secrets* and *Cinderella Love* than to have the radio set to a top pop station? For love comic fans in the 1950s, these were the tunes they would have been listening to as they dreamed of the bliss to come.

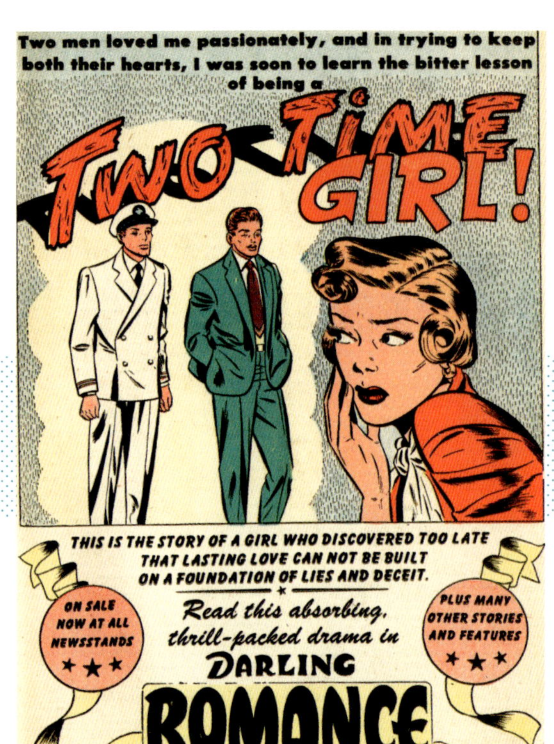

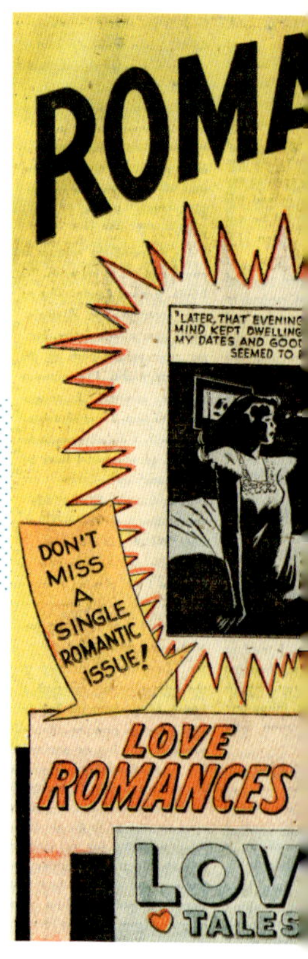

1950

1. "Goodnight Irene"
   Gordon Jenkins and the Weavers
2. "Mona Lisa"
   Nat King Cole
3. *Third Man* theme
   Anton Karas
4. "Sam's Song"
   Gary and Bing Crosby
5. "Chattanoogie Shoe Shine Boy"
   Red Foley
6. "Music, Music, Music"
   Teresa Brewer
7. "It Isn't Fair"
   Sammy Kaye and Don Cornell
8. "Simple Melody"
   Gary and Bing Crosby
9. "Harbor Lights"
   Guy Lombardo
10. *Third Man* theme
    Guy Lombardo

1951

1. "Too Young"
   Nat King Cole
2. "Because of You"
   Tony Bennett
3. "Come On-a My House"
   Rosemary Clooney
4. "How High the Moon"
   Les Paul and Mary Fordy
5. "If"
   Perry Como
6. "On Top of Old Smoky"
   The Weavers
7. "Cold, Cold Heart"
   Tony Bennett
8. "Be My Love"
   Mario Lanza
9. "Loveliest Night of the Year"
   Mario Lanza
10. "Tennessee Waltz"
    Patti Page

1952

1. "Blue Tango"
   Leroy Anderson
2. "Cry"
   Johnnie Ray
3. "Wheel of Fortune"
   Kay Starr
4. "Half as Much"
   Rosemary Clooney
5. "Auf Wiederseh'n, Sweetheart"
   Vera Lynn
6. "You Belong to Me"
   Jo Stafford
7. "Wish You Were Here"
   Eddie Fisher and Hugo Winterhalter
8. "I Went to Your Wedding"
   Patti Page
9. "Here in My Heart"
   Al Martino
10. "Delicado"
    Percy Faith

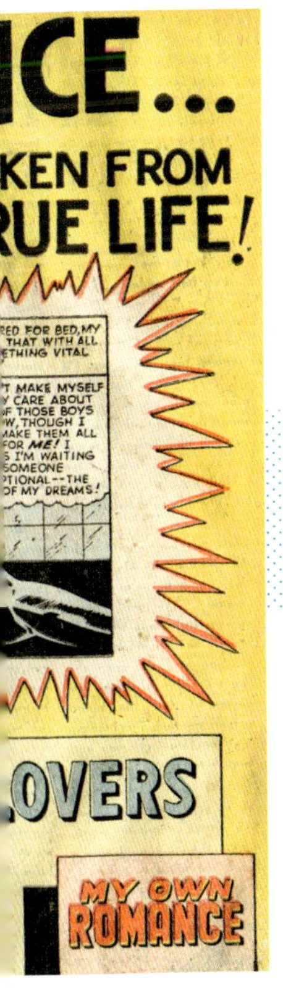

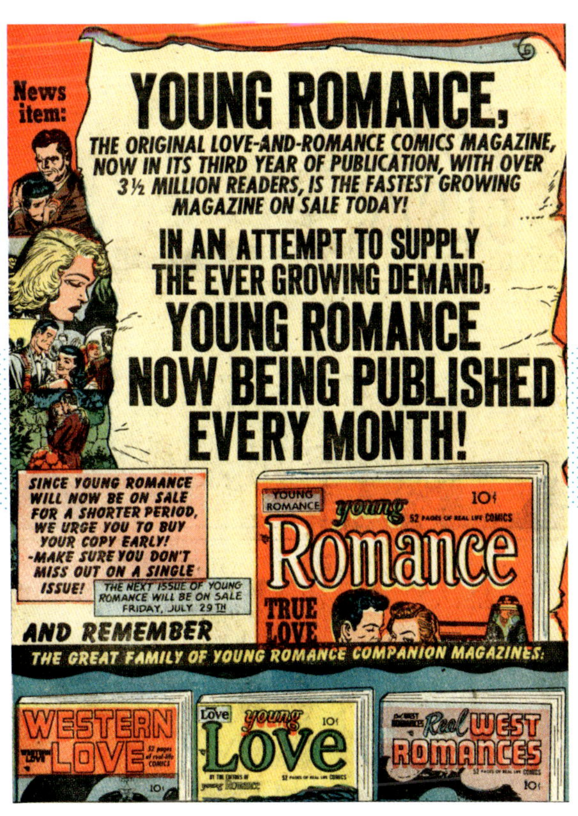

WHAT DID SHE WANT?
LIFE SLAPPED HER CRUELLY, AGAIN AND AGAIN--HER BRUISED YOUNG HEART WAS NO MATCH FOR THE TORMENTS OF FEAR AND SHAME!
I can't stand it any longer! This world is no place for softies, for innocent suckers, for simpering goody-goodies! I'm going out on my own! I'll get what I want at any price!!
THE SENSATIONAL STORY OF AN UNSELFISH GIRL DOMINATED BY A SELFISH MOTHER!
CONFESSIONS OF A MISSING GIRL
THE SHOCK OF A LIFE-TIME AWAITS YOU IN THE TERRIFIC CLIMAX!
DON'T MISS
ON SALE MAY 16th!
"CAN FIRST LOVE BE TRUE LOVE"
FIRST LOVE

1953

1 "Song from Moulin Rouge"
Percy Faith

2 "You, You, You"
The Ames Brothers

3 "Doggie in the Window"
Patti Page

4 "I'm Walking Behind You"
Eddie Fisher

5 "Vaya con Dios"
Les Paul and Mary Ford

6 "Till I Waltz Again with You"
Teresa Brewer

7 "Don't Let the Stars Get in Your Eyes"
Perry Como

8 "No Other Love"
Perry Como

9 "April in Portugal"
Guy Lombardo

10 "I Believe"
Frankie Laine

1954

1 "Hey There"
Rosemary Clooney

2 "Wanted"
Perry Como

3 "Little Things Mean a Lot"
Kitty Kallen

4 "Sh-Boom"
The Crew Cuts

5 "Make Love to Me"
Jo Stafford

6 "Oh! My Papa"
Eddie Fisher

7 "I Get So Lonely"
The Four Knights

8 "Three Coins in the Fountain"
The Four Aces

9 "Secret Love"
Doris Day

10 "That's Amore"
Dean Martin

1955

1 "Cherry Pink and Apple Blossom White"
Perez Prado

2 "Rock Around the Clock"
Bill Haley and His Comets

3 "Autumn Leaves"
Roger Williams

4 "Sixteen Tons"
Tennessee Ernie Ford

5 "The Ballad of Davy Crockett"
Bill Hayes

6 "The Yellow Rose of Texas"
Mitch Miller

7 "Sincerely"
The McGuire Sisters

8 "Moments to Remember"
The Four Lads

9 "Love Is a Many-Splendored Thing"
The Four Aces, feat. Al Alberts

10 "Unchained Melody"
Les Baxter

LETTERS of LOVE

ARE YOU STUMPED ON THE BUMPY ROAD TO LOVE? INSTEAD OF LETTING YOUR PROBLEM SIMMER INSIDE, SEND A LETTER TO CLAIRE CURTIS, WHO WILL ANSWER AS MANY AS POSSIBLE ON THESE PAGES...... ANSWERS GLEANED FROM YEARS OF EXPERIENCE AS A COUNSELOR OF LOVE!

Dear Miss Curtis,

I have a difficult problem, but I want to be practical about it, because I can't spend my life mooning over the man I have lost. I have gone with him for two years, and love him more than I could love anyone else. He has left me and is going to marry another woman. Everything I see or touch reminds me of him. I run into him occasionally and it is more than I can bear. I can't pry myself away from memories of our happiness together. What shall I do? How can I free myself?

B.W.-Des Moines, Ia.

DEAR B.W.

NATURALLY THE ASSOCIATIONS OF YOUR PAST ROMANCE DISTURB YOU--BUT YOU ARE RIGHT, YOU MUST BE PRACTICAL. IF YOU THINK YOUR LIFE HAS ENDED WITH HIS LEAVING, YOU MUST MAKE A NEW LIFE. IF IT IS POSSIBLE FOR YOU TO FIND NEW FRIENDS AND INTERESTS, WE WOULD ADVISE YOU TO DO SO. IT WILL BE A SLOW, DIFFICULT PROCESS, BUT YOU OWE IT TO YOURSELF TO MAKE THE EFFORT, AS LONG AS YOUR LOVE FOR THIS MAN HAS ASSUMED SUCH PROPORTIONS IN YOUR LIFE. REMEMBER THAT THERE ARE OTHER MEN LOOKING FOR A GIRL SUCH AS YOU TO LOVE. LIFE GOES ON, AND YOU MUST [illegible] YOURSELF TO WITHDRAW FROM [illegible]

Dear Miss Curtis, *Providence, R.I.*

I am twenty and have been going with a young doctor for three years. I want to marry him, but he says he has too many years ahead of him with little or no income. He thinks marriage now would spoil our chances for future happiness, because he would be away so much and we would have hardly any money. He is interning in Philadelphia, and I would like to go there and work, so I could at least see him. Do you think this would be wise?

A.M.K.

DEAR A.M.K.

AT TWENTY YOU MAY STILL BE IN NEED OF THE HELPFUL AND LOVING GUIDANCE OF YOUR PARENTS. HAVE YOU TALKED IT OVER WITH THEM?

I BELIEVE IT WOULD BE BEST IF YOU WERE TO REMAIN AT HOME UNTIL YOUR YOUNG MAN COMPLETES HIS INTERNSHIP. THEN, IF HE STILL LOVES YOU, HE WILL UNDOUBTEDLY ASK YOU TO JOIN HIM. IN THE MEANTIME, SEE OTHER MEN. YOU MAY MEET A MAN WHO WILL OFFER YOU LOVE AND MARRIAGE, WHICH WOULD BE MUCH MORE CONCRETE THAN THE INDEFINITE PROMISES OF HAPPINESS THE YOUNG DOCTOR HAS OFFERED YOU FOR THE FUTURE!

Dear Miss Curtis, *Dade City, Fla.*

The only way to be popular in the crowd I go around with is to be free with my kisses! After one date a fellow won't ask a girl out again unless she is willing to kiss him, even though she obviously can't know him very well at such an early stage. I'm considered an awful prude and miss out on a lot of dates. What shall I do?

A.F.E.

DEAR NFE

ARE YOU CERTAIN THERE IS NOT A BOY IN YOUR CROWD WHO WON'T DATE A GIRL AGAIN UNLESS SHE KISSES HIM ON THE FIRST DATE? IF THERE ISN'T, THEN YOU SEEM TO BE IN A VERY FAST CROWD.

BECAUSE YOU DO NOT HAVE THE SAME IDEAS, YOU ARE ONLY HARMING YOURSELF BY EVEN WISHING YOU WERE POPULAR WITH THEM. YOU ARE NOT A PRUDE, BUT A SENSIBLE YOUNG GIRL WITH HEALTHY, NORMAL CONVICTIONS. WATER SEEKS ITS OWN LEVEL, AND IF YOU DISASSOCIATE YOURSELF FROM YOUR PRESENT CROWD, BOYS WHO FEEL AS YOU DO.. THAT KISSES HAVE MEANING AND ARE NOT TO BE GIVEN TO ANY CASUAL DATE..WILL BE EASIER TO FIND!

Dear Miss Curtis -

I am twenty-two and engaged to a man who is twenty-five. He lives and works in another state. We plan to be married in six months, but I have just met a wonderful man that seems to have all the qualities my fiancé lacks. However, he is a professional baseball player and travels all over the country. He likes me, but I doubt if anything definite will come of our relationship. Yet, knowing him has made me realize the defects in our engagement. I am terribly confused. Would it be crazy to break our engagement just because I've met another man who doesn't even want to marry me?

W. S.
Los Gatos, Calif.

DEAR W.S.,

IT WOULD BE "CRAZY," AS YOU PUT IT, TO BREAK YOUR ENGAGEMENT BECAUSE OF THIS OTHER MAN, BUT IT WOULD BE WISE TO BREAK IT FOR YOUR OWN SAKE. IF YOU ARE SO GREATLY ATTACHED TO ANOTHER MAN, DESPITE THE FACT THAT YOUR MARRIAGE IS SOON TO TAKE PLACE, YOU ARE NOT READY TO SETTLE DOWN AND ACCEPT THE RESPONSIBILITIES OF MARRIED LIFE. I WOULD ADVISE YOU TO HAVE A LONG TALK WITH YOURSELF. DO YOU SINCERELY LOVE YOUR FIANCE? ARE YOU JUST INFATUATED WITH THIS NEWCOMER? PERHAPS YOUR FIANCE IS REALLY NOT THE MAN FOR YOU. WHEN YOU MARRY, W.S., YOU MUST DO SO WITH THE IDEA THAT IT WILL BE FOREVER!

Dear Miss Curtis,

Recently I started going out with a man who was engaged to a girl I knew slightly. He is very attractive, and we always have a wonderful time together. But he tells me that he is still in love with the girl he was engaged to, and that she broke the engagement. But he also tells me how much I mean to him. Yet I know that if this girl would ask him to come back, he'd return to her in a second. I like him too much, I guess, and am overly sensitive when he tells me about his ex-fiancée. Yet I think that maybe, if I keep going with him, I may replace her in his feelings. What shall I do?

Plainfield, N.J. B.L.K.

DEAR B.L.K.,

THIS MAN WITH WHOM YOU FEEL YOU ARE IN LOVE WOULD OBVIOUSLY NOT, AT THIS TIME, MAKE A GOOD HUSBAND. HE MAY FEEL THAT YOU MEAN A LOT TO HIM, BUT HE SHOWS LACK OF CONSIDERATION FOR YOUR FEELINGS WHEN HE TALKS TO YOU ABOUT ANOTHER GIRL. HOWEVER, YOU MAY BE THANKFUL THAT HE HAS TOLD YOU THE TRUTH. YOU MUST FORGET ABOUT A SERIOUS RELATIONSHIP AND BE ON GUARD AGAINST TOO GREAT AN ATTACHMENT FOR HIM, AND, AT THE SAME TIME, ENJOY HIS COMPANY. IN THIS WAY, YOU MAY BE OF HELP TO HIM IN OVERCOMING HIS CONFUSION OF THE HEART, AND IF HE IS THE RIGHT MAN FOR YOU, HE WILL FORGET ABOUT THE OTHER GIRL AND FIND YOU ARE THE ONE HE LOVES!

WHY NOT WRITE CLAIRE CURTIS A LETTER ABOUT YOUR LOVE PROBLEM TODAY? SEND IT TO:

CLAIRE CURTIS
SUITE 1404
350 FIFTH AVENUE
NEW YORK 1, NEW YORK

Bibliography

Andrews, Robert. *The New Penguin Dictionary of Modern Quotations.* New York: Penguin Books, 2003.

Berman, Louis A. *Proverb Wit & Wisdom.* New York: Perigee, 1997.

Goulart, Ron. *The Great Comic Book Artists.* New York: St. Martin's Press, 1986.

Maltin, Leonard. *Leonard Maltin's 2009 Movie Guide.* New York: Plume, 2009.

Nolan, Michelle. *Love on the Racks: A History of American Romance Comics.* Jefferson, North Carolina: McFarland & Company, 2008.

Overstreet, Robert. *The Official Overstreet Comic Book Price Guide*, 39th edition. New York: House of Collectibles, 2009, and Timonium, Maryland: Gemstone, 2009.

Oxford Dictionary Book of Quotations, The, Third Edition. New York: Oxford University Press, 1979, 1980.

Robbins, Trina. *From Girls to GRRRLZ: A History of [Women's] Comics from Teens to Zines.* San Francisco: Chronicle Books, 1999.

Sherrin, Ned. *Oxford Dictionary of Humorous Quotations*, Third Edition. New York: Oxford University Press, 2005, 2007.

Sikov, Ed. *Screwball: Hollywood's Madcap Romantic Comedies.* New York: Crown, 1989.

Simon, Joe, with Jim Simon. *The Comic Book Makers.* New York: Crestwood/II Publications, 1990.

Simon, Joe, and Jack Kirby. *Real Love: The Best of the Simon and Kirby Romance Comics*: 1940s–1950s. Forestville, California: Eclipse Books, 1988.

Tripp, Rhoda Thomas. *The International Thesaurus of Quotations.* New York: Thomas Crowell, 1970.

www.allgreatquotes.com/elizabeth_taylor_quotes.shtml. Accessed June 13, 2010.

www.thinkexist.com/quotes/Warren_Beatty/; thinkexist.com/quotes/bette_davis/2.html; thinkexist.com/quotations/marriage/. Accessed June 13, 2010.

Thanks to

Elizabeth Sullivan, editor extraordinaire, who won every single argument and made me like it. Or else.

Nicole Hughes, for the careful reads.

Gary Dolgoff, who helped me locate many of the comic book treasures that lie within.

And the various girls who subjected me to agonizing love over the course of this wondrous life (commencing in 1956 at age five): Susan, Laurel, Susan (another one), Debbie, Julie, Susan (yeah, another one), Julie (ditto), Frieda (who really shouldn't have slept with my best friend, but it wasn't entirely her fault), Ulrika, Brett, Holly, Linda, Susan (gosh, there are a lot of you out there!), and of course Jean, after whom I never so much as looked at another woman—except maybe for Adrianna Lima.

Credits

 Page 4 and **pages 18–19**: *Stories of Romance* #9 (December 1956), cover (detail); **page 14**: *Our Love Story* #5 (June 1970), cover; **page 15**: unknown issue, circa 1949, house ad for "America's Most Thrilling Western Romances"; **pages 16–17**: *My Own Romance*, issue unknown, circa 1951, "Straight from the Heart!" letters column; **page 22, top left**: *Lovers* #70 (September 1955), cover; **page 22, bottom left**: *Stories of Romance* #12 (June 1957), cover; **page 24, left**: *True Tales of Love* #27 (December 1956), cover; **page 24, right**: *Love Romances* #52 (October 1955), cover; **page 25**: *My Own Romance* #53 (August 1956), cover (detail); **page 43**: *Love Tales* #44 (January 1951), cover (detail); **pages 45–51**: *Love Tales* #39 (December 1949), "With Hate in My Heart"; **pages 52–58**: *Best Love* #36 (April 1950), "I Craved His Kisses"; **page 71**: *My Own Romance* #76 (July 1960), cover; **page 74**: *Best Love* #36 (April 1950), "Loveless Marriage" (splash page); **pages 75–82**: *Rangeland Love* #2 (March 1950), "The Trail of the Purple Sage"; **pages 107–113**: unknown issue, circa 1950, "Was I a Wicked Wife?"; **pages 115–122**: *My Love* #4 (April 1950), "I Was Engaged to a Puppet!"; **page 154, bottom right**: *My Own Romance* #63 (May 1958), cover; **pages 158–164**: *Best Love* #33 (or #34) (August 1949), "The Man I Couldn't Love!"

Pages 206–207:
UNKNOWN ISSUE
circa 1951